JSP 2.0:
The Complete Reference

Phil Hanna

McGraw-Hill/Osborne

New York   Chicago   San Francisco
Lisbon   London   Madrid   Mexico City
Milan   New Delhi   San Juan
Seoul   Singapore   Sydney   Toronto

The *McGraw·Hill* Companies

McGraw-Hill/Osborne
2600 Tenth Street
Berkeley, California 94710
U.S.A.

To arrange bulk purchase discounts for sales promotions, premiums, or fund-raisers, please contact **McGraw-Hill/**Osborne at the above address. For information on translations or book distributors outside the U.S.A., please see the International Contact Information page immediately following the index of this book.

JSP 2.0: The Complete Reference

1234567890 CUS CUS 0198765432

ISBN 0-07-222437-1

Publisher
  Brandon A. Nordin

Vice President & Associate Publisher
  Scott Rogers

Editorial Director
  Wendy Rinaldi

Project Editors
  Katie Conley
  Carolyn Welch

Technical Editor
  Karl Moss

Copy Editor
  Robert Campbell

Proofreaders
  Robin Small
  Susie Elkind

Indexer
  Valerie Robbins

Computer Designers
  Kathleen Fay Edwards
  John Patrus
  Apollo Printing Services

Illustrators
  Melinda Moore Lytle
  Michael Mueller
  Lyssa Wald

Series Design
  Peter F. Hancik

This book was composed with Corel VENTURA™ Publisher.

To the officers and members
of Engine 16 and Ladder 7,
Fire Department of New York.

About the Author

Phil Hanna has more than 20 years of
experience as a programmer, systems architect,
analyst, and project manager. He has
developed network-based software at IBM,
and served as a consultant to Chase Manhattan
Bank. He is the author of *Instant Java Servlets*
and *JSP: The Complete Reference,* and works as a
software developer for SAS Institute.

Contents

Part II

Elements of JSP

Part III

JSP Tag Extensions

Part IV

JSP Applications

Acknowledgments

It would not have been possible to write this book without the collaboration and support of a number of people.

I would first like to thank Wendy Rinaldi, Editorial Director at McGraw-Hill/ Osborne, who conceived of this project and worked with me to shape the scope and approach. Her unique mix of confidence, patience, drive, and wit pulled the whole project through many obstacles and into the light of day. Thanks also to Katie Conley and Carolyn Welch, my long-suffering project editors; to Bob Campbell for his careful copyediting; and especially to Karl Moss, my technical editor, who provided timely feedback, useful suggestions, and valuable encouragement.

I owe a great debt of gratitude to Jim Adams, Chris Bailey, William Bloemeke, Bryan Boone, Alan Carter, Denise Griffith, Pat Herbert, Larry Isaacs, Franny Kelly, Rich Main, David Malkovsky, Sandra Malkovsky, Sharon Martin, Mark McCue, Carol Rigsbee, Carlo Rossi, Perry Scherman, and Richard Wilson for their help in countless ways.

I am very grateful for the support of Mark Little, Alan Eaton, and Keith Collins of SAS Institute, who made it possible for me to undertake this project.

Most of all, and more than ever, I would like to thank my dear wife Mary, my children Eleanor and John, and my mother-in-law Ann Jordan, for their support, encouragement, kindness, and patience.

Preface

The first wave of a new technology is often outpaced by the expectations it generates. Those riding the second wave benefit from the experience of their predecessors and the real value emerges. This has been the case with Java. Client-side browser applications (applets) have encountered limitations in three areas:

- Browser incompatibilities
- Security overkill
- Performance problems due to long download times

The emergence of server-side Java has changed all this. Java Servlets and JavaServer Pages (JSP) provide a secure, robust, and platform-independent technology for bringing the power of Java to e-commerce and enterprise Web computing. This being the case, interest in JSP is flourishing and the demand for JSP skills is running high. Nearly all the Fortune 500 companies now have or will soon deploy server-side Java applications.

The purpose of this book is to provide a complete reference to JSP technology, starting with the Web programming environment and elements of JSP, then proceeding to a deeper examination of advanced topics.

How This Book Is Organized

This book consists of four parts, starting with high-level overviews and proceeding to a deeper examination of topics.

Part I, "The Web Programming Environment"

The four chapters in the opening section of the book provide an introduction to the Web as a programming environment and introduce servlets, JavaServer Pages (JSP), and HTTP, the Web network protocol.

- **Chapter 1, "Evolution of the Web Application"**
  This chapter describes how the application programming model has evolved as the Web has matured, and how experience with each phase has driven requirements for the next.

- **Chapter 2, "Overview of the Hypertext Transfer Protocol (HTTP)"**
  This chapter introduces the underlying language of the Web client/server model, the Hypertext Transfer Protocol (HTTP). It develops the basic concepts critical to understanding the Web programming environment.

- **Chapter 3, "Introduction to Servlets"**
  Servlet technology is the foundation on which JSP is built. The intimate connection between JSP and servlets is explained in this overview chapter. The essential features that they share are outlined and demonstrated.

- **Chapter 4, "JSP Overview"**
  Chapter 4 provides an overview of JavaServer Pages (JSP) as a server-side scripting environment, a description of the JSP container, and several tutorial examples. Only the basics are covered here; Part II considers the topic in depth.

Part II, "Elements of JSP"

This part deals with the syntax and semantics of JSP, equipping the reader with the skills necessary to create working code. Topics include basic syntax, scriptlets, expressions, declarations, including files, forwarding requests, and specifying page behavior.

- **Chapter 5, "JSP Syntax and Semantics"**
  This chapter covers the basic syntax of JavaServer Pages, describing how they merge HTML templates and Java code. It introduces the page directive and gives examples of each of its attributes.

- **Chapter 6, "Expressions, Scriptlets, and Declarations"**
  This section considers the basic model of incorporating Java code fragments into a JSP page. It covers legal and illegal uses and describes how the code

fragments are composed by the translator into a working servlet. It explores how declarations make advanced functionality available to a JSP page.

- **Chapter 7, "Request Dispatching"**
  This chapter discusses how HTTP requests can be handled by more than one server-side component. It describes two methods for including other files, and it explains why one method may be preferable to another. It covers how to use the `<jsp:forward>` action to pass a request on to another JSP page for processing.

- **Chapter 8, "Session and Thread Management"**
  HTTP is a stateless protocol, but JSP pages can use HTTP sessions to overcome this limitation. This chapter explores the issues involved and describes techniques available to the developer. Servlet threading models are also discussed.

- **Chapter 9, "Application Event Listeners"**
  Event listeners allow code to be invoked at significant points in the application lifecycle. This chapter discusses servlet context, session, and servlet request listeners, providing detailed examples of their use.

- **Chapter 10, "Filters"**
  JSP 2.0 provides the ability to apply filters to requests and responses. This chapter covers the filter lifecycle, wrapping requests and responses, the filter environment, and filter configuration.

Part III, "JSP Tag Extensions"

This section deals with the heart of the JSP 2.0 tag extension mechanism. Topics include an overview of JSP custom tags, the JSP Standard Tag Library (JSTL), the JSP Expression Language (EL), and JSP fragments.

- **Chapter 11, "Introduction to Custom Tags"**
  Basic concepts of custom tags and tag libraries are covered in this chapter. Topics include the tag lifecycle, tag handlers, tag library descriptors, and validators.

- **Chapter 12, "Expression Language"**
  A core new feature of JSP 2.0 is the JSP Expression Language (EL). Originally designed for use in the JSP Standard Tag Library (JSTL), it has been adopted as an official standard in both the JSP and JSTL specifications. This chapter covers EL in depth.

- **Chapter 13, "The JSP Standard Tag Library (JSTL)"**
  This chapter presents an overview of the key features of the JSP Standard Tag Library (JSTL). Topics include the core tag library, with its data access, iteration, and conditional logic, the XML parsing, flow control, and transformation library, the SQL database access library, and the internationalization library.

- **Chapter 14, "Simple Tag Extensions, Tag Files, and JSP Fragments"**
  JSP 2.0 makes it possible to develop custom tags in JSP itself, without having to write Java code. This chapter shows how to use JSP fragments, tag files, and the new SimpleTag interface.

Part IV, "JSP Applications"

The final part of the book looks at how JSP works with JDBC, XML, and other major components of the Java enterprise environment. Includes detailed coverage of debugging and deployment.

- **Chapter 15, "Database Access with JDBC"**
  Most JSP pages of any consequence need to access a database. This section includes a comprehensive look at Java database connectivity and how it can be used in Web-based applications.

- **Chapter 16, "JSP and XML"**
  XML has emerged as the universal language for structured data storage and interchange. In addition, since JSP 1.2, JSP pages can be written entirely in XML. This chapter examines how JSP can use XML for both input and output. Topics include XML parsers, the Java XML API, the Document Object Model (DOM) and Simple API for XML (SAX) architectures, and XSLT.

- **Chapter 17, "JSP Testing and Debugging"**
  Debugging techniques are frequently ignored in programming tutorials but are indispensable knowledge. JavaServer Pages present their own challenges. This chapter outlines a basic methodology that can be applied and the tools that are available.

- **Chapter 18, "Deploying Web Applications"**
  Chapter 18 describes how to move JSP pages out of the development environment into a production Web environment. It includes detailed coverage of the deployment descriptor, web.xml.

- **Chapter 19, "Case Study: A Product Support Center"**
  The book concludes with a detailed case study that brings together elements discussed throughout the book. The application is a Web-based system for managing a technical support center. The Model-View-Controller (MVC) architecture is illustrated.

Finally, there is an appendix, which covers the Servlet 2.4 and JSP 2.0 application programming interface.

The Lyric Note

Most of the examples in this book are set in the context of a hypothetical company—The Lyric Note. This is an Internet-based music company that sells books, gifts, sheet music, music software, and musical instruments. I have populated it with fifty employees working in eleven departments, and a large product catalog.

Servlet and JSP API Levels

As this book is written, there are proposed final drafts of the Servlet 2.4 and JSP 2.0 specifications, as well as very early code for the Jakarta Tomcat 5.0 reference implementation. Since these specifications are not yet final, there are very likely changes in the version you are using that are not reflected in the book. For detailed reference, consult the official specifications at http://jcp.org. The servlet specification is JSR 154, and the JSP 2.0 specification is JSR 152.

Updates

Errata, examples, and updates can be found on my Web site at http://www.philhanna.com.

The Complete Reference

Part I

The Web Programming Environment

The
Complete
Reference

Chapter 1

Evolution of the
Web Application

3

One of the most remarkable things about the World Wide Web is that it wasn't originally conceived as an application environment. Yet today, Web applications are the mainstay of most Internet use—in particular, of e-commerce use. This chapter briefly traces the origins of the World Wide Web, Web applications, and associated technologies, setting the context for more detailed technical exploration in the remainder of the book.

Birth of the Web

The World Wide Web and its associated *Hypertext Transfer Protocol (HTTP)* grew out of work done at the European Laboratory for Particle Physics (CERN) in 1990. Tim Berners-Lee developed HTTP as a networking protocol for distributing documents and wrote the first Web browser. The system was used at CERN and other high-energy physics laboratories and universities in 1991 and 1992, and grew steadily in popularity. In 1993, the advent of the Mosaic browser led to the explosion of commercial Web use. In five years, more than 650,000 Web servers were in use worldwide, with uncounted millions of users.

Growth of the Web Programming Model

The idea of using the Web as an application environment developed over time, with each stage of technology serving as a springboard for new ideas. The first operational model had the Web server simply serving up documents on request. In this environment, the content doesn't change unless a human author supplies a new version of a document. The client/server interaction is illustrated in Figure 1-1.

HTTP is a simple request/response protocol in which a Web browser asks for a document (typically using a GET command), and the Web server returns the document in the form of an HTML data stream preceded by a few descriptive headers. Chapter 2 examines HTTP in greater detail.

What quickly became apparent is that if humans could revise the documents handled by the Web server, so could a text-processing program such as a Perl script. The Web browser is unaware of the difference because the result of an HTTP request is still an HTML data stream. What's more, the browser can send more than just a request—it can send parameters, either by embedding them in the URL or by sending a data stream with the request. This suggests that an HTTP request can be interpreted as a database query and the query results can be used to build an HTML document dynamically. With the development of the NCSA HTTPd Web Server came a new specification designated the *Common Gateway Interface (CGI)*.

A CGI program is invoked by the Web server in response to certain types of requests, usually requests for documents in a particular directory or filenames having a particular extension, such as .cgi. The request parameters are passed as key/value pairs, and the request headers, as environment variables. The program reads these parameters and headers, performs the application task at hand (typically accessing a

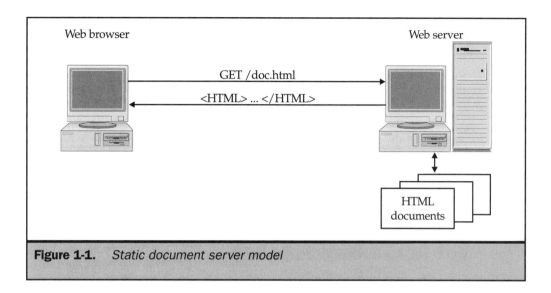

Figure 1-1. *Static document server model*

database to do so), and then generates an HTTP response. The response is sent back to the requesting Web browser as if it were an ordinary static document. Figure 1-2 illustrates the process flow.

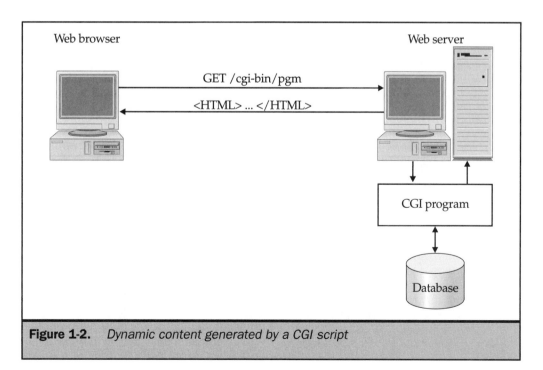

Figure 1-2. *Dynamic content generated by a CGI script*

CGI is convenient, but it has one big drawback. Ordinarily, CGI spawns a new process for each HTTP request.[1] This isn't a problem when traffic volume is low, but it creates a great deal of overhead when the traffic level increases. This being the case, CGI in general doesn't scale well.

A significant improvement came with the release in 1997 of the Java Servlet API, followed quickly by the *JavaServer Pages (JSP)* API. These related technologies bring the full power of Java to the Web server, with database connectivity, network access, and multithreaded operations, and, notably, a different process model. Servlets and JSP pages operate from a single instance that remains in memory and uses multiple threads to service requests simultaneously. As Figure 1-3 shows, servlets and JSP pages can make use of the full *Java 2 Enterprise Edition (J2EE)* environment for sophisticated, robust applications.

The Shift from Client-Side to Server-Side Solutions

The Web application model has evolved as the Web has matured, and experience with each phase has driven requirements for the next. The initial wave of client-side Java in the form of applets was phenomenally popular but led to some disappointment as reality intruded. Considerable incompatibilities occurred between browsers, downloads over slow modems were lengthy, and security restrictions limited applet usefulness. Because of this, applet development slowed,[2] and server-side Java has been the biggest growth area.

Server-side Java has none of the restrictions of the applet environment. No browser inconsistencies occur, because the browser isn't required to host a Java virtual machine. The browser only has to render HTML, which even the oldest browsers do reasonably well. Also, no client-side setup is involved, and no download of large class files. Likewise, security considerations are limited to those already handled by the Web server, which is typically in a closed environment with controls in place.

JSP has proved to be a successful server-side technology and an excellent base for developing Web applications. The remainder of this book explores JSP in depth to demonstrate why this is so.

---

[1] Improvements on this exist, such as FastCGI, which handles all requests from a single persistent process.

[2] Many observers believe client-side Java is poised for a comeback. The Java plug-in eliminates browser inconsistencies and allows Swing components to be used. Java Web Start allows applications to be deployed easily over the Web. Moreover, high-speed Internet connections are making download time less of a consideration.

THE WEB PROGRAMMING
ENVIRONMENT

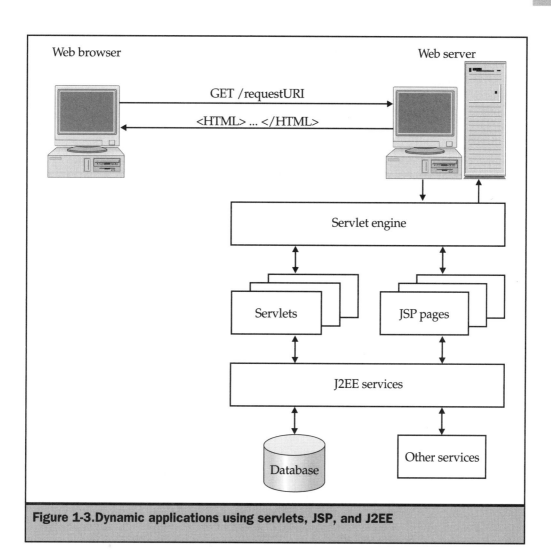

Figure 1-3.Dynamic applications using servlets, JSP, and J2EE

Chapter 2

Overview of the Hypertext Transfer Protocol (HTTP)

This chapter introduces the underlying language used by the Web client/server model. In doing so, it develops the basic concepts critical to understanding the Web programming environment. The chapter presents several examples of Web browsers and servers using this language to communicate.

What Is HTTP?

Whereas *Hypertext Markup Language (HTML)* is the language used to describe the insides of Web documents, *Hypertext Transfer Protocol (HTTP)* is the language used to describe how these documents are sent over the Internet. The key to understanding Web programming is understanding this protocol and the environment in which it operates.

A Language for Requesting Documents over the Internet

HTTP prescribes the rules by which browsers make requests and servers supply responses. This set of rules, or *protocol*, includes ways to

- Ask for a document by name
- Agree on the data format
- Determine who the user is
- Decide how to handle outdated resources
- Indicate the results of a request

and other useful functions.

HTTP consists of a set of commands written as lines of ordinary ASCII text. When you use a Web browser, you don't enter the HTTP commands directly. Instead, when you type a URL or click a hyperlink, the browser translates your action into HTTP commands that request the document from the server specified in the URL. The Web server finds the document and sends it back to the browser, where it's displayed, along with its associated graphics and other hyperlinks.

The HTTP Specification

Internet standards are usually specified in a *Request for Comments (RFC)* published by the *Internet Engineering Task Force (IETF)*. These RFCs are widely accepted by the Internet research and development community. Because they're standards documents, they tend to be written in formal language, like that of a legal document. This makes them unsuitable as tutorials, but invaluable for reference.

RFCs are numbered and never change when issued. If a standard is updated, a new RFC is issued. Being standards, RFCs are widely available on the Internet. The official online reference is `http://www.ietf.org/rfc.html`.

Several RFCs deal with HTTP, as shown in Table 2-1.

RFC Document Number	Contents
RFC 1945	A description of HTTP version 1.0
RFC 2068	The initial description of version 1.1
RFC 2616	The current HTTP/1.1 specification
RFC 2817	Upgrading to TLS Within HTTP/1.1

Table 2-1.   *RFCs Defining HTTP Standards*

Unless otherwise specified, this book uses the HTTP/1.1 standard as documented in RFC 2616.

HTTP Request Model

The specification describes HTTP as a stateless request/response protocol whose basic operation is as follows:

1. A client application, such as a Web browser, opens a socket to the Web server's HTTP port (80, by default).

2. Through the connection, the client writes an ASCII text request line, followed by zero or more HTTP headers, an empty line, and any data that accompanies the request.

3. The Web server parses the request and locates the specified resource.

4. The server writes a copy of the resource to the socket, where it's read by the client.

5. The server closes the connection.

Figure 2-1 illustrates this basic operation.

A key consideration is this model is *stateless*. This means in handling a request, the Web server doesn't remember anything about previous requests from the same client. The protocol is simply a request ("please give me this document") and a response ("OK, here it is"). Obviously, this imposes limitations on application programming, which typically requires a great deal of back-and-forth conversation, as well as complex objects that must be initialized and have their state maintained.

The way around this is to have the server assign an identifier to the session represented by a set of client requests, and to have the client remember the identifier and supply it to the server with each request. This technique is explored in depth in Chapter 11.

Let's examine each of these steps in greater detail.

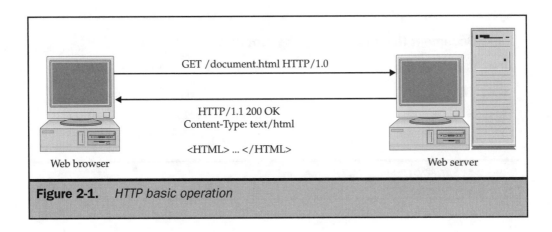

Figure 2-1.   *HTTP basic operation*

Connecting to the Web Server

A Web server operates by listening for requests on a well-known port number. The default is port 80, although any available port can be used. If a Web server listens on a different port, URLs that refer to this server must include a colon and the port number immediately after the server name. For example,

```
http://www.mycompany.com/mypath.html
```

refers to an HTML document known to a Web server running on the www.mycompany.com host on the default port 80. If the server is running on port 4311 instead, the URL looks like this:

```
http://www.mycompany.com:4311/mypath.html
```

Why bother with alternate port numbers, especially because they introduce that ugly URL syntax? Because this allows more than one server to be running on a single host. An experimental Web server with different capabilities may need to coexist with the main server. A servlet engine, for example, may provide a mini–HTTP server for development and testing of servlets and JSP pages. Web servers often provide some means of hiding this alternate syntax by mapping the URLs to a different namespace.

A client, such as a Web browser, initiates an HTTP request by opening a TCP/IP socket to the Web server port, and then opening input and output streams over the socket. In Java terms, this would amount to a few lines of code:

```
Socket socket = new Socket("www.mycompany.com", 80);
InputStream istream = socket.getInputStream();
OutputStream ostream = socket.getOutputStream();
```

The parameters required to open the socket are the Web server host name and the port number. The server host name is extracted from the URL, while the port number is either implied or also extracted from the URL. The output stream is used to send HTTP commands to the Web server; the input stream is used to read the response.

Sending the HTTP Request

Once the socket connection is made, the Web browser writes an HTTP command to request the document. A request has up to four parts.

The first part is the *request line*. This consists of three tokens, separated by spaces: the request method, the request URI, and the HTTP version. The following shows a typical request line:

```
GET /mypath.html HTTP/1.0
```

In this example, the request method is GET, the URI is /mypath.html, and the HTTP version is HTTP/1.0.

The HTTP specification defines eight possible methods, shown in Table 2-2. Of all these methods, the vast majority of requests use either GET or POST. These two methods are the only ones considered in this book.

Method	Description
GET	A simple request to retrieve the resource identified in the URI.
HEAD	The same as GET, except the server doesn't return the requested document. The server returns only the status line and headers.
POST	A request for the server to accept data that will be written to the client's output stream.
PUT	A request for the server to store the data in the request as the new contents of the specified URI.
DELETE	A request for the server to delete the resource named in the URI.
OPTIONS	A request for information about what request methods the server supports.
TRACE	A request for the Web server to echo the HTTP request and its headers.
CONNECT	A documented but currently unimplemented method reserved for use with a tunneling proxy.

Table 2-2. *HTTP Request Methods*

The second token on the request line is the *Uniform Resource Identifier (URI)*. This identifies the document or other resource being requested. For all practical purposes, this corresponds to the URL without the leading `http://` and host name. In the example of http://www.mycompany.com/mypath.html, the request URI is `/mypath.html`.

The last token on the line is the HTTP version. This indicates the highest level of the HTTP specification the client application understands. The allowable values are `HTTP/1.0` and `HTTP/1.1`.

After the request line come any request headers. These are key/value pairs, one pair per line, with the key and the value separated by a colon (`:`). After the last request header is written, an empty line consisting of only a carriage return and a line feed is sent. This informs the server that no more headers follow. Even if no headers exist, this empty line must be sent, so that the server doesn't look for any more headers.

Request headers inform the server further about the identity and capabilities of the client. Some typical request headers are listed in Table 2-3.

For HTTP `POST` requests, the request may include data. For example, HTML form fields are transmitted as a string of key/value pairs separated by the ampersand character. If data is present, it is common to see both the `Content-Type` and `Content-Length` request headers used.

Server Acceptance of the Request

When a client connects to the Web server's listening port, the server accepts the connection and handles the request. In most cases, it does so by starting a thread to process the request, so that it can continue to service new requests.

Handling the request means different things depending on the URI. If the URI represents a static document, the server opens the document file and prepares to copy its contents back to the client. If the URI is a program name, such as a CGI script, servlet, or JSP page, and the server is configured to handle such a request, the server prepares to invoke the program or process.

Request Header	Description
User-Agent	The vendor and version of the client.
Accept	A list of content types the client recognizes.
Content-Length	The number of bytes of data appended to the request.

Table 2-3. *HTTP Request Headers*

The HTTP Response from the Server

By whatever means the server processes the request, the result is the same—an HTTP response. Similar to a request, a response consists of up to four parts: a status line, zero or more response headers, an empty line signaling the end of the headers, and the data that makes up the response.

The status line consists of up to three tokens:

■ The *HTTP version*. Just as the client indicates the highest version it can understand, so the server indicates its capabilities.

■ The *response code*. This is a three-digit numeric code that indicates whether the request succeeded or failed and, if it failed, the reason why.

■ An *optional response description*, which is a human-readable explanation of the response code.

A typical HTTP response status line looks like this:

```
HTTP/1.0 200 OK
```

which indicates a successful retrieval of the requested document according to the 1.0 level of the HTTP specification.

After the status line come the response headers, with an empty line as the delimiter. Like request headers, these indicate the capabilities of the server and identify details about the response data.

The last part of the response is the requested data itself, typically an HTML document or image stream. After the data is sent, the server closes its end of the connection.

 Examples

A look at several examples can make this clearer. A simple case of a GET request would be what happens when a URL is typed in a browser address line or a hyperlink is clicked. If you type http://www.lyricnote.com/simple.html into your Web browser's address field, the browser opens a socket connection to the www.lyricnote.com host on port 80, and then it writes the line

```
GET /simple.html HTTP/1.0
```

followed by an empty line. The Web server returns the following:

```
HTTP/1.1 200 OK
Content-Type: text/html
Content-Length: 315
```

```
Connection: close
Date: Fri, 01 Mar 2002 05:18:12 GMT
Server: Apache Tomcat/4.0.2 (HTTP/1.1 Connector)
Last-Modified: Fri, 01 Mar 2002 05:18:02 GMT

<html>
<head>
<title>Simple Document</title>
</head>
<body>
<h3>Welcome</h3> to <b>The Lyric Note</b>,
the best Internet source for
<ul>
<li>sheet music</li>
<li>musical instruments</li>
<li>books on musical topics</li>
<li>music software, and</li>
<li>musical gift items</li>
</ul>
</body>
</html>
```

The browser first parses the status line and sees the status code indicating that the request was successful. The browser then parses each of the response headers, which inform it about the type (HTML) and length (315 bytes) of response data that is being sent. The browser reads the HTML, formats it according to the syntax and semantics of HTML, and displays it in the browser window, as shown in Figure 2-2.

Nested Requests

An HTML document may contain references to other resources that need to be loaded when the document is loaded. For example, images are often embedded in the page with the HTML <img> tag. JavaScript files or external style sheets may also be required. The Web browser (not the server) recognizes these cases and makes additional requests for the other resources.

This bears repeating. The Web server doesn't read through the HTML that it serves, recognize an <img> tag, and then start sending the bytes of the image file. The Web server simply sends back the resource that was requested in one operation. If, a few milliseconds later, the browser requests an image file, the server returns this in a separate operation. The Web browser does all this under the covers, so the user is unaware that several requests are involved.

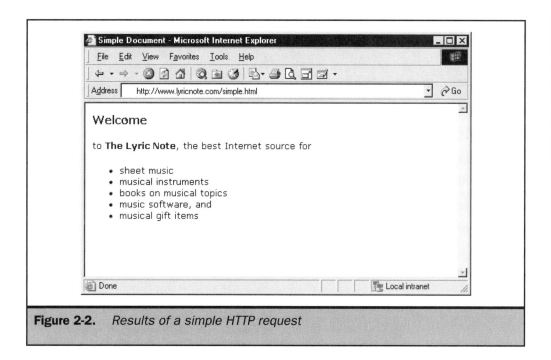

Figure 2-2.   *Results of a simple HTTP request*

To augment the previous example slightly, suppose you open `http://www.lyricnote.com/compound.html`. The browser again opens a socket connection to `www.lyricnote.com` port 80 and requests the HTML document,

```
GET /compound.html HTTP/1.0
```

which results in the following response:

```
HTTP/1.1 200 OK
Content-Type: text/html
Content-Length: 439
Connection: close
Date: Fri, 01 Mar 2002 05:18:52 GMT
Server: Apache Tomcat/4.0.2 (HTTP/1.1 Connector)
Last-Modified: Fri, 01 Mar 2002 05:14:44 GMT

<html>
<head>
<title>Compound Document</title>
```

```
<link rel="stylesheet" href="lyricnote.css">
</head>
<body>
<img src="images/logo.png">
<hr color="#005a9c" align="left" width="500">
<h3>Welcome</h3> to <b>The Lyric Note</b>,
the best Internet source for
<ul>
<li>sheet music</li>
<li>musical instruments</li>
<li>books on musical topics</li>
<li>music software, and</li>
<li>musical gift items</li>
</ul>
</body>
</html>
```

Note that although the page includes an image and a style sheet, their *contents* are not included in the response—only the bare HTML that refers to them, as you can verify by viewing the HTML source in your browser.

As the browser is parsing the HTML, it encounters the style sheet request:

```
<link rel="stylesheet" href="lyricnote.css">
```

and makes a second HTTP request, interpreting the value of the href attribute as a URL relative to the current request (http://www.lyricnote.com/compound.html):

```
GET /lyricnote.css HTTP/1.0
```

The Web server retrieves the style sheet and returns it to the client:

```
HTTP/1.1 200 OK
Content-Type: text/css
Content-Length: 73
Connection: close
Date: Fri, 01 Mar 2002 05:19:43 GMT
ETag: "73-1014959584710"
Server: Apache Tomcat/4.0.2 (HTTP/1.1 Connector)
Last-Modified: Fri, 01 Mar 2002 05:13:04 GMT

h3 {
```

```
    font-size: 20px;
    font-weight: bold;
    color: #005A9C;
}
```

The browser interprets the style sheet and applies the font size, weight, and color styles to the <h3> tag. Next, it encounters an <img> tag,

```
<img src= "images/logo.png" >
```

and makes a request for the logo,

```
GET /images/logo.png HTTP/1.0
```

which causes the Web server to respond with the image data stream:

```
HTTP/1.1 200 OK
Content-Type: image/png
Content-Length: 1280
Connection: close
Date: Fri, 01 Mar 2002 05:20:53 GMT
Server: Apache Tomcat/4.0.2 (HTTP/1.1 Connector)
Last-Modified: Fri, 22 Sep 2000 02:34:07 GMT

(Binary image data here)
```

Finally, the browser renders the completed page, as shown in Figure 2-3.

Summary

This chapter introduces HTTP, the set of rules by which requests are made and responses are returned. Understanding these rules is crucial to proper development and troubleshooting. It is important to understand that HTTP is stateless, meaning HTTP doesn't by itself retain knowledge from one request to the next. The JSP environment provides robust ways to remedy this.

Another key consideration is that both browsers and servers can be replaced by work-alike software. Applications, applets, and programs written in other languages can act as clients, and diagnostic tools can play the role of server. Because all they need to do is provide the same HTTP request and response streams a browser and a Web server would use, these other applications are indistinguishable from the real thing. You'll exploit this capability in later chapters.

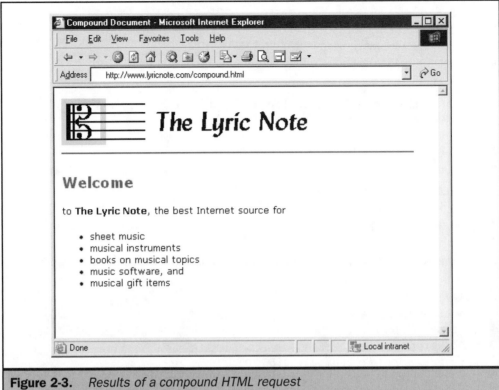

Figure 2-3. Results of a compound HTML request

Chapter 3

Introduction to Servlets

To understand JavaServer Pages, it's necessary to understand their underlying technology—Java servlets. *Servlets* are Java classes that extend the functionality of a Web server by dynamically generating Web pages. A runtime environment known as a *servlet container* manages servlet loading and unloading, and works with the Web server to direct requests to servlets and to send output back to Web clients.

Since their introduction in 1997, servlets have become the dominant environment for server-side Java programming and a widely used portal into application servers. They offer several key advantages:

- **Performance**   Older technologies such as the *Common Gateway Interface* (*CGI*) typically start a new process to handle each incoming request. In the days when the Web was primarily a repository for academic and scientific research, there wasn't very much traffic and this approach worked well. Servlets, by contrast, are loaded when first requested, and stay in memory indefinitely. The servlet engine loads a single instance of the servlet class and dispatches requests to it using a pool of available threads. The resulting performance improvement is considerable.

- **Simplicity**   Client-side Java applets run in a virtual machine provided by the Web browser. This introduces compatibility issues that increase complexity and limit the functionality that applets can provide. Servlets simplify this situation considerably because they run in a virtual machine in a controlled server environment and require only basic HTTP to communicate with their clients. No special client software is required, even with older browsers.

- **HTTP Sessions**   Although HTTP servers have no built-in capability to remember details of a previous request from the same client, the Servlet API provides an `HttpSession` class that overcomes this limitation.

- **Access to Java Technology**   Servlets, being Java applications, have direct access to the full range of Java features, such as threading, network access, and database connectivity.

JSP pages, which are automatically translated into servlets, inherit all these advantages. Both servlets and JSP pages are key components of the Java 2 Enterprise Edition (J2EE).

This chapter provides an overview of how servlets work. It examines the primary servlet objects and their application programming interface.[1] It discusses the servlet engine, the servlet lifecycle, servlet threading models, and how servlets can maintain persistent state between requests. This chapter also includes an annotated example of a servlet.

---

[1]   For detailed and authoritative information about servlets, see the Java Servlet Specification 2.3, available at http://www.jcp.org/aboutJava/communityprocess/final/jsr053/.

Servlet Lifecycle

Like their client-side applet counterparts, servlets provide methods that are called when specific events occur in a larger context. Programming in this environment involves writing predefined methods (sometimes known as *callback* methods), which are called as required by a managing program.

An applet, for example, provides methods such as `init()`, `start()`, `paint()`, `stop()`, and `destroy()`, which are called by the applet runtime environment in response to actions the user takes. The `java.applet.Applet` base class provides default implementations for all these methods; you only override those that occur during events with which you are concerned. You would write an `init()` method, for instance, if you have GUI components that need to be created.

Similarly, servlets operate in the context of a request and response model managed by a servlet engine. The engine does the following:

- Loads a servlet when it is first requested.

- Calls the servlet's `init()` method.

- Handles any number of requests by calling the servlet's `service()` method.

- When shutting down, calls the `destroy()` method of each active servlet.

As with applets, there are standard base classes `javax.servlet.GenericServlet` and `javax.servlet.http.HttpServlet` that implement the servlet callback methods. *Servlet programming, then, consists of subclassing one of these classes and overriding the necessary method to accomplish the specific task at hand.* The following sections examine each of these lifecycle methods.

init

When a request for a servlet is received by the servlet engine, it checks to see if the servlet is already loaded. If not, the servlet engine uses a class loader to get the particular servlet class required, and then invokes its constructor to get an instance of the servlet. After the servlet is loaded, but before it services any requests, the servlet engine calls an initialization method with the following signature:

```
public void init(ServletConfig config)
    throws ServletException
```

This method is called only once, just before the servlet is placed into service. The `ServletConfig` object provides access to the servlet context (discussed later in this chapter) and to any initialization parameters coded for the servlet. To maintain a reference to the servlet context, the `config` object must be stored as an instance variable, a task that's done by the `init(ServletConfig)` method in `GenericServlet`. For this reason, it's important to call `super.init(config)` within the `init()` method of any subclass.

Alternatively, if your servlet is a subclass of `GenericServlet`, you can use the no-argument `init()` method:

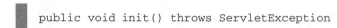

```
public void init() throws ServletException
```

This convenience method is called automatically from within `GenericServlet`'s `init(ServletConfig)` method, after the `config` parameter is already safely tucked away. This ensures that the parameter is not inadvertently lost.

Inside the `init()` method, the servlet can perform any necessary startup tasks, such as establishing database connections. If any errors occur that make the servlet unable to handle requests, it should throw an `UnavailableException`. `UnavailableException` is a subclass of `ServletException` that can optionally include a number of seconds the servlet is expected to be unavailable. If the time is not specified, the servlet is assumed to be permanently unavailable, which ensures that no requests will be directed to the servlet.

service

After the `init()` method completes successfully, the servlet is able to accept requests. By default, only a single instance of the servlet is created, and the servlet container dispatches each request to the instance in a separate thread. The servlet method that's called has the following signature:

```
public void service(
    ServletRequest request,
    ServletResponse response)
throws ServletException, IOException
```

The `ServletRequest` object is constructed by the servlet container and acts as a wrapper for information about the client and the request. This includes the identity of the remote system, the request parameters, and any input stream associated with the request. Similarly, the `ServletResponse` object provides the means for a servlet to communicate its results back to the original requester. It includes methods for opening an output stream and for specifying the content type and length.

As important as the `service()` method is, it's rarely used directly. This is because most servlets are designed to operate in the HTTP environment, for which there's a specialized `javax.servlet.http` package.

Rather than extending `javax.servlet.GenericServlet` directly, most servlets extend its subclass `javax.servlet.http.HttpServlet`. This subclass provides specialized methods corresponding to each HTTP request method: GET requests are handled by doGet(), POST requests by doPost(), and so on. The signatures for these methods use HTTP-specific versions of the request and response objects:

```
public void doGet(
    HttpServletRequest request,
    HttpServletResponse response)
  throws ServletException, IOException
```

The service(Request, Response) method in HttpServlet casts the request and response objects into their HTTP-specific counterparts, and then calls service(HttpServletRequest, HttpServletResponse). This method examines the request and calls the appropriate doGet(), doPost(), or other method. A typical HTTP servlet, then, includes an override to one or more of these subsidiary methods, rather than an override to service().

destroy

The servlet specification allows a servlet container to unload a servlet at any time. This may be done to conserve system resources or in preparation for servlet container shutdown. The servlet container notifies each loaded servlet this is about to happen by calling its destroy() method. By overriding destroy(), you can release any resources allocated during init().

 Note   *Calling destroy() yourself won't actually unload the servlet. Only the servlet container can cause this to happen. There is no architected way for a servlet to unload itself programmatically.*

Example: Kilometers per Liter to Miles per Gallon Servlet

Let's look at a simple servlet. K2MServlet, shown in the following, creates a fuel efficiency conversion table that expresses kilometers per liter in terms of miles per gallon.

```
package com.jspcr.servlets;

import java.io.*;
import java.text.*;
```

```java
import java.util.*;
import javax.servlet.*;
import javax.servlet.http.*;

/**
 * Prints a conversion table of miles per gallon
 * to kilometers per liter
 */
public class K2MServlet extends HttpServlet
{
    /**
     * Numeric format used to display temperatures
     */
    private static final DecimalFormat FMT
        = new DecimalFormat("#0.00");

    /**
     * Factor to convert from km/l to mi/gal
     */
    private static final double CONVERSION_FACTOR = 2.352145;

    /**
     * Handles a GET request
     */
    public void doGet(
            HttpServletRequest request,
            HttpServletResponse response)
        throws ServletException, IOException
    {
        // Set up for creating HTML output

        response.setContentType("text/html");
        PrintWriter out = response.getWriter();

        // Generate heading

        out.println
            ( "<html>"
            + "<head>"
```

```
           + "<title>Fuel Efficiency Conversion Chart</title>"
           + "</head>"
           + "<body>"
           + "<center>"
           + "<h1>Fuel Efficiency Conversion Chart</h1>"
           + "<table border='1' cellpadding='3' cellspacing='0'>"
           + "<tr>"
           + "<th>Kilometers per Liter</th>"
           + "<th>Miles per Gallon</th>"
           + "</tr>"
           );

    // Generate table

    for (double kmpl = 5; kmpl <= 20; kmpl += 1.0) {
        double mpg = kmpl * CONVERSION_FACTOR;
        out.println
           ( "<tr>"
           + "<td align='right'>" + FMT.format(kmpl) + "</td>"
           + "<td align='right'>" + FMT.format(mpg) + "</td>"
           + "</tr>"
           );
    }

    // Generate footer

    out.println
       ( "</table>"
       + "</center>"
       + "</body>"
       + "</html>"
       );
    }
}
```

Nestled among the import statements at the beginning of the program are these two statements:

```
import javax.servlet.*;
import javax.servlet.http.*;
```

These statements inform the compiler that we will be using classes from the general and HTTP-specific servlet packages. import statements are not strictly required, but they make it possible to refer to classes without specifying their fully qualified names.

Next, the class declaration:

```
public class K2MServlet extends HttpServlet
```

A servlet is required at a minimum to implement the javax.servlet.Servlet interface. To simplify servlet writing, the servlet API provides a basic implementation of this interface called GenericServlet. It also supplies an HTTP-specific subclass HttpServlet, which is the base class most commonly used for servlets.

```
public void doGet(
    HttpServletRequest request,
    HttpServletResponse response)
  throws ServletException, IOException
```

Our servlet has no special requirement for startup or termination actions, so it only overrides one method—doGet(). This will be invoked from the HttpServlet superclass service() method if the request method is GET.

```
response.setContentType("text/html");
```

Before writing any results back to the client, we need to specify any HTTP headers we want to send. In our case, the only one is Content-Type, which we set to text/html.

```
PrintWriter out = response.getWriter();
```

Creating an HTML page consists of writing HTML statements to an output stream associated with the HTTP request. This output stream can be obtained from the response object using either its getOutputStream() or getWriter() methods, depending on whether a binary stream or character output is to be written, respectively. It is important to note that a servlet must choose one or the other of these methods; it cannot call both. Because we're writing ordinary HTML, we'll use getWriter() to obtain a character writer.

All that remains is to print the text of our HTML table. The header and footer are generated simply by writing strings of HTML to the output writer. We calculate and print the table rows in a loop over the desired range. In each iteration of the loop, we calculate the miles per gallon equivalent of kilometers per liter by multiplying by a conversion factor.[1]

```
for (double kmpl = 5; kmpl <= 20; kmpl += 1.0) {
    double mpg = kmpl * CONVERSION_FACTOR;
    out.println
      ( "<tr>"
      + "<td align='right'>" + FMT.format(kmpl) + "</td>"
      + "<td align='right'>" + FMT.format(mpg) + "</td>"
      + "</tr>"
      );
}
```

To run the servlet, we first need to compile it. For this to be successful, the classes in the servlet API must be in the compiler's classpath. These classes are typically found in a JAR file distributed with the servlet container. In Tomcat 4, for example, this is `servlet.jar` in the `$CATALINA_HOME/common/lib` directory. The official JAR file can also be downloaded from `http://java.sun.com/products/servlet/download.html`.

Next, depending on the servlet container, it might be necessary to describe the servlet in the Web application deployment descriptor `/WEB-INF/web.xml`. For a simple servlet, this might consist only of a `<servlet>` tag with its child `<servlet-name>` and `<servlet-class>` elements. In this case, the entry looks like this:

```
<?xml version="1.0" ?>
<web-app>
    ...
    <servlet>
        <servlet-name>K2M</servlet-name>
        <servlet-class>com.jspcr.servlets.K2MServlet</servlet-class>
    </servlet>
    ...
</web-app>
```

Note   *<servlet> entries in web.xml must be coded in a specific order with respect to other elements. See Chapter 17 for details or examine the web-app_2.3.DTD.*

---

[1]   The conversion factor was calculated from tables published by the U. S. National Institute of Standards, NIST Handbook 44, Appendix C. (See http://ts.nist.gov/ts/htdocs/230/235/appxc/appxc.htm)

It is also possible to specify a mapping of URIs to servlets with the `<servlet-mapping>` element in `web.xml`. In most cases, modifying the `web.xml` file requires either the Web application or the servlet container to be restarted before any changes take effect.

Finally, the servlet can be invoked using a URL of this form:

```
http://<servername>/<webappname>/servlet/<servletname>
```

The results can be seen in Figure 3-1.

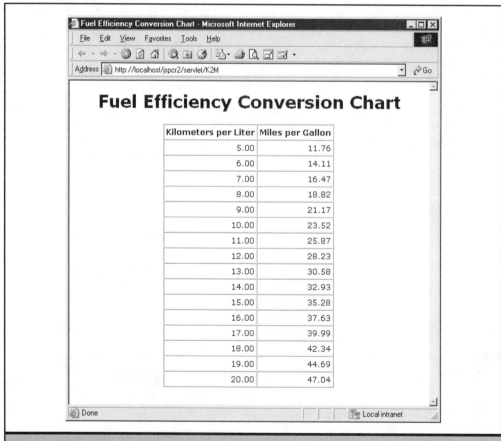

Figure 3-1. *Kilometers per liter to miles per gallon output*

Servlet Classes

This section outlines several important classes from the `javax.servlet` and `javax.servlet.http` packages. Since this is an introductory chapter, only the more commonly used classes and methods are described. Full details can be found in either the Servlet specification or the JavaDoc. The latter can be browsed online at `http://java.sun.com/products/servlet/2.3/javadoc/index.html`.

Servlet

The basic servlet abstraction is the `javax.servlet.Servlet` interface, shown in Table 3-1. It prescribes the set of methods that must be implemented by a servlet class for it to be recognized and managed by a servlet container. Its primary purpose is to supply the lifecycle methods `init()`, `service()`, and `destroy()`.

The servlet API provides a concrete implementation of the `Servlet` interface named `GenericServlet`, described in Table 3-2. This class supplies default

Method	Description
`void init(ServletConfig config) throws ServletException`	Called once by the servlet container after a servlet is loaded, just before it's placed into service. If `init()` throws an `UnavailableException`, the servlet is then taken out of service. A servlet should provide some way to store the `config` object to implement the `getServletConfig()` method (see `GenericServlet`).
`ServletConfig getServletConfig()`	Returns the `ServletConfig` object passed to the servlet's `init()` method.
`void service(ServletRequest request, ServletResponse response) throws ServletException, IOException`	Handles the request described in the `request` object, using the `response` object to return its results to the requester.
`String getServletInfo()`	Returns a string that can describe the servlet. Intended for use by administrative tools that need to provide a human-readable description.
`void destroy()`	Called by the servlet container when the servlet is about to be unloaded.

Table 3-1.   *Methods in the `servlet` Interface*

Method	Description
`void destroy()`	Writes a log entry consisting of the word "`destroy`".
`String getInitParameter (String name)`	Returns the value of the initialization parameter with the specified name. Does so by calling `config.getInitParameter(name)`.
`Enumeration getInitParameterNames()`	Returns an `Enumeration` of all the initialization parameters coded for this servlet, calling `config.getInitParameterNames()` to obtain the list. If no initialization parameters were supplied, returns an empty `Enumeration` (not null).
`ServletConfig getServletConfig()`	Returns the `ServletConfig` object that was passed to the `init()` method.
`ServletContext getServletContext()`	Returns the `ServletContext` referred to in the `config` object.
`String getServletInfo()`	Returns an empty string ("").
`void init(ServletConfig config) throws ServletException`	Stores the `config` object in an instance variable, writes a log entry consisting of the word "init", and then calls the convenience method `init()`.
`void init() throws ServletException`	Can be overridden to handle servlet initialization. Automatically called at the end of `init(ServletConfig config)`, after the `config` object has been stored. A concession to servlet authors who, like me, always forget to call `super.init(config)`.
`void log(String msg)`	Writes an entry to the servlet log, invoking the servlet context's `log()` method to do so. The servlet's name is added to the beginning of the message text.
`void log(String msg, Throwable t)`	Writes an entry and a stack trace to the servlet log. This method is also a pass-through to the corresponding method in `ServletContext`.
`abstract void service(Request request, Response response) throws ServletException, IOException`	Called by the servlet container to service the request described by the request object. This is the only abstract method in `GenericServlet`, hence, it's the only one that must be overridden by subclasses.
`String getServletName()`	Returns the servlet name as specified in the Web application deployment descriptor (`web.xml`).

Table 3-2.   *Methods in the `GenericServlet` interface*

implementations of all the interface methods except service(). This means you can write a basic servlet simply by extending GenericServlet and writing a custom service() method.

In addition to the Servlet interface, GenericServlet also implements ServletConfig, which handles initialization parameters and the servlet context, providing convenience methods that delegate to the ServletConfig object that was passed to init().

Although the servlet API allows for expansion to other protocols, the current version supports only protocol-independent servlets[2] and HTTP servlets. Because virtually all servlets operate in the Web server environment, few servlets extend GenericServlet directly. It's more common for servlets to extend its HTTP-specific subclass HttpServlet, described in Table 3-3. See Chapter 2 for an introduction to HTTP.

HttpServlet implements service() by calling methods specific to the HTTP request method. That is, for DELETE, HEAD, GET, OPTIONS, POST, PUT, and TRACE, it calls doDelete(), doHead(), doGet(), doOptions(), doPost(), doPut(), and doTrace(), respectively. It also casts the request and response objects used by these methods into their HTTP-specific subclasses, described later in this section.

Method	Description
void doGet(HttpServletRequest request, HttpServletResponse response) throws ServletException, IOException	Called by the servlet container to process an HTTP GET request. Input parameters, HTTP headers, and the input stream (if any) can be obtained from the request object, and response headers and the output stream from the response object.
void doPost(HttpServletRequest request, HttpServletResponse response) throws ServletException, IOException	Called by the servlet container to process an HTTP POST request. No different from doGet() from the standpoint of obtaining parameters and input data or returning the response.
void doPut(HttpServletRequest request, HttpServletResponse response) throws ServletException, IOException	Called by the servlet container to process an HTTP PUT request. The request URI in this case indicates the destination of the file being uploaded.

Table 3-3. *Methods in the HttpServlet Class*

---

[2] What might a protocol-independent servlet be? Perhaps one that doesn't service requests at all, but simply launches background threads from its init() method and kills them in destroy(). This could be used to emulate Windows NT services or Unix daemon processes.

Method	Description
void doDelete(HttpServletRequest request, HttpServletResponse response) throws ServletException, IOException	Called by the servlet container to process an HTTP DELETE request. The request URI indicates the resource to be deleted.
void doOptions(HttpServletRequest request, HttpServletResponse response) throws ServletException, IOException	Called by the servlet container to process an HTTP OPTIONS request. Returns an Allow response header indicating the HTTP methods supported by this servlet. It's unlikely that a servlet will need to override this method because the HttpServlet method already implements the functionality required by the HTTP specification.
void doTrace(HttpServletRequest request, HttpServletResponse response) throws ServletException, IOException	Called by the servlet container to process an HTTP TRACE request. Causes the request headers to be echoed as response headers. It's unlikely that a servlet will need to override this method because the HttpServlet method already implements the functionality required by the HTTP specification.
void service(HttpServletRequest request, HttpServletResponse response) throws ServletException, IOException	An intermediate method called by service(Request request, Response response) with HTTP-specific request and response objects. This is the method that actually directs the request to doGet(), doPost(), and so forth. It shouldn't be necessary to override this method.
void service(Request request, Response response) throws ServletException, IOException	Casts the request and response objects to their HTTP-specific subclasses and invokes the HTTP-specific service() method.

Table 3-3. *Methods in the HttpServlet Class* (continued)

Note *The methods that handle GET, POST, PUT, and DELETE by default return an error indicating the requested method is not supported, so a servlet explicitly needs to override the methods it supports.*

Servlet Request

The `ServletRequest` interface encapsulates the details of the client request. A generic version exists that is protocol-independent and a subinterface exists that is HTTP-specific.

Generic Request

The protocol-independent version shown in Table 3-4 has methods for

- Finding the host name and IP address of the client.
- Retrieving request parameters.
- Getting and setting attributes.
- Getting the input and output streams.

Method	Description
Object getAttribute (String name)	Returns the request attribute with the specified name, or null if it doesn't exist. Attributes can be those set by the servlet container or those explicitly added with setAttribute(). The latter method is useful in connection with a RequestDispatcher object.
Enumeration getAttributeNames()	Returns an Enumeration of the names of all attributes in this request. Returns an empty Enumeration if no attributes exist.
String getCharacterEncoding()	Returns the character encoding used by this request.
void setCharacterEncoding (String enc)	Overrides the request's character encoding.
int getContentLength()	Specifies the length of the input stream, if any. If not known, returns -1.
String getContentType()	Returns the MIME type of the request body (if there is one). This indicates whether the input stream is text, images, form data, or something else. This provides a clue to the programmer concerning whether to read it with an InputStream or an InputReader.
ServletInputStream getInputStream() throws IOException	Returns the (binary) input stream associated with this request, if any. Either getInputStream() or getReader() may be called, but not both.

Table 3-4. *Methods in the* `ServletRequest` *Class*

Method	Description
String getParameter (String name)	Returns the specified input parameter, or null, if it doesn't exist.
Enumeration getParameterNames()	Returns a possibly empty Enumeration of the names of all parameters in this request.
String[] getParameterValues (String name)	Returns an array of values for the specified input parameter name, or null, if no values exist. Useful in the case of parameters that can have multiple values (the HTTP checkbox element, for example).
String getProtocol()	Returns the name and version of the protocol used by this request.
String getScheme()	Returns the substring of the request URL up to, but not including, the first colon (http, for example).
String getServerName()	Returns the host name of the server processing the request.
int getServerPort()	Returns the port number on which the receiving host is listening.
BufferedReader getReader() throws IOException	Returns a character reader for input data associated with this request. Either this method or getInputStream() may be called, but not both.
String getRemoteAddr()	Returns the numeric IP address of the client host.
String getRemoteHost()	Returns the name of the client host, if known.
void setAttribute (String name, Object obj)	Stores a reference to the specified object in the request under the specified name.
void remoteAttribute (String name)	Removes the specified attribute from the request.
Locale getLocale()	Returns the client's preferred locale, if known, else null.
Enumeration getLocales()	Returns an Enumeration of the client's preferred locales, if known; otherwise, returns the server's preferred locale.
boolean isSecure()	Returns true if the request was made using a secure channel, such as HTTPS.
RequestDispatcher getRequestDispatcher (String name)	Returns a RequestDispatcher object for the specified resource name. See Chapter 7 for details about request dispatching.

Table 3-4.   *Methods in the ServletRequest Class* (continued)

HTTP-specific request

The `HttpServletRequest` subinterface in Table 3-5 adds methods to handle

- Reading and writing HTTP headers
- Getting and setting cookies
- Getting path information
- Identifying the HTTP session, if any

Method	Description
`String getAuthType()`	If the servlet is protected by an authentication scheme, such as HTTP Basic Authentication, returns the name of the scheme.
`String getContextPath()`	Returns the prefix of the URI that designates the servlet context (Web application).
`Cookie[] getCookies()`	Returns an array of the cookies associated with this request.
`long getDateHeader (String name)`	A convenience version of `getHeader()` that converts its output to a `long` value suitable for constructing a `Date` object.
`String getHeader(String name)`	Returns the value of the specified HTTP header, if it was supplied with this request. The name is case-insensitive.
`Enumeration getHeaderNames()`	Returns an Enumeration of the names of all HTTP headers supplied with this request.
`Enumeration getHeaders (String name)`	Returns an Enumeration of the values of all HTTP headers of the specified type supplied with this request. Useful for headers that can have multiple values.
`int getIntHeader(String name)`	A convenience version of `getHeader()` that converts its output to an `int` value.
`String getMethod()`	Returns the HTTP request method (for example, `GET`, `POST`, and so forth).

Table 3-5.   *Methods in the `HttpServletRequest` Interface*

Method	Description
`String getPathInfo()`	Returns any additional path information specified in the URL.
`String getPathTranslated()`	Returns any additional path information specified in the URL, translated into a real path.
`String getQueryString()`	Returns the query string—that portion of the URL following the "?", if any.
`String getRemoteUser()`	Returns the name of the remote user, if the user has been authenticated, else `null`.
`String getRequestedSessionId()`	Returns the session ID returned by the client.
`String getRequestURI()`	Returns the portion of the URL beginning with "/" and the context, up to, but not including, any query string.
`String getServletPath()`	Returns the substring of the request URI that follows the context.
`HttpSession getSession()`	Convenience method that calls `getSession(true)`.
`HttpSession getSession (boolean create)`	Returns the current HTTP session, creating a new one if one doesn't exist and the `create` parameter is `true`.
`Principal getPrincipal()`	Returns a `java.security.Principal` object representing the current user if the user has been authenticated, else `null`.
`boolean isRequestedSessionIdFromCookie()`	Returns `true` if the requested session ID was supplied by a Cookie object, `false` otherwise.
`boolean isRequestedSessionIdFromURL()`	Returns `true` if the requested session ID was encoded in the request URL, `false` otherwise.
`boolean isRequestedSessionIdValid()`	Returns `true` if the session ID returned by the client is still valid.
`boolean isUserInRole(String role)`	Returns `true` if the currently authenticated user is associated with the specified role. Returns `false` if not, or if the user isn't authenticated.

Table 3-5.   *Methods in the `HttpServletRequest` Interface* (continued)

Servlet Response

The function of the *servlet response* object is to convey results generated by a servlet back to the client that made the request. A ServletResponse operates mainly as a wrapper for an output stream, as well as information about its content type and length. It's created by the servlet container and passed to the servlet as the second parameter of the service() method.

Generic response

Like the servlet request, the servlet response has both a generic protocol-independent interface and an HTTP-specific one. Table 3-6 describes the methods available in the generic version.

HTTP-specific response

The HTTP-specific subinterface HttpServletResponse adds methods for manipulating the status code, status message, and response headers. This allows the response, for example, to be used to send cookies or to redirect the user to another URL. It also provides for encoding the HTTP session ID in URLs written to a Web page. Table 3-7 describes the methods in HttpServletResponse.

Besides additional methods, HttpServletResponse also defines integer constants for each possible HTTP response code.

Servlet Context

A *servlet context* is a very useful interface supplied by the servlet container to provide services to a Web application. The servlets in the Web application can use the servlet context to get

- The capability to store and retrieve attributes between invocations, and to share these attributes with other servlets.

- The capability to read the contents of files and other static resources in the Web application.

- A means to dispatch requests to each other.

- A facility for logging errors and informational messages.

The servlet context has a name (the name of the Web application it belongs to), which is uniquely mapped to a directory in the file system.

A servlet can get a reference to the servlet context by invoking the getServletContext() method on the ServletConfig object that was passed to

Method	Description
`void flushBuffer()` `throws IOException`	Sends the contents of the output buffer to the client. Because HTTP requires headers to be sent before content, calling this method sends the status line and response headers, committing the request.
`int getBufferSize()`	Returns the buffer size used by the response, or 0 if buffering isn't in effect.
`String getCharacterEncoding()`	Returns the name of the character encoding used for the response. Unless explicitly set otherwise, this corresponds to ISO-8859-1.
`Locale getLocale()`	Returns the locale used for the response. Unless modified with `setLocale()`, this defaults to the server's locale.
`OutputStream getOutputStream()` `throws IOException`	Returns a stream that can be used to write binary output to be returned to the client. Either this method or `getWriter()` can be called, but not both.
`Writer getWriter()` `throws IOException`	Returns a character writer that can be used to write text output to be returned to the client. Either this method or `getOutputStream()` can be called, but not both.
`boolean isCommitted()`	Returns `true` if the status and response headers have already been sent back to the client. Setting headers in the response after it's committed has no effect.
`void reset()`	Clears the output buffer as well as any response headers. Causes an `IllegalStateException` if the response has already been committed.
`void setBufferSize` `(int nBytes)`	Sets the minimum buffer size for the response. The actual buffer size may be larger and can be obtained by a call to `getBufferSize()`. If any output has already been written, this method throws an `IllegalStateException`.
`void setContentLength` `(int length)`	Sets the length of the content body.
`void setContentType` `(String type)`	Sets the content type. In HTTP servlets, this sets the `Content-Type` header.
`void setLocale` `(Locale locale)`	Sets the locale to be used in the response. In HTTP servlets, this may affect the `Content-Type` header value.

Table 3-6.   *Methods in the* `ServletResponse` *Interface*

Method	Description
`void flushBuffer() throws IOException`	Sends the contents of the output buffer to the client. Because HTTP requires headers to be sent before content, calling this method sends the status line and response headers, committing the request.
`int getBufferSize()`	Returns the buffer size used by the response, or 0 if buffering isn't in effect.
`String getCharacterEncoding()`	Returns the name of the character encoding used for the response. Unless explicitly set otherwise, this corresponds to ISO-8859-1.
`Locale getLocale()`	Returns the locale used for the response. Unless modified with `setLocale()`, this defaults to the server's locale.
`OutputStream getOutputStream() throws IOException`	Returns a stream that can be used to write binary output to be returned to the client. Either this method or `getWriter()` can be called, but not both.
`Writer getWriter() throws IOException`	Returns a character writer that can be used to write text output to be returned to the client. Either this method or `getOutputStream()` can be called, but not both.
`boolean isCommitted()`	Returns `true` if the status and response headers have already been sent back to the client. Setting headers in the response after it's committed has no effect.
`void reset()`	Clears the output buffer as well as any response headers. Causes an `IllegalStateException` if the response has already been committed.
`void resetBuffer()`	Clears the output data in the response buffer, but not the HTTP headers or status code.
`void setBufferSize (int nBytes)`	Sets the minimum buffer size for the response. The actual buffer size may be larger and can be obtained by a call to `getBufferSize()`. If any output has already been written, this method throws an `IllegalStateException`.
`void setContentLength (int length)`	Sets the length of the content body.
`void setContentType (String type)`	Sets the content type. In HTTP servlets, this sets the `Content-Type` header.
`void setLocale (Locale locale)`	Sets the locale to be used in the response. In HTTP servlets, this may affect the `Content-Type` header value.

Table 3-7. *Methods in the* `HttpServletResponse` *Interface*

init(). If the servlet subclasses GenericServlet directly or indirectly, it can use the inherited convenience method getServletContext().[3]

Table 3-8 outlines the methods provided by ServletContext.

Method	Description
Object getAttribute (String name) void setAttribute (String name, Object obj)	Returns the object bound to the specified name in the servlet context or binds an object using the specified name. Such objects are global, from the standpoint of the Web application, because they can be accessed by the same servlet at another time or by any other servlet in the context.
Enumeration getAttributeNames()	Returns an Enumeration of the names of all attributes stored in the servlet context.
ServletContext getContext (String uripath)	Returns the servlet context that is mapped to another URI on the same server. The URI must be an absolute path beginning with "/".
String getInitParameter (String name)	Returns the value of the specified context-wide initialization parameter. This isn't the same as the method of the same name in ServletConfig, which applies only to specific servlet for which it is coded. Instead, it's a parameter that applies to all servlets in the context.
Enumeration getInitParameterNames()	Returns a (possibly empty) Enumeration of the names of all the context-wide initialization parameters.
int getMajorVersion() int getMinorVersion()	Returns the major and minor version numbers of the level of the servlet API supported by this context.
String getMimeType(String fileName)	Returns the MIME type of the specified filename. Typically based on the file extension, rather than the contents of the file itself (which needn't necessarily exist). May return null if the MIME type is unknown.

Table 3-8. *Methods in the ServletContext Interface*

---

[3] JSP pages have it even easier - a reference to the servlet context is automatically stored in the implicit variable application.

Method	Description
RequestDispatcher getNamedDispatcher (String name) RequestDispatcher getRequestDispatcher (String path)	Returns a RequestDispatcher for the servlet or JSP page having the specified name or path, or null if the RequestDispatcher cannot be created. The path, if specified, must begin with "/" and be relative to the top of the servlet context.
String getRealPath(String path)	Given a URI, returns the absolute path in the file system the URI corresponds to, or null if the mapping cannot be made.
URL getResource(String path) InputStream getResourceAsStream (String path)	Returns a URL corresponding to the specified absolute path relative to the servlet context, or an input stream for reading that URL. Returns null if no such resource exists.
String getServerInfo()	Returns the name and version number of the servlet container.
void log(String message) void log(String message, Throwable t)	Writes a message to the servlet log, including a stack trace, if a Throwable parameter is supplied.
void removeAttribute (String name)	Removes the specified attribute from the servlet context.

Table 3-8.   *Methods in the* ServletContext *Interface* (continued)

Threading Models

To provide robust performance in a large-scale environment, servlets can be configured to run in several different threading environments. The term *threading model* refers to the strategy used by the servlet container in servicing requests simultaneously. The servlet specification provides for two threading models, which are discussed in this section.

Default Threading Model

By default, the servlet container loads only a single instance of a servlet. Requests serviced by the servlet are run in separate threads, but share the same instance. This enables applications to be responsive and scalable, since it requires fewer resources and uses them more efficiently.

However, since there is only a single instance, there is also only one set of instance variables. This fact has several implications, most notably that *instance variables are not thread safe.* For example, look at the following servlet:

```java
package com.jspcr.servlets;

import java.io.*;
import java.sql.*;
import java.util.*;
import javax.servlet.*;
import javax.servlet.http.*;

/**
 * Bad example.  Don't try this at home.
 */
public class ColliderServlet extends HttpServlet
{
    /**
     * The database connection - a BAD idea here
     * because it is a shared instance variable.
     */
    private Connection con;

    /**
     * Handles GET requests
     */
    public void doGet(
          HttpServletRequest request,
          HttpServletResponse response)
       throws ServletException, IOException
    {
       try {
          Class.forName("sun.jdbc.odbc.JdbcOdbcDriver");
          con = DriverManager.getConnection("jdbc:odbc:someDataSource");
          // ... run some lengthy database operation here
          con.close();
       }
       catch (Exception e) {
          throw new ServletException(e.getMessage());
       }
    }
}
```

Consider what happens when two requests arrive in separate threads a few hundred milliseconds apart. The first one opens the database connection and stores a reference to it in the con instance variable. It then uses the connection to perform a table update or some other database operation. Meanwhile, the second request arrives and opens another connection and stores a reference to it in the same con instance variable. If the first operation finishes and tries to do another database operation, it no longer has its original connection object—it only knows about the second one. Bad things then happen when it tries to use the second connection.

The same type of problem with instance variables can occur in servlets that call other methods from within their service method. If these other methods try to access the servlet request, response, or any object created in the service method that has been saved in an instance variable, there's no way to guarantee a request in another thread won't corrupt the variables by storing references to its own objects in them.[4]

The safest approach is simply not to use instance variables, only local variables defined inside the service method. While this differs from conventional programming, it should not be viewed as a deficiency in the servlet capabilities. Servlets are not, after all, general-purpose programs. They are specifically designed to run in a stateless request and response environment and allow the programmer to exploit that environment fully.

SingleThreadModel

Although the single instance multiple thread model is the default, a servlet can change this behavior by implementing SingleThreadModel. This interface, which has no methods, informs the servlet container that it should create a pool of instances and allocate each incoming request to its own instance and thread. This guarantees no two requests *handled by the same instance* will overlap in their execution of the service method. Thus, instance variables can only be affected by one request at a time, making them thread safe. Note, because multiple instances may exist, however, there's nothing to prevent them from executing concurrently in different threads. If they access external resources like files or database connections, therefore, they can still come into conflict.

Although SingleThreadModel is a supported option, my own view is that it should be avoided. There are very few situations in which SingleThreadModel solves a problem that couldn't be handled better by other means. More often, it seems to be used as a brute-force fix for a bad design.

HTTP Sessions

Although navigating through a Web page may seem like a conversation between client and server, in most cases, it isn't. Typically, a Web client requests an HTML document, which is located by the server and transmitted back to the client. If image links are in the HTML, the client (if it's a Web browser) will make additional requests to the server

---

[4]   This particular problem can be solved by using a private class (essentially a data structure) to hold all objects of interest, and then passing this class as a parameter to the subsidiary methods.

for each image. If the user clicks a hyperlink in the page, the client issues a new HTTP request for it, but all this happens one request at a time. Between each request, the server moves on to handle other requests, forgetting all about the first client. No back-and-forth exchange of commands and data occurs, only a request followed by a response and a disconnect.[5]

For basic downloading of static documents, this is adequate. However, applications like shopping carts or iterative search engines need to maintain active objects on the server that are associated with particular clients. It may take several requests to build these objects. In this case, a need exists to keep track of to which client the objects are bound.

Several approaches can be used to solve this problem. Most of them involve maintaining the object itself on the server, assigning it a unique key the client is asked to remember. In each subsequent related request, the client passes back the key, which enables the server to reestablish the context.

This is similar to booking an airline ticket over the telephone. The ticket agent asks the customer for her name, address, and flight information, entering all this into a data entry application that assigns a confirmation number, which is reported back to the customer. Later on, if the customer needs to call back and change anything, she supplies the confirmation number, which allows the ticket agent to access and update the original record.

Back to the Web application session problem. How can the client browser be induced to remember and supply the key when required? There are several possibilities:

- **Cookies**   The server can send a `Set-Cookie` header in its initial response, with the session ID as the value of the cookie.[6] On subsequent requests, the client can return the value with a Cookie header. However, individual users might choose to turn off their browser's cookie capability, so this technique isn't guaranteed to work.

- **Appending the session ID to the URL**   For hyperlinks in Web pages created by a dynamic process, the session ID can be encoded as a request parameter in the URL. This doesn't require cookies to be enabled, but it does require every clickable URL to be so encoded. If one is overlooked (an easy thing to do), the session link is lost.

---

[5]   HTTP 1.1 does provide a means for connections to persist for a few seconds, so that, for example, HTML and associated images located on the same server can be downloaded efficiently. This requires both the client and server to know about the capability and to request it explicitly. The request/response protocol itself, however, is the same.

[6]   Cookies are name/value pairs sent by a Web server that have a specified life span. Client browsers store cookies and return them automatically each time the browser requests a page from the same domain. More details about cookies can be found in RFC 2109 (see http://www.ietf.org/rfc/rfc2109.txt).

■ **Hidden fields**   If the application consists of a series of HTML forms using `submit` buttons for navigation, the session ID can be stored as a hidden field that is retrieved with `request.getParameter()`. Obviously, this only works if the forms are all dynamically generated.

The HttpSession Interface

The servlet API provides a convenient wrapper around these various techniques called an *HTTP Session*. A hashtable-like interface named `javax.servlet.http.HttpSession` has `setAttribute()` and `getAttribute()` methods that store and retrieve objects by name. Associating a name with an object is often referred to as *binding* the name to the attribute.

`HttpSession` provides a session ID key that a participating client stores and returns on subsequent requests in the same session. The servlet container looks up the appropriate session object and makes it available to the current request. Table 3-9 lists the methods available in `HttpSession`.

Method	Description
`Object getAttribute(String name)` `void setAttribute(String name, Object value) void removeAttribute (String name)`	Stores an object in the session under the specified name, or returns or removes an object by that name that was previously stored.
`Enumeration getAttributeNames()`	Returns an `Enumeration` of the names of all attributes currently bound to the session.
`long getCreationTime()` `long getLastAccessedTime()`	Returns a long integer representing the date and time at which the session was created or last accessed. The integer is in the form used by the `java.util.Date()` constructor.
`String getId()`	Returns the session ID, a unique key assigned by the servlet container.
`int getMaxInactiveInterval()` `void setMaxInactiveInterval (int seconds)`	Sets or returns the maximum number of seconds the session will be kept alive if no interaction occurs with the client.
`void invalidate()`	Causes the session to expire and unbinds any objects in it.
`boolean isNew()`	Returns `true` if the client hasn't yet joined the session. This is true when the session is first created and the session ID is passed to the client, but the client hasn't made a second request that includes the session ID.

Table 3-9.   *Methods in the `HttpSession` Interface*

The API also provides an HttpSessionBindingListener interface. Objects that implement this interface must provide valueBound() and valueUnbound() methods, which get invoked when the objects are added to or removed from an HttpSession.

Summary

Java servlets are extensions to a Web server that allow Web content to be created dynamically in response to a client request. They are managed by a servlet container, which loads and initializes them, passes them a number of requests for servicing, and then unloads them. Servlets have key advantages over other server-side programming environments:

- Better performance because they remain resident and can run in multiple threads simultaneously
- Simplicity because they require no client software installation other than a Web browser
- Session tracking
- Access to Java technology, including threading, networking, and database connectivity

Servlets operate in a fixed lifecycle, providing callback methods to a servlet container for being initialized, handling requests, and terminating. The API provides two threading models: the default being a single instance running multiple threads, and the alternative single threaded model.

The principal classes and interfaces in the servlet API are

- The Servlet interface, which prescribes the callback methods that must be implemented.
- GenericServlet, a base class that implements the Servlet interface methods.
- HttpServlet, an HTTP-specific subclass of GenericServlet.
- ServletRequest, which encapsulates information about the client request.
- ServletResponse, which provides access to an output stream for results to be returned to the client.
- The ServletContext interface, which allows a group of servlets to interoperate with each other in a Web application.

Servlets are the underlying technology for JSP pages. Understanding them is vital to forming the mental model required to develop and debug in the JSP environment.

The Complete Reference

Chapter 4

JSP Overview

A *JavaServer page (JSP)* is a template for a Web page that uses Java code to generate an HTML document dynamically. JSPs are run in a server-side component known as a JSP container, which translates them into equivalent Java servlets. For this reason, servlets and JSP pages are intimately related. What's possible in one is, in large part, also possible in the other, although each technology has its individual strengths.

Because they are servlets, JSP pages have all the advantages of servlets:

- They have better performance and scalability than ordinary CGI scripts because they are persistent in memory and multithreaded.

- No special client setup is required.

- They have built-in support for HTTP sessions, which makes application programming possible.

- They have full access to Java technology—network awareness, threads, and database connectivity—without the limitations of client-side applets.

But, in addition, JSP pages have advantages of their own:

- They are automatically recompiled when necessary.

- Because they exist in the ordinary Web server document space, no special URL mapping is required to address them.

- Because JSP pages are HTML-like, they have greater compatibility with Web development tools.

This chapter provides an overview of JSP as a server-side scripting environment. It describes the JSP container operations and walks through a complete example. Only the basics are covered here; the four chapters of Part II consider JSP pages in-depth.

How JSP Works

A JSP page exists in three forms or versions, as illustrated in Figure 4-1.

- **JSP source code**   This is the version the developer actually writes. It consists of a text file with an extension of `.jsp`, and contains a mix of HTML template code, Java language statements, and JSP directives and actions that describe how to generate a Web page to service a particular request.

- **Java source code**   The JSP container translates the JSP source code into the source code for an equivalent Java servlet as needed. This source code is typically saved in a work area and is often helpful for debugging.

- **Compiled Java class**   Like any other Java class, the generated servlet code is compiled into byte codes in a `.class` file, ready to be loaded and executed.

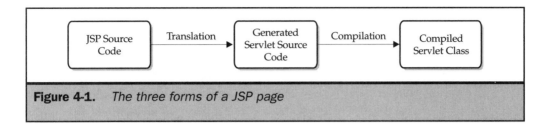

Figure 4-1. *The three forms of a JSP page*

The JSP container manages each of these forms of the JSP page automatically, based on the timestamps of each file. In response to an HTTP request, the container checks to see if the .jsp source file has been modified since the .java source was last compiled. If so, the container retranslates the JSP source into Java source and recompiles it.

Figure 4-2 illustrates the process used by the JSP container. When a request for a JSP page is made, the container first determines the name of the class corresponding to the .jsp file. If the class doesn't exist or if it's older than the .jsp file (meaning the JSP source has changed since it was last compiled), then the container creates Java source code for an equivalent servlet and compiles it. If an instance of the servlet isn't already running (or if the servlet was newly generated), the container loads the servlet class and creates an instance. Finally, the container dispatches a thread to handle the current HTTP request in the loaded instance.

A Basic Example

To illustrate how JSP works, let's look at the same example used in the preceding chapter—converting kilometers per liter to miles per gallon. Here's the JSP page:

```
<%@ page session="false" %>
<%@ page import="java.io.*" %>
<%@ page import="java.text.*" %>
<%@ page import="java.util.*" %>


<%-- Prints a conversion table of miles per gallon
     to kilometers per liter --%>

<%!
   private static final DecimalFormat FMT
      = new DecimalFormat("#0.00");
   private static final double CONVERSION_FACTOR = 2.352145;
```

```
%>
<html>
<head>
<title>Fuel Efficiency Conversion Chart</title>
</head>
<body>
<center>
<h1>Fuel Efficiency Conversion Chart</h1>
<table border='1' cellpadding='3' cellspacing='0'>
<tr>
    <th>Kilometers per Liter</th>
    <th>Miles per Gallon</th>
</tr>
<%
    for (double kmpl = 5; kmpl <= 20; kmpl += 1.0) {
        double mpg = kmpl * CONVERSION_FACTOR;
%>
    <tr>
        <td align='right'><%= FMT.format(kmpl) %></td>
        <td align='right'><%= FMT.format(mpg) %></td>
    </tr>
<% } %>
</table>
</center>
</body>
</html>
```

Comparing this to the K2MServlet from Chapter 3, first note the JSP is shorter—38 lines versus 77 lines for the servlet. In addition, it looks more like a Web page. Much of the HTML is recognizable as ordinary HTML. Also, to the Java programmer, it's apparent that there is a loop of some kind that produces the individual rows of the table. Finally, sets of special characters appear to mark the boundaries between Java code and HTML template data. Don't worry if you don't understand what they are— we'll cover that fully in Chapters 5 and 6.

If you invoke this JSP page from a Web browser, you see the table shown in Figure 4-3, which, not surprisingly, is the same as what the Chapter 3 servlet produced.

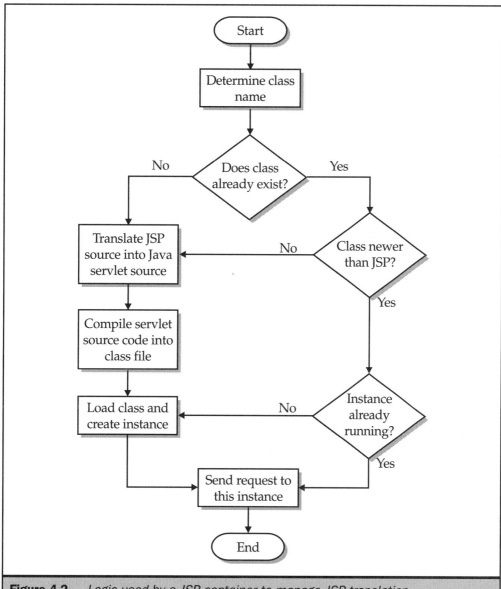

Figure 4-2. *Logic used by a JSP container to manage JSP translation*

To make the JSP-to-servlet relationship clearer, look at the `.java` source code generated by the JSP container. This code will differ greatly, depending on which container is used and the implementation approach it takes. The code listed here is what was generated by Tomcat 4 (reformatted slightly for readability):

```java
package org.apache.jsp;

import java.io.*;
import java.text.*;
import java.util.*;
import javax.servlet.*;
import javax.servlet.http.*;
import javax.servlet.jsp.*;
import org.apache.jasper.runtime.*;

public class K2M$jsp extends HttpJspBase
{
    private static final DecimalFormat FMT
        = new DecimalFormat("#0.00");
    private static final double CONVERSION_FACTOR = 2.352145;

    static {}

    public K2M$jsp( ) {}

    private static boolean _jspx_inited = false;

    public final void _jspx_init()
        throws org.apache.jasper.runtime.JspException {}

    public void _jspService(
            HttpServletRequest request,
            HttpServletResponse response)
        throws java.io.IOException, ServletException
    {
        JspFactory _jspxFactory = null;
        PageContext pageContext = null;
        ServletContext application = null;
        ServletConfig config = null;
        JspWriter out = null;
        Object page = this;
        String _value = null;
        try {
```

```java
      if (_jspx_inited == false) {
         synchronized (this) {
            if (_jspx_inited == false) {
               _jspx_init();
               _jspx_inited = true;
            }
         }
      }
      _jspxFactory = JspFactory.getDefaultFactory();
      response.setContentType
         ("text/html;charset=ISO-8859-1");
      pageContext = _jspxFactory.getPageContext
         (this, request, response, "", false, 8192, true);

      application = pageContext.getServletContext();
      config = pageContext.getServletConfig();
      out = pageContext.getOut();
      out.write("\r\n");
      out.write("\r\n");
      out.write("\r\n");
      out.write("\r\n\r\n");
      out.write("\r\n\r\n");
      out.write("\r\n<html>\r\n<head>\r\n<title>Fuel "
         + "Efficiency Conversion Chart</title>\r\n</head>"
         + "\r\n<body>\r\n<center>\r\n<h1>Fuel Efficiency "
         + "Conversion Chart</h1>\r\n<table border='1' "
         + "cellpadding='3' cellspacing='0'>\r\n<tr>"
         + "\r\n    <th>Kilometers per Liter</th>"
         + "\r\n    <th>Miles per Gallon</th>\r\n</tr>\r\n");

   for (double kmpl = 5; kmpl <= 20; kmpl += 1.0) {
      double mpg = kmpl * CONVERSION_FACTOR;
      out.write("\r\n    <tr>\r\n       <td align='right'>");
      out.print( FMT.format(kmpl) );
      out.write("</td>\r\n       <td align='right'>");
      out.print( FMT.format(mpg) );
      out.write("</td>\r\n    </tr>\r\n");
   }
   out.write("\r\n</table>\r\n</center>\r\n</body>"
      + "\r\n</html>\r\n");
}
catch (Throwable t) {
   if (out != null && out.getBufferSize() != 0)
```

```
                    out.clearBuffer();
            if (pageContext != null)
                pageContext.handlePageException(t);
        }
        finally {
            if (_jspxFactory != null)
                _jspxFactory.releasePageContext(pageContext);
        }
    }
}
```

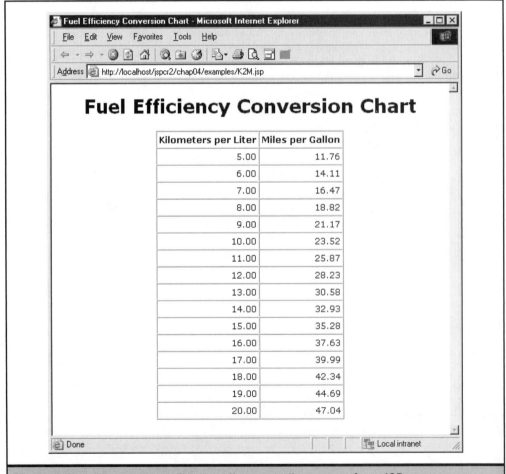

Figure 4-3.   *Kilometers per liter to miles per gallon output from JSP page*

A bit mechanical, as if it were generated by a computer program (which, of course, it was), but still recognizable as a servlet, especially the middle part, which differs little from the K2MServlet source code in Chapter 3.

As you will see, building a mental model of this process is the key to successful JSP development and debugging. With this backdrop, let's proceed to Part II and explore the elements of JSP more deeply.

The Complete Reference

Part II

Elements of JSP

The Complete Reference

Chapter 5

JSP Syntax and Semantics

The purpose of this chapter is to give an overview of the basic components used in JavaServer Pages, to describe how they are written, and to explain what they do. This chapter reviews the JSP development model and then introduces each JSP element and considers how the element is used in this overall design. The chapter concludes with an annotated example that illustrates the use of each element. In covering this material, our concern is with the following:

- **Syntax** The coding structure used to represent the element so that the JSP compiler recognizes it

- **Semantics** The meaning of the element to the JSP container—what happens when it is used

Each of the JSP elements described in this chapter is covered in greater detail in the remaining chapters of Part II.

The JSP Development Model

Recall from Chapter 4 that a JSP page exists in three forms:

1. The `.jsp` source file containing HTML statements and JSP elements
2. The Java source code for a servlet program
3. The compiled Java class

To understand how JSP elements operate, it is important to build a mental model of how these three objects are created and the relationship among them. First, the JSP developer writes a `.jsp` source file and stores it somewhere in the document file system of a Web server or Web application. In this respect, the `.jsp` source file is no different from an ordinary HTML file. The URL by which it is known to the network is the same, except its filename ends in `.jsp` instead of `.html`.

Next, when the `.jsp` URL is invoked for the first time, the JSP container reads the `.jsp` file, parses its contents, and generates the source code for an equivalent Java servlet. It then compiles the servlet and creates a `.class` file.

Finally, the JSP container loads the servlet class and uses it to service the HTTP request. The middle step (generating the servlet source code) is repeated for later requests only if the `.jsp` file has been modified.

In this design, JSP elements can affect how the JSP container operates during two operational phases:

- **Translation time** Generating the Java servlet source code from a `.jsp` file
- **Request time** Invoking the servlet to handle an HTTP request

Keeping this model in mind will help you understand the syntactical units of a JSP page and what their capabilities are.

Components of a JSP Page

A `.jsp` file can contain JSP elements, fixed template data, or any combination of the two. JSP elements are instructions to the JSP container about what code to generate and how it should operate. These elements have specific start and end tags that identify them to the JSP compiler. Template data is everything else that is not recognized by the JSP container. Template data (usually HTML) is passed through unmodified, so the HTML that is ultimately generated contains the template data exactly as it was coded in the `.jsp` file.

There are three types of JSP elements:

- Directives
- Scripting elements, including expressions, scriptlets, and declarations
- Actions

Let's consider each of these elements in more detail.

Directives

Directives are instructions to the JSP container that describe what code should be generated. They have the general form

> *<%@ directive-name [attribute="value" attribute="value" ...] %>*

Zero or more spaces, tabs, and newline characters can appear after the opening <%@ and before the ending %>, and one or more whitespace characters can appear after the directive name and between attributes/value pairs. The only restriction is that the opening <%@ tag must be in the same physical file as the ending %> tag.

The JSP 1.2 specification describes three standard directives available in all compliant JSP environments:

- page
- include
- taglib

Although the specification declares that no custom directives can be used in the JSP 1.2 environment, this leaves open the possibility that user-defined directives may be included in a later specification.

The next three sections provide an overview of each of these directives.

The page Directive

The *page directive* is used to specify attributes for the JSP page as a whole. It has the following syntax:

> *<%@ page [attribute="value" attribute="value" ...] %>*

where the attributes are any of those listed in Table 5-1.

Attribute	Value
language	The language used in scriptlets, expressions, and declarations. In JSP 1.2, the only valid value for this attribute is java.
extends	The fully qualified name of the superclass of this JSP page. This must be a class that implements the HttpJspPage interface. The JSP specification warns against the use of this attribute without fully understanding its implications.
import	A comma-separated list of one or more *package.** names and/or fully qualified class names. This list is used to create corresponding import statements in the generated Java servlet. The following packages are automatically included and need not be specified: java.lang.* java.servlet.* java.servlet.jsp.* java.servlet.http.*
session	*true* or *false,* indicating whether the JSP page requires an HTTP session. If the value is true, then the generated servlet will contain code that causes an HTTP session to be created (or accessed, if it already exists). The default value is *true.*
buffer	Specifies the size of the output buffer. Valid entries are *nnn*kb or none, where *nnn* is the number of kilobytes allocated for the buffer. The default value is 8kb.
autoFlush	*true* if the buffer should be automatically flushed when it is full, or *false* if a buffer overflow exception should be thrown. The default value is *true.*
isThreadSafe	*true* if the page can handle simultaneous requests from multiple threads, or *false* if it cannot. If *false,* the generated servlet declares that it implements the SingleThreadModel interface.
info	A string that will be returned by the page's getServletInfo() method.

Table 5-1. *Attributes of the Page Directive*

Attribute	Value
isErrorPage	*true* if this page is intended to be used as another JSP's error page. In that case, this page can be specified as the value of the errorPage attribute in the other page's page directive. Specifying *true* for this attribute makes the *exception* implicit variable available to this page. The default value is *false.*
errorPage	Specifies the URL of another JSP page that will be invoked to handle any uncaught exceptions. The other JSP page must specify isErrorPage="true" in its page directive.
contentType	Specifies the MIME type and, optionally, the character encoding to be used in the generated servlet.
pageEncoding	Specifies the character encoding for the JSP page itself.

Table 5-1.   *Attributes of the Page Directive* (continued)

More than one page directive can be in a file and the attributes specified collectively apply to the whole file, but no attribute can be specified more than once, with the exception of the import attribute.

Let's consider each of these attributes in a little more detail.

language   The JSP architecture allows room for it to be extended as a general framework for server-side scripting. For this reason, it supports a language attribute in the page directive. The value specified (which is java by default) applies to all declarations, expressions, and scriptlets in the current translation unit, including any files specified in an include directive. All JSP 1.2–compliant containers must support the value java for the language attribute. No other language is supported in the JSP 1.2 specification, although individual JSP engines may do so.

Although the specification allows for other languages to be used, it imposes some restrictions. The language must support the Java Runtime Environment to the extent that it allows access to the standard implicit object variables, to JavaBeans get and set methods, and to public methods of Java classes.

Obviously, any JSP pages written in a language not explicitly required by the JSP specification most likely won't be portable between JSP containers of different vendors.

extends   Ordinarily, the JSP container supplies the parent class for any servlet it generates from a JSP page. However, the specification allows you to subclass a different parent class. You do this by specifying its fully qualified name in the extends attribute of the page directive. This lets you provide additional behavior to a family of JSP pages without explicitly coding the behavior in the page.

The JSP specification urges caution when using this capability because it may prevent the JSP container from providing vendor-specific performance and reliability enhancements. For example, the standard JSP parent class used by JRun provides methods for determining dependencies and their last modification times. Similarly, Tomcat implements a parent class that stores a reference to a specialized class loader. If you use a different parent class, it ought to provide important functionality that outweighs these features.

For a class to be used as the superclass for JSP pages, it must implement one of the following interfaces:

- `javax.servlet.jsp.JspPage` A generic interface, not necessarily for use with HTTP. Few servlets implement this interface directly.

- `javax.servlet.jsp.HttpJspPage` Intended for JSP pages that operate under the HTTP protocol, this interface is an extension of `JspPage`.

These interfaces define three methods you must implement, which are described in Table 5-2.

Method	Description
`public void jspInit()`	Method called automatically from the servlet `init()` method when the JSP page is loaded. Although you must implement this method, your implementation needn't do anything. The method is designed as a placeholder to be overridden by JSP page subclasses for any initialization work they need to do.
`public void jspDestroy()`	The counterpart of `jspInit()`, this method is automatically called from the servlet's `destroy()` method when a JSP page class is unloaded.
`public void _jspService(request, response) throws ServletException, IOException`	This method is the heart of the JSP request processing logic. It must not be explicitly defined in the JSP page because it is the work of the JSP container to generate the method from the JSP's scriptlets, expressions, and directives. This method is typically declared to be `abstract` in the JSP parent class.

Table 5-2.   *Methods That Must Be Declared by JSP Superclasses*

The exact types of the request and response parameters in the `_jspService` method are dictated by the protocol they support. For the HTTP environment, these types are `javax.servlet.http.HttpServletRequest` and `javax.servlet.http.HttpServletResponse`. If you are implementing a different protocol, you need to define request and response classes to be used in the method signature.

`HttpJspPage` extends `JspPage` to provide HTTP-specific behavior. `JspPage`, in turn, extends `javax.servlet.Servlet`.

The JSP superclass must adhere to and implement the JSP protocol. This requires that:

- The `init()` method must call `jspInit()`.

- The `destroy()` method must call `jspDestroy()`.

- The `service()` method must cast its request and response parameters into their protocol-specific classes and invoke `_jspService()`.

This implementation can be direct, or the superclass can itself extend a class that provides the implementation, such as `javax.servlet.http.HttpServlet`.

Suitably warned and cautious, if you still want to proceed, here's a complete example. Suppose you have a family of JSP pages that all access a common database. If the JSP pages did not have to bother with loading the JDBC driver and establishing a database connection, this might simplify matters. The following servlet can both perform those functions and be used as the parent class of the family of JSP pages:

```
package com.jspcr.servlets;

import java.io.*;
import java.sql.*;
import javax.servlet.*;
import javax.servlet.http.*;
import javax.servlet.jsp.*;

/**
 * An example of a JSP superclass that can be selected with
 * the <code>extends</code> attribute of the page
 * directive.  This servlet automatically loads the
 * JDBC-ODBC driver class when initialized and establishes
 * a connection to the USDA nutrient database.
 */
public abstract class NutrientDatabaseServlet
    extends HttpServlet
    implements HttpJspPage
{
    protected Connection con;
```

```java
/**
 * Initialize a servlet with the driver
 * class already loaded and the database
 * connection established.
 */
public void init(ServletConfig config)
    throws ServletException
{
    super.init(config);
    try {
        Class.forName("sun.jdbc.odbc.JdbcOdbcDriver");
        con = DriverManager.getConnection("jdbc:odbc:usda");
    }
    catch (Exception e) {
        throw new UnavailableException(e.getMessage());
    }

    jspInit();
}

/**
 * Closes the database connection when
 * the servlet is unloaded.
 */
public void destroy()
{
    try {
        if (con != null) {
            con.close();
            con = null;
        }
    }
    catch (Exception ignore) {}

    jspDestroy();
    super.destroy();
}

/**
 * Called when the JSP is loaded.
 * By default does nothing.
 */
public void jspInit() {}
```

```
/**
 * Called when the JSP is unloaded.
 * By default does nothing.
 */
public void jspDestroy() {}

/**
 * Invokes the JSP's _jspService method.
 */
public final void service(
      HttpServletRequest request,
      HttpServletResponse response)
    throws ServletException, IOException
{
    _jspService(request, response);
}

/**
 * Handles a service request.
 */
public abstract void _jspService(
      HttpServletRequest request,
      HttpServletResponse response)
    throws ServletException, IOException;
}
```

In the example, the driver name and database URL are hard-coded. In a production environment,[1] these values could be configurable parameters.

import The `import` attribute is used to describe the fully qualified names of classes used in the JSP page. This makes it possible for the classes to be referred to by their class names without the package prefix. This is an optional attribute.

The value of an `import` attribute can be

■ A comma-separated list of package names, each terminated with the wildcard string ".*"

and/or

■ A fully qualified class name

---

[1] Actually, in a production environment, you would probably use a connection pool, but this example is simplified to illustrate the concept.

These names are converted directly to import statements in the generated Java servlet. The syntax is fairly flexible. To import all classes in the `java.io`, `java.sql` and `java.util` packages, for example, you can use any of the following:

```
<%@ page import= "java.io.*,java.sql.*,java.util.*"  %>
```

or on individual lines (because newlines count as whitespace inside the string):

```
<%@ page import="
   java.io.*,
   java.sql.*,
   java.util.*
    "%>
```

or using separate page directives:

```
<%@ page import= "java.io.*"   %>
<%@ page import= "java.sql.*"   %>
<%@ page import= "java.util.*"   %>
```

All these generate the same Java code, apart from differences in whitespace:

```
import java.io.*;
import java.sql.*;
import java.util.*;
```

Note, importing classes does not involve loading anything; it is simply a shorthand way of letting you use class names inside your Java methods without having to specify the package to which they belong. If you import `java.util.*`, you can write

```
Vector names = new Vector();
```

instead of

```
java.util.Vector names = new java.util.Vector();
```

which affects only the Java compiler, not the runtime class image. You can import thousands of classes, but only those you actually refer to will be required at runtime.

The default import list consists of four packages:

- `java.lang`
- `javax.servlet`
- `javax.servlet.http`
- `javax.servlet.jsp`

You do not need to supply an import statement for classes in these packages; you also do not need to qualify them with their package names.

 Remember, `import` is the only attribute of the page directive that can be specified more than once.

session   The `session` attribute of the page directive indicates whether the page requires an HTTP session. Two values are possible:

- `session="true"` if the page needs an HTTP session. This is the default value.
- `session="false"` if no HTTP session is required. If this is specified, the `session` implicit variable is undefined and will cause a translation error if used.

If your JSP page does not require a session, it is valuable from a performance standpoint to specify `session="false"`, so unnecessary sessions will not be created, using up memory and CPU cycles.

Chapter 8 describes HTTP sessions and session management in detail.

buffer and autoFlush   The `buffer` and `autoFlush` attributes are used to describe the output buffering model the JSP will employ. The `buffer` attribute can have the value "none", indicating all output will be written directly to the servlet response object's output stream, or it can have an integer value with a "kb" suffix. In the latter case, output is stored in memory in a buffer of the specified size. Depending on whether `autoFlush` is "true" or "false," when the buffer is full, either the output will be flushed or a buffer overflow exception will be thrown. The default buffer size is 8kb. Table 5-3 summarizes the results of each combination of values for the two attributes.

isThreadSafe   By default, servlet engines load a single instance of a servlet and use a pool of threads to service individual requests. This means two or more threads can be executing the same servlet methods simultaneously. If the servlet has instance variables, and if no provision is made to synchronize access, the threads can collide and interfere with each others' access to the variables.

The servlet API provides a way around this—the *SingleThreadModel* interface. This interface has no methods; it simply marks a servlet as requiring a dedicated thread for

Buffer	AutoFlush	Effect
none	true	Characters are written to the servlet response output stream as soon as they are generated.
none	false	An illegal combination. autoFlush="false" is meaningless if buffering is not in effect.
8kb	true	An 8,192-byte buffer is used. When this buffer is filled, it is automatically flushed. This is the default value.
8kb	false	An 8,192-byte buffer is used. When this buffer is filled, an exception is thrown.
*size*kb	true	A *size* times 1,024-byte buffer is used. When this buffer is filled, it is automatically flushed.
*size*kb	false	A *size* times 1,024-byte buffer is used. When this buffer is filled, an exception is thrown.

Table 5-3. *Effects of Each Combination of buffer and autoFlush Values*

each instance of the servlet.[2] The isThreadSafe attribute of the page directive provides a means for causing SingleThreadModel to be associated with a JSP page.

If you specify isThreadSafe="true", you are asserting that you take care of any possible thread conflicts, so the JSP container can safely dispatch multiple requests to the servlet simultaneously. If the value is "false", then the JSP container generates a servlet that implements SingleThreadModel. If not specified, the value of isThreadSafe is "true".

Note *SingleThreadModel is of limited value because it prevents thread conflicts only within an instance of a servlet. Nothing can prevent the JSP container from loading multiple instances of a servlet, each with a dedicated thread. In this case, competition for external resources such as databases and file locks is obviously still unregulated. Careful planning and thorough understanding of the issues is the only sure design guideline.*

info The info attribute of the page directive lets you specify descriptive information about the JSP page, for example:

<%@ page info="Shopping Cart Checkout Page" %>

---

[2] Chapter 8 discusses threading issues in more detail.

The value of this attribute is compiled into the class and is available by means of the servlet's `getServletInfo()` method. This allows servlet engines to provide a useful description for their servlets in an administrative interface.

contentType and pageEncoding   A JSP page ordinarily generates HTML output, but other content types can also be produced. By specifying the `contentType="value"` attribute in the `page` directive, you can cause an HTTP `Content-Type` header to be returned to the requesting application. If you do not specify `contentType`, `"text/html"` is assumed.

In addition, you can indicate that the JSP page itself is written in some character encoding other than ISO-8859-1. You use the `pageEncoding` attribute to specify the value for this.

errorPage and isErrorPage   If an exception occurs while a JSP page is being evaluated, the servlet engine typically dumps a stack trace to the browser. This may be helpful
to the programmer during development, but it is undesirable in a commercial Web application. JSP offers a simple and convenient solution that requires the coordinated use of two attributes: `errorPage` and `isErrorPage`.

A JSP page can indicate that a specific error page should be displayed when it throws an uncaught exception,

    <%@ page errorPage="error_url" %>

where *error_url* is the URL of another JSP page in the same servlet context. That JSP page must use the following attribute in its `page` directive:

    <%@ page isErrorPage="true" %>

An error page has access to the exception through the `exception` implicit variable.[3] It can extract the error message text with `exception.getMessage()`, displaying or logging it as necessary. It can also generate a stack trace with `exception.printStackTrace()`.

The include Directive

The *include directive* merges the contents of another file at translation time into the `.jsp` source input stream, much like a `#include` C preprocessor directive. The syntax is

    <%@ include file="filename" %>

---

[3]   This is the *only* circumstance in which the JSP page has access to this variable.

where *filename* is an absolute or relative pathname interpreted according to the current servlet context. Examples would be

```
<%@ include file="/header.html" %>
<%@ include file="/doc/legal/disclaimer.html" %>
<%@ include file="sortmethod" %>
```

The include directive contrasts with the `<jsp:include>` action described later in this chapter, which merges the output of another file at request time into the response output stream. Either element can be used to include standard headers and footers or other common text in JSP pages. Chapter 7 examines both approaches in detail.

The taglib Directive

The *taglib* directive makes custom actions available in the current page through the use of a tag library. The syntax of the directive is

<%@ taglib uri="*tagLibraryURI*" prefix="*tagPrefix*" %>

where the attributes are those listed in Table 5-4.

For example, if the following directive is used,

```
<%@ taglib uri="/tlds/FancyTableGenerator.tld" prefix="ft" %>
```

and if `FancyTableGenerator.tld` defines a tag named `table`, then the page can contain tags of the following type:

```
<ft:table>
...
</ft:table>
```

JSP tag extensions are considered in detail in Chapters 11-14.

Attribute	Value
URI	The URL of a Tag Library Descriptor.
Prefix	A unique prefix used to identify custom tags used later in the page.

Table 5-4.   *Attributes of the Taglib Directive*

Comments

The JSP specification provides two means of including comments in a JSP page: one for hidden comments only visible in the JSP page itself and one for comments included in the HTML or XML output generated by the page. The former type has the syntax

```
<%-- This is a hidden JSP comment --%>
```

and the latter looks like this:

```
<!-- This is included in the generated HTML -->
```

When the JSP compiler encounters the start tag `<%--` of a JSP comment, it ignores everything from that point in the file until it finds the matching end tag`--%>`. This means JSP comments can be used to disable (or "comment out") sections of the JSP page. This is a time-honored technique for temporarily enabling and disabling parts of a program without making major modifications to the source code. In addition, however, it means JSP comments cannot be nested, because the end tag of an inner comment would be interpreted as marking the end of the outer comment.

The other comment type uses the normal HTML or XML comment tag. Comments of this type are passed through unaltered to the response output stream and are included in the generated HTML. They are invisible in the browser window but can be seen by invoking the View Source menu option.

If the purpose of a comment is to enlighten the person viewing it, then the second comment type seems less useful than the first: it is found in HTML generated by a program which is typically never seen by a human. However, because these HTML comments are computer-generated, they can incorporate version numbers, dates, and other identifying numbers that may be useful to technical support personnel in troubleshooting applications. For example, these three lines included in a JSP page

```
<!--
   Remote address was <%= request.getRemoteAddr() %>
-->
```

would record the remote address of the user making a Web request without cluttering the output. If something goes wrong with the application, technical support personnel can instruct the user to view the generated HTML source and report the identifying data.

Expressions

JSP provides a simple means for accessing the value of a Java variable or other expression and merging that value with the HTML in the page. The syntax is

```
<%= exp %>
```

where *exp* is any valid Java expression. The expression can have any data value, as long as it can be converted to a string. This conversion is usually done simply by generating an out.print() statement. For example, the JSP code

```
The current time is <%= new java.util.Date() %>
```

may generate the servlet code

```
out.write("The current time is ");
out.print( new java.util.Date() );
out.write("\r\n");
```

Tip   *Understanding what code is generated can help you remember not to put a semicolon inside an expression.*

Chapter 6 discusses expressions in more detail.

Scriptlets

A *scriptlet* is a set of one or more Java language statements intended to be used to process an HTTP request. The syntax of a scriptlet is

<% *statement;* [*statement;* ...] %>

The JSP compiler simply includes the contents of scriptlet verbatim in the body of the _jspService() method. A JSP page may contain any number of scriptlets. If multiple scriptlets exist, they are each appended to the _jspService() method in the order in which they are coded. This being the case, a scriptlet may contain an open curly brace that is closed in another scriptlet. Consider the following JSP page, which produces a Fahrenheit to Celsius temperature conversion table:

```
<%@ page import="java.text.*" session="false"%>
<html>
<head>
<title>Scriptlet Example</title>
</head>
<body>
<table border="0" cellpadding="3">
<tr>
    <th>Fahrenheit</th>
    <th>Celsius</th>
</tr>
```

```
<%
   NumberFormat fmt = new DecimalFormat("###.000");
   for (int f = 32; f <= 212; f += 20) {
      double c = ((f - 32) * 5) / 9.0;
      String cs = fmt.format(c);
%>
   <tr>
      <td align="RIGHT"><%= f %></td>
      <td align="RIGHT"><%= cs %></td>
   </tr>
<%
   }
%>
</table>
</body>
</html>
```

The example code contains two scriptlets: one for the main body of the loop and one for the closing curly brace. Between the two scriptlets is the HTML markup for a single table row, using JSP expressions to access the values. The generated servlet code converts the scriptlets and what is between them to this:

```
   NumberFormat fmt = new DecimalFormat("###.000");
   for (int f = 32; f <= 212; f += 20) {
      double c = ((f - 32) * 5) / 9.0;
      String cs = fmt.format(c);
      out.write("\r\n   <tr>\r\n      <td align=\"RIGHT\">");
      out.print( f );
      out.write("</td>\r\n      <td align=\"RIGHT\">");
      out.print( cs );
      out.write("</td>\r\n   </tr>\r\n");
   }
```

which produces the following output:

```
Fahrenheit   Celsius
        32      .000
        52    11.111
        72    22.222
        92    33.333
       112    44.444
```

ELEMENTS OF JSP

```
132      55.556
152      66.667
172      77.778
192      88.889
212     100.000
```

Scriptlets are explored at length in Chapter 6.

Declarations

Like scriptlets, *declarations* contain Java language statements, but with one big difference: scriptlet code becomes part of the _jspService() method, whereas declaration code is incorporated into the generated source file *outside* the _jspService() method. The syntax of a declaration section is

<%! *statement* [*statement* ...] %>

Declaration sections can be used to declare class or instance variables, methods, or inner classes. Unlike scriptlets, they have no access to the implicit objects described in the next section. If you use a declaration section to declare a method that needs to use the request object, for example, you need to pass the object as a parameter to the method.

The following shows an example of a JSP page that uses a declaration section:

```
<%@ page
     errorPage="ErrorPage.jsp"
     import="java.io.*"
     import="java.util.*"
%>

<%
   Enumeration enames;
   Map map;
   String title;

   // Print the request headers

   map = new TreeMap();
   enames = request.getHeaderNames();
   while (enames.hasMoreElements()) {
      String name = (String) enames.nextElement();
```

```
        String value = request.getHeader(name);
        map.put(name, value);
    }
    out.println(createTable(map, "Request Headers"));

    // Print the session attributes

    map = new TreeMap();
    enames = session.getAttributeNames();
    while (enames.hasMoreElements()) {
        String name = (String) enames.nextElement();
        String value = "" + session.getAttribute(name);
        map.put(name, value);
    }
    out.println(createTable(map, "Session Attributes"));

%>

<%-- Define a method to create an HTML table --%>

<%!
    private static String createTable(Map map, String title)
    {
        StringBuffer sb = new StringBuffer();

        // Generate the header lines

        sb.append("<table border='1' cellpadding='3'>");
        sb.append("<tr>");
        sb.append("<th colspan='2'>");
        sb.append(title);
        sb.append("</th>");
        sb.append("</tr>");

        // Generate the table rows

        Iterator imap = map.entrySet().iterator();
        while (imap.hasNext()) {
            Map.Entry entry = (Map.Entry) imap.next();
            String key = (String) entry.getKey();
            String value = (String) entry.getValue();
            sb.append("<tr>");
```

```
        sb.append("<td>");
        sb.append(key);
        sb.append("</td>");
        sb.append("<td>");
        sb.append(value);
        sb.append("</td>");
        sb.append("</tr>");
    }

    // Generate the footer lines

    sb.append("</table><p></p>");

    // Return the generated HTML

    return sb.toString();
  }
%>
```

This JSP page collects data for two tables: the HTTP headers passed to the request object and the session attributes. The desired output for each is a nicely formatted HTML table. Of course, the tables could be created while iterating through the data rows, but this would require duplicating the formatting code. Instead, a private static method named createTable() is used; it is passed a reference to a Map object containing the key/value pairs and the table caption.

Chapter 6 discusses declarations in greater detail.

Implicit Objects

Although scriptlets, expressions, and HTML template data are all incorporated into the _jspService() method, the JSP container writes the skeleton of the method itself, initializing the page context and several useful variables. These variables are implicitly available inside scriptlets and expressions (but not declarations). They can be accessed like any other variable, but they do not have to be declared first. For example, the HttpServletRequest object passed to _jspService() is available in the variable named request, as shown in the following scriptlet:

```
<%
    String accountNumber = request.getParameter("acct");
    if (accountNumber == null) {
        // ... handle the missing account number problem
```

```
    }
%>
```

Table 5-5 provides a complete list of implicit variables.

Additional implicit variables can be created by means of a tag library. See Chapter 13 for discussion of this topic.

Standard Actions

Actions are high-level JSP elements that create, modify, or use other objects. Unlike directives and scripting elements, actions are coded using strict XML syntax:

<tagname [attr="value" attr="value" ...] > ... </tag-name>

ELEMENTS OF JSP

Variable Name	Value
request	The ServletRequest or HttpServletRequest being serviced.
response	The ServletResponse or HttpServletResponse that will receive the generated HTML output.
pageContext	The PageContext object for this page. This object is a central repository for attribute data for the page, request, session, and application.
session	If the JSP page uses an HttpSession, it is available here under the name session.
application	The servlet context object.
out	The character output stream used to generate the output HTML.
config	The ServletConfig object for this servlet context.
page	A reference to the JSP page itself.
exception	An uncaught exception that causes the error page to be invoked. This variable is available only to pages with isErrorPage="true".

Table 5-5.   *Implicit Variables*

or, if the action has no body, an abbreviated form:

<tagname [attr="value" attr="value" ...] />

XML syntax requires the following:

- Every tag must have a matching end tag or use the short form /> previously shown.

- Attribute values must be placed in quotes.

- Tags must nest properly: <A><B> . . . </B></A> is legal, but <A><B> . . . </A></B> is not.

Seven standard actions are available in all JSP 1.2–compliant environments. Table 5-6 outlines the syntax.

Tag Name	Description
<jsp:useBean>	Declares a JavaBean instance and associates it with a variable name. Syntax is <jsp:useBean id="*name*" [type="*type*"] [class="*class*"] [beanName="*beanName*"] [scope="*page* | *request* | *session* | *application*"]> ...</jsp:useBean>
<jsp:setProperty>	Sets the values of one or more properties of a bean previously declared with <jsp:useBean>. Syntax is <jsp:setProperty name="*id*" *prop-expression* /> where *prop-expression* is one of the following: property="*" property="*propName*" property="*propName*" param="*parameterName*" property="*propName*" value="*value*" property="*propName*" value=<%= *expression* %>

Table 5-6. *Standard Actions*

Tag Name	Description
`<jsp:getProperty>`	Returns the value of the specified property of a bean. Syntax is <jsp:getProperty name="*id*" property="*name*" />
`<jsp:include>`	Invokes another resource and merges its output stream with the JSP page output stream. Syntax is <jsp:include page="*URL*" flush="true|false " /> or, if parameters need to be passed: <jsp:include page="*URL*" flush="true|false"> <jsp:param ... /> <jsp:param ... /> ... <jsp:param ... /> </jsp:include>
`<jsp:forward>`	Forwards this HTTP request to another JSP page or servlet for processing. Syntax is <jsp:forward page="*URL*" /> or, if parameters need to be passed: <jsp:forward page="*URL*"> <jsp:param ... /> <jsp:param ... /> ... <jsp:param ... /> </jsp:forward>
`<jsp:param>`	Binds a value to a name and passes the binding to another resource invoked with `<jsp:include>` or `<jsp:forward>`. Syntax is <jsp:param name="*name*" value="*value*" />

Table 5-6. *Standard Actions (continued)*

Tag Name	Description
`<jsp:plugin>`	Used to generate the appropriate HTML linkage for downloading the Java plugin: <jsp:plugin type="*bean | applet*" code="*objectCode*" codebase="*objectCodebase*" { align="*alignment*" } { archive="*archiveList*" } { height="*height*" } { hspace="*hspace*" } { jreversion="*jreversion*" } { name="*componentName*" } { vspace="*vspace*" } { width="*width*"} { nspluginurl="*url*" } { iepluginurl="*url*" } > { <jsp:params> { <jsp:param name="*name*" value="*value*" /> }+</jsp:params> }}</jsp:plugin>

Table 5-6.   *Standard Actions (continued)*

Tag Extensions

In addition to the standard actions listed in Table 5-6, the JSP author can write custom tags to extend JSP functionality of JSP. Chapter 11 is devoted to tag extensions.

A Complete Example

An example of a JSP page that incorporates all the elements introduced here concludes this chapter. The page is named `Echo.jsp`. Its sole function is to pass back to the client browser an HTML table containing the HTTP request headers the browser sent. The listing is shown in the following:

```
<%@ page import="java.util.*" %>
<html>
```

```
    <head>
       <title>Echo</title>
       <style>
       <jsp:include page="style.css" flush="true"/>
       </style>
    </head>
    <body>
       <h1>HTTP Request Headers Received</h1>
       <table border="1" cellpadding="4" cellspacing="0">
       <%
          Enumeration eNames = request.getHeaderNames();
          while (eNames.hasMoreElements()) {
             String name = (String) eNames.nextElement();
             String value = normalize(request.getHeader(name));
       %>
          <tr><td><%= name %></td><td><%= value %></td></tr>
       <%
          }
       %>
       </table>
    </body>
</html>
<%!
    private String normalize(String value)
    {
       StringBuffer sb = new StringBuffer();
       for (int i = 0; i < value.length(); i++) {
          char c = value.charAt(i);
          sb.append(c);
          if (c == ';')
             sb.append("<br>");
       }
       return sb.toString();
    }
%>
```

When `Echo.jsp` is first invoked, the servlet container (Tomcat 4, in this case)
creates the following Java source code:[4]

---

[4]   The code has been slightly reformatted for legibility.

```
package org.apache.jsp;

import java.util.*;
import javax.servlet.*;
import javax.servlet.http.*;
import javax.servlet.jsp.*;
import org.apache.jasper.runtime.*;

public class Echo$jsp extends HttpJspBase
{
    private String normalize(String value)
    {
        StringBuffer sb = new StringBuffer();
        for (int i = 0; i < value.length(); i++) {
            char c = value.charAt(i);
            sb.append(c);
            if (c == ';')
                sb.append("<br>");
        }
        return sb.toString();
    }

    static {}
    public Echo$jsp( ) {}

    private static boolean _jspx_inited = false;

    public final void _jspx_init()
        throws org.apache.jasper.runtime.JspException {}

    public void _jspService(
            HttpServletRequest request,
            HttpServletResponse response)
        throws java.io.IOException, ServletException
        {
            JspFactory _jspxFactory = null;
            PageContext pageContext = null;
            HttpSession session = null;
            ServletContext application = null;
            ServletConfig config = null;
            JspWriter out = null;
            Object page = this;
            String _value = null;
```

```
try {
   if (_jspx_inited == false) {
      synchronized (this) {
         if (_jspx_inited == false) {
            _jspx_init();
            _jspx_inited = true;
         }
      }
   }
   _jspxFactory = JspFactory.getDefaultFactory();
   response.setContentType
      ("text/html;charset=ISO-8859-1");
   pageContext = _jspxFactory.getPageContext
      (this, request, response, "", true, 8192, true);

   application = pageContext.getServletContext();
   config = pageContext.getServletConfig();
   session = pageContext.getSession();
   out = pageContext.getOut();
   out.write
      ("\r\n<html>\r\n"
      + "   <head>\r\n"
      + "      <title>Echo</title>\r\n"
      + "      <style>\r\n         ");

   {
      String _jspx_qStr = "";
      JspRuntimeLibrary.include
            (request,
             response,
             "style.css" + _jspx_qStr,
             out,
             true);
      if ("true".equals
         (request.getAttribute
         ("javax.servlet.forward.seen")))
         return;
   }
   out.write
      ("\r\n      </style>\r\n"
      + "   </head>\r\n"
      + "   <body>\r\n   "
```

```
                    + "    <h1>HTTP Request Headers Received</h1>\r\n"
                    + "        <table"
                        + " border=\"1\""
                        + " cellpadding=\"4\""
                        + " cellspacing=\"0\">\r\n        ");

            Enumeration eNames = request.getHeaderNames();
            while (eNames.hasMoreElements()) {
                String name = (String) eNames.nextElement();
                String value = normalize(request.getHeader(name));
                out.write("\r\n            <tr><td>");
                out.print( name );
                out.write("</td><td>");
                out.print( value );
                out.write("</td></tr>\r\n        ");
            }
            out.write("\r\n"
                    + "        </table>\r\n"
                    + "    </body>\r\n"
                    + "</html>\r\n");
            out.write("\r\n");
        }
        catch (Throwable t) {
            if (out != null && out.getBufferSize() != 0)
                out.clearBuffer();
            if (pageContext != null)
                pageContext.handlePageException(t);
        }
        finally {
            if (_jspxFactory != null)
                _jspxFactory.releasePageContext(pageContext);
        }
    }
}
```

Let's consider the JSP page and the generated code section by section.

A Page Directive

The JSP page begins with a page directive indicating the page uses the `java.util` package:

```
<%@ page import= java.util.  %>
```

This directive shows up in the servlet source code at the beginning of its list of imported classes:

```
...
import java.util.*;
import javax.servlet.*;
import javax.servlet.http.*;
import javax.servlet.jsp.*;
import org.apache.jasper.runtime.*;
```

A <jsp:include> Action

The page uses a style sheet to set the look and feel of the output. The style sheet is incorporated using a <jsp:include> action:

```
<jsp:include page="style.css" flush="true"/>
```

The <jsp:include> action causes the following style sheet to be read at request time:

```
body {
    font: Sans-Serif 12px;
    background-color: #FEFEF2;
};
h1 { font-size: 130% }
```

Scriptlet

There are two scriptlets on the page, with HTML template data located before, between, and after them. The HTML data

```
<html>
    <head>
        <title>Echo</title>
        <style>
...
```

is passed through unchanged by means of write statements:

```
out.write
    ("\r\n<html>\r\n"
+ "    <head>\r\n"
+ "        <title>Echo</title>\r\n"
+ "        <style>\r\n        ");
...
```

Then the first scriptlet is simply copied to the servlet:

```
Enumeration eNames = request.getHeaderNames();
while (eNames.HasMoreElements()) {
    String name = (String) eNames.nextElement();
    String value = normalize(request.getHeaderName());
```

Notice the code fragment has an unclosed curly brace on the second line. The matching brace is supplied by the second scriptlet.

JSP Expressions

During each iteration of the loop, the scriptlet extracts a header name and header value from the request object. Rather than printing these values using out.write(), the page author switches back into HTML mode and uses JSP expression tags,

```
%>
    <tr><td><%= name %></td><td><%= value %></td></tr>
<%
```

which generates the following servlet code:

```
        out.write("\r\n        <tr><td>");
        out.print( name );
        out.write("</td><td>");
        out.print( value );
        out.write("</td></tr>\r\n        ");
```

A Declaration

Header values that are lists can be very long and cause the table width to be distorted. You can get around this problem by scanning the header value for semicolons and inserting <br> tags wherever they are found. This function is performed by a method called normalize(), which is found at the end of the JSP file:

```
<%!
   private String normalize(String value)
   {
      StringBuffer sb = new StringBuffer();
      for (int i = 0; i < value.length(); i++) {
         char c = value.charAt(i);
         sb.append(c);
         if (c == ';')
            sb.append("<br>");
      }
      return sb.toString();
   }
%>
```

As was the case with the two scriptlets, the declaration code is copied verbatim to the generated servlet, except it is not placed inside the _jspService() method. Instead, it is written inside the class block, but outside any other method, near the beginning of the servlet:

```
   private String normalize(String value)
   {
      StringBuffer sb = new StringBuffer();
      for (int i = 0; i < value.length(); i++) {
         char c = value.charAt(i);
         sb.append(c);
         if (c == ';')
            sb.append("<br>");
      }
      return sb.toString();
   }
```

The resulting output is shown in Figure 5-1.

ELEMENTS OF JSP

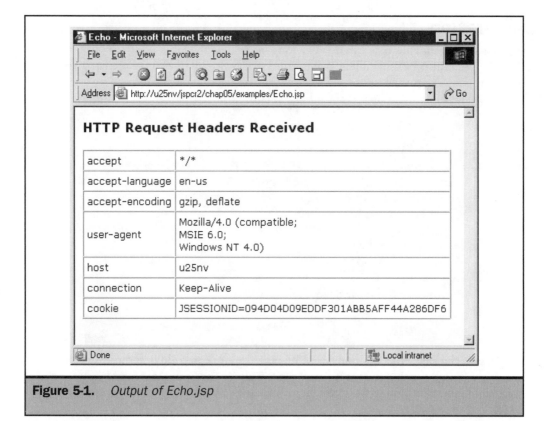

Figure 5-1.   *Output of Echo.jsp*

Summary

The JSP development environment provides a means for generating HTML pages dynamically with server-side Java programming. The syntax allows most of the HTML to be coded directly, with sections marked off for Java code that controls the page generation. There is support for including other resources, both static and dynamic. JavaBeans are fully integrated into the framework, and custom tags allow functionality to be encapsulated and made available to nonexpert page authors.

The key point this chapter makes is this: a mental model of the JSP development cycle is crucial to understanding how to create and debug Web applications. Knowledge of what happens at translation time (static resources are included via the <%@ include %> directive, for example) versus request time (dynamic request dispatching with <jsp:include>) provides insight into which features to use and when to use them. The remaining chapters of Part II discuss each of these features of the application model in more detail.

The Complete Reference

Chapter 6

Expressions, Scriptlets, and Declarations

The preceding chapter provided an overview of JSP syntax and semantics. While the syntax is not difficult to learn, mastering it doesn't teach you everything you need to know. Understanding JSP requires building a mental model of how it operates, how and when Java source code is generated, and when classes are compiled and loaded.

In this chapter, part of that mental model is clarified by exploring three scripting elements: expressions, scriptlets, and declarations. You will see how the JSP container combines template text and JSP scripting elements to generate a Java method that handles user requests. You will also see how a JSP page gets access to the Web environment in which it is used, and how it communicates its results.

Note *As of JSP 1.2, JavaServer Pages can also be written and deployed entirely as XML documents. This creates some interesting possibilities for automatically generating JSP source code. The XML syntax is covered in Chapter 16. In this chapter, we'll use only the traditional JSP syntax.*

Expressions

A JSP *expression* is simply a Java[1] language expression in a JSP page set off from its surrounding HTML by the delimiters <%= and %>, as the following shows:

```
<%= expression %>
```

For example, an expression can be a primitive numeric value,

```
Simple math: 2 + 2 = <%= 2 + 2 %>
```

which produces the output:

```
Simple math: 2 + 2 = 4
```

or a more elaborate expression involving method calls,

```
The Java virtual machine vendor is
<em><%= System.getProperty("java.vm.vendor") %></em>
```

which produces the output:

```
The Java virtual machine vendor is Sun Microsystems Inc.
```

---

[1] In theory, JSP pages could be written in other languages, as envisioned in the JSP specification. As of this writing, with a few experimental exceptions, Java is the only supported language. That is why the technology is called JavaServer Pages (JSP), not Language Independent Server Pages (LISP) or Any Old Language Server Pages (AOLSP).

An expression can create new objects and manipulate them. This code creates a `Date` object and passes it to the `format()` method of a new `SimpleDateFormat` object,

```
Today is
<%=
    new java.text.SimpleDateFormat("MMMM d, yyyy")
    .format(new java.util.Date())
%>
```

which produces (on the appropriate day, of course):

```
Today is June 28, 2003
```

The Java expression between the `<%=` and `%>` delimiters can be as complex as desired, the only requirement being that it must be capable of being evaluated as a `java.util.String`, either directly or through the invocation of its `toString()` method or a `String.valueOf()` method.

Note *Expressions must not end in a semicolon. They must consist solely of what can legally appear on the right side of an assignment statement between the equal sign and the ending semicolon.*

Scriptlets

A *scriptlet* is a set of Java programming statements embedded in an HTML page. The statements are distinguished from their surrounding HTML by being placed between `<%` and `%>` markers, as the following shows:

<% *statement; [statement; ...]* %>

Whitespace is permitted after the `<%` and before the `%>`, so the previous scriptlet could also be written as:

<%
statement;
[statement; ...]
%>

Here is an example of a JSP page that uses a scriptlet to generate a table of ASCII characters:

```
<html>
<body>
<center>
<h1>ASCII Table</h1>
```

```
<table border="0" cellpadding="0" cellspacing="0">
<%
    StringBuffer sb = new StringBuffer();
    sb.append("<tr>");
    sb.append("<th width=\"40\"> </th>");
    for (int col = 0; col < 16; col++) {
        sb.append("<th>");
        sb.append(Integer.toHexString(col));
        sb.append("</th>");
    }
    sb.append("</tr>");
    for (int row = 0; row < 16; row++) {
        sb.append("<tr>");
        sb.append("<th>");
        sb.append(Integer.toHexString(row));
        sb.append("</th>");
        for (int col = 0; col < 16; col++) {
            char c = (char)(row * 16 + col);
            sb.append("<td width=\"32\" align=\"center\">");
            sb.append(c);
            sb.append("</td>");
        }
        sb.append("</tr>");
    }
    out.println(sb);
%>
</table>
</center>
</body>
</html>
```

There are five lines of HTML, followed by the scriptlet open delimiter <%, a number of lines of Java code, the scriptlet closing delimiter %>, and then the HTML lines needed to close the document. When invoked, the page produces the output shown in Figure 6-1.

The following section describes how these scripting elements are handled by the JSP container.

Expression and Scriptlet Handling by the JSP Container

When it encounters a new or revised JSP page, the JSP container parses it and creates the source code for an equivalent Java servlet.[2] The expressions, scriptlets, and HTML template data found in the page are used by the JSP container to create Java source code

---

[2]   Servlets are discussed at length in Chapter 3.

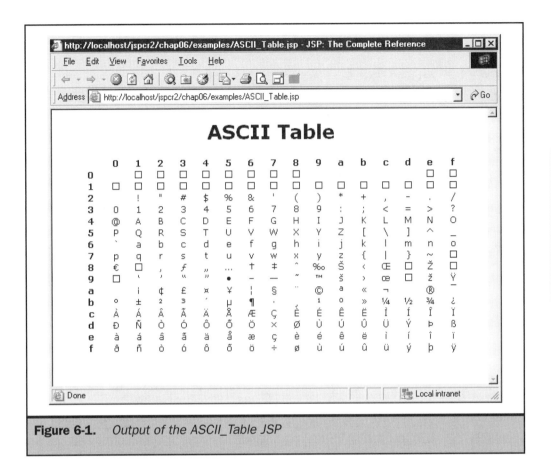

Figure 6-1. *Output of the ASCII_Table JSP*

for a method named `_jspService()`. This method corresponds to the `service()` method of a servlet, or the more commonly used `doGet()` and `doPost()` methods. `_jspService()` is automatically generated by the container. The JSP author must not define it explicitly.

Note *The JSP specification does not dictate the exact form of the generated servlet. The details are left up to the JSP container vendor, and the implementations vary widely. To avoid any confusion, the examples shown in this book are taken from the Apache Tomcat 4 reference implementation.*

The generated _jspService() method consists of up to three types of statements, depending on the contents of the JSP page:

- Code to handle HTML template data and expressions
- The contents of any scriptlets
- Container-generated initialization and exit code

Let's examine each of these and see how they are handled.

HTML Template Data and Expressions

Any characters in the JSP page not inside a JSP element (a directive, expression, scriptlet, or action) are considered part of a fixed HTML template. The JSP container creates out.write() or out.print() statements that write these characters to the response output stream. For example, this code

```
<li>Cash and Marketable Securities</li>
```

might be converted to this:

```
out.write("<li>Cash and Marketable Securities</li>\r\n");
```

If the HTML template needs to contain any literal <% or %> strings, they must be treated specially to avoid confusing the JSP container. The JSP specification indicates this can be done by writing <\% instead of <% and %\> instead of %>. The container generates code to write the intended <% or %> in the output stream.

> **Note** *JSP containers typically generate one long out.write() statement for each uninterrupted stretch of fixed HTML data. The examples in this book take the liberty of breaking long character strings into multiple out.write() statements for the sake of readability.*

Besides fixed HTML data, the template also may contain JSP expressions that are evaluated at runtime in and printed with an out.write() statement. Expressions are considered in the next section.

Scriptlet Contents

Anything found between <% and %> tags is copied verbatim to the _jspService() method. Hence, these lines in a JSP page, which produce the output shown in Figure 6-2,

```
<table border="0" align="center" width="50%">
<tr>
   <th align="right">Celsius</th>
```

```
        <th align="right">Fahrenheit</th>
</tr>
<%
    for (int c = 0; c <= 100; c += 10) {
        int f = 32 + 9*c/5;
        out.print("<tr>");
        out.print("<td align=\"right\">" + c + "</td>");
        out.print("<td align=\"right\">" + f + "</td>");
        out.print("</tr>");
    }
%>
</table>
```

are transformed by the Tomcat JSP container into the following lines in the
_jspService() method:

```
    // HTML
    // begin [file="c2f.jsp";from=(0,0);to=(5,0)]
        out.write("<table border=\"0\" align=\"center\""
            + " width=\"50%\">\r\n<tr>\r\n"
            + "    <th align=\"right\">Celsius</th>\r\n"
            + "    <th align=\"right\">Fahrenheit</th>\r\n"
            + "</tr>\r\n");
    // end
    // begin [file="c2f.jsp";from=(5,2);to=(13,0)]
        for (int c = 0; c <= 100; c += 10) {
            int f = 32 + 9*c/5;
            out.print("<tr>");
            out.print("<td align=\"right\">" + c + "</td>");
            out.print("<td align=\"right\">" + f + "</td>");
            out.print("</tr>");
        }
    // end
    // HTML
    // begin [file="c2f.jsp";from=(13,2);to=(15,0)]
        out.write("\r\n</table>\r\n");
    // end
```

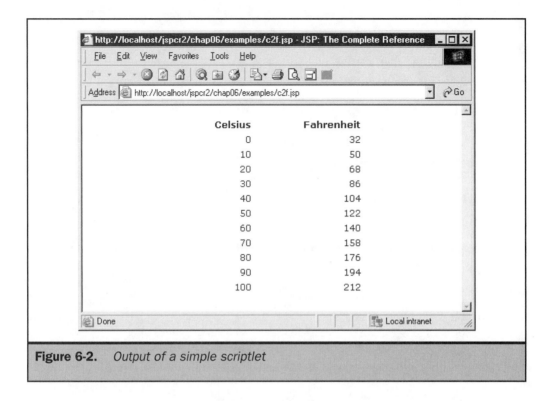

Figure 6-2. *Output of a simple scriptlet*

The HTML markup for the table is found in the `out.write()` statements, and the scriptlet contents appear unaltered in the body of the method. The Tomcat-generated servlet contains comments that indicate which lines of the JSP file correspond to which lines in the servlet.

If there are multiple scriptlets in a page, they are copied to the generated servlet in the order they are encountered. Thus, no functional difference exists between writing this code,

```
<%
    for (int i = 0; i < 10; i++) {
        out.println(i);
    }
%>
```

and this,

```
<%    for (int i = 0; i < 10; i++) { %>
<%        out.println(i); %>
<%    } %>
```

except for several newline characters generated in the latter case (which occur because they are technically considered fixed HTML data).

Because multiple scriptlets are concatenated and placed into the same method, syntactical units can be started in one scriptlet and completed in another, as illustrated by the opening and closing curly braces in the `for` statement. This also means variables defined in any scriptlet are treated as local variables of the `_jspService()` method and retain their value from one scriptlet or expression to the next. In other words, you can do this:

```
<%
    int value = 3;
%>
<p>The value is <%= value %>.</p>
<%
    value += 2;
%>
<p>After adding 2, the value is <%= value %>.</p>
```

and get this output:

```
The value is 3.
After adding 2, the value is 5.
```

Container-Generated Initialization and Exit Code

In addition to code that the JSP page author writes, `_jspService()` begins and ends with statements that initialize and release objects needed in the method. The exact code generated is implementation-dependent and specific to the JSP container vendor. In the case of the Celsius-to-Fahrenheit example previously given, Tomcat generates the following initialization and exit code:

```
public void _jspService(
     HttpServletRequest request,
     HttpServletResponse response)
   throws java.io.IOException, ServletException
{
   // ... Initialization code generated by Tomcat ...
```

```
JspFactory _jspxFactory = null;
PageContext pageContext = null;
HttpSession session = null;
ServletContext application = null;
ServletConfig config = null;
JspWriter out = null;
Object page = this;
String  _value = null;
try {
    if (_jspx_inited == false) {
        synchronized (this) {
            if (_jspx_inited == false) {
                _jspx_init();
                _jspx_inited = true;
            }
        }
    }
    _jspxFactory = JspFactory.getDefaultFactory();
    response.setContentType
        ("text/html;charset=ISO-8859-1");
    pageContext = _jspxFactory.getPageContext
        (this, request, response, "", true, 8192, true);

    application = pageContext.getServletContext();
    config = pageContext.getServletConfig();
    session = pageContext.getSession();
    out = pageContext.getOut();

    // ... Your code appears here ...

}

// ... Exit code generated by Tomcat JSP container

catch (Throwable t) {
    if (out != null && out.getBufferSize() != 0)
        out.clearBuffer();
    if (pageContext != null)
        pageContext.handlePageException(t);
}
```

```
finally {
    if (_jspxFactory != null)
        _jspxFactory.releasePageContext(pageContext);
    }
}
```

You can see that a number of objects are created before the JSP author's code is added. The meaning of these objects is the subject of the next section.

Implicit Objects and the JSP Environment

The scriptlets and expressions written in a JSP page do not stand alone as a complete program—they need an environment in which to operate. The JSP container provides this environment and makes it accessible to the page author through what are called *implicit objects.* These objects are created by container-generated statements at the beginning of the `_jspService()` method and are assigned predetermined names that are the same in all JSP pages. There are nine of these objects, as listed in Table 6-1.

Object	Description
request	The HttpServletRequest object that was passed to _jspService().
response	The HttpServletResponse object that was passed to _jspService().
pageContext	A means of accessing page, request, session, or application attributes.
session	The current HttpSession object, if one exists.
application	The ServletContext object.
out	The JspWriter response output stream object.
config	The servlet configuration object.
page	A reference to the current instance of the JSP class itself.
exception	An uncaught exception (valid in error pages only).

Table 6-1.   *Implicit Objects Available Within Scriptlets and Expressions*

These variables can be accessed simply by using their predetermined names like any other variable. One of these variables has already been used in the examples in this chapter—the `JspWriter out` variable,

```
<%
    out.println("<code>out</code> is an <i>");
    out.println(out.getClass().getName());
    out.println("</i> object.");
%>
```

which produces this output when run under Tomcat 4:

```
out is an org.apache.jasper.runtime.JspWriterImpl object.
```

The JSP implicit objects provide the context in which an HTTP request is serviced. The following sections consider each of these objects. For a complete list of the methods each object implements, consult the API documentation for the class.

request

The `request` variable contains a reference to the `HttpServletRequest` object passed in the first parameter of the generated `_jspService()` method. This object encapsulates the details of the HTTP request generated by the Web browser or other client—its parameters, attributes, headers, and data. Some of its more useful methods are listed in Table 6-2.

response

The `response` variable provides access to the other side of the HTTP transaction. This object encapsulates the output returned to the HTTP client, providing the page author with

Method	Description
String getHeader(String *name*)	Returns the value of the specified HTTP header, or `null` if the header is not present in the request.
Enumeration getHeaderNames()	Returns an enumeration of all HTTP headers present in the request.
String getParameter(String *name*)	Given the name of a single-valued form parameter, returns its value.

Table 6-2. *Some Useful Methods of the* `request` *Object*

Method	Description
Enumeration getParameterNames()	Returns an enumeration of the names of all form parameters passed to this request.
HttpSession getSession(boolean *create*)	Returns the current `HttpSession` object. If one does not exist, either creates a new one or returns `null`, depending on the *create* flag.

Table 6-2.   *Some Useful Methods of the* `request` *Object* (continued)

a means for setting response headers and the status code. It also has methods for accessing the response output stream, but the JSP specification prohibits directly accessing this stream. All JSP response output must be written using the `out` implicit variable. Methods provided by the `HttpServletResponse` object include those listed in Table 6-3.

Method	Description
String getHeader(String *name*)	Returns the value of the specified HTTP header, or `null` if the header is not present in the request.
Enumeration getHeaderNames()	Returns an enumeration of all HTTP headers present in the request.
String getParameter(String *name*)	Given the name of a single-valued form parameter, returns its value.
Enumeration getParameterNames()	Returns an enumeration of the names of all form parameters passed to this request.
HttpSession getSession(boolean *create*)	Returns the current `HttpSession` object. If one does not exist, either creates a new one or returns `null`, depending on the *create* flag.

Table 6-3.   *Some Useful Methods of the* `response` *Object*

pageContext

As Figure 6-3 illustrates, JSP code operates within a hierarchy of environments. A single HTTP request, for example, may be serviced by multiple JSP pages: one that produces heading information and another that generates detailed output. Similarly, multiple HTTP requests may be part of a larger HTTP session that starts with a login request, proceeds through some user selection requests, and then commits the work to a database. Finally, the set of all HTTP sessions in a servlet context may share a connection pool or other common objects.

Each of the layers in this hierarchy is restricted to attributes that apply at that level. The JSP specification provides for a `PageContext` object that keeps track of attributes at four levels:

- The JSP page
- The HTTP request
- The HTTP session
- The overall application

A `PageContext` object is automatically initialized and assigned to a variable named `pageContext` at the beginning of the `_jspService()` method. This object provides search and update capability for attributes at each of the four levels, as described in Table 6-4. It also provides methods that forward requests to other resources and include the output of other resources.

session

HTTP is a stateless protocol, which means it doesn't remember from one request to the next anything about previous requests. However, Web applications frequently involve more than one request. For example, an application may begin with some kind of user identification and validation that must be propagated through several other Web pages. The continuity required for this type of application must be provided by something other than the Web server.

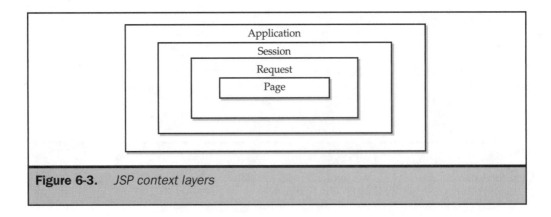

Figure 6-3.   *JSP context layers*

Method	Description
Object findAttribute (String *name*)	Searches for an attribute object with the specified name in the page, request, session, and application scopes, in that order, returning the first one found, or null, if none is found.
Object getAttribute (String *name*, int *scope*)	Returns the attribute object with the specified name in the given scope. The *scope* parameter value should be selected from among the PAGE_CONTEXT, REQUEST_CONTEXT, SESSION_CONTEXT, and APPLICATION_CONTEXT constants provided in the PageContext class.
void removeAttribute (String *name*, int *scope*)	Removes the attribute object having the specified name in the given scope.
void setAttribute (String *name*, Object *value*, int *scope*)	Stores an object as a named attribute in the given scope. The *scope* parameter value should be selected from among the PAGE_CONTEXT, REQUEST_CONTEXT, SESSION_CONTEXT, and APPLICATION_CONTEXT constants defined in the PageContext class.

Table 6-4.   *Some Useful Methods of the pageContext Object*

Several approaches can be taken to accommodate this need, depending on the requirements of the application. Chapter 8 explores a number of these alternatives in detail, including:

■ Hidden fields

■ Cookies

■ URL rewriting

■ HTTP sessions

The last item mentioned is of interest here. An HttpSession is an object similar to a Map or a Hashtable that is associated with a single Web browser session. It persists between HTTP requests and can store named objects of any kind. By default, the JSP container creates an HttpSession object or accesses the currently active one at the beginning of the _jspService() method. This object is assigned to a variable named session.

ELEMENTS OF JSP

| Note | *If you do not need to retain objects between requests, you should turn off automatic session creation by specifying* session="false" *in the* page *directive. Doing so can improve performance by reducing the number of objects that the servlet engine has to keep track of. Because a session persists until it times out (typically 30 minutes later) or it is explicitly invalidated, the impact on performance can be considerable.* |

Table 6-5 outlines several useful methods in the session object.

Remember, the pageContext object can also be used to get and set attributes in the session in the same manner as the session.getAttribute() and session.setAttribute() methods.

application

The application implicit object encapsulates a view of the collection of all servlets, JSP pages, HTML pages, and other resources in a Web application. This object implements the javax.servlet.ServletContext interface and is automatically constructed at the beginning of the _jspService() method. It provides information about the server version, any application-wide initialization parameters, and the absolute paths of resources within the application. This object also provides a means for logging messages. Some of its more useful methods are described in Table 6-6.

Method	Description
Object getAttribute (String *name*)	Returns the object with the specified name, if it exists in the session.
Enumeration getAttributeNames()	Returns an enumeration of the names of all the objects stored in the session.
String getId()	Returns the unique session ID. This ID must be stored by the client (Web browser) between requests and passed back to the JSP container to identify which session is required.
int getMaxInactiveInterval()	Returns the maximum number of seconds the session stays active between user requests. The JSP container closes the session if no activity occurs over that length of time.
void invalidate()	Closes the session and unbinds all its objects.
void setAttribute (String *name*, Object *value*)	Stores an object in the session under the specified name.

Table 6-5.   *Some Useful Methods of the* session *Object*

Method	Description
Enumeration getAttributeNames()	Returns an enumeration of the names of all objects stored in the servlet context.
Object getAttribute (String *name*)	Returns an object with the specified name that was stored with the application's `setAttribute()` method.
void setAttribute (String *name*, Object value)	Binds an object to the application under the specified name. This will cause any servlet context listeners to be notified.
void removeAttribute (String *name*)	Removes the specified object binding from the application. This will cause any servlet context listeners to be notified.
String getInitParameter (String *name*)	Returns the value of the specified application-wide initialization parameter.
Enumeration getInitParameterNames()	Returns an enumeration of the names of all application-wide initialization parameters.
String getRealPath (String *path*)	Converts a path in the context of the Web application to an absolute path in the file system, if possible.
URL getResource (String *path*)	Returns the URL (if any) mapped to the specified path in the application. The path must begin with a "/" and is relative to the root of the application.
InputStream getResourceAsStream (String *path*)	Similar in operation to `getResource()`, but returns an opened input stream to the resulting URL.
void log (String *msg*)	Writes a message to the log file associated with this application.

Table 6-6. *Some Useful Methods of the `application` Object*

As is the case with the `page`, `request`, and `session` implicit objects, attributes of the `application` object can be manipulated with methods in the `pageContext` object. Initialization parameters are discussed in a later section of this chapter.

out

The whole purpose of a JSP page is to produce some output and send it back to the user on the other end of the socket connection. As you saw earlier in this chapter, fixed HTML template data and JSP expressions are written by automatically generated `out.write()` and/or `out.print()` method calls. The `out` variable is initialized with a reference to a `javax.servlet.jsp.JspWriter` object early in the `_jspService()` method. You can have all output generated in this manner, or you can write explicitly to the `out` object in scriptlets. Thus, the JSP page

```
<%
    String[] colors = {"red", "green", "blue"};
    for (int i = 0; i < colors.length; i++) {
%>
<p><%= colors[i] %></p>
<%
    }
%>
```

is functionally equivalent to this one:

```
<%
    String[] colors = {"red", "green", "blue"};
    for (int i = 0; i < colors.length; i++) {
        out.print("<p>" + colors[i] + "</p>");
    }
%>
```

Besides the `write()` methods common to all `java.io.Writer` objects, the `out` object provides methods for querying and manipulating the output buffer, as shown in Table 6-7.

Method	Description
void clear()	Clears the output buffer. If the buffer contents have already been transmitted to the client, this method will cause an `IOException` to be thrown.
void clearBuffer()	Simliar to `clear()`, but does not throw an exception if the buffer has already been flushed.

Table 6-7.   *Some Useful Methods of the out Object*

Method	Description
void flush()	Forces buffered data to be written to the output stream.
int getBufferSize()	Returns the size of the output buffer in bytes, or zero if the writer is unbuffered.
int getRemaining()	Returns the number of bytes remaining before buffer overflow occurs.
void print (*type value*)	A variety of methods to write objects of the specified primitive or object type. No newline character is added at the end.
void println (*type value*)	Similar to print(), but adds a newline character at the end.

Table 6-7.   *Some Useful Methods of the* `out` *Object* (Continued)

ELEMENTS OF JSP

config

Besides application-wide initialization parameters that are made available through the `application` object, individual servlet mappings (and, therefore, JSP pages) can have initialization parameters. The `config` implicit object provides methods for accessing these parameters, the servlet context (application), and the servlet name, as detailed in Table 6-8.

Method	Description
String getInitParameter(String *name*)	Returns the value of the specified servlet initialization parameter, or null, if the named parameter does not exist.
Enumeration getInitParameterNames()	Returns a list of the names of all initialization parameters for this servlet.
ServletContext getServletContext()	Returns a reference to the servlet context (same as the *application* implicit variable).
String name getServletName()	Returns the name of the generated servlet.

Table 6-8.   *Some Useful Methods of the* `config` *Object*

page

The page implicit object is a variable containing a reference to the current servlet instance, essentially just an alias for the this variable. This object is not typically useful to JSP page authors.

exception

The object referred to by the implicit exception variable is any instance of java.lang.Throwable that has been thrown, but not caught, by a catch block in the JSP page. The exception variable is valid only if the <%@ page %> directive has the isErrorPage=*"true"* attribute. This attribute is discussed in more detail in Chapter 17.

Initialization Parameters

Initialization parameters are external name/value pairs that can be read by a JSP page. They can be used in the same manner as string constants, but they have the added advantage that they can be modified without requiring the program that uses them to be recompiled. This makes initialization parameters especially useful for storing installation and configuration data, such as HTTP proxy server names, application color schemes, or installation directory names.

These parameters can be specified at the individual JSP and servlet level or for all the JSP pages in an application. In either case, initialization parameters are declared in the application's web.xml file.[3] For JSP and servlet level access, this is accomplished by adding one or more <init-param> elements to the appropriate <servlet> element, as the following shows:

```
<servlet>

    <servlet-name>Food</servlet-name>
    <jsp-file>/Chap06/examples/Food.jsp</jsp-file>

    <init-param>
        <param-name>DRIVER_NAME</param-name>
        <param-value>sun.jdbc.odbc.JdbcOdbcDriver</param-value>
    </init-param>

    <init-param>
        <param-name>DATABASE_URL</param-name>
        <param-value>jdbc:odbc:usda</param-value>
    </init-param>

</servlet>
```

---

[3] The web.xml file and other configuration and deployment issues are discussed in Chapter 18.

In this example, `Food.jsp` is a JSP page (not shown here) that accesses a database of nutrition information. Rather than containing hardcoded values for the JDBC driver name and database URL, the JSP page gets these values from initialization parameters using the `getInitParameter()` method:

```
String driverName = getInitParameter("DRIVER_NAME");
if (driverName == null)
   throw new ServletException
   ("No DRIVER_NAME parameter was specified");

String databaseURL = getInitParameter("DATABASE_URL");
if (databaseURL == null)
   throw new ServletException
   ("No DATABASE_URL parameter was specified");

Class.forName(driverName);
Connection con = DriverManager.getConnection(databaseURL);
```

Database access parameters are likely needed in several places within a Web application. Rather than having duplicate values in the `web.xml` file, commonly used values can be specified at the application level. This is done with the `<context-param>` element:

```
<context-param>
   <param-name>DRIVER_NAME</param-name>
   <param-value>sun.jdbc.odbc.JdbcOdbcDriver</param-value>
</context-param>

<context-param>
   <param-name>DATABASE_URL</param-name>
   <param-value>jdbc:odbc:usda</param-value>
</context-param>
```

The JSP code for accessing the values is almost the same, except the application object's `getInitParameter()` method is called:

```
String driverName =
   application.getInitParameter("DRIVER_NAME");
if (driverName == null)
   throw new ServletException
   ("No DRIVER_NAME parameter was specified");
```

```
String databaseURL =
    application.getInitParameter("DATABASE_URL");
if (databaseURL == null)
    throw new ServletException
    ("No DATABASE_URL parameter was specified");

Class.forName(driverName);
Connection con = DriverManager.getConnection(databaseURL);
```

Declarations

The previous sections covered JSP expressions and scriptlets. Along with fixed HTML template data, these two element types share a common environment—they exist within the _jspService() method of a generated Java servlet. While this is adequate for most request processing, it imposes some restrictions on the servlet's capability. This chapter introduces JSP declarations, which allow the JSP author to write Java code that operates outside the _jspService() method.

What Is a Declaration?

Similar to a scriptlet, a JSP *declaration* consists of Java source code embedded within an HTML page. Declarations are set off from the rest of the page by special opening and closing tags, as the following shows:

<%! *java statements* %>

The syntax of a declaration is identical to that of a scriptlet, with one exception: the opening delimiter is <%!, rather than <%.

Like a scriptlet, the code inside the declaration delimiters is copied verbatim to the generated Java servlet. The essential difference is *where* the code is placed: scriptlets are copied to the inside of the _jspService() method, whereas declarations are written outside the method as top-level members of the enclosing class. Understanding this distinction can help develop your mental model of how JSP works and can help explain unexpected behavior.

Where Declaration Code Is Generated

An example of how code for a declaration is generated would make this clearer. Consider the following JSP page that uses a scriptlet to display the current time:

```
<%@ page import="java.text.*,java.util.*" %>
<%
    DateFormat fmt = new SimpleDateFormat("hh:mm:ss aa");
```

```
    String now = fmt.format(new Date());
%>
The time is <%= now %>
```

Let's call this page ShowTimeS.jsp (*S* for *scriptlet*). When the page is invoked, it displays the current time:

```
The time is 10:45:28 PM
```

If the user refreshes the page, the time is incremented, as expected:

```
The time is 10:45:35 PM
The time is 10:45:37 PM
The time is 10:45:38 PM
```

Now consider the same JSP written with a declaration rather than a scriptlet. This page is named ShowTimeD.jsp (*D* for *declaration*):

```
<%@ page import= java.text.*,java.util.*  %>
<%!
   DateFormat fmt = new SimpleDateFormat("hh:mm:ss aa");
   String now = fmt.format(new Date());
%>
The time is <%= now %>
```

The only difference between ShowTimeS.jsp and ShowTimeD.jsp is that line two in ShowTimeD.jsp starts with <%! instead of <%, making it a declaration rather than a scriptlet.

When ShowTimeD.jsp is invoked, it, likewise, displays the current time:

```
The time is 10:47:26 PM
```

But look what happens when the page is refreshed:

```
The time is 10:47:26 PM
The time is 10:47:26 PM
The time is 10:47:26 PM
```

The time is not changing. Why not? The answer can be found in the generated servlet source code for each page. Here is the scriptlet version:

```java
package org.apache.jsp;

import java.text.*;
import java.util.*;
import javax.servlet.*;
import javax.servlet.http.*;
import javax.servlet.jsp.*;
import org.apache.jasper.runtime.*;

public class ShowTimeS$jsp extends HttpJspBase
{
    static {}
    public ShowTimeS$jsp( ) {}
    private static boolean _jspx_inited = false;
    public final void _jspx_init()
        throws org.apache.jasper.runtime.JspException {}

    public void _jspService
            (HttpServletRequest request,
            HttpServletResponse response)
        throws java.io.IOException, ServletException
    {
        JspFactory _jspxFactory = null;
        PageContext pageContext = null;
        HttpSession session = null;
        ServletContext application = null;
        ServletConfig config = null;
        JspWriter out = null;
        Object page = this;
        String _value = null;
        try {
            if (_jspx_inited == false) {
                synchronized (this) {
                    if (_jspx_inited == false) {
                        _jspx_init();
                        _jspx_inited = true;
                    }
                }
            }
```

```
      _jspxFactory = JspFactory.getDefaultFactory();
      response.setContentType("text/html;charset=ISO-8859-1");
      pageContext = _jspxFactory.getPageContext
          (this, request, response, "", true, 8192, true);
      application = pageContext.getServletContext();
      config = pageContext.getServletConfig();
      session = pageContext.getSession();
      out = pageContext.getOut();
      out.write("\r\n");

      // begin [file="ShowTimeS.jsp";from=(1,2);to=(4,0)]

          DateFormat fmt = new SimpleDateFormat("hh:mm:ss aa");
          String now = fmt.format(new Date());

      // end

      out.write("\r\nThe time is ");
      out.print( now );
      out.write("\r\n");
    }
  catch (Throwable t) {
      if (out != null && out.getBufferSize() != 0)
          out.clearBuffer();
      if (pageContext != null)
          pageContext.handlePageException(t);
    }
  finally {
      if (_jspxFactory != null)
          _jspxFactory.releasePageContext(pageContext);
    }
  }
}
```

and here is the declaration version:

```
package org.apache.jsp;

import java.text.*;
import java.util.*;
import javax.servlet.*;
```

```java
import javax.servlet.http.*;
import javax.servlet.jsp.*;
import org.apache.jasper.runtime.*;

public class ShowTimeD$jsp extends HttpJspBase
{
    // begin [file="ShowTimeD.jsp";from=(1,3);to=(4,0)]

        DateFormat fmt = new SimpleDateFormat("hh:mm:ss aa");
        String now = fmt.format(new Date());

    // end

    static {}
    public ShowTimeD$jsp( ) {}
    private static boolean _jspx_inited = false;
    public final void _jspx_init()
        throws org.apache.jasper.runtime.JspException {}

    public void _jspService
            (HttpServletRequest request,
            HttpServletResponse response)
        throws java.io.IOException, ServletException
    {
        JspFactory _jspxFactory = null;
        PageContext pageContext = null;
        HttpSession session = null;
        ServletContext application = null;
        ServletConfig config = null;
        JspWriter out = null;
        Object page = this;
        String _value = null;
        try {
            if (_jspx_inited == false) {
                synchronized (this) {
                    if (_jspx_inited == false) {
                        _jspx_init();
                        _jspx_inited = true;
                    }
                }
            }
            _jspxFactory = JspFactory.getDefaultFactory();
```

```
            response.setContentType("text/html;charset=ISO-8859-1");
            pageContext = _jspxFactory.getPageContext
                (this, request, response, "", true, 8192, true);
            application = pageContext.getServletContext();
            config = pageContext.getServletConfig();
            session = pageContext.getSession();
            out = pageContext.getOut();
            out.write("\r\n");
            out.write("\r\nThe time is ");
            out.print( now );
            out.write("\r\n");
        }
        catch (Throwable t) {
            if (out != null && out.getBufferSize() != 0)
                out.clearBuffer();
            if (pageContext != null)
                pageContext.handlePageException(t);
        }
        finally {
            if (_jspxFactory != null)
                _jspxFactory.releasePageContext(pageContext);
        }
    }
}
```

Other than the program names, the only difference between the two servlets is the location of the two scripting lines. In the scriptlet version, they are found in the middle of the _jspService() method, making the fmt and now variables local to that method. In the declaration version, however, they appear as the first entries inside the class. This makes the two variables *instance* variables, which are initialized when the servlet instance is first created and never updated. We will see shortly that this is not only undesirable, it's also dangerous.

Primary Uses for Declarations

Declarations can contain any valid Java code, but they are most commonly used in three contexts:

- **Variable declarations** Both class and instance variables can be declared and initialized.

- **Method definitions**   Duplicate or overly complex scriptlet code can be restructured into a main routine that calls other methods.

- **Inner classes**   Additional classes can be defined and made available to scriptlets, expressions, and other declaration code.

Variable Declarations

As illustrated in the preceding examples, declarations can be used to define and initialize variables. The variables will be available to scriptlets, expressions, and other declarations. These can be class variables (marked with the `static` keyword), as in the following example,

```
<%!
    static final String[] COLORS = {
        "#CA9A26",
        "#3BF428",
        "#F7E339",
        "#FF40FF",
    };
%>
<%
    for (int i = 0; i < COLORS.length; i++) {
        String color = COLORS[i];
%>
<div style="background-color: <%= color%>;
            font-size: 12pt;
            font-weight: bold;">
    This is color <%= color %>
</div>
<% } %>
```

or instance variables, as the following shows:

```
<%@ page import="java.text.*" %>
<%@ page import="java.util.*" %>

<%! int count; %>
<%
    String requestTime =
        new SimpleDateFormat("hh:mm:ss a").format(new Date());
```

```
   count = 0;
   for (int i = 0; i < 10; i++) {
%>
Request at <%= requestTime %> count = <%= ++count %><br>
<%
       Thread.sleep(250);
   }
%>
```

In either case, the variable declaration is copied verbatim into the generated servlet as a top-level member of the enclosing class.

Thread Safety and Instance Variables

The preceding instance variable example contains a subtle flaw. Each time it services a request, it sets the count variable to zero and then enters a loop of ten iterations, incrementing the count and displaying it along with the request object hash code. When first tested, it might look like the output shown in Figure 6-4.

But look what happens when two people request the JSP page at about the same time (now you know why we added the Thread.sleep(250): to introduce enough of a delay to allow for the collision). Figures 6-5 and 6-6 show two requests being handled simultaneously.

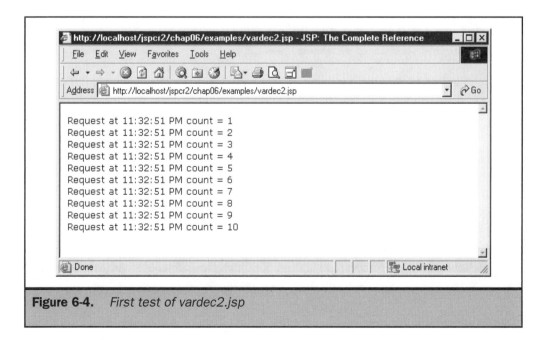

Figure 6-4. *First test of vardec2.jsp*

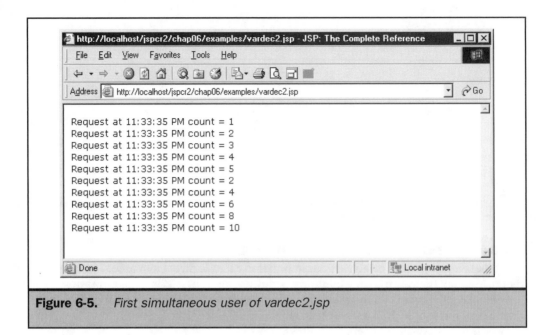

Figure 6-5. First simultaneous user of vardec2.jsp

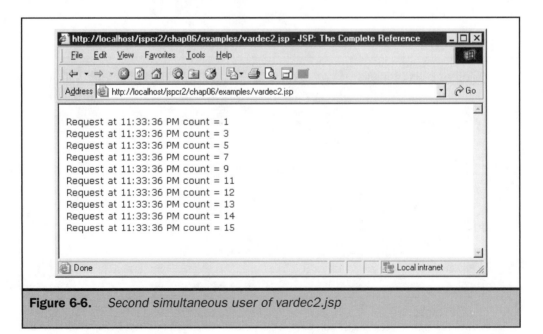

Figure 6-6. Second simultaneous user of vardec2.jsp

The first request starts off normally enough for the first five lines. But then the count drops back to 2, and appears to increment by 2 for the rest of the loop. Similarly, the second request starts at 1 but then skips the even numbers up to 12. An examination of the generated source code (edited for clarity) shows what the problem is:

```
package org.apache.jsp;

import java.text.*;
import java.util.*;
import javax.servlet.*;
import javax.servlet.http.*;
import javax.servlet.jsp.*;
import org.apache.jasper.runtime.*;

public class vardec2$jsp extends HttpJspBase
{
    int count;

    // ...

    public void _jspService
        (HttpServletRequest request,
         HttpServletResponse response)
      throws java.io.IOException, ServletException
    {

        // ...

        String requestTime =
            new SimpleDateFormat("hh:mm:ss a").format(new Date());

        count = 0;
        for (int i = 0; i < 10; i++) {
            out.write("\r\nRequest at ");
            out.print( requestTime );
            out.write(" count = ");
            out.print( ++count );
            out.write("<br>\r\n");
            Thread.sleep(250);
        }
```

```
        out.write("\r\n");

        // ...
    }
}
```

The source of the problem is that `count` is an instance variable, not a local variable in the `_jspService()` method. Recall that JSP pages are compiled as servlets, which, by default, run as a single instance with separate threads to handle each request. This being the case, any instance variables are automatically shared between all request-handling threads. In the example, the first request got as far as 5, but then the thread that handled the second request entered `_jspService()` and reset the shared `count` variable back to zero. As the loop progressed, the two threads alternated every 125 milliseconds or so, each incrementing the value.

Chapter 11 discusses this problem and explores several solutions. The conclusion presenting itself here is that variable declarations in a JSP page are best used to handle *read-only* variables.

Method Definitions

A more common use for declarations is to define additional methods. The syntax is no different than for any other method definitions, except for the `<%!` and `%>` delimiters:

```
<%!
    public int sum(int a, int b)
    {
        return a + b;
    }
%>
```

As with variable declarations, method definitions are copied verbatim into the generated servlet as top-level members outside the `_jspService()` method:

```
public class methdef1 extends HttpJspBase
{
    // begin [file="methdef1.jsp";from=(0,3);to=(5,0)]

        public int sum(int a, int b)
        {
```

```
            return a + b;
        }
    // end

    // ...

    public void _jspService(
        HttpServletRequest request,
        HttpServletResponse  response)
      throws IOException, ServletException
    {
        // ...
    }
}
```

A typical method definition in a JSP declaration would be for a utility method that reformats strings produced by a scriptlet. Consider the following JSP page that displays the value of several system properties in an HTML table:

```
<%@ page session="false" %>
<html>
<head>
<title>Selected System Properties</title>
</head>
<body>
<h1>Selected System Properties</h1>
<table border="1" cellpadding="3" cellspacing="0">
<%
    final String[] propNames = {
        "java.awt.printerjob",
        "java.class.path",
        "java.class.version",
        "java.ext.dirs",
        "java.library.path",
    };
    for (int i = 0; i < propNames.length; i++) {
        String name = propNames[i];
        String value = System.getProperty(name);
```

```
%>
<tr>
   <td align="left" valign="top"><%= name %></td>
   <td align="left" valign="top"><%= value %></td>
</tr>
<% } %>
</body>
</table>
</html>
```

The output of the JSP page is shown in Figure 6-7. The problem with this table is that several of the values are quite long, with no embedded spaces. This means the right-hand table cell is too long to be displayed in the window.

A simple solution for this is to shorten the property value strings. One quality the offending members have in common is that they consist of a list of several values separated by semicolons. These can be shortened by inserting a <br> tag after each semicolon so that the list will be displayed on multiple lines. This will make the table width requirement no larger than the widest list entry. This could be done with inline code in the scriptlet, but a more readable solution would be to use a `normalize()` method that applies the necessary transformation. That way, the `<%= value %>`

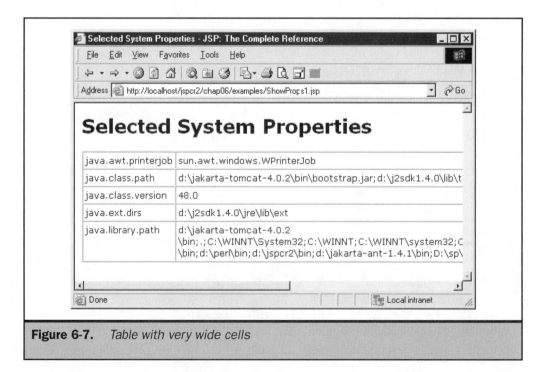

Figure 6-7. *Table with very wide cells*

expression could simply be written `<%= normalize(value) %>`. The following shows the method declaration:

```
<%!
   private static final String normalize(String s)
   {
      StringBuffer sb = new StringBuffer();
      for (int i = 0; i < s.length(); i++) {
         char c = s.charAt(i);
         sb.append(c);
         if (c == ';')
            sb.append("<br>");
      }
      return sb.toString();
   }
%>
```

This time, when the same properties are displayed, the table fits within a more reasonable window size (see Figure 6-8).

Overriding jspInit and jspDestroy

In the preceding example, the string manipulation could have been done with inline code in the scriptlet, rather than by a method call. In some circumstances, that is not possible. For example, if resources need to be acquired or threads started when a JSP page is loaded, these functions should be performed in the context of the servlet `init()` and `destroy()` methods.

The JSP 1.2 Specification expressly forbids page authors from overriding any of the servlet lifecycle methods directly, including `init()` and `destroy()`. However, it provides two special methods named `jspInit()` and `jspDestroy()` that accomplish the same purpose. These methods are called automatically from within `init()` and `destroy()`, and they have empty definitions in the parent JSP page implementation. In Tomcat, for example, the base JSP class `org.apache.jasper.runtime.HttpJspBase` defines `init()` and `jspInit()` as follows:

```
public final void init(ServletConfig config)
   throws ServletException
   {
      super.init(config);
      jspInit();
   }

public void jspInit()
```

ELEMENTS OF JSP

```
{
}
```

Similarly, it defines `destroy()` and `jspDestroy()` as follows:

```
public final void destroy()
{
    jspDestroy();
}
public void jspDestroy()
{
}
```

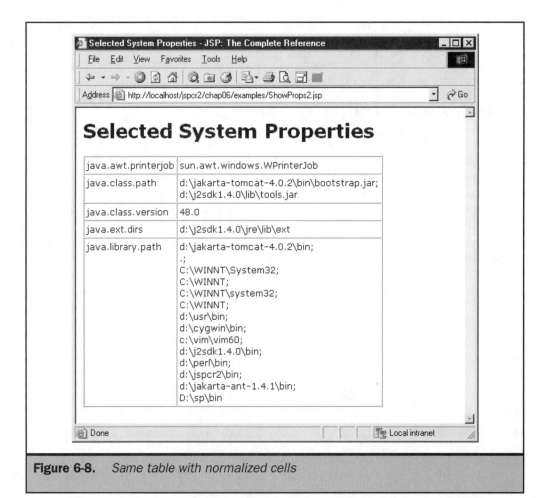

Figure 6-8. *Same table with normalized cells*

The use of the `final` keyword ensures `init()` and `destroy()` themselves cannot be overridden. This, in turn, guarantees `jspInit()` and `jspDestroy()` will always be called. To add something to the initialization phase of a JSP, the necessary code should be entered in a JSP declaration:[4]

```
public void jspInit()
{
    TimerThread t = new TimerThread();
    t.start();
}
```

Access to Implicit Objects

Unlike scriptlets and expressions, declarations have no access to the implicit objects described earlier. The reason for this is apparent when you remember that methods in declarations are defined outside the `_jspService()` method. Therefore, if a declaration method needs access to one or more of these objects, the objects must be passed somehow from `_jspService()`. You can do this in several ways:

- Pass the objects as individual parameters. This is easy to do but tends to become unwieldy if more than a few parameters are necessary.

- Pass the `pageContext` implicit object as a parameter. From the page context, all the other variables can be accessed indirectly.

- Pass a structure containing all the variables of interest as a single parameter.

Summary

JSP pages provide several means for incorporating Java code in the handling of requests: expressions, scriptlets, and declarations. JSP *expressions* are simply Java-language expressions that yield a string value (or can be converted into one). Expressions are enclosed in `<%=` and `%>` delimiters. Whatever is between the delimiters is made the argument of an `out.print()` or `out.write()` method. For this reason, expressions must not end in a semicolon. *Scriptlets* are Java code fragments designed to operate inside the `_jspService()` method and are marked by the `<%` and `%>` delimiters. The programming statements in a scriptlet are copied directly into the Java source code of the generated servlet.

---

[4]   Curiously enough, the JSP 1.2 specification makes no provision for throwing an exception from `jspInit()`, even though `init()` itself can do so. This seems to be an oversight in the specification. What can be done if the JSP detects a fatal error during the `jspInit()`, say, failure to connect to a database?

To give it linkage to the JSP container, a JSP page has access to a number of implicit objects. These are automatically initialized objects that have predefined variable names. These variables are

- `request`
- `response`
- `pageContext`
- `session`
- `application`
- `out`
- `config`
- `page`
- `exception`

The last variable (`exception`) is available only to pages with the `isErrorPage="true"` attribute in their page directive.

Like a scriptlet, a JSP *declaration* is used to incorporate Java statements into a JSP page. The key difference between the two is *where* the JSP container writes the code in the generated servlet. With a scriptlet, the code becomes part of the `_jspService()` method, whereas code in a declaration becomes top-level code in the servlet class. This distinction is important to understand because it affects the context in which the code operates.

Declarations have three primary uses:

- **Variable declarations**   Both class and instance variables can be defined, although care must be taken to ensure that write access to the variables is synchronized, because servlets, by default, are multithreaded. The most practical use of variable declarations is for static final constants.

- **Method definitions**   Additional methods can be added to the generated servlet by means of JSP declarations. Because the generated code is not inside the `_jspService()` method, however, it does not have access to the implicit variables (`request`, `response`, `out`, and so forth). These variables must be explicitly passed to the method if they are to be used. Declarations can be used to override the `jspInit()` and `jspDestroy()` methods.

- **Inner classes**   Declarations provide a convenient means for writing inner classes. A typical inner class might be a data structure for passing a set of variables between methods in the generated servlet.

The Complete Reference

Chapter 7

Request Dispatching

In large-scale Web development projects, having HTTP requests handled by more than one server-side component is often desirable. There are several reasons for this:

- **Eliminating redundancy**   Many features of a Web site are common to all pages, such as headers and footers, navigation bars, and other elements of the look and feel. Rather than duplicate the HTML that generates these features, being able to write them once and use them in a number of places is useful.

- **Separating content and presentation**   Because Java can be used freely in any part of a JSP, you can easily end up with code that both generates information and presents it, perhaps reading from a database, performing calculations, and generating HTML tables. Changing both the logic and the appearance of the page may be necessary later. Such code can quickly become overly complex. It makes more sense to separate the pure Java code that accesses the database and applies business logic from the JSP code that creates an output Web page.

- **Combining JSP and servlet technologies**   To facilitate separating content and presentation, you may wish to use servlets to handle the pure Java aspects of request processing and JSP pages to render the results.

This chapter examines features of the JSP environment that allow requests to be forwarded and the contents or output of other resources to be included. The chapter also discusses how the `RequestDispatcher` class works and concludes with a comparison of two JSP development models.

Anatomy of Request Processing

The servlet container that handles servlet and JSP requests can be part of the Web server itself (referred to as the *in-process* model). Most JSP and servlet containers include a simple HTTP server that can run in standalone mode, which is useful for development and testing. This model is illustrated in Figure 7-1.

A more robust alternative is the *out-of-process* model, shown in Figure 7-2. In this case, the Web server contains a component referred to as a *connector*. The connector intercepts

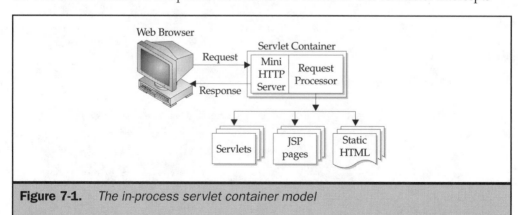

Figure 7-1.   *The in-process servlet container model*

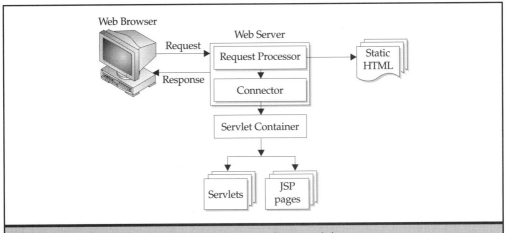

Figure 7-2.   *The out-of-process servlet container model*

servlet requests and passes them on to the servlet container by an implementation-dependent protocol servlet container. Other requests are handled by the Web server as usual.

When the servlet container receives a request, it assembles all the details about the request into an `HttpServletRequest` object. These details include the request headers, the URI, the query string, any parameters sent, and so on. Similarly, it initializes an `HttpServletResponse` object that can hold response headers and the response output stream. It then invokes the servlet's `service()` method (the `_jspService()` method, if the servlet is a JSP), passing it references to the two objects, as shown in Figure 7-3.

A simple JSP can extract what it needs from the request object, perform the necessary calculations and other logic, and then create output using the response

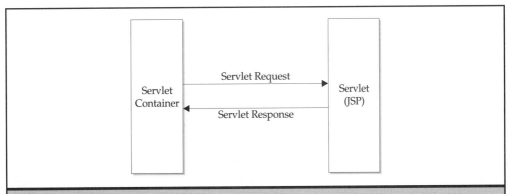

Figure 7-3.   *Servlet container passing request and response objects to a servlet*

object. The remainder of this chapter examines how larger and more complex Web applications can operate on these request and response objects, passing them through more than one servlet or JSP.

Including Other Resources

HTML itself does not have a direct means for including data from other files in its output. This is unfortunate, because a great deal of HTML markup is common to a number of pages in a typical Web site—corporate logos, copyright notices, navigation links, and other features. Besides these static sources of text and images, you may have dynamic content that needs to be included. JSP provides two means of incorporating such data:

- The **<%@ include %> directive** is used to copy static text into the JSP source code before it is transformed into Java servlet source code and compiled. Typically, this text is HTML code, but it can be anything that could appear in a JSP page.

- The **<jsp:include> action** causes the servlet container to invoke another URL and merge its output with that of the original JSP page.

| Note | *A key point to remember in building a mental model is that the <%@ include %> directive is performed once, at compilation time, whereas the <jsp:include> action is performed each time a request is made. If you keep this clearly in mind, you won't be confused about why you can't specify a runtime expression for the <%@ include %> filename.* |

The next two sections describe each of these JSP components and how they operate.

The include Directive

The syntax of the include directive is as follows:

<%@ include file="*filename*" %>

The included filename must be a relative URL specification, meaning it contains only path information, not protocol or server information. As a consequence, only resources in the current servlet context can be included by this means.

If the filename begins with "/", it is considered to be absolute with respect to the top of the servlet context. Otherwise, the filename is considered to be relative to the current JSP page. For example, if a Web application has a products subdirectory and the products/search.jsp page contains the directive

```
<%@ include file="/includes/header.inc" %>
```

then the file that would be included is *<path>*/includes/header.inc, where *<path>* is the Web application root directory (i.e., the docBase attribute of the application's <Context> element in server.xml, if you are using Tomcat 4). If, instead, the directive is

```
<%@ include file="includes/header.inc" %>
```

then the file would be *<path>*/products/includes/header.inc.

How It Works

When a <%@ include %> directive is encountered, the JSP container reads the specified file and merges its contents into the JSP source code currently being parsed. For example, if flavors.jsp contains

```
<h3>Flavors</h3>
Our most popular flavors are:
<%@ include file="flavor_list.html" %>
Try them all!
```

and if flavor_list.html contains

```
<ol>
<li>Chocolate</li>
<li>Strawberry</li>
<li>Vanilla</li>
</ol>
```

the HTML sent to the Web browser is exactly the same as if flavors.jsp contained this:

```
<h3>Flavors</h3>
Our most popular flavors are:
<ol>
<li>Chocolate</li>
<li>Strawberry</li>
```

```
<li>Vanilla</li>
</ol>
Try them all!
```

We can see the interleaving of the two files in the servlet source code generated by Tomcat:[1]

```
// begin [file="flavors.jsp";from=(0,0);to=(2,0)]
   out.write("<h3>Flavors</h3>\r\n"
      + "Our most popular flavors are:\r\n");
// end

// begin [file="flavor_list.html";from=(0,0);to=(5,0)]
   out.write("<ol>\r\n"
      + "<li>Chocolate</li>\r\n"
      + "<li>Strawberry</li>\r\n"
      + "<li>Vanilla</li>\r\n"
      + "</ol>\r\n");
// end

// begin [file="flavors.jsp";from=(2,38);to=(4,0)]
   out.write("\r\nTry them all!\r\n");
// end
```

Other than the filename change in the comment, there is no way to tell that the ordered list was not simply coded in the original JSP page. In this respect, the `<%@ include %>` directive is similar to the C language `#include` preprocessor directive.

Effect of Changes in an Included File

What happens if the `flavor_list.html` file is modified? The JSP 1.2 specification makes no specific provision for notifying the JSP container that an included file has changed, although it does encourage it, and a robust JSP container should do so.

The key point to remember is that *the file included is the file that exists at compilation time, because this is when the `<%@ include %>` directive is processed.* This implies that:

1. The filename cannot be a runtime expression.

2. The included file must exist at compilation time.

---

[1]   Generated source code examples have been slightly reformatted for readability.

In addition to being used to copy HTML, the `include` directive can be used to include Java source code as a declaration section. However, this is almost always a bad idea, for several reasons:

- The JSP 1.2 specification does not guarantee pages that include code in this manner will be notified if the code changes. This creates significant maintenance problems.

- The included code uses the namespace of the including page, so you need to exercise care to ensure that no duplicate variable definitions occur.

- Nobody but you (and eventually not even you) will be able to find the bugs that get introduced this way.

The <jsp:include> Action

In contrast to the `include` directive, the `jsp:include` action is interpreted each time a request is made. The syntax of this action is

<jsp:include page="*resourcename*" flush="true" />

The included resource name must be a relative URL specification, containing only path information. The resource name is mapped to the current servlet context in the same way as the filename in an `include` directive. If the name begins with "/", it refers to a path beginning at the top of the servlet context; otherwise, it is interpreted as a path relative to the directory containing the calling JSP. The flush attribute (which is mandatory) is used to indicate whether to force the output buffer used by the `JspWriter` to be written to the client before the resource is included. The only valid value in JSP 1.1 was *true*; however, JSP 1.2 supports both the *true* and *false* options.

How It Works

The <jsp:include> action is parsed by the JSP compiler, but rather than being executed at compilation time, it is converted into Java code that invokes the named resource at request time. The resource can be a static data source, such as an HTML file or a dynamic source, such as a JSP page or a servlet. Returning to our ice cream flavors example, suppose `flavors2.jsp` contains

```
<h3>Flavors</h3>
Our most popular flavors are:
<jsp:include page="/FlavorList" flush="true"/>
Try them all!
```

where `FlavorList` is a *servlet* that extracts the favorite flavors from a database or some other dynamic source:

```java
package com.jspcr.servlets;

import java.io.*;
import java.net.*;
import java.sql.*;
import java.util.*;

import javax.servlet.*;
import javax.servlet.http.*;

/**
 * Returns the list of the most popular flavors
 */
public class FlavorListServlet extends HttpServlet
{
    public static final String JDBC_DRIVER =
        "sun.jdbc.odbc.JdbcOdbcDriver";

    public static final String URL =
        "jdbc:odbc:IceCream";

    public void doGet(
            HttpServletRequest request,
            HttpServletResponse response)
        throws ServletException, IOException
    {
        PrintWriter out = response.getWriter();

        Connection con = null;
        try {

            // Connect to the ice cream database

            Class.forName(JDBC_DRIVER);
            con = DriverManager.getConnection(URL);

            // Run a query to get the top flavors

            Statement stmt = con.createStatement();
```

```
    String sql =
        "SELECT  RANK, NAME"
        + "   FROM flavors"
        + "   WHERE (RANK <= 3)"
        + "   ORDER BY RANK" ;

    ResultSet rs = stmt.executeQuery(sql);

    // Print as an ordered list

    out.println("<ol>");
    while (rs.next()) {
        int rank = rs.getInt(1);
        String name = rs.getString(2);
        out.println("   <li>" + name + "</li>");
    }
    out.println("</ol>");
}
catch (SQLException e) {
    throw new ServletException(e.getMessage());
}
catch (ClassNotFoundException e) {
    throw new ServletException(e.getMessage());
}

// Close the database

finally {
    if (con != null) {
        try { con.close(); }
        catch (SQLException ignore) {}
    }
}
}
}
```

When `flavors2.jsp` is invoked, it produces the following output:

```
<h3>Flavors</h3>
Our most popular flavors are:
<ol>
```

```
   <li>Espresso Chip</li>
   <li>Orange Cream</li>
   <li>Peanut Butter</li>
</ol>
Try them all!
```

The resulting HTML may look similar, but the underlying mechanism is completely different, as can be seen in the source code of the servlet Tomcat generates:

```
// begin [file="flavors2.jsp";from=(0,27);to=(3,0)]
   out.write("<h3>Flavors</h3>\r\n"
   + "Our most popular flavors are:\r\n");
// end

// begin [file="flavors2.jsp";from=(3,0);to=(3,46)]
   {
      String _jspx_qStr = "";
      JspRuntimeLibrary.include
         (request,
         response,
         "/FlavorList" + _jspx_qStr,
         out,
         true);
      if ("true".equals(request.getAttribute
         ("javax.servlet.forward.seen")))
         return;
   }
// end

// begin [file="flavors2.jsp";from=(3,46);to=(5,0)]
   out.write("\r\nTry them all!\r\n");
// end
```

Rather than containing the ordered list of flavors, the JSP contains code that invokes the JspRuntimeLibrary.include() method to run the servlet that accesses the database. The output of the servlet is included in the JSP output and the JSP resumes control. Whereas the include *directive* is similar to the C language #include preprocessor directive, the <jsp:include> *action* is more like a C language function call.

Restrictions

A JSP page invoked by a <jsp:include> action has access to all the implicit objects available to the calling JSP, including the response object. It can write to and flush the out object, but it cannot set response headers. For example, you can neither specify a different content type nor use a <jsp:include> action to handle authentication with the WWW-Authenticate header.

Runtime Features

Because a <jsp:include> is evaluated at runtime, the page it refers to can be supplied in a runtime expression, rather than being hardcoded. The following JSP page is designed to be a comprehensive view of an HTTP servlet request. Rather than being a long, scrolling list of attribute names and values, the page simulates a tabbed dialog box, with attributes broken down into logical groups and radio buttons along the top used to select which group to show.

```
<%@ page import= java.util.*  %>
<%!
   // Table row colors

   static final String[] COLORS = {"#E0E0E0", "#F0F0F0"};

   // Array of tab codes, labels, and JSP names

   public static final String[][] TABS = {
      {  "HD",
         "Headers",
         "ShowRequestHeaders.jsp"},

      {  "PM",
         "Parameters",
         "ShowParameters.jsp"},

      {  "SR",
         "ServletRequest Methods",
         "ShowServletRequestMethodValues.jsp"},

      {  "HR",
         "HttpServletRequest Methods",
         "ShowHttpServletRequestMethodValues.jsp"},
   };
%>
<html>
<head>
```

```jsp
<title>Show Request</title>
</head>
<body>
<h2>Show Request</h2>
<form>
<table border="0" cellpadding="3" cellspacing="0">

   <%-- Radio buttons for selecting the page --%>

   <tr>
      <td align="left">
<%
   String which = request.getParameter("which");
   if (which == null)
      which = TABS[0][0];
   String jspToRun = null;
   for (int i = 0; i < TABS.length; i++) {
      String tabCode  = TABS[i][0];
      String tabLabel = TABS[i][1];
      String tabJSP   = TABS[i][2];
      String CHECKED  = "";
      if (which.equals(tabCode)) {
         CHECKED = "CHECKED";
         jspToRun = tabJSP;
      }
%>
   <input name="which" type="RADIO" value="<%= tabCode %>"
         <%= CHECKED %> onClick="this.form.submit()"
         ><%= tabLabel %>
<%
   }
%>
      <p>
      </td>
   </tr>

   <tr>
      <td align="center" valign="top">

      <%-- Page showing details of the request --%>

      <jsp:include page="<%= jspToRun %>" flush="true"/>
```

```jsp
    <%-- Resulting table --%>

    <table border="1" cellpadding="3" cellspacing="0" width="600">
    <tr>
       <th colspan="2" align="left" bgcolor="#000000">
          <font size="+1" color="#ffffff">
          <%= request.getAttribute("_table_title") %>
          </font>
       </th>
    </tr>
    <tr>
       <th width="200" align="left">Name</th>
       <th width="400" align="left">Value</th>
    </tr>
    <%
       Map entries = (Map)
          request.getAttribute("_table_entries");
       Iterator iNames = entries.keySet().iterator();
       int row = 0;
       while (iNames.hasNext()) {
          String name = (String) iNames.next();
          Object value = entries.get(name);
    %>
    <tr bgcolor="<%= COLORS[row % 2] %>">
       <td align="left" valign="top"><b><%= name %></b></td>
       <td align="left" valign="top"><%= value %></td>
    </tr>
    <%
          row++;
       }
    %>
    </table>
    <p>
    </td>
   </tr>

</table>
</form>
</body>
</html>
```

ELEMENTS OF JSP

The categories available for display are coded in a static `String` array. For each category, a two-character abbreviation exists: a label and the name of a JSP page that will extract the desired data. The array specifies four categories of attributes:

- Request headers
- Parameters
- Methods in `ServletRequest`
- Methods in `HttpServletRequest`

The string array provides all the information needed to generate the page. The radio buttons are contained in a self-referring HTML form and are generated in a loop, with the two-character abbreviation used as the VALUE attribute and the label as the visible text. When a radio button is clicked, the form is submitted, with the value of the button supplying the value of the `which` parameter. Figure 7-4 shows the initial display, which is the request headers category.

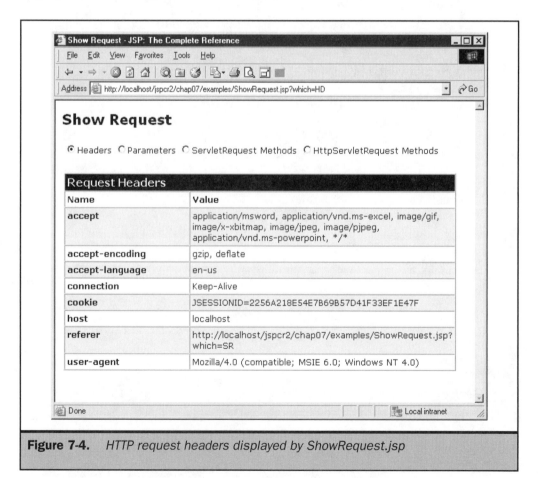

Figure 7-4. *HTTP request headers displayed by ShowRequest.jsp*

When another radio button is clicked (for example, the `ServletRequest Methods` button), a different table appears in the body of the table (see Figure 7-5).

`ShowRequest.jsp` determines which radio button was clicked and selects the corresponding JSP filename from the string array. This filename is then passed in a JSP expression to the `<jsp:include>` action:

```
<jsp:include page="<%= jspToRun %>" flush="true" />
```

Each of the individual table generating pages creates a list of attribute names and values, and writes them to a `java.util.Map` object that is stored as a request attribute.

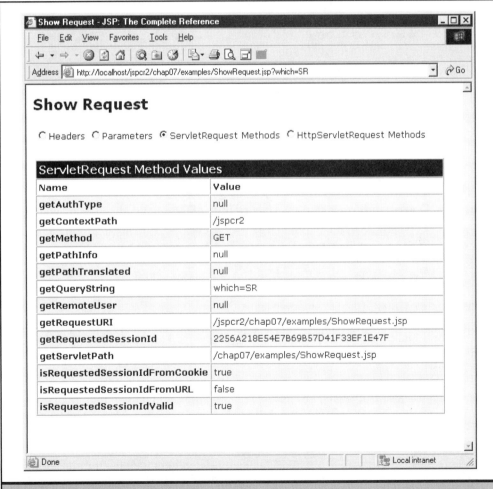

Figure 7-5. *Servlet request methods shown in the third tab of ShowRequest.jsp*

The table heading string is also stored as a request attribute. When the included JSP completes, the map is retrieved from the request attribute and rendered in an HTML table. The JSP that generates the Request Headers tab is shown here:

```
<%@ page import="java.util.*" %>
<%
    Enumeration eNames = request.getHeaderNames();
    if (eNames.hasMoreElements()) {
        String title = "Request Headers";
        Map entries = new TreeMap();
        while (eNames.hasMoreElements()) {
            String name = (String) eNames.nextElement();
            String value = request.getHeader(name);
            entries.put(name, value);
        }
        request.setAttribute("_table_title", title);
        request.setAttribute("_table_entries", entries);
    }
%>
```

This capability to select a page to be included based on runtime information is a useful characteristic of JSP-based Web applications because it allows complex processing to be built on table-driven logic.

Passing Parameters to the Included JSP

Parameters can be passed to JSP pages that are invoked through `<jsp:include>` actions to provide additional customization. The syntax in this case would be

```
<jsp:include page="pageName" flush="true">
<jsp:param name="name_1" value="value_1" />
<jsp:param name="name_2" value="value_2" />
...
<jsp:param name="name_n" value="value_n" />
</jsp:include>
```

The parameters are passed to the included JSP the same as ordinary form parameters, and can be retrieved with `request.getParameter(name)`. If the parameter name is the same as one the JSP is already using, both values are passed and can be retrieved as an array of strings using `getParameterValues(name)`.

The following JSP illustrates how this technique can be used. It includes the same page twice, using different parameters each time:

```
<%
    // Diameter of the earth in kilometers

    int distance = 12756;
%>

<h4>Diameter of the Earth in SI (Metric) Units</h4>
<jsp:include page="ShowDiameter.jsp" flush="true">
    <jsp:param name="dist" value="<%= distance %>" />
    <jsp:param name="units" value="SI" />
</jsp:include>

<h4>Diameter of the Earth in U.S. Customary Units</h4>
<jsp:include page="ShowDiameter.jsp" flush="true">
    <jsp:param name="dist" value="<%= distance %>" />
    <jsp:param name="units" value="US" />
</jsp:include>
```

Two parameters are passed:

- **dist**   The distance in kilometers.
- **units**   "SI" if metric units are desired, "US" otherwise.

The ShowDiameter.jsp page retrieves the kilometer distance, converts it to an integer, and finds the mile equivalent. Then, based on the unit of measure code passed in the units parameter, it displays the distance in either SI or U.S. units:

```
<%
    String dist = request.getParameter("dist");
    int kilometers = Integer.parseInt(dist);
    double miles = kilometers / 1.609344;

    String units = request.getParameter("units");
```

```
    if (units.equals("SI")) {
    %> Diameter = <%= kilometers %> km <%
    }
    else {
    %> Diameter = <%= miles %> miles <%
    }
%>
```

Figure 7-6 shows the results.

Retrieving the Original URI

When a page is invoked in a `<jsp:include>` action, it uses the same request object as its including page, which means that `request.getRequestURI()` and `request.getServletPath()` return the path to the page originally handling the

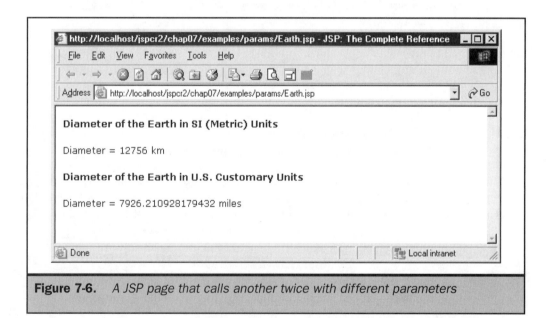

Figure 7-6.   *A JSP page that calls another twice with different parameters*

request, not the current page. The equivalent values for the included page, however, are available as attributes of the request. This is illustrated in `ShowPath1.jsp`:

```
<html>
<head>
<title>Retrieving the Original URI</title>
</head>
<body>
<pre>
In ShowPath1.jsp:

    request.getRequestURI() =
        <%= request.getRequestURI() %>

    request.getServletPath() =
        <%= request.getServletPath() %>

</pre>
<jsp:include page="ShowPath2.jsp" flush="true"/>
</body>
</html>
```

and the page it includes, `ShowPath2.jsp`:

```
<pre>
In ShowPath2.jsp:

    request.getRequestURI() =
        <%= request.getRequestURI() %>

    request.getServletPath() =
        <%= request.getServletPath() %>

    javax.servlet.include.request_uri =
        <%= request.getAttribute
        ("javax.servlet.include.request_uri") %>
```

```
javax.servlet.include.servlet_path =
   <%= request.getAttribute
   ("javax.servlet.include.servlet_path") %>
</pre>
```

The output of the two pages is shown in Figure 7-7. Note that in ShowPath2, the getRequestURI() and getServletPath() methods still reflect the main URI (ShowPath1.jsp) but that the included page (ShowPath2.jsp) can be determined by looking at specific request attributes. The set of attributes that can be retrieved in this fashion is listed in Table 7-1.

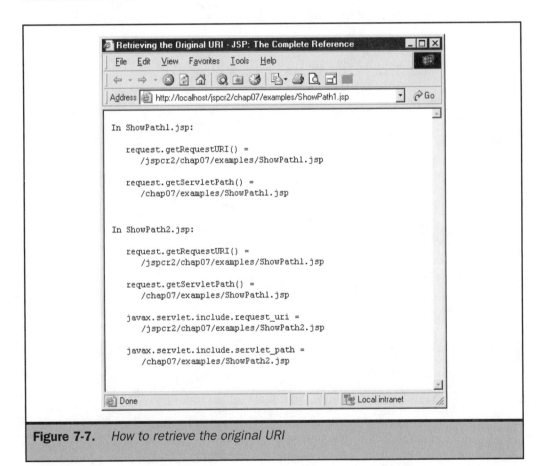

Figure 7-7. *How to retrieve the original URI*

Attribute Name	Equivalent Method
`javax.servlet.include.request_uri`	`request.getRequestURI()`
`javax.servlet.include.context_path`	`request.getContextPath()`
`javax.servlet.include.servlet_path`	`request.getServletPath()`
`javax.servlet.include.path_info`	`request.getPathInfo()`
`javax.servlet.include.query_string`	`request.getQueryString()`

Table 7-1.   *Request Attributes That Describe an Included JSP Page*

ELEMENTS OF JSP

Which Method to Use

The include directive and the `<jsp:include>` action perform similar functions, and each has its advantages. The decision to use one or the other should take into account whether the inclusion needs to be done at runtime. Table 7-2 compares the two options:

Criterion	`<%@ include %>`	`<jsp:include>`
Compilation time	Slower—resource must be parsed.	Slightly faster.
Execution time	Slightly faster.	Slower—resource must be resolved each time.
Flexibility	Less—page name is fixed.	More—page can be chosen at runtime.

Table 7-2.   *Advantages and Disadvantages of Each Include Method*

Forwarding Requests

To facilitate splitting a Web application into content and presentation, the JSP environment provides the `<jsp:forward>` action, which allows requests to be forwarded from one page to another, or to a servlet. The syntax is

<jsp:forward page="*page*" />

where `page` is a URI relative to the current page, or an absolute URI with respect to the top of the servlet context. Like `<jsp:include>`, the `<jsp:forward>` action can use a runtime expression for the page name. Similarly, it can pass parameters to the new JSP using the following syntax:

<jsp:forward page="*page*">
<jsp:param name="*name_1*" value="*value_1*" />
<jsp:param name="*name_2*" value="*value_2*" />
...
<jsp:param name="*name_n*" value="*value_n*" />
</jsp:forward>

When a `<jsp:forward>` action is executed, the named page is loaded and the current page is terminated. The new page has access to the request and response objects, and it is expected to create all the output because the forwarding page cannot write any output. Table 7-3 describes what happens when output buffering is or is not enabled, and when the buffer has been filled or not.

Buffering Enabled	Buffer Filled	Action
no	N/A	If any output has been written, an IllegalStateException is thrown.
yes	no	Buffer is cleared before forwarding.
yes	yes	IllegalStateException is thrown.

Table 7-3. *Buffering Actions*

The following code shows a typical use for request forwarding—to separate content from presentation. The first JSP page is GetFoodGroups.jsp, which reads a list of food groups from the USDA Nutrient Database:

```jsp
<%@ page import="java.io.*" %>
<%@ page import="java.sql.*" %>
<%@ page import="java.util.*" %>
<%@ page import="com.jspcr.forward.*" %>
<%
    // Load the driver class and establish a connection

    Class.forName
        ("sun.jdbc.odbc.JdbcOdbcDriver");

    Connection con = DriverManager.getConnection
        ("jdbc:odbc:usda");

    // Run a database query to get the list of food groups

    Statement stmt = con.createStatement();
    String sql =
        " SELECT    FdGp_Cd, FdGp_Desc"
      + " FROM      fd_group"
    ;
    ResultSet rs = stmt.executeQuery(sql);

    // Store the results as a list of FoodGroup objects

    List fglist = new ArrayList();
    while (rs.next()) {
        String code = rs.getString(1);
        String desc = rs.getString(2);
        FoodGroup fg = new FoodGroup(code, desc);
        System.out.println("DEBUG: code=" + code + ",desc=" + desc);
        fglist.add(fg);
    }
```

ELEMENTS OF JSP

```
    rs.close();
    stmt.close();
    con.close();

    // Store the list as a request attribute

    request.setAttribute("com.jspcr.forward.FoodGroups", fglist);

    // Now forward the request

%><jsp:forward page="ShowFoodGroups.jsp" />
```

As the food groups records are read, they are stored in a `List` structure. The list is saved as an attribute in the request. When all the records have been extracted from the database, the request is forwarded to `ShowFoodGroups.jsp`, which retrieves the list and writes it as an HTML table:

```
<%@ page import="java.io.*,java.util.*,com.jspcr.forward.*" %>

<html>
<head>
<title>Show Food Groups</title>
<style>
    body, td {
        background-color: #FFFFFF;
        font: 8pt Sans-Serif;
    }
</style>
</head>
<body>
<center>
<h3>Food Groups</h3>

<%-- Get the list of FoodGroup objects
        that was created by database calls --%>
```

```
<%
   List fglist = (List) request.getAttribute
      ("com.jspcr.forward.FoodGroups");
   if (fglist == null)
      throw new ServletException
         ("No com.jspcr.forward.FoodGroups attribute");
   Iterator igroups = fglist.iterator();
%>

<table border="1" cellpadding="3" cellspacing="0">
<tr><th>Code</th><th>Description</th></tr>

<%-- Loop through the list and print each item --%>

<%
   while (igroups.hasNext()) {
      FoodGroup fg = (FoodGroup) igroups.next();
%>
<tr>
   <td><%= fg.getCode() %></td>
   <td><%= fg.getDescription() %></td>
</tr>
<%
   }
%>
</center>
</body>
</table>
```

ShowFoodGroups.jsp has the advantage that it can be tested in isolation, without having to be connected to a database. A stub JSP for testing purposes can be written. As long as it populates the List attribute, ShowFoodGroups.jsp is unaware that it is not dealing with a database. The results are shown in Figure 7-8.

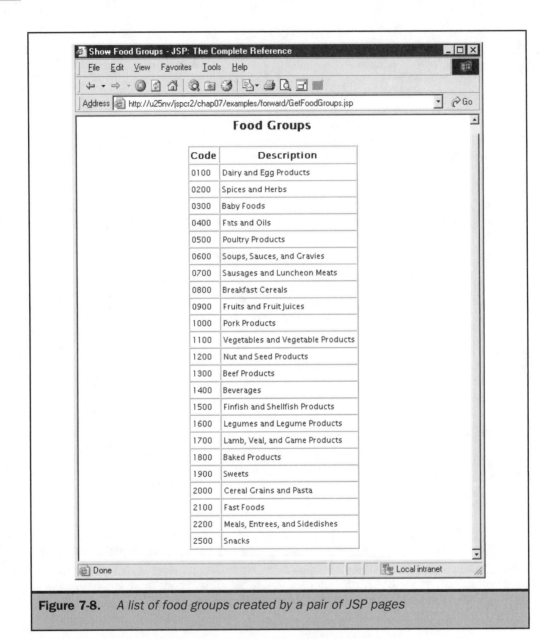

Figure 7-8. *A list of food groups created by a pair of JSP pages*

The RequestDispatcher Object

The underlying mechanism for both <jsp:include> and <jsp:forward> is the
javax.servlet.RequestDispatcher class. In the food groups example from

the preceding section, the <jsp:forward> action is translated into the following by Tomcat:

```
if (true) {
 out.clear();
 String _jspx_qfStr = "";
 pageContext.forward("ShowFoodGroups.jsp" + _jspx_qfStr);
 return;
}
```

The Tomcat implementation of pageContext, in turn, invokes a Request Dispatcher to handle the forwarding:

```
public void forward(String relativeUrlPath)
        throws ServletException, IOException
    {
        ...
        String path = getAbsolutePathRelativeToContext(relativeUrlPath);
        context.getRequestDispatcher(path).forward(request, response);
        ...
    }
```

You can create a RequestDispatcher in three ways:

1. ServletContext.getRequestDispatcher(String *path*)

   - The path must be absolute with respect to the context.
   - A dispatcher for a resource in another servlet context can be created if its context is known. The context can be obtained with context.getContext(*otherContext*).

2. ServletContext.getNamedDispatcher(String *name*)

   - The *name* parameter refers to a servlet alias, rather than a physical pathname.
   - A servlet can get its own name with config.getServletName().

3. ServletRequest.getRequestDispatcher(String *name*)

   - The path can be absolute with respect to the context, or relative with respect to the page. This is the essential difference between this method and the first method.

Request Dispatching vs. Redirection

Much of what is done by a request dispatcher can also be done by having a JSP or servlet write a "Moved Temporarily" or "Moved Permanently" status code and the URL of the next JSP or servlet written in the Location header. The difference is redirection involves a cooperating client to work, whereas request dispatching is handled entirely on the server side, with no client interaction.

Model 1 vs. Model 2

These are all handy features, but they are underused if they are only used hit-or-miss for headers and footers. They can, instead, be part of a well-coordinated architecture. If you read JSP newsgroups, you often encounter references to the Model 1 and Model 2 architectures, two different approaches to the structure of a Web application introduced in the original JSP 0.92 specification.

In a Model 1 application, JSP does it all:

- The user requests a JSP page.
- JSP performs calculations, database access, and so forth.
- The JSP page renders its output with HTML.

The Java code necessary to do all this work can be written directly in the form of scriptlets, or it can be contained in JavaBeans.

A Model 2 application follows the *Model-View-Controller (MVC)* paradigm. MVC is an object-oriented programming concept prominently featured in the Smalltalk language. It describes a logical partitioning of an application into three parts:

- **Model** is the logical "inner" representation. It has no visible output, no outside representation at all. For this reason, it can be run equally well in a servlet, a standalone GUI, or a batch test program. For example, the model for a chess game may include an array representing the board, numbers representing each of the pieces, and some encoding of the rules.

- **View** is a presentation layer for a model, with little or no programming logic. It reads from already populated structures and displays them. In our chess example, the view would be the screen representation of the game, possibly with alternating colors and ornately carved pieces.

- **Controller** provides user input and directions to a model. In the chess example, the controller would be the keyboard.

In the case of a Model 2 Web application, all user requests are referred to a single URL, a servlet sometimes called a *dispatcher* (the **controller**). This servlet looks in the request's path information for an indication of what it needs to do. There may be a table of actions and names of JSP pages to handle each of them. These action handlers constitute the **model** of the application. They may access a database or perform other calculations, and then populate JavaBeans or other classes with the results. Finally, they invoke JSP pages (the **view**) to present their output.

Which of these models is superior? Model 1 is easier to throw together quickly, but it doesn't scale. Too much is packaged together, and it becomes unwieldy as the application grows. Model 2 scales much better and also allows specialists to write different parts of the application:

- Java programmers can write the model and controller.
- User interface specialists can write JSP pages that do nothing but display output.

The Jakarta Struts web application framework is a comprehensive implementation of the Model 2 architecture. You can find all the details at http://jakarta.apache.org/struts/index.html.

Summary

A number of situations exist in which splitting the processing of an HTTP request is advantageous. JSP provides two general capabilities to support this:

- Including other resources, with either `<%@ include %>` or `<jsp:include>`.
- Forwarding a request using `<jsp:forward>`.

Included resources can be either static (like HTML) or dynamic (like a JSP or servlet). The capability to forward requests provides the basis for table-driven applications.

Two general development architectures exist, commonly referred to as Model 1 and Model 2. Model 1 uses JSP pages to accept user input, to access databases as needed, and to format its output. Model 2 follows the MVC paradigm, allowing complex projects to be separated as necessary between groups of people who specialize in one layer or another.

ELEMENTS OF JSP

The Complete Reference

Chapter 8

Session and Thread Management

The *Hypertext Transfer Protocol (HTTP)* was originally designed for distributing documents and images over the World Wide Web. As such, it uses a fairly simple communication model. A client makes a request for a document, the server responds with the document or some error code, and the transaction is complete. The server doesn't retain any knowledge of the request. The next time the client makes a request, the server has no way of distinguishing it from any other client. For this reason, HTTP is said to be a *stateless* protocol.

Unfortunately, few applications fit this single request/response model. In most cases, several requests are required for any meaningful work to be done. For example, an application may have one Web page that prompts for a user ID and password, and then a search page that requests keywords to look up in a product database, followed by a list of matching products, a detailed product information page, a shopping cart checkout page, and an order summary page. Each of these pages depends on the previous pages and also depends on the server knowing the state of the application for that client at that time. What's worse, the user on the client end of the application may go forward or backward through the pages, or go to another Web page entirely, never telling the server that the session is over or what to do with any partial work. A related difficulty is that some server processes take a long time—longer than a Web server can afford to wait if it's to maintain reasonable performance.

These aren't new problems. *Common Gateway Interface (CGI)* programs and online transaction processing systems have been dealing with these same issues for years. The techniques applied in those environments still work in the Servlet/JSP environment, but the Java Servlet API has a built-in mechanism that provides a clean, easy-to-use solution: *HTTP sessions*.

This chapter explores two key aspects of making the JSP model fit the application model: session management and thread management. It discusses four techniques for session tracking, focusing primarily on the HTTP session API, examining how sessions are created, how they manage objects, and how they are terminated. The chapter then explores Java's built-in support for multithreaded applications and the available servlet threading models, concluding with a section covering application considerations with respect to object lifecycle and visibility.

Session Tracking

Because the Web server doesn't remember clients from one request to the next, the only way to maintain a session is for clients to keep track of it. You can accomplish this in two basic ways:

- Have the client remember all session-related data and send it back to the server as needed.

- Have the server maintain all the data, assign an identifier to it, and have the client remember the identifier.

The first approach is simple to implement and requires no special capabilities on the part of the server. This approach can entail transmitting large amounts of data back and forth, however, which might degrade performance. Another problem is server-side objects, such as database and network connections, have to be reinitialized with every request. For these reasons, this approach is best suited for long-term persistence of small amounts of data, such as user preferences or account numbers.

The second approach offers more functionality. Once a server initiates a session and the client accepts it, the server can build complex, active objects and maintain large amounts of data, requiring only a key to distinguish between sessions. Most of the discussions in this chapter focus on this approach.

So, how can we get the client to remember data and return it to the Web server? Four techniques are commonly used:

- Hidden fields
- URL rewriting
- Cookies
- The HTTP session API

The following sections describe each technique in detail.

Hidden Fields

HTML forms support input elements with a type of HIDDEN. *Hidden fields* are passed along with other form parameters in the HTTP request sent to the Web server, but they don't have any visual representation. They serve only to include literals or constant values with a request. A similar technique is used with CICS and mainframe transaction monitors to supply transaction codes. In principle, hidden fields can be used in ordinary HTML Web pages, but being hard-coded, they aren't much use for session tracking purposes. They are more useful in dynamically generated Web pages created by server processes like CGI, servlets, or JSP.

Hidden fields are well suited to back-and-forth conversational applications that don't require a great deal of data storage or object initialization. An example would be the well-known number-guessing game included in the Tomcat examples folder. This game selects a random integer between 1 and 100, and then asks the user to guess it. After each guess, the game tells the user whether the guess was too low, too high, or exactly right.[1]

The set of JSP pages presented in the following example make up a game that does the opposite: it asks the user to think of a number between 1 and 100, and then guesses the number, relying on the user to indicate whether each guess is too low, too high, or exactly right. The program uses a binary search to find the number.

---

[1]   If you play these programs against each other in separate windows, you can watch them politely comment on each other's progress.

ELEMENTS OF JSP

The JSP pages use hidden fields to keep track of what's happening in the game—its "state." These fields include the current "too low" and "too high" guesses, and the number of guesses made so far. Based on this state, it displays the appropriate form.

■ `Start.jsp` The initial form, listed here and shown in Figure 8-1, explains the game and sets up the variables to be used. These include the state, the number of guesses, the highest value known to be too low, and the lowest value known to be too high. The variables are all stored as hidden fields in the form.

```
<%@ page session="false" %>
<html>
<head>
<title>Number Guess Guesser</title>
</head>
<body>
<h1 style="font-size: 130%">Number Guess Guesser</h1>
<form action="NextGuess.jsp">
<p> Think of a number between 1 and 100, and I'll try to
guess it.  Click OK when ready. </p>
<input type="submit" value="OK" />
<input type="hidden" name="lo" value="0" />
<input type="hidden" name="hi" value="101" />
<input type="hidden" name="count" value="1" />
</form>
</body>
</html>
```

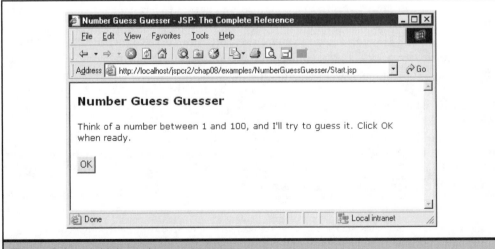

Figure 8-1.   *Initial number guess page*

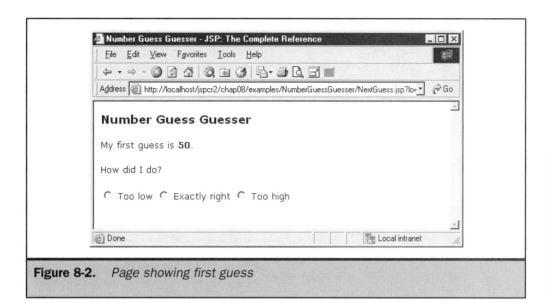

Figure 8-2. *Page showing first guess*

■ NextGuess.jsp   After the user clicks the OK button, the program retrieves the too-low and too-high parameters and uses the average of the two as its next guess. The form presents the user with three radio buttons to indicate whether the guess is too low, too high, or exactly right, as shown in Figure 8-2. The low and high values, the user result selection, and the incremented number of guesses are stored again as hidden fields.

```
<%@ page session="false" %>
<%-- Get current state from hidden fields --%>
<%
    int hi = Integer.parseInt(request.getParameter("hi"));
    int lo = Integer.parseInt(request.getParameter("lo"));
    int count = Integer.parseInt(request.getParameter("count"));
%>
<%-- Next guess is the average of high and low --%>
<%
    int guess = (hi + lo) / 2;
%>
<html>
<head>
<title>Number Guess Guesser</title>
</head>
<body>
<h1 style="font-size: 130%">Number Guess Guesser</h1>
<form action="CheckResults.jsp">
```

```
<p>
   My <%= (count == 1)
             ? "first guess"
             : "guess number " + count %>
   is <b><%= guess %></b>.
</p>
<p>
   How did I do?
</p>
<input type="radio"
       name="result"
       value="tooLow"
       onClick="submit()"> Too low </input>

<input type="radio"
       name="result"
       value="justRight"
       onClick="submit()"> Exactly right </input>

<input type="radio"
       name="result"
       value="tooHigh"
       onClick="submit()"> Too high </input>
</p>

<%-- Store current state in hidden fields --%>

<input type="hidden" name="lo" value="<%= lo %>" />
<input type="hidden" name="hi" value="<%= hi %>" />
<input type="hidden" name="count" value="<%= count + 1 %>" />

</form>
</body>
</html>
```

■ CheckResults.jsp   Based on what the user specified in the radio buttons, the nonvisual JSP page in the following listing updates either the too-low or the too-high value with the new lower or upper bounds, and forwards the request to one of three JSP pages.

```jsp
<%@ page session="false" %>
<%-- Get current state from hidden fields --%>
<%
   int hi = Integer.parseInt(request.getParameter("hi"));
   int lo = Integer.parseInt(request.getParameter("lo"));
   int count = Integer.parseInt(request.getParameter("count"));
%>
<%-- Which button did the user click? --%>
<%
   String result = request.getParameter("result");
   if (result.equals("justRight")) {
%>
<jsp:forward page="IWin.jsp"/>
<%
   }
   else if ((hi - lo) <= 1) {
%>
<jsp:forward page="Cheater.jsp"/>
<%
   }
   else {
      int guess = (hi + lo) / 2;
      if (result.equals("tooLow"))
         lo = guess;
      else
         hi = guess;
%>
<%-- Replace the values of the low and high parameters --%>
<jsp:forward page="NextGuess.jsp">
   <jsp:param name="lo" value="<%= lo %>"/>
   <jsp:param name="hi" value="<%= hi %>"/>
</jsp:forward>
<%
   }
%>
```

ELEMENTS OF JSP

If the guess is not exact, the NextGuess.jsp page again displays the known upper and lower bounds and its next guess, narrowing the upper and lower bounds each time. Figures 8-3 and 8-4 illustrate the process.

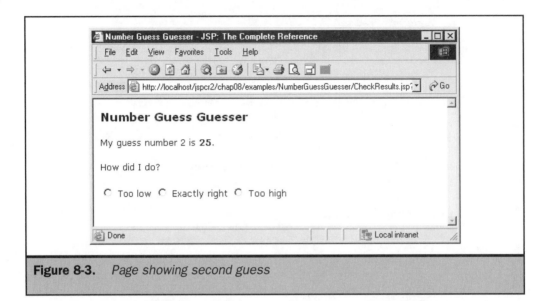

Figure 8-3. *Page showing second guess*

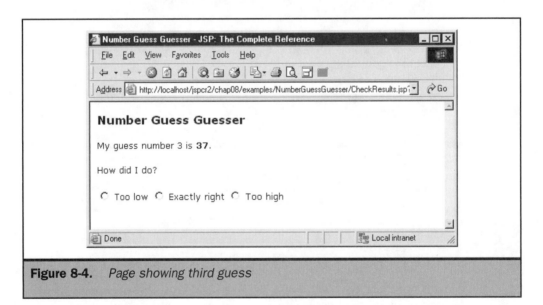

Figure 8-4. *Page showing third guess*

■ IWin.jsp   If the guess was exactly right, the program congratulates itself and prompts for whether to play again, as shown in Figure 8-5.

```jsp
<%@ page session="false" %>
<%-- Get current state from hidden fields --%>
<%
   int count = Integer.parseInt(request.getParameter("count"));
%>
<html>
<head>
<title>Number Guess Guesser</title>
</head>
<body>
<h1 style="font-size: 130%">Number Guess Guesser</h1>
<p>
   I win, and after only <%= count - 1 %> guesses!
</p>
<form action="Start.jsp">
<input type="submit" value="Play again" />
</form>
</body>
</html>
```

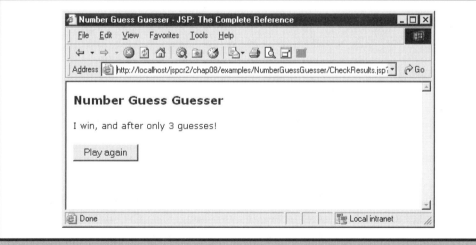

Figure 8-5.   *Winning guess page*

■ `Cheater.jsp`   If the low and high bounds are too close, the user is politely accused of cheating. A random message is chosen from an array of strings, and the page shown in Figure 8-6 is displayed.

```jsp
<%@ page session="false" %>
<%-- Get current state from hidden fields --%>
<%
    int hi = Integer.parseInt(request.getParameter("hi"));
    int lo = Integer.parseInt(request.getParameter("lo"));
%>
<html>
<head>
<title>Number Guess Guesser</title>
</head>
<body>
<h1 style="font-size: 130%">Number Guess Guesser</h1>
<%= lo %> is too low, and <%= hi %> is too high.
<%
    String[] text = {
        "Are we cheating, perhaps?",
        "Did we forget our number, hmm?",
        "Perhaps we clicked the wrong button?",
        "What happened?",
        "What gives?",
    };
    int r = (int) (Math.random() * text.length);
    String message = text[r];
%>
<%= message %>
<form action="Start.jsp">
<input type="submit" value="Play again" />
</form>
</body>
</html>
```

The problem with hidden fields is that they can only be used in HTML forms. If the user clicks a hyperlink and leaves the page, the hidden fields are lost, unless the technique described in the next section—URL rewriting—is also employed.

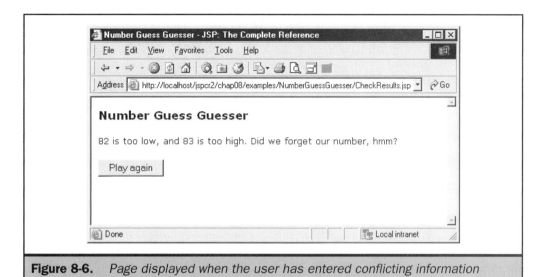

Figure 8-6.   *Page displayed when the user has entered conflicting information*

URL Rewriting

A URL can have parameters appended to it that are sent along with the request to the Web server. These parameters are name/value pairs having the following syntax:

```
http://server/MyPage.jsp?name1=value1&name2=value2&...
```

When the JSP page receives the request, it can read the values with

```
String value1 = request.getParameter("name1");
String value2 = request.getParameter("name2");
...
```

Note that the techniques for retrieving a hidden field and a form parameter are exactly the same: a call to getParameter(). This simplifies the refactoring process if the form changes over time.

Dynamically generated Web pages can take advantage of this facility to store session data in URLs that are written to the page as hyperlinks. This allows the client to remind the server of all values necessary to put the server application into the required state.

A simple example would be a counter that indicates the number of times a user has accessed a page during the current session, as shown in the following listing:

```
<%@ page session="false" %>
<html>
<head>
<title>Page Counter Using URL Rewriting</title>
<style type="text/css">
h1 { font-size: 130%; }
</style>
</head>
<body>
<h1>Page Counter Using URL Rewriting</h1>
<%
    int count = 0;
    String parm = request.getParameter("count");
    if (parm != null)
        count = Integer.parseInt(parm);
    if (count == 0) {
%> This is the first time you have accessed this page. <%
    }
    else if (count == 1) {
%> You have accessed the page once before.<%
    }
    else {
%> You have accessed the page <%= count %> times before.<%
    }
%>
<p>
    Click <a href="Counter.jsp?count=<%=count + 1 %>">here</a>
    to visit the page again.
</p>
</body>
</html>
```

When the user requests the page for the first time using nothing but the basic URL, no count parameter exists, and therefore, the integer count variable is set to zero:

At the bottom of the page is a hyperlink that invokes the same `counter.jsp` page again, but this time with a `count` parameter with a value one greater than the current count:

Each time the page is reinvoked, the counter is updated and the message changes.

This technique is guaranteed to work in all browser environments and security settings, but that's about its only advantage. The technique tends to degrade performance if large amounts of data are stored. The URLs can become very large, possibly exceeding the size accepted by the Web server. Additionally, the URLs aren't secure, being visible in the browser address window and in Web server logs. The requirement that every URL on the page has to be rewritten entails a lot of tedious code, and it's easy to overlook a URL in the process. Nevertheless, for simple applications, URL rewriting is reliable and easy to implement.

 Manually appending parameters to hyperlink URLs isn't commonly done. More common is to use the HTTP Session API to do the URL rewriting; in this case, only a session ID is appended. HTTP sessions are covered later in this chapter.

Cookies

The most widely used technique for *persistent* client data storage involves HTTP cookies. A *cookie* is a small, named data element the server passes to a client with a `Set-Cookie` header as part of the HTTP response. The client is expected to store the cookie and return it to the server with a `Cookie` header on subsequent requests to the same server. Along with the name and value, the cookie may contain

- An expiration date, after which the client is no longer expected to retain the cookie. If no date is specified, the cookie expires as soon as the browser session ends.

- A domain name, such as `servername.com`, which restricts the subset of URLs for which the cookie is valid. If unspecified, the cookie is returned with all requests to the originating Web server.

- A path name that further restricts the URL subset.

- A `secure` attribute, which, if present, indicates that the cookie should be returned only if the connection uses a secure channel, such as SSL.

Details of the original Netscape cookie specification can be found at http://home.netscape.com/newsref/std/cookie_spec.html. The official Internet standards documents covering cookies are RFC 2109 and RFC 2965, which can be found at http://www.ietf.org/rfc.html.

Figure 8-7 illustrates how cookies are set and retrieved with HTTP requests and responses. First, the Web browser requests a page from the Web server. No cookies are involved at this point. When the server responds with the requested document, it sends a `Set-Cookie` header assigning the value `fr` to a cookie named `language`. The cookie is set to expire in one year. The browser reads this header, extracts the cookie information, and stores the name/value pair in its cookie cache, along with the Web server's domain and default path. Later, when the user visits the page again, the browser recognizes that it previously received a cookie from this server and the cookie hasn't yet expired, and, therefore, sends the cookie back to the server.

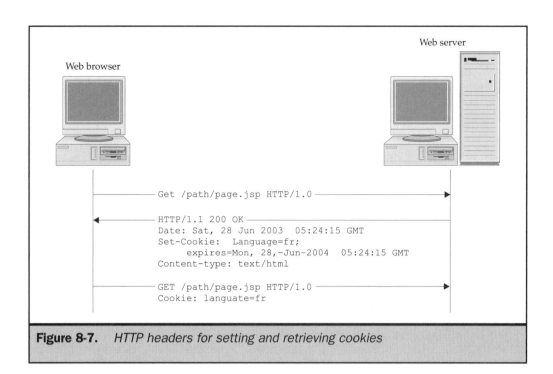

Figure 8-7. *HTTP headers for setting and retrieving cookies*

One advantage of cookies over other persistence schemes is that they can retain their values after the browser session is over, even after the client computer is rebooted. This makes cookies well suited for maintaining users' preferences, such as language.

The application shown in the following code enables the user to select the desired language by clicking a hyperlink. The selection causes a cookie containing the preferred language to be sent to the client. The next time the user visits the site, the browser automatically sends the cookie back to the server and the user's preferred language is used in the page.

```
<%@ page session="false"
        import="java.io.*,
                java.net.*,
                java.util.*" %>
<html>
<head>
<title>Using Cookies to Store Preferences</title>
<style><%= STYLESHEET %></style>
</head>
<body>
<table border="0" cellspacing="3" width="500">
```

```jsp
   <%-- Company logo --%>
   <tr><td>
      <img src="images/lyric_note.png">
   </td></tr>

   <%-- Language preference bar --%>
   <tr><td class="LB">
      <%= getLanguageBar(request) %>
   </td></tr>

</table>

   <%-- Localized greeting --%>
   <h1><%= getGreeting(request) %></h1>

   <%-- Store language preference in a persistent cookie --%>
   <% storeLanguagePreferenceCookie(request, response); %>

</body>
</html>
<%!
   // ========================================
   //    Helper methods included here for
   //    clarity.  A better choice would be
   //    to put them in beans or a servlet.
   // ========================================

   /**
    * The CSS stylesheet
    */
   private static final String STYLESHEET =
      "h1 { font-size: 130%; }\n"
      + ".LB {\n"
      + "    background-color: #005A9C;\n"
      + "    color: #FFFFFF;\n"
      + "    font-size: 90%;\n"
      + "    font-weight: bold;\n"
      + "    padding: 0.5em;\n"
      + "    text-align: right;\n"
      + "    word-spacing: 1em;\n"
      + "}\n"
      + ".LB a:link, .LB a:active, .LB a:visited {\n"
```

```
        + "    text-decoration: none;\n"
        + "    color: #FFFFFF;\n"
        + "}\n";

/**
 * Creates the language preference bar
 */
private String getLanguageBar
    (HttpServletRequest request)
        throws IOException
{
    String thisURL = request.getRequestURL().toString();
    StringBuffer sb = new StringBuffer();
    appendLink(sb, thisURL, Locale.ENGLISH);
    appendLink(sb, thisURL, Locale.GERMAN);
    appendLink(sb, thisURL, Locale.FRENCH);
    appendLink(sb, thisURL, Locale.ITALIAN);
    String languageBar = sb.toString();
    return languageBar;
}


/**
 * Helper method to create hyperlinks
 */
private void appendLink
    (StringBuffer sb, String thisURL, Locale locale)
        throws UnsupportedEncodingException
{
    if (sb.length() > 0)
        sb.append(" ");

    String language = locale.getLanguage();

    sb.append("<a href=\"");
    sb.append(thisURL);
    sb.append("?language=");
    sb.append(URLEncoder.encode(language, "UTF-8"));
    sb.append("\">");
    sb.append(locale.getDisplayName(locale));
    sb.append("</a>\n");
}
```

```java
/**
* Gets the greeting message appropriate for
* this locale
*/
private String getGreeting
    (HttpServletRequest request)
{
    Locale locale = getLocaleFromCookie(request);
    ResourceBundle RB = ResourceBundle.getBundle
        ("com.jspcr.sessions.welcome", locale);
    String greeting = RB.getString("greeting");
    return greeting;
}

/**
* Determines the locale to use, in the following
* order of preference:
*
* 1. Language parameter passed with request
* 2. Language cookie previously stored
* 3. Default locale for client
* 4. Default locale for server
*/
private Locale getLocaleFromCookie
    (HttpServletRequest request)
{
    Locale locale = null;
    String language = request.getParameter("language");
    if (language != null)
        locale = new Locale(language);
    else {
        Cookie[] cookies = request.getCookies();
        if (cookies != null) {
            for (int i = 0; i < cookies.length; i++) {
                Cookie cookie = cookies[i];
                String name = cookie.getName();
                if (name.equals("language")) {
                    language = cookie.getValue();
                    locale = new Locale(language);
                    break;
                }
            }
```

```
        }
        if (locale == null)
            locale = request.getLocale();
    }
    return locale;
}


/**
 * Stores the language preference
 * in a persistent cookie
 */
private void storeLanguagePreferenceCookie
    (HttpServletRequest request, HttpServletResponse response)
{
    Locale locale = getLocaleFromCookie(request);
    String name = "language";
    String value = locale.getLanguage();
    Cookie cookie = new Cookie(name, value);
    final int ONE_YEAR = 60 * 60 * 24 * 365;
    cookie.setMaxAge(ONE_YEAR);
    response.addCookie(cookie);
}
%>
```

The JSP page first checks to see if a `language` parameter was included with the request. This would be the case if the user had clicked one of the hyperlinks on the language preference bar to get here. Otherwise, the JSP scans the request headers for existing cookies and uses a resource bundle[2] to get the greeting message in the appropriate language. The response prepared includes a cookie that stores the preferred language code for one year.

The JSP page originally comes up in the default locale, as shown in Figure 8-8.

If the user clicks the French hyperlink, the page stores the preference in a cookie and displays the French version of the page, seen in Figure 8-9. If the user visits the site the next day, the language preference is remembered and applied.

The main problem with cookies is that users can and do turn off their browser's cookie support, usually for privacy reasons. This means that the application must be prepared to do its work some other way if it cannot use cookies.

---

[2] A `java.util.ResourceBundle` object is a means for a program to retrieve messages and other strings in different languages so that the program can be used in multiple locales without requiring any changes. Several implementations of `ResourceBundle` exist, the most common of which uses an ordinary `.properties` file to store the message text.

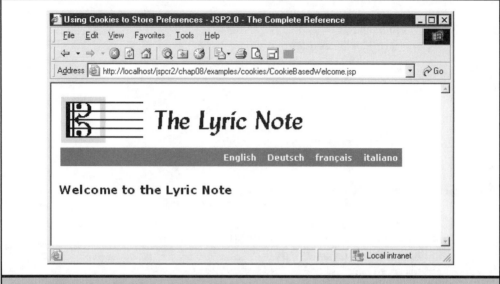

Figure 8-8. *Detail of the LyricNote home page showing language selection bar*

Figure 8-9. *French version of the LyricNote home page*

The Session API

So far, we've examined two general approaches to session tracking, both of which involve the client remembering the state:

- Have the client store all session data and return it to the server with each request.
- Have the client store a session identifier and have the server handle the rest.

While the first method may be easier to implement, the second, in general, offers more flexibility and scalability. We have seen that hidden fields, URL rewriting, and cookies can all be used to support either method, to some extent. But most servlets and JSP pages that need to use sessions can take advantage of a higher-level approach: the *HttpSession* API.

There are seven[3] classes in the `javax.servlet.http` package that comprise the session API, listed here in alphabetical order:

- **HttpSession**   An interface that acts like a `Map` or `Hashtable`, able to store and retrieve objects by name. A session is created by a call to `HttpServletRequest.getSession()` and persists until it times out or is shut down by a servlet participating in the session. Incoming HTTP requests that carry the session identifier are automatically associated with the session.

- **HttpSessionActivationListener**   An interface that can be implemented by objects bound to a session that need to be notified when the session is about to be activated or passivated. This interface is discussed in more detail in Chapter 9.

- **HttpSessionAttributeListener**   An interface that can be implemented by a listener class at the application-wide level. The listener will be notified when any session attribute in any session is added, removed, or changed. This interface is discussed in more detail in Chapter 9.

- **HttpSessionBindingEvent**   An event object passed to the `valueBound()` and `valueUnbound()` methods of an `HttpSessionBindingListener`. The event has methods for returning the session and the name under which the listener was bound to the session.

- **HttpSessionBindingListener**   An interface that allows an object to know when it has been stored in a session or removed from one. The interface has two callback methods, `valueBound()` and `valueUnbound()`, which the object must implement to receive the binding notifications.

- **HttpSessionEvent**   A superinterface of `HttpSessionBindingEvent` that provides a reference to a session object. This interface is used by methods in the

---

[3]   There is an eighth class, `HttpSessionContext`, but it has been deprecated since the Servlet 2.1 API days because of security considerations.

HttpSessionListener and HttpSessionActivationListener classes. Chapter 9 will provide more details.

- **HttpSessionListener** An interface implemented by application-wide objects that want to be notified when new sessions are created and old ones destroyed. This interface is discussed more fully in Chapter 9.

The following sections discuss how these classes can be used.

Creating Sessions

A servlet indicates it wants to use a session by calling the getSession() or getSession(boolean create) methods in HttpServletRequest, as shown here:

```
HttpSession session = request.getSession(true);
```

The getSession() method with no parameters is a convenience method that simply calls getSession(true). The create parameter indicates whether the servlet container should create a new session if one doesn't already exist. If the parameter is false, the servlet or JSP page can operate only with an existing session. In either case, the request is examined to see if it contains a valid session ID. If so, the servlet container returns a reference to the session object, which can then be used to store and retrieve session attributes.

A JSP page uses the page directive to indicate whether or not to use a session:

```
<%@ page session="true|false" %>
```

with the default value being true.

In a JSP page, session creation is automatic, unless it is suppressed in the page directive. At the beginning of the _jspService() method in the generated servlet, the PageContext object is created and initialized. The fifth parameter passed to JspFactory.getPageContext() boolean value that indicates whether a session is required. If this value is true, then as part of the initialization, the getPageContext() method calls request.getSession(true). The newly created or accessed session is returned to the generated servlet when it calls pageContext.getSession(). The session is then accessible to the rest of the JSP page as the implicit variable session, as this example shows:

```
public void _jspService(
     HttpServletRequest request,
     HttpServletResponse response)
   throws IOException, ServletException
{
   ...
```

```
pageContext = _jspxFactory.getPageContext
      (this, request, response, "", true, 8192, true);
   application = pageContext.getServletContext();
   config = pageContext.getServletConfig();
   session = pageContext.getSession();
   out = pageContext.getOut();
   ...
}
```

By contrast, a page that doesn't use a session gets initialized like this:

```
public void _jspService(
      HttpServletRequest request,
      HttpServletResponse response)
   throws IOException, ServletException
{
   ...
   pageContext = _jspxFactory.getPageContext
      (this, request, response, "", false, 8192, true);
   application = pageContext.getServletContext();
   config = pageContext.getServletConfig();
   out = pageContext.getOut();
   ...
}
```

Note   *If you do not need a session in a JSP page, you should suppress the automatic creation using the page directive:*

```
<%@ page session="false" %>
```

This relieves the servlet container from having to create and maintain a session when it isn't needed. The memory and CPU requirements for unnecessary sessions can be significant.

Joining a Session

When the session is first created, the client (Web browser) doesn't yet know about it. When the session ID has been sent to the client and the client sends it back in the next request, the client is said to *join* the session. A servlet or JSP page can detect whether this has happened with the isNew() method:

```
HttpSession session = request.getSession();
if (session.isNew()) {
```

```
    // Create an empty shopping cart
}
```

The `session.isNew()` method is true if the session is newly created and the client hasn't yet been informed or if the client has been informed but chooses not to participate.

Session Tracking Mechanisms

The servlet container tries to use cookies to keep track of the session ID. In the HTTP response written by a servlet that created a session, a `Set-Cookie` header containing the session ID is in a cookie named `JSESSIONID`.

```
Set-Cookie: JSESSIONID=rkbg6z27j1;Path=/jspcr2
```

If the client accepts the cookie, the client returns it in subsequent requests:

```
Cookie: JSESSIONID=rkbg6z27j1
```

If this happens, the client request can be associated with the session with no special considerations on the part of the servlet. If the client doesn't accept cookies, however, the session is lost. To prevent this, the servlet API has a fallback mechanism: It uses URL rewriting if cookies fail. This is slightly more complicated for the programmer because it means all URLs written by the servlet must have the session ID appended.

But, because this is unnecessary and expensive if the client accepts cookies, the URL rewriting should be done only if you definitely know the cookie technique fails. Fortunately, the servlet API has methods that encapsulate all this logic. The `HttpServletResponse` class has `encodeURL()` and `encodeRedirectURL()` methods that add the session ID to a URL only if necessary.

Note that `encodeRedirectURL()` should be used with URLs passed to the `response.sendRedirect()` method:

```
String loginPage = response.encodeRedirectURL
    ("/login.jsp");
response.sendRedirect(loginPage);
```

and `encodeURL()` should be used with all others:[4]

```
String myURL = response.encodeURL
    ("/servlet/nextServlet");
```

---

[4] There are two methods because it is possible that the requirements for each type of link may be different. However, the Tomcat 4 reference implementation is identical for both methods.

```
out.println("Click"
    + " <a href=\"" + myURL + "\">"
    + "here"
    + "</a> to continue");
```

When the `encodeURL()` or `encodeRedirectURL()` method is used, and when `session.isNew()` is true, the session ID is always embedded in the URL. After the first response from the client, the servlet container determines whether the session ID was returned in a cookie. If not, the servlet container continues to append the ID to URLs passed through the encoding methods. Otherwise, it switches to using cookies only and the encoding methods return unmodified URL strings. This makes testing all the possibilities unnecessary for the programmer.

Although the servlet container takes care of all these details for you, you must remember to encode *all* the URLs on a page, otherwise the session will be lost if the user clicks an unencoded URL.

Storing and Retrieving Objects from Sessions

Objects are bound to a session with the `setAttribute()` method:

```
session.setAttribute("com.jspcr.sessions.myapp.user", userID);
```

The name under which an object is bound can be any unique string. Because sessions are shared between all servlets and JSP pages in the current HTTP session, however, it makes sense to use a name that won't conflict with other applications. A common technique is to choose names prefixed with the package name or fully qualified class name of the servlet or JSP page.

Any kind of object can be stored in a session, but because sessions may be serialized, a good idea is to have session objects implement `java.io.Serializable`. Note, too, only objects can be stored, not primitives like `int`, `char`, or `double`. To store these primitives, you must use their object wrappers `Integer`, `Character`, or `Double`.

Objects can be retrieved from a session with the `getAttribute()` method:

```
String userID = (String) session.getAttribute(
    "com.jspcr.sessions.myapp.user");
```

ELEMENTS OF JSP

Like a `Map` or `Hashtable`, a session stores only objects, so when they're retrieved, they must be cast into the appropriate type. Primitives contained in wrapper classes must be extracted by the methods provided in the wrapper class:

```
Integer countObject = (Integer) getAttribute("count");
int count = countObject.intValue();
```

Usually, if you stored an attribute in a session, you know its name and type, and you can request it directly in this manner. You can also get a list of attribute names, however, from the `getAttributeName()` method:

```
out.println("Objects in this session:");
out.println("<pre>");
Enumeration enames = session.getAttributeNames();
while (enames.hasMoreElements()) {
    String name = (String) enames.nextElement();
    Object value = session.getAttribute(name);
    out.println(name + " = " + value);
}
out.println("</pre>");
```

When an object is no longer needed, it can be removed from the session with `removeAttribute()`:

```
session.removeAttribute("jspcr.sessions.myapp.user");
```

This happens automatically when the session is closed, but situations may occur when an attribute needs to be removed earlier than this.

Destroying Sessions

Once created, a session ordinarily persists until it times out or is shut down. *Timeout* refers to the maximum length of time between requests that the session will remain valid. This is an important consideration because the server has no way of knowing whether a client has finished working with a session, other than by being told explicitly or by waiting a fixed length of time.

This bears repeating. The link between a client and Web server is a logical session, not a persistent connection. If the user goes to a different page or shuts down the browser, the server doesn't get a signal of any kind. For all it knows, you are going to be coming back with another request soon. Unless the application gives some indication that it is done, the only thing that can shut down a session is timeout.

The default timeout interval can be set in the deployment descriptor `web.xml`:

```
<web-app>
   ...
   <session-config>
      <session-timeout> 30 </session-timeout>
   </session-config>
   ...
</web-app>
```

The interval is specified as a number of minutes, 30 being the default. The value entered here applies to all sessions in the application unless they individually override it.

Some applications that use scarce resources such as database connections may choose to time out sooner. These applications can use the setMaxInactiveInterval() method to select a shorter time period:

```
session.setMaxInactiveInterval(180);
```

The argument supplied to setMaxInactiveInterval() is a number of seconds.[5] The previous example uses 180 seconds or three minutes. The current value can be obtained with getMaxInactiveInterval(). To indicate that the session should never time out, use the value –1.

In some cases, you know of an event that should mark a definite end to the session. In these cases, the invalidate() method can be used:

```
session.invalidate();
```

This method marks the session as being inactive and unbinds all objects bound to it. For example, in a shopping cart application that uses a session to store items being ordered, after the checkout logic writes the order to a database, the session should be destroyed so that, if the user purchases more items, the old session contents won't still be there.

Examples Revisited

The session API can handle all the session tracking tasks described earlier in this chapter. In this section, we'll redo two of the examples to show how they can be done using the session API approach.

Hidden Fields Example: The Number Guesser

The number guesser developed in the hidden fields section can be simplified by moving all the hidden fields into an object stored in an HTTP session. In this example, we use

---

[5]   The API is a bit inconsistent here. Why use minutes in the deployment descriptor and seconds in the session API?

a simple, externally defined class named `GameState`, which keeps track of the guesses known to be too high and too low, as well as the number of guesses.

```java
package com.jspcr.sessions;

/**
 * Holds the number guesser application state
 */
public class GameState
{
    private int tooLow;
    private int tooHigh;
    private int count;

    /**
     * Initializes the state
     */
    public GameState()
    {
        tooLow = 0;
        tooHigh = 101;
        count = 1;
    }

    /**
     * Returns the greatest integer known to be too low.
     */
    public int getTooLow()
    {
        return tooLow;
    }

    /**
     * Sets the "tooLow" value
     * @param tooLow the tooLow
     */
    public void setTooLow(int tooLow)
    {
        this.tooLow = tooLow;
    }

    /**
```

```
 * Returns the least integer known to be too high.
 */
public int getTooHigh()
{
   return tooHigh;
}

/**
 * Sets the tooHigh
 * @param tooHigh the tooHigh
 */
public void setTooHigh(int tooHigh)
{
   this.tooHigh = tooHigh;
}

/**
 * Returns the number of guesses so far
 */
public int getCount()
{
   return count;
}

/**
 * Returns the next guess, which is the average of the
 * too high and too low values.
 */
public int getNextGuess()
{
   return (getTooHigh() + getTooLow()) / 2;
}

/**
 * Updates the lower bound
 */
public void guessIsTooLow()
{
   setTooLow(getNextGuess());
}

/**
```

```
   * Updates the upper bound
   */
  public void guessIsTooHigh()
  {
     setTooHigh(getNextGuess());
  }

  /**
   * Adds 1 to the count
   */
  public void incrementCount()
  {
     count++;
  }

  /**
   * Returns true if the upper and lower bounds
   * leave no room for further guesses between them.
   * This can only happen if the user gave conflicting
   * information
   */
  public boolean boundsAreTooClose()
  {
     return (getTooHigh() - getTooLow()) <= 1;
  }

  /**
   * Returns a randomly chosen message politely accusing
   * the user of cheating.
   */
  public String getCheaterMessage()
  {
     String[] text = {
        "Are we cheating, perhaps?",
        "Did we forget our number, hmm?",
        "Perhaps we clicked the wrong button?",
        "What happened?",
        "What gives?",
     };
     int r = (int) (Math.random() * text.length);
     String message = text[r];
     return message;
  }
}
```

The logic remains the same, but where hidden fields were written to the HTML form, their values are now stored in the `GameState` object that's bound to the session. This simplifies the JSP pages considerably, taking out almost all the Java code.

The `Start.jsp` page causes the `GameState` bean to be created and bound to a session:

```
<%@ page session="true" %>
<%@ page import="com.jspcr.sessions.*" %>

<jsp:useBean id="state"
             class="com.jspcr.sessions.GameState"
             scope="session"/>

<html>

<head>
<title>Number Guess Guesser</title>
<style type="text/css">
   h1 { font-size: 130%; }
</style>
</head>

<body>
<h1>Number Guess Guesser</h1>
<form action="NextGuess.jsp">
<p>
   Think of a number between 1 and 100, and I'll try to
   guess it.  Click OK when ready.
</p>
<input type="submit" value="OK" />
</form>
</body>

</html>
```

The `NextGuess.jsp` page no longer calculates the number guess directly. It retrieves the state object from the session and uses `<jsp:getProperty>` to get its `nextGuess` property (using the `getNextGuess()` method under the covers—the standard JavaBeans access mechanism).

```
<%@ page session="true" %>
<%@ page import="com.jspcr.sessions.*" %>
```

```
<%-- Get current state from session --%>

<jsp:useBean id="state"
             class="com.jspcr.sessions.GameState"
             scope="session"/>

<html>

<head>
<title>Number Guess Guesser</title>
<style type="text/css">
   h1 { font-size: 130%; }
</style>
</head>

<body>
<h1>Number Guess Guesser</h1>
<form action="CheckResults.jsp">
<p>
   My guess is
   <b><jsp:getProperty name="state" property="nextGuess"/></b>.
   How did I do?
</p>

<input type="radio"
       name="result"
       value="tooLow"
       onClick="submit()"> Too low </input>

<input type="radio"
       name="result"
       value="justRight"
       onClick="submit()"> Exactly right </input>

<input type="radio"
       name="result"
       value="tooHigh"
       onClick="submit()"> Too high </input>
</p>
</form>
</body>

</html>
```

The CheckResults.jsp page is completely nonvisual. It gets the state bean from the session, determines what happened in the previous page, and forwards the request to the appropriate next page.[6] In contrast to the hidden fields version, the logic in this case resides entirely in the state bean. The bean has methods that can be used to

- Determine if the user has given consistent information.
- Specify that the guess is too high and update the upper bound.
- Specify that the guess is too low and update the lower bound.
- Increment the number of guesses.

```jsp
<%@ page session="true" %>
<%@ page import="com.jspcr.sessions.*" %>

<%-- Get current state from session --%>

<jsp:useBean id="state"
             class="com.jspcr.sessions.GameState"
             scope="session"/>

<%-- Which button did the user click? --%>

<%
   String nextPage = "NextGuess.jsp";

   String result = request.getParameter("result");

   if (result.equals("justRight"))
      nextPage = "IWin.jsp";

   else if (state.boundsAreTooClose())
      nextPage = "Cheater.jsp";

   else {
      if (result.equals("tooLow"))
         state.guessIsTooLow();
      else
         state.guessIsTooHigh();
```

---

[6] If you're familiar with the Model-View-Controller (MVC) design pattern, you'll recognize this as the role of the controller, for which a servlet is usually better suited. We'll cover the MVC architecture in Chapter 19.

```
        state.incrementCount();
    }

    pageContext.forward(nextPage);
%>
```

The Cheater.jsp page is also simplified:

```
<%@ page session="true" %>

<%-- Get current state from session --%>

<jsp:useBean id="state"
             class="com.jspcr.sessions.GameState"
             scope="session"/>
<html>

<head>
<title>Number Guess Guesser</title>
<style type="text/css">
    h1 { font-size: 130%; }
</style>
</head>

<body>
<h1>Number Guess Guesser</h1>

<jsp:getProperty name="state" property="tooLow"/>

is too low, but

<jsp:getProperty name="state" property="tooHigh"/>

is too high.

<jsp:getProperty name="state" property="cheaterMessage"/>

<form action="Start.jsp">
<input type="submit" value="Play again" />
</form>
</body>
```

```
</html>

<% session.removeAttribute("state"); %>
```

The only Java code this page uses is on the last line, in which the state bean is removed from the session when a new game starts. This is also the case with the IWin.jsp page, which uses <jsp:getProperty> with the state bean to get the number of guesses that it took:

```
<%@ page session="true" %>

<%-- Get current state from session --%>

<jsp:useBean id="state"
             class="com.jspcr.sessions.GameState"
             scope="session"/>
<html>

<head>
<title>Number Guess Guesser</title>
<style type="text/css">
   h1 { font-size: 130%; }
</style>
</head>

<body>
<h1>Number Guess Guesser</h1>
<p>
   I win, and after only
   <jsp:getProperty name="state" property="count"/>
   guesses!
</p>

<form action="Start.jsp">
<input type="submit" value="Play again" />
</form>
</body>

</html>

<% session.removeAttribute("state"); %>
```

URL Rewriting Example: The Page Counter

Similarly, the page counter developed in the URL rewriting section can use an HTTP session to store the count variable. Because int is a primitive, we need to use the Integer object wrapper and call its intValue() method to get the actual value.

```
<%@ page session="true" %>
<html>
<head>
<title>Cookie-Based Page Counter</title>
<style type="text/css">
h1 { font-size: 130% }
</style>
</head>
<body>
<h1>Cookie-Based Page Counter</h1>
<%
    int count = 0;
    Integer parm = (Integer) session.getAttribute("count");
    if (parm != null)
        count = parm.intValue();
    session.setAttribute("count", new Integer(count+1));
    if (count == 0) {
%> This is the first time you have accessed this page. <%
    }
    else if (count == 1) {
%> You have accessed the page once before.<%
    }
    else {
%> You have accessed the page <%= count %> times before.<%
    }
%>
<p>
    Click <a href=
'<%= response.encodeURL("CookieCounter.jsp")%>'>here</a>
    to visit the page again.
</p>
</body>
</html>
```

Each time the page is refreshed, the count is incremented and stored in the session in a new Integer wrapper. Notice that the hyperlink the user clicks to redisplay the page uses `response.encodeURL()` to ensure that the session tracking works, regardless of whether the browser accepts cookies.

Session Binding Listeners

The session API provides a means for objects to keep track of when they are added or removed from a session. An object that wants to receive notification of these events can implement the `HttpSessionBindingListener` interface. Implementing classes must provide two methods:

- `public void valueBound(HttpSessionBindingEvent event)`
- `public void valueUnbound(HttpSessionBindingEvent event)`

In each case, an instance of `HttpSessionBindingEvent` is passed to the methods. The event parameter has methods for retrieving the session and for determining the name by which the object was bound to the session.

The main advantage gained by session-binding listeners is that they can free the resources they acquire, regardless of whether the client explicitly closes the application or the session times out. This makes the interface useful for managing database connections. JDBC 2.0 provides for connection pooling, but many drivers don't yet implement it. In this case, a session-resident connection that knows enough to disconnect itself is a workable alternative.

The following example illustrates the technique. `BoundConnection` is a wrapper around a `java.sql.Connection` object and implements `HttpSessionBindingListener`, so it can close the connection after it's no longer in use:

```
package com.jspcr.jdbc;

import java.io.*;
import java.sql.*;
import java.text.*;
import java.util.*;
import javax.servlet.*;
import javax.servlet.http.*;


/**
 * A wrapper for a <code>Connection</code>
 * object that is aware it is in an HTTP session.
```

```
 * This enables it to shut down the connection
 * when the session is destroyed.
 */
public class BoundConnection
    implements HttpSessionBindingListener, Serializable
{
    private transient Connection connection;

    /**
     * Creates a new <code>BoundConnection</code> object
     * for the specified connection.
     * @param con the connection
     */
    public BoundConnection(Connection con)
    {
        this.connection = con;
    }

    /**
     * Returns the underlying connection
     */
    public Connection getConnection()
    {
        return connection;
    }

    /**
     * Called when the <code>BoundConnection</code>
     * is stored in an HTTP session
     * @param event the binding event
     */
    public void valueBound(HttpSessionBindingEvent event)
    {
        trace("bound", event);
    }

    /**
     * Called when the <code>BoundConnection</code>
     * is removed from an HTTP session
     * @param event the unbinding event
     */
    public void valueUnbound(HttpSessionBindingEvent event)
```

```
{
   if (connection != null)
      try {
         connection.close();
         connection = null;
      }
      catch (SQLException e) {
         e.printStackTrace();
      }
   trace("unbound", event);
}

/**
* Prints a trace message
*/
private void trace(String s, HttpSessionBindingEvent event)
{
   HttpSession session = event.getSession();

   java.util.Date now =
      new java.util.Date(System.currentTimeMillis());
   java.util.Date last =
      new java.util.Date(session.getLastAccessedTime());

   SimpleDateFormat fmt = new SimpleDateFormat("hh:mm:ss");
   StringBuffer sb;

   sb = new StringBuffer();
   sb.append("TRACE: ");
   sb.append(fmt.format(now));
   sb.append(" session ");
   sb.append(session.getId());
   sb.append(" last accessed time ");
   sb.append(fmt.format(last));
   System.err.println(sb.toString());

   sb = new StringBuffer();
   sb.append("TRACE: ");
   sb.append(fmt.format(now));
   sb.append(" session ");
   sb.append(session.getId());
   sb.append(" connection " );
```

```
         sb.append(s);
         System.err.println(sb.toString());
   }
}
```

The `BoundConnection` constructor stores a `Connection` object as a private instance variable and makes it available through a `getConnection()` method. `BoundConnection` implements the two `HttpSessionBindingListener` methods: `valueBound()` and `valueUnbound()`. In each of them, it writes a trace message, so a record exists of when the connection is bound or unbound. The key feature is the `valueUnbound()` method, which closes the underlying connection.

Note *The `BoundConnection` object implements `Serializable` because sessions may be serialized, especially in distributable applications. This makes marking the `Connection` instance variable as `transient` necessary so that the servlet container won't attempt to serialize it. The caller of `getConnection()`, therefore, needs to check the value returned for null and, if necessary, create a new `BoundConnection`.*

A JSP page that uses `BoundConnection` can, therefore, invoke it when the session begins, giving it a newly opened database connection. When a `BoundConnection` is stored in the session, its `valueBound()` method is triggered. Subsequent requests in the same session can simply retrieve the `BoundConnection` from the session and call its `getConnection()` method to get the underlying `java.sql.Connection`. The reusable `connect.jsp` module shown next implements this logic.

```
<%@ page import="java.sql.*" %>
<%@ page import="com.jspcr.jdbc.*" %>
<%
   // If there is not already a connection bound to this
   // session, create one

   if (session.getAttribute("bcon") == null) {

      String driver =
         application.getInitParameter("jdbc.driver");
      String url =
         application.getInitParameter("jdbc.url.internal");

      Class.forName(driver);
      Connection con = DriverManager.getConnection(url);
```

```
        // Bind the connection to this session

        BoundConnection bcon = new BoundConnection(con);
        session.setAttribute("bcon", bcon);

        // Set the timeout interval to three minutes

        session.setMaxInactiveInterval(180);
    }
%>
```

In addition to creating the BoundConnection when necessary, connect.jsp sets the
session timeout interval to three minutes.

The application shown next uses a BoundConnection to provide quick access
for repeated database queries. ComposerSearch.jsp prompts for a nationality and
century, and then searches the LyricNote composer database and displays the results.
It includes connect.jsp to do the actual connection and session binding work.

```
<%@ page session="true" %>
<%@ page import="com.jspcr.jdbc.*" %>
<%@ page import="java.sql.*" %>
<%
    // Get form parameters or use defaults

    String nationality = request.getParameter("nationality");
    if (nationality == null)
        nationality = "";

    String yearRange = request.getParameter("yearRange");
    if (yearRange == null)
        yearRange = "1901-2000";
%>
<html>
<head>
<title>Composer Search</title>
<style type="text/css">
h1 { font-size: 130%; }
</style>
</head>
<body>
<center>
```

```
<h1>Composer Search</h1>
<form method="POST">
<b>Nationality:</b>
<input type="text" name="nationality" value="<%= nationality %>">
<b>Century:</b>
<select name="yearRange">
<%
    // Create the century option list

    for (int century = 16; century <= 20; century++) {
        int fromYear = (century - 1) * 100 + 1;
        int toYear = century * 100;
        StringBuffer sb = new StringBuffer();
        sb.append("<OPTION");
        if (yearRange.startsWith("" + fromYear))
            sb.append(" SELECTED");
        sb.append(" VALUE='");
        sb.append(fromYear);
        sb.append("-");
        sb.append(toYear);
        sb.append("'>");
        sb.append(century);
        sb.append("th Century</OPTION>");
        out.println(sb);
    }
%>
</select>
<input type="submit" value="Search">
</form>
<%
    // If values were entered in the form, display results

    if (!nationality.equals("")) {
%>

<%-- Get the bound connection --%>

<jsp:include page="connect.jsp" flush="true"/>

<table border="0" cellpadding="1" cellspacing="1">
<%
        BoundConnection bcon = (BoundConnection)
```

```
         session.getAttribute("bcon");
     Connection con = bcon.getConnection();
     String sql = ""
        + " SELECT    lname, fname, born, died"
        + " FROM      composers"
        + " WHERE     nationality = ?"
        + " AND       ((born between ? and ?)"
        + " OR        (died between ? and ?))"
        + " ORDER BY born, lname"
        ;
     PreparedStatement pstmt = con.prepareStatement(sql);

     int fromYear = Integer.parseInt(yearRange.substring(0, 4));
     int toYear = Integer.parseInt(yearRange.substring(5));

     pstmt.setString(1, nationality);
     pstmt.setInt(2, fromYear);
     pstmt.setInt(3, toYear);
     pstmt.setInt(4, fromYear);
     pstmt.setInt(5, toYear);
     ResultSet rs = pstmt.executeQuery();
     while (rs.next()) {
        String lname = rs.getString(1);
        String fname = rs.getString(2);
        int born = rs.getInt(3);
        int died = rs.getInt(4);
%>
<tr>
   <td><%= fname %> <%= lname %></td>
   <td><%= born %>-<%= died %></td>
</tr>
<%
     }
     rs.close();
     pstmt.close();
%>
</table>
<%
   }
%>
</center>
</body>
</html>
```

To access the session-resident connection, all the application needs to do is retrieve the bcon session attribute, cast it to a `BoundConnection`, and call its `getConnection()` method. Notice it's unnecessary to close the connection explicitly—that's the whole purpose of the bound connection. The close is done automatically when three minutes have expired with no further requests from the client. The resulting Web page, seen in Figure 8-10, can be used for repeated queries, with a new connection required only for the first one.

The trace entries in the System.err log show the `BoundConnection` lifecycle in the HTTP session:

```
TRACE: 07:55:00 session 8720188469 last accessed time 07:55:00
TRACE: 07:55:00 session 8720188469 connection bound
TRACE: 07:59:38 session 8720188469 last accessed time 07:56:38
TRACE: 07:59:38 session 8720188469 connection unbound
```

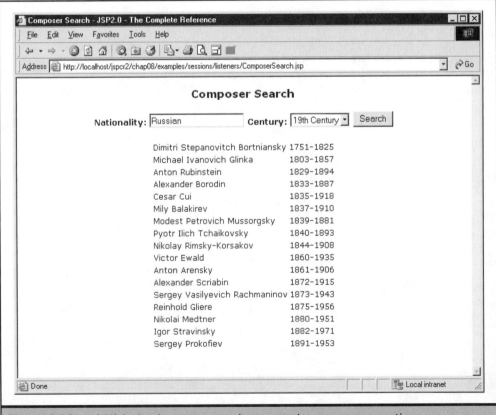

Figure 8-10.   *A Web database query using a session-aware connection*

The connection was bound to the session at 07:55:00 and used one or more times, the last time being 07:56:38. Three minutes later, at 07:59:38, the session timed out, unbinding the BoundConnection object. This, in turn, caused the valueUnbound() method to be called, which closed the underlying connection.

Thread Management

Servlets and JSP pages have a significant advantage over older server-side technologies because they are loaded into memory and run as single instances in a multithreaded environment. This benefit comes with a trade-off, however. The multithreaded model introduces difficulties that don't exist in simpler application models. For example, if a servlet has instance variables, they can potentially be accessed simultaneously from different requests. If both requests write to the variables, their values may be unpredictable.

Fortunately, because the servlet container is written in Java, it can take advantage of Java's built-in support for multithreaded applications. In this section, you learn about some basic threading concepts, examine two servlet threading models, and consider an efficient multithreaded application.

Threading Concepts

A *thread* is a single sequential flow of control with its own stack and program counter. Programs that use multiple threads appear to be doing more than one thing at a time. A thread is able to operate independently of other threads in the same process while, at the same time, sharing all the process objects.

The Web server itself is an example of where threads can be useful. A simple Web server operates as follows:

1. Creates a ServerSocket and invokes its accept() method to wait for HTTP clients requests.

2. Gets the client Socket object returned by the accept() method and starts a separate thread to handle its request.

3. Returns to step 1 to accept more requests at the same time the last one is being processed by the other thread.

Java in general (not only in JSP pages) makes creating and using multiple threads easy. Both the language and the class libraries are built from the ground up with threads in mind. java.lang.Object, the ultimate base class of all objects, has methods for synchronizing thread operations, which are inherited by every Java object.

A thread is represented by an instance of the java.lang.Thread class. A new Thread object isn't actually associated with an underlying operating system thread until its start() method is called, which allows its characteristics (name, priority, and so forth) to be set before it starts. After start() is called, an operating system thread is created by the Java virtual machine and this thread begins executing the thread's run() method. A Thread continues to run until its run() method returns or its interrupt() method is called.

ELEMENTS OF JSP

Creating Threads by Subclassing java.util.Thread

You can use several different techniques to start a new thread. The first is to subclass java.lang.Thread itself and override its run() method. Objects of this class can then be created and started individually. The following ThreadExample1.java illustrates this technique. It uses a subclass of Thread called CounterThread to count to eight, printing the thread name and time for each iteration, and waiting a random length of time between iterations.

```java
import java.text.*;
import java.util.*;

/**
 * A class that demonstrates simple multithreading
 */
public class ThreadExample1
{
    public static void main(String[] args)
    {
        /**
         * Create, name, and start two counter threads
         */

        Thread t1 = new CounterThread();
        t1.setName("A");
        t1.start();

        Thread t2 = new CounterThread();
        t2.setName("B");
        t2.start();
    }
}

/**
 * A thread that counts to eight, waiting
 * a random length of time between iterations.
 */
class CounterThread extends Thread
{
    /**
     * Date format used in message. Includes milliseconds.
     */
```

```
public static final SimpleDateFormat FMT
   = new SimpleDateFormat("hh:mm:ss.SSS aa");

/**
 * Starts the run method in a new thread
 */
public void start()
{
   System.out.println("Starting " + getName());
   super.start();
}

/**
 * Where the counter loop takes place.
 */
public void run()
{
   for (int i = 0; i < 8; i++) {
      try {
         sleep((long) (Math.random() * 500 + 100));
      }
      catch (InterruptedException e) {
         break;
      }
      System.out.println
         (FMT.format(new Date())
         + " Thread " + getName()
         + ": Count = " + i);
   }
   System.out.println("Leaving " + getName());
}
}
```

The mainline launches two `CounterThread` instances named A and B. The following program output shows both threads execute simultaneously and occasionally overlap in their iterations:

```
Starting A
Starting B
09:48:52.442 PM Thread B: Count = 0
09:48:52.582 PM Thread B: Count = 1
```

```
09:48:52.682 PM Thread A: Count = 0
09:48:52.962 PM Thread B: Count = 2
09:48:53.243 PM Thread A: Count = 1
09:48:53.303 PM Thread B: Count = 3
09:48:53.393 PM Thread A: Count = 2
09:48:53.653 PM Thread B: Count = 4
09:48:53.874 PM Thread B: Count = 5
09:48:53.964 PM Thread A: Count = 3
09:48:54.214 PM Thread B: Count = 6
09:48:54.385 PM Thread A: Count = 4
09:48:54.405 PM Thread B: Count = 7
Leaving B
09:48:54.755 PM Thread A: Count = 5
09:48:55.186 PM Thread A: Count = 6
09:48:55.496 PM Thread A: Count = 7
Leaving A
```

Creating Threads by Implementing Runnable

The second technique is to have a class implement the Runnable interface. In this
case, the class must provide its own run() method and also create a Thread object
to do the actual work. The class must pass a reference to itself (using the this variable)
in the Thread constructor. The following ThreadExample2.java shows this
technique in operation. Modeled closely after ThreadExample1, it creates two threads
and passes each of them its this variable. Note that both threads can run the same
run() method simultaneously.

```java
import java.text.*;
import java.util.*;

/**
 * A class that demonstrates simple multithreading
 * using the Runnable interface.
 */
public class ThreadExample2 implements Runnable
{
    public static void main(String[] args)
    {
        new ThreadExample2();
    }

    public ThreadExample2()
    {
```

```
    /**
     * Start two Runnable threads each using this run method.
     */

    Thread t1 = new Thread(this);
    t1.setName("A");
    t1.start();

    Thread t2 = new Thread(this);
    t2.setName("B");
    t2.start();
  }

  /**
   * Date format used in message. Includes milliseconds.
   */

  public static final SimpleDateFormat FMT
     = new SimpleDateFormat("hh:mm:ss.SSS aa");

  /**
   * Where the counter loop takes place.
   */
  public void run()
  {
    Thread t = Thread.currentThread();
    System.out.println("Starting " + t.getName());
    for (int i = 0; i < 8; i++) {
       try {
          t.sleep((long) (Math.random() * 500 + 100));
       }
       catch (InterruptedException e) {
          break;
       }
       System.out.println
          (FMT.format(new Date())
          + " Thread " + t.getName()
          + ": Count = " + i);
    }
    System.out.println("Leaving " + t.getName());
  }
}
```

The output from `ThreadExample2` is similar to the output from `ThreadExample1`:

```
Starting A
Starting B
10:17:00.098 PM Thread B: Count = 0
10:17:00.229 PM Thread B: Count = 1
10:17:00.309 PM Thread A: Count = 0
10:17:00.369 PM Thread B: Count = 2
10:17:00.629 PM Thread A: Count = 1
10:17:00.669 PM Thread B: Count = 3
10:17:00.799 PM Thread B: Count = 4
10:17:01.000 PM Thread A: Count = 2
10:17:01.320 PM Thread A: Count = 3
10:17:01.340 PM Thread B: Count = 5
10:17:01.641 PM Thread A: Count = 4
10:17:01.901 PM Thread B: Count = 6
10:17:02.041 PM Thread A: Count = 5
10:17:02.161 PM Thread B: Count = 7
Leaving B
10:17:02.382 PM Thread A: Count = 6
10:17:02.592 PM Thread A: Count = 7
Leaving A
```

One disadvantage of using the `Runnable` interface is that it's a class with only one `run()` method and so can only perform one kind of background operation, no matter how many threads it creates. An application that does animation and also listens to a socket or input stream, for instance, cannot do so by implementing `Runnable` directly.

A simple variation on this technique is to use an anonymous inner class that implements `Runnable`. The advantages of this approach are these:

■ Each thread can have its own `run()` method and perform different operations.

■ The thread code stays in close visual proximity to the method in which it's used.

The following listing illustrates the anonymous inner class approach:

```
import java.text.*;
import java.util.*;

/**
 * A class that demonstrates simple multithreading
 * using the Runnable interface implemented by
 * an anonymous class.
```

```
*/
public class ThreadExample3
{
    public static void main(String[] args)
    {
        // Anonymous runnable thread 1

        new Thread(new Runnable() {

            public void run() {
                for (int i = 0; i < 8; i++) {
                    ThreadExample3.sleep(600, 100);
                    int n = (int) (Math.random() * flavors.length);
                    System.out.println("A: " + flavors[n]);
                }
            }

            private String[] flavors
                = { "Chocolate", "Strawberry", "Vanilla", };

        }).start();

        // Anonymous runnable thread 2

        new Thread(new Runnable() {

            public void run() {
                for (int i = 0; i < 16; i++) {
                    ThreadExample3.sleep(300, 50);
                    int n = (int) (Math.random() * 100);
                    System.out.println("B: " + n);
                }
            }

        }).start();
    }

    /**
     * Utility method that sleeps for a random amount
     * of time.
     */
    private static void sleep(int mean, int lowLimit)
```

```
    {
        try {
            long delay = (long)(Math.random() * mean + lowLimit);
            Thread.currentThread().sleep(delay);
        }
        catch (InterruptedException ignore) {}
    }
}
```

which produces output like the following:

```
B: 21
B: 54
B: 57
A: Chocolate
B: 38
B: 80
B: 26
A: Chocolate
A: Strawberry
B: 14
B: 75
A: Vanilla
B: 46
B: 66
A: Strawberry
B: 86
B: 73
B: 80
A: Vanilla
B: 85
B: 12
B: 94
A: Strawberry
A: Strawberry
```

If you're not familiar with this anonymous inner class syntax, just remember that anywhere you can write this:

```
new MyClass()
```

you can also write this:

```
new MyInterface() { ... method definitions ... } );
```

which is functionally equivalent to this:

```
class MyInterfaceImpl() implements MyInterface {
    ... method definitions ...
}
new MyInterfaceImpl();
```

Even though it looks as if you're using new to create an instance of an interface, you're really just using it to create an instance of an unnamed class that the compiler supplies with your method implementations. If you don't refer to the class elsewhere, it makes your code a bit more clear.

Creating Threads with Timer and TimerTask

Java 2 introduced a third technique for starting threads, the java.util.Timer and java.util.TimerTask classes. The Timer class acts as a scheduler of delayed or repeated tasks. These tasks must extend the TimerTask class and provide a run() method. Tasks are scheduled for execution with the Timer.scheduleTask() method in one of its several forms. Unlike in the other two approaches, the TimerTask run() method doesn't normally contain an execution loop, because Timer can automatically schedule repeated task execution. The following TimerExample.java shows the counter example done with Timer and TimerTask.

```
import java.text.*;
import java.util.*;

/**
 * A class that demonstrates simple multithreading
 * using <code>java.util.Timer</code>
 */
public class TimerExample
{
    /**
     * Creates and runs an instance of the timer example.
     */
    public static void main(String[] args)
```

```
{
    new TimerExample().run();
}

private Timer timer;
private int taskCount;

/**
 * Runs two timer tasks
 */
public void run()
{
    // Create a timer to control the timer tasks

    timer = new Timer();

    // Keep track of how many tasks have been
    // created so that we can shut down the
    // timer.

    taskCount = 0;

    // Create two timer tasks and schedule
    // their execution at half-second intervals,
    // delaying the second one's start by 250 ms

    TimerTask t1 = new CounterTimerTask("A", this);
    taskCount++;
    timer.schedule(t1, 0, 500);

    TimerTask t2 = new CounterTimerTask("B", this);
    taskCount++;
    timer.schedule(t2, 250, 500);
}

/**
 * Callback method that allows scheduled tasks to
 * notify us when they are done.
 */
public synchronized void done()
{
    taskCount--;
```

```
        if (taskCount <= 0)
            timer.cancel();
    }
}

/**
 * A TimerTask that counts to eight
 */
class CounterTimerTask extends TimerTask
{
    /**
     * Date format used in message. Includes milliseconds.
     */
    public static final SimpleDateFormat FMT
        = new SimpleDateFormat("hh:mm:ss.SSS aa");

    private String name;
    private int counter;
    private TimerExample parent;

    public CounterTimerTask(String name, TimerExample parent)
    {
        this.name = name;
        this.counter = 0;
        this.parent = parent;
    }

    /**
     * Where the counter loop takes place.
     */
    public void run()
    {
        if (counter == 0)
            System.out.println("Starting " + name);

        System.out.println
            (FMT.format(new Date())
            + " Thread " + name
            + ": Count = " + counter);

        counter++;
        if (counter >= 8) {
```

```
            System.out.println("Leaving " + name);
            cancel();
            parent.done();
        }
    }
}
```

The `CounterTimerTask` object keeps track of the number of times it has been called and invokes its own `cancel()` method when it reaches the iteration limit. It then calls the `TimerExample done()` method so that the reference count can be decremented and the timer thread can be shut down gracefully. Because `TimerExample` uses a fixed schedule for each task, the counter messages alternate in approximate quarter- second intervals:

```
Starting A
11:40:24.865 PM Thread A: Count = 0
Starting B
11:40:25.125 PM Thread B: Count = 0
11:40:25.366 PM Thread A: Count = 1
11:40:25.626 PM Thread B: Count = 1
11:40:25.866 PM Thread A: Count = 2
11:40:26.127 PM Thread B: Count = 2
11:40:26.367 PM Thread A: Count = 3
11:40:26.627 PM Thread B: Count = 3
11:40:26.868 PM Thread A: Count = 4
11:40:27.128 PM Thread B: Count = 4
11:40:27.369 PM Thread A: Count = 5
11:40:27.629 PM Thread B: Count = 5
11:40:27.869 PM Thread A: Count = 6
11:40:28.130 PM Thread B: Count = 6
11:40:28.370 PM Thread A: Count = 7
Leaving A
11:40:28.630 PM Thread B: Count = 7
Leaving B
```

Synchronizing Threads

Multithreaded applications often have operations that must be performed by only one thread at a time or operations that require multiple threads to act cooperatively. To accomplish this, a means for protecting critical sections of code must exist, so that two threads don't run them simultaneously.

To see why this is necessary, consider the following example of a program that issues invoice numbers to a billing application. The last invoice number used is stored in a text file. A new invoice number is assigned in a method that reads the file, adds one to the invoice number, and writes it back to disk. The program starts five threads to simulate multiple online users accessing the invoice numbering routine at random times. The invoice handling in this demonstration consists of simply printing the name of the thread and the invoice number it has been assigned. See if you can spot the bug:

```java
import java.io.*;
import java.net.*;
import java.util.*;

/**
 * An illustration of a thread synchronization problem
 */
public class SynchronizationTest implements Runnable
{
    public static void main(String args[])
    {
        new SynchronizationTest();
    }

    /**
     * Creates a new SynchronizationTest object that starts
     * five invoice handling threads.
     */
    public SynchronizationTest()
    {
        Thread[] threads = {
            new Thread(this, "A"),
            new Thread(this, "B"),
            new Thread(this, "C"),
            new Thread(this, "D"),
            new Thread(this, "E"),
        };
        for (int i = 0; i < threads.length; i++)
            threads[i].start();
    }

    /**
     * Simulates handling ten invoices. This method
     * will be run by each of the five threads.
```

```java
*/
public void run()
{
   try {
      for (int i = 0; i < 10; i++) {
         handleInvoice();
         Thread.sleep((long) (Math.random()*500));
      }
   }
   catch (InterruptedException ignore) {
   }
   catch (IOException e) {
      e.printStackTrace();
   }
}

/**
 * The invoice handling method (with a subtle bug)
 */
public void handleInvoice()
   throws IOException
{
   Thread t = Thread.currentThread();

   // Get the last used invoice number from invoice.dat

   BufferedReader in =
      new BufferedReader(
      new FileReader("invoice.dat"));
   int invoiceNumber = Integer.parseInt(in.readLine());
   in.close();

   // Add 1 to get the current invoice number

   invoiceNumber++;
   System.out.println
      (t.getName() + " handles invoice " + invoiceNumber);

   // Update the invoice number

   PrintWriter out =
      new PrintWriter(
      new FileWriter("invoice.dat"));
   out.println(invoiceNumber);
```

```
    out.flush();
    out.close();
  }
}
```

The program may run several times without any problems, assigning consecutive invoice numbers to each thread. But after a while, output like this appears:

```
A handles invoice 68401
B handles invoice 68402
C handles invoice 68403
D handles invoice 68404
E handles invoice 68405
E handles invoice 68406
D handles invoice 68407
A handles invoice 68408
D handles invoice 68409
B handles invoice 68410
B handles invoice 68411
E handles invoice 68412
C handles invoice 68412
B handles invoice 68413
D handles invoice 68414
E handles invoice 68415
B handles invoice 68416
B handles invoice 68417
A handles invoice 68418
```

Invoice number 68412 appears twice in the list, assigned to both thread E and thread C. What happened?

The problem is this: during the time interval from when the invoice number is read to when it is rewritten in the `invoice.dat` file, it's possible for another thread executing the same method to read the file and get the old number. This thread can then increment it and update the file, but it can then have a duplicate invoice number.

To prevent this, Java provides a means for getting an exclusive lock on an object respected by all threads. This locking mechanism is called *synchronization* and is triggered by the keyword `synchronized`. Individual blocks of code can be synchronized using this syntax:

```
synchronized (object) {
  // code to be synchronized
}
```

where *object* is a reference to any object. Entire methods can be synchronized by using the synchronized keyword as a method modifier, for example,

```
public synchronized void myMethod() {
    // code to be synchronized
}
```

which is functionally equivalent to the following:

```
public void myMethod() {
    synchronized(this) {
        // code to be synchronized
    }
}
```

When a thread encounters a synchronized block, it first attempts to obtain the lock on the specified object. If the thread is successful, it executes the block and releases the lock. If the thread cannot obtain the lock, it waits until the lock is available, acquires the lock for itself, executes the block, and releases the lock. The Java virtual machine ensures these operations are performed by only one thread at a time.

In the invoice handling example, the duplicate invoice problem can be eliminated by synchronizing the handleInvoice() method:[7]

```
public synchronized void handleInvoice() throws IOException
{
    // Read the file, increment the invoice number,
    // and update the file.
    ...
}
```

For the sake of performance, it's important not to synchronize any more code than necessary, because this forces threads to walk single file through the synchronized section. The entire handleInvoice() needn't be synchronized, just the code from where the file is opened for reading to where it's closed for writing.

---

[7]   Assuming, of course, that you have total control of the file. Synchronization protects you only from your own Java virtual machine, not from other processes that access the file. JDK 1.4 introduces the java.nio.channels.FileLock class, which can be used for more robust locking.

Servlet Threading Models

The servlet API takes advantage of Java's built-in support for multithreading to ensure responsive request handling and good throughput. In doing so, it offers some flexibility in how threads are used. The process whereby requests are dispatched to one or more threads is called the *servlet threading model.* You can choose from two models:

- Multiple threads running a single servlet instance, which is the *default threading model.*

- Multiple instances, each running in their own thread. This is referred to as the *single-thread model.*

Let's consider the implications of operating in each model.

Default Threading Model

In the default model, only a single instance of the servlet (or JSP) is loaded.[8] The servlet container maintains a pool of threads, assigning them to requests as they arrive. Each thread runs the appropriate service method, typically doGet() or doPost(). During periods of peak activity, many requests may be running simultaneously through the same servlet methods, but because each thread has its own instruction pointer and stack for local variables, no conflict occurs between requests. Figure 8-11 illustrates the default model, showing three requests being handled by three threads.

The default model provides good throughput, but some restrictions exist. Because there is only one servlet instance, only one copy of any instance variable exists. If no precautions are taken and the code allows the variables to be written, one thread can overwrite a value needed by another. In Figure 8-11, for example, Request 2 is running at the same time as both Request 1 and Request 3. If they are all in the doGet() method writing to an instance variable and, later, reading it, their writes and reads could possibly overlap. Also, if the doGet() or doPost() method calls subroutines, it must pass all necessary objects as parameters because it cannot rely on instance variables to retain their value from the time they are written until the time the subroutine reads them.

For this reason, avoid using instance variables, unless they are read-only. This may sound like a restriction, but it's simply a different point of view. The real unit of work, after all, is the request, not the servlet instance. Objects of any kind can be stored as request attributes in a completely thread-safe manner:

```
public void doGet(
      HttpServletRequest request,
```

---

[8]   Actually, one per servlet name. Several servlet names may be associated with the same servlet class in the web.xml deployment descriptor. See Chapter 18 for details.

```
        HttpServletResponse response)
    throws ServletException, IOException
{
    ...
    openConnection(request);
    runQuery(request);
    ...
}

public void openConnection(HttpServletRequest request)
    throws SQLException
{
    request.setAttribute
        ("connection", DriverManager.getConnection(...));
}

public void runQuery(HttpServletRequest request)
    throws SQLException
{
    Connection con = (Connection)
        request.getAttribute("connection");
    Statement stmt = con.createStatement();
    ResultSet rs = stmt.executeQuery("SELECT ...");
    request.setAttribute("resultSet", rs);
}
```

Likewise, you can synchronize critical sections of code in a servlet method, although care must be exercised to avoid synchronizing too much and adversely affecting performance.

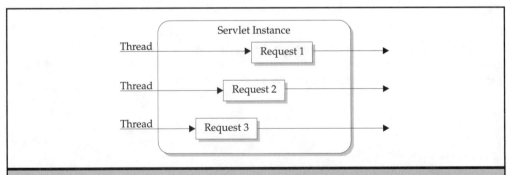

Figure 8-11.   *Default threading model: one instance with multiple threads*

Single-Threaded Model

The alternative to the default model is the single-threaded model. In this environment, the servlet container guarantees that only one request at a time is running the service method of a servlet instance. To use this model, a servlet must implement the `SingleThreadModel` interface. No methods are in this interface; it simply marks the servlet as requiring this threading treatment. In a JSP page, this model is selected by means of the `page` directive:

```
<%@ page isThreadSafe="false" %>
```

This causes the generated servlet to specify it implements `SingleThreadModel`.

Only one thread at a time can execute the `doGet()` or `doPost()` method of a single-threaded servlet, so this means instance variables are thread-safe. But the servlet container is free to create as many instances of the servlet as it needs to maintain adequate performance. This mode of operation is illustrated in Figure 8-12, which shows Request 3 waiting until Request 1 is completely finished before it runs, but Request 2 running in a different instance at the same time as the others.

Caution *I cover `SingleThreadModel` here only for completeness, not because I think it's a good idea to use it. `SingleThreadModel` is the source of much confusion and is often resorted to in an attempt to fix a faulty design. You can find messages posted to Java newsgroups complaining that network or database connections aren't properly isolated, despite the fact that they're used in a servlet that implements `SingleThreadModel`. And it's easy to see why: the only thing that's made thread-safe is the servlet instance itself. But, because multiple instances exist, external resources aren't protected from simultaneous access. It is difficult to find any compelling advantages afforded by the single-threaded model. Given a little planning and judicious synchronization, the default model is usually a better choice.*

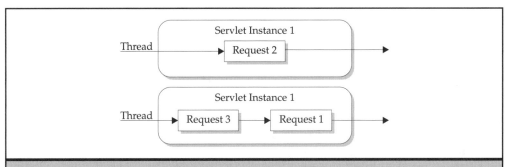

Figure 8-12. *Multiple servlet instances in the single-threaded model*

ELEMENTS OF JSP

Multithreaded Applications

Running more than one thread at a time is often the best way to accomplish a server-side task. One case is running an automatically started background process, not attached to any specific request, similar to a Unix daemon or a Windows NT service. This can easily be done in a servlet environment, using the following technique:

1. Have the init() method start a thread that performs the desired task. This may consist of opening a socket to service requests or periodically reading a Web page for dynamically updated data, such as stock quotes or news headlines. Maintain a reference to the thread in the servlet context.

2. Use the doGet() method strictly for commands, administrative tasks, and status reporting. Providing a command that can shut down or restart the background thread is usually desirable.

3. In the destroy() method, close the thread after releasing any resources it's using.

The servlet (or JSP) can be designated as load-on-startup in the deployment descriptor, so that it runs whenever the servlet container is running, without requiring a user to be logged on. Because the servlet container itself can typically be run as a daemon or service, this amounts to being able to write such processes as Java servlets.

Another beneficial use of multithreading is for handling long-running requests, such as complex data analysis or other project-like requests. If a client requests a server process that takes a considerable amount of time, both the client and the servlet container simply wait until it finishes. This needn't be the case, though.

Consider how print spooling works. A user can click the Print button in a word processing application and experience only a slight pause while the print request is queued. Usually, some message about which printer has received the request appears and possibly a job ID identifying the print request. The spooled output then waits on a queue for the printer to become available, but the user is free to continue writing the document or to perform any other tasks. Those other tasks may include monitoring the print queue status, holding and releasing jobs, changing their priority, canceling them, and so forth.

A JSP page can operate similarly. Instead of running a complex task in the current thread, it can launch a background thread, keeping a reference to the thread as a session attribute. The user can receive notification that the request has been queued and is being serviced. The JSP page may also provide displays that show the status of the request and enable the user to hold, release, or cancel it. When the request completes, the JSP page can provide a hyperlink that enables the results to be viewed. Extremely long-running requests handled by extremely clever JSP pages might even have their results e-mailed to the user.

Long-Running Requests with Status Messages

A variation on this technique can be used to provide the user with a status screen indicating the request is being processed, which is replaced by the results when the request is complete. The key to the technique is using a background session-scoped thread to do the work and using the <META HTTP-EQUIV="REFRESH"> HTML tag to have the Web browser automatically monitor the status.

In the following example, the user is logging on and requesting authentication by means of time-consuming simulated database operation. While the authentication request is being processed, the user sees an "Authenticating, please wait..." message. When the request is complete, this message is replaced with the results of the authentication. Meanwhile, the servlet container is free to handle other requests without waiting for the authentication request to complete.

The basic conversation between client and server in this session is as follows:

Client: Please authenticate me. UserID=MyUserID, password=****
Server: OK, call me back in two seconds for status.
Client: (*two seconds later*) Are you done?
Server: No, call me back in two seconds for status.
Client: (*two seconds later*) Are you done?
Server: No, call me back in two seconds for status.
Client: (*two seconds later*) Are you done?
Server: Yes, you are authenticated (*or not*).

The user needn't request the updated status manually. HTML provides a client-side automatic means of periodically updating a page:

<META HTTP-EQUIV="REFRESH" CONTENT="*seconds*; URL=*url*">

The presence of this particular <META> tag in an HTML document causes the browser to wait the specified number of seconds, and then redirect to the specified URL. This feature is commonly used to indicate a Web site has moved and the user is going to be automatically forwarded to the new address.

The following JSP implements this protocol using a background worker thread that simulates the database authentication delay.

```
<%--
    A JSP page that displays status messages during a
    long-running request and does not tie up server
    resources waiting for the request to complete.
```

```
--%>
<%

    // See if there is an authentication worker thread running

    WorkerThread worker = (WorkerThread)
        session.getAttribute("worker");

    // If not, create a new one and start the authentication

    if (worker == null) {
        String userID = request.getParameter("userID");
        String password = request.getParameter("password");
        worker = new WorkerThread(userID, password);
        session.setAttribute("worker", worker);
    }

    // Now display either the "please wait" screen
    // or the "user authenticated" screen

    if (!worker.isDone()) {
        String url = request.getRequestURL().toString();
        url = response.encodeURL(url);
%>
<html>
<head>
<title>Please Wait</title>
<meta http-equiv="REFRESH" content="2; URL=<%= url %>">
</head>
<body>
Authenticating, please wait...
</body>
</html>
<%
    }
    else {
%>
<html>
<head><title>Done</title></head>
<body>
Authentication complete.
<%= worker.isAuthenticated() ? " You pass!" : " You fail!" %>
</body>
</html>
```

```
<%

    // Done with worker

    session.invalidate();

  }
%>
<%!
/**
* A background thread that performs a potentially
* long-running task (authentication from a database).
*/
public class WorkerThread implements Runnable
{
   private boolean done;
   private boolean authenticated;
   private Thread kicker;

   public WorkerThread(String userID, String password)
   {
      done = false;
      authenticated = false;
      kicker = new Thread(this);
      kicker.start();
   }

   public boolean isDone()
   {
      return done;
   }

   public boolean isAuthenticated()
   {
      return authenticated;
   }

   public void run()
   {
      // Do the work here

      try {

         // Pretend to do something that takes five seconds
```

```
        for (int i = 0; i < 5; i++)
           Thread.sleep(1000);

        // Randomly authenticate 80% of all users

        authenticated = (Math.random() > 0.2);

        // We are done

        done = true;
      }
   catch (InterruptedException ignore) {}
   finally {
      kicker = null;
   }
  }
 }
%>
```

Application Considerations

The JSP environment offers a rich set of alternatives for mapping application characteristics to the HTTP environment. The main consideration is *object scope,* that is, the period of time during which an attribute is valid. The page context defines four scopes:

- page
- request
- session
- application

Each scope has its own lifecycle, and attributes can be stored in any of them. Objects in a particular scope are accessible to both JSP pages and servlets in the same servlet context. The task of the developer is to choose the object scope that matches the object use requirements.

Page scope is equivalent to the lifetime of the _jspService() method in a single JSP page. A user ID string, for example, can be given this page scope as follows:

```
pageContext.setAttribute
   ("userID", userID, PageContext.PAGE_SCOPE);
```

or simply

```
pageContext.setAttribute("userID", userID);
```

Corresponding `getAttribute()` methods exist for retrieving the object.

Why bother storing objects in the page context with page scope when they are already accessible simply as Java variables? The main context for this is JSP custom tags, which use the page context to communicate between tag handlers and the JSP page. See Chapter 11 for details about JSP custom tags.

Request scope is almost the same as page scope, but it includes other JSP pages or servlets invoked by `<jsp:include>` or `<jsp:forward>`. Attributes can be set in the request directly:

```
request.setAttribute("userID", userID);
```

or by means of the page context:

```
pageContext.setAttribute
    ("userID", userID, PageContext.REQUEST_SCOPE);
```

The effect of the two method calls is identical; the `pageContext.setAttribute()` method simply calls `request.setAttribute()`. Request scope is appropriate for objects associated with a single request, possibly set in a servlet and used in a JSP page to which a `RequestDispatcher` forwards the request.

Session scope is used by multiple requests that identify themselves with the same session ID and are associated with an active `HttpSession` with that ID. Attributes can be set in the `session` object directly:

```
session.setAttribute("userID", userID);
```

or by means of the page context:

```
pageContext.setAttribute
    ("userID", userID, PageContext.SESSION_SCOPE);
```

Session scope is appropriate when all three of the following requirements are present:

- The application requires multiple HTTP requests.
- Data needs to persist between requests.
- One or more server-side objects must persist in a particular state across requests.

As considered in this chapter, alternatives such as hidden fields, URL rewriting, and cookies exist when HTTP sessions aren't required.

Application scope is the common namespace for all servlets and JSP pages in a Web application. It persists between requests automatically; no session is required. Static initialization parameters can be set in application scope by using `<context-param>` in the `web.xml` deployment descriptor:

```
<context-param>
    <param-name>jdbc.driver</param-name>
    <param-value>sun.jdbc.odbc.JdbcOdbcDriver</param-value>
</context-param>

<context-param>
    <param-name>jdbc.url</param-name>
    <param-value>jdbc:odbc:composers</param-value>
</context-param>
```

These static parameters can be retrieved in a servlet or JSP page with the servlet context `getInitParameter()` method:

```
String driver = application.getInitParameter("jdbc.driver");
String url = application.getInitParameter("jdbc.url");
```

Objects can be stored in and retrieved from application scope with the same methods as the other three scopes:

```
pageContext.setAttribute
    ("userID", userID, PageContext.APPLICATION_SCOPE);
```

or

```
application.setAttribute("userID", userID);
```

Application scope is most useful for objects that need to persist between requests, for objects that must be visible to all users of the application, or for objects that need to be shared between other servlets and JSP pages.

Summary

The Web application model doesn't automatically map into the HTTP protocol. HTTP is *stateless*, not remembering anything about the client from one request to the next. The Web browser environment also introduces complications—in an application, each page depends on its predecessors, but a user may browse pages out of order and leave an application without signaling she is done.

The solution to the problem is to have the client (browser) remember certain details and remind the server each time it makes a request. This can involve the client managing all the data but, in practice, it's more common to see the client remember only an identifier of some kind and have the server use that to retrieve the rest of the data from a database. This virtual conversation (virtual because no persistent connection is involved) is commonly called a *session*.

This chapter deals with four techniques for session management:

- **Hidden fields in HTML forms**   These are simple to use, but can be transmitted only with an HTML form. If the user clicks a hyperlink, the hidden fields (and, therefore, the session) are lost.

- **URL rewriting**   This involves appending the session identifier to all URLs generated by the JSP page. Performance-wise, this technique can be expensive.

- **Cookies**   Small named data elements are sent to the client and returned to the server when the page is revisited. Cookies have the advantage that they can persist for an arbitrary length of time, even after the client computer is turned off. The disadvantage is some users turn off cookie support because of concerns for privacy.

- **The session API**   The servlet container can create an `HttpSession` object that acts as a repository for named objects that persist between requests from the same client in the same application. The client remembers the ID of the session either with cookies or URL rewriting. The servlet container determines which of these techniques the client accepts and adjusts accordingly.

Sessions can be shut down programmatically, or they can time out according to a configurable period of inactivity. The session API provides a means for objects to know when they have been bound or unbound from a session.

JSP pages, because they run in a pure Java environment, have full access to Java's support for multithreaded applications. This chapter discusses basic thread concepts, such as how to create, start, and synchronize them, and then considers the two servlet threading models. Two examples of Web applications using multiple threads are presented.

Even though dynamic content wasn't planned for in the original HTTP protocol, the protocol has proved to be quite capable of extension. Building on this flexibility, the session API provides the framework for making HTTP work in the Web application environment.

The Complete Reference

Chapter 9

Application Event Listeners

A s the servlet architecture has matured, more of its components have become standardized. For example, there was at first no standard means for servlet configuration, at least none that was spelled out in the servlet specification. Each vendor used a different approach; some had .properties files, others used Apache-like .conf files. Eventually, "best practices" emerged, and a standard Web application structure became part of the specification.

A similar evolutionary path happened with event listeners. Originally, only the servlet container itself knew about the application lifecycle, that is, when servlets, sessions, or contexts were started or stopped. Over time, as applications became more sophisticated, developers found the need for more access to these lifecycle events. To fill this need, *application event listeners* were added to the servlet specification.

Application event listeners are Java classes that allow code to be invoked at significant points in the application lifecycle. This chapter discusses servlet context, session, and servlet request listeners, and provides detailed examples of their use.

Beyond Session Binding Listeners

One type of event listener, HttpSessionBindingListener, has been available since the earliest versions of the Servlet API. This is an interface that objects can implement to receive notification when they are added to or removed from an HttpSession. The Servlet 2.3 API extended this capability with HttpSessionActivationListener, which notifies objects in distributable applications when their session has been activated or is about to be passivated.[1]

The main characteristic of these two listener interfaces is that they only allow objects to know about their *own* events; being bound or unbound, activated or passivated. The Servlet 2.3 API, however, introduced the notion of independent, asynchronous objects at the Web application level that could listen for session-wide or application-wide events. Servlet 2.4 adds an additional level—the servlet request.

In the following sections, we'll see where these asynchronous listeners can be used, and what types of events they can monitor.

Event Scope

As you may recall from Chapter 6, there is a hierarchy of four environments or *scopes* in which events can occur:

- page   The individual JSP page.
- request   The HTTP request, which may be handled by several JSP pages through the request dispatcher mechanism.

---

[1]   Activation and passivation refer to sessions being serialized and deserialized as they are transferred between virtual machines. In this case, transient objects like threads and database connections need to be recreated, which is where the activation listener methods become useful.

- `session` An HTTP session, which may consist of a login page, several requests, and a database update.
- `application` The overall Web application, corresponding to one servlet context.

The Servlet 2.4 API provides listeners for events in the request, session, and application scopes. Page scope is not included, because it's not significantly different from request scope in terms of events of interest.

In each of these environments, similar kinds of events can occur. The environment can be created and destroyed, and possibly activated and passivated. These are referred to as *lifecycle* events. In addition, objects can be stored in each of these scopes and retrieved by name, much like a `Hashtable` or `Map`, using the `setAttribute()`, `getAttribute()`, and `removeAttribute()` methods. These are known as *attribute change* events. The Servlet API allows you to monitor both lifecycle and attribute change events by implementing one or more of the *event listener interfaces*, which are the subject of the next section.

Event Listener Interfaces

If you've done any Java GUI or JavaBeans programming, you've most likely run into event listeners. These are Java interfaces that you can implement and register with a source of events. For example, a `JButton` click event can be handled by creating a class that implements `ActionListener`, and then registering that class with the button's `addActionListener()` method. When the button is clicked, it fires an action event, which causes the action listener's `actionPerformed()` method to be called. The parameter to `actionPerformed()` is an object that provides information about the click event and the component that was its source.

Similarly, event listeners in the Servlet 2.4 API are Java interfaces that receive notification when lifecycle or attribute change events occur. Table 9-1 briefly describes each of these eight interfaces.

Interface	Description
`ServletContextListener`	Called when the application starts or stops.
`HttpSessionListener`	Called when a session starts or stops.
`ServletRequestListener`	Called when a request is about to be handled or immediately after it has been handled.

Table 9-1. *Event Listener Interfaces in the Servlet 2.4 API*

ELEMENTS OF JSP

`HttpSessionActivationListener`	Called when a session is activated or passivated.
`HttpSessionBindingListener`	Called when an object is bound to or unbound from a session.
`ServletContextAttributeListener`	Notified when an application-wide attribute changes.
`HttpSessionAttributeListener`	Notified when a session attribute changes.
`ServletRequestAttributeListener`	Notified when a request attribute changes.

Table 9-1. *Event Listener Interfaces in the Servlet 2.4 API* (continued)

You can have as many or as few listeners as you want, and more than one listener of a particular type.

How It Works

Developing and deploying event listeners is not difficult. There are four steps involved:

1. Write a class that implements one or more of the listener interfaces. This consists of adding the keyword `implements` and the interface name to the class declaration, and then implementing the methods required by the interface.

2. Add a `<listener>` entry to the `web.xml` deployment descriptor. This entry must contain a `<listener-class>` child entry with the fully qualified name of your listener class. This has the form:

   ```
   <listener>
       <listener-class> your.class.name </listener-class>
   </listener
   ```

   You can have multiple `<listener>` entries, one after the other. These entries must be placed after any `<filter>` and `<filter-mapping>` entries, and before any `<servlet>` and `<servlet-mapping>` entries in the `web.xml` file.[2]

---

[2] The order of elements in the `web.xml` file is clearly spelled out in the XML schema *web-app_2_4.xsd*. You can download this file from *http://java.sun.com/xml/ns/j2ee/web-app_2_4.xsd*. It's well worth looking at whenever you have questions about the syntax of the deployment descriptor.

3. At Web application startup time, the servlet container reads the `<listener>` entries in the order they are coded, creates instances of the specified classes, and registers each of them as a listener for its particular events of interest.

4. When the events occur, the servlet container calls the appropriate method in each registered listener, passing it an indication of what happened and a reference to the servlet context, session, or request to which it happened.

This process differs slightly from the Java GUI model in that you don't explicitly call `addMyListener()` anywhere—the servlet container does that on your behalf according to the `<listener>` entries in the deployment descriptor. Likewise, you don't create the listener objects with `new`. Instead, the servlet container creates the instances it requires with `Class.forName().newInstance()` or the equivalent. For this reason, you must ensure that your listener class has a zero-argument default constructor.

 Although a servlet, like any other class, can implement a listener interface, a servlet instance may not act as a listener, since the two object types have different lifecycles.

Listeners for Lifecycle Events

In this section, we'll examine each of the five lifecycle interfaces in more detail.

ServletContextListener

A servlet context listener gets called when the Web application starts (before any requests are handled) and when it ends (after all the servlets are destroyed). It must implement the two methods shown here.

Method	Description
void `contextInitialized` (ServletContextEvent)	Called when the Web application is ready to process requests.
void `contextDestroyed` (ServletContextEvent)	Called when the Web application is about to be shut down.

Each of these methods is called with a `ServletContextEvent` parameter, which provides access to the servlet context through its `getServletContext()` method. Possible uses for servlet context listeners include:

■ Logging application start and stop events (although this is probably adequately handled by the container's own logging mechanism).

■ Starting another server that is used by this application.

■ Refreshing a snapshot of some data source that doesn't change frequently but is expensive or impractical to access in real time, such as an extract from a data warehouse.

Later in this chapter, we'll see an example of a servlet context listener that monitors currency exchange rates.

HttpSessionListener

A session listener is notified whenever new sessions are created and whenever they end, either by being invalidated or timing out. Note that this is more than what a `HttpSessionBindingListener` does, since an `HttpSessionListener` listens to *all* sessions in the application. The methods it must implement are listed here.

Method	Description
void sessionCreated (HttpSessionEvent)	Called when an HTTP session is created.
void sessionDestroyed (HttpSessionEvent)	Called when an HTTP session is invalidated or when it times out.

Since these methods receive a `HttpSessionEvent` parameter, they can get the session object, and in turn the servlet context object, if necessary. Access to the servlet context allows you to use context attributes to communicate globally between your listener and your servlets.

Like the servlet context listener, a session listener can be used for logging. In this case, it makes more sense, because server logs do not adequately record when *sessions* start and stop; only individual requests. To track how applications are being used, a session listener is useful. The examples section in this chapter includes a session listener that monitors start and stop times for sessions and records them in a database. This could be used to analyze peak access times and average session duration.

ServletRequestListener

The Servlet 2.4 API introduced a new listener interface, `ServletRequestListener`. Classes that implement this interface receive notification when a request is about to be handled (when it comes into scope) or right after it has been handled (when it is about to go out of scope). Its methods, which are listed in this table, are passed an event object that has references to both the servlet request and servlet context objects.

Method	Description
void requestInitialized (ServletRequestEvent)	Called when a request is about to be handled.
void requestDestroyed (ServletRequestEvent)	Called after a request has been handled and is about to be destroyed.

In addition to the uses described for servlet context and session listeners, a request listener can examine the request headers. Unlike filters (described in Chapter 10), request listeners are asynchronous, not part of the request processing chain. This means they can be used for noninvasive processes that do not hold up the request. One example might be monitoring for access by particular client addresses, to signal possible denial of service attacks.

HttpSessionActivationListener

Introduced in Servlet 2.3, the session activation listener interface provides for notification when a session is activated or passivated. This is of interest primarily for Web applications marked as distributable in the deployment descriptor. Passivation refers to the process of serializing a session prior to moving it to another virtual machine, and activation refers to the reverse process of deserializing the session in the new virtual machine. Session activation listeners must implement the two methods listed here.

Method	Description
void sessionDidActivate (HttpSessionEvent)	Called when a session has just been activated.
void sessionWillPassivate (HttpSessionEvent)	Called when a session is about to be passivated.

This listener is really an extension to the capabilities of a session binding listener, in that the listener object belongs to the session being activated or passivated. It receives notifications only about its own session. It is common to see classes that implement both interfaces, since their semantics are similar.

HttpSessionBindingListener

Chapter 8 introduced the session binding listener in connection with the BoundConnection example. This interface (the oldest of the listener interfaces) can be implemented by objects that need to know when they are bound to a session or unbound from it. This allows them to start and stop threads, database connections, and other transient objects. This table lists the two methods that must be implemented.

Method	Description
void valueBound (HttpSessionBindingEvent)	Notifies an object that it has been stored in a session. The event parameter gives access to the session object and the name by which the object is bound.
void valueUnbound (HttpSessionBindingEvent)	Notifies an object that it has been removed from a session, either explicitly with the removeAttribute() method or by virtue of the session being invalidated or timing out.

ELEMENTS OF JSP

Listeners for Attribute Change Events

The application, session, and request scopes each can store objects by name, in the same manner that a `Hashtable` or a `Map` does. Objects are bound with the `setAttribute()` method and unbound with the `removeAttribute()` method found in each scope object. An object can also be unbound by another `setAttribute()` using the same name but a different value. When these attribute changes happen, you can receive notification by implementing the attribute listener for the corresponding scope. This section describes the three attribute listener interfaces.

ServletContextAttributeListener

An instance of a class that implements `ServletContextAttributeListener` is notified whenever an object is bound or unbound from the application context. The notification consists of a call to one of the three callback methods described here.

Method	Description
void attributeAdded (ServletContextAttributeEvent)	Called when a new attribute is added to the servlet context.
void attributeReplaced (ServletContextAttributeEvent)	Called when an object is bound to the servlet context with the name of an existing attribute.
void attributeRemoved (ServletContextAttributeEvent)	Called when an object is unbound from the servlet context.

Each of these methods is passed an event object as a parameter. This event object provides `getName()` and `getValue()` methods whose interpretation varies according to the method:

- When an attribute is added to the servlet context, `getValue()` returns the object that was added.
- When an attribute is removed, `getValue()` returns the removed object.
- When an attribute is replaced by another under the same name, `getValue()` returns the old object.

HttpSessionAttributeListener

A session attribute listener is notified whenever an object is bound to or removed from an HTTP session. `HttpSessionAttributeListener`, is similar to the `HttpSessionBindingListener`, but it operates on all sessions in the application (from the outside looking in), not on the object being bound or unbound (from the inside looking out). The listener is notified by one of the three callback methods described in this table.

Method	Description
void attributeAdded (HttpSessionBindingEvent)	Called when a new attribute is added to a session.
void attributeReplaced (HttpSessionBindingEvent)	Called when an object is bound to a session with the name of an existing attribute.
void attributeRemoved (HttpSessionBindingEvent)	Called when an object is unbound from a session.

In each case, the method is called after the event takes place (add, remove, or replace). The event parameter provides methods that can retrieve the session object, the attribute name, and the attribute value, with semantics like those of the ServletContextAttributeListener.

The examples section of this chapter shows how a session attribute listener can be used to trigger the start and stop of an expensive external resource.

ServletRequestAttributeListener

Completing the set of interfaces is ServletRequestAttributeListener, which is new with the Servlet 2.4 API. As you might expect, this listener receives notification whenever an attribute is added, deleted, or changed in any servlet request in the Web application. Its methods are shown here.

Method	Description
void attributeAdded (ServletRequestAttributeEvent)	Called when a new attribute is added to a request.
void attributeReplaced (ServletRequestAttributeEvent)	Called when an object is bound to a request with the name of an existing attribute.
void attributeRemoved (ServletRequestAttributeEvent)	Called when an object is unbound from a request.

Clearly, this listener can expect a lot of traffic. You probably won't be interested in every attribute change event; more likely, you'll be looking for a specific attribute name.

One example would be unhandled JSP page exceptions. When this occurs, the servlet container stores the exception in the servlet request under the name javax.servlet.jsp.jspException and then forwards the request to the error page. If you check for an attribute of that name in a ServletRequestAttributeListener, you can provide system-wide additional logging for the exception beyond what the error page returns to the browser.

Examples of Application Event Listeners

So much for abstract descriptions—let's see some actual code! In this section, we'll look at three event listeners:

- A servlet context event listener that downloads and caches currency exchange rates.

- A session listener that logs session start and stop times to a database.

- A session attribute listener that activates an expensive metered resource only when needed.

Currency Exchange Rate Cache

Servlets often acquire resources in their init() method that are used throughout the servlet instance lifetime. There may be background threads that are launched in the servlet's init() method and shut down in its destroy(). But what about resources that are shared by several servlets? Which servlet should initialize the resource? We don't usually know which servlet will be called first. This sounds like a perfect candidate for a servlet context listener.

Suppose we have a JSP-based financial application that requires access to currency exchange rates, and that the rates are provided by a Web service. The rates need to be updated periodically by a background process, but only while the financial application is running. The ServletContextListener interface provides the hooks for starting and stopping such a background process.

For modularity and ease of testing, we'll separate this function into two classes, one to download and cache the rates, and another to listen for the start and stop events. Here is the class that implements the rate download and caching function:

```
package com.jspcr.listeners.currency;

import java.io.*;
import java.net.*;
import java.util.*;

/**
 * Downloads currency exchange rates from some source
 * and makes them available through method calls.
 */
public class RateCache implements Serializable
{
    /**
     * Map of from/to currency code to their
     * exchange rate.
     */
    private Map rateMap;
```

```
/**
 * Time at which rates were last updated
 */
private Date lastUpdateTime;

// ==========================================
//    Constructor
// ==========================================

/**
 * Creates a new RateCache
 */
public RateCache()
{
    rateMap = new HashMap();
}


// ==========================================
//    Instance methods
// ==========================================

/**
 * Updates the map with the most recent values
 */
public void refresh()
{
    // Simulate downloading the rates.  Here we just use
    // random values that fall within a plausible range.
    // A robust implementation would also require
    // synchronization so that rates would not be in an
    // inconsistent state while the refresh is going on.

    rateMap.clear();

    Object[][] rates = {
        {"USD","EUR",new Double(0.95),new Double(1.05)},
        {"USD","GBP",new Double(0.60),new Double(0.80)},
        {"USD","JPY",new Double(99.0),new Double(130.0)},
    };
    for (int i = 0; i < rates.length; i++) {

        String fromCurrency = (String) rates[i][0];
        String toCurrency = (String) rates[i][1];
        String key = fromCurrency + toCurrency;
```

```
            double lo = ((Double) rates[i][2]).doubleValue();
            double hi = ((Double) rates[i][3]).doubleValue();
            double range = hi - lo;
            double rate = Math.random() * range + lo;

            rateMap.put(key, new Double(rate));
        }

        // Note the time of last update

        lastUpdateTime = new Date();
    }

    /**
     * Returns the specified rate
     */
    public Double getExchangeRate
        (String fromCurrency, String toCurrency)
    {
        String key = fromCurrency + toCurrency;
        Double rate = (Double) rateMap.get(key);
        return rate;
    }

    /**
     * Returns the time of last update
     */
    public Date getLastUpdateTime()
    {
        return lastUpdateTime;
    }
}
```

The RateCache class provides a refresh() method that can be called to cause
the latest set of exchange rates to be downloaded,[3] and two accessor methods,
getExchangeRate() and getLastUpdateTime(). The rate cache will be stored in
the servlet context so that it is accessible to the JSP financial application. However, it

---

[3]   The means by which the rates are obtained is not shown here, although there are numerous Web
      sites that contain such data, most of which come with serious-sounding warnings about
      commercial reuse.

has no knowledge that it is being used in a servlet environment, and it can operate equally well in a standalone batch program (such as a unit test suite).

The heartbeat of the application is maintained by the `DownloadTimer` class, which implements `ServletContextListener` in order to be notified when the JSP financial application starts and stops. It performs three tasks:

1. When the JSP Web application starts, `DownloadTimer` creates an instance of the `RateCache` class and stores it in the servlet context.

2. It next starts a thread that invokes the rate cache `refresh()` method every 20 minutes (this can obviously be made a configurable parameter).

3. When the Web application is shut down, the rate cache object is removed from the servlet context and the timer thread is stopped.

```java
package com.jspcr.listeners.currency;

import java.io.*;
import java.net.*;
import java.util.*;
import javax.servlet.*;

/**
 * A servlet context listener that downloads currency exchange
 * rates every 20 minutes, but only while this Web application is
 * running.
 */
public class DownloadTimer implements ServletContextListener
{
    /**
     * Constant for twenty minutes (in milliseconds)
     */
    public static final long REFRESH_RATE = 20 * 60 * 1000;

    /**
     * Name of the rate cache attribute in the servlet context
     */
    public static final String CACHE_ATTRIBUTE =
        "com.jspcr.listeners.currency.rateCache";

    /**
     * The rate cache object
     */
    private RateCache cache;

    /**
     * Timer thread
     */
```

```java
private Thread timer;

/**
 * The servlet context used for logging messages
 */
private transient ServletContext context;

// ==========================================
//    These two methods implement the
//    ServletContextListener interface
// ==========================================

/**
 * Called when the Web application is ready to service
 * requests.
 */
public void contextInitialized(ServletContextEvent sce)
{
    context = sce.getServletContext();
    context.log("DownloadTimer: Starting download timer");

    // Create a rate cache that will maintain a
    // set of exchange rates.

    cache = new RateCache();

    // Store the rate cache in the servlet context

    context.setAttribute(CACHE_ATTRIBUTE, cache);

    // Schedule an update for every twenty minutes

    Runnable task = new Runnable() {
        public void run() {
            while (cache != null) {
                context.log("DownloadTimer: updating rates");
                cache.refresh();
                try {
                    Thread.sleep(REFRESH_RATE);
                }
                catch (InterruptedException e) {
                    break;
                }
            }
        }
    };
```

```
         // Start the timer

         timer = new Thread(task);
         timer.start();
      }

      /**
       * Called when the Web application is about to be shut down.
       */
      public void contextDestroyed(ServletContextEvent sce)
      {
         context = sce.getServletContext();
         context.log("DownloadTimer: Stopping download timer");

         // Remove the rate cache object from the servlet context

         context.removeAttribute(CACHE_ATTRIBUTE);

         // Stop the periodic download

         cache = null;
         timer.interrupt();
      }
   }
```

To access the rate quotation service, a servlet or JSP page simply retrieves the
RateCache object from the servlet context and calls its getExchangeRate() and
getLastUpdateTime() methods. The DollarToEuro.jsp page shown here
illustrates the technique:

```
<%@ page session="false" %>
<%@ page import="java.util.*" %>
<%@ page import="java.text.*" %>
<%@ page import="com.jspcr.listeners.currency.*" %>

<html>

<head>
<title>
   Dollar to Euro Exchange Rate
</title>
</head>

<body style="font-family: Verdana; font-size: 9pt;">
<h1 style="font-size: 130%;">
```

```
    Dollar to Euro Exchange Rate
</h1>
<%
    // Get the rate cache from the servlet context

    String attrKey = DownloadTimer.CACHE_ATTRIBUTE;
    Object attribute = application.getAttribute(attrKey);
    if (attribute == null) {
%>
<em>The rate service is not currently running</em>
<%
    }
    else {
        RateCache rateCache = (RateCache) attribute;

        // Get the rate itself from the cache

        attribute = rateCache.getExchangeRate("USD", "EUR");
        if (attribute == null) {
%>
<em>The rate is currently unavailable.</em>
<%
        }
        else {
            double rate = ((Double) attribute).doubleValue();
            NumberFormat rateFmt = NumberFormat.getNumberInstance();
            String rateString = rateFmt.format(rate);

            // Get the time of last update

            Date lastUpdate = rateCache.getLastUpdateTime();
            DateFormat timeFmt =
                DateFormat.getTimeInstance(DateFormat.LONG);
            String timeString = timeFmt.format(lastUpdate);
%>
The rate as of <%= timeString %> was <%= rateString %>
<%
        }
    }
%>
</body>
</html>
```

The results can be seen in Figure 9-1.

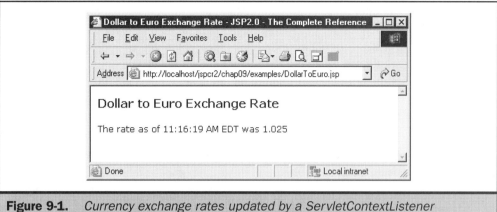

Figure 9-1.   *Currency exchange rates updated by a ServletContextListener*

Session Log

Web server logs have long been used for data mining, but they have limitations. One
in particular is that you can't easily determine which requests are part of a larger
application, a single session for one user. This kind of logging can of course be done
by Web applications themselves, but a more elegant solution is to implement that
functionality in a separate module that can be turned on or off.

This section illustrates how a session listener can be used to obtain the start and
stop times of each session in the application, and to log the results in a database.
The traffic counter class listed here implements both HttpSessionListener (to
monitor the start and stop times) and ServletContextListener (to start and
stop the database connection that it uses).

```
package com.jspcr.listeners.traffic;

import java.io.*;
import java.sql.*;
import java.util.*;
import java.util.Date;
import javax.naming.*;
import javax.sql.*;
import javax.servlet.*;
import javax.servlet.http.*;

/**
 * A session listener that keeps track of the start time
 * and duration of each session.  It also implements
 * <code>ServletContextListener</code> so that it can
```

```java
 * start and stop the database connection it uses.
 */
public class Counter implements
    HttpSessionListener, ServletContextListener
{
    /**
     * Table of active sessions
     */
    private Map activeSessionMap = new HashMap();

    /**
     * The database connection
     */
    private Connection con;

    /**
     * The statement object used to update the database
     */
    private PreparedStatement stmt;

    // ==========================================
    //     These two methods implement the
    //     HttpSessionListener interface
    // ==========================================

    /**
     * Logs the start of a session
     */
    public void sessionCreated(HttpSessionEvent se)
    {
        HttpSession session = se.getSession();

        // Save the creation time in the active session map

        String id = session.getId();
        Date created = new Date();
        activeSessionMap.put(id, created);
    }

    /**
     * Logs the end of a session
     */
```

```java
public void sessionDestroyed(HttpSessionEvent se)
{
   HttpSession session = se.getSession();

   // Retrieve the creation time from the active session map

   String id = session.getId();
   Date created = (Date) activeSessionMap.get(id);
   if (created == null) {
      // Ignore sessions whose start time we don't know
      return;
   }

   // Add a row to the session log table for this session

   Date destroyed = new Date();
   synchronized(this) {
      try {
         stmt.setString(1, id);
         stmt.setTimestamp(2, new Timestamp(created.getTime()));
         stmt.setTimestamp(3, new Timestamp(destroyed.getTime()));
         stmt.executeUpdate();
      }
      catch (SQLException e) {
         e.printStackTrace();
      }
   }
}


// =========================================
//    These two methods implement the
//    ServletContextListener interface
// =========================================

/**
* Called when the Web application is ready to service
* requests.
*/
public void contextInitialized(ServletContextEvent sce)
{
   // Log the application start event
```

```java
ServletContext context = sce.getServletContext();
context.log("Counter: Opening connection");

try {

    // Get a database connection from a data source
    // specified in the deployment descriptor

    Context ctx = new InitialContext();
    DataSource ds = (DataSource) ctx.lookup
        ("java:comp/env/jdbc/SessionLog");
    con = ds.getConnection();

    // Precompile an SQL statement that will add
    // entries to the database

    String SQL = "INSERT INTO session_log VALUES(?,?,?)";
    stmt = con.prepareStatement(SQL);
}
catch (NamingException e) {
    e.printStackTrace();
}
catch (SQLException e) {
    e.printStackTrace();
}
}

/**
* Called when the Web application is about to be shut down.
*/
public void contextDestroyed(ServletContextEvent sce)
{
    // Log the application end event

    ServletContext context = sce.getServletContext();
    context.log("Counter: Closing connection");

    // Shut down the database objects

    if (stmt != null) {
        try { stmt.close(); }
        catch (SQLException e) {
```

```
                e.printStackTrace();
            }
        }
        if (con != null) {
            try { con.close(); }
            catch (SQLException e) {
                e.printStackTrace();
            }
        }
    }
}
```

The `contextInitialized()` method is invoked when the application starts. It starts a database connection using a data source specified in the deployment descriptor. It also creates a `PreparedStatement` that will be used for logging the session time events. Whenever a session starts, the `sessionCreated()` method is called, which stores the session start time in a map using the session ID as the key. When the session ends, `sessionDestroyed()` retrieves the start time and logs the event in the database. Finally, when the application shuts down, the `contextDestroyed()` method closes the prepared statement and connection objects.

Controlling an Expensive Shared Resource

Web services that are billed according to connection time can be expensive to maintain when they are not being used. Suppose you have a news feed that can be shared by several applications, but that can be shut down whenever it is not being used at all. This can be handled by keeping a reference count of the number of active users, and shutting down the connection whenever the count reaches zero, as illustrated in the `NewsController` session attribute listener class:

```
package com.jspcr.listeners.attributes;

import java.io.*;
import java.net.*;
import java.util.*;
import javax.servlet.*;
import javax.servlet.http.*;

/**
 * A session attribute listener that controls the
 * starting and stopping of a shared news feed.
```

```java
 * The news server is active only while there are
 * one or more sessions using it.
 */
public class NewsController
    implements HttpSessionAttributeListener
{
    /**
     * Name of attribute that triggers startup and
     * shutdown of news server
     */
    public static final String ATTRIBUTE_NAME
        = "com.jspcr.listeners.attributes.newsfeed";

    /**
     * Number of sessions using the news server
     */
    private int referenceCount = 0;

    // =============================================
    //     These three methods implement the
    //     HttpSessionAttributeListener interface
    // =============================================

    /**
     * Called when an attribute has been added to a session.
     */
    public void attributeAdded(HttpSessionBindingEvent se)
    {
        String name = se.getName();
        if (name.equals(ATTRIBUTE_NAME)) {
            synchronized(this) {
                if (referenceCount == 0) {
                    startNewsServer();
                }
                referenceCount++;
            }
        }
    }

    /**
     * Called when an attribute has been replaced in a session.
     */
```

```
public void attributeReplaced(HttpSessionBindingEvent se)
{
}

/**
* Called when an attribute has been removed from a session.
*/
public void attributeRemoved(HttpSessionBindingEvent se)
{
   String name = se.getName();
   if (name.equals(ATTRIBUTE_NAME)) {
      synchronized(this) {
         referenceCount--;
         if (referenceCount == 0) {
            stopNewsServer();
         }
      }
   }
}

// ===========================================
//    Methods controlling the shared
//    news feed
// ===========================================

/**
* Starts the news server
*/
public void startNewsServer()
{
   // ... not shown here
}

/**
* Stops the news server
*/
public void stopNewsServer()
{
   // ... not shown here
}
}
```

ELEMENTS OF JSP

Summary

Event listeners allow code to be invoked at noteworthy points in the application lifecycle. These are classes that implement one or more of the listener interfaces provided by the Servlet 2.4 API:

- `ServletContextListener`
- `HttpSessionListener`
- `ServletRequestListener`
- `HttpSessionActivationListener`
- `HttpSessionBindingListener`
- `ServletContextAttributeListener`
- `HttpSessionAttributeListener`
- `ServletRequestAttributeListener`

Listeners fall into two categories: *lifecycle* and *attribute change.* In addition, there are two listener perspectives: that of an object being bound or unbound (represented by `HttpSessionActivationListener` and `HttpSessionBindingListener`), which receives notification of its own events, and that of an external observer listening for all events of the specified type in a Web application (represented by all the others).

The external observer listeners are registered with the servlet container by entries in the `web.xml` deployment descriptor and can be called when:

- A request, session, or Web application starts or stops, or
- Attributes are added, deleted, or change in any of these three scopes.

Listener classes provide a convenient place for shared functionality and can be a valuable tool in economic use of Web resources.

The Complete Reference

Chapter 10

Filters

In the Unix shell programming environment, pipes and filters have proved to be popular and highly useful tools. For example, a programmer can string together a few commands like this:

```
find -name '*.java' | sed 's/\/[^\/]*$//' | sort -u
```

to make a one-line program[1] that builds a list of packages from a directory tree of Java source code. Each of the commands is a building block that takes the output of the previous one, transforms it in some way, and then passes it on to the next command in the chain.

Similarly, the servlet API makes it possible to apply a set of filters to requests handled by a servlet container. These filters can be used to convert data formats, to provide authentication, to support testing and debugging, and to effect other useful transformations. They can be used to modify the incoming request, the response data, or both. Simple filters can be chained together to accomplish sophisticated tasks, refactoring code that would otherwise clutter up servlets and JSP pages.

This chapter examines how filters work, how they are configured, and how they can be used. It describes the filter objects provided by the servlet API and the methods they support. Several complete examples illustrate the concepts and provide a starting point for building your own filter toolkit.

Filter Overview

A filter is simply a Java class that implements the three methods of the `javax.servlet`
`.Filter` interface. It is not explicitly instantiated by the programmer, but rather by the servlet container, which needs to know only the filter class name and to which requests it should be applied. As Figure 10-1 illustrates, the servlet container passes requests to the filter, which can access and modify the request headers and data as necessary to perform the filtering function. The filter then passes the request to the next filter or resource in the pipeline. After the request is finally handled (whether by a servlet or a static resource such as an HTML file), the filter can access and modify the response and return it to the client.

As you might expect, it is very common to see more than one filter handling a request and/or response. Figure 10-2 shows two filters arranged as an output pipeline, first sorting the lines of text returned from the Web resource, then converting these lines to an HTML table. We'll return to this figure later in the chapter when we actually implement these two filters.

Filters are very much like their servlet cousins, in that they both process requests and return responses in a Web container. However, a servlet can only be the endpoint in a processing chain; a filter can be an endpoint or a middleware component. Moreover, a

---

[1] A one-line program that is shorter than the sentence it took to describe it, by the way.

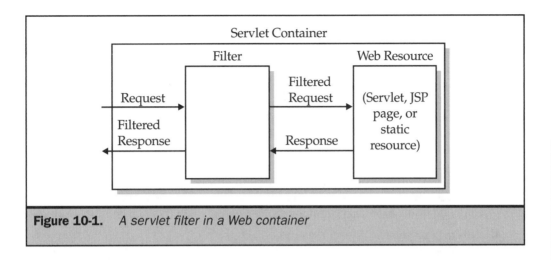

Figure 10-1.   *A servlet filter in a Web container*

single filter can be applied with different parameters and modes of operation to one or many servlets, making it a useful building block for robust and full-featured applications.

The Filter Lifecycle

As I mentioned earlier, a programmer does not create a filter directly by invoking a constructor in a program somewhere. Instead, the filter is declared in the servlet container in the web.xml deployment descriptor, where its name, its class, and the requests to

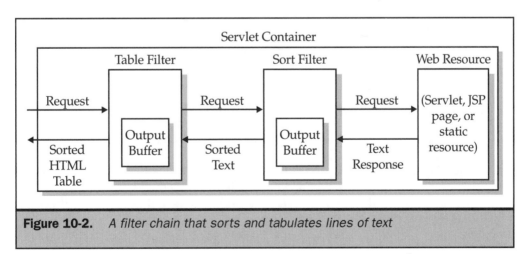

Figure 10-2.   *A filter chain that sorts and tabulates lines of text*

which it should be applied are described. The servlet container in turn manages events in the filter's lifecycle, which consists of three stages:

- **Initialization** When starting a servlet context (i.e., a Web application), the container examines its web.xml deployment descriptor for a list of filters to be created. As it encounters each one, the container uses the filter's configured class name as a parameter in a call to Class.forName().newInstance(), or some equivalent code. After ensuring that the object implements the required javax.servlet.Filter interface, the container invokes the filter's init() method. In this method, the programmer can do any necessary initialization, such as acquiring a database connection, opening a socket, setting a counter, etc. The container will not ask the filter to do anything else until it has either returned, thrown an exception, or timed out.

- **Filtering requests** After being initialized, the filter is ready to handle requests. The Web container will know in which request-handling pipelines the filter should participate and will dispatch requests to the filter's doFilter() method. If there are multiple filters that apply to the same set of requests, the container will chain the filters together in the order in which they are declared in the web.xml deployment descriptor. This method receives a reference to the servlet request, the servlet response, and an object called a FilterChain. The filter chain is a container-managed object that maintains an ordered list of filters. The filter can optionally modify the request (not really, but we'll get to that shortly) and then tell the filter chain to call the doFilter() method of the next filter in the chain. The last link in the chain is the servlet or static resource being accessed. Its response is passed back to the immediate prior filter, which is blocking on the doFilter() call. This filter can modify the response and pass it back to its nearest upstream neighbor, and so on until the final response is sent back to the original requesting client. Note that the filter can reject a request if necessary by simply not calling filterChain.doFilter(). This may be the sole function of an authentication filter, for example.

- **Termination** The time-reversed counterpart of initialization is termination. When the Web application is about to be shut down, or when the filter is about to be taken out of service for any other reason (such as passivation or load balancing), the container will call the filter's destroy() method. This provides the filter with the opportunity to release any resources it has acquired and otherwise prepare to be shut down. Note that this method will not be called if any threads are still running the doFilter() method, unless a timeout period has expired.[2]

---

[2] Note as well that it is the container that controls the filter lifecycle, not the filter. A filter cannot shut itself down by calling its own destroy() method. Once an instance is assimilated into the container's overall function, it can be prolonged indefinitely. Its technical distinctiveness has been added to the container's, and it will adapt to service requests as needed.

If you think this sounds similar to the servlet lifecycle, you're correct. Both filters and servlets have `init()` and `destroy()` methods, and both are multithreaded in their service routines. That being the case, the same caveats about instance variables and thread safety that apply to servlets apply to filters as well. You may wish to review the servlet threading model discussion in Chapter 8 for more details.

A Simple Example

To get a clearer mental model of filters, let's look at a simple example. This will be a basic logging filter that writes entries to the servlet container's log file when it is started and stopped, and when it handles requests. The concepts illustrated in this example will be

- Use of the `init()` and `destroy()` methods
- Accessing the servlet context
- Passing a request on to the next entity in the filter chain

```
package com.jspcr.filters;

import java.io.*;
import javax.servlet.*;
import javax.servlet.http.*;

/**
 * Simple class that illustrates the basic operation of a filter
 */
public class LoggingFilter implements Filter
{
    /**
     * Saved reference to filter configuration
     */
    private FilterConfig config;

    /**
     * Called when filter is initialized
     */
    public void init(FilterConfig config)
        throws ServletException
    {
        this.config = config;
        log("Initialized");
    }
```

```
/**
 * Called when filter is shut down
 */
public void destroy()
{
    log("Destroyed");
}

/**
 * Called when filter is invoked
 */
public void doFilter(
        ServletRequest request,
        ServletResponse response,
        FilterChain chain)
    throws IOException, ServletException
{
    HttpServletRequest httpRequest =
        (HttpServletRequest) request;

    log(httpRequest.getServletPath());

    chain.doFilter(request, response);
}

/**
 * Convenience method that writes a message to the servlet log
 */
public void log(String msg)
{
    config.getServletContext().log("LoggingFilter: " + msg);
}
}
```

First note that in addition to the classes it needs for its application-specific functions, the filter class needs to import classes that make up the filter API:

```
import javax.servlet.*;
import javax.servlet.http.*;
```

These are the same packages that you import in a servlet class.

Unlike servlets, which typically extend a standard class such as GenericServlet or HttpServlet, filters have no generic base class, only a simple interface with three methods. In order to indicate to the container that it is a filter, the class declares that it implements the Filter interface:

```
public class LoggingFilter implements Filter
```

The first method of interest is init():

```
public void init(FilterConfig config)
    throws ServletException
{
    this.config = config;
    log("Initialized");
}
```

This method is called once by the Web container when the filter is about to be placed into service. It takes one parameter, a FilterConfig object. Like its servlet counterpart, ServletConfig, the filter configuration object provides access to the filter name, the servlet context, and any initialization parameters that exist in web.xml for this filter. Our simple example does not use initialization parameters, but it does need to access the servlet context object to call its log() method. Filters typically store a reference to the FilterConfig object as an instance variable so that its functions are available after the init() method returns.

The logging function itself is a method with a one-line body:

```
config.getServletContext().log("LoggingFilter: " + msg);
```

The logging could be done inline without the method call, but it is usually a good idea to have a convenience method that formats messages consistently. If you need to change the format or add a timestamp, you need only change it in one place.

The heart of the filter is the doFilter() method:

```
public void doFilter(
        ServletRequest request,
        ServletResponse response,
        FilterChain chain)
    throws IOException, ServletException
{
    HttpServletRequest httpRequest =
        (HttpServletRequest) request;
```

ELEMENTS OF JSP

```
        log(httpRequest.getServletPath());
        chain.doFilter(request, response);
    }
```

Analogous to the `doGet()` or `doPost()` method of a servlet, this method is called by the container to invoke the filtering function on the specified request. The parameter list and exceptions thrown are similar to those of the servlet methods, with two differences:

1. The request and response parameters are the generic versions, not `HttpServletRequest` and `HttpServletResponse`. If you need to access their HTTP-specific methods, you need to ascertain that they are instances of the HTTP versions and cast them accordingly.

2. There is a third parameter: `FilterChain chain`. This is a container-handled object that has exactly one purpose: to allow a filter to call the next entity in the filter chain (which may be another filter or the static or dynamic resource at the end of the chain). You can't look forward or backward in the filter chain with this object; you can only invoke your immediate downstream neighbor. Moreover, there is no way to tell if the next entity in the chain is a filter or the target resource. All you know is that it will supply a method that accepts parameters implementing the `ServletRequest` and `ServletResponse` methods.

Finally, when the filter is shut down, its `destroy()` method is called. In our case, all we do is log the event:

```
public void destroy()
{
    log("Destroyed");
}
```

After compiling the filter class (remembering to include `servlet.jar` in the class path!) and placing it wherever the container looks for its servlet and listener classes, we need to describe it in `web.xml`:

```
<web-app>
    ...
    <filter>
        <filter-name>Logger</filter-name>
```

```
        <description>
            Simple filter that logs its actions
        </description>
        <filter-class>
            com.jspcr.filters.LoggingFilter
        </filter-class>
    </filter>
    ...
    <filter-mapping>
        <filter-name>Logger</filter-name>
        <url-pattern>/chap10/examples/*</url-pattern>
    </filter-mapping>
    ...
</web-app>
```

The `<filter>` entry assigns a name to the filter (which is made available to the filter through the `config.getFilterName()` method, if necessary) and specifies the fully qualified class name. Then one or more `<filter-mapping>` elements link a particular filter (using the name previously described) with the requests it handles. This can be a specific servlet by name, or a wildcard pattern. In our case, we want the filter invoked for all requests for resources in the `/chap10/examples` directory or any of its subdirectories.

When we restart the Web application or the servlet container as a whole, we'll get results similar to these in the servlet log file.[3]

```
2002-07-30 23:06:46 LoggingFilter: Initialized
2002-07-30 23:07:01 LoggingFilter: /chap10/examples/Hello.html
2002-07-30 23:07:09 LoggingFilter: Destroyed
```

Developing and Deploying a Filter

Now that you have a general idea of what a filter is, how it operates, and how it can be used, it's time to get into more of the specifics. In this section, we'll consider how to develop a filter and place it in service. We'll examine the filter API and the object model it uses, and then look at the `web.xml` deployment descriptor entries it uses.

---

[3]   If you're using the Tomcat reference implementation, the log file is found in $CATALINA_HOME/
      logs, or wherever specified in the appropriate `<Logger>` entry in Tomcat's `server.xml`
      configuration file.

The Filter API

The object model provided by the filter API is very simple. It consists of only three interfaces, two of which are implemented entirely by the container. Let's look at each interface.

javax.servlet.Filter

The main interface is `javax.servlet.Filter`. Because it is an interface, it doesn't have a constructor, only three methods for which you need to provide an implementation, either directly or through a subclass. Table 10-1 lists the methods.

Method	Description
`void init(FilterConfig)` `throws ServletException`	Called exactly once for a filter instance, when it is about to be placed into service. No requests will be passed to this filter until it successfully completes this method. If a fatal error occurs, you can throw a `ServletException` or one of its subclasses to tell the Web container not to send you any requests. You need to store the filter configuration object in an instance variable if you need to use it later during filtering or termination.
`void doFilter` `(ServletRequest,` `ServletResponse,` `FilterChain) throws` `IOException,` `ServletException`	Called by the Web container when a request needs to be filtered. The method has access to the request and response object, as well as the ability to invoke the next entity in the filter chain (with `chain.doFilter()`). It can abort the request by not calling `chain.doFilter()`, or it can throw an exception if it encounters a fatal error.
`void destroy()`	Called when the filter is about to be shut down, allowing it to release any resources it has acquired. No more requests will be passed to this filter once its `destroy()` method has been called.

Table 10-1. Methods in the javax.servlet.Filter Interface

javax.servlet.FilterChain

The filter chain interface is the simplest of the whole lot, consisting of exactly one method, described here.

Method	Description
void doFilter (ServletRequest, ServletResponse)	Called by you from within your doFilter() method. Invokes the next filter chain entity, which may be another filter or the static or dynamic resource at the end of the chain.

When a filter is called, it is passed a request/response object pair and a reference to a filter chain. An application will typically do the following in its doFilter() method:

1. Modify the request object's headers or data if necessary before passing it on to the next filter.

2. Call the FilterChain object's doFilter(ServletRequest, ServletResponse) method and wait for the call to return. This will invoke the downstream portion of the filter chain, including its return voyage with the response.

3. Modify the response object's headers and/or data if necessary before returning, which in turn completes the previous filter's call to FilterChain.doFilter().

Steps 1 and 3 don't tell the whole story—you can't actually modify a servlet request or response. What you *can* do is to provide a replacement request or response that you pass on to the next filter chain entity. This is a bit complicated and will be covered in the next section.

javax.servlet.FilterConfig

The last interface in the API is FilterConfig. This is a close analog to ServletConfig and has almost exactly the same methods, listed in Table 10-2. It is passed to the filter as a parameter to its init() method and should be saved as an instance variable if it will be needed later.

Servlet Request and Response Wrappers

There's a problem, however. You can't really modify servlet requests or servlet responses, because they don't surface methods that let you set much of anything. What's more, the parameters passed to your doFilter() method are Java *interfaces*, not classes. To be sure, there are underlying implementation objects that correspond to these interfaces, but you don't necessarily know what they are or that they will be the same in another servlet container. All you know is that the request and response objects, whatever their classes, implement the ServletRequest and ServletResponse interfaces, respectively.

Method	Description
String getFilterName()	Returns the value of the `<filter-name>` element for this filter as it appears in `web.xml`.
ServletContext getServletContext()	Returns the servlet context, which in turn provides access to context attributes and methods.
String getInitParameter (String name)	Returns the value of the named initialization parameter. Parameters are specified with `<init-param>` elements nested in the `<filter>` entry in `web.xml`, using exactly the same syntax as servlet initialization parameters.
Enumeration getInitParameterNames()	Returns a `java.util.Enumeration` that provides the names of all the filter initialization parameters. In conjunction with `getInitParameter(String name)`, this method can be used to get both the names and the values.

Table 10-2.   *Methods in the javax.servlet.FilterConfig Interface*

This minimalism itself contains the solution to the problem. You can't modify these objects to any extent, but you *can* provide look-alike replacements that you write. As long as you pass an instance of a class that implements ServletResponse, it can be any class you want to develop. Since your next downstream neighbor filter is called with just interfaces as parameters, it can't really tell that you've made a switch.

To make this nontrivial task easier, the servlet API provides four concrete classes that implement the necessary interfaces, listed in Table 10-3.

The two examples at the end of this chapter make this clearer.

Configuring a Filter

In the example at the beginning of the chapter, we briefly touched on the `<filter>` and `<filter-mapping>` elements in the `web.xml` deployment descriptor. Table 10-4 describes these two elements and their required subelements.

Class	Description
ServletResponse Wrapper	A class in the `javax.servlet` package that implements `ServletResponse`. By default, it delegates all of its interface implementation methods to the underlying response object. To filter a response coming back upstream, you need to replace it with a `ServletResponseWrapper` subclass instance before you call `doFilter()`. That way, the downstream filter will operate on your custom response object, including its custom output stream.
ServletRequest Wrapper	The request counterpart of `ServletResponse Wrapper`. It delegates everything to the underlying request except methods that your custom subclass overrides.
HttpServletResponse Wrapper	The HTTP-specific version of `ServletResponse Wrapper`, which it extends.
HttpServletRequest Wrapper	The HTTP-specific version of ServletRequestWrapper.

Table 10-3. *Servlet Request and Response Wrapper Classes*

Element	Description
<filter>	Declares the filter to the container. Must have <filter-name> and <filter-class> subelements. Optional elements include <icon>, <display-name>, <description>, and <init-param>.
<filter-name>	A unique name you assign to the filter.
<filter-class>	The fully qualified name of the filter class.

Table 10-4. *Entries for Filters in the web.xml Deployment Descriptor*

Element	Description
`<init-param>`	The `<filter>` element has one of these for each initialization parameter it supports. `<init-param>` must have `<param-name>` and `<param-value>` subelements. Identical to the corresponding elements for servlet init params.
`<filter-mapping>`	Maps a filter instance to a `<url-pattern>` or `<servlet-name>` by the name specified by the `<filter-name>` element. May contain zero or more `<dispatcher>` elements.
`<url-pattern>`	A regular expression that describes which requests the filter should be applied to. The Servlet 2.4 API describes the syntax in detail.
`<servlet-name>`	The unique name of a servlet described elsewhere in this `web.xml` descriptor.
`<dispatcher>`	An optional child element of `<filter-mapping>` that specifies how it operates under a request dispatcher. Valid values are: REQUEST: if direct client requests are supported FORWARD: if the matching URL pattern or servlet name is invoked because a `RequestDispatcher` called `forward()` INCLUDE: if the matching URL pattern or servlet name is invoked because a `RequestDispatcher` called `include()` There can be any number of dispatcher elements nested within the `<filter-mapping>` element, using any combination of the values described here.

Table 10-4. *Entries for Filters in the web.xml Deployment Descriptor* (continued)

A Request Filter Example

The simple logging filter presented at the beginning of this chapter was really little more than an event listener. It affected neither the request nor the response. To do any significant filtering, we need to modify the data stream in one or both directions.

The example we'll consider next is one that changes the request, but not the response. Suppose a legacy Web application such as a CGI script supports only HTTP POST, not HTTP GET. We may not be able to change the application; it may have been written in C and the source code may be unavailable.

Recall that GET requests pass parameters in the request URL, appending them as encoded key/value pairs. The server-side CGI script will receive this in the QUERY_STRING environment variable. A POST request, by contrast, passes the parameter string as an input stream, providing a `Content-Length` HTTP header that indicates the length of the stream.

In this section, we'll develop a `PostFilter` class that transforms a GET into a POST. First, however, we'll write a base class that implements the Filter interface. This provides a minor convenience in that our derived subclasses don't have to implement dummy versions of `init()` and `destroy()`. Here is a listing of `BaseFilter`:

```java
package com.jspcr.filters;

import java.io.*;
import java.net.*;
import java.util.*;
import javax.servlet.*;
import javax.servlet.http.*;

/**
 * Generic filter that passes requests on to the next resource
 * in the filter chain.  Intended as a base class from which
 * more useful filters are derived.
 */
public class BaseFilter implements Filter
{
    protected FilterConfig config;

    /**
     * Called when the filter is placed into service.
     * @param config the filter configuration object
     * @exception ServletException if a fatal error occurs
     */
    public void init(FilterConfig config)
        throws ServletException
    {
        this.config = config;
    }
```

```
/**
 * Called when the filter is about to be shut down.
 */
public void destroy()
{
}

/**
 * Convenience method to write a message to the servlet log
 */
protected void log(String msg)
{
    config.getServletContext().log(msg);
}

/**
 * Passes the request and response unmodified along the
 * filter chain. Subclasses should override this method
 * to perform any required filtering.
 * @param request the original request object
 * @param response the original response object
 * @exception IOException if an I/O error occurs
 * @exception ServletException if an application error occurs.
 */
public void doFilter(
        ServletRequest request,
        ServletResponse response,
        FilterChain chain)
    throws IOException, ServletException
{
    // Pass the request on to the next processor in the
    // filter chain.

    chain.doFilter(request, response);
}
}
```

Before we implement the transformation filter, let's get a little more detail about what we need to do. We'll write two HTML forms that are identical except for the method attribute of the <form> tag (GET or POST). We'll provide a few parameters to make it more realistic. Let's suppose that this is a form used to specify user preferences. For the server-side action component, we'll use a JSP page that echoes back the form parameters and selected request headers in tabular form. Here is the HTML for the GET form:

```html
<html>
<head>
<title>User Preferences (using GET)</title>
<style type="text/css">
body  { font-family: Verdana; font-size: 10pt; }
h1    { font-size: 130%; }
.note { font-size: 110%;
        font-style: italic;
        font-weight: bold; }
</style>
<base href="http://localhost/jspcr2/"/>
</head>
<body>
<div class="note">
   (Using HTTP GET)
</div>
<h1>User Preferences</h1>
<form method="GET" action="chap10/examples/postonly/Echo.jsp">
   <p>
      Text editor:
      <input type="radio" name="editor" value="vim" checked="1">
         vim
      </input>
      <input type="radio" name="editor" value="emacs">
         emacs
      </input>
      <input type="radio" name="editor" value="other">
         other
      </input>
   </p>
   <p>
      Programming language:
      <select name="language">
         <option value="Java">Java</option>
      </select>
   </p>
   <p>
      <input type="submit" value="Save"/>
      <input type="reset" value="Clear"/>
   </p>
</form>
</body>
</html>
```

The POST form is identical except for using "POST" everywhere "GET" appears.

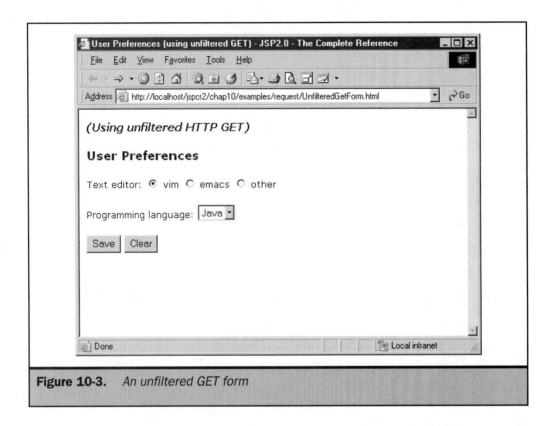

Figure 10-3. *An unfiltered GET form*

The GET form looks like Figure 10-3 when displayed in the browser, and its parameters and headers are listed in Figure 10-4.

The corresponding POST form is shown in Figure 10-5, with results in 10-6. Comparing Figures 10-4 and 10-6, we note several differences:

- The content length for POST is 24, whereas the GET has –1 to indicate that there is no input stream content.

- The content-type is null for GET and application/x-www-form-urlencoded for POST.

- GET has a query string; POST does not.

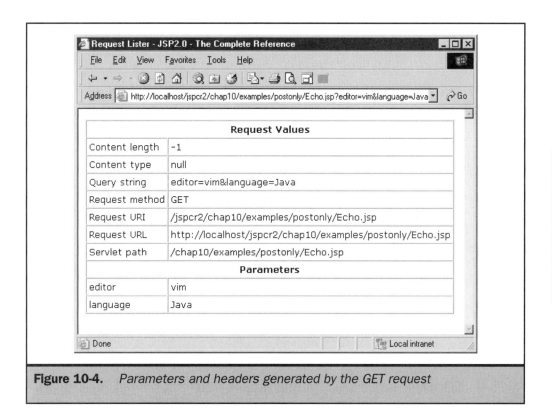

Figure 10-4. *Parameters and headers generated by the GET request*

In order to transform the GET request into a POST, we'll have to reconcile all these differences. The filter that does this is shown here:

```
package com.jspcr.filters;

import java.io.*;
import java.net.*;
import java.util.*;
import javax.servlet.*;
import javax.servlet.http.*;
```

```java
/**
 * Filter that converts an HTTP GET request to an equivalent
 * HTTP POST.
 */
public class PostFilter extends BaseFilter
{
    /**
     * Converts GET requests to POST requests.
     * @param request the original request object
     * @param response the original response object
     * @exception IOException if an I/O error occurs
     * @exception ServletException if an application error occurs.
     */
    public void doFilter(
            ServletRequest request,
            ServletResponse response,
            FilterChain chain)
        throws IOException, ServletException
    {
        // Cast the request so that we can get its
        // HTTP-specific attributes

        HttpServletRequest httpRequest =
            (HttpServletRequest) request;

        // If this is a GET request, create a custom
        // wrapper and substitute it for the actual
        // request

        if (httpRequest.getMethod().equalsIgnoreCase("GET")) {
            request = new PostWrapper(httpRequest);
        }

        // Pass the request on to the next processor in the
        // filter chain.

        chain.doFilter(request, response);
    }

    /**
     * Request wrapper that overrides the methods necessary
     * to make the request look like a POST:
     *
     * <ul>
```

```
*     <li>Adds a <code>content-type</code> header</li>
*     <li>Adds a <code>content-length</code> header</li>
*     <li>Adds a <code>cache-control</code> header</li>
*     <li><code>getMethod()</code> returns POST</li>
*     <li><code>getQueryString()</code> returns
*      <code>null</code></li>
* </ul>
*
* All other methods are automatically delegated to
* the wrapped request.
*/
public class PostWrapper
    extends HttpServletRequestWrapper
{
    private String queryString;
    private InputStream queryStream;

    private ServletInputStream inputStream;
    private BufferedReader reader;
    private int contentLength;

    /**
     * Creates a new <code>PostWrapper</code>
     * for the specified request
     */
    public PostWrapper(HttpServletRequest request)
    {
        super(request);

        // Save the query string and note its length

        queryString = request.getQueryString();
        byte[] buffer = queryString.getBytes();
        queryStream = new ByteArrayInputStream(buffer);
        contentLength = buffer.length;
    }

    /**
     * Returns the specified header, which may be one of those
     * added to make this a POST request.
     * @param name the header name
     */
    public String getHeader(String name)
    {
```

```java
      String header = null;

      if (name.equalsIgnoreCase("content-type"))
         header = "application/x-www-form-urlencoded";
      else if (name.equalsIgnoreCase("content-length"))
         header = String.valueOf(contentLength);
      else if (name.equalsIgnoreCase("cache-control"))
         header = "no-cache";
      else {
         HttpServletRequest request =
            (HttpServletRequest) getRequest();
         header = request.getHeader(name);
      }
      return header;
   }

   /**
   * Returns all the values of a particular header
   * @param name the header name
   */
   public Enumeration getHeaders(String name)
   {
      Enumeration enumHeaders = null;

      if (name.equalsIgnoreCase("content-type")) {
         Vector v = new Vector();
         v.addElement("application/x-www-form-urlencoded");
         enumHeaders = v.elements();
      }
      else if (name.equalsIgnoreCase("content-length")) {
         Vector v = new Vector();
         v.addElement(String.valueOf(contentLength));
         enumHeaders = v.elements();
      }
      else if (name.equalsIgnoreCase("cache-control")) {
         Vector v = new Vector();
         v.addElement("no-cache");
         enumHeaders = v.elements();
      }
      else {
         HttpServletRequest request =
            (HttpServletRequest) getRequest();
         enumHeaders = request.getHeaders(name);
      }
```

```
         return enumHeaders;
      }

      /**
       * Returns the names of all the headers in the request,
       * including the augmented ones.
       */
      public Enumeration getHeaderNames()
      {
         Vector vnames = new Vector();
         HttpServletRequest request =
            (HttpServletRequest) getRequest();
         Enumeration e = request.getHeaderNames();
         while (e != null && e.hasMoreElements()) {
            vnames.addElement(e.nextElement());
         }
         vnames.addElement("content-type");
         vnames.addElement("content-length");
         vnames.addElement("cache-control");
         return vnames.elements();
      }

      /**
       * Returns an input stream over the request body,
       * which actually comes from the query string.
       * @exception IOException if an I/O error occurs
       * @exception IllegalStateException if getReader()
       * was already called
       */
      public ServletInputStream getInputStream()
         throws IOException
      {
         if (inputStream != null)
            return inputStream;

         if (reader != null)
            throw new IllegalStateException
               ("getReader() was already called");

         inputStream = new ServletInputStream()
         {
            public int read() throws IOException
            {
               return queryStream.read();
```

```
      }
   };

   return inputStream;
}


/**
 * Returns a character reader over the request body.
 * @exception IOException if an I/O error occurs
 * @exception IllegalStateException if getInputStream()
 * was already called
 */
public BufferedReader getReader()
   throws IOException
{
   if (reader != null)
      return reader;

   if (inputStream != null)
      throw new IllegalStateException
         ("getInputStream() was already called");

   reader = new BufferedReader(
         new StringReader(queryString));

   return reader;
}


/**
 * Returns the length of the query string
 */
public int getContentLength()
{
   return contentLength;
}


/**
 * Returns the <code>content-type</code> header.
 */
public String getContentType()
{
   return getHeader("content-type");
}
```

```
/**
 * Returns POST to indicate the HTTP method
 */
public String getMethod()
{
   return "POST";
}


/**
 * Suppresses the return of the real query string
 * so that this looks like a POST request
 */
public String getQueryString()
{
   return null;
}
   }
}
```

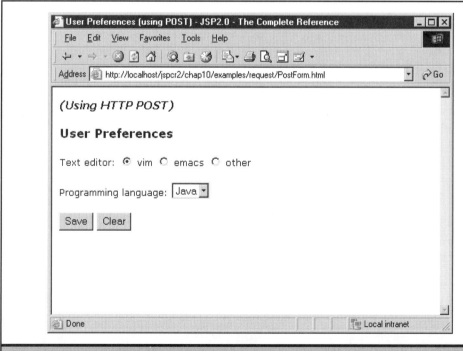

Figure 10-5. *An unfiltered POST form*

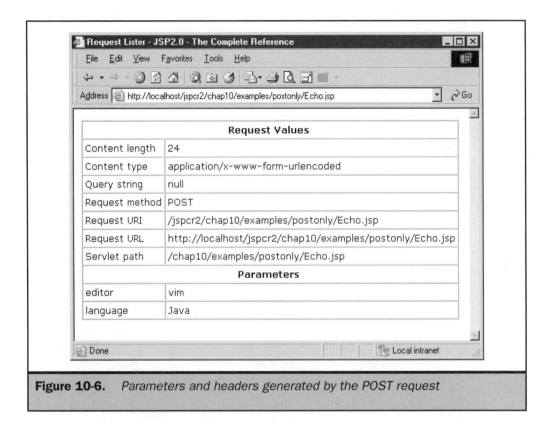

Figure 10-6. *Parameters and headers generated by the POST request*

The init() and destroy() implementations are inherited from the BaseFilter superclass. The only interface implementation method we provide is doFilter(). All it does is the following:

1. It casts the request into an HttpServletRequest variable so that we can use its HTTP-specific methods (like getMethod()).

2. If the request is a GET, it creates an instance of an HttpServletRequestWrapper subclass in an inner class.

3. It calls the next filter or other entity on the filter chain. The class will block on the doFilter() until the downstream filter's doFilter() method completes.

Nothing special needs to be done with the output.

The wrapper class needs to override a few methods to switch from a long URL to an input stream for the parameters.

- The methods `getQueryString()`, `getContentType()`, `getContent Length()`, and `getMethod()` have to report the implied values.

- Since `HttpServletRequest` provides direct access to the request headers, we need to make them return the same modified values. Again, this is not done by actually changing the headers returned from the endpoint, but by overriding the access methods.

- Since POST requires an input stream, we need to create one that will return the encoded parameter data. An added wrinkle here is that downstream filters may call either `getInputStream()` or `getWriter()`—we have no control over which one, and the two are mutually exclusive. We solve this by storing the original query string and returning either a `BufferedReader` or a `ServletInputStream` that uses the string as the data source.

When we've made these changes and declared the filter and filter mapping in `web.xml`, we get the results shown in Figure 10-7 from the filtered GET form.

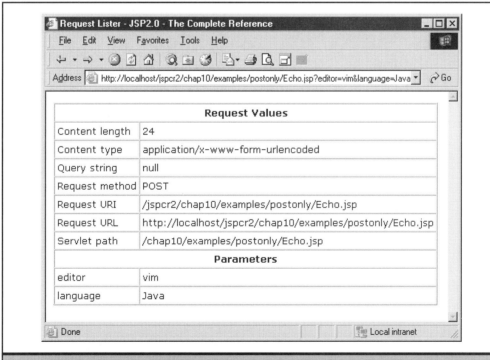

Figure 10-7. *Parameters and headers from the converted GET form*

A Response Filter Example

It is more common to filter responses rather than requests—responses host most of the data of interest. Our final example is that of a filter chain that transforms the response in two stages:

1. Sorting an ordinary comma-separated values file
2. Rendering the sorted results in an HTML table

Response filtering is the mirror image of request filtering: you must provide a wrapper for the response object and an output stream that buffers its data so that you can transform it. You'll create this buffered output stream before calling `doFilter()`, and the next downstream filter will use it instead of writing directly to the client.

This buffering of the output data is common enough that it makes sense to create a separate class that can be used for the purpose. Listed here is `BufferedResponse Wrapper`:

```
package com.jspcr.filters;

import java.io.*;
import java.net.*;
import java.util.*;
import javax.servlet.*;
import javax.servlet.http.*;

/**
 * A servlet response wrapper that buffers its output
 * and makes it available to the upstream filter
 */
public class BufferedResponseWrapper
    extends HttpServletResponseWrapper
{
    private ByteArrayOutputStream byteBuffer;
    private CharArrayWriter charBuffer;
    private ServletOutputStream outputStream;
    private PrintWriter writer;
    private ServletContext context;

    /**
     * Creates a new <code>BufferedResponseWrapper</code>
     */
    public BufferedResponseWrapper
```

```java
         (ServletResponse response, ServletContext context)
   {
      super((HttpServletResponse) response);
      this.context = context;
   }


   /**
    * Writes a message to the servlet log file
    */
   public void log(String message)
   {
      context.log("BufferedResponseWrapper: " + message);
   }


   /**
    * Returns a binary output stream
    */
   public ServletOutputStream getOutputStream()
      throws IOException
   {
      if (writer != null) {
         String errmsg = "getWriter() was already called";
         throw new IllegalStateException(errmsg);
      }

      if (outputStream == null) {

         // Create a subclass of ServletOutputStream
         // that delegates everything to a
         // ByteArrayOutputStream

         byteBuffer = new ByteArrayOutputStream();
         outputStream = new ServletOutputStream() {
            public void write(int c) throws IOException {
               byteBuffer.write(c);
            }
         };
      }

      return outputStream;
   }
```

```java
/**
 * Returns a character writer
 */
public PrintWriter getWriter()
   throws IOException
{
   if (outputStream != null) {
      String errmsg = "getOutputStream() was already called";
      throw new IllegalStateException(errmsg);
   }

   if (writer == null) {
      charBuffer = new CharArrayWriter();
      writer = new PrintWriter(charBuffer);
   }

   return writer;
}

/**
 * Returns the contents of the buffer as a string
 */
public String getBufferAsString()
   throws IOException
{
   String buffer = null;

   if (charBuffer != null) {
      writer.flush();
      charBuffer.flush();
      buffer = charBuffer.toString();
   }
   else if (byteBuffer != null) {
      outputStream.flush();
      byteBuffer.flush();
      buffer = byteBuffer.toString();
   }
   else
      buffer = "";

   return buffer;
}
```

```
/**
 * Returns the contents of the buffer as a byte array
 */
public byte[] getBufferAsByteArray()
   throws IOException
{

   byte[] buffer = null;

   if (byteBuffer != null) {
      outputStream.flush();
      byteBuffer.flush();
      buffer = byteBuffer.toByteArray();
   }
   else if (charBuffer != null) {
      writer.flush();
      charBuffer.flush();
      buffer = charBuffer.toString().getBytes();
   }
   else
      buffer = new byte[0];

   return buffer;
}
}
```

This is a subclass of `HttpServletResponseWrapper`, which delegates all of the API methods to the underlying `HttpServletResponse`. The only methods we override are `getOutputStream()` and `getWriter()`. Again, these are mutually exclusive calls. Since we don't know which method downstream filters will use, we need to support both. We'll use a `ByteArrayOutputStream` for binary data and a `CharArrayWriter` for characters. We'll provide `getBufferAsString()` and `getBufferAsString()` methods so that we can read either buffer in either form.

Now let's look at the sort filter:

```
package com.jspcr.filters;

import java.io.*;
import java.net.*;
import java.util.*;
import javax.servlet.*;
import javax.servlet.http.*;
```

ELEMENTS OF JSP

```java
/**
 * Filter that sorts the lines of its response data
 */
public class SortFilter extends BaseFilter
{
    public void doFilter(
            ServletRequest request,
            ServletResponse response,
            FilterChain chain)
        throws IOException, ServletException
    {
        // Create a servlet response wrapper that will
        // buffer the response data so that it can be
        // sorted

        BufferedResponseWrapper wrappedResponse =
            new BufferedResponseWrapper
                (response, config.getServletContext());

        // Pass the request on to the next entry in
        // the filter chain

        chain.doFilter(request, wrappedResponse);

        // After the request is processed, retrieve
        // the output lines from the wrapper object
        // and sort them

        // Split the buffer into a list of individual lines

        BufferedReader in =
            new BufferedReader(
            new StringReader(
            wrappedResponse.getBufferAsString()));

        List list = new ArrayList();

        while (true) {
            String line = in.readLine();
            if (line == null)
                break;
            list.add(line);
```

```
        }
        in.close();

        // Use the collections framework to sort the list

        Collections.sort(list);

        // Write the sorted list, using the original response
        // object to send results back to the requesting client

        response.setContentType("text/plain");
        PrintWriter out = response.getWriter();

        for (Iterator it = list.iterator(); it.hasNext(); ) {
            String line = (String) it.next();
            out.println(line);
        }
        out.flush();
    }
}
```

Again we extend `BaseFilter` so that we don't have to bother with the `init()` and `destroy()` methods. Also, we'll use our `BufferedResponseWrapper` to handle the buffering. After returning from `chain.doFilter()`, the unfiltered response data is available by calling the wrapped response object's `getBufferAsString()` method, reading it into a `java.util.List`. The Collections framework provides a convenient sort method. After the sort, we use the original response object to return the results.

The second filter (`CSVFilter`) is one that takes comma-separated values data and creates an HTML table:

```
package com.jspcr.filters;

import java.io.*;
import java.net.*;
import java.util.*;
import javax.servlet.*;
import javax.servlet.http.*;

/**
* Filter that converts a comma-separated-values stream
* to an HTML table
```

```java
*/
public class CSVFilter extends BaseFilter
{
    public void doFilter(
        ServletRequest request,
        ServletResponse response,
        FilterChain chain)
      throws IOException, ServletException
    {
        // Create a servlet response wrapper that will
        // buffer the response data so that it can be
        // converted to HTML

        BufferedResponseWrapper wrappedResponse =
            new BufferedResponseWrapper
                (response, config.getServletContext());

        // Pass the request on to the next entry in
        // the filter chain

        chain.doFilter(request, wrappedResponse);

        // After the request is processed, retrieve
        // the output lines from the wrapper object.

        String buffer = wrappedResponse.getBufferAsString();
        BufferedReader in =
            new BufferedReader(new StringReader(buffer));

        int nRows = 0;
        int nCols = 0;

        StringBuffer htmlBuffer = new StringBuffer();

        while (true) {
            String line = in.readLine();
            if (line == null)
                break;
            nRows++;

            // We use a regular expression to split the line
            // along comma boundaries. A robust application
```

```java
        // would need to take into account commas contained
        // inside quoted strings.

        // NOTE: the String.split(regex) method requires
        // JDK 1.4 or greater

        String[] tokens = line.split(",");

        // When the first row of data is read, count
        // the columns so that we can generate the
        // table header

        if (nRows == 1) {
            nCols = tokens.length;
            htmlBuffer.append("<table");
            htmlBuffer.append(" border='1'");
            htmlBuffer.append(" cellpadding='3'");
            htmlBuffer.append(" cellspacing='0'>\n");
        }


        // Write the table cells

        htmlBuffer.append("<tr>\n");
        int col = 0;
        while ((col < tokens.length) && (col < nCols)) {
            htmlBuffer.append("<td>");
            htmlBuffer.append(tokens[col]);
            htmlBuffer.append("</td>\n");
            col++;
        }
        while (col < nCols) {
            htmlBuffer.append("<td> </td>\n");
            col++;
        }
        htmlBuffer.append("</tr>\n");
    }

// Close the table

if (nRows > 0)
    htmlBuffer.append("</table>\n");
```

```
        // Use the original response object to send
        // converted results back to the requesting client

        response.setContentType("text/html");
        response.setContentLength(htmlBuffer.length());
        PrintWriter out = response.getWriter();
        out.print(htmlBuffer);
        out.flush();
    }
}
```

This filter is very similar to the previous one, but it has one additional complication: the content length changes. Therefore, we have to buffer all the output we generate so that we know the length.

The order of the filters is very important. Remember that the servlet container will chain them together in the order listed in web.xml. Examining Figure 10-2 again, we see that the order of application for responses is the reverse of that of requests. In order to sort the response first, then the CSV-to-Table generation, we need to specify the CSV filter first in web.xml.

So how does this work? Suppose the filter endpoint is a static resource, a file named Reindeer.csv:

```
Dasher,the quickest
Dancer,the most agile
Prancer,the most spirited
Vixen,the cleverest
Comet,the brightest
Cupid,the happiest
Donner,the loudest
Blitzen,the lightest
```

After invoking SortFilter, it looks like this:

```
Blitzen,the lightest
Comet,the brightest
Cupid,the happiest
Dancer,the most agile
Dasher,the quickest
Donner,the loudest
Prancer,the most spirited
Vixen,the cleverest
```

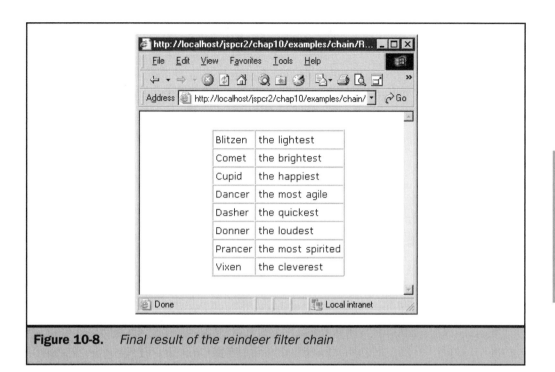

Figure 10-8.   *Final result of the reindeer filter chain*

And finally, after `CSVFilter`, it looks like the table shown in Figure 10-8.

Summary

Filters are Java components that process requests in a Web container, modifying either the input or the output. Like servlets, they operate on a request and response object pair. Typically, however, they do not generate content on their own, but rather they modify content produced by another resource. Simple filters can be chained together to provide more sophisticated processing.

The filter API consists of three interfaces:

- `javax.servlet.Filter`
- `javax.servlet.FilterChain`
- `javax.servlet.FilterConfig`

Of the three, only the first is implemented by the developer. The others are provided by the servlet container.

Since request and response objects cannot really be modified for filtering purposes, the filter API also specifies four concrete classes that wrap the servlet request and response, delegating by default all methods to the underlying request or response.

Filters have long been popular in diverse programming environments—in the Unix shell, in SAX-based XML parsing, in Ant build tasks, and many others. It is likely that servlet filters will also become a necessary part of servlet and JSP development toolkits.

The
Complete
Reference

Part III

JSP Tag Extensions

The Complete Reference

Chapter 11

Introduction to Custom Tags

The JavaServer Pages 1.1 specification significantly enhanced the JSP architecture by making it possible to extend the page authoring environment with custom tags. *Custom tags* (also referred to as tag extensions) are user-developed XML-like additions to the syntax and semantics of a JSP page. Collections of tags are organized into *tag libraries* that can be packaged as JAR files, enabling their functionality to be easily distributed and installed over any JSP-compliant servlet container.

Since JSP 1.1, there have been several notable developments. The JSP 1.2 specification added a number of new features to the tag extension framework:

- Better validation and error handling
- Listener classes
- Support for iteration

Tag libraries have matured in JSP 2.0 with the development of the JSP Standard Tag Library (JSTL). JSTL greatly simplifies the work of developing Web applications with JSP, offering standard tags for control flow, XML processing, database access, and internationalization.

But to use JSTL to its best advantage, you need to understand the basics about custom tags. This chapter introduces their roles and advantages. It gives an extended, step-by-step example of how to write and deploy a custom tag and then proceeds to the details of tag libraries, the tag library descriptor, the tag extension API, and tag handlers.

Note *The JSP 2.0 specification and reference implementation were not final at the time of this writing. To the extent possible, the information in this chapter describes how JSP 2.0 tag extensions are expected to work; in some cases, however, you'll see JSP 1.2 examples. If you run into difficulties, consult the version of the specification that matches your JSP container.*

Why Custom Tags?

Most programmers can write ordinary HTML, and most Web designers can learn to write simple JSP pages. But really good HTML with navigation, browser detection, image handling, and forms interaction requires a knowledgeable author—a specialist.[1] Likewise, Java programming that accesses databases, handles transactions, and communicates with sockets is beyond what could be expected from an HTML author.

Custom tags provide a means for bridging the gap between the two specialties. Java programmers can provide application functionality in convenient packages that Web designers can use as building blocks. While JavaBeans can also encapsulate code, they are most useful as repositories for attributes. Notions of iteration, nesting, or cooperative actions are difficult to express with beans. Custom tags enable a higher-level application-specific approach to JSP development.

---

[1] Bring up http://www.cnn.com or http://www.msnbc.com and view the HTML source. How much of it do you think you could write by hand?

For example, a database query written with custom tags might look like the following:

```
<db:connect url="mydatabase">

    <db:runQuery>
        SELECT    *
        FROM      FD_GROUP
        WHERE     FdGp_Desc LIKE '%F%'
        ORDER BY FdGp_Cd
    </db:runQuery>

    <table border="1" cellpadding="3" cellspacing="0">
        <tr><th>Food Group Code</th><th>Description</th></tr>
    <db:forEachRow>
        <tr>
            <td><db:getField name="FdGp_Cd"/></td>
            <td><db:getField name="FdGp_Desc"/></td>
        </tr>
    </db:forEachRow>
    </table>

</db:connect>
```

where `connect`, `runQuery`, `forEachRow`, and `getField` are application-oriented custom tags.

All the logic in the preceding example could have been written with scriptlets embedded in the JSP page. For example, the equivalent code for the `<db:connect>` tag might include loading the driver class, opening a connection to the database (possibly getting an existing connection from a pool), setting up `Statement` and `ResultSet` objects, and handling any of several exceptions that might be thrown. Also possible would be to incorporate most of the logic in a JavaBean, although scriptlet code would still be required for looping over the result set. Neither alternative is as convenient as packaging the logic into a set of HTML-like tags whose function is readily apparent to both Web designers and servlet developers.

Besides the separation of content and presentation, other benefits of custom tags include

■ **Simplicity** It's significantly easier to express a complex task as a cooperating set of subtasks with their own attributes and control flow than it is to write it as a monolithic block of code. Not only is this easier to code, it's easier to understand. In the preceding database query, for example, it's easy to guess correctly what the scope of the database connection is, that an implied result set is created by the `<db:runQuery>` block, and that `<db:forEachRow>` iterates over this result set.

■ **Opportunity for code reuse** There may be hundreds of database queries in a Web application. Sharing scriptlet code is difficult without resorting to `<%@ include %>` directives that obscure the logic and may have undesirable side effects. Tag libraries make it easier to package standard code and share it throughout an application.

■ **Suitability for authoring tools** *Integrated development environments (IDEs)* can see scriptlet blocks only as blocks of ASCII text. Custom tags, however, by virtue of having a Tag Library Descriptor, lend themselves to being managed by a development tool that can display their descriptions, validate their attributes, and so on.

To get a better idea of how to develop custom tags, let's take a simple example and walk through its development step by step.

Developing Your First Custom Tag

Resisting the temptation to write a "Hello, World!" tag, we will develop an example of a marginally useful component—a custom tag that retrieves the name and version of the Web server. The implementation of this tag, as well as all the other tags we develop, will follow the same four basic steps:

1. Define the tag.
2. Write the entry in the Tag Library Descriptor.
3. Write the tag handler.
4. Use the tag in a JSP page.

Step 1: Define the Tag

To start, we need to define the syntax of the tag clearly. This involves answering such questions as

■ What is the name of the tag? As we will see later on, custom tags are always used with a namespace qualifier, so it isn't necessary to make tag names globally unique.

■ What attributes does it have? For example, the HTML `<table>` tag has the optional attributes `border`, `cellpadding`, `cellspacing`, and `width` (among others). Custom tags can define any number of required or optional attributes, which are passed to the tag handler when the tag is evaluated.

■ Will the tag define scripting variables? The standard action `<jsp:useBean id="xyz" class="com.jspcr.beans.XYZBean">`, for example, causes a variable named xyz of type `com.jspcr.beans.XYZBean` to be defined. This variable is then available to the `<jsp:getProperty>` and `<jsp:setProperty>` actions, as well as to Java code in any scriptlets or expressions that follow. Custom tags can create scripting variables in the same manner.

■ Does the tag do anything special with the body contained between its start and end tags? The HTML `<table>` tag expects table rows and table cells before its terminating `</table>` end tag. Each of these elements rely on information provided by related elements above them in the evaluation stack. Custom tag applications can likewise feature nested tags that cooperatively perform some function. The tag body can also contain non-JSP data (such as SQL statements) that are evaluated by the tag.

In the case of the first example tag, there isn't much to do. We'll call the tag `getWebServer`. It has no attributes because it doesn't need to be configured differently in different JSP pages. The tag defines no scripting variables, simply returning the string containing the Web server name in place of the `getWebServer` tag. Finally, the tag has no body to be considered because its entire function is contained in its start tag.

Step 2: Create the TLD Entry

A *Tab Library Descriptor (TLD)* is an XML document that defines the names and attributes of a collection of related tags. Here is the TLD we will use with the `getWebServer` example tag:

```xml
<?xml version="1.0"?>

<!DOCTYPE taglib PUBLIC
    "-//Sun Microsystems, Inc.//DTD JSP Tag Library 1.2//EN"
        "http://java.sun.com/dtd/web-jsptaglibrary_1_2.dtd">

<taglib xmlns="http://java.sun.com/JSP/TagLibraryDescriptor">
    <tlib-version>1.0</tlib-version>
    <jsp-version>1.2</jsp-version>
    <short-name>diag</short-name>
    <tag>
        <name>getWebServer</name>
        <tag-class>
            com.jspcr.taglibs.diag.GetWebServerTag
        </tag-class>
        <body-content>empty</body-content>
    </tag>
</taglib>
```

The format of the TLD has changed with each update of the JSP specification, but the most recent version will accept JSP 1.1 and JSP 1.2 TLDs for backward compatibility. A TLD maps a tag name,

```
<name>getWebServer</name>
```

to a fully qualified class name,

```
<tag-class>
    com.jspcr.taglibs.diag.GetWebServerTag
</tag-class>
```

The JSP container uses this mapping to create the appropriate servlet code when it evaluates the custom tag at compile time.

We will give this file the name diagnostics.tld. For the purposes of this example, the only thing we need to worry about is copying the file to the right place. A TLD can be placed anywhere in the Web application directory system, but putting it under the WEB-INF directory makes sense because it won't be made available for direct public access. By convention, TLDs are often installed in a directory named /WEB-INF/tlds.

If there is a Web application named test, for example, then diagnostics.tld would be found in /test/WEB-INF/tlds/. Written as a URI relative to the servlet context, this would be /WEB-INF/tlds/diagnostics.tld.

Step 3: Write the Tag Handler

A tag's action is implemented in a Java class known as a *tag handler*. Instances of tag handlers are created and maintained by the JSP container, and predefined methods in these classes are called directly from a JSP page's generated servlet.

In the sample tag, we need to get the name of the Web server (for example, Apache, Microsoft IIS, and so forth). The servlet API doesn't provide an obvious way to get this information. The request object tells a lot about the Web client and the servlet context knows about the servlet container, but neither of these objects appears to know what software product happens to be listening on port 80. However, this information is provided by the Web server itself when it sends the HTTP response back to the Web client. The approach we'll take is to make a dummy HTTP request ourselves within the tag handler and then extract the server information from the HTTP headers that are returned.

Here is the complete source code for the tag handler:

```
package com.jspcr.taglibs.diag;

import javax.servlet.http.*;
import javax.servlet.jsp.*;
```

```
import javax.servlet.jsp.tagext.*;
import java.io.*;
import java.net.*;

/**
* Handler for the <code>getWebServer</code> tag
*/
public class GetWebServerTag extends TagSupport
{
    public int doStartTag() throws JspException
    {
        try {

            // Get server host and port number from
            // the page context.

            HttpServletRequest request =
                (HttpServletRequest) pageContext.getRequest();

            String host = request.getServerName();
            int port = request.getServerPort();

            // Make an HTTP request to the web server
            // that will cause it to send back the
            // server information we need.

            URL url = new URL("http", host, port, "/");
            HttpURLConnection con = (HttpURLConnection)
                url.openConnection();
            con.setRequestMethod("OPTIONS");
            String webserver = con.getHeaderField("server");

            // Write it to the output stream

            JspWriter out = pageContext.getOut();
            out.print(webserver);
        }
        catch (IOException e) {
            throw new JspException(e.getMessage());
        }
        return SKIP_BODY;
    }
}
```

Let's look at the source code in detail to see what we expect it to do.

```
package com.jspcr.taglibs.diag;
```

The first line identifies the package name. It isn't strictly necessary to place the code in a package, but it helps to organize related classes and makes for more meaningful Javadoc documentation. Besides, some JSP containers don't correctly generate `import` statements for custom tags, so classes without a package name can cause compilation errors in the generated servlet.

```
import javax.servlet.http.*;
import javax.servlet.jsp.*;
import javax.servlet.jsp.tagext.*;
import java.io.*;
import java.net.*;
```

Simple tag handlers usually need to import only the `javax.servlet.jsp` and `javax.servlet.jsp.tagext` packages, as well as the `java.io.IOException` class. In this case, we need the `HttpServletRequest` class from `javax.servlet.http`, as well as several classes from `java.net`.

```
public class GetWebServerTag extends TagSupport
```

A tag handler needs to implement either the `Tag`, `IterationTag`, or `BodyTag` interface, all of which are in the `javax.servlet.jsp.tagext` package. `BodyTag` is a subinterface of `IterationTag`, which in turn is a subinterface of `Tag`. While the tag author is free to implement these interfaces directly, it usually is more convenient to extend one of the default implementation classes `TagSupport` or `BodyTagSupport`, overriding only those methods needed for the task at hand. The example tag requires neither a tag body nor loop control, so we simply extend the `TagSupport` class.

```
public int doStartTag() throws JspException
```

This method is called when the start tag is encountered, after any attributes it specifies have been set in the tag handler, but before the body of the tag is processed. In this case, no body and no attributes exist, so all the code will be contained in the `doStartTag()` method. Note, the method lets you throw a `JspException` if the code runs into trouble. Because we will be accessing network classes that can throw a `java.io.IOException`, we enclose the entire method in a `try ... catch` block that converts this to a `JspException` for handling by the JSP container. Note, likewise, the method returns an integer return code (more about this shortly).

```
HttpServletRequest request =
   (HttpServletRequest) pageContext.getRequest();
```

To send an HTTP request to the Web server, we need to know the host name and port number of the request we received. This information can be found in the request object, which can be obtained from the `pageContext` object. The observant reader will notice that `pageContext` is nowhere defined in this class. This is because it's defined as a `protected` field in the `TagSupport` superclass, which makes it accessible to subclasses like ours.[2] This variable is set just before `doStartTag()` is called when the `TagSupport.setPageContext()` method is called:

```
String host = request.getServerName();
int port = request.getServerPort();

// Make an HTTP request to the web server
// that will cause it to send back the
// server information we need.

URL url = new URL("http", host, port, "/");
HttpURLConnection con = (HttpURLConnection)
   url.openConnection();
con.setRequestMethod("OPTIONS");
String webserver = con.getHeaderField("server");
```

We use the four-argument constructor of `java.net.URL` that takes a protocol name, server name, port number, and path; from this, we get an `HttpURLConnection` object. Because we don't actually care about the contents of any particular file, we specify the `OPTIONS` method rather than `GET` or `POST`. We could also use `HEAD`, which is essentially the same as `GET` but returns only headers. Occasionally, however, Web servers report that `HEAD` is not a supported method. `OPTIONS` should work for any `HTTP/1.1`- compliant Web server (after all, its purpose is to return a list of request methods the Web server *does* support). Invoking the connection object's `getHeaderField()` method causes the request to be sent and the appropriate HTTP header in the response to be read.

```
JspWriter out = pageContext.getOut();
out.print(webserver);
```

---

[2]   Reading the source code for `TagSupport` and `BodyTagSupport` is helpful. These are fairly small classes, and it's instructive to see where the page context and body content variables come from, and how `findAncestorWithClass` works. The source is available from http://cvs.apache.org/viewcvs/jakarta-servletapi-5/.

After capturing the desired information in the `webserver` variable, we can simply write it to the current servlet output stream, which we can obtain from the page context. The effect is that the `getServer` tag used in the JSP page is replaced by the server information obtained from the HTTP request.

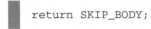

```
return SKIP_BODY;
```

Finally, we exit from the method returning the integer constant `SKIP_BODY`, which is defined in the `Tag` interface. Because we have defined this tag to have no body, there's no need to evaluate it, and the JSP page will throw a runtime exception if any other return code is specified.

Compiling the Sample Code

This completes the tag handler. The source code file must be named `GetWebServerTag`
`.java`, and its compiled class must have the fully qualified name `com.jspcr.taglibs`
`.diag.GetWebServerTag`. An easy way to ensure this is to create the appropriate set of directories under the Web application's `/WEB-INF/classes` directory,

```
/WEB-INF/classes/com/jspcr/taglibs/diag
```

and place the `.java` source file in the `diag` directory. The program can be compiled from the `/WEB-INF/classes` directory with the command

```
javac com/jspcr/taglibs/diag/GetWebServerTag.java
```

with appropriate provision being made for having the `servlet.jar` file somewhere in the classpath. This should put a `GetWebServerTag.class` file in the same directory as `GetWebServerTag.java`. If this doesn't happen, check to make sure the `package` statement has been entered correctly as shown in the listing.

Step 4: Incorporate the Tag into a JSP Page

At this point, the tag is ready to be used. The following JSP page (`ShowServer.jsp`) demonstrates how this is done:

```
%@ page session="false" %>
<%@ taglib prefix="diag"
            uri="http://www.jspcr.com/taglibs/diagnostics"
            %>
<html>
<head>
<title>Basic Example of a Custom Tag</title>
<style>
```

```
h1 { font-size: 140% }
</style>
</head>
<body>
<h1>Basic Example of a Custom Tag</h1>
The Web server is <diag:getWebServer/>
</body>
</html>
```

The taglib Directive

The first line specifies that no JSP session is required for this page:

```
<%@ page session="false" %>
```

Since the default is "true" and JSP sessions are expensive in terms of system usage, it is a good idea always to specify session="false" unless you know that you need a session.

Next comes the taglib directive:

```
<%@ taglib prefix="diag"
           uri="http://www.jspcr.com/taglibs/diagnostics"
           %>
```

This directive must appear in the JSP page before any of the custom tags it refers to are used. The top of the page is a good place.

What does the URI attribute of the taglib directive refer to? It looks like a URL used by a Web server, but actually, it's just a unique name that identifies the namespace used by the tag library. It can refer to an actual TLD file that is accessible through HTTP, but it can also be mapped to a file on the server in the web.xml deployment descriptor. In this example, the entry in web.xml would be this:

```
<web-app>
   ...
   <taglib>
      <taglib-uri>http://www.jspcr.com/taglibs/diagnostics</taglib-uri>
      <taglib-location>/WEB-INF/tlds/diagnostics.tld</taglib-location>
   </taglib>
   ...
</web-app>
```

The `<taglib-uri>` element contains the unique identifier you will use in your JSP pages, and the `<taglib-location>` element is the servlet-context-relative path to the actual TLD.

Note that you can also use the TLD path directly in the JSP page:

```
<%@ taglib prefix="diag" uri="/WEB-INF/tlds/diagnostics.tld"%>
```

You'll probably want to use this form during development, because changing it doesn't involve changing the `web.xml` file.

How to Use the Tag in the JSP Page

The rest of the Web page is traditional HTML, with the exception of the line on which the custom tag is specified:

```
The Web server is <diag:getWebServer/>
```

When `ShowServer.jsp` is first invoked, the JSP container uses information from the `taglib` directive to locate the tag library descriptor and to identify where its tags are used on this page. When the generated servlet receives a request, it produces HTML something like this:

```
<html>
<head>
<title>Basic Example of a Custom Tag</title>
<style>
h1 { font-size: 140% }
</style>
</head>
<body>
<h1>Basic Example of a Custom Tag</h1>
The Web server is Apache Coyote/1.0
</body>
</html>
```

depending, of course, on the actual Web server involved. The results are shown in Figure 11-1.

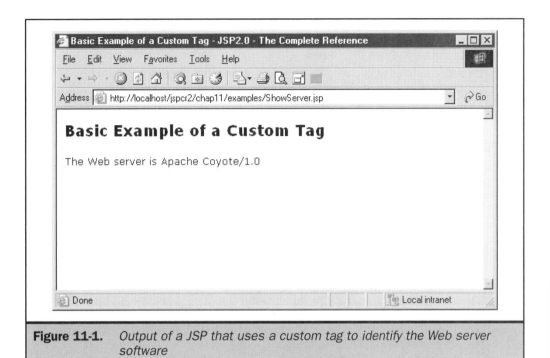

Figure 11-1. *Output of a JSP that uses a custom tag to identify the Web server software*

It is worth noting that custom tags used in JSP pages must conform to strict XML rules:

1. All tags must be completed, either by a matching end tag,

```
<diag:name>
...
</diag:name>
```

or by the shortcut form, if there's no body:

```
<diag:name/>
```

2. All attributes must be quoted, even numeric ones:

```
<diag:for id="I" start="1" end="10">
...
</diag:for>
```

3. Nested tags cannot overlap. The following

```
<diag:A>
<diag:B>
</diag:A>
</diag:B>
```

is illegal.

4. Case is significant in tag and attribute names.

How Tag Handlers Work

A *tag handler* is a Java class that performs the action of a custom tag by implementing a set of predefined methods that a JSP container calls. In this section, we will learn about the structure of a tag handler, the interfaces it implements, its lifecycle, and how it works with attributes and scripting variables. We also look at cooperating and nested tags, and show how they can interact. To start, however, let's review how the JSP container translates and invokes a JSP page.

What the JSP Container Does

Recall that a JSP page exists in three forms:

- **The .jsp file**   The original source file the page author writes, which may include HTML, scriptlets, expressions, declarations, action tags, and directives.
- **The .java file**   Java source code for a servlet that's equivalent to the .jsp file. This servlet is generated by the JSP container.
- **The .class file**   The compiled form of the generated Java servlet.

When a JSP page is requested by an HTTP client, the JSP container checks the modification dates of the .jsp and .java files. If the .java file doesn't exist or if it's older than the .jsp file (as it would be if the JSP page had been modified), the JSP container re-creates the Java servlet and compiles it. During this step, the following transformations take place:

- The <%@ page %>, <%@ include %>, and <%@ taglib %> directives supply translation-time information to the JSP container.
- JSP expressions and lines of HTML get translated into out.print() statements inside the _jspService() method in the order they occur.
- Scriptlets are copied verbatim into _jspService().

- Declarations are copied verbatim into the source code outside of
  `_jspService()`.

- Standard JSP actions such as `<jsp:include>`, `<jsp:useBean>`, and `<jsp:setProperty>` are translated into the runtime logic that performs their function.

- Custom actions (custom tags) are expanded into Java statements that call methods in their corresponding tag handler.

Tag-Related Code Generated by the Container

The container uses the `taglib` directives to locate Tag Library Descriptors (TLDs) and to match them to custom tags used in the page according to the tag prefix used. For example, if the directive is

```
<%@ taglib prefix="db"
    uri="/WEB-INF/tlds/database.tld" %>
```

then the container reads the `database.tld` file to get a list of tags it describes and the name of the tag handler class associated with each one. When it encounters a tag later in the page with a namespace prefix,

```
<db:connect url="mydatabase">
```

it looks in the tag library associated with "db" for a tag with the name "connect". The container uses information about the tag's structure, which it finds in the TLD, to generate a series of Java statements that accomplish the tag's function. In the case of the db:connect tag previously shown, this might include

1. Code to create an instance of the `connect` tag handler or obtain one from a pool.

2. Code to pass the `connect` tag handler a reference to the `pageContext` object. This is a useful feature because it gives the tag handler access to the JSP page's `Request`, `Response`, `HttpSession`, `ServletContext`, and output stream objects. It also means the tag handler can get or set attributes at any level the page context manages.

3. Code to pass a reference to the parent tag, if db:connect is nested within another custom tag.

4. A call to the `connect` tag handler's `setUrl()` method, passing the "mydatabase" value.

5. A call to a method named `doStartTag()`, which the `connect` tag handler implements to perform any action that takes place when its start tag is encountered (more about this shortly).

What a Tag Handler Does

In the body of a JSP page, a custom tag may look like this:

```
<app:mail from="Accounting Manager" to="Staff" >
   <app:subject>Expense Reports</app:subject>
   Please be sure to submit all expense reports before
   the fifteenth day of the month to allow sufficient
   processing time.  Thanks.
</app:mail>
```

The components of this tag include

- A start tag, <app:mail ...>, with zero or more attributes
- An end tag, </app:mail>
- The lines between the start and end tags, known as the *body* of the tag, which may include ordinary text or other JSP statements.[3]

In transforming the tag into servlet code, the container invokes the tag handler for each of these components, using the pageContext object to share attributes to the handler. The invocation of these methods is sometimes referred to as the tag handler's *lifecycle*.

For this to work, a tag handler must implement one of three interfaces:

- **javax.servlet.jsp.tagext.Tag**   For simple tags that don't operate on their bodies.
- **javax.servlet.jsp.tagext.IterationTag**   For tags that need to be able to evaluate their bodies multiple times (looping over the values of an array, for example). IterationTag is a subinterface of Tag.
- **javax.servlet.jsp.tagext.BodyTag**   For tags that need to operate on the content of their bodies. BodyTag is a subinterface of IterationTag.

These interfaces specify the lifecycle methods the tag handler must provide.

The API also provides two support classes—TagSupport and BodyTagSupport— that act as the default implementation of the corresponding interfaces. Most tag handlers extend these support classes rather than implementing the interfaces directly, although the interfaces aren't particularly complex. One benefit of using a support class is you can override only the methods you need to change, allowing the support class to handle the rest, much like an adapter class in Java AWT or Swing development. In addition, the support class can take care of saving the page context and body content objects in protected variables, so subclasses can simply access them.

---

[3]   A tag is not required to have a body. A tag may simply perform its function in accordance with the attributes specified in the start tag. In this case, the shorthand <tag ... /> notation is commonly used.

Tag Libraries

Custom tags are implemented and distributed in a structure known as a *tag library*, also referred to as a *taglib.* A tag library is a collection of classes and meta-information that includes

- **Tag handlers**   Java classes that implement the functionality of custom tags
- **Tag extra information classes**   Optional classes that supply the JSP container with logic for validating tag attributes and creating scripting variables
- **A tag library validator**   An optional class that can be used for translation-time validation of a JSP page
- **A tag library descriptor (TLD)**   An XML document that describes the properties of the individual tags and the tag library as a whole

The components of a tag library can be installed anywhere they are accessible to the JSP container. The tag handler, tag extra information, and tag library validator classes need to be located where they can be found by the JSP container class loader. The tag library descriptor can be located anywhere.

For ease of deployment, however, the JSP 1.2 specification mandates that the JSP container must accept a tag library packaged as a JAR file having a certain fixed structure. In such a JAR file, the classes should be in a directory tree starting at the root that matches their package structure, and the TLD must be a file that meets three conditions:

1. It must be in the `/META-INF` directory in the JAR file.
2. Its name must end in `.tld`.
3. It must have a `<uri>...</uri>` element. The contents of this element will match the `uri` attribute of the `<%@ taglib %>` directive in pages that use the tag library.

This means a tag library can be deployed simply by copying its JAR file to the `/WEB-INF/lib` directory. Or, the classes can be unzipped into the `/WEB-INF/classes` directory and the TLD can be placed in another Web-accessible location. This is typically a directory named `/WEB-INF/tlds`, although this is only a convention, not a requirement.

The Tag Library Descriptor (TLD)

The tag library configuration information needed by a JSP container is stored in a *tag library descriptor (TLD).* A TLD is an XML document that describes the individual tags in the library, their tag handlers and attributes, as well as version and identifying information about the library as a whole.

TLD Elements

The *document type definition (DTD)* for a JSP 1.2 tag library descriptor can be found at http://java.sun.com/dtd/web-jsptaglibrary_1_2.dtd. The corresponding XML Schema for JSP 2.0 TLDs is found at http://java.sun.com/ xml/ns/j2ee/ web-jsptaglibrary_2_0 .xsd. There are several minor differences between the 1.2 and 2.0 formats; for more details, look at the DTD or schema for your version.

A valid TLD consists of a single `<taglib>` element having certain subelements:

- **tlib-version**   A required element containing the version number of the tag library. This is a dotted decimal number consisting of up to four groups of digits separated by decimal points, such as "1.0", or "1.3.045".

- **jsp-version**   A required element identifying the minimal level of the JSP specification required to support the tag library. For example, for JSP version 1.2, this would be "1.2".

- **short-name**   A short descriptive name that identifies the tag library. A JSP authoring tool might use this name as a default prefix for tags from this library. The DTD prescribes that this name should have no whitespace and must begin with an alphabetic character; however, the restriction about whitespace seems widely ignored in practice. shortname is a required element.

- **uri**   An optional element that defines a unique URI, which identifies this library. This is often the URL of the location from which the latest version of the taglib can be downloaded, but it can be any well-formed URI.

- **display-name**   An optional element in which descriptive information about the tag library is entered. This is intended for human viewing in a JSP authoring tool.

- **validator**   If specified, it's the fully qualified name of a class that can syntax-check JSP pages that use this library. The class has access to the intermediate XML format of the JSP page.

- **listener**   Contains a `<listener-class>` subelement with the fully qualified name of a `ServletContextListener`, `ServletContextAttributeListener`, `HttpSessionActivationListener`, or `HttpSessionAttributeListener` that the JSP container will automatically instantiate and register. There can be any number of `<listener>` elements defined here, including zero.

- **tag**   An element that can appear one or more times in a TLD. Tag elements describe the individual tags that comprise the library.

A `tag` element itself consists of up to 12 types of subelements:

- **description**   Text that describes the function of the tag.

- **display-name**   A name by which the tag can be identified in IDE tools.

- **icon**   An optional large and/or small icon name.

- **name**   The tag name as it will be used in a JSP page. Together with a namespace prefix that identifies the tag library, the name uniquely identifies a tag to the JSP container.

- **tag-class**   A required element consisting of the fully qualified name of the tag handler that implements the tag.

- **tei-class**   An optional element consisting of the fully qualified name of the *tag extra information (TEI)* class used by this tag, if any. A TEI class provides information about scripting variables the tag handler creates, as well as any validations that can be performed on tag attributes.

- **body-content**   Optionally describes how the tag handler uses its body content. The possible values are

empty	The tag body must be empty.
JSP	The tag body consists of other JSP elements.
tagdependent	The tag body is interpreted by the tag itself, with no JSP transformations.

- **info**   Optional human-readable descriptive information about the tag.

- **attribute**   Optional information about attributes that can be coded when the tag is used in a JSP page. This entry is described more fully in the "Defining Tag Attributes" section later in this chapter.

The taglib Directive

The purpose of the taglib directive is to specify the location of the TLD and assign it a short alias (prefix) that distinguishes its tags on this page. Its syntax is as follows:

```
<%@ taglib prefix="tag prefix" uri="taglibURI" %>
```

where the two attributes are

tag prefix	A name, unique on this page, used to identify tags from this library. If the prefix is diag, for example, then any tag from this tag library used on this page should be written as <diag:xxx>, where xxx is the tag name. The prefix can be any valid XML name token, although Sun Microsystems reserves the prefixes jsp, jspx, java, javax, servlet, sun, and sunw.

taglibURI   The URI of the tag library itself. This can be an absolute path name beginning with / that is interpreted relative to the top of the Web application as in the preceding example. Or, it can be a URL that acts as a symbolic name for the TLD. In this case, the name must be mapped to the actual TLD by means of a <taglib> entry in the web.xml file.

The Tag Handler API

The following section describes the methods associated with the Tag interface and the TagSupport class.

The Tag Interface

Table 11-1 lists the lifecycle methods that must be supported by classes implementing the Tag interface.

Method	Description
public void setPageContext (PageContext ctx)	The generated servlet calls this method first before requiring the handler to do anything else. The implementing class should save the context variable so that it's available at any point in the tag lifecycle. From the page context, the tag handler can access all the JSP implicit objects and can get and set attributes in any scope.
public void setParent (Tag parent)	Enables a tag to find the tag above it in the evaluation stack. Called immediately after setPageContext.
public Tag getParent()	Returns the parent tag.
public int doStartTag() throws JspException	Called after the page context, parent, and any attributes coded on the start tag have been set. The return code indicates whether the JSP implementation servlet should evaluate the tag body (EVAL_BODY_INCLUDE) or not (SKIP_BODY). The method can throw a JspException to indicate a fatal error.

Table 11-1. *Methods in the Tag Interface*

Method	Description
`public int doEndTag()` `throws JspException`	Called when the end tag has been encountered. The return code indicates whether the JSP implementation servlet should continue with the rest of the page (EVAL_PAGE) or not (SKIP_PAGE). The method can throw a `JspException` to indicate a fatal error.
`public void release()`	Guaranteed to be called before page exit. Allows the tag handler to release any resources it holds and reset its state so that it can be reused, if necessary.

Table 11-1.   *Methods in the Tag Interface* (continued)

The interface also includes four constants that represent the possible return code from the `doStartTag()` and `doEndTag()` methods:

- **EVAL_BODY_INCLUDE**   When returned by `doStartTag()`, indicates that the page implementation servlet should evaluate the tag body.
- **SKIP_BODY**   When returned by `doStartTag()`, indicates that the servlet should ignore the body of this tag.
- **EVAL_PAGE**   When returned by `doEndTag()`, indicates that the rest of the page should be evaluated as usual.
- **SKIP_PAGE**   When returned by `doEndTag()`, indicates that the rest of the page should be skipped.

The TagSupport Class

The class `javax.servlet.jsp.tagext.TagSupport` is a concrete class that implements the `Tag` interface. In addition to the interface, the `TagSupport` class provides the additional methods listed in Table 11-2.

Extending this class rather than directly implementing the interface is usually advantageous. In addition to providing default implementations for all the required methods and storing the `pageContext` variable, `TagSupport` offers several convenience methods. The method `findAncestorWithClass()` is particularly useful for supporting nested tags. An *outer tag,* for example, can manage a set of objects as instance variables, providing public accessors that make these objects accessible to *inner tags.* The database tag example later in this chapter illustrates the technique.

Method	Description
`public static Tag findAncestorWithClass (Tag thisTag, Class cls)`	Looks in the runtime tag stack for the desired parent tag handler. A tag handler can provide methods that child tags within its scope can call.
`public void setId(String id)` `public String getId()`	Stores or retrieves the name specified in the `id` attribute.
`public void setValue (String name, Object o)` `public Object getValue (String name)`	Stores or retrieves a value under the given name in a local hashtable.
`public void removeValue (String name)`	Removes the named value from the local hashtable.
`public Enumeration getValues()`	Returns a `java.util.Enumeration` of the keys in the hashtable.

Table 11-2. *Additional Methods in the TagSupport Class*

The Tag Handler Lifecycle

The flowchart in Figure 11-2 describes the events in the life of a tag handler. The process shown in the flowchart corresponds to the Java code the JSP container generates for a tag when the JSP page is translated into a servlet. Knowing when each of your tag handler methods will be called, and what the state of the page and container will be, is important. Understanding this protocol can help you write code that works the way you expect. Also important is to remember that the tag itself doesn't exist in the generated servlet at runtime—the tag has been replaced by equivalent code that sets attributes and calls methods in the tag handler.

Let's consider each step in the flowchart.

The Flowchart

To start, the generated servlet needs to create an instance of the tag handler class. It usually does so by invoking a method in a factory class that is part of the JSP container. The factory class may maintain a pool of tag handler instances so that it can reuse tag handlers that are no longer active.

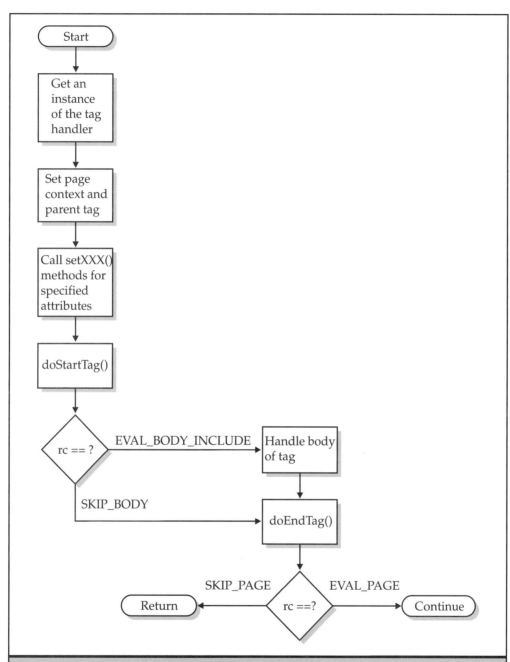

Figure 11-2.   *Flowchart of the tag handler lifecycle*

Next, the tag handler instance is initialized and made aware of the state of the servlet in which it exists. The servlet does this by calling two methods in the tag handler:

`setPageContext(PageContext ctx)`	The `PageContext` object contains references to all the JSP implicit objects and provides access to attributes at the page, request, session, and application level. When the servlet calls this method, the tag handler should save the context in an instance variable so that it will be available to all the handlers' methods. Note, the `TagSupport` base class does this automatically.
`setParent(Tag parent)`	Tags in a JSP page may be nested, that is, contained within the body of another tag. Immediately after `setPageContext()` is called, the servlet calls `setParent()`, passing a reference to the tag that contains this one, if any. If the tag isn't nested, the parameter will be null. Having access to enclosing tags makes it possible for a tag to call methods in any of its parents, which makes cooperative action practical. The `TagSupport` class also saves this variable automatically.

If a tag supports attributes, the runtime values of these attributes are passed to the tag handler by means of setter methods, which the handler must supply. For example, the database connection tag at the beginning of this chapter

```
<db:connect url="mydatabase">
```

has one attribute, named `url`. Its tag handler must have a method with the signature

```
public void setUrl(String value)
```

that stores the value of the `url` attribute, most likely in a private instance variable. For each attribute *xxx* coded in the start tag, the generated servlet will have a set*Xxx*(value) method call. These calls are located immediately after the `setParent()` call.

At this point, the tag handler's `doStartTag()` method is called. The page context and parent tag have already been set, as have all the tag's attributes. The method can read these variables and perform whatever calculations and operations necessary to implement the tag's functionality. It can access the servlet output writer by calling `pageContext.getOut()`. It can change the values of scripting variables in the JSP page by setting attributes in the page context. If any fatal errors are encountered, the method should throw a `JspException`.

The `doStartTag()` method must return an integer return code, either `SKIP_BODY` or `EVAL_BODY_INCLUDE`. If the return code from `doStartTag()` is `EVAL_BODY_INCLUDE`, then the body of the tag is handled as usual. If the return code is `SKIP_BODY`, everything in the original JSP page up to this tag's end tag is ignored.

After the tag body is either evaluated or ignored, the tag handler's `doEndTag()` method is invoked. Like `doStartTag()`, this method must return an integer return code that indicates how to proceed. If the value is `EVAL_PAGE`, the rest of the page is evaluated; if it's `SKIP_PAGE`, the servlet code executes an immediate return from `_jspService()`.

Defining Tag Attributes

A custom tag can have any number of *attributes*, which are name/value pairs coded in the start tag when it's used in a JSP page. For example, the tag

```
<opera:role name="Papageno" range="baritone"
            description="a bird-catcher"/>
```

has three attributes: `name`, `range`, and `description`. Attributes may be required or optional, and their values can be coded as string literals or supplied at request time using JSP expressions (if the tag allows this).

For each attribute a tag supports, its tag handler must supply two things:

- An instance variable to store the attribute
- One or more `setAttrname()` methods, where `Attrname` is the attribute name with the first letter capitalized

For the preceding example tag, the tag handler might look like this:

```
/**
 * RoleTag
 */
public class RoleTag extends TagSupport
{
    // Three attributes:

    private String name;
```

```
private String range;
private String description;

// ... and their setter methods:

public void setName(String nameFromJSPTag)
{
    name = nameFromJSPTag;
}

public void setRange(String rangeFromJSPTag)
{
    range = rangeFromJSPTag;
}

public void setDescription(String descriptionFromJSPTag)
{
    description = descriptionFromJSPTag;
}

public int doStartTag() throws JspException
{
    try {
        JspWriter out = pageContext.getOut();
        out.println("<TR>");
        out.println("<TD>" + name + "</TD>");
        out.println("<TD>" + range + "</TD>");
        out.println("<TD>" + description + "</TD>");
        out.println("</TR>");
    }
    catch (IOException e) {
        throw new JspException(e.getMessage());
    }
    return SKIP_BODY;
}
}
```

The JSP container generates code in the JSP servlet to take attribute values coded in a custom tag and sends them to the tag handler. It does this by calling the set*Attrname*() methods for each attribute. This is done after the page context and parent tag have been set, but just before `doStartTag()` has been called. For example, suppose a JSP page uses the `<opera:role>` tag as follows:

```
<%@ page session="false" %>
<%@ taglib prefix="opera" uri="/WEB-INF/tlds/opera.tld" %>

<HTML>
<HEAD><TITLE>The Magic Flute</TITLE></HEAD>

<BODY>
<H2>The Magic Flute</H2>
<H3>Dramatis Personae</H3>
<TABLE BORDER="1" CELLPADDING="3" CELLSPACING="0">
<TR><TH>Role</TH><TH>Range</TH><TH>Description</TH>

<opera:role name="Tamino" range="Tenor"
            description="an Egyptian prince"/>

<opera:role name="Pamina" range="Soprano"
            description="daughter of the Queen of the Night"/>

<opera:role name="Papageno" range="Baritone"
            description="a bird-catcher"/>

<opera:role name="Queen of the Night" range="Soprano"
            description="die Sternflammende Königin"/>

<opera:role name="Sarastro" range="Bass"
            description="High Priest of Isis and Osiris"/>

</TABLE>
</BODY>
</HTML>
```

The generated servlet (again using JRun as the container) would then handle each of the `<opera:role>` tags with code similar to the following:

```
RoleTag roleTag = (RoleTag)
   JRunJSPStaticHelpers.createTagHandler
   (pageContext, "RoleTag");
```

```
roleTag.setPageContext(pageContext);
roleTag.setParent(null);

roleTag.setRange("Baritone");
roleTag.setName("Papageno");
roleTag.setDescription("a bird-catcher");


roleTag.doStartTag();
```

The property setter method is all that's required for a tag to support an attribute, but more information can be specified in the TLD. The `<tag>` element can include any number of `<attribute>` elements in the following form:

```
<attribute>
    <name>attributeName</name>
    <required>true|false</required>
    <rtexprvalue>true|false</rtexprvalue>
</attribute>
```

Only the attribute name is required; the other two elements are optional and default to `false`.

If `<required>true</required>` is specified, then the attribute must be coded everywhere the tag is used or a fatal translation error will occur. Otherwise, the attribute is optional. The tag handler should take care to handle the case where the attribute hasn't been specified, in which case the instance variable will be null.

If `<rtexprvalue>true</rtexprvalue>` is specified, then the attribute value may be specified with a request time expression. Attributes coded in this manner have the form

```
attribute="<%= scriptlet_expression %>"
```

where the quotes may include nothing but the JSP expression. In addition to making it possible to supply a value for the attribute at runtime, this also causes the type of the expression to be preserved. In other words,

```
date="<%= new java.util.Date() %>"
```

would result in the generated servlet code

```
tag.setDate(new java.util.Date());
```

which would cause the tag handler's `public void setDate(Date date)` method to be invoked, rather than `public void setDate(String date)`.

The IterationTag Interface

Frequently, an HTML page contains repeated information, such as rows in a table that are populated from a database query. To support this functionality, the tag extension API provides a second tag interface, `javax.servlet.jsp.tagext.IterationTag`.

`IterationTag` extends the `Tag` interface with one additional method:

```
public int doAfterBody()
```

Like `doStartTag()` and `doEndTag()`, `doAfterBody()` is a lifecycle method that is invoked at a certain point in the execution of the tag. In this case, it is called after every evaluation of the tag and provides the tag handler a point at which to determine whether to evaluate the tag again or exit from the loop. The choice is expressed in the return value of `doAfterBody()`:

- **EVAL_BODY_AGAIN**   Indicates that the tag body should be evaluated again.
- **SKIP_BODY**   Indicates that the loop is complete.

In the example of a tag that generates table rows from a database query, the tag handler might get a reference to a JDBC `ResultSet` object and repeat this logic:

1. Invoke the `ResultSet next()` method to advance to the next row. If `next()` returns `false`, the method would return `SKIP_BODY`.
2. Extract the fields from the current row and write the appropriate HTML to generate a table row.
3. Return `EVAL_BODY_AGAIN` to cause the generated servlet to loop back to step 1.

For most applications of `IterationTag`, you will probably find it easier to use the JSTL iteration capabilities. This is the subject of Chapters 12 and 13.

The Body Tag Handler API

Simple tags are useful components that perform their function entirely within their start tag. However, the real power of custom tags results from their capability to interact with their tag body. This makes it possible for a custom tag to

- Postprocess its body text, perhaps sorting it, making an HTML table from it, or filtering out characters like "<" and ">", replacing them with their HTML-safe equivalents "`&lt;`" and "`&gt;`".

■ Define new implicit objects and create scripting variables for them.

■ Cooperate with nested tags to perform complex operations.

Tags that operate on their body are an extension of the tags discussed so far in this chapter. They implement a subinterface of `javax.servlet.jsp.tagext.Tag`, known as `javax.servlet.jsp.tagext.BodyTag`. As was the case with the `TagSupport` class, a base class implementation of `BodyTag` also exists, called `BodyTagSupport`.

BodyContent

When the JSP container generates code for a tag that has a body, it saves and restores the object that represents the current servlet output writer. Before the body of the tag is processed, a new output writer is created—this one an instance of the `BodyContent` class. While the body is being evaluated, the `out` scripting variable as well as the value returned by `pageContext.getOut()` both refer to the new writer object. If several levels of nesting exist, the writers are saved on a stack, so each level has its own writer.

`BodyContent` is a subclass of `javax.servlet.jsp.JspWriter`, but differs from its superclass in that its contents aren't automatically written to the servlet output stream. Instead, they're accumulated in what amounts to a string buffer. After the tag body is completed, the original `JspWriter` is restored, but the `BodyContent` object is still available in `doEndTag()` in the `bodyContent` variable. Its contents can be retrieved with its `getString()` or `getReader()` method, modified as necessary, and written to the restored `JspWriter` output stream to be merged with the page output. Table 11-3 lists the additional methods that `BodyContent` provides.

Method	Description
`public void flush() throws IOException`	Overrides the `JspWriter.flush()` method so that it always throws an exception. Flushing a `BodyContent` writer is not valid because it isn't connected to an actual output stream to which it could be written.
`public void clearBody()`	Resets the `BodyContent` buffer to empty. This can be useful if the body is being written to the enclosing writer in `doAfterBody()`.

Table 11-3. *Additional Methods in the BodyContent Class*

Method	Description
`public Reader getReader()`	Returns a reader for the body content after it has been evaluated. This reader can be passed to other classes that can process a `java.io.Reader`, such as `StreamTokenizer`, `FilterReader`, or an XML parser.
`public String getString()`	Returns a string containing the body content after it has been evaluated.
`public void writeOut(Writer w)`	Writes the body content to the specified output writer.
`public JspWriter getEnclosingWriter()`	Returns the writer object (possibly another `BodyContent`) next higher in the stack.

Table 11-3.   *Additional Methods in the BodyContent Class* (continued)

Why does the JSP container create this elaborate structure for custom tag output? We already learned the JSP container allows output to be postprocessed and filtered, but it's also because not all body content is intended to produce output. For example, in the earlier database query

```
<db:runQuery>
    SELECT    *
    FROM      FD_GROUP
    WHERE     FdGp_Desc LIKE '%F%'
    ORDER BY FdGp_Cd
</db:runQuery>
```

the body is not HTML at all, but a character string representing an SQL statement. This would presumably be read with the `Body-content.getString()` method and passed to a JDBC statement object whose output would be written to the Web page. This is automatically possible because the `Body-content` object stores its output in a buffer rather than writing it.

The BodyTag Interface

Tags that interact with their body content have a slightly more complex lifecycle, so they require a few more methods in their tag handlers. For this reason, an extension of the Tag interface called BodyTag exists, which inherits all the methods required by Tag, but adds three new ones having to do with body handling. Table 11-4 describes the interface.

In addition to the three new methods, the BodyTag interface also defines one new integer constant, EVAL_BODY_BUFFERED, which when returned by doStartTag(), causes a new BodyContent object to be created and associated with this tag handler. When returned by doAfterBody(), it causes the JSP servlet to evaluate the body again after updating any scripting variables controlled by this tag. This makes it possible for a tag handler to loop through a list of elements, evaluating the body for each one.

The BodyTagSupport Class

As was the case with the Tag interface, BodyTag has a default implementation class called javax.servlet.jsp.tagext.BodyTagSupport. This class extends TagSupport, but with a few subtle changes. Table 11-5 describes the public methods implemented by BodyTagSupport.

Method	Description
public void setBodyContent (BodyContent out)	Invoked by the JSP servlet after the current JspWriter has been pushed and a new BodyContent writer has been created. This occurs just after doStartTag().
public void doInitBody() throws JspException	A lifecycle method called after setBodyContent(), but just before the body is evaluated. If the body is evaluated multiple times, this method is called only once.
public int doAfterBody() throws JspException	A lifecycle method called after the body has been evaluated, but while the BodyContent writer is still active. This method must return either EVAL_BODY_TAG or SKIP_BODY. If the return code is EVAL_BODY_TAG, the body is evaluated again and doAfterBody() is called again.

Table 11-4.   *Methods in the BodyTag Interface*

Method	Description
`public int doStartTag()` `throws JspException`	Overrides `doStartTag()` in `TagSupport`, returning `EVAL_BODY_TAG` by default instead of `SKIP_BODY`.
`public int doEndTag()` `throws JspException`	Invokes `doEndTag()` in `TagSupport`, returning its result.
`public void setBodyContent (BodyContent out)`	Stores the new body content object in a protected variable named `bodyContent`. Subclasses can access this variable directly.
`public void doInitBody()` `throws JspException`	Does nothing by default. Intended to be overridden by subclasses that need to perform initialization before the body is evaluated.
`public int doAfterBody()` `throws JspException`	Called by the JSP servlet after each time the body has been evaluated. The body content object is still active. This method must return either `SKIP_BODY` or `EVAL_BODY_TAG`, which causes the body to be evaluated again and `doAfterBody()` to be called again.
`public void release()`	Sets the `bodyContent` variable to `null` and then calls `super.release()`. An overriding method must call `super` `.release()` as well; otherwise, `bodyContent` may not be available for garbage collecting.
`public BodyContent getBodyContent()`	Returns the `bodyContent` variable. Subclasses already have access to the protected variable, but this method allows unrelated tag handler classes to send output to this body content.
`public JspWriter getPreviousOut()`	A convenience method that calls `getEnclosingWriter()` on the `bodyContent` variable and returns the result.

Table 11-5.   *Methods in BodyTagSupport*

Body tag handlers are free to implement the `BodyTag` interface directly, but `BodyTagSupport` is usually a more convenient base class.

Summary

Custom tags are an elegant, robust method of extending the JSP authoring environment, allowing development teams to provide a toolkit of application-specific JSP tags that can be used by page designers who aren't proficient in Java programming. A tag's functionality is implemented by a Java class called a *tag handler*, which provides methods that are called by the JSP container at various points in the tag's lifecycle. Sets of related tags can cooperate to accomplish complex tasks. Collections of tag handlers and configuration information are packaged in *tag libraries*, which have a vendor-independent structure and can be deployed with a minimum of effort.

JSTL and its expression language will have a big impact on how JSP tags are used. It is likely that much future tag development will use that framework. This is the subject of the next two chapters.

Chapter 12

Expression Language

J SP has sometimes been criticized for making it difficult to keep content and presentation separate, since it allows Java code and HTML to be freely intermingled. This is true as far as it goes, although it is certainly possible to write bad code in any language. But as the division of labor between Web designers and Java programmers becomes more prevalent, it is valuable to have tools that do not require expert skills in both areas. The Java language is powerful, but not all of its capabilities are required for typical Web applications. For this reason, the JSP *Expression Language* may be a simpler choice in many cases.

What Is EL?

The *JSP Expression Language (EL)* is a simple, special-purpose language designed for the Web application environment. In contrast to general-purpose programming languages like Java, EL has only enough syntax and semantics to take one or more values, perform some operations on them, and return the results. It has no if-then logic or looping constructs, only the equivalent of the right-hand side of an assignment statement (i.e., <var> = <expr>)—which is why it is appropriately named *Expression* Language.

EL was originally developed in connection with the *JSP Standard Tag Library (JSTL)*, but as of JSP 2.0, it has been incorporated into JSP itself, and is part of the official JSP specification. For backward compatibility with earlier JSP versions, EL can be enabled or disabled:

- Application-wide by default if a Servlet 2.4-format web.xml deployment descriptor is used.

- For an individual JSP page by means of the isELEnabled attribute of the page directive.

- For a group of files within an application by means of the <el-enabled> element. This is a subelement of the <jsp-property-group> element in the <jsp-config> section of a deployment descriptor.

EL can be used inside the attributes of a JSP or HTML tag as well as in the main body of a JSP page (i.e., the template text).

EL Syntax

An EL expression is recognized by the JSP translator as anything that starts with a dollar sign and left curly brace and ends with a right curly brace:

${*expression*}

Whatever is inside the curly braces is evaluated at runtime and sent to the JSP output stream in place of the ${...}. You can use an expression as the entire value of an attribute:

```
<a href="${someURL}">
```

or combine it with literal text:

```
<a href="http://www.lyricnote.com/users/${empno}">
```

or with other expressions:

```
<a href="${someURL}/users/${empno}">
```

Likewise, you can use expressions in the HTML (template) text:

```
<h1>A Simple Mathematical Fact</h1>
Two plus two equals ${2 + 2}.
```

In the example just given, the output stream sent to the browser would be:

```
<h1>A Simple Mathematical Fact</h1>
Two plus two equals 4.
```

Literals and Variables

Values can be supplied to EL either as literals or as variables. Literals look like what you would expect them to look like:

- **booleans** `${true}` and `${false}`
- **integers** `${68412}`
- **floating point numbers** With a decimal point `${3.14159265358979}` or in exponential notation `${9.3e+7}`
- **strings** Enclosed either with quotation marks `${"Hello"}` or apostrophes `${'Goodbye'}`
- **The null value** `${null}`

Variables are referred to by name and correspond either to named attributes in one of the four JSP scopes (page, request, session, application) or to implicit objects, using reserved keywords. It is important to note that variables are resolved dynamically by means of a `VariableResolver` object, rather than by any explicit means defined in the language. JSP 2.0 includes the default variable resolver that enables EL in JSP pages.

JSP pages are converted into Java servlet source code. For ordinary scriptlets, expressions, and declarations, this conversion is done simply by copying their contents into the generated source code. Obviously, this won't work for EL expressions, because they typically aren't syntactically valid Java expressions. Instead, the original string value of the EL expression is preserved in the generated source code and passed to the variable resolver at runtime.

Implicit Objects

A number of EL variables are automatically defined, similar to the implicit objects that relate to the page context environment. Table 12-1 gives the complete list.

Variable Name	Description
pageContext	The JSP `PageContext` object.
pageScope	A `java.util.Map` providing values for named attributes in page scope.
requestScope	A `java.util.Map` providing values for named attributes in request scope.
sessionScope	A `java.util.Map` providing values for named attributes in session scope.
applicationScope	A `java.util.Map` providing values for named attributes in application scope.
param	A `java.util.Map` that links parameter names to their `ServletRequest.getParameter(String name)` values.
paramValues	A `java.util.Map` that links parameter names to `String` arrays corresponding to `ServletRequest.getParameterValues(String name)`.
header	A `java.util.Map` of HTTP header names to their values (using `ServletRequest.getHeader(String name)`).
headerValues	A `java.util.Map` of HTTP header names to `String` arrays corresponding to `ServletRequest.getHeaders(String)`.
cookie	A `java.util.Map` that maps a cookie name to a `Cookie` object.
initParam	A `java.util.Map` of *context* (not *servlet*) initialization parameter names to values.

Table 12-1.   *Implicit Objects Available to EL Expressions*

Extracting Property Values

Properties of JavaBeans (which are stored as scoped attributes by JSP) can be accessed using the dot (.) or bracket ([]) operators. If you're familiar with JavaScript, you'll recognize the syntax:

> ${*beanName.propertyName*}

or

> ${*beanName["propertyName"]*}

The dot operator takes two arguments, the first being the name of a variable and the second, the name of a property of the object represented by that variable. So, for example, to get the `phoneNumber` property of a `customer` object (which would be `customer.getPhoneNumber()` in Java terminology), you would write

> ${*customer.phoneNumber*}

The bracket syntax is more general in that it enables you to specify an expression that evaluates to the property name. In most cases, this expression is simply a string:

> ${*customer["phoneNumber"]*}

although a computed value is equally valid. If the property value is itself an object with properties, the dot or bracket operators can be nested:

> ${*customer.phoneNumber.areaCode*}

In keeping with its goal of simplicity, EL uses intelligent default values when a property does not exist: zero for arithmetic properties, empty for strings, etc.

Operators

Like any programming language, EL has built-in operators that use one or more values to produce another. There are four types of operators: arithmetic, relational, logical, and the `empty` operator.

Arithmetic

Arithmetic operators are the traditional ones:

- **Addition** `${a + b}`
- **Subtraction** `${a - b}`
- **Multiplication** `${a * b}`
- **Division** `${a / b}`
- **Modulo** `${a % b}` or `${a mod b}`

Thus, the code in the following listing:

```
<%
    pageContext.setAttribute("a", new Integer(10));
    pageContext.setAttribute("b", new Integer(3));
%>
a = ${a}, b = ${b}:
<table>
    <tr> <td>a + b = </td> <td>${a + b}</td> </tr>
    <tr> <td>a - b = </td> <td>${a - b}</td> </tr>
    <tr> <td>a * b = </td> <td>${a * b}</td> </tr>
    <tr> <td>a / b = </td> <td>${a / b}</td> </tr>
    <tr> <td>a % b = </td> <td>${a % b}</td> </tr>
    <tr> <td>a mod b = </td> <td>${a mod b}</td> </tr>
</table>
```

produces the output

```
a = 10, b = 3:
a + b = 13
a - b = 7
a * b = 30
a / b = 3.3333333333333335
a % b = 1
a mod b = 1
```

Operator precedence works in the usual manner:

```
${2 + 3 * 4} = ${2 + 12} = 14
```

and parentheses can be used to override the order of evaluation:

```
${(2 + 3) * 4} = ${5 * 4} = 20
```

Relational

Numeric or string values can be compared with the traditional relational operators:

- **Greater than** >
- **Less than** <
- **Equals** ==
- **Greater than or equals** >=

- **Less than or equals** `<=`
- **Not equals** `!=`

To use relational operators inside attribute values (where the "<" character is prohibited), you can use the escape sequence `&lt;` for "less than." In addition, there is an alternate form for all relational operators:

- **Greater than** `gt`
- **Less than** `lt`
- **Equals** `eq`
- **Greater than or equals** `ge`
- **Less than or equals** `le`
- **Not equals** `ne`

The nostalgic reader will recognize this as "Fortran" syntax.

Logical

Boolean values, whether literals, variables, or boolean-valued expressions, can be used with the three standard logical operators:

- `and` (or `&&`)
- `or` (or `||`)
- `not` (or `!`)

Thus, the following code

```
<%
    Map map = new HashMap();
    map.put("speed", new Float(500));
    map.put("power", new Float(1000));
    pageContext.setAttribute("flyingObject", map);
    pageContext.setAttribute("speedingBullet", new Float(400));
    pageContext.setAttribute("locomotive", new Float(800));
%>
${
    (flyingObject.speed gt speedingBullet)
        and
    {flyingObject.power gt locomotive)
}
```

produces the value `true`.

This example, like others in this chapter, uses JSP scriptlets with embedded Java code to explicitly set attributes in the page context. This is not the usual way values used by EL are set; it's only used for illustrative purposes here. The next chapter, which introduces the JSP Standard Tag Library, describes the environment more commonly used.

Empty

The last operator we'll consider is the `empty` operator. This is a handy means for detecting a null or empty value. It is coded as a unary prefix operator. To test an object named "obj", the syntax is

```
${empty obj}
```

and the evaluation is done as follows:

1. If `obj` is null, the value is `true`.

2. If `obj` is the empty string `""`, the value is `true`.

3. If `obj` is an empty array, map, or list, the value is `true`.

In all other cases, `${empty obj}` is false.

Functions

EL's built-in operators provide the most commonly used functionality. For specialized needs, however, you can define external functions. These functions can then be used anywhere in an EL expression that variables, literals, or other values can be used. In this section, we'll show a complete example of how to develop and deploy a custom EL function.

Function Implementation Class

Like custom tags, functions are implemented in Java classes and registered in a TLD. There are no special requirements for the implementation class itself, but the implementation function must be a public static method.

For example, suppose our LyricNote.com Web site needs a currency conversion routine for quoting product prices online. There are any number of ways to implement this, but let's try an EL function. The Java code for the implementation class looks like this:

```java
package com.jspcr.el;

/**
 * Expression language functions dealing with currency conversion
 */
public class Currency
```

```
{
    /**
    * Converts amount from one currency to another
    */
    public static double convert(double amount,
                String fromCurrency,
                String toCurrency)
    {
        // A real function might access a database or
        // web service.  Here, we simply return a
        // plausible calculated value.

        return amount * 1.44;
    }
}
```

Nothing complicated about this: there is a public static method named `convert()` that takes a currency amount and two currency codes. The method computes the equivalent amount in the target currency and returns it as a `double`. There are no restrictions on how this can be done; it may be by means of a database query or a call to a Web service. That part is not important in our example; let's just assume it's done by some well-defined technique.

Registering the Function

In order to make the function available to a Web application through EL, we need to register it in a *tag library descriptor (TLD)*. In this respect, a function is treated similarly to a custom tag. Moreover, the purpose of the TLD entry is the same: to map a function name to a method in a class.

For our currency conversion function, we'll create a TLD named `currency.tld` that contains the following:

```xml
<?xml version="1.0" encoding="UTF-8" ?>

<taglib xmlns="http://java.sun.com/xml/ns/j2ee"
        xmlns:xsi="http://www.w3.org/2001/XMLSchema-instance"
        xsi:schemaLocation=
    "http://java.sun.com/xml/ns/j2ee web-jsptaglibrary_2_0.xsd"
        version="2.0">

    <description>
        EL functions supporting currency conversions
```

```
    </description>
    <tlib-version>
        1.0
    </tlib-version>
    <short-name>
        currency
    </short-name>
    <uri>
        /currency
    </uri>

    <function>
        <description>
            Converts first currency to another
        </description>
        <name>
            convert
        </name>
        <function-class>
            com.jspcr.el.Currency
        </function-class>
        <function-signature>
            double convert(double, java.lang.String, java.lang.String)
        </function-signature>
    </function>

</taglib>
```

In addition to the elements common to all TLDs, there are entries specific to the function declaration. These are described in Table 12-2.

Element	Description
`<function>`	Introduces the function declaration. Contains the subelements described in the following rows.
`<name>`	The name to be assigned to the function. This is the name that will be used inside the EL expressions that use this function.

Table 12-2. *Elements in the TLD Definition of an EL Function*

Element	Description
`<function-class>`	The fully qualified name of the Java class containing the function's implementation.
`<function-signature>`	The signature of the function as it would be declared in a Java class. Two things are noteworthy about the entry: 1.) The parameters are listed as class names only, not class names and dummy variable names. 2.) Class names must be fully qualified, even those in the java.lang package.

Table 12-2. *Elements in the TLD Definition of an EL Function* (continued)

The implementation class must be made available to the JSP container by any of the usual means. Typically, this is a jar file in the /WEB-INF/lib directory of the Web application.

The TLD itself should be registered with the Web application by means of the `<taglib>` entry in the web.xml deployment descriptor:

```
<jsp-config>
   <taglib>
      <taglib-uri>
         http://www.jspcr.com/taglibs/currency
      </taglib-uri>
      <taglib-location>
         /WEB-INF/tlds/currency.tld
      </taglib-location>
   </taglib>
</jsp-config>
```

Invoking the Custom Function

Once the function is implemented and registered, it can be used in an EL expression in a JSP page. To associate the function with a page, you need to first declare the TLD and associate it with a prefix (just as you would a custom tag library):

```
<%@ taglib prefix="curr"
           uri="http://www.jspcr.com/taglibs/currency" %>
```

Then within the page, you can invoke the function as follows:

```
${curr:convert(dollars, "USD", "CHF")}
```

When the function is evaluated, the JSP container will locate the implementation class by means of the TLD, then invoke the method in that class that is mapped to the named function.

Summary

JSP 2.0 provides a new method of writing expressions in a JSP page: a simplified *Expression Language (EL)* that is suitable for use by nonprogrammers. EL is a special-purpose language that operates only in a Web application. EL has read-only access to objects bound as attributes in any of the JSP scopes (page, request, session, and application). It can extract the named properties of these objects using a straightforward syntax similar to JavaScript.

EL expressions are delimited by curly braces, with a dollar sign immediately preceding the left curly brace:

${*expression*}

An expression can contain any of the following:

- Variable names, which refer to attributes in one of the JSP scope contexts
- Reserved keywords, which provide access to servlet parameters, HTTP headers, Cookies, etc.
- Numeric, boolean, or string literals
- Property accessors, which are the dot and bracket operators
- Arithmetic operators for addition, subtraction, multiplication, division, and remainders
- Relational operators used to compare two values
- Logical operators and, or, and not
- The empty operator

In addition to built-in operators, EL can be extended with user-defined functions. These functions must be implemented as public static methods in a Java class, which must be registered with the Web application in a TLD.

EL becomes more useful in the context of the JSP standard tag library, which is the subject of the next chapter.

The Complete Reference

Chapter 13

The JSP Standard Tag Library (JSTL)

As a technology matures and more people rely on it, the need for standardization becomes greater. Standards make it possible to have electrical outlets supply power to hundreds of interchangeable devices, railroad cars that run on any set of tracks, and bottle openers that handle soft drinks from any manufacturer. In addition, standards make it possible for many groups of people to work together on different aspects of a large project. Moreover, standards can reduce costs by allowing solutions to common problems to be shared.

JSP is no exception to this rule. With greater use has come greater need for shared solutions to common programming problems: iteration, XML processing, database access, etc. Many tag libraries from different sources exist that work in this domain, but if you have to distribute each one with your Web application, it becomes cumbersome for the user and adds to the learning curve.

The *JSP Standard Tag Library (JSTL)* solves this problem, essentially by extending the JSP "language" to include basic operations that are common to most Web applications. Its widespread acceptance makes it possible for designers to develop JSP pages that can be used in any JSP 2.x–compliant servlet container. In this chapter, we'll examine the custom tags that JSTL provides and see how they can be used in a Web application.

Getting Started with JSTL

JSTL was originally a stand alone part of the Jakarta taglibs project, but has been standardized by the Java Community Process (see JSR 052 at http://jcp.org). It is not technically part of the JSP specification,[1] but for practical purposes, you can probably assume that it will be available in most Web applications. JSTL implementations are used in Sun's Java Web Services Developer Pack, Sun ONE Studio 4, and are expected to be part of Java Server Faces as well.

You can download the JSTL specification from http://jcp.org/aboutJava/community process/final/jsr052, and the Jakarta implementation from http://jakarta.apache.org/taglibs/doc/standard-doc/intro.html. Installing the implementation software is quite straightforward; at a minimum, you can just drag and drop the jar files[2] directly into your application's /WEB-INF/lib directory.

JSTL consists of four families of tags:

---

[1]   The fact that the main JSTL package names start with javax.servlet.jsp.jstl should be a big hint that JSTL should henceforth be considered part of JSP.

[2]   There are quite a few jar files distributed with the Jakarta implementation because the Jakarta taglibs project involves more than JSTL. If you are working with JDK 1.4 or later, you probably need only `jstl.jar` and `standard.jar`.

- **core**   General purpose "programming" tags that let you get and set variables, loop through a collection, and write to the output stream.
- **xml**   Tags that parse, generate, and transform XML.
- **sql**   Database access tags, including connection support, transactions, queries, and updates.
- **fmt**   Tags for formatting numbers and dates, and for localizing internationalized text.

This chapter includes syntax and descriptive information about each tag, as well as examples of how JSTL tags can be used in a Web application.

Using JSTL in a JSP Page

To use JSTL tags in a JSP page, you need to include a `taglib` directive, the same as you would for any other tag library. For JSTL, the `uri` and `prefix` attributes are as described in Table 13-1.

You can, of course, use any prefix you like, but the ones listed in Table 13-1 are used consistently in the JSTL documentation and are more likely to be interpreted correctly by other developers.

There are actually two different tag libraries for each group, one for use with the JSP Expression Language (EL) and one for JSP 1.2–style expressions. You use the URIs shown in Table 13-1 with EL; for JSP 1.2 expressions, use the URI with `_rt` appended to it as shown in Table 13-2.

To get some idea how this works, let's look at an example of a JSP page written with JSTL. The Fahrenheit-to-Celsius temperature conversion table we worked on in Chapter 5 is a simple choice. Don't worry about understanding all the tags yet; they are all explained in more detail later in the chapter.

taglib	uri	prefix
core	`http://java.sun.com/jstl/core`	c
xml	`http://java.sun.com/jstl/xml`	x
sql	`http://java.sun.com/jstl/sql`	sql
fmt	`http://java.sun.com/jstl/fmt`	fmt

Table 13-1.   *The uri and prefix Attributes for JSTL Tag Libraries*

taglib	uri	prefix
core	http://java.sun.com/jstl/core_rt	c_rt
xml	http://java.sun.com/jstl/xml_rt	x_rt
sql	http://java.sun.com/jstl/sql_rt	sql_rt
fmt	http://java.sun.com/jstl/fmt_rt	fmt_rt

Table 13-2. *Attributes for JSTL Tag Libraries with JSP 1.2 Expressions*

```jsp
<%@ page session="false" %>
<%@ taglib uri="http://java.sun.com/jstl/core" prefix="c" %>
<%@ taglib uri="http://java.sun.com/jstl/fmt"  prefix="fmt" %>

<html>
<head>
<title>Temperature Conversion Table</title>
<style>
   body, td, th {
      font-family: Tahoma, Sans-Serif;
      font-size: 10pt;
   }
   h1 { font-size: 140%; }
   h2 { font-size: 120%; }
</style>
</head>

<body>
<center>
<h1>Temperature Conversion Table</h1>
<h2><i>(Powered by JSTL)</i></h2>
<table border="1" cellpadding="3" cellspacing="0">
   <tr>
      <th align="right" width="100">Fahrenheit</th>
      <th align="right" width="100">Celsius</th>
   </tr>
   <c:forEach var="f" begin="32" end="212" step="20">
     <tr>
         <td align="right"> ${f} </td>
         <td align="right">
```

```
                <fmt:formatNumber pattern="##0.000">
                    ${(f - 32) * 5 / 9.0}
                </fmt:formatNumber>
            </td>
        </tr>
    </c:forEach>
</table>
</center>
</body>
</html>
```

The logic is fairly easy to follow. We need to loop through a range of Fahrenheit temperatures from 32 to 212 in increments of 20. For each temperature, we convert to Celsius[3] by subtracting 32 and multiplying by 5/9. The conversion calculation is done with an EL expression (see Chapter 12 for a refresher if you need it). We then generate a table row with cells for the Fahrenheit and Celsius measurements, with the Celsius number formatted to three decimal positions.

This task requires two JSTL tags: one to do the loop (`<c:forEach>`) and one to format the Celsius value (`<fmt:formatNumber>`). To make the tags accessible, we need to declare their tag library URIs and the prefix we'll use to refer to them. That is the function of the two `taglib` directives at the top of the page. The `<c:forEach>` tag has attributes that accept the start, end, and increment of the loop, and declare the name of the variable representing the current observation. Within the body of this tag, we calculate the required value and format it with `<fmt:formatNumber>`, which accepts a pattern that operates like `java.text.DecimalFormat`. Figure 13-1 shows the results.

There is no Java code visible anywhere on the page. To a significant extent, the combination of JSTL and EL in a JSP container make it possible to separate the responsibilities of the programmer and the Web designer.

In the remainder of this chapter, we'll consider each of the four JSTL tag libraries, describing each of their tags, its syntax and attributes. In most cases, there is more than one syntax given for the tag, usually because the tag can be used with multiple object types. The attribute section for each tag describes all possible attributes, but the syntax key is essential for figuring out which ones are valid in which combinations.

Core Tags

The foundation of JSTL is the core taglib, which provides access to application objects and programming logic. There are three groups of actions in this library: general-purpose tags, conditional tags, and URL-related tags.

---

[3]   The Celsius temperature system uses the properties of water as its calibration points. Water freezes at 0 degrees Celsius and boils at 100 degrees.

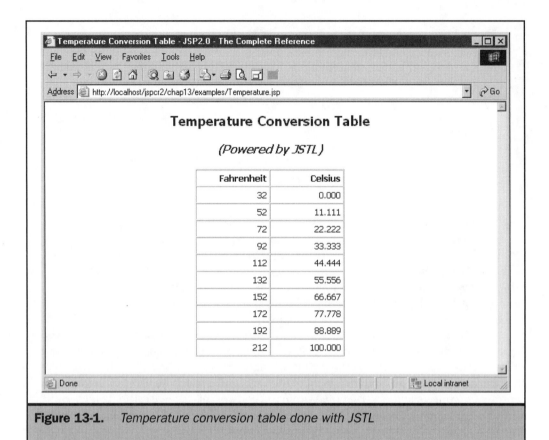

Figure 13-1. *Temperature conversion table done with JSTL*

General-Purpose Actions

This group contains tags for getting and setting variables, for writing their values to the output stream, and for catching exceptions.

<c:out>

The <c:out> tag evaluates an expression, which may be supplied in an attribute value or contained in the tag body. The resulting value is written to the current JSP output stream.[4]

---

[4] This tag is not particularly necessary unless you need its specialized escapeXml or default operations. Otherwise, you can simply write the EL expression that you would have used in the value attribute without bothering with the enclosing <c:out> tag. This is a relic of early JSTL, which allowed EL to be used inside attribute values only.

Syntax

Without a body

```
<c:out value="value"
       [escapeXml="{true|false}"]
       [default="defaultValue"]
       />
```

With a body

```
<c:out value="value" [escapeXml="{true|false}"]>
    default value
</c:out>
```

Attributes

- **value**   The variable or expression to be evaluated.
- **escapeXml**   If true, converts the XML-confusing characters <, >, &, ', and " to their character-entity equivalents <, >, &, ', ". The default value is true.
- **default**   Value to be written if the input value is null. The default value can also be specified in the body of the tag (second syntax). This is useful if you have a complex calculation that involves other tags.

<c:set>

Sets the value of a variable or property.

Syntax

Using an attribute value

```
<c:set value="value"
       var="varName"
       [scope="{page|request|session|application}"]
       />
```

Using a tag body

```
<c:set var="varName"
       [scope="{page|request|session|application}"]>
    body content
</c:set>
```

Using an attribute value to set a property value

```
<c:set value="value"
       target="target"
       property="propertyName"
       />
```

Using a tag body to set a property value

```
<c:set target="target" property="propertyName">
   body content
</c:set>
```

Attributes

- **value**   The expression to be evaluated.
- **var**   If specified, stores the resulting value in a scoped variable of that name.
- **scope**   The scope for var (page, request, session, or application).
- **target**   An expression that evaluates to the target object to be set, either a JavaBean or a java.util.Map (an expression, not the *name* of the object).
- **property**   The name of the property to be set.

`<c:remove>`

Removes a variable from the specified scope (page, by default).

Syntax

```
<c:remove var="varName"
          [scope="{page|request|session|application}"]
          />
```

Attributes

- **var**   The name of the variable to be removed.
- **scope**   The variable scope.

`<c:catch>`

Catches exceptions thrown by any tag in its body. This bypasses the default error handler provided by the JSP container.

Syntax

```
<c:catch [var="varName"]>
   nested actions
</c:catch>
```

Attributes

- **var**   The optional name of a variable to contain the thrown exception. You can test this value for null later on to determine if the body of the <c:catch> tag executed cleanly.

Conditional and Iterator Actions

This group contains tags that provide if-then, switch-case, and looping capability.

<c:if>

Determines the value of the test attribute (a boolean variable or expression). If the value is true, the body of the <c:if> tag is executed.

Syntax
Without body content

```
<c:if test="testCondition"
      var="varName"
      [scope="{page|request|session|application}"]
      />
```

Syntax
With body content

```
<c:if test="testCondition"
      [var="varName"]
      [scope="{page|request|session|application}"]>
   body content
</c:if>
```

Attributes

- **test**   The boolean variable or expression.
- **var**   A variable name by which the result of the test can be saved for later use. This allows you to avoid unnecessarily duplicating a test.
- **scope**   The scope for the variable.

`<c:choose>`

Roughly the equivalent of the Java `switch` statement, with two exceptions:

1. The conditions controlling each case can be logically unrelated, full boolean expressions. They do not have to refer to the same variable.
2. The default case (see `<c:otherwise>`) is not always executed as a last resort as it is in Java or C. It will be executed any time all the cases preceding it in document order have unsatisfied conditions.

Syntax

```
<c:choose>
    body content (<c:when> and <c:otherwise>)
</c:choose>
```

`<c:when>`

The tag that encloses a single case within a `<c:choose>` action.

Syntax

```
<c:when test="testCondition">
    body content
</c:when>
```

Attributes

- **test** The condition that, if it evaluates to `true`, will cause the body of the `<c:when>` tag to be executed.

`<c:otherwise>`

Equivalent to the default case in a Java or C switch statement, i.e., a `<c:when>` with an unconditional `true` test.

Syntax

```
<c:otherwise>
    conditional block
</c:otherwise>
```

`<c:forEach>`

A general-purpose looping tag. Works either as an iterator over a collection or as a fixed loop over a range of numbers.

Syntax
Iterate over a collection of objects

```
<c:forEach items="collection"                \
            [var="varName"]
            [varStatus="varStatusName"]
            [begin="begin"]
            [end="end"]
            [step="step"]>
    body content
</c:forEach>
```

Syntax
Iterate a fixed number of times

```
<c:forEach [var="varName"]
            [varStatus="varStatusName"]
            begin="begin"
            end="end"
            [step="step"]>
    body content
</c:forEach>
```

Attributes

- **var** The name of a variable that represents the current iteration item. Its data type depends on the collection over which it's iterating. For a `java.util.Map`, this is a `Map.Entry` object, which has `key` and `value` properties you can test with an EL expression.

- **items** A `Collection`, `Map`, or array.

- **varStatus** If specified, this is the name of an object that implements the `javax.servlet.jsp.jstl.core.LoopTagStatus` interface. The properties of this object (which you can get with an EL expression) describe where we are inside a loop (first item, last item) and the number of objects in the collection.

- **begin** An optional starting index for the loop.

- **end** An optional ending index for the loop.

- **step** An optional increment for the loop (the default is 1).

`<c:forTokens>`

Loops over the tokenized elements of a string. Equivalent to using a `StringTokenizer` to create a list and then calling `<c:forEach>` on the list.

Syntax

```
<c:forTokens items="stringOfTokens"
             delims="delimiters"
             [var="varName"]
             [varStatus="varStatusName"]
             [begin="begin"]
             [end="end"]
             [step="step"]>
    body content
</c:forEach>
```

Attributes

- **var** The name of a variable that represents the current iteration item.
- **items** The string to be tokenized.
- **delims** The delimiter or delimiters (equivalent to the delimiters in a StringTokenizer).
- **varStatus** Same as in `<c:forEach>`.
- **begin** Same as in `<c:forEach>`.
- **end** Same as in `<c:forEach>`.
- **step** Same as in `<c:forEach>`.

Networking Tags

This final group in the core taglib consists of tags that operate on URLs.

`<c:import>`

A generalization of `<jsp:include>` that can be used for URLs in other Web applications, not just those in the same servlet context.

Syntax

The resource to be included

```
<c:import url="url"
          [context="context"]
          [var="varName"]
          [scope="{page|request|session|application}"]
          [charEncoding="charEncoding"]>
    optional body content
</c:import>
```

Syntax
The resource

```
<c:import url="url"
        [context="context"]
        varReader="varReaderName"
        [charEncoding="charEncoding"]>
   body content where varReader is consumed by another action
</c:import>
```

Attributes

- **url**   The URL of the resource to import.
- **context**   An optional name of the foreign context (application).
- **var**   The name of the variable that will store the results, if specified.
- **scope**   The scope of the var variable.
- **charEncoding**   The character encoding used for the reader in syntax 2.
- **varReader**   The name of a reader object from which the content can be read.

`<c:url>`

Creates a URL, possibly with a session ID embedded, as would be done with `HttpServletResponse.encodeURL()` or `encodeRedirectURL()`.

Syntax
Without body content

```
<c:url value="value"
      [context="context"]
      [var="varName"]
      [scope="{page|request|session|application}"]
      />
```

Syntax
With query string parameters

```
<c:url value="value"
      [context="context"]
      [var="varName"]
      [scope="{page|request|session|application}"]>
   <c:param> subtags
</c:url>
```

JSP TAG EXTENSIONS

Attributes

- **value** The URL to be rewritten, potentially with the session ID.
- **context** The name of another Web application.
- **var** The name of the variable that will receive the new value.
- **scope** The variable scope.

`<c:redirect>`

Sends an HTTP redirect to the client (Web browser).

Syntax
Without body content

```
<c:redirect url="value" [context="context"]/>
```

Syntax
With query string parameters

```
<c:redirect url="value" [context="context"]>
   <c:param> subtags
</c:redirect>
```

Attributes

- **url** The URL of the resource to which the client is being redirected.
- **context** The other Web application name, if not this one.

`<c:param>`

Adds request parameters to a URL. Only valid inside the scope of `<c:import>`, `<c:url>`, `<c:redirect>`.

Syntax
The value specified in the attribute

```
<c:param name="name" value="value"/>
```

Syntax
The value specified in the tag body

```
<c:param name="name">
   parameter value
</c:param>
```

Attributes

- **name** The query string parameter name.
- **value** The parameter value.

Example

Let's revisit the `NumberGuesserGuesser` application from Chapter 8. You may recall that this was the other side of the number guesser sample application that is distributed with Tomcat. This time, we'll write it with JSTL.

The `GameState` class changes slightly to make it more bean-like:

```
package com.jspcr.el.sessions;

import java.io.Serializable;

/**
* Holds the number guesser application state using the
* following properties:
* <ul>
* <li>lowerLimit - highest value so far known to be too low</li>
* <li>upperLimit - lowest value so far known to be too high</li>
* <li>count - number of guesses so far</li>
* <li>nextGuess - readonly integer property</li>
* <li>userCheating - true if the upper and lower limits
*                    leave no room for further guesses.
*                    This can only happen if the user
*                    is cheating.</li>
* <li>cheaterMessage - returns a randomly chosen message
*                    accusing the user of cheating.</li>
* </ul>
*/
public class GameState implements Serializable
{
   // lowerLimit property

   private int lowerLimit = 0;

   public int getLowerLimit() {
      return lowerLimit;
   }

   public void setLowerLimit(int lowerLimit) {
      this.lowerLimit = lowerLimit;
```

```
   }

   // upperLimit property

   private int upperLimit = 101;

   public int getUpperLimit() {
      return upperLimit;
   }

   public void setUpperLimit(int upperLimit) {
      this.upperLimit = upperLimit;
   }

   // count property

   private int count = 1;
   public int getCount() {
      return count;
   }
   public void setCount(int count) {
      this.count = count;
   }

   // nextGuess property

   public int getNextGuess() {
      return (getUpperLimit() + getLowerLimit()) / 2;
   }

   // userCheating property

   public boolean getUserCheating()
   {
      return (getUpperLimit() - getLowerLimit()) <= 1;
   }

   // cheaterMessage

   public String getCheaterMessage()
   {
      String[] text = {
```

```
            "Are we cheating, perhaps?",
            "Did we forget our number, hmm?",
            "Perhaps we clicked the wrong button?",
            "What happened?",
            "What gives?",
        };
        int r = (int) (Math.random() * text.length);
        String message = text[r];
        return message;
    }
}
```

The only change to the `Start.jsp` page is a different package name:

```
<%@ page import="com.jspcr.el.sessions.*" %>

<jsp:useBean id="gameState"
            class="com.jspcr.el.sessions.GameState"
            scope="session"/>

<html>
<head>
    <title>Number Guess Guesser</title>
    <link rel="stylesheet" type="text/css" href="style.css"/>
</head>
<body>
    <h1>Number Guess Guesser</h1>
    <form action="NextGuess.jsp">
        <p>
            Think of a number between 1 and 100,
            and I'll try to guess it.
            Click OK when ready.
        </p>
        <input type="submit" value="OK" />
    </form>
</body>
</html>
```

The `gameState` bean is created here and bound to the session, from which it will be accessible to all the other JSP pages. When the OK button is clicked, the `NextGuess.jsp` page is invoked.

NextGuess.jsp changes little in the JSTL version, simply using an EL expression instead of a <jsp:getProperty>:

```
<%@ taglib prefix="c" uri="http://java.sun.com/jstl/core" %>
<html>
<head>
    <title>Number Guess Guesser</title>
    <link rel="stylesheet" type="text/css" href="style.css"/>
</head>
<body>
<h1>Number Guess Guesser</h1>
<form action="CheckResults.jsp">
<p>
    My guess is <b>${sessionScope.gameState.nextGuess}</b>. How did I do?
</p>
<p>
<input type="radio"
       name="result"
       value="tooLow"
       onClick="submit()"> Too low </input>

<input type="radio"
       name="result"
       value="justRight"
       onClick="submit()"> Exactly right </input>

<input type="radio"
       name="result"
       value="tooHigh"
       onClick="submit()"> Too high </input>
</p>
</form>
</body>
</html>
```

Here is the IWin.jsp page:

```
<%@ taglib prefix="c" uri="http://java.sun.com/jstl/core" %>
<html>
<head>
    <title>Number Guess Guesser</title>
    <link rel="stylesheet" type="text/css" href="style.css"/>
</head>

<body>
    <h1>Number Guess Guesser</h1>
    <p>
```

```
      I win, and after only
      <b>${sessionScope.gameState.count}</b>
      guesses!
   </p>

   <c:remove var="gameState" scope="session"/>

   <form action="Start.jsp">
      <input type="submit" value="Play again" />
   </form>

</body>
</html>
```

The only changes are the use of an EL expression to display the count, and the use of `<c:remove>` to dispose of the old game state bean. The same is true of `Cheater.jsp`:

```
<%@ taglib prefix="c" uri="http://java.sun.com/jstl/core" %>
<html>
<head>
   <title>Number Guess Guesser</title>
   <link rel="stylesheet" type="text/css" href="style.css"/>
</head>

<body>
<h1>Number Guess Guesser</h1>
   <p>
      <b>${sessionScope.gameState.lowerLimit}</b> is too low, but
      <b>${sessionScope.gameState.upperLimit}</b> is too high.
   </p>

   <p>
      ${sessionScope.gameState.cheaterMessage}
   </p>

   <c:remove var="gameState" scope="session"/>

   <form action="Start.jsp">
      <input type="submit" value="Play again" />
   </form>

</body>
</html>
```

The CheckResults.jsp page, which handles the conversation flow, is completely different:

```jsp
<%@ taglib prefix="c" uri="http://java.sun.com/jstl/core" %>

<c:set var="state" value="${sessionScope.gameState}"/>
<c:set var="nextPage" value="NextGuess.jsp"/>

<c:choose>
    <c:when test="${param.result == 'justRight'}">
        <c:set var="nextPage" value="IWin.jsp"/>
    </c:when>
    <c:when test="${state.userCheating}">
        <c:set var="nextPage" value="Cheater.jsp"/>
    </c:when>
    <c:otherwise>
        <c:set var="nextGuess" value="${state.nextGuess}"/>
        <c:set var="count" value="${state.count}"/>
        <c:choose>
            <c:when test="${param.result == 'tooLow'}">
                <c:set target="${state}"
                       property="lowerLimit"
                       value="${nextGuess}"/>
                <c:set target="${state}"
                       property="count"
                       value="${count + 1}"/>
            </c:when>
            <c:otherwise>
                <c:set target="${state}"
                       property="upperLimit"
                       value="${nextGuess}"/>
                <c:set target="${state}"
                       property="count"
                       value="${count + 1}"/>
            </c:otherwise>
        </c:choose>
    </c:otherwise>
</c:choose>

<jsp:forward page="${nextPage}"/>
```

We first use <c:set> to get a simple reference to the game state object and then use another <c:set> to set the default next page. The main body of the page is then a <c:choose> block. If the user indicates that the guess was exactly right, the "next page" variable is set to IWin.jsp. Otherwise, if the upper and lower limits are too close, the user is warned about his or her cheating ways via the Cheater.jsp page. If this is not the case, the button clicked by the user is interrogated to find out whether the preceding guess was too high or two low. Finally, the request is forwarded to the next page.

In the real world, this functionality would be handled by a servlet. It is done in JSTL here just to show how the conditional tags work.

Refer to Figures 8-1 through 8-6 to see the result.

XML Tags

The XML taglib can be used for parsing, writing, or transforming XML. If you are a beginner with XML, you might want to read Chapter 16 first.

To use this tag library, you'll need to copy the jaxen and saxpath jar files from the JSTL distribution to your /WEB-INF/lib directory.

Core Actions

This section covers the basic parsing and XPath tags in the XML taglib.

<x:parse>

Parses an XML document.

Syntax
A document specified by a String or Reader object

```
<x:parse xml="XMLDocument"
        {
            var="var" [scope="scope"] |
            varDom="var" [scopeDom="scope"]
        }
        [systemId="systemId"]
        [filter="filter"]
        />
```

Syntax
A document specified by the tag body

```
<x:parse {
        var="var" [scope="scope"] |
        varDom="var" [scopeDom="scope"]
```

```
        }
        [systemId="systemId"]
        [filter="filter"]>
    XML Document to parse
</x:parse>
```

Attributes

- **xml**   A literal XML string.
- **systemId**   The system identifier used in parsing the document.
- **filter**   An optional source filter.
- **var/varDom**   The parsed document object, which may be a DOM object or something else (which allows non-DOM parsers to be used).
- **scope/scopeDom**   The scope of the var or varDom variable.

`<x:out>`

Evaluates the XPath expression in the select attribute and writes the result to the servlet output stream. This is the counterpart of <c:out>, but it uses XPath instead of EL as the expression language.

Syntax

```
<x:out select="XPathExpression" [escapeXml="{true|false}"]/>
```

Attributes

- **select**   An XPath expression.
- **escapeXml**   See <c:out>.

`<x:set>`

Same as <x:out>, but stores its results in a variable.

Syntax

```
<x:set select="XPathExpression"
       var="varName"
       [scope="{page|request|session|application}"]
       />
```

Attributes

- **select** An XPath expression.
- **var** A variable to hold the results.
- **scope** The scope for the variable.

Flow Control Actions

This important group includes the basic programming constructs for conditionals: if-then, switch-case, and for-each in the context of XML. See the corresponding tags in the core library for details.

`<x:if>`

Evaluates the XPath expression in the select attribute. If the value is true, writes its tag body.

Syntax
Without body content

```
<x:if select="XPathExpression"
    var="varName"
    [scope="{page|request|session|application}"]
  />
```

Syntax
With body content

```
<x:if select="XPathExpression"
    [var="varName"]
    [scope="{page|request|session|application}"]>
  body content
</x:if>
```

`<x:choose>`

Marks the beginning of a conditional section, corresponding to a Java switch statement.

Syntax

```
<x:choose>
  body content (<x:when> and <x:otherwise> subtags)
</x:choose>
```

JSP TAG EXTENSIONS

`<x:when>`

One of the case blocks in an `<x:choose>`.

Syntax

```
<x:when select="XPathExpression">
   body content
</x:when>
```

`<x:otherwise>`

Represents the last alternative within an <x:choose> action.

Syntax

```
<x:otherwise>
   conditional block
</x:otherwise>
```

`<x:forEach>`

Evaluates the given XPath expression and repeats its nested body content over the result, setting the context node to each element in the iteration.

Syntax

```
<x:forEach[var="varName"] select="XPathExpression">
   body content
</x:forEach>
```

Transform Actions

The last group in the XML `taglib` is an interface to XSLT, which allows you to transform XML to HTML, text, or different XML.

`<x:transform>`

Transforms an XML document with an XSLT transformation.

Syntax
Without body

```
<x:transform xml="XMLDocument"
             xslt="XSLTStylesheet"
             [xmlSystemId="XMLSystemId"]
             [xsltSystemId="XSLTSystemId"]
             [{
```

```
                        var="varName" [scope="scopeName"] |
                        result="resultObject"
                   }]
                   />
```

Syntax
With a body for parameters

```
<x:transform xml="XMLDocument"
             xslt="XSLTStylesheet"
             [xmlSystemId="XMLSystemId"]
             [xsltSystemId="XSLTSystemId"]
             [{
                var="varName" [scope="scopeName"] |
                result="resultObject"
             }]>
   <x:param> actions
</x:transform>
```

Syntax
With a body for the input document and possibly parameters

```
<x:transform xslt="XSLTStylesheet"
             xmlSystemId="XMLSystemId"
             xsltSystemId="XSLTSystemId"
             [{
                var="varName" [scope="scopeName"] |
                result="resultObject"
             }] >
   XML Document to parse
   optional <x:param> actions
</x:transform>
```

Attributes

- **xml**   A string version of an XML document to be transformed.
- **xslt**   A reference to an XSLT stylesheet. This can be either a string containing the actual XML, a reader of some kind, or a JAXP Source object.
- **xmlSystemId**   The system identifier of the XML document.
- **xsltSystemId**   The system identifier of the XSLT stylesheet.
- **var**   A name given to the DOM object generated from the parsing.
- **scope**   The scope for this variable.
- **result**   A JAXP Result object to hold the transformation output.

`<x:param>`

Sets transformation parameters. Only valid inside `<x:transform>`.

Syntax
The value specified in the attribute

```
<x:param name="name" value="value"/>
```

Syntax
The value specified in the tag body

```
<x:param name="name">
   parameter value
</x:param>
```

Attributes

- **name**   Parameter name.
- **value**   Parameter value.

Example

Here is a sample XML document (TheBirds.xml) that we'll use in this example:

```
<?xml version="1.0"?>
<song>
   <title>The Birds</title>
   <words-by>Hilaire Belloc</words-by>
   <music-by>Benjamin Britten</music-by>

   <track name="Voices">
      <time-signature>2/2</time-signature>
      <tempo>Andante con Moto</tempo>
      <measure>
         <rest duration="1"/>
      </measure>
   </track>

   <track name="Piano">
      <time-signature>2/2</time-signature>
```

```
      <tempo>Andante con Moto</tempo>
      <measure>
         <note duration="8" value="e" octave="2"/>
         <note duration="8" value="g#" octave="2"/>
         <note duration="8" value="c#" octave="3"/>
         <note duration="8" value="g#" octave="3"/>
         <note duration="2" value="f#" octave="3"/>
      </measure>
   </track>
</song>
```

This example is simple; we'll just parse the document and create a table from some of its top-level elements:

```
<%@ taglib prefix="c" uri="http://java.sun.com/jstl/core" %>
<%@ taglib prefix="x" uri="http://java.sun.com/jstl/xml" %>

<x:parse var="doc">
   <c:import url="TheBirds.xml"/>
</x:parse>

<table border="1" cellpadding="5" cellspacing="0">
   <tr>
      <td>Song title:</td>
      <td><x:out select="$doc/song/title"/></td>
   </tr>
   <tr>
      <td>Words by:</td>
      <td><x:out select="$doc/song/words-by"/></td>
   </tr>
   <tr>
      <td>Music by:</td>
      <td><x:out select="$doc/song/music-by"/></td>
   </tr>
</table>
```

The results are shown in Figure 13-2. The only tricky part is the treatment of expressions—the XML taglib uses XPath, not EL, as its base. See Chapter 16 if you are not well versed in XML or XPath.

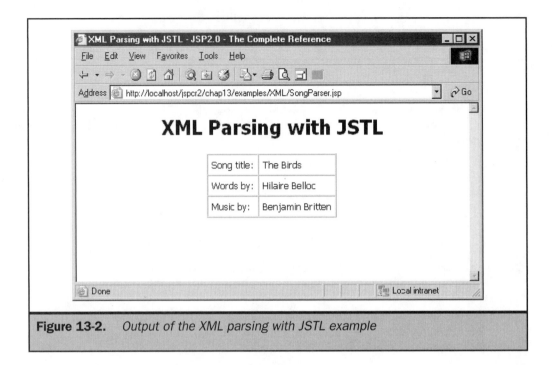

Figure 13-2. *Output of the XML parsing with JSTL example*

SQL Tags

The SQL taglib provides access to relational database systems through JDBC.

Data Extraction and Manipulation Tags

This section covers query and update actions.

<sql:query>

Executes an SQL query.

Syntax

Without a tag body

```
<sql:query sql="sqlQuery"
           var="varName"
           [scope="{page|request|session|application}"]
           [dataSource="dataSource"]
           [maxRows="maxRows"]
           [startRow="startRow"]
           />
```

Syntax
With a tag body, used to supply parameters

```
<sql:query sql="sqlQuery"
           var="varName"
           [scope="{page|request|session|application}"]
           [dataSource="dataSource"]
           [maxRows="maxRows"]
           [startRow="startRow"]>
   <sql:param> actions
</sql:query>
```

Syntax
With a body to specify both

```
<sql:query var="varName"
           [scope="{page|request|session|application}"]
           [dataSource="dataSource"]
           [maxRows="maxRows"]
           [startRow="startRow"]>
   query
   optional <sql:param> actions
</sql:query>
```

Attributes

- **sql**   The SQL that will be used to run the query.
- **dataSource**   A JNDI datasource.
- **maxRows**   The maximum number of rows to be included in the query result.
- **startRow**   The starting row number.
- **var**   The name of a variable to hold the query result.
- **scope**   The scope of the variable.

`<sql:update>`
A general tag for running any SQL command that does not produce a result set.

Syntax
Without a body

```
<sql:update sql="sqlUpdate"
           [dataSource="dataSource"]
```

```
          [var="varName"]
          [scope="{page|request|session|application}"]
          />
```

Syntax
With a body for update parameters

```
<sql:update sql="sqlUpdate"
          [dataSource="dataSource"]
          [var="varName"]
          [scope="{page|request|session|application}"]>
    <sql:param> actions
</sql:update>
```

Syntax
With a body for an update statement and optional update parameters

```
<sql:update [dataSource="dataSource"]
          [var="varName"]
          [scope="{page|request|session|application}"]>
    update statement
    optional <sql:param> actions
</sql:update>
```

Attributes

- **sql**   The SQL statement as literal text.
- **dataSource**   A JNDI datasource.
- **var**   The name of a variable to hold results.
- **scope**   The scope of the variable.

DataSource Tags

This group of actions deals with getting and releasing transactions and connections.

`<sql:transaction>`

Specifies the commit boundaries of a transaction.

Syntax

```
<sql:transaction [dataSource="dataSource"]
                 [isolation="
                     read_committed |
```

```
                             read_uncommitted |
                             repeatable_read |
                             serializable"]>
    <sql:query> and <sql:update> statements
</sql:transaction>
```

Attributes

- **dataSource**   A JNDI data source.
- **isolation**   The transaction isolation level, if different from one that the DataSource has been configured with.

`<sql:setDataSource>`

Binds a datasource to a variable name.

Syntax

```
<sql:setDataSource
     {
         dataSource="dataSource" |
         url="jdbcUrl"
         [driver="driverClassName"]
         [user="userName"]
         [password="password"]
     }
     [var="varName"]
     [scope="{page|request|session|application}"]
     />
```

Attributes

- **dataSource**   A JNDI datasource.
- **driver**   The JDBC driver class name.
- **url**   The JDBC database URL.
- **user**   The user ID.
- **password**   The password.
- **var**   The name of the result variable.
- **scope**   The scope of the exported variable.

`<sql:param>`

Sets the values of the substitution parameters in an SQL prepared statement.

Syntax

A parameter value specified in an attribute

```
<sql:param value="value"/>
```

Syntax

A parameter value specified in the body content

```
<sql:param>
   parameter value
</sql:param>
```

Attributes

- ■ value   The parameter value.

`<sql:dateParam>`

An `<sql:param>` that works with dates.

Syntax

```
<sql:dateParam value="value" type="[timestamp|time|date]"/>
```

Attributes

- ■ **value**   A date value.
- ■ **type**   Either "date", "time", or "timestamp".

Formatting Tags

The last library we'll consider is the formatting taglib. This consists of tags that handle internationalization, locales, time zones, number formatting, and date formatting.

Internationalization (i18n) Actions

This section includes the tags that work with locales and resource bundles.

`<fmt:setLocale>`

Sets the configured locale.

Syntax

```
<fmt:setLocale value="locale"
               [variant="variant"]
               [scope="{page|request|session|application}"]
               />
```

Attributes

- ■ **value**   The printable representation of a locale.
- ■ **variant**   The locale variant.
- ■ **scope**   The scope of the locale configuration variable.

<fmt:bundle>

Creates a resource bundle.

Syntax

```
<fmt:bundle basename="basename" [prefix="prefix"]>
   body content
</fmt:bundle>
```

Attributes

- ■ **basename**   Resource bundle resource name.
- ■ **prefix**   The prefix for the value of the message key of any <fmt:message> action.

<fmt:setBundle>

Sets the resource bundle.

Syntax

```
<fmt:setBundle basename="basename"
               [var="varName"]
               [scope="{page|request|session|application}"]
               />
```

Attributes

- ■ **basename**   The resource bundle base name.
- ■ **var**   The name of a variable to hold the resulting bundle.
- ■ **scope**   The scope of the var variable.

<fmt:message>

Looks up a message in a resource bundle by key.

Syntax

Without a body

```
<fmt:message key="messageKey"
             [bundle="resourceBundle"]
```

```
            [var="varName"]
            [scope="{page|request|session|application}"]
            />
```

Syntax
With a body for parameters

```
<fmt:message key="messageKey"
            [bundle="resourceBundle"]
            [var="varName"]
            [scope="{page|request|session|application}"]>
    <fmt:param> subtags
</fmt:message>
```

Syntax
With a body for key and optional message parameters

```
<fmt:message [bundle="resourceBundle"]
            [var="varName"]
            [scope="{page|request|session|application}"]>
    key
    optional <fmt:param> subtags
</fmt:message>
```

Attributes

- **key**   The message key.
- **bundle**   The resource bundle.
- **var**   The name of the result variable.
- **scope**   The scope of the variable.

`<fmt:param>`

Used to supply a value of the `<fmt:message>` action.

Syntax
Using an attribute

```
<fmt:param value="messageParameter"/>
```

Syntax
Using the tag body

```
<fmt:param>
    body content
</fmt:param>
```

Attributes

- **value**   The parameter value.

`<fmt:requestEncoding>`

Sets the character encoding used by the request.

Syntax

```
<fmt:requestEncoding [value="charsetName"]/>
```

Attributes

- **value**   The character set name.

Date and Number Formatting Actions

Date actions include those that work with times, timestamps, dates, and time zones.

`<fmt:timeZone>`

A simple wrapper for a temporary time zone object. Applies to all dates in the tag body.

Syntax

```
<fmt:timeZone value="timeZone">
    body content
</fmt:timeZone>
```

Attributes

- **value**   The time zone.

`<fmt:setTimeZone>`

Binds the specified time zone to a variable.

Syntax

```
<fmt:setTimeZone value="timeZone"
                 [var="varName"]
                 [scope="{page|request|session|application}"]
                 />
```

Attributes

- **value**   The time zone.
- **var**   A variable name to receive the time zone.
- **scope**   The scope of var.

<fmt:formatNumber>

Performs number formatting based on java.text.Format.

Syntax
Without a body

```
<fmt:formatNumber
      value="numericValue"
      [type="{number|currency|percent}"]
      [pattern="customPattern"]
      [currencyCode="currencyCode"]
      [currencySymbol="currencySymbol"]
      [groupingUsed="{true|false}"]
      [maxIntegerDigits="maxIntegerDigits"]
      [minIntegerDigits="minIntegerDigits"]
      [maxFractionDigits="maxFractionDigits"]
      [minFractionDigits="minFractionDigits"]
      [var="varName"]
      [scope="{page|request|session|application}"]
      />
```

Syntax
With a body to specify the numeric value to be formatted

```
<fmt:formatNumber
      [type="{number|currency|percent}"]
      [pattern="customPattern"]
      [currencyCode="currencyCode"]
      [currencySymbol="currencySymbol"]
```

```
          [groupingUsed="{true|false}"]
          [maxIntegerDigits="maxIntegerDigits"]
          [minIntegerDigits="minIntegerDigits"]
          [maxFractionDigits="maxFractionDigits"]
          [minFractionDigits="minFractionDigits"]
          [var="varName"]
          [scope="{page|request|session|application}"]>
     numeric value to be formatted
</fmt:formatNumber>
```

Attributes

- **value**   The number to be formatted.
- **type**   Number, currency, or percentage.
- **pattern**   An optional formatting pattern.
- **currencyCode**   The currency code for the destination locale.
- **currencySymbol**   The currency symbol (e.g., dollar sign).
- **groupingUsed**   Whether to use commas (or the equivalent).
- **maxIntegerDigits**   See `java.text.DecimalFormat`.
- **minIntegerDigits**   See `java.text.DecimalFormat`.
- **maxFractionDigits**   See `java.text.DecimalFormat`.
- **minFractionDigits**   See `java.text.DecimalFormat`.
- **var**   The name of a variable to store the result.
- **scope**   The scope of this variable.

`<fmt:parseNumber>`

The opposite of `<fmt:formatNumber>`. Parses a number or date.

Syntax
Without a body

```
<fmt:parseNumber
      value="numericValue"
      [type="{number|currency|percent}"]
      [pattern="customPattern"]
      [parseLocale="parseLocale"]
      [integerOnly="{true|false}"]
      [var="varName"]
      [scope="{page|request|session|application}"]
      />
```

Syntax

With a body containing the numeric value to be parsed

```
<fmt:parseNumber
      [type="{number|currency|percent}"]
      [pattern="customPattern"]
      [parseLocale="parseLocale"]
      [integerOnly="{true|false}"]
      [var="varName"]
      [scope="{page|request|session|application}"]>
   numeric value to be parsed
</fmt:parseNumber>
```

Attributes

- **value**   The string to be parsed.
- **type**   Number, currency, or percentage.
- **pattern**   A custom formatting pattern.
- **parseLocale**   An optional parsing locale.
- **integerOnly**   If true, indicates that just the integer portion of the given value should be parsed.
- **var**   The name of a variable to hold the result.
- **scope**   The scope of var.

`<fmt:formatDate>`

Formats a date in the manner used by `java.text.DateFormat`.

Syntax

```
<fmt:formatDate
      value="date"
      [type="{time|date|both}"]
      [dateStyle="{default|short|medium|long|full}"]
      [timeStyle="{default|short|medium|long|full}"]
      [pattern="customPattern"]
      [timeZone="timeZone"]
      [var="varName"]
      [scope="{page|request|session|application}"]
      />
```

Attributes

- **value** The date and/or time to be formatted.
- **type** Whether to format the date, the time, or both.
- **dateStyle** A predefined formatting style for dates.
- **timeStyle** A predefined formatting style for times.
- **pattern** A custom formatting style for dates and times.

`<fmt:parseDate>`

Parse date strings into `Date` objects.

Syntax
Without a body

```
<fmt:parseDate
    value="dateString"
    [type="{time|date|both}"]
    [dateStyle="{default|short|medium|long|full}"]
    [timeStyle="{default|short|medium|long|full}"]
    [pattern="customPattern"]
    [timeZone="timeZone"]
    [parseLocale="parseLocale"]
    [var="varName"]
    [scope="{page|request|session|application}"]
    />
```

Syntax
With a body supplying the date

```
<fmt:parseDate
    [type="{time|date|both}"]
    [dateStyle="{default|short|medium|long|full}"]
    [timeStyle="{default|short|medium|long|full}"]
    [pattern="customPattern"]
    [timeZone="timeZone"]
    [parseLocale="parseLocale"]
    [var="varName"]
    [scope="{page|request|session|application}"]>
    date value to be parsed
</fmt:parseDate>
```

JSP TAG EXTENSIONS

Attributes

- **value**   The date string to be parsed.
- **type**   Date, time, or both.
- **dateStyle**   The date style, as used with `java.util.SimpleDateFormat`.
- **timeStyle**   The time style, as used with `java.util.SimpleDateFormat`.
- **pattern**   A custom formatting pattern.
- **timeZone**   The time zone implied for the date.
- **parseLocale**   The default locale.
- **var**   The name of a variable to receive the new Date object.
- **scope**   The variable scope.

Summary

This chapter covered the preliminary release of JSTL in the JSP 2.0 environment. It outlines the motivation for JSTL and who can benefit from using it. There are four `taglibs` that compose JSTL:

1. Core programming constructs
2. XML parsing and transformation
3. SQL for relational database access
4. Formatting (I18N)

The chapter gives information about the syntax and attributes of each one. For detailed information about any tag, please see the JSTL or JSP specifications.

The Complete Reference

Chapter 14

Simple Tag Extensions, Tag Files, and JSP Fragments

As useful as JSP custom tags are, their configuration and development environment is fairly complex. JSP scriptlets and declarations complicate things with a raft of assumptions about the tag lifecycle. Because tag handlers can be cached, the developer needs to consider attribute state between invocations. In addition, tag development and testing generally involves frequent restarts of the Web application because of tag library descriptor changes.

JSP 2.0 introduces several features that make things simpler. The *JSP Standard Tag Library (JSTL)* and *Expression Language (EL)* reduce the amount of Java code a JSP page needs to use, sometimes to zero. Moreover, custom tags have a new, simpler protocol: *Simple Tag Extensions.* These tag handlers generally need to implement only a single method called `doTag()`, rather than the three or four lifecycle methods required by classic tag handlers. They can be written in two ways:

- In Java, by implementing the `SimpleTag` interface.
- In pure JSP syntax, using tag files.

Simple tags extensions have access to the body of a tag in the form of an object that implements the `JspFragment` interface. In this chapter, we'll examine JSP fragments, the `SimpleTag` interface, and tag files, developing an example in both Java and JSP syntax.

Note *The JSP 2.0 specification and API were still undergoing last-minute changes after the proposed final draft. The examples in this chapter were done with the most recent version of the reference implementation available. Do not use them in JSP code to run a nuclear power plant without checking the final specification.*

JSP Fragments

A JSP fragment is an object that represents a chunk of JSP code that can be invoked as needed by a tag handler. The fragment object is an instance of the `javax.servlet.jsp.tagext.JspFragment` class, which has only one method:

```
public void invoke(Writer out) throws JspException, IOException
```

You can use any `java.io.Writer` subclass for the `out` parameter. For example, you could create a `StringWriter` to capture the output, manipulate it further, and then send it to the output stream. You can also set the `out` parameter to `null`, in which case the current `JspContext.getOut()` writer will be used.

The JSP container provides the implementation of the `JspFragment` class. You should not need to write an implementing class.

Fragments Used as Tag Bodies

A JSP fragment can be the body of a custom tag, one that implements the `SimpleTag` interface:

```
<my:environment>
   <table>
      <tr>
         <th>Name</th>
         <th>Value</th>
      </tr>
      <c:forEach items="${env}" var="entry">
         <tr>
            <td> ${entry.name} </td>
            <td> ${entry.value} </td>
         </tr>
      </c:forEach>
   </table>
</my:environment>
```

In this example, if `<my:environment>` is a tag whose handler implements `SimpleTag` (or if it is a tag defined by a JSP tag file, which we'll examine shortly), then `<table>`, `</table>`, and all the HTML and JSP elements between them constitute the JSP fragment. An object representing this fragment will be passed to the tag handler, which can invoke it zero or more times and send its output to the JSP output stream.

Fragments Used as Attribute Values

A JSP fragment can also be the value of an attribute of a custom tag or JSP standard action. For example, the properties of a JavaBean could be set with a mix of static and dynamic operations like this:

```
<jsp:useBean id="report" class="com.jspcr.report.BalanceSheet">

   <jsp:setProperty name="report" property="title"
       value="Balance Sheet"/>

   <jsp:setProperty name="report" property="date">
      <jsp:attribute name="value">
         <my:dateCalculator/>
      </jsp:attribute>
   </jsp:setProperty>

</jsp:useBean>
```

Here, the `title` property is set from a fixed string in the `value` attribute. The `date` property, however, is calculated at runtime by some hypothetical custom tag `<my:dateCalculator/>`. You can't use a custom tag directly in an attribute value, but you can use it in the body of a `<jsp:attribute>` tag, which then becomes the

JSP TAG EXTENSIONS

value of the value attribute in the containing <jsp:setProperty> tag. Note that <jsp:attribute> works only for JSP tags, not for ordinary HTML, which is simple text from the standpoint of the JSP container.

The alternative to <jsp:attribute> in the preceding example might involve an intermediate variable and the Expression Language, as shown here:

```
<jsp:useBean id="report" class="com.jspcr.report.BalanceSheet">

   <jsp:setProperty name="report" property="title"
         value="Balance Sheet"/>

   <c:set var="date">
      <my:dateCalculator/>
   </c:set>

   <jsp:setProperty name="report" property="date"
         value="${date}"/>

</jsp:useBean>
```

The SimpleTag Interface

The Tag, BodyTag, and IterationTag interfaces used in the JSP 1.1 and 1.2 API[1] are still supported in JSP 2.0; however, as JSP has matured, it has become apparent that they can be fairly complex to develop and implement. New in JSP 2.0 are the SimpleTag interface and its SimpleTagSupport default implementation. This interface has two key simplifications:

1. In place of the doStartTag(), doInitBody(), doAfterBody(), and doEndTag() lifecycle methods, there is only one: doTag().

2. SimpleTag objects are not cached; they are newly created for each invocation.

Rather than providing callbacks for each point in the evaluation of a tag, you get the whole tag at once, body and attributes. Attributes are passed with individual setter methods as usual, but the body is made available as a JspFragment object.

SimpleTag does not extend the Tag interface; instead, both interfaces extend the new JspTag interface, a marker interface that defines no methods. This complicates the idea of parent tags a bit, since the Tag getParent() and setParent() methods explicitly use Tag as their data type. For this reason, the JSP 2.0 API includes a

---

[1]   These tag handlers are euphemistically referred to as "classic" tag handlers in the JSP 2.0 specification.

Method	Description
`void doTag() throws JspException, IOException`	Called by the JSP container to invoke the tag handler.
`JspTag getParent()`	Returns the containing tag, if one exists.
`void setParent(JspTag tag)`	Provides the tag handler with a reference to the containing tag.
`void setJspContext(JspContext ctx)`	Passes the JSP context object to the tag handler.
`void setJspBody(JspFragment body)`	Makes the tag body available to the tag handler as a JSP fragment.

Table 14-1.   *Methods in the SimpleTag Interface*

`TagAdapter` class that wraps a `SimpleTag` and makes it operate like a classic custom tag. The `PageContext` class has also been refactored to separate the attribute handling methods from the servlet- and HTTP-specific methods. The attribute handling is now in `JspContext`, which is the immediate superinterface of `PageContext`.

Table 14-1 lists the methods that comprise the `SimpleTag` interface.

SimpleTag Lifecycle

The semantics of the `SimpleTag` interface are similar to those of the classic tag interface, with the main difference being that the handler drives the logic rather than supplying callbacks that are invoked by the calling servlet. The lifecycle consists of the following steps, in this order:

1. The JSP container creates the tag handler by calling its zero-argument constructor. `SimpleTag` objects are not cached, so their attributes are not polluted by previous incantations.

2. The container calls `setJspContext()`, passing the JSP context object. This provides the tag handler with access to the page attributes, expression evaluator, and variable resolver. The default `SimpleTagSupport` helper class will automatically store this reference; if you extend `SimpleTag` directly, you'll need to do the same.

3. The container calls the tag handler's `setParent()` method, enabling a tag to interact with its containing tag(s). This is useful in tag collaboration in which you want to use implicit contextual relationships rather than scripting variables.

`SimpleTagSupport` provides the basic get and set handling of the parent object. It also provides a `findAncestorWithClass()` method analogous to the one provided by `BodyTagSupport`.

4. For each attribute X coded in this invocation of the tag, the container calls the corresponding `setX()` method.

5. The tag body is passed as a JSP fragment in the `setJspBody()` method.

6. Finally, the container calls `doTag()`. Note that there is no return value as in `doStartTag()` or `doEndTag()`. If you need to skip the rest of the page, you throw a `SkipPageException`.

SimpleTag Interface Example

To make things a little clearer, let's rework an example from Chapter 13, the Fahrenheit-to-Celsius conversion table. You may recall that we used the JSTL `<c:forEach>` tag to loop over a range of temperatures, converting Fahrenheit to Celsius with an Expression Language (EL) calculation. Here, we'll use a `SimpleTag` handler to do the iteration, and a JSP fragment to create the HTML table rows. This may or may not be any simpler, but it is a workable illustration of the `SimpleTag` technique.

```
<%@ page session="false" %>
<%@ taglib prefix="jspcr" uri="/WEB-INF/chap14.tld" %>
<html>
   <head>
      <title>Temperature Conversion Table (SimpleTag)</title>
      <link rel="stylesheet" type="text/css" href="style.css"/>
   </head>
   <body>
      <center>
      <h1>Temperature Conversion Table</h1>
      <h2><i>(Powered by SimpleTags)</i></h2>
      <table border="1" cellpadding="3" cellspacing="0">
         <tr>
            <th align="right" width="100">Fahrenheit</th>
            <th align="right" width="100">Celsius</th>
         </tr>
         <jspcr:toCelsius from="32" to="212" by="20">
            <tr>
               <td align="right">${f}</td>
               <td align="right">${c}</td>
            </tr>
         </jspcr:toCelsius>
```

```
      </table>
      </center>
   </body>
</html>
```

The custom tag is `toCelsius`, which takes three attributes:

- **from**   The starting temperature in degrees Fahrenheit
- **to**   The ending temperature
- **by**   The loop increment value

The body of the tag consists of the HTML tags that generate one row of the table, with cells for the temperature in both scales. This will be passed as a `JspFragment` object to the tag handler, which will invoke it after doing the necessary calculation and formatting. Here is the tag handler:

```
package com.jspcr.simpletags;

import java.io.*;
import java.text.*;
import java.util.*;
import javax.servlet.*;
import javax.servlet.jsp.*;
import javax.servlet.jsp.tagext.*;

/**
* Simple tag handler that calculates the Celsius equivalent
* of a range of Fahrenheit temperatures and invokes a
* JSP fragment to display them.
*/
public class F2CSimpleTag extends SimpleTagSupport
{
    /**
    * Attributes (from, to, by) and their getters
    * and setters
    */
    private int from;
    public int getFrom() { return from; }
    public void setFrom(int from) { this.from = from; }

    private int to;
```

```
public int getTo() { return to; }
public void setTo(int to) { this.to = to; }

private int by;
public int getBy() { return by; }
public void setBy(int by) { this.by = by; }

/**
 * Default constructor
 */
public F2CSimpleTag()
{
    super();
}

/**
 * Processs the tag invocation
 */
public void doTag() throws JspException, IOException
{
    DecimalFormat fmt = new DecimalFormat("##0.00");

    for (
        int degrees = getFrom();
        degrees <= getTo();
        degrees += getBy())
    {
        // Calculate the Celsius value

        double c = (degrees - 32) * 5 / 9.0;

        // Create the variables used by the JSP fragment

        JspContext ctx = getJspContext();
        ctx.setAttribute("f", String.valueOf(degrees));
        ctx.setAttribute("c", fmt.format(c));

        // Invoke the fragment

        JspFragment fragment = getJspBody();
        fragment.invoke(null);
```

```
        }
    }
}
```

The getter and setter methods for the three attributes are the same as you would write for a classic tag handler. The real difference is the doTag() method, which does the following:

- Creates a DecimalFormatter for the Celsius temperature. The Fahrenheit values in this case are all integers, so there are no particular formatting requirements.

- Iterates over the range of temperatures in a for loop, performing the following steps for each loop iteration:

  - Calculates the Celsius temperature.

  - Creates f and c variables as attributes in the page context. Note that these must be objects, not int or double primitives. Here, we convert both of them to strings, f with String.valueOf() and c with the formatter's format() method. These variables must be declared in the tag library descriptor to make them available to the JSP page.

  - Calls getJspBody() to get the JSP fragment that encapsulates the tag body, then executes it by calling its invoke() method. We use null as the parameter to invoke() so that the output will go to the JSP output stream. We could also use a StringWriter or some other java.io.Writer to capture the output rather than passing it on to the output stream.

The last thing we need to do is write the TLD:

```
<?xml version="1.0" encoding="UTF-8" ?>

<taglib
    xmlns="http://java.sun.com/xml/ns/j2ee"
    xmlns:xsi="http://www.w3.org/2001/XMLSchema-instance"
    xsi:schemaLocation=
    "http://java.sun.com/xml/ns/j2ee web-jsptaglibrary_2_0.xsd"
    version="2.0">

    <description>Tag handlers for Chapter 14</description>
    <tlib-version>1.0</tlib-version>
    <short-name>Chap14</short-name>
    <uri>/Chap14</uri>
```

```
<tag>
    <description>Generates F2C table</description>
    <name>toCelsius</name>
    <tag-class>com.jspcr.simpletags.F2CSimpleTag</tag-class>
    <body-content>JSP</body-content>

    <attribute>
        <name>from</name>
        <required>true</required>
    </attribute>

    <attribute>
        <name>to</name>
        <required>true</required>
    </attribute>

    <attribute>
        <name>by</name>
        <required>true</required>
    </attribute>

    <variable>
        <name-given>f</name-given>
    </variable>

    <variable>
        <name-given>c</name-given>
    </variable>

</tag>

</taglib>
```

The format of the TLD is covered in Chapter 11. It is also helpful to review the documentation incorporated in the XML schema if you have detailed questions about some element. Briefly, the key elements here are the tag name, the tag handler class name, and the attribute and variable definitions.

Once you've compiled the tag handler and copied the TLD to the /WEB-INF directory, you should see the results shown in Figure 14-1.

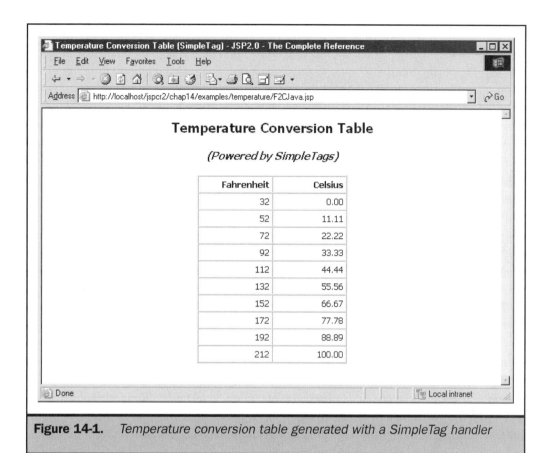

Figure 14-1. *Temperature conversion table generated with a SimpleTag handler*

Tag Files

It gets even better—you can write `SimpleTag` handlers entirely in JSP, with no Java code or even a TLD. This capability is provided by *tag files*.

A tag file is a text file in a slightly modified JSP format, one that allows you to define a single custom tag and specify the attributes it supports and any scripting variables it creates. Certain JSP directives and actions are valid only in JSP pages or in tag files; most are available in both. Here are the highlights:

- The `<%@ page %>` directive is not valid in tag files because they are not JSP pages. The equivalent directive for tag files is `<%@ tag %>`, whose attributes are listed in Table 14-2.

Attribute	Description
display-name	Short name for the tag, intended for use by tools.
body-content	How the tag body should be interpreted: "empty", "tagdependent", or "scriptless".
dynamic-attributes	True if the tag supports attributes whose names are supplied at runtime.
small-icon	Filename for a 16 × 16 icon representing this tag.
large-icon	Filename for a 32 × 32 icon representing this tag.
description	You guessed it.
example	An optional syntax string.
language	Same as the tag directive language attribute.
import	Same as the tag directive import attribute.
pageEncoding	Same as the tag directive pageEncoding attribute.
isScriptingEnabled	Same as the tag directive isScriptingEnabled attribute.
isELEnabled	Same as the tag directive isELEnabled attribute.

Table 14-2.   *Attributes of the tag Directive (all optional)*

- An `<%@ attribute %>` directive is specified for each attribute supported by the tag. See Table 14-3 for details.
- Similarly, a `<%@ variable %>` directive is used for each scripting variable defined. Table 14-4 lists the details of the variable directive.
- The `<jsp:invoke fragment="name">` action is used to run a named JSP fragment.[2]
- The `<jsp:doBody/>` action does the same as `<jsp:invoke/>`, except that it operates on the tag body rather than a named fragment.

---

[2]   The exact syntax and semantics of `<jsp:invoke>` were unstable at the time of this writing. See the final JSP 2.0 specification.

Attribute	Description
name	The attribute name as it appears in the tag.
required	(Optional) True if the attribute is required. Default is true.
fragment	(Optional) True if the attribute must contain a `JspFragment`. Forces `rtexprvalue` to be `true` and `type` to be `javax.servlet.jsp.tagext.JspFragment`. Default is `false`.
rtexprvalue	(Optional) True if the attribute may contain a runtime expression. Default is `false`.
type	(Optional) The class name of the attribute's type. Defaults to `java.lang.String`.
description	(Optional) Attribute description.

Table 14-3. *Attributes of the attribute Directive*

Attribute	Description
name-given	The name of the scripting variable that will be visible to the invoking script. Either this attribute or `name-from-attribute` must be specified, but not both.
name-from-attribute	Name of the attribute containing the variable name. Either this attribute or `name-given` must be specified, but not both.
variable-class	(Optional) Name of the variable's class. Defaults to `java.lang.String`.
scope	(Optional) The scope of the variable definition: `AT_BEGIN`, `AT_END`, or `NESTED`. Default is `NESTED`.
declare	(Optional) True if the JSP container should generate a declaration for this variable in the generated servlet code. Default is true.
fragment	(Optional) Name of an attribute of type `JspFragment` whose value should be synchronized with this variable.
description	(Optional) The variable description.

Table 14-4. *Attributes of the variable Directive*

Tag File Configuration and Usage

A tag file can reside either in the /META-INF/tags directory of a jar file in /WEB-INF/
lib, or directly in the /WEB-INF/tags directory (or one of its subdirectories). The
name of the file (minus its .tag extension) becomes the name of the tag as it's used in
a JSP page. The <%@ taglib %> directive is slightly different:

```
<%@ taglib prefix="prefix" tagdir="/WEB-INF/tags" %>
```

where tagdir points to the *directory* in which the tag file resides (not the file itself).
Thus, if the tag name is connect, the tag file would be

```
$webapp/WEB-INF/tags/connect.tag
```

and a JSP page that uses it would contain the following:

```
<%@ taglib prefix="db" tagdir="/WEB-INF/tags"
...
<db:connect/>
```

Tag File Example

We conclude this chapter with the same example as for SimpleTag, this time written
in JSP as a tag file. The JSP page is exactly the same except for the taglib directive at
the top of the page:

```
<%@ taglib prefix="jspcr" tagdir="/WEB-INF/tags" %>
```

This illustrates one of the strengths of the SimpleTag interface: it makes the
implementation of the tag transparent. The same tag can be written in either JSP or
Java without involving significant rework on the part of the page author.

The tag file looks like this:

```
<%-- Declare the JSTL taglibs being used --%>

<%@ taglib prefix="c" uri="http://java.sun.com/jstl/core_rt" %>
<%@ taglib prefix="fmt" uri="http://java.sun.com/jstl/fmt_rt" %>

<%-- Declare the attributes use by the custom tag --%>

<%@ attribute name="from" %>
```

```
<%@ attribute name="to" %>
<%@ attribute name="by" %>

<%-- Declare variables used in this tag handler --%>

<%@ variable name-given="f" %>
<%@ variable name-given="c" %>

<%-- Loop over the range of temperatures specified --%>

<c:forEach var="degrees" begin="${from}" end="${to}" step="${by}">

   <%-- Set the values of the variables used
        in the JSP fragment --%>

   <c:set var="f" value="${degrees}"/>
   <c:set var="c">
      <fmt:formatNumber pattern="##0.00">
         ${(f - 32) * 5 / 9.0}
      </fmt:formatNumber>
   </c:set>

   <%-- Invoke the JSP fragment --%>

   <jsp:doBody/>

</c:forEach>
```

The substance and actions of the tag file are similar to the SimpleTag version. The tag file contains:

- The taglib directives for the JSTL libraries used in the tag handler
- Attribute declarations for the three attributes supported by the tag
- Variable declarations for the two scripting variables (f and c)
- A <c:forEach> loop over the specified range
- For each iteration, <c:set> actions to make variables available to the JSP fragment when it is invoked
- A <jsp:doBody/> tag to cause the fragment to be invoked

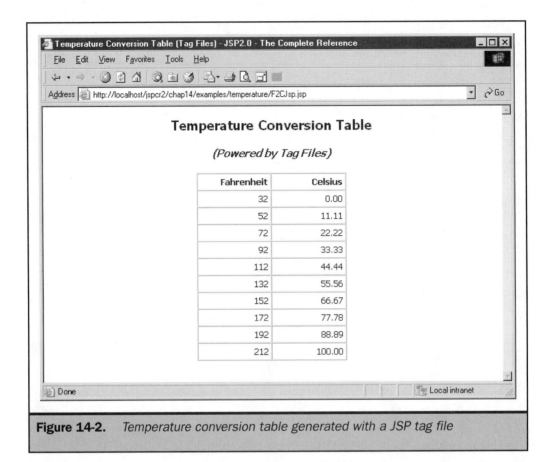

Figure 14-2. *Temperature conversion table generated with a JSP tag file*

No TLD is required for this tag; it need only be copied to the /WEB-INF/tags directory of the Web application to be made available. The results, shown in Figure 14-2, are the same as for the SimpleTag version.

Summary

JSP custom tags are quite useful but can be complicated to develop. JSP 2.0 introduces a new SimpleTag interface, which makes it possible to separate content and presentation more easily than before. Simple tags can be written in two ways:

1. In Java by implementing SimpleTag or extending SimpleTagSupport
2. In JSP using tag files

Armed with these tools, tag developers and page authors can apply their skills to develop robust and modular components for the Web application environment.

The
Complete
Reference

Part IV

JSP Applications

The Complete Reference

Chapter 15

Database Access with JDBC

The corporate database is the heart of the business, and most JSP pages of any consequence need access to it. Web sites for online retailers make their catalogs available for browsing. Theater Web pages may list show times and movie information. Search engines prompt for keywords and return sets of matching links.

In addition to read-only access, many JSP pages act as front ends to applications that store data as well. In a shopping cart checkout function, lists of items to be ordered must be converted into transactions that are processed by other systems: order fulfillment, shipping, and accounting.

Java provides a comprehensive and general-purpose means for handling database use with a technology known as JDBC. *JDBC* makes communication possible with a wide variety of database management systems using SQL.[1] This chapter contains an overview of JDBC and how it can be used in Web-based applications. It covers JDBC drivers, how to connect to a database, how to execute SQL statements, and how to read their results. It describes JDBC's mechanisms for robust transaction handling and connection pooling. Throughout the chapter, complete examples are given to illustrate key points.

Overview of JDBC

JDBC is an application programming interface between Java programs and database management systems. Like Oracle's *Oracle Call Interface (OCI)* or Microsoft's *Open Database Connectivity (ODBC)*, JDBC is a call-level interface. This means a program uses method or function calls to access its features, as opposed to embedded SQL statements, which are translated by a precompiler.

A programmer uses a Java class known as a *JDBC driver* to connect to a database. Hundreds of JDBC drivers exist—at least one for each widely used database, whether commercial or shareware. A special JDBC driver, known as the *JDBC-ODBC bridge*, makes using ODBC as an intermediary possible, which makes the vast number of ODBC drivers usable from JDBC.

The great advantage of JDBC is that it provides a standard interface to all database management systems. JDBC queries that work on an Oracle database require few or no changes to work with DB2, or SQL Server, or any other database. The few differences that remain usually have to do with data type names and support for certain operation types. Even these differences can usually be resolved programmatically using metadata provided by the JDBC connection.

JDBC also eases the transition from legacy systems to Web-enabled applications. Embedded SQL products, which have been around since the early 1980s, for the most part use SQL statements and operations that can be duplicated by JDBC calls. The syntax and semantics of SQL statements in a batch mainframe COBOL application require few changes when the applications are converted to Java.

---

[1] SQL is a topic large enough to fill several books. One of the best is SQL: *The Complete Reference,* by James R. Groff & Paul N. Weinberg, published by Osborne/McGraw-Hill, ISBN 0-07-211845-8.

JDBC API Versions

Like any other successful programming environment, JDBC has evolved since its early days. It emerged in early 1996 as an add-on to the JDK. With the aid of the JDBC-ODBC bridge, it quickly leveraged the pervasive acceptance of Microsoft's ODBC API to establish itself as a widely available and supported database API. Version 1.1 was included as a standard package (the java.sql package) with JDK 1.1. The Java 2 JDK included JDBC 1.2, which is the base level that you can usually assume is supported by all JDBC drivers.

The JDBC 2.0 Core API is the most full-featured level that is widely used, and it is the basis for all the examples in this chapter. Although JDBC 3.0 is officially part of the Java 2 SDK 1.4, few database drivers support it yet, but that will no doubt change over time.

In practice, the particular set of supported features varies from driver to driver and database to database. The main thing to keep in mind is that JDBC supports a wide variety of forms of metadata access that can tell you exactly which features are supported by the database and driver you are using. This allows you to write robust code that can adapt to its operating environment.

Basic JDBC Operations

Working with JDBC isn't difficult. Depending on the task to be performed, usually only four steps are required:

1. Load a JDBC driver for your DBMS. This typically involves only a `Class.forName()` statement specifying the driver class name.

2. Use that driver to open a connection to a particular database. This is done with a call to a static `getConnection(url)` method to the `DriverManager` class. The `url` argument is in a specific form that indicates the driver type and the data source to use.

3. Issue SQL statements through the connection. Once the connection is established, it can be used to create `Statement` objects through which SQL commands can be made.

4. Process result sets returned by the SQL operations. The `ResultSet` interface provides methods to step through each row and get the values of each column.

Not shown but very important—close all the JDBC objects, including the connection, statement, result set, etc.) Figure 15-1 illustrates these four steps.

Since JDBC 2.0, there is a bit more flexibility. Using *Java Naming and Directory Interface (JNDI)*, an application can look up a `DataSource` object by name from a naming service, rather than hard-coding the driver class name and database URL. Additionally, result sets have more capabilities. They can be accessed in random order rather than sequentially from start to finish. They can be updated and have the updates propagated back to the underlying table. They can also be dynamically linked to their base table(s) so that changes

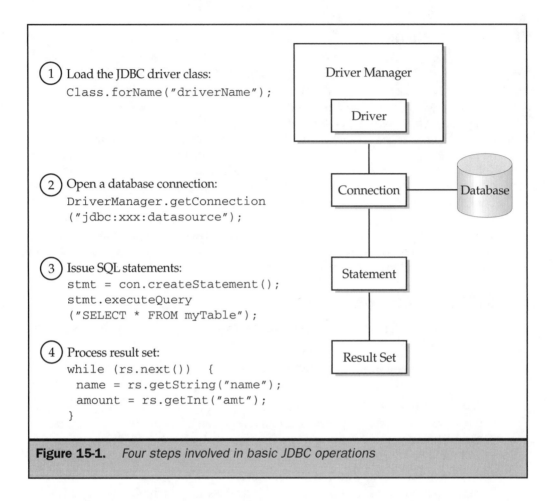

Figure 15-1. *Four steps involved in basic JDBC operations*

there are reflected concurrently in the result set. Figure 15-2 shows the basic steps involved in database access through a JNDI data source.

Essential JDBC Classes

The JDBC interface is contained in the java.sql and javax.sql packages. It consists mainly of interfaces rather than concrete classes because each vendor's implementation is specific to their particular database protocol. The core API in java.sql consists of 18 interfaces, seven classes, and four exception types. The server-side javax.sql API adds another 12 interfaces and two classes. Many of these classes are of interest

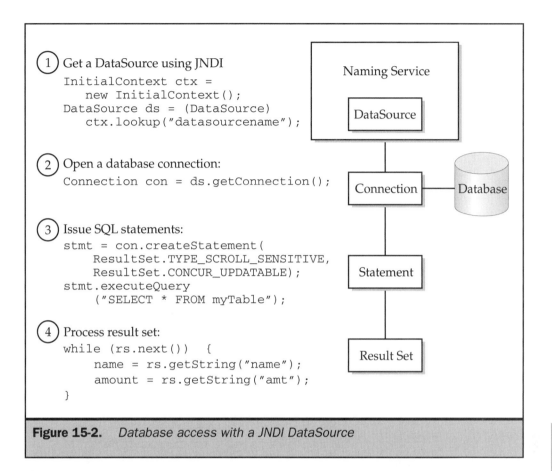

```
1  Get a DataSource using JNDI
   InitialContext ctx =
      new InitialContext();
   DataSource ds = (DataSource)
      ctx.lookup("datasourcename");

2  Open a database connection:
   Connection con = ds.getConnection();

3  Issue SQL statements:
   stmt = con.createStatement(
       ResultSet.TYPE_SCROLL_SENSITIVE,
       ResultSet.CONCUR_UPDATABLE);
   stmt.executeQuery
       ("SELECT * FROM myTable");

4  Process result set:
   while (rs.next())   {
       name = rs.getString("name");
       amount = rs.getString("amt");
   }
```

Naming Service

DataSource

Connection — Database

Statement

Result Set

Figure 15-2. *Database access with a JNDI DataSource*

primarily to JDBC driver developers. A smaller subset of these is more commonly used, as outlined in the following:

- **Connection** An active link to a database through which a Java program can read and write data, as well as explore the database structure and capabilities. A Connection object is created by a call to either DriverManager.get Connection() or DataSource.getConnection().

- **Statement** An object that allows SQL statements to be sent through a connection and retrieves the result sets and update counts they produce. Three types of statements exist, each one a specialization of its predecessors:

  - **Statement** Used to execute static SQL strings. A Statement is created with Connection.createStatement().

- **PreparedStatement** An extension of Statement that uses precompiled SQL, possibly with dynamically set input parameters. PreparedStatement objects are often used in a loop with SQL insert operations. They are created with Connection.prepareStatement(*sqlstring*).

- **CallableStatement** A PreparedStatement that invokes a stored procedure. Not all database management systems support stored procedures, but for those that do, CallableStatement provides a standard invocation syntax.

- **ResultSet** An ordered set of table rows produced by an SQL query or a call to certain metadata functions. A ResultSet is most often encountered as the return value of a Statement.executeQuery(*sqlstring*) method call. The JDBC API provides methods for iterating through the rows of a ResultSet and for extracting the column values.

- **DatabaseMetaData** An interface containing numerous methods that provide information about the structure and capabilities of a database. The DatabaseMetaData object is returned by the getMetaData() method of a Connection object.

- **ResultSetMetaData** An interface that describes the columns of a ResultSet. This can be obtained by calling the result set's getMetaData() method. It contains methods that describe the number of columns, as well as each column's name, display size, data type, and class name.

- **DriverManager** A class that registers JDBC drivers and supplies connections that can handle specific JDBC URLs. The only method commonly used is the static DriverManager.getConnection(), in one of its three forms, which returns an active Connection object bound to the specified JDBC URL.

- **SQLException** The base exception class used by the JDBC API. SQLException has methods that can supply the SQLState value any vendor-specific error code. It can also be linked to another SQLException if more than one exception occurred.

One of the stated goals of the JDBC API was that it should be simple and easy to master. Learning these seven classes and three or four of their main methods can easily be done in a few days, which has helped to make JDBC a popular and well-accepted technology.

A Simple JDBC Example

Let's consider an example of JDBC used in a JSP page. Our hypothetical LyricNote company maintains an internal employee database containing two tables: departments and employees. These tables were created with the following SQL statements:

```
CREATE TABLE departments (
    deptno      CHAR(2),
    deptname    CHAR(40),
```

```
    deptmgr      CHAR(4)
);
```

and

```
CREATE TABLE employees (
    empno        CHAR(4),
    lname        CHAR(20),
    fname        CHAR(20),
    hiredate     DATE,
    ismgr        BIT,
    deptno       CHAR(2),
    title        CHAR(50),
    email        CHAR(32),
    phone        CHAR(4)
);
```

Note   *The SQL shown here was used with the MySQL database. While SQL is fairly standard, the data type names in particular vary between implementations, as does the syntax of the data type declarations. If you are designing for a specific database, you may choose not to worry about this. If you need a more generic solution (at the cost of a little more complexity), you can use the DatabaseMetaData class described later in this chapter to make your SQL adapt to its environment. An excellent reference in this regard is* Java Servlets, 2nd Edition, *by Karl Moss, published by McGraw-Hill/Osborne, ISBN 0-07-1351884.*

Our example JSP page displays a list of departments identifying their manager's name, title, telephone number, and e-mail address. The SQL to assemble this list is as follows:

```
SELECT    D.deptname, E.fname, E.lname, E.title, E.email, E.phone
FROM      departments D, employees E
WHERE     D.deptmgr = E.empno
ORDER BY D.deptname
```

The D and E prefixes are pseudotable names used to qualify column names, so the DBMS can distinguish which table supplies which columns.

The complete source code for ShowDept.jsp is

```
<%@ page session="false" %>
<%@ page import="java.sql.*" %>
```

JSP APPLICATIONS

```
<%@ page import="java.util.*" %>

<html>
<head>
<title>Department Managers</title>
</head>
<body style="font-size: 9pt;">
<img src="images/lyric_note.png" border="0"/>
<hr/>
<h1 style="font-size: 130%;">
   Department Managers
</h1>
<%
   String DRIVER = "org.gjt.mm.mysql.Driver";
   String URL = "jdbc:mysql://localhost/lyricnote";

   // Open a database connection

   Class.forName(DRIVER);
   Connection con = null;
   try {

      con = DriverManager.getConnection(URL);

      // Get department manager information

      String sql = ""
         + " SELECT    D.deptname, E.fname, E.lname,"
         + "           E.title, E.email, E.phone"
         + " FROM      departments D, employees E"
         + " WHERE     D.deptmgr = E.empno"
         + " ORDER BY D.deptname"
         ;

      Statement stmt = con.createStatement();
      ResultSet rs = stmt.executeQuery(sql);
%>
<dl>
<%
      while (rs.next()) {
         String dept  = rs.getString(1);
         String fname = rs.getString(2);
```

```
            String lname = rs.getString(3);
            String title = rs.getString(4);
            String email = rs.getString(5);
            String phone = rs.getString(6);
%>
<dt><b><%= dept %></b></dt>
<dd>
   <%= fname %> <%= lname %>, <%= title %><br>
   (919) 555-0822 x<%= phone %>, <%= email %>
</dd>
<%
        }
        rs.close();
        rs = null;

        stmt.close();
        stmt = null;
    }
    finally {
        if (con != null) {
            con.close();
        }
    }
%>
</dl>
</body>
</html>
```

Let's examine each section.
To begin with, there are three page directives:

```
<%@ page session="false" %>
<%@ page import="java.sql.*" %>
<%@ page import="java.util.*" %>
```

We explicitly request that no HTTP session should be created. This should be done in all JSP pages that don't require access to a session, because it saves the server resources required to establish and maintain the session.

After the HTML that creates the page headings, a scriptlet interrogates the LyricNote internal database and displays the results. It begins with the declaration of two string constants that define the JDBC driver name and database URL.[2] For convenience, keep this information isolated in a declarations section for ease of modification:

```
String DRIVER = "org.gjt.mm.mysql.Driver";
String URL = "jdbc:mysql://localhost/lyricnote";
```

The real work begins with the next statements:

```
Class.forName(DRIVER);
Connection con = null;
try {
    con = DriverManager.getConnection(URL);
    ...
}
```

The `Class.forName()` call causes the JDBC driver class to be loaded. According to the JDBC specification, drivers must include a static initialization section that causes an instance to be created and registered with the driver manager. A peek at the source code for MM.MySQL will verify that it complies with this requirement. A few ill-behaved drivers fail to do this, and in that case, invoking the `newInstance()` method on the driver class is necessary. The `DriverManager` class provides the actual connection in response to the call to its static `getConnection()` method.

Note that the `con` variable that holds a reference to the connection is declared and assigned a `null` value. Then the rest of the page is enclosed in a `try {...}` block followed by

```
finally {
    if (con != null) {
        con.close();
    }
}
```

The reason for this is that once opened, the connection needs to be closed, regardless of whether any errors occur or exceptions are thrown. This can be guaranteed by the `finally { ... }` block. Including a `catch` block is unnecessary. If it is not present,

---

[2]   The examples in this book use the MySQL database, version 3.23.51, and the MM.MySQL 2.0.14 JDBC driver. MySQL is a widely used, open source, free, fast, and full-featured database server that you can download from http://www.mysql.com. There are several JDBC drivers available for MySQL; MM.MySQL is freely available at http://mmmysql.sourceforge.net. The combination of this DBMS and driver is very popular.

exceptions will be thrown to the calling method. In our case, the default exception handler for the Web page is good enough.

Once the connection is established, the SQL query can be run. For this, we call the `Connection` object's `createStatement()` method to obtain a `Statement` object, on which we can invoke the `executeQuery()` method.

```
String sql = ""
   + " SELECT    D.deptname, E.fname, E.lname,"
   + "           E.title, E.email, E.phone"
   + " FROM      departments D, employees E"
   + " WHERE     D.deptmgr = E.empno"
   + " ORDER BY D.deptname"
   ;

Statement stmt = con.createStatement();
ResultSet rs = stmt.executeQuery(sql);
```

The `executeQuery()` method returns a `ResultSet`. We read each row of this set by invoking its `next()` method in a loop:

```
while (rs.next()) {
        String dept  = rs.getString(1);
        String fname = rs.getString(2);
        String lname = rs.getString(3);
        String title = rs.getString(4);
        String email = rs.getString(5);
        String phone = rs.getString(6);
%>
<dt><b><%= dept %></b></dt>
<dd>
   <%= fname %> <%= lname %>, <%= title %><br/>
   (919) 555-0822 x<%= phone %>, <%= email %>
</dd>
<%
        }
```

Inside the loop, we extract each column value with the `ResultSet.getString` (*columnNumber*) method, and then format and print the department name, manager name, title, telephone number, and e-mail lines.

Finally, we close all the JDBC objects we created and set their references to `null`, so that they can be garbage collected.

```
rs.close();
rs = null;

stmt.close();
stmt = null;
```

The Connection object is closed in the finally { . . . } block previously discussed.

The finished product is shown in Figure 15-3.

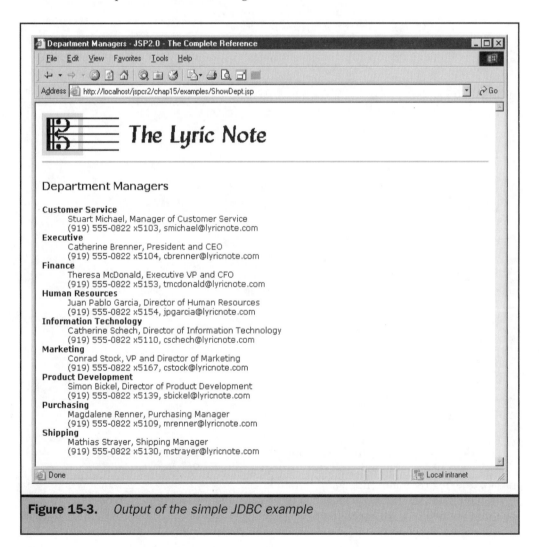

Figure 15-3. *Output of the simple JDBC example*

JDBC Drivers

To insulate programs from the specifics of particular database protocols, JDBC uses a middle layer composed of a `DriverManager` class and one or more JDBC drivers. A *driver* is Java class, usually supplied by the database vendor, which implements the `java.sql.Driver` interface. The primary function of the driver is to connect to a database and return a `java.sql.Connection` object.

Drivers aren't called directly by application programs. Instead, they're registered with the `DriverManager`, which determines the appropriate driver for a particular connection request and makes the connection through it.

Hundreds of JDBC drivers exist, covering virtually all database management systems. Most of them can be downloaded from vendor Web sites. A searchable list can be found at http://industry.java.sun.com/products/jdbc/drivers.

The next section discusses the four JDBC driver types, the special case of the JDBC-ODBC bridge, and the mechanics of registering a driver.

Driver Types

The JDBC specification classifies drivers as being one of four types, according to their architecture. These types are

- **Type 1—JDBC-ODBC bridge**   Drivers of this type connect to databases through an intermediate ODBC driver. Several drawbacks are involved with this approach, so Sun describes it as being experimental and appropriate for use only where no other driver is available. Both Microsoft and Sun provide type 1 drivers.

- **Type 2—Native API, partly Java**   Similar to a JDBC-ODBC bridge, type 2 drivers use native methods to call vendor-specific API functions. These drivers are also subject to the same limitations as the JDBC-ODBC bridge, in that they require native library files to be installed on client systems, which must be configured to use them.

- **Type 3—Pure Java to database middleware**   Type 3 drivers communicate using a network protocol to a middleware server, which, in turn, communicates to one or more database management systems.

- **Type 4—Pure Java direct to database**   Drivers of this type call directly into the native protocol used by the database management system.

The architecture of each of the four driver types is shown in Figure 15-4.

What difference does the driver type make? From the standpoint of the application programmer, not much. The classifications mean more to the system architect. Type 1 and type 2 drivers require native code to be installed and configured on client systems. Type 4 drivers may not be suitable if the DBMS is behind a firewall. Likewise, each of the four driver types has its own performance characteristics, but the application programming interface is exactly the same in all four cases.

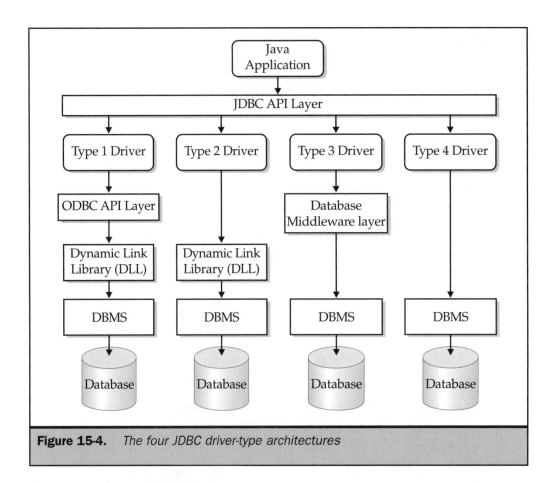

Figure 15-4.   *The four JDBC driver-type architectures*

The JDBC-ODBC Bridge

The type 1 JDBC-ODBC bridge driver requires special considerations. First, the JDBC-ODBC bridge driver is limited to the capabilities of the underlying ODBC driver, which is single-threaded and may, therefore, perform poorly under a heavy load. You cannot tell from within your Java class whether the underlying ODBC driver is thread-safe or not. Also, the bridge requires native code library JdbcOdbc.dll to be installed on the client system. Finally, to be of any use, the JDBC-ODBC bridge driver requires an ODBC data source to be configured. These restrictions make it unsuitable for applets intended for use on the external internet. Sun recommends the bridge be used only for experimental purposes when no other JDBC driver is available.

On the other hand, the JDBC-ODBC bridge offers several significant advantages. Because JSP pages aren't operating in the applet environment, they have none of these limitations. ODBC is widely supported, so using the bridge makes possible access to a wide variety of existing systems for which data sources are already configured. Likewise, ODBC-enabled database products, such as Microsoft Access and FoxBase, are widely available. In my opinion, these features make the JDBC-ODBC bridge a useful tool for learning JDBC.

To use the JDBC-ODBC bridge in a Java application, you need to configure a suitable ODBC data source. On Windows systems, you do this through the Control Panel ODBC Data Sources application. You should configure the data source as a System DSN, not a User DSN, because the JSP engine is typically running under a system user profile. The driver class name is `sun.jdbc.odbc.JdbcOdbcDriver` if the Sun JVM is being used or `com.ms.jdbc.odbc.JdbcOdbcDriver` for the Microsoft virtual machine. The database URL used in the `getConnection()` statement is `jdbc:odbc:dsn`, where *dsn* is the data source name.

Microsoft supplies ODBC drivers for its Access database product, as well as dBase, Excel, FoxPro, and a number of others, including a text driver that can use ordinary text files (.txt and .csv) as a simple database system.

Registering a Driver

To use a JDBC driver, you must first register it with the driver manager. You can accomplish this in several ways, but each involves calling `DriverManager.registerDriver()`, directly or indirectly.

Automatic Registration by the Driver Class

The most common approach is simply to load the driver class:

```
try {
    Class.forName("MyJdbcDriver");
}
catch (ClassNotFoundException e) {
    // Report the exception
}
```

A driver class loaded in this fashion should create an instance of itself and register it with the driver manager, using logic similar to the following:

```
static {
    PrintStream log = DriverManager.getLogStream();
    if (log != null)
        log.println("MyJdbcDriver class loaded");
    MyJdbcDriver driver = new MyJdbcDriver();
    try {
        DriverManager.registerDriver(driver);
```

```
    }
    catch (SQLException e) {
        if (log != null)
            log.println("Unable to register driver");
    }
}
```

Creating a Driver Instance

Some older drivers have been known to omit the required static initialization, doing the registration in their constructor instead. In that case, creating an instance of the driver is necessary, using the following method:

```
try {
    Class.forName("MyJdbcDriver").newInstance();
}
catch (ClassNotFoundException e) {
    // Report the exception
}
catch (InstantiationException e) {
    // Report the exception
}
catch (IllegalAccessException e) {
    // Report the exception
}
```

Using the jdbc.drivers System Property

Another approach to driver registration is to put the driver name in the jdbc.drivers system property. This is a colon-delimited list of driver class names, which DriverManager loads during its initialization. For example, a standalone Java application that uses this approach might be invoked as follows:

```
java -Djdbc.drivers=org.gjt.mm.mysql.Driver MyProgram
```

Direct Registration

Some JDBC driver vendors, notably Oracle, recommend explicitly creating an instance of the driver and registering it with the driver manager:

```
DriverManager.registerDriver(
    new oracle.jdbc.driver.OracleDriver());
```

Using a JNDI DataSource

Since JDBC 2.0, you can make connections through a `DataSource` object that is registered with a JNDI service provider. This functionality is typically offered by the servlet container itself. Tomcat, for example, provides a means for defining JDBC data sources at the Web server level. An upcoming section gives more details about how to configure and use a `DataSource`.

Connecting to a Database with DriverManager

After a driver is loaded and registered, it can be used to create database connections. `DriverManager` provides three methods for doing this:

```
Connection con = DriverManager.getConnection(String url)
Connection con = DriverManager.getConnection
(String url, String userID, String password)
Connection con = DriverManager.getConnection
(String url, Properties prop)
```

Internally, `DriverManager` uses the same private worker method to handle each of these methods.

The driver manager maintains a list of registered drivers. When its `getConnection()` method is invoked, it interrogates each driver in turn to see if it will accept the specified URL. The driver manager does this by calling the driver's `connect()` method, which returns either `null` if the driver cannot accept the URL or an active `Connection` object if it can.

As noted previously, you can use a `DataSource` instead of `DriverManager` to establish connections:

```
DataSource ds = (DataSource) ctx.lookup(...);
Connection con = ds.getConnection();
```

In this case, the URL parameter isn't used, because it's stored in the naming service. The factory object that creates the data source calls the driver's `connect()` method directly to get a connection.

The JDBC Database URL

The key argument to `DriverManager.getConnection()` is a *JDBC URL*, which is a string with three components separated by semicolons:

<protocol>:*<subprotocol>*:*<subname>*

where

- *protocol* is always jdbc.

- *subprotocol* is a vendor-specific string that identifies the driver to be used. The driver indicates whether it can handle that subprotocol when asked by the driver manager. For example, the JDBC-ODBC bridge uses the reserved value odbc as its subprotocol. This value is intended to be unique across all driver vendors. Sun Microsystems acts as an informal registrar of JDBC subprotocols.

- *subname* identifies the specific database to connect to. This string contains whatever the driver needs to identify the database. It may also contain connection parameters the database needs.

Examples of JDBC URLs are

```
jdbc:odbc:usda
```

This would indicate an ODBC data source named usda that is accessed by the JDBC-ODBC bridge driver.

```
jdbc:mysql://localhost:3306/lyricnote
```

MM.MySQL interprets the *subname* shown here as the database server host, server port number, and database name:

```
"jdbc:oracle:thin:@"
    + "(DESCRIPTION="
    + "(ADDRESS=(HOST=u25nv)"
    + "(PROTOCOL=tcp)"
    + "(PORT=4311))"
    + "(CONNECT_DATA=(SID=music)))"
```

This is a lengthy connection string that might be used with the Oracle thin client driver.

Connecting to a Database Using a JNDI DataSource

The advantage of this approach is that driver class names and database URLs are stored in the naming service, rather than being hard-coded in application programs. Only the data source name is required. The sample JSP page associated with Figure 15-3 earlier in this chapter could have its connection logic replaced with the following:

```
InitialContext initCtx = new InitialContext();
Context ctx = (Context) initCtx.lookup("java:comp/env");
DataSource ds = (DataSource) ctx.lookup("jdbc/LyricNote");
Connection con = null;
try {
   con = ds.getConnection();
   ...
}
finally {
   if (con != null)
      con.close();
}
```

> **Note** *JSP pages using a DataSource for JDBC connections must import javax.sql.* and javax.naming.* or else fully qualify the references to InitialContext, Context, and DataSource.*

To use this approach, you need to configure several items. First, in your web.xml deployment descriptor for the application, you need to specify a resource reference, as illustrated here:

```
<resource-ref>
   <description>
      Data source for LyricNote database
   </description>
   <res-ref-name>jdbc/LyricNote</res-ref-name>
   <res-type>javax.sql.DataSource</res-type>
   <res-auth>Container</res-auth>
</resource-ref>
```

The resource reference provides the name by which a connection factory will be known to the Web application. The name is appended to the prefix java:comp/env to uniquely identify a resource (the database) that can be accessed through JNDI.[3] That is, if res-ref-name is jdbc/LyricNote, you would use lookup("java:comp/env/jdbc/LyricNote") from the JNDI initial context and cast the result to a DataSource.

The res-type element specifies a fully qualified class name that indicates the type of object that is referred to. This allows the JNDI service provider to invoke the correct object factory to get the resource. In the preceding example, the type is javax.sql.DataSource.

---

[3] If you are not familiar with JNDI, don't be intimidated. It is really no more complicated than navigating through a filesystem with the java.io.File listFiles() method. There is a good tutorial at http://java.sun.com/products/jndi/tutorial/trailmap.html.

You use the `res-auth` element to indicate whether your application contacts the resource manager directly or delegates this to the Web container (the values are `Application` or `Container`, respectively). This configuration in `web.xml` is the same for all Web containers.

The next step is container-specific. You need to equate the resource reference to the specific database and connection parameters it uses. This information is used by the Web container's implementation of the JNDI `InitialContext` interface from which your program obtains a data source.

In the Tomcat reference implementation, this is done by adding resource configuration elements to the `server.xml` file:

```xml
<Resource name="jdbc/LyricNote" auth="Container"
    type="javax.sql.DataSource"/>

<ResourceParams name="jdbc/LyricNote">
    <parameter>
        <name>factory</name>
        <value>org.apache.commons.dbcp.BasicDataSourceFactory</value>
    </parameter>

    <parameter>
        <name>maxActive</name>
        <value>100</value>
    </parameter>

    <parameter>
        <name>maxIdle</name>
        <value>30000</value>
    </parameter>

    <parameter>
        <name>maxWait</name>
        <value>100</value>
    </parameter>

    <parameter>
        <name>username</name>
        <value>author</value>
    </parameter>

    <parameter>
        <name>password</name>
        <value>goodness</value>
```

```
      </parameter>

      <parameter>
         <name>driverClassName</name>
         <value>org.gjt.mm.mysql.Driver</value>
      </parameter>

      <parameter>
         <name>url</name>
         <value>jdbc:mysql://localhost:3306/lyricnote</value>
      </parameter>

   </ResourceParams>
```

Note *Versions of Tomcat prior to 4.1 by default used a Tyrex EnabledDataSource to handle all javax.sql.DataSource resources. According to Tyrex (http://tyrex.exolab.org/tomcat.html): "... Tomcat only supports tyrex.resource.jdbc.xa.EnabledDataSource which means that JDBC data sources are not supported and there is limited connection pool support. EnabledDataSource only supports JDBC 1.1 connections."*
Tomcat 4.1 has upgraded the Tyrex version that it uses, and it also supports the Jakarta Commons connection pooling data source. The Jakarta Commons jar files are included in the Tomcat 4.1 distribution, but you can also download them directly and apply them to earlier Tomcat configurations. Also, your driver vendor may provide its own DataSource implementation (MM.MySQL does).

This looks more complicated than it really is. All it amounts to is specifying a name and data type, together with the factory name and the parameters it requires, which will probably change very little from application to application. The whole process is very clearly explained in the Tomcat documentation (see http://jakarta.apache.org/tomcat/tomcat-4.1-doc/index.html).

A big advantage of using a `DataSource` is that advanced database features like connection pooling and distributed transactions can be implemented entirely with changes to bindings in the naming service. No changes to the JSP source code are required.

Note *The examples in this chapter typically use the `DataSource` approach, rather than `Class.forName()` and `DriverManager.getConnection()`. Both techniques work, and although data sources are slightly more complicated to configure, they require fewer changes to your source code when you change database vendors, drivers, or pooling characteristics. If you are experimenting with an example and having configuration trouble, you can certainly switch to the driver manager approach.*

As was the case with driver registration, it is possible to use a `DataSource` from a naming service to hide the details of the JDBC URL.

The Statement Interfaces

The SQL language consists of statements that create, manipulate, and extract data from a relational database. JDBC provides an object-oriented representation of these SQL statements that encapsulates their text, execution status, and results. Not surprisingly, this representation is called the `java.sql.Statement` interface. Statement objects can be used to send any of the following types of SQL commands to a database:

- A data definition command such as CREATE TABLE or CREATE INDEX
- A data manipulation command such as INSERT or UPDATE
- A SELECT statement for performing a query

Data manipulation commands return a count of the number of rows modified, whereas a SELECT statement returns a set of rows known as a result set.

The Statement interface has two specialized subinterfaces that extend its capabilities: PreparedStatement, which uses precompiled SQL, and CallableStatement, which invokes stored procedures. The following section discusses all three types of statements and how they are used.

Statement

The base interface is `java.sql.Statement`. Because this is an interface, it doesn't have a constructor; instead, it's obtained from the connection object with `createStatement()`. A typical example is this:

```
DataSource ds = ...
Connection con = null;
try {

    con = ds.getConnection();        Statement stmt = con.createStatement();
    ...
    stmt.close();
}
finally {
    if (con != null)
        con.close();
}
```

JDBC 2.0 introduced an additional form of `createStatement()` that takes parameters indicating whether its result sets should be scrollable or not and whether they reflect concurrent changes in the underlying table. The section on result sets later in this chapter describes these features in more detail.

Once a statement is created, it can be used to execute commands. Four methods exist for doing this: executeUpdate, executeQuery, execute, and executeBatch. The choice of which method to use depends on the expected results:

- **executeQuery** is used to execute an SQL SELECT statement and to return a result set.

- **executeUpdate** is intended for use with the SQL INSERT, UPDATE, or DELETE statements, or with data definition statements such as CREATE TABLE. It returns a count of the number of rows updated or deleted.

- **execute** can be used for either purpose but is intended for those statements that return either an update count, multiple result sets, or some combination. It returns a boolean flag that indicates whether its result was an update count or a result set. Additional methods are available that navigate through results.

- **executeBatch** allows multiple update statements to be executed in a batch. The update counts are returned in an array.

The following examples[4] illustrate each of these methods. The database is from our fictional music publishing company, the LyricNote.

The executeQuery Method

This example uses a SELECT statement to display all sheet music titles in the product catalog that are Telemann concertos:

```
<%@ page session="false" %>
<%@ page import="java.sql.*,javax.naming.*,javax.sql.*" %>
<html>
<head><title>Query Example</title></head>
<body>
<h1>Query Example</h1>
<%
    // Get the data source using JNDI

    InitialContext initCtx = new InitialContext();
    Context ctx = (Context) initCtx.lookup("java:comp/env");
    DataSource ds = (DataSource) ctx.lookup("jdbc/LyricNote");

    // Define these objects outside the "try" block so that
    // they can be closed in the "finally" block

    Connection con = null;
    Statement stmt = null;
    ResultSet rs = null;
```

---

[4]   The examples are embedded in JSP pages to make them easy to experiment with, not because this is a particularly efficient or maintainable approach. In a production application, you would likely use a servlet or an auxiliary bean class.

```
try {

    // Get a connection from the data source
    // and a statement from the connection

    con = ds.getConnection();
    stmt = con.createStatement();

    // Run the SQL query that selects the products
    // of interest

    rs = stmt.executeQuery(
            "SELECT  itemcode, description"
        + " FROM     products"
        + " WHERE    description like 'Telemann% Concerto%'");

    // Loop through the result set printing each line

    out.println("<pre>");
    out.println("ITEMCODE    DESCRIPTION");
    out.println("--------    -----------");

    while (rs.next()) {
        String itemCode = rs.getString(1);
        String description = rs.getString(2);
        out.println(itemCode + "      " + description);
    }

    out.println("</pre>");
}
finally {

    // Close the open JDBC objects

    if (rs != null) rs.close();
    if (stmt != null) stmt.close();
    if (con != null) con.close();
}
%>
</body>
</html>
```

The process of getting values from the result set is explained later in this chapter.

No doubt, when you look at the results in Figure 15-5, you'll immediately spot an error. Yes, Telemann's first double horn concerto was in the key of F, not F#!

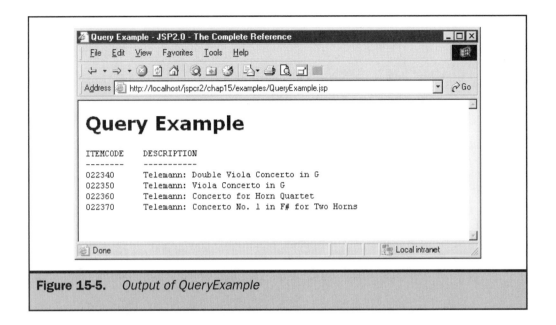

Figure 15-5.   *Output of QueryExample*

The executeUpdate Method

In this example, we'll fix the erroneous product description with an SQL UPDATE
statement invoked by the `executeUpdate` method. When successfully executed,
the program prints the old and new descriptions and the number of rows updated.

```
<%@ page session="false" %>
<%@ page import="java.sql.*,javax.naming.*,javax.sql.*" %>
<html>
<head><title>Update Example</title></head>
<body>
<h1>Update Example</h1>
<pre>
<%
    // Get the data source using JNDI

    InitialContext initCtx = new InitialContext();
    Context ctx = (Context) initCtx.lookup("java:comp/env");
    DataSource ds = (DataSource) ctx.lookup("jdbc/LyricNote");

    // Define these objects outside the "try" block so that
    // they can be closed in the "finally" block

    Connection con = null;
    Statement stmt = null;
```

```
ResultSet rs = null;

try {

    // Get a connection from the data source
    // and a statement from the connection

    con = ds.getConnection();
    stmt = con.createStatement();

    // Get the description from the erroneous listing

    rs = stmt.executeQuery(
          "SELECT   description"
        + " FROM     products"
        + " WHERE    itemcode = '022370'");
    rs.next();
    String description = rs.getString(1);

    // Display the original value and close the result set

    out.println("Original description:    " + description);
    rs.close();

    // Change F# to F (note: the String.replaceFirst()
    // method requires JDK 1.4 or later)

    description = description.replaceFirst("in F#", "in F");

    // Run the SQL update statement to correct
    // the description

    int nRows = stmt.executeUpdate(
          " UPDATE    products"
        + " SET       description = '" + description + "'"
        + " WHERE     itemcode = '022370'"
        );
```

```
                // Print the update count

                out.println("Number of rows updated:     " + nRows);

                // Show the new description

                rs = stmt.executeQuery(
                    "SELECT  description"
                  + " FROM    products"
                  + " WHERE   itemcode = '022370'");
                rs.next();
                description = rs.getString(1);

                // Display the new value

                out.println("Updated description:     " + description);
            }
            finally {

                // Close any open JDBC objects

                if (rs != null) rs.close();
                if (stmt != null) stmt.close();
                if (con != null) con.close();
            }
        %>
        </pre>
        </body>
        </html>
```

The example first gets the original description for item 022370 using another SQL SELECT statement run with executeQuery(). It then modifies the description and invokes an SQL UPDATE statement for that one row using executeUpdate(). The number of rows updated (one, in this case) is returned by executeUpdate(). Finally, the program reruns the query to allow us to verify that the change was made successfully. Messages are logged for each step, as shown in Figure 15-6.

JSP APPLICATIONS

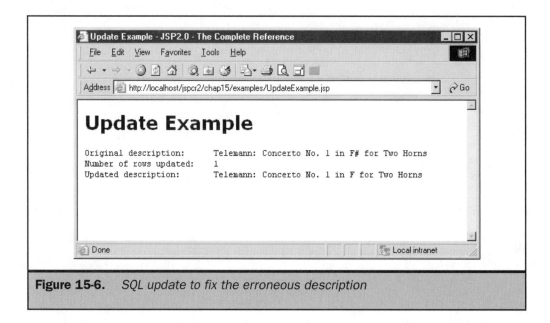

Figure 15-6. *SQL update to fix the erroneous description*

The execute Method

Although the `execute` method can be used for either queries or updates, it's strictly necessary only for operations that may return multiple results. The `Statement` interface provides methods for determining what has been returned and for processing the results. The most common use for `execute` is for processing unknown SQL strings, such as in this example, which reads and processes SQL statements from a file named "`data.sql`". Here is the data file:

```
SELECT    description
FROM      products
WHERE     description LIKE "Vivaldi% in C minor%" ;

DELETE
FROM      products
WHERE     itemcode = 'bogus' ;
```

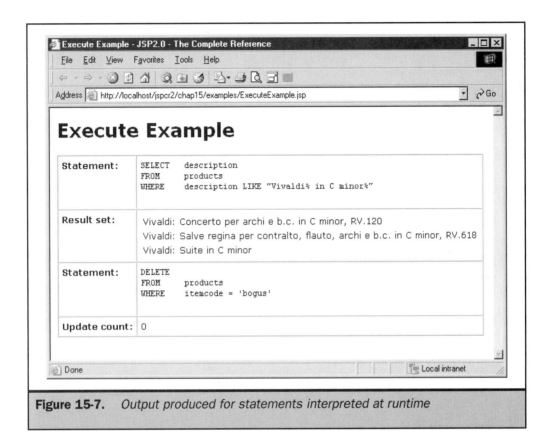

Figure 15-7.   *Output produced for statements interpreted at runtime*

Our JSP application will read the file a character at a time, stopping each time it encounters a semicolon, and there invoking the `execute()` method to process the SQL statement. Figure 15-7 shows the results:

```
<%@ page session="false" %>
<%@ page import="java.io.*" %>
<%@ page import="java.net.*" %>
<%@ page import="java.sql.*" %>
<%@ page import="javax.naming.*" %>
<%@ page import="javax.sql.*" %>
<html>
```

```
<head><title>Execute Example</title></head>
<body>
<h1>Execute Example</h1>
<%
    // Get the data source using JNDI

    InitialContext initCtx = new InitialContext();
    Context ctx = (Context) initCtx.lookup("java:comp/env");
    DataSource ds = (DataSource) ctx.lookup("jdbc/LyricNote");

    // Define these objects outside the "try" block so that
    // they can be closed in the "finally" block

    Connection con = null;
    Statement stmt = null;
    ResultSet rs = null;

    try {

        // Get a connection from the data source
        // and a statement from the connection

        con = ds.getConnection();
        stmt = con.createStatement();

        // Read SQL statements from a file

        URL dataURL = application.getResource("/examples/data.sql");

        BufferedReader in =
            new BufferedReader(
            new InputStreamReader(
            dataURL.openStream())));

        StringBuffer sb = new StringBuffer();

        out.println("<table border='1'"
                    + "  cellpadding='5'"
                    + "  cellspacing='0'>");

        while (true) {
```

```java
// Read characters into a string buffer until
// a semicolon marking the end of the statement

int c = in.read();
if (c == -1)
   break;

if (c != ';') {
   sb.append((char) c);
   continue;
}

// Get the line to be executed and reset the
// string buffer so it can be reused

String line = sb.toString().trim();
sb.setLength(0);

// Execute the line as an SQL statement

out.println("<tr valign='top'>");
out.println("<td> <b>Statement:</b> </td>");
out.println("<td> <pre>" + line + "</pre> </td>");
out.println("</tr>");

boolean hasResultSet = stmt.execute(line);
while (true) {

   if (hasResultSet) {

      // Get the result set from the statement
      // and print it in a table

      rs = stmt.getResultSet();

      out.println("<tr valign='top'>");
      out.println("<td><b>Result set:</b></td>");
      out.println("<td>");
      out.println("<table border='0'>");

      ResultSetMetaData rmd = rs.getMetaData();
      int nColumns = rmd.getColumnCount();
```

```
                while (rs.next()) {
                    out.println("<tr>");
                    for (int i = 0; i < nColumns; i++) {
                        int col = i+1;
                        String value = rs.getString(col);
                        out.println("<td>" + value + "</td>");
                    }
                    out.println("</tr>");
                }

                out.println("</table>");
                out.println("</td>");
                out.println("</tr>");

                rs.close();
                rs = null;
            }
            else {
                int count = stmt.getUpdateCount();
                if (count == -1)
                    break;
                out.println("<tr valign='top'>");
                out.println("<td><b>Update count:</b></td>");
                out.println("<td>" + count + "</td>");
                out.println("</tr>");
            }

            // See if there are any more results

            hasResultSet = stmt.getMoreResults();
        }
    }
    in.close();
}
finally {

    out.println("</table>");

    // Close any open JDBC objects

    if (rs != null) rs.close();
    if (stmt != null) stmt.close();
    if (con != null) con.close();
```

```
    }
%>
</body>
</html>
```

The initial return code from `execute` is a boolean value that is true if the statement execution produced a result set. If not, the update count can be obtained with `Statement.getUpdateCount()`. If the update count is –1, then no more results exist. Otherwise, the `Statement.getMoreResults()` method can be called to cycle through the next result set or update count. It returns a boolean value with the same interpretation as the one returned by `execute`.

The executeBatch Method

JDBC 2.0 introduced the capability to submit a group of update statements to be executed as a batch. In some cases, this can represent a significant performance improvement. The methods used in connection with batch updates are these:

- **clearBatch** resets a batch to the empty state.
- **addBatch** adds an update statement to the batch.
- **executeBatch** submits the batch and collects update counts.

Not all drivers support batch updates. Those that do indicate this by returning `true` from their `DatabaseMetaData.supportsBatchUpdates()` method. MySQL and the MM.MySQL driver fully support batch updates.

In the following example, the LyricNote `composers` database is updated with a table of composers who lived to at least the age of 90. Here is the input file:

```
Auber,Daniel Francois,90
Copland,Aaron,91
Gossec,Francois-Joseph,96
Rodrigo,Joaquin,99
Ruggles,Carl,96
Sibelius,Jean,93
Stravinsky,Igor,90
Widor,Charles-Marie,94
```

and here is the JSP page:

```
<%@ page session="false" %>
<%@ page import="java.io.*" %>
```

```jsp
<%@ page import="java.net.*" %>
<%@ page import="java.sql.*" %>
<%@ page import="javax.naming.*" %>
<%@ page import="javax.sql.*" %>
<html>
<head><title>Batch Update Example</title></head>
<body>
<h1>Batch Update Example</h1>
<pre>
<%
    // Get the data source using JNDI

    InitialContext initCtx = new InitialContext();
    Context ctx = (Context) initCtx.lookup("java:comp/env");
    DataSource ds = (DataSource) ctx.lookup("jdbc/LyricNote");

    // Define these objects outside the "try" block so that
    // they can be closed in the "finally" block

    Connection con = null;
    Statement stmt = null;

    try {

        // Get a connection from the data source
        // and a statement from the connection

        con = ds.getConnection();
        stmt = con.createStatement();

        // Clear the over90 table if it exists
        // and create a new one

        stmt.executeUpdate("DROP TABLE IF EXISTS over90");
        stmt.executeUpdate(
            "CREATE TABLE over90 ("
            + "    lastName        CHAR(20),"
            + "    firstName       CHAR(20),"
            + "    age             INTEGER)"
            );

        // Set up for handling all-or-nothing transaction

        con.setAutoCommit(false);
```

```
// Tell the database we're going to use a batch update

stmt.clearBatch();

// Read lines from a comma-separated-values file

URL dataURL = application.getResource
   ("/examples/over90.csv");

BufferedReader in =
   new BufferedReader(
   new InputStreamReader(
   dataURL.openStream()));

out.println("Reading lines from " + dataURL);
out.println();
int nLines = 0;
while (true) {
   String line = in.readLine();
   if (line == null)
      break;
   nLines++;
   out.println(nLines + ": " + line);

   // Split the input line into three tokens

   String[] tokens = line.split(",");
   if (tokens.length != 3)
      throw new IOException("Bad input data");

   String lastName = tokens[0];
   String firstName = tokens[1];
   String age = tokens[2];

   // Add an SQL INSERT statement to the batch

   final String QUOTE = "'";

   String insertSQL = "INSERT INTO over90 VALUES ("
      + QUOTE + lastName + QUOTE + ","
      + QUOTE + firstName + QUOTE + ","
      + age + ")" ;

   stmt.addBatch(insertSQL);
}
```

```
      in.close();

      // Now execute the batch

      out.println();
      out.println("Starting batch update");
      int[] rowsInserted = stmt.executeBatch();

      // There should have been one row updated for
      // every statement in the batch

      int n = rowsInserted.length;
      int sum = 0;
      for (int i = 0; i < n; i++)
         sum += rowsInserted[i];

      out.println();
      out.println(n + " rows inserted");

      // If all updates were good, commit the transaction

      if (sum == n) {
         out.println("Committing transaction");
         con.commit();
      }

      // Otherwise, rollback

      else {
         out.println("Rolling back transaction");
         con.rollback();
      }
   }
   finally {

      // Close any open JDBC objects

      if (stmt != null) stmt.close();
      if (con != null) con.close();
   }
%>
</pre>
</body>
</html>
```

The procedure is fairly straightforward. After obtaining a data source and database connection as usual, we run some SQL that creates the `over90` table. We set the autocommit mode to `false`, because we want to define the transaction boundaries explicitly. We call `stmt.clearBatch()` to ensure we don't have any leftover updates. After opening the input text file as a URL, we read and log each line. After splitting the line into three fields (for last name, first name, and age), we convert it to an SQL INSERT statement and call `stmt.addBatch()` to add it to the list. At end of file, the batch is ready to go, so we call `stmt.executeBatch()`, which returns an array of integers representing the update counts. There is one element in the array for each entry in the batch. Since we are inserting one row per line, the sum of the update count array should be the same as the number of rows. If all is well, we commit the batch as a whole. Otherwise, we can roll back the entire transaction. See Figure 15-8 for the results.

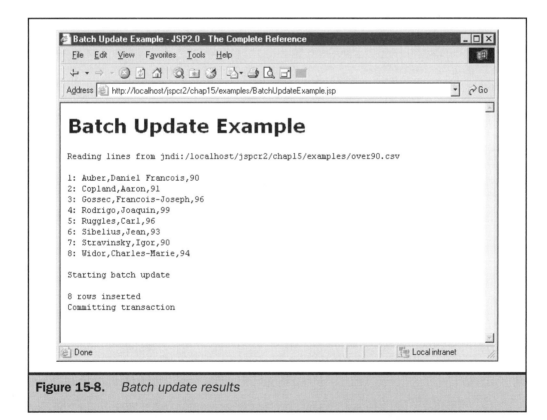

Figure 15-8. *Batch update results*

PreparedStatement

java.sql.PreparedStatement is a subinterface of Statement that uses precompiled SQL.[5] This may result in performance improvements if the statement is used repeatedly. A PreparedStatement differs from Statement in that its execute methods don't take an SQL string as a parameter. Instead, the SQL string is specified when the PreparedStatement is created, as shown here:

```
PreparedStatement pstmt = con.prepareStatement(sqlstring);
```

The string to be executed may contain substitution parameters, which are indicated by the presence of a question mark (?) in the string. These parameters act as placeholders in the statement and must be filled in with values before they are executed. To do this, the API provides a number of set*XXX*() methods, where *XXX* is the Java data type.

The batch update example, which created and loaded a table of composers who lived to at least the age of 90, could also be written with a PreparedStatement that is executed in a loop, as shown here:

```
<%@ page session="false" %>
<%@ page import="java.io.*" %>
<%@ page import="java.net.*" %>
<%@ page import="java.sql.*" %>
<%@ page import="javax.naming.*" %>
<%@ page import="javax.sql.*" %>
<html>
<head><title>Prepared Statement Example</title></head>
<body>
<h1>Prepared Statement Example</h1>
<pre>
<%
    // Get the data source using JNDI

    InitialContext initCtx = new InitialContext();
    Context ctx = (Context) initCtx.lookup("java:comp/env");
    DataSource ds = (DataSource) ctx.lookup("jdbc/LyricNote");

    // Define these objects outside the "try" block so that
    // they can be closed in the "finally" block
```

---

[5] At least, the JDBC specification says that the SQL is precompiled. I have encountered drivers that do not actually do this. About the only thing you can count on is that the PreparedStatement syntax is supported.

```
Connection con = null;
Statement stmt = null;
PreparedStatement pstmt = null;

try {

   // Get a connection from the data source
   // and a statement from the connection

   con = ds.getConnection();
   stmt = con.createStatement();

   // Clear the over90 table if it exists
   // and create a new one

   stmt.executeUpdate("DROP TABLE IF EXISTS over90");
   stmt.executeUpdate(
      "CREATE TABLE over90 ("
      + "    lastName       CHAR(20),"
      + "    firstName      CHAR(20),"
      + "    age            INTEGER)"
      );
   stmt.close();
   stmt = null;

   // Prepare a statement that will handle the update

   pstmt = con.prepareStatement
      ("INSERT INTO over90 VALUES(?, ?, ?)");

   // Read lines from a comma-separated-values file

   URL dataURL = application.getResource
      ("/examples/over90.csv");

   BufferedReader in =
      new BufferedReader(
      new InputStreamReader(
      dataURL.openStream()));

   out.println("Reading lines from " + dataURL);
   out.println();
```

```
        int nLines = 0;
        int totalRowCount = 0;
        while (true) {
            String line = in.readLine();
            if (line == null)
                break;
            nLines++;
            out.println(nLines + ": " + line);

            // Split the input line into three tokens

            String[] tokens = line.split(",");
            if (tokens.length != 3)
                throw new IOException("Bad input data");

            String lastName = tokens[0];
            String firstName = tokens[1];
            int age = Integer.parseInt(tokens[2]);

            // Set the parameters in the prepared statement

            pstmt.setString(1, lastName);
            pstmt.setString(2, firstName);
            pstmt.setInt(3, age);

            // Insert the row in the table

            int rowCount = pstmt.executeUpdate();
            out.println(rowCount + " record added");
            totalRowCount += rowCount;
        }

        in.close();

        out.println();
        out.println(totalRowCount + " rows inserted");
    }
    finally {

        // Close any open JDBC objects

        if (pstmt != null) pstmt.close();
        if (stmt != null) stmt.close();
```

```
         if (con != null) con.close();
    }
%>
</pre>
</body>
</html>
```

The results are shown in Figure 15-9.

Consider several key points in the code. First, the statement needs to be created with substitution parameters:

```
    pstmt = con.prepareStatement
        ("INSERT INTO over90 VALUES(?, ?, ?)");
```

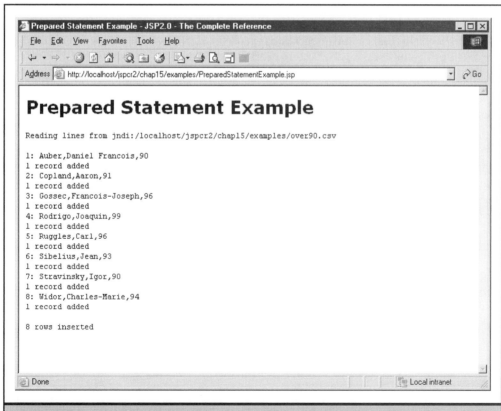

Figure 15-9.   *Output of the over90 query using a PreparedStatement*

There are three question marks, one for each column in the table. There is no difference in use between numeric and string parameters. Both are coded simply as question marks, with no embedded quotes or apostrophes needed.

To use the values that were read from the file in the INSERT statement, employ the setString() and setInt() methods:

```
pstmt.setString(1, lastName);
pstmt.setString(2, firstName);
pstmt.setInt(3, age);
```

The first parameter to the set*XXX*() methods is the column number, which starts at 1 for the first column, 2 for the second, and so on. The second parameter is the value to be inserted.

set*XXX*() methods exist for all data types, as well as two special ones: setObject() and setNull(). Type conversions into any JDBC data type can be made with setObject(), which takes a third parameter:

```
pstmt.setObject(int column, Object value, int typeNumber)
```

where *typeNumber* is a static integer constant defined in java.sql.Types. Similarly, setNull() can be used to store the appropriate null type in a parameter:

```
pstmt.setNull(int column, int typeNumber)
```

Using Prepared Statements to Avoid Dynamic Syntax Errors

While the primary motivation for using prepared statements is performance, another subtle advantage exists. Suppose you want to make a JSP page that can run queries against the LyricNote product database. The page includes a form in which a search argument can be entered. This argument is extracted from the request parameters, and an SQL statement is then constructed on the fly. Here is part of the JSP page showing how the SQL is constructed:

```
ResultSet rs = stmt.executeQuery(
  " SELECT    itemcode, description"
  + " FROM      products"
  + " WHERE     prodtype = 'SM'"
  + " AND       description like '%" + searchFor + "%'"
  );
```

When the JSP page is used to search for works by Stravinsky, it returns the results shown in Figure 15-10.

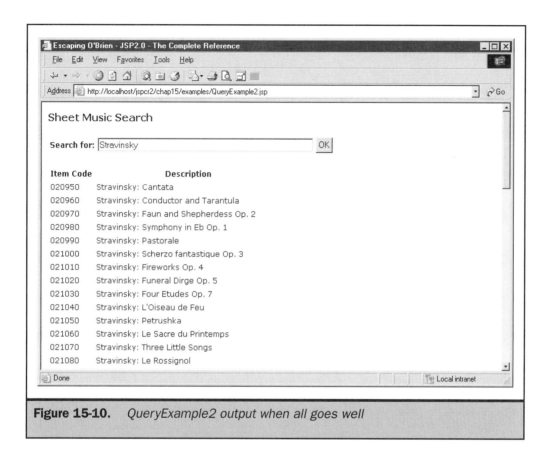

Figure 15-10. *QueryExample2 output when all goes well*

If, however, you search specifically for Stravinsky's *L'Histoire du Soldat,* you get the nasty error screen shown in Figure 15-11.

What happened? Well, consider the SQL that gets created:

```
SELECT    itemcode, description
FROM      products
WHERE     prodtype = 'SM'
AND       description like '%L'Histoire du Soldat%'
```

The word *L'Histoire* has an embedded apostrophe, so when the LIKE clause is evaluated, it terminates too soon, viewing '%L' as the operand it is trying to match. Whatever follows is parsed as if it were SQL, which causes the error.

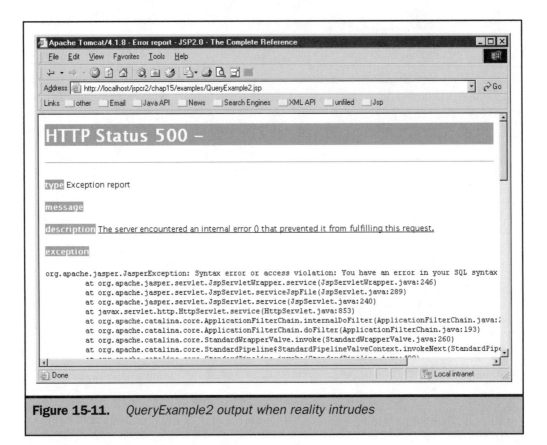

Figure 15-11.   *QueryExample2 output when reality intrudes*

This problem can be avoided by scanning user input for embedded apostrophes and replacing them with a safe alternative, but this is more complicated than it sounds. This technique, referred to as *escaping characters,* varies in different databases and SQL dialects. A JDBC-architected way exists to indicate the escape character, but this adds complexity everywhere user input has to be handled.

A simpler and cleaner way to handle this is to use a `PreparedStatement` with a substitution parameter. The statement creation code needs to be changed to this:

```
PreparedStatement pstmt = con.prepareStatement(
    " SELECT    itemcode, description\n"
  + " FROM      products\n"
  + " WHERE     prodtype = 'SM'\n"
  + " AND       description like ?"
);
```

```
pstmt.setString(1, "%" + searchFor + "%");
ResultSet rs = pstmt.executeQuery();
```

The operand of the LIKE clause is now simply a question mark, and the search argument is now added dynamically at runtime. The query now works with any type of input, regardless of its meaning in SQL, as seen in Figure 15-12.

CallableStatement

A further refinement of PreparedStatement is embodied in java.sql.CallableStatement. This interface is used to invoke stored procedures, if the database supports them.[6] Oracle, for example, allows procedures to be written in PL/SQL. Queries written in Microsoft Access can be invoked through the JDBC-ODBC bridge as stored procedures.

Like its immediate superinterface PreparedStatement, a CallableStatement is created with an explicit command string that gets precompiled:

```
CallableStatement cstmt = con.prepareCall(escapeString);
```

It also uses question marks to indicate substitution parameters. The syntax of a stored procedure call used with CallableStatement is as follows:

```
{? = call procedureName(?, ?, ..., ?)}
```

If you imagine a variable name everywhere you see a question mark in this syntax, you'll understand what goes where. If there is no return value from the procedure, the "? =" should be omitted. Similarly, if there are no input parameters, the "(?, ?, ..., ?)" is not used.

Because CallableStatement extends PreparedStatement, it uses the same methods for setting substitution parameter values:

```
String sql = "{call myproc(?, ?)}";
CallableStatement cstmt = con.prepareCall(sql);
cstmt.setString(1, "New York");
cstmt.setDouble(2, "19.73");
cstmt.executeQuery();
```

If any of the parameters are used for output or input/output, their types must be registered with CallableStatement.registerOutParameter() before the call

---

[6]   Few, if any, noncommercial databases support stored procedures.

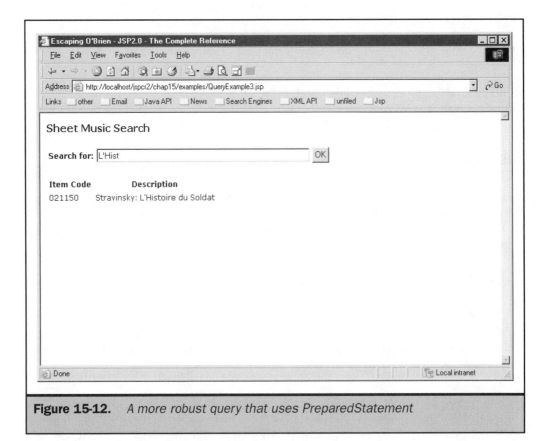

Figure 15-12. *A more robust query that uses PreparedStatement*

is executed. Their values can be retrieved with the same get*XXX*() methods used by
PreparedStatement.

Stored Procedures in Microsoft Access

Microsoft Access supports queries written in SQL or developed with its own design
wizard. These queries can be invoked by name using the JDBC-ODBC bridge and
a CallableStatement. Figure 15-13 shows the design view of a query that creates
a list of composers born during a specified year interval. The beginning and ending years
are input parameters to the query.

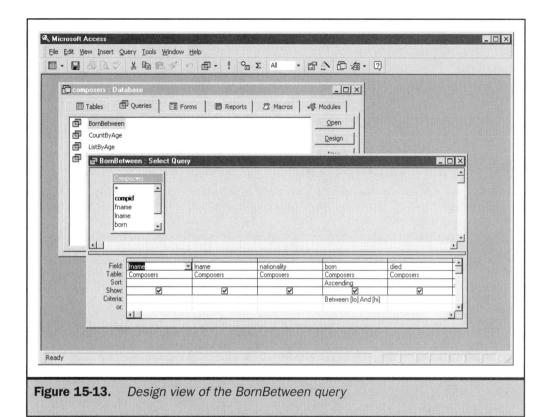

Figure 15-13.   *Design view of the BornBetween query*

You can toggle between the design view, the SQL view (see Figure 15-14), and the datasheet or output view. When run using 1891–1900 as the year interval, 12 records are selected. The results are shown in Figure 15-15.

This query can be run from a JSP page using `CallableStatement`, as illustrated in the following listing. The steps the JSP page performs are as follows:

1. Prompts for the beginning and ending year in an HTML form.

2. Connects to the Access database through the JDBC-ODBC bridge.

3. Creates a `CallableStatement` that calls the query.

4. Sets the beginning and ending year parameters from the form values.

5. Executes the query.

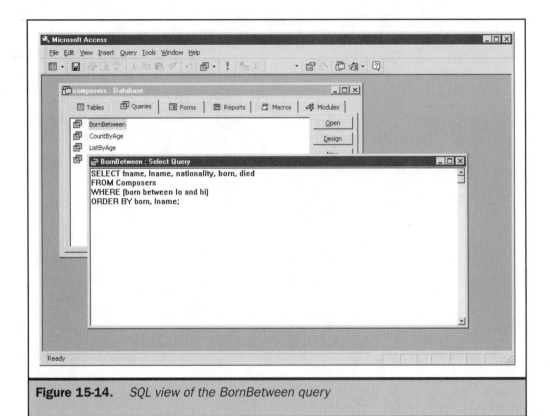

Figure 15-14.   *SQL view of the BornBetween query*

6. Displays the results in an HTML table.

```
<%@ page session="false" %>
<%@ page import="java.sql.*" %>
<html>
<head>
<title>Callable Statement Example</title>
<style type="text/css">
body, td, th {
    font-family: Verdana;
    font-size: 9pt;
    text-align: center;
}
h1 { font-size: 130%; }
</style>
</head>
<body>
```

```
<h1>Select Composers by Year Born</h1>
<form>
<table>
<%
    // Get beginning and ending years

    String param1 = request.getParameter("lo");
    if (param1 == null)
        param1 = "";

    String param2 = request.getParameter("hi");
    if (param2 == null)
        param2 = "";
%>
<tr>
    <td>Year range:
        <input type="TEXT" name="lo" size="4" value="<%= param1 %>">

        and

        <input type="TEXT" name="hi" size="4" value="<%= param2 %>">
        <input type="SUBMIT" value="Search">
    </td>
</tr>
</table>
</form>
<%
    if (!param1.equals("") && (!param2.equals(""))) {

        int lo = Integer.parseInt(param1);
        int hi = Integer.parseInt(param2);

        Connection con = null;
        CallableStatement cstmt = null;
        ResultSet rs = null;
        try {

            // Load the driver

            Class.forName("sun.jdbc.odbc.JdbcOdbcDriver");

            // Connect to the composers database

            con = DriverManager.getConnection
                ("jdbc:odbc:composers");
```

```
            // Set up callable procedure

            String sql = "{call BornBetween(?, ?)}";
            cstmt = con.prepareCall(sql);
            cstmt.setInt(1, lo);
            cstmt.setInt(2, hi);
            rs = cstmt.executeQuery();
%>
    <table border=1 cellpadding=3 cellspacing=0>
    <tr>
       <th>Name</th>
       <th>Nationality</th>
       <th>Lived</th>
    </tr>
<%
            // Print the result set

            while (rs.next()) {
                String fname = rs.getString(1);
                String lname = rs.getString(2);
                String nationality = rs.getString(3);
                int yearBorn = rs.getInt(4);
                int yearDied = rs.getInt(5);
%>
    <tr>
       <td><%= fname %> <%= lname %></td>
       <td><%= nationality %></td>
       <td><%= yearBorn %>-<%= yearDied %></td>
    </tr>
<%
        }
%>
    </table>
<%
        }
        finally {
            if (rs != null) rs.close();
            if (cstmt != null) cstmt.close();
            if (con != null) con.close();
        }
    }
%>
</body>
</html>
```

Figure 15-15. *Datasheet view of the BornBetween query*

The results are as shown in Figure 15-16.

Of course, because the query itself is SQL-based, couldn't you just execute the equivalent SQL inside the JSP page with an ordinary `Statement`? Perhaps, but several good reasons exist why you may choose not to do this:

- The query has already been written and tested in the native Microsoft Access environment. Hundreds of queries may already be developed, with little justification for conversion.

- If the query is modified in its original form, the changes are automatically reflected in the Web-based version.

- The query may use database features that work within Access but aren't supported through the ODBC and JDBC-ODBC bridge layers.

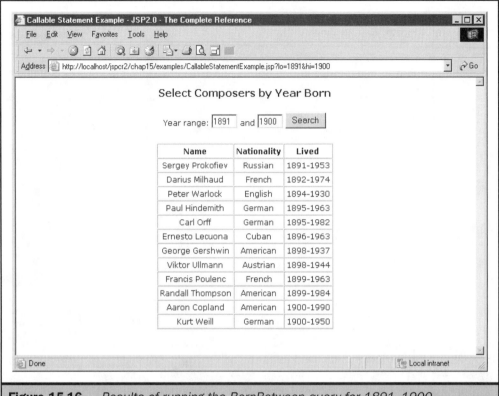

Figure 15-16. *Results of running the BornBetween query for 1891–1900*

Result Sets

A *result set* is an ordered list of table rows, represented in JDBC with the
java.sql.ResultSet interface. Result sets are produced by executeQuery() or by
certain metadata method calls. Once it is created, the data in a result set can be extracted
as follows:

1. Move to the desired row, by calling the ResultSet.next() method or by one
   of the richer sets of methods provided by JDBC 2.0—absolute(), relative(),
   next(), previous(), first(), last(), beforeFirst(), or afterLast().

2. Retrieve desired column values with ResultSet.get*XXX*(columnNumber)
   or ResultSet.get*XXX*(columnName), where *XXX* is the JDBC data type.

The following is a simple example, with a JSP page that searches the LyricNote
composer database for those born in Ireland:

```
<%@ page session="false" %>
<%@ page import="java.sql.*" %>
<%@ page import="javax.sql.*" %>
<%@ page import="javax.naming.*" %>
<html>
<head>
<title>Irish Composers</title>
<style type="text/css">
body, td, th { font-family: Verdana; font-size: 9pt; }
h1 { font-size: 130%; }
</style>
</head>
<body>
<h1>Irish Composers</h1>
<table border="0" cellpadding="3" cellspacing="1">
<%
    // Get the data source using JNDI

    InitialContext initCtx = new InitialContext();
    Context ctx = (Context) initCtx.lookup("java:comp/env");
    DataSource ds = (DataSource) ctx.lookup("jdbc/LyricNote");

    // Define these objects outside the "try" block so that
    // they can be closed in the "finally" block

    Connection con = null;
    Statement stmt = null;
    ResultSet rs = null;

    try {

        // Connect to the database

        con = ds.getConnection();
        stmt = con.createStatement();

        // Execute a query to select Irish composers

        String sql =
            "SELECT lname, fname, born, died"
            + " FROM composers"
            + " WHERE nationality = 'Irish'";
        rs = stmt.executeQuery(sql);

        // Loop through each row of the result set

        while (rs.next()) {
```

```
        // Extract the two string values and two
        // integer values from the current row

        String lastName = rs.getString(1);
        String firstName = rs.getString(2);
        int born = rs.getInt(3);
        int died = rs.getInt(4);

        // Print a table row with the values
        %>
        <tr>
           <td><%= firstName %> <%= lastName %></td>
           <td><%= born %>-<%= died %></td>
        </tr>
        <%
      }
   }

   // Close any open database objects

   finally {
      if (rs != null) rs.close();
      if (stmt != null) stmt.close();
      if (con != null) con.close();
   }
%>
</table>
</body>
</html>
```

A ResultSet object is created when the Statement executes a query. The JSP page reads each row by using the next() method and then extracts each column value with getString() or getInt(). The results are shown in Figure 15-17.

A number of getXXX() methods can be called on a ResultSet object. Table 15-1 contains the complete list.

Two versions of each getXXX() method exist: one that takes an integer column number (1, 2, ...) and one that takes a column name string. Accessing columns by number can be slightly more efficient, although column names make maintenance easier when the order of fields changes.

JDBC 2.0 introduced significant new features in result sets, which are discussed in the next three sections.

Scrollable Result Sets

Originally, result sets could be navigated in only one direction (forward) and starting at only one point (the first row). Since JDBC 2.0, the programmer has a great deal more flexibility. The cursor (row pointer) can be manipulated as if it were an array index. Methods exist for reading both forward and backward, for starting from any row, and for testing the current cursor location. Table 15-2 lists the available navigation methods.

Figure 15-17. *A simple example of result set processing*

Method	Description
getArray	Returns an SQL array.
getAsciiStream	Returns an opened `java.io.InputStream` of ASCII characters. Translation to ASCII (if necessary) is handled by the JDBC driver.
getBigDecimal	Returns a `java.math.BigDecimal`.
getBinaryStream	Returns an opened `java.io.InputStream`. No translation is done on the stream.
getBlob	Returns a `java.sql.Blob` (*Binary Large OBject*).
getBoolean	Returns a `true` or `false` value.
getByte	Returns a single byte.
getBytes	Returns an array of bytes.
getCharacterStream	Returns a `java.io.Reader` character stream.
getClob	Returns a `java.sql.Clob` (*Character Large OBject*).
getDate	Returns a `java.sql.Date` (a subclass of `java.util.Date`).
getDouble	Returns a double value.

Table 15-1. *getXXX() Methods Provided by ResultSet*

Method	Description
getFloat	Returns a float value.
getInt	Returns an integer value.
getLong	Returns a long integer value.
getObject	Returns a `java.lang.Object`.
getRef	Returns a `java.sql.Ref`, which is a reference to an SQL structured type value.
getShort	Returns a short integer value.
getString	Returns a string.
getTime	Returns a `java.sql.Time` value.
getTimestamp	Returns a `java.sql.Timestamp` value, which includes time in nanoseconds.
getURL	Returns a `java.net.URL` value.

Table 15-1. *getXXX() Methods Provided by ResultSet* (continued)

Method	Description
`boolean next()`	Advances the cursor to the next row.
`boolean previous()`	Moves the cursor back one row.
`boolean first()`	Moves the cursor to the first row.
`boolean last()`	Moves the cursor to the last row.
`void beforeFirst()`	Moves the cursor before the first row, usually in anticipation of calling `next()`.
`void afterLast()`	Moves the cursor after the last row, usually in anticipation of calling `previous()`.

Table 15-2. *JDBC 2.0 Navigation Methods for Scrollable Result Sets*

Method	Description
`boolean absolute(int row)`	Moves the cursor to the specified row. Specifying a negative number moves the cursor relative to the end of the result set; `absolute(-1)` is the same as `last()`.
`boolean relative(int row)`	Moves the cursor forward or backward the number of rows specified.
`boolean isBeforeFirst()`	True if the cursor is before the first row.
`boolean isAfterLast()`	True if the cursor is after the last row.
`boolean isFirst()`	True if the cursor is positioned on the first row.
`boolean isLast()`	True if the cursor is positioned on the last row.

Table 15-2. *JDBC 2.0 Navigation Methods for Scrollable Result Sets* (continued)

To use scrollable result sets, the `Statement` object must be created with parameters that indicate the specific capabilities requested. For this reason, there are two new forms of the `Connection.createStatement()` method:

```
public Statement createStatement(
    int resultSetType,
    int resultSetConcurrency)
throws SQLException

public Statement createStatement(
    int resultSetType,
    int resultSetConcurrency,
    int resultSetHoldability)
throws SQLException
```

where *resultSetType* indicates the type of scrolling to be used, *resultSetConcurrency* indicates whether the result set can be updated, and *resultSetHoldabililty* specifies whether to close cursors when a commit is done. These parameters take their values from constants in `ResultSet`, as shown in Table 15-3.

Constant	Meaning
TYPE_FORWARD_ONLY	JDBC 1.0–style navigation in which the cursor starts at the first row and can only move forward.
TYPE_SCROLL_INSENSITIVE	All cursor positioning methods are enabled; the result set doesn't reflect changes made by others in the underlying table.
TYPE_SCROLL_SENSITIVE	All cursor positioning methods are enabled; the result set reflects changes made by others in the underlying table.
CONCUR_READ_ONLY	The result set won't be updatable.
CONCUR_UPDATABLE	Rows can be added and deleted, and columns can be updated.
HOLD_CURSORS_OVER_COMMIT	Do not close cursors after a commit is done.
CLOSE_CURSORS_AT_COMMIT	Close cursors when a commit is done.

Table 15-3. *Constants in ResultSet That Can Be Used to Describe Scrollable Result Sets*

The following JSP page is an example of using a scrollable result set to display only the last page of a potentially lengthy query:

```jsp
<%@ page session="false" %>
<%@ page import="java.sql.*" %>
<%@ page import="java.text.*" %>
<%@ page import="java.util.*" %>
<%@ page import="javax.naming.*" %>
<%@ page import="javax.sql.*" %>
<%!
    private static final NumberFormat PRICE_FMT
        = NumberFormat.getCurrencyInstance();
%>
<html>
<head>
<title>Scrollable Example</title>
<style type="text/css">
body, td, th {
```

```
      font-family: Verdana;
      font-size: 9pt;
}
h1 {
      font-size: 130%;
}
</style>
</head>
<body>
<img src="images/lyric_note.png" border="0">
<div><hr/></div>
<%
   InitialContext initCtx = new InitialContext();
   Context ctx = (Context) initCtx.lookup("java:comp/env");
   DataSource ds = (DataSource) ctx.lookup("jdbc/LyricNote");

   // Declare JDBC objects outside the "try" block

   Connection con = null;
   Statement stmt = null;
   ResultSet rs   = null;

   try {
      con = ds.getConnection();

      stmt = con.createStatement(
         ResultSet.TYPE_SCROLL_INSENSITIVE,
         ResultSet.CONCUR_READ_ONLY);

      rs = stmt.executeQuery(
            " SELECT   itemcode, price, description"
         + " FROM     products"
         + " WHERE    prodtype = 'IN'"
         + " ORDER BY description"
         );

      // Calculate number of rows

      rs.last();
      int nRows = rs.getRow();

      // Back up ten rows
```

JSP APPLICATIONS

```
        rs.relative(-10);

        // Now print last page of result set
%>
<h1>
    Musical Instruments -
        Items <%= rs.getRow() + 1 %>
        through <%= nRows %>
</h1>
<table border="1" cellpadding="5" cellspacing="0">
<tr><th>Item</th><th>Price</th><th>Description</th></tr>
<%
    while (rs.next()) {
        String itemcode = rs.getString(1);
        double price = rs.getDouble(2);
        String description = rs.getString(3);
%>
<tr>
    <td><%= itemcode %></td>
    <td align="RIGHT"><%= PRICE_FMT.format(price) %></td>
    <td><%= description %></td>
</tr>
<%
    }
    }
    finally {
        if (rs != null) { rs.close(); rs = null; }
        if (stmt != null) { stmt.close(); stmt = null; }
        if (con != null) { con.close(); con = null; }
    }
%>
</table>
</body>
</html>
```

The `Statement` object is opened such that the result sets it creates are scrollable, but not updatable. Having these properties, the `ResultSet` can be asked how many rows it contains, which wasn't possible in JDBC 1.0. By positioning the cursor at the last row and issuing a `relative(-10)` method call, the last ten rows in the result set can be isolated and printed. Figure 15-18 shows the results.

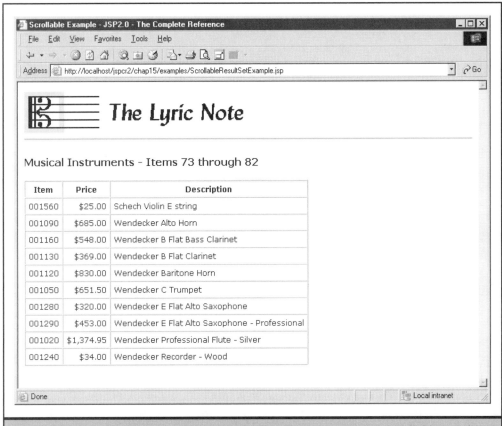

Figure 15-18. *Showing the last page of a lengthy query using a scrollable result set*

Updatable Result Sets

Since JDBC 2.0, updating columns in a result set is possible, both to add new rows and to delete existing rows. In each of these cases, the corresponding rows in the underlying table are then also updated.

For a result set to be updated, it must have been produced by a Statement object created with a concurrency type of ResultSet.CONCUR_UPDATABLE. JDBC 2.0 provides update*XXX*() methods, where *XXX* is the JDBC data type, similar to the existing get*XXX*() methods. These methods take a column number or column name parameter, and a value parameter, as illustrated in the following example:

```
double mySalary = rs.getDouble("SALARY");
```

```
mySalary *= 2.0;
rs.updateDouble("SALARY", mySalary);
rs.updateString("HOME_PHONE", unlisted);
rs.updateRow();
```

The updated values aren't automatically replicated in the underlying table until `updateRow()` is called. The updates can be canceled explicitly with `ResultSet.cancelRowUpdates()` if `updateRow()` hasn't yet been called or implicitly if a cursor movement method is called before `updateRow()`.

New rows can be added to the result set and the underlying table with `insertRow()`. This involves a special cursor position known as the *insert row*. The following example illustrates how this works:

```
rs.moveToInsertRow();
rs.setString("employeeid", "M1205");
rs.setString("firstName", "Maria");
rs.setString("lastName", "Alicia");
rs.insertRow();
rs.moveToCurrentRow();   // Return to where we were
```

In like fashion, rows in a result set and its underlying table can be deleted with `deleteRow()`. To do so, the cursor must be positioned at the row to be deleted, as shown here:

```
rs.last(); // Delete the last row    rs.deleteRow();
```

RowSets

The `javax.sql` package contains a `RowSet` interface, which extends and generalizes `java.sql.ResultSet` so that it can be detached from its database connection. This can be useful for *Personal Digital Assistant (PDA)* applications that cannot easily maintain a connection and have a limited amount of memory. `RowSets` are still in their infancy. Sun Microsystems has three early access implementations of the interface that can be used to explore their capabilities:

- **CachedRowSet** A serializable, disconnectable `RowSet` that can be populated from a JDBC result set.

- **JdbcRowSet** A connected `RowSet` also populated from a JDBC result set, which behaves according to the JavaBeans model.

- **WebRowSet** A subclass of `CachedRowSet` that can write its contents as an XML document.

Using Metadata

JDBC provides a rich set of *metadata*—data about data—for database connections and result sets. This section describes these two interfaces, how instances of them are obtained, and highlights of what information they can provide.

Database Metadata

Information about a JDBC connection can be obtained with
`Connection.getMetaData()`. This method returns an instance of
`java.sql.DatabaseMetaData`, an interface that has more methods
(165 in all) than any other class or interface in the `java.sql` and `javax.sql`
packages. These methods describe the features the database supports, what tables
it contains, and what columns are in these tables. Using metadata, differences in
the SQL language and capabilities of database systems can be minimized.

Viewing all the information a `DatabaseMetaData` object provides can be
instructional. Because so many methods are in the interface, coding all the individual
calls by hand is tedious. For this purpose, it is easier to use reflection to list all the
metadata methods. Here's how the technique works.

First, let's create a helper class `MetaDataEvaluator` that does the introspection:

```
package com.jspcr.jdbc.tools;

import java.lang.reflect.*;
import java.util.*;

/**
 * Evaluates the simple accessor methods of an object
 */
public class MetaDataEvaluator
{
    private Object obj;
    private Map methodMap = new TreeMap();
    private Object[] NO_PARMS = new Object[0];

    /**
     * Creates a new <code>MetaDataEvaluator</code>
     * for the specified object
     * @param obj the object
     */
    public MetaDataEvaluator(Object obj)
    {
        this.obj = obj;
        Class cls = obj.getClass();
        Method[] methods = cls.getMethods();
```

```
        for (int i = 0; i < methods.length; i++) {
            Method method = methods[i];
            if (method.getParameterTypes().length == 0) {
                Class returnType = method.getReturnType();
                if (
                    returnType.equals(String.class) ||
                    returnType.equals(Boolean.TYPE) ||
                    returnType.equals(Integer.TYPE)
                    )
                {
                    methodMap.put(method.getName(), method);
                }
            }
        }
    }

    /**
     * Returns an iterator over the set of method names
     */
    public Iterator getMethodNames()
    {
        return methodMap.keySet().iterator();
    }

    /**
     * Returns the value of the specified method
     * when evaluated on the object. For simplicity,
     * no exception reporting is done.
     * @param name the method name
     */
    public Object getMethodValue(String name)
    {
        Object value = null;
        Method method = (Method) methodMap.get(name);
        if (method != null) {
            try {
                value = method.invoke(obj, NO_PARMS);
            }
            catch (Throwable ignore) {}
        }
        return value;
    }
}
```

MetaDataEvaluator accepts an object in its constructor, then enumerates all of its simple accessor methods—those that have no parameters and return a String, boolean, or int. It has a getMethodNames() method that returns an iterator over the names, and a getMethodValue() method that evaluates the method against the object and returns the result.

Next, let's create a simple form that prompts for the necessary parameters:

- Driver class
- Database URL
- User ID (optional)
- Password (optional)

The form is displayed in Figure 15-19.

```html
<html>
<head>
<title>Metadata Explorer Form</title>
</head>
<body>
<h1 style="font-size: 130%;">Metadata Explorer</h1>
<form method="POST" action="MetaDataExplorer.jsp">
<table border="0" cellpadding="3" cellspacing="1">
<tr>
   <td>Driver class:</td>
   <td><input name="driverName" type="text" size=32></td>
</tr>
<tr>
   <td>Database URL:</td>
   <td><input name="url" type="text" size=32></td>
</tr>
<tr>
   <td>User ID:</td>
   <td><input name="userid" type="text" size=16></td>
</tr>
<tr>
   <td>Password:</td>
   <td><input name="password" type="password" size=16></td>
</tr>
<tr>
   <td> </td>
   <td><input type="submit" value="Connect"></td>
</tr>
</table>
</form>
</body>

</html>
```

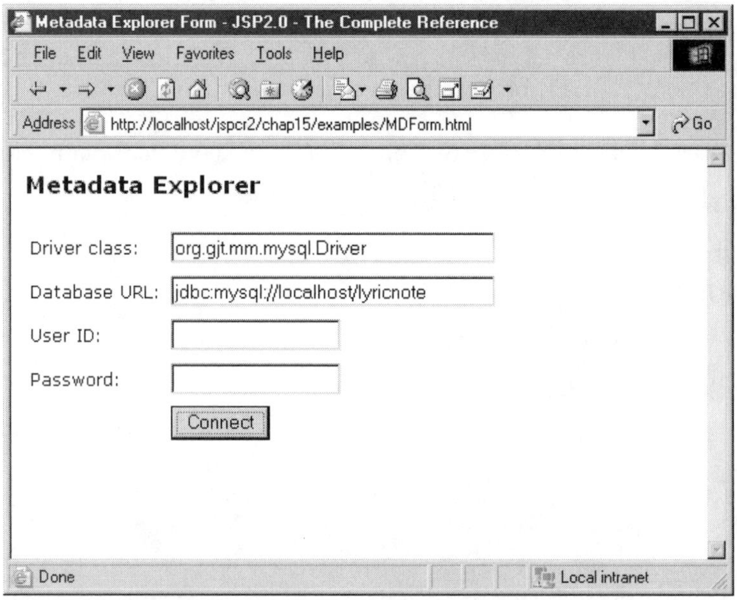

Figure 15-19. *Parameter input form for MetaDataExplorer.jsp*

The form captures the input parameters and then invokes the MetaDataExplorer.jsp shown here to invoke the helper class and render the results:

```
<%@ page session="false" %>
<%@ page import="com.jspcr.jdbc.tools.*" %>
<%@ page import="java.sql.*" %>
<%@ page import="java.util.*" %>
<html>
<head>
<title>Metadata Explorer</title>
<style type="text/css">
body, td, th {
    font-family: Verdana;
    font-size: 9pt;
}
th {
    text-align: left;
}
```

```
h1 {
   font-size: 130%;
   text-align: center;
}
</style>
</head>
<%
   // Get required driver name parameter

   String driverName = request.getParameter("driverName");
   if (driverName == null)
      driverName = "";
   driverName = driverName.trim();

   // Get required database URL parameter

   String url = request.getParameter("url");
   if (url == null)
      url = "";
   url = url.trim();

   // Get optional userID parameter

   String userID = request.getParameter("userID");
   if (userID == null)
      userID = "";
   userID = userID.trim();

   // Get optional password parameter

   String password = request.getParameter("password");
   if (password == null)
      password = "";
   password = password.trim();

   Class.forName(driverName);
   Connection con = null;
   try {

      con = DriverManager.getConnection(url, userID, password);
      DatabaseMetaData md = con.getMetaData();
      MetaDataEvaluator mde = new MetaDataEvaluator(md);
```

```
        out.println("<body>");
        out.println("<h1>Metadata Explorer for "
            + md.getDatabaseProductName()
            + " "
            + md.getDatabaseProductVersion()
            + "<br/>"
            + "[" + driverName + "]"
            + "</h1>"
            );
        out.println("<table border='1'"
                        + " cellpadding='3'"
                        + " cellspacing='0'>");
        out.println("<tr><th>Method</th><th>Value</th></tr>");

        for (Iterator it = mde.getMethodNames(); it.hasNext(); ) {
            String name = (String) it.next();
            Object value = mde.getMethodValue(name);
            out.println("<tr>");
            out.println("<td>" + name + "</td>");
            out.println("<td>" + value + "</td>");
            out.println("</tr>");
        }
    }
    finally {
        if (con != null)
            con.close();
    }
%>
</table>
</body>
</html>
```

When run against a MySQL database with the MM.MySQL driver, `MetaDataExplorer` produces the output partially listed in Figure 15-20.

ResultSetMetadata

In addition to `DatabaseMetaData` for database connections, `ResultSetMetaData` also gets information about the columns of a result set. This interface consists of one

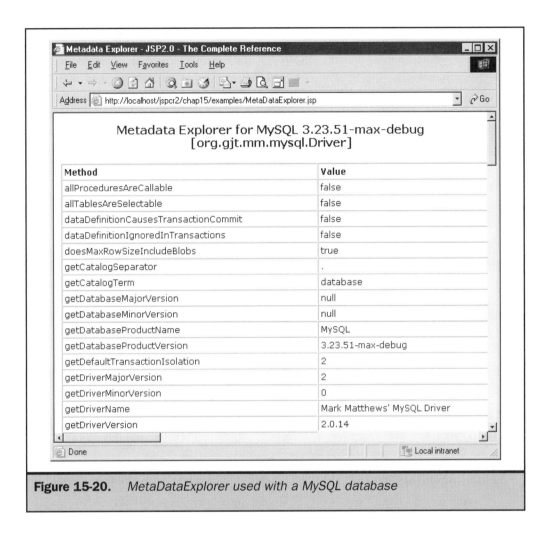

Figure 15-20.   *MetaDataExplorer used with a MySQL database*

method to get the number of columns—getColumnCount()—and 20 other methods
that describe individual columns.

To obtain a ResultSetMetaData object, a program invokes the
ResultSet.getMetaData() method, and then invokes its methods, passing
it a column number parameter. As is the case with ResultSet, the column numbers
start with 1.

Table 15-4 describes the methods available in ResultSetMetaData.

JSP APPLICATIONS

Method	Description
getColumnCount()	Returns the number of columns in each row of the result set.
getCatalogName(int col)	Returns the catalog name of the table from which the specified column is drawn.
getColumnClassName(int col)	Returns the fully qualified Java type name of the specified column.
getColumnDisplaySize(int col)	Returns the maximum display width for the specified column.
getColumnLabel(int col)	Returns the label for the specified column.
getColumnName(int col)	Returns the name of the specified column.
getColumnType(int col)	Returns the type of the specified column in a form corresponding to java.sql.Types.
getColumnTypeName(int col)	Returns the column data type as a string.
getPrecision(int col)	Returns number of decimal positions.
getScale(int col)	Returns the number of digits to the right of the decimal point.
getSchemaName(int col)	Returns the schema name of the column's table.
getTableName(int col)	Returns the name of the column's underlying table.
isAutoIncrement(int col)	True if the column is automatically numbered.
isCaseSensitive(int col)	True if the column's case matters.
isCurrency(int col)	True if the column is a cash value.
isDefinitelyWritable(int col)	True if a write to the specified column will definitely succeed.
isNullable(int col)	Returns a constant indicating whether the column can have a null value.
isReadOnly(int col)	True if the result set is read-only.

Table 15-4. *Methods Available in ResultSetMetaData*

Method	Description
isSearchable(int col)	True if this column can be used in a where clause.
isSigned(int col)	True if the column value is signed numeric.
isWritable(int col)	True if a write to the specified column may succeed.

Table 15-4.   *Methods Available in ResultSetMetaData* (continued)

Summary

Almost all nontrivial JSP applications require access to a database. Java provides a standard API known as JDBC. JDBC allows a wide variety of database systems to be accessed using standard SQL statements in an object-oriented framework. To use JDBC, a driver must be available for the database. Drivers exist for virtually all commercial databases, as well as a JDBC-ODBC bridge for using ODBC data sources.

JDBC has only a few key objects, which makes it easy to learn. The Connection object maintains an active link to a database. The three types of Statement objects allow SQL statements to be executed through the connection and capture the results in a ResultSet object. A large volume of information about connections and result sets can be obtained from the DatabaseMetaData and ResultSetMetaData objects.

A number of JDBC 2.0 features were discussed throughout this chapter, including:

■ **DataSource**   JDBC driver names and URLs can be stored in a name service and retrieved using JNDI.

■ **Connection pooling**   A data source provider can offer connection pooling, allowing connections to be activated and recycled, usually with a significant performance improvement. This capability is configured entirely in the naming service and requires no changes to applications.

■ **Scrollable result sets**   JDBC 1.0 allowed only forward navigation through a result set starting at the first record. JDBC 2.0 provides methods for forward and backward navigation, as well as relative and absolute cursor positioning.

■ **RowSets**   Disconnected result sets can be made to conform to the JavaBeans model.

■ **BatchUpdates**   Transactions can be grouped and sent to the database as a unit.

The final draft of JDBC 3.0 was released with JDK 1.4. Its new features include

■ Enhanced control of commit/rollback transaction boundaries
■ Configurability for connection pools
■ Better interface to parameters in prepared and callable statements

JDBC has continued to evolve through several releases with enhanced features and promises to continue as the dominant database access technology for Java programming.

Chapter 16

JSP and XML

ince its origin in the World Wide Web Consortium (W3C) in 1996 and its adoption as a W3C recommendation in 1998, the *Extensible Markup Language (XML)* has established itself as the universal language for structured data storage and interchange. XML is used for Web site content management, business to business data exchange, and applications as diverse as architecture, financial reporting, and music. XML is the foundation of Microsoft's .NET architecture, and the basis of SOAP (Simple Object Access Protocol). In addition to applications, XML tools and extensions are finding their way into all aspects of programming.

This chapter examines some ways in which XML can be incorporated into Web applications. After an overview section, it discusses the two XML parser models, and then XSL transformations. All three technologies are illustrated in three solutions to the same HTML creation task. The XML syntax for JSP pages is also covered.

XML Overview

XML is a system of describing structured data with a user-defined set of markup tags. XML isn't a language itself, but a system of defining special-purpose languages. It looks superficially like HTML, which marks sections of a Web document with predefined <ul>, <li>, <table>, and other tags. The difference is that HTML has a fixed set of tags, whereas XML enables you to design any set of tags necessary to describe your data.

For example, a song for voice and piano might be represented in part like this:

```
<?xml version="1.0"?>
<song>
    <title>The Birds</title>
    <words-by>Hilaire Belloc</words-by>
    <music-by>Benjamin Britten</music-by>

    <track name="Voices">
        <time-signature>2/2</time-signature>
        <tempo>Andante con moto</tempo>
        <measure>
            <rest duration="1"/>
        </measure>
        <measure>...</measure>
    </track>

    <track name="Piano">
        <time-signature>2/2</time-signature>
        <tempo>Andante con moto</tempo>
```

```
<measure>
   <note duration="8" value="e" octave="2"/>
   <note duration="8" value="g#" octave="2"/>
   <note duration="8" value="c#" octave="3"/>
   <note duration="8" value="g#" octave="3"/>
   <note duration="2" value="f#" octave="3"/>
</measure>
<measure>...</measure>
   </track>
</song>
```

Note, this representation of the song is entirely structural—it has nothing to do with how the song will appear. Indeed, the same XML document might be used for generating the printed sheet music and for synthesizing the tones in a MIDI player.

The Problem XML Solves

Earlier text-processing formats often didn't distinguish between content and presentation. RTF (Rich Text Format), for example, has codes for structural data like tables and lists, as well as for fonts and graphics. HTML suffers from the same problem. Elements like <table>, <tr>, and <td> with specific width and height attributes are commonly used to influence physical layout in a Web page, rather than to group related items in tabular format.

But there's a problem with this approach. Tags originally designed to convey structural information are misused, simply for their side effects, such as using <ul> to cause indentation. As new output formats are needed, the formatting information contained in the document can become useless.

XML, by contrast, focuses entirely on structure. Specific data elements can be clearly identified and extracted by text search applications. If an XML document needs to be rendered on a Web browser, it can be programmatically converted to HTML using an XSL stylesheet. If the document needs to be used in a transaction processing system, it can be parsed by an XML parser, which extracts the specific fields that make up the transaction. The XML document can be browsed as a tree structure or collapsed into relational database tables. So long as the application using the document knows the language in which it's written, the application can find and extract the data it needs.

In this sense, using XML content translated into HTML for presentation is like using the familiar MVC (model-view-controller) design pattern. The XML document serves as the *model*, having no display-oriented features and no browser dependencies to clutter it up. The HTML version is the *view*, perhaps combining with a Cascading Stylesheet (CSS) to provide fine-grained control over the look and feel. The *controller* is the transformation process, typically an XSL stylesheet applied by the Web container.

XML Syntax

XML is simple, and the rules governing its syntax are easy to learn. An XML document consists of elements, each of which has a start tag, a body, and an end tag, as the following illustrates:

```
<tempo>Andante con moto</tempo>
```

The *start tag* `<tempo>` consists of a tag name enclosed in the less-than and greater-than characters. The *end tag* `</tempo>` is the same as the start tag, but with a forward slash following the opening greater-than character. The *body* consists of everything between the start tag and the end tag. This may include ordinary text or other XML elements.

A start tag may include *attributes,* which are *name="value"* pairs coded inside the start tag after the name, but before the closing greater-than character:

```
<track name="voices"> ... </track>
```

Attributes in XML *must* be enclosed in single or double quotes.

If the body of an element is empty, an abbreviated form of the start and end tags can be used. In this form, the forward slash from the end tag is moved into the start tag just before the closing greater-than character, and then the body and end tags are omitted. Therefore, the following two forms are functionally equivalent:

```
<rest duration="1"></rest>
<rest duration="1"/>
```

Elements can be nested inside each other to any depth:

```
<song>
   <track>
      <measure>...</measure>
   </track>
</song>
```

but their end tags must appear in the exact opposite order in which the start tags appear. That is, elements cannot overlap. The following is illegal:

```
<b><i>Do not do this!</b></i>
```

An XML document, therefore, must consist of exactly one outer element, called the *document element,* which may contain any number of properly nested inner elements.

For complete details on XML syntax, consult the XML 1.0 specification, second edition, found in the W3C Recommendation of October 6, 2000. The current version of this document can be found at http://www.w3.org/TR/REC-xml.

A bit of history is instructive here. XML's predecessor is SGML, the Standard Generalized Markup Language. SGML is a powerful system for describing markup language, but its complexity has somewhat limited its widespread use. In 1996, a working group of the W3C set about to design a compatible replacement for SGML, adopting a number of welcome simplifications, from which XML emerged. Any valid XML document is by construction a valid SGML document as well.

The significance is that HTML, which is a specific markup language defined in SGML, is "almost" XML. Capitalizing on this similarity, the W3C has reformulated the HTML definition in XML, resulting in XHTML, which is a highly regular and syntactically exact HTML subset. XHTML documents are both valid HTML (correctly rendered by existing Web browsers) and valid XML (amenable to automatic parsing and generation). With few exceptions, this book uses XHTML in all its sample code. The only difference you may have noticed is that all elements have matching end tags and all elements and attributes have lowercase names. The potential value of XHTML and the ease with which it can be written make it well worth switching to.

The Document Type Definition

XML isn't just a free-form group of tags. Clearly, applications that use an XML document for input need to know what elements it can contain, how these elements can be nested or repeated, what attributes are allowed, and so on. Likewise, applications that generate XML documents (as well as humans composing documents with a text editor) need to know the same structural information. This is the role of the *document type definition (DTD)*.

A DTD is the definition of the tags and attributes allowed in a specific document type. For example, a DTD for memo documents might define the `<memo>`, `<from>`, `<to>`, `<subject>`, `<text>`, and `<paragraph>` tags, indicate `<paragraph>` elements can appear only inside `<text>` elements, and prescribe that `<from>` and `<to>` are required, while the rest are optional. Then applications that generate memo documents can ensure they generate only syntactically correct versions. Likewise, validation tools can read human-generated memo documents and determine whether they adhere to the syntax. This means applications on the receiving end can be relied on to understand the document and process it correctly.

An XML document indicates the DTD it uses and where to find it with a `<!DOCTYPE>` tag immediately before the document element:

```
<?xml version="1.0"?>
<!DOCTYPE song SYSTEM "song.dtd">
<song>
...
</song>
```

The DTD can also be embedded in the document itself

```
<?xml version="1.0"?>
<!DOCTYPE song [
...
]>
<song>
...
</song>
```

or it can be kept in a public repository:

```
<?xml version="1.0"?>
<!DOCTYPE song PUBLIC publicid systemid>
<song>
...
</song>
```

in which the public ID is an official "name" for the DTD and the system ID is a URI that points to its location.

A DTD isn't required, but if present, the document must adhere to it. In the language of the XML specification, a document is said to be *well formed* if it adheres to the syntactical rules (all elements closed, no nested elements, all attributes in quotes). If the document has a DTD, it is said to be *valid* if it is well formed and adheres to the DTD. To put it another way, you can think of a well-formed document as being *syntactically* correct, and a valid document as being both syntactically and *semantically* correct.

The DTD for our `song` document type looks like this:

```
<!ELEMENT    song     (title?,words-by?,music-by?,track+)>
<!ELEMENT    title    (#PCDATA)>
<!ELEMENT    words-by (#PCDATA)>
<!ELEMENT    music-by (#PCDATA)>
<!ELEMENT    track    (time-signature|tempo|measure)*>
<!ATTLIST    track
    name     CDATA    #IMPLIED>
<!ELEMENT    time-signature (#PCDATA)>
<!ELEMENT    tempo    (#PCDATA)>
<!ELEMENT    measure  (note|rest)+>
<!ELEMENT    note     EMPTY>
<!ATTLIST    note
    duration CDATA    #IMPLIED
    value    CDATA    #IMPLIED
```

```
   octave    (1|2|3|4|5|6|7|8) #REQUIRED>
<!ELEMENT  rest     EMPTY>
<!ATTLIST  rest
   duration CDATA    #IMPLIED>
```

A DTD consists of a list of elements and attributes. Each element definition gives the element name followed by a rigorous description of the elements it can contain, their order, whether they are required, and whether they can be repeated. This description may take several forms:

- Ordinary text is indicated as (#PCDATA), for *parsed character data*.
- Allowable subelements are listed in order, separated by commas.
- Mutually exclusive elements are separated by the logical OR symbol, |.
- Subelements and parenthesized lists of subelements can be followed by a repetition count: ? meaning zero or one occurrences, * for zero or more, and + for one or more.
- Elements that cannot contain a body are described as EMPTY.

For example, the <song> element is allowed to contain the optional <title>, <words-by>, and <music-by> elements, followed by one or more <track> elements:

```
<!ELEMENT   song     (title?,words-by?,music-by?,track+)>
```

Subelements, if present, must occur only in the order specified. The <measure> element is defined as containing at least one <note> or <rest> element, followed by any number of repetitions of <note> or <rest>:

```
<!ELEMENT   measure  (note|rest)+>
```

and the <time-signature> element may contain only ordinary text:

```
<!ELEMENT   tempo    (#PCDATA)>
```

Note *This element ordering requirement is a common source of errors in the web.xml deployment descriptor. I frequently need to consult the DTD to get the syntax right. For example, the DTD shows that initialization parameters for a servlet must be coded in the <servlet> block, just after <servlet-class> and before <load-on-startup>. Although not all Web containers validate the deployment descriptor against the DTD, you are asking for trouble if you ignore it. For maximum portability, follow the DTD.*

The attributes an element can have are listed in an `<!ATTLIST>` tag containing the element name, followed by groups of three tokens for each attribute, designating the attribute name, type, and default value. For example, the `<note>` element is described in the following as having optional `duration` and `value` attributes, as well as a required `octave` attribute that can take integer values from 1 to 8:

```
<!ATTLIST   note
   duration CDATA     #IMPLIED
   value    CDATA     #IMPLIED
   octave   (1|2|3|4|5|6|7|8) #REQUIRED>
```

If the DTD syntax looks intimidating, don't worry. Unless you're a document definition specialist, you'll rarely be called on to write one. The informal description given in this section is intended to give you the basic ability to read a DTD. For a rigorous definition, consult the XML specification.

XML Schema

My earlier comment about the element ordering restriction in `web.xml` points out an artifact of the limitations of the DTD "language," not an essential characteristic of the Web container's configuration. DTDs often impose restrictions that don't need to be there. Additionally, they don't handle namespaces correctly, and they are somewhat foreign to the spirit of XML, not being valid XML themselves.

A new approach from the W3C that addresses these problems is XML Schema, available in two parts at http://www.w3.org/TR/xmlschema-1 and http://www.w3.org/TR/xmlschema-2. XML Schema is a definition language for describing the structure of an XML document. An XML Schema is itself written in XML, so it can be read and manipulated by the rich set of tools that exist for XML. It also employs a more powerful syntax for describing the order in which elements occur, their minimum and maximum number of occurrences, and the attributes they can have.

We'll only consider a very high-level overview of XML Schema here. The official specification is over 300 pages long and may tax the comprehension of all but devoted computer scientists. Beginning with Servlet 2.4 and JSP 2.0, however, the deployment descriptor is officially defined only in terms of an XML schema, not a DTD. At a minimum, you need to be able to read a schema, even if you have no need to write one.

Elements of an XML Schema

There are quite a number of elements defined in XML Schema, but you can get by with recognizing just a few:

- **`<xs:element>`** Is used to define elements. It has attributes that can describe the minimum and maximum number of occurrences of this element in a given context. The body of an `<xs:element>` can describe what it contains and in what order.

- **<xs:attribute>** Is used to define individual attributes. XML Schema offers a flexible approach to defining attributes, much like element definition. Attributes can also be described by top-level standalone elements in a schema, and used by reference elsewhere. This allows you to define a common attribute in one place.

- **<xs:simpleType>** Marks the beginning of the definition of a type that has no attributes and only text content.

- **<xs:complexType>** Marks the beginning of the definition of any other type, that is, one that has some combination of attributes and child elements.

- **<xs:restriction>** Is used to define new types in terms of others, much like subclassing in object-oriented terms.

- **<xs:choice>** Describes a set of subelements an element can contain.

- **<xs:sequence>** Describes a set of subelements in a particular order.

The xs: namespace prefix, by the way, is a convention, not a requirement. You can define any other prefix you like using an xmlns attribute in your schema. Unless you have a compelling reason to do so, however, why make it more complicated than it already is?

An XML Schema Example

To get a more concrete idea of what an XML schema looks like, let's convert the song.dtd from the preceding section. Written as an equivalent schema, it might look like this:

```
<?xml version="1.0"?>
<xs:schema xmlns:xs="http://www.w3.org/2001/XMLSchema">

   <xs:element name="song">
      <xs:complexType>
         <xs:sequence>
            <xs:element ref="title" minOccurs="0"/>
            <xs:element ref="words-by" minOccurs="0"/>
            <xs:element ref="music-by" minOccurs="0"/>
            <xs:element ref="track" maxOccurs="unbounded"/>
         </xs:sequence>
      </xs:complexType>
   </xs:element>

   <xs:element name="title" type="xs:string"/>
   <xs:element name="words-by" type="xs:string"/>
   <xs:element name="music-by" type="xs:string"/>

   <xs:element name="track">
      <xs:complexType>
         <xs:choice minOccurs="0" maxOccurs="unbounded">
```

```xml
            <xs:element ref="time-signature"/>
            <xs:element ref="tempo"/>
            <xs:element ref="measure"/>
        </xs:choice>
        <xs:attribute name="name" type="xs:string"/>
    </xs:complexType>
</xs:element>

<xs:element name="time-signature" type="xs:string"/>
<xs:element name="tempo" type="xs:string"/>

<xs:element name="measure">
    <xs:complexType>
        <xs:choice maxOccurs="unbounded">
            <xs:element ref="note"/>
            <xs:element ref="rest"/>
        </xs:choice>
    </xs:complexType>
</xs:element>

<xs:element name="note">
    <xs:complexType>
        <xs:attribute name="duration" type="xs:string"/>
        <xs:attribute name="value" type="xs:string"/>
        <xs:attribute name="octave" use="required">
            <xs:simpleType>
                <xs:restriction base="xs:string">
                <xs:enumeration value="1"/>
                <xs:enumeration value="2"/>
                <xs:enumeration value="3"/>
                <xs:enumeration value="4"/>
                <xs:enumeration value="5"/>
                <xs:enumeration value="6"/>
                <xs:enumeration value="7"/>
                <xs:enumeration value="8"/>
                </xs:restriction>
            </xs:simpleType>
        </xs:attribute>
    </xs:complexType>
</xs:element>

<xs:element name="rest">
```

```
        <xs:complexType>
            <xs:attribute name="duration" type="xs:string"/>
        </xs:complexType>
    </xs:element>

</xs:schema>
```

Even though it's more verbose than the corresponding DTD, you should have little trouble understanding it if you take it a piece at a time. The song element, described in the DTD like this:

```
<!ELEMENT song (title?,words-by?,music-by?,track+)>
```

consists of optional title, words-by, and music-by elements, followed by one or more track elements. In schema form, this becomes:

```
<xs:element name="song">
    <xs:complexType>
        <xs:sequence>
            <xs:element ref="title" minOccurs="0"/>
            <xs:element ref="words-by" minOccurs="0"/>
            <xs:element ref="music-by" minOccurs="0"/>
            <xs:element ref="track" maxOccurs="unbounded"/>
        </xs:sequence>
    </xs:complexType>
</xs:element>
```

with the order and cardinality (number) clearly indicated. Note that only the song element is being defined in this block. Its subelements are pointed to by the ref attribute in each <xs:element> child.

The measure element illustrates how to describe alternative elements. In the DTD, it looks like this:

```
<!ELEMENT measure (note|rest)+>
```

indicating that it contains at least one of the note or rest elements, and optionally more. In schema form, this is expressed as:

```
<xs:element name="measure">
    <xs:complexType>
```

```
      <xs:choice maxOccurs="unbounded">
          <xs:element ref="note"/>
          <xs:element ref="rest"/>
      </xs:choice>
   </xs:complexType>
</xs:element>
```

Enumerated values, such as the (1|2|3|4|5|6|7|8) allowed for the octave attribute of the note element, are expressed as subtypes defined with <xs:restriction> and <xs:enumeration>, and so on.

XML Schema is still in its early stages of acceptance, and not all tools recognize it or handle it properly. It is likely, however, that it will become more widespread as its advantages are established.

XML Processing Models

To use an XML document in an application, you need to parse it. An XML *parser* reads a document and separates it into start tags, attributes, body contents, and end tags. The parser has an application programming interface that enables you to extract the elements you need without the complexity of interpreting the input stream yourself.

Two generally accepted XML parser models exist:

- **DOM**   Document Object Model
- **SAX**   Simple API for XML

The following sections consider each of these models.

Document Object Model (DOM)

The *Document Object Model (DOM)* is the W3C standard representation of a document in memory. Rather than just strings of text, DOM represents a document as a tree of nodes. The tree can be traversed in any order, nodes can be added and deleted, and the modified DOM tree can be saved as a new document.

The DOM specification has different versions, referred to as *levels. DOM Level 1* was the core feature set, providing the means for creating and accessing document elements. *DOM Level 2*, which was approved as a W3C recommendation on November 13, 2000, adds support for namespaces and events. The *DOM Level 3* working draft defines a load and save protocol, validation, more event handling, and an XPath interface.

DOM isn't just a standard, but an *Application Programming Interface (API)* as well. The W3C publishes a list of interfaces that compose the org.w3c.dom package. Different vendors, then, supply parsers that implement these interfaces.

The DOM API consists of four categories of classes and interfaces:

- Nodes
- Node collections
- Metadata
- Exceptions

Node Interfaces

The basic unit of interest in DOM is the *node.* Everything in an XML document—individual elements, attributes in a start tag, comments, element text, and the document as a whole—is a node. Table 16-1 lists the methods in the `Node` interface.

In DOM Level 2, `Node` has two new methods—`isSupported()` and `hasAttributes()`—and now contains the `normalize()` method, which was previously part of the `Element` interface.

Method	Description
`Node appendChild(Node newChild)` `throws DOMException`	Adds a new child node to the current node.
`Node cloneNode(boolean deep)`	Makes a copy of the node. If `deep` is true, recursively clones all subtrees under this node. Otherwise, clones the current node.
`NamedNodeMap getAttributes()`	Returns the named attributes of this node, if the node is an `Element`. Otherwise, returns `null`.
`NodeList getChildNodes()`	Returns the list of all immediate child nodes.
`Node getFirstChild()`	Returns the first child node, or `null`, if this node isn't an `Element`.
`Node getLastChild()`	Returns the last child node, or `null`, if this node isn't an `Element`.
`Node getNextSibling()`	Returns the next child of the same parent, or `null`, if the parent node isn't an `Element`.

Table 16-1. *Methods in the Node Interface*

Method	Description
String getNodeName()	Returns the name of the node, for named nodes types like Element, Attr, and Entity. For unnamed types like Text, CDATAsection, and Comment, returns #text, #cdata-section, and #comment, respectively.
int getNodeType()	Returns an integer constant that indicates this node's specific type. The value returned is one of the following constants defined in the Node interface: ATTRIBUTE_NODE CDATA_SECTION_NODE COMMENT_NODE DOCUMENT_FRAGMENT_NODE DOCUMENT_NODE DOCUMENT_TYPE_NODE ELEMENT_NODE ENTITY_NODE ENTITY_REFERENCE_NODE NOTATION_NODE PROCESSING_INSTRUCTION_NODE TEXT_NODE
String getNodeValue()	For attributes and text-type nodes, returns the text, otherwise null.
Document getOwnerDocument()	Returns the Document node for the document in which this node occurs.
Node getParentNode()	Returns the immediate parent node, or null, if this is a Document, DocumentFragment, or Attr node. New nodes that haven't yet been added to a document may also have a null parent node.

Table 16-1.   *Methods in the Node Interface* (continued)

Method	Description
Node getPreviousSibling()	Returns the previous child of the same parent, or null, if the parent node isn't an Element.
boolean hasChildNodes()	Returns true if this node has a nonempty list of child nodes.
Node insertBefore(Node *child*, Node *beforeNode*)	Inserts a new child node before the specified node. beforeNode may be null, in which case the child node is appended to the end of the list.
Node removeChild(Node *child*) throws DOMException	Removes the specified node from the list of child nodes. Throws an exception if the node isn't a child of the current node.
Node replaceChild(Node *newChild*, Node *oldChild*) throws DOMException	Removes *oldChild* and replaces it with *newChild*. Throws an exception if the node isn't a child of the current node.
void setNodeValue(String *value*) throws DOMException	Sets the value of the current node.

Table 16-1.   *Methods in the Node Interface* (continued)

Node has 13 specialized subinterfaces that correspond to particular nodes types, which can appear in an XML document. These interfaces are listed in Table 16-2.

Interface	Description
Attr	An attribute of an Element node. Attr has methods for retrieving the name and value of the attribute. In DOM Level 2, the Attr interface includes a getOwnerElement() method.

Table 16-2.   *Subinterfaces of Node for Specific Node Types*

Interface	Description
CDATASection	A text node enclosed with the `<![CDATA[ ... ]]>` escape syntax in the XML document. CDATA sections are parsed verbatim without being evaluated. They allow document content to contain characters and strings that, otherwise, would be interpreted as XML.
CharacterData	A common superinterface for the three text-containing node types: Text, Comment, and CDATASection. Provides methods for getting and setting the character contents, as well as determining the length of the data.
Comment	A node containing an XML comment. The Comment value doesn't include the `<!--` and `-->` delimiters, only the text of the comment, including whitespace.
Document	The Document node represents the XML document as a whole. Only one Document node is in a DOM instance. DOM Level 2 adds support for namespaces to the Document interface.
DocumentFragment	A temporary node used to build a subtree of a Document node. This interface has no methods.
DocumentType	A node representing the `<!DOCTYPE>` element at the beginning of the document. This interface provides methods for getting the DTD name, entities, and notations defined in the DTD.
Element	The most common subinterface of Node. Represents an XML start tag, body, and end tag. In addition to the methods it inherits from Node, Element has methods for setting and retrieving the attributes that appear in the start tag. In DOM Level 2, Element includes numerous namespace-aware methods.
Entity	An external component used in an XML document, such as an image file. DOM level 1 provides only minimal support for this node type.

Table 16-2. *Subinterfaces of Node for Specific Node Types (continued)*

Interface	Description
EntityReference	A reference (name or pointer) to an unevaluated Entity. This interface acts simply as a placeholder in the document; it defines no methods.
Notation	Represents a notation declared in the DTD. Notations describe the format of external entities.
Processing Instruction	A processor-specific instruction in the XML document. Processing instructions employ the syntax <?<target> [<data>]?>.
Text	A Text node contains the character content of an element body.

Table 16-2. *Subinterfaces of Node for Specific Node Types* (continued)

Node Collection Interfaces

Various DOM API methods return collections of nodes, either ordered lists or maps of names to nodes. Two interfaces represent these collections: NodeList, shown in Table 16-3, and NamedNodeMap, in Table 16-4.

The NamedNodeMap interface in DOM Level 2 supports qualified item names in namespaces.

Method	Description
int getLength()	Returns the number of nodes in the list.
Node item(int n)	Returns the nth node in the list, where nodes are numbered 0, 1, ...

Table 16-3. *Methods Defined by the NodeList Interface*

Method	Description
int getLength()	Returns the number of nodes in the list.
Node item(int *n*)	Returns the *n*th node in the list, where nodes are numbered 0, 1, ...
Node getNamedItem(String *name*) void setNamedItem(Node *item*) void removeNamedItem(String *name*)	Gets, sets, or removes the node having the specified name. getNamedItem() returns null if the node doesn't exist in the collection.

Table 16-4. *Methods Defined by the NamedNodeMap Interface*

Node Metadata

XML features can be version-specific. To determine the DOM configuration, DOM has an interface that enables you to query which features it supports. This interface is named DOMImplementation. Currently, it consists of a single method

```
boolean hasFeature(String feature, String version)
```

which returns true if the specified level of the specified feature is supported. DOM Level 2 adds two new methods to DOMImplementation to support creating documents.

Exceptions

DOM defines a single exception class named DOMException. This is a subclass of RuntimeException, which means the compiler won't require methods that can throw this exception to declare it or to enclose it in a try/catch block.

Simple API for XML (SAX)

SAX provides a different approach to parsing. Rather than creating a tree from an XML document, a SAX parser reads through the file and notifies registered listeners when certain parsing events occur. These events include

- The beginning of a document
- Reading a start tag at the beginning of a new element
- Reading an end tag at the end of an element
- Reading text in the body of an element

- Reading comments
- Reaching the end of a document

A SAX interface defines methods for all these events. An application that wants to handle particular events can implement one or more of the methods, and then register as a handler for the document. When the events occur, the handler's method(s) are then invoked with values from the element currently being parsed. This makes SAX ideal for filtering-type applications that require little or no document context.

Like DOM, the SAX API continues to evolve. SAX 1.0 emerged in May 1998 from design discussions on the XML-DEV mailing list. The SAX 2.0 specification was published in May 2000. While SAX isn't an official W3C specification, it's widely accepted and usually offered alongside DOM in most parsers. In fact, DOM parsers are often built over SAX parsers and the JAXP `DocumentBuilder` interface for DOM uses several SAX classes.

The main improvement in SAX 2.0 is support for namespaces. *Namespaces* are groups of tags with a common prefix that distinguishes them from other tags that may have the same name. This allows packages of XML tags to be defined without worrying about colliding with similarly named tags.

In API terms, SAX 2.0 deprecates the `Parser`, `DocumentHandler`, and `AttributeList` interfaces, replacing them with the namespace-aware `XMLReader`, `ContentHandler`, and `Attributes` interfaces, respectively.

The SAX Parser

The basic SAX interface is `XMLReader`. An implementation of the SAX API would supply a concrete class that implements `XMLReader`. This interface defines methods that register the various handler classes to be used and defines two forms of the `parse()` method, as shown in Table 16-5.

Method	Description
`void parse(InputSource is) throws SAXException, IOException`	Causes the parser to begin parsing the document supplied by the specified input source.
`void parse(String systemId) throws SAXException, IOException`	Causes the parser to begin parsing the document referred to in the specified system ID. This can be a filename or a fully resolved URL.
`void setContentHandler (ContentHandler handler)`	Registers a content handler for this parser.

Table 16-5.   *Methods in the SAX XMLReader Interface*

Method	Description
void setDTDHandler(DTDHandler *handler*)	Registers a DTD handler for this parser.
void setEntityResolver(EntityResolver *resolver*)	Registers an entity resolver for this parser. An EntityResolver can be used to locate external entities in custom ways.
void setErrorHandler(ErrorHandler *handler*)	Registers an error handler for custom error handling.
Object getProperty(String *name*) void setProperty(String *name*, Object *value*)	Gets or sets a property object for the parser. This facility is used to supply implementation-specific objects to parsers without requiring the API to support them directly. The name of the property is a fully qualified URI that typically identifies the parser vendor and the property name. The URI is not actually a pointer to any location; it is just a unique identifier.
boolean getFeature(String *name*) void setFeature(String *name*, boolean *value*)	Similar to properties, these are yes-or-no values that can be used to enable or disable parser features.

Table 16-5. *Methods in the SAX XMLReader Interface* (continued)

Handlers

Four interfaces handle parsing events:

- **ContentHandler** defines callback methods for the start and end of a document, for the start and end of every XML element, for the text of the document, and for whitespace, comments, and processing instructions.

- **ErrorHandler** defines callbacks for fatal, recoverable, and warning errors.

- **EntityResolver** allows custom handling of external entities, such as document type definitions.

- **DTDHandler** receives notifications of notation declarations and unparsed entity declarations in a document type definition.

Of these, you'll most often employ only the first, ContentHandler. An application can implement this interface, and then register itself with the parser using the setContentHandler() method to begin receiving callbacks. The methods in ContentHandler are described in Table 16-6.

Method	Description
void setDocumentLocator (Locator *locator*)	Informs the content handler about the Locator to be used during parsing. Locator provides line and column number information useful during parsing errors. You should save a reference to this object if you intend to use it later.
void startDocument() throws SAXException	Called when the parser starts parsing a new document.
void endDocument() throws SAXException	Called when the parser has finished parsing a document.
void startElement(String *namespaceURI*, String *localName*, String *qName*, Attributes *attrs*) throws SAXException	Called when the parser encounters the beginning of a new element tag. The parameters passed include the tag name and the name/value attribute pairs. If namespaces are being used, the namespace URI and local name will give the element name; otherwise, the qualified name (qName) will generally provide it. Parser vendors are not always consistent on this point.
void endElement(String *namespaceURI*, String *localName*, String *qName*) throws SAXException	Called when the end tag for the current element is parsed. The parameters are the same as those of startElement, except that there are no attributes.
void characters(char[] *ch*, int *start*, int *len*) throws SAXException	This method is called with the XML parser and reads character data in the text of an element. The character data is passed in the *ch* array starting at *start* for length *len*. Conveniently, a String constructor uses these same three fields, and StringBuffer has an append() method with the same parameters.
void startPrefixMapping(String *prefix*, String *URI*) throws SAXException	Called when the parser finds a new namespace declaration.

Table 16-6. *Methods Defined by ContentHandler*

Method	Description
void endPrefixMapping(String *prefix*, String *URI*) throws SAXException	Called when a namespace declaration goes out of scope.
void ignorableWhitespace(char[] *ch*, int *start*, int *len*) throws SAXException	This method is called with the XML parser and reads nonsignificant character data. The character data is passed in the *ch* array starting at *start* for length *len*.
void processingInstruction (String *target*, String *data*) throws SAXException	Called when a processing instruction is encountered.
void skippedEntity(String *name*) throws SAXException	Called when the parser bypasses an entity reference in a document, such as &copyright;, either because it has no definition of it or because it is an external entity.

Table 16-6. *Methods Defined by ContentHandler* (continued)

In addition to the four handler interfaces, the SAX API provides a default implementation—named DefaultHandlerf—or all four of them. An application would typically subclass DefaultHandler and implement only those necessary methods. Often, this consists of just the startElement(), characters(), and endElement() methods.

Parsing XML

In this section, we'll develop complete examples of how to read XML in applications, with both DOM and SAX. First, however, we'll cover a slightly higher-level API that makes this all easier.

JAXP

One of the consequences of developing interface-based vendor-implemented APIs is that the original API rarely covers everything, and so vendors implement the rest each in their own way. An example is that DOM itself doesn't provide any means for actually creating a Document object to begin with, or any way to write it out as XML. Parser vendors provided various means for doing this. This means that if you change parsers, you need to change and recompile a number of your classes.

The Java Community Process addresses this issue by providing a common layer that hides the differences. This layer is known as *JAXP* (Java API for XML Processing). JAXP is a very thin layer, consisting primarily of a few factory classes that are controlled by system properties. Properly used, JAXP makes your code (nearly) independent of the underlying parser implementation.

The DOM and SAX sections following describe the specific JAXP factory interfaces they use.

Parsing with DOM

A typical DOM-oriented application creates an instance of a DOM parser, and then instructs it to parse an XML input source to create the DOM tree. Once the tree is created, the application can navigate through it, examining its contents and extracting what it needs.

Under JAXP, an application creates an instance of `DocumentBuilderFactory`, optionally sets its `namespaceAware` and/or `validating` properties, and then uses the factory to obtain an instance of the parser. The factory finds a DOM parser class that matches the required features.

So, to parse an XML document with DOM, an application can do this:

```
DocumentBuilderFactory factory =
    DocumentBuilderFactory.newInstance();
DocumentBuilder builder = factory.newDocumentBuilder();
Document document = builder.parse(fileName);
Element root = document.getDocumentElement();
```

Let's look at an example of XML parsing with DOM in a JSP page. The following XML document was extracted from the LyricNote product catalog, possibly as the result of a database query. It consists of a list of musical instruments identified by a product code. For each instrument, the document contains the price, the quantity on hand, the name of the manufacturer, and a product description. The list is abbreviated here; the full list has 82 entries.

```
<?xml version="1.0"?>

<products>

    <product code="001000">
        <product-type>IN</product-type>
        <price>537.00</price>
        <on-hand>48</on-hand>
        <manufacturer>Clemens-Altman</manufacturer>
```

```
      <description>Silver Flute - Student</description>
   </product>

   <product code="001010">
      <product-type>IN</product-type>
      <price>876.00</price>
      <on-hand>83</on-hand>
      <manufacturer>Gabriel</manufacturer>
      <description>Silver Flute</description>
   </product>

   ...

   <product code="001790">
      <product-type>IN</product-type>
      <price>165.50</price>
      <on-hand>94</on-hand>
      <manufacturer>Roush and Sons</manufacturer>
      <description>Cello case (1/2 size)</description>
   </product>

</products>
```

The JSP parses the document and extracts only products whose manufacturer is
Clemens-Altman. It arranges this subset in an HTML table, with columns for the
product code, the description, and the price. Because the document consists of a set
of product elements, a logical approach is to parse the document and convert it into
a collection of Product objects. The Product object will have fields corresponding
to the XML elements in each product block.

The following code shows the Java interface that describes the Product object:

```
package com.jspcr.xmlsamples;

import java.io.*;

/**
 * A data structure that represents a product in
 * the LyricNote catalog
 */
public interface Product extends Serializable
{
```

```
    public String getCode();
    public String getType();
    public double getPrice();
    public String getManufacturer();
    public String getDescription();
}
```

To provide access to the parsed collection of `Product` objects, we'll define a Java interface that provides an iterator:

```
package com.jspcr.xmlsamples;

import java.io.*;
import java.util.*;

/**
 * Container for a list of <code>Product</code> objects.
 * Parses an XML input stream and fills the list by creating
 * <code>Product</code> objects from the XML.
 */
public interface ProductList
{
    /**
     * Returns an iterator over the product list.
     * @exception IOException if an I/O error occurs
     * while constructing the list
     */
    public Iterator iterator() throws IOException;
}
```

At this point, we'll cheat a little bit and pretend that we had the foresight to develop a general-purpose implementation of this interface, rather than a DOM-specific one. It turns out that this implementation will be the base class that we'll use for both DOM and SAX versions:

```
package com.jspcr.xmlsamples;

import java.io.*;
import java.util.*;

/**
```

```java
 * Default implementation of <code>ProductList</code>
 * interface. This serves as a common parent for the
 * DOM and SAX versions.
 */
public abstract class AbstractProductList
    implements ProductList
{
   /**
    * The constructed list of products
    */
   private List list;

   /**
    * Hard-coded URL - in a real application, this would be
    * a read/write property
    */
   protected String inputURL =
       "http://localhost/jspcr2/chap16/XMLSource";

   // ==========================================
   //    Public interface - this is what
   //    implements ProductList
   // ==========================================

   /**
    * Returns an iterator over the product list.
    * @exception IOException if an I/O error occurs
    */
   public Iterator iterator() throws IOException
   {
      if (list == null)
         list = loadProductList();

      return list.iterator();
   }

   // ==========================================
   //    Abstract methods - must be implemented
   //    by subclasses
   // ==========================================

   /**
    * Loads the product list from the input URL.
```

```
     * @exception IOException if an I/O error occurs
     */
    protected abstract List loadProductList() throws IOException;

    // =========================================
    //    Protected inner class defined here
    //    so that it can be used by subclasses
    // =========================================

    /**
     * Implementation of the Product interface.
     */
    protected static class ProductImpl implements Product
    {
        protected String code;
        protected String type;
        protected double price;
        protected String manufacturer;
        protected String description;

        public String getCode() { return code; }
        public String getType() { return type; }
        public double getPrice() { return price; }
        public String getManufacturer() { return manufacturer; }
        public String getDescription() { return description; }
    }
}
```

The `iterator()` method uses what is known as "lazy instantiation." The first time it is called, it calls another method to parse the XML and create the product list. It then saves a reference to the product list so that it can bypass reloading the data. In this case, the method that loads the list is declared to be `abstract`, so the DOM and SAX subclasses will have to implement their own versions. In addition, this parent class provides a concrete implementation of the `Product` interface that can be used by subclasses. There is no need to make this class public, because the `Product` interface is all that clients will ever be allowed to use.

Now let's look at the DOM-specific subclass of `AbstractProductList`, which simply needs to implement the `loadProductList()` method:

```
package com.jspcr.xmlsamples;

import java.io.*;
```

```
import java.net.*;
import java.util.*;
import javax.xml.parsers.*;
import org.w3c.dom.*;
import org.xml.sax.*;

/**
 * An extension of AbstractProductList that loads data from
 * an XML DOM tree.
 */
public class DOMProductList extends AbstractProductList
{
    /**
     * DOM-specific implementation of loadProductList.
     */
    protected synchronized List loadProductList()
        throws IOException
    {
        List list = new ArrayList();
        try {

            // Use JAXP to parse the input stream
            // into a DOM tree

            DocumentBuilderFactory factory =
                DocumentBuilderFactory.newInstance();
            DocumentBuilder builder = factory.newDocumentBuilder();
            Document doc = builder.parse(inputURL);
            Element root = doc.getDocumentElement();

            // Extract the <product> elements, create Product
            // objects from them, and add them to the list.

            NodeList nodes = root.getElementsByTagName("product");

            for (int i = 0, n = nodes.getLength(); i < n; i++) {

                Element elemProduct = (Element) nodes.item(i);
                ProductImpl product = new ProductImpl();
                product.code = elemProduct.getAttribute("code");

                for ( Node node = elemProduct.getFirstChild();
                      node != null;
```

```
                    node = node.getNextSibling()) {

            if (node.getNodeType() == Node.ELEMENT_NODE) {

                Element element = (Element) node;

                String tagName = element.getNodeName();
                String text = getElementText(element);

                if (tagName.equals("product-type"))
                    product.type = text;

                else if (tagName.equals("price"))
                    product.price = Double.parseDouble(text);

                else if (tagName.equals("manufacturer"))
                    product.manufacturer = text;

                else if (tagName.equals("description"))
                    product.description = text;
            }
        }

        list.add(product);
    }
}
catch (SAXException e) {
    throw new IOException
        ("parsing exception: " + e.getMessage());
}
catch (ParserConfigurationException e) {
    throw new IOException
        ("parsing exception: " + e.getMessage());
}

return list;
}

/**
* Helper method that extracts the text of an element
*/
private static String getElementText(Element element)
{
```

```
          StringBuffer sb = new StringBuffer();

          for ( Node node = element.getFirstChild();
                node != null;
                node = node.getNextSibling()) {

             if (node.getNodeType() == Node.TEXT_NODE) {
                Text textNode = (Text) node;
                sb.append(textNode.getData());
             }
          }
          return sb.toString().trim();
       }
   }
```

Among other things, this class illustrates how to use JAXP to create a DOM tree from an XML input source. After ensuring that you import the JAXP packages (`javax.xml.parsers.*`), the first thing you do is create a document builder factory. You do this with a factory method that checks system properties to see which vendor's factory class you're using:

```
   DocumentBuilderFactory factory = DocumentBuilderFactory.newInstance()
```

Next, you ask the factory to give you a document builder:

```
   DocumentBuilder builder = factory.newDocumentBuilder();
```

This document builder can be used to create a new DOM document object, either by parsing an XML document or just creating a new one from scratch:

```
   // To parse an XML document:
   Document doc = builder.parse(uri);

   // To create an empty DOM tree:
   Document doc = builder.newDocument();
```

There are several flavors of each of these methods; the JAXP documentation describes them in detail. Mostly, they provide convenience implementations for the different forms your input may take.

The remainder of this method consists of code that invokes methods to navigate through the `Document` object, collect product data, and create a list of `Product` objects.

It first uses the document's `getElementsByTagName()` method to get a `NodeList` of `product` nodes. The outer loop then iterates through the node list and constructs `Product` objects.

The `code` field is easy to get because it's an attribute of the product element. All you have to do is call the element's `getAttribute("code")` method. The other fields are slightly more complicated because their values are in text nodes beneath subelements of `product`. Our approach is to loop through the child nodes of the `product` element, comparing the node name in each to the field names we need to populate. This loop can be done several ways:

- Call the `getChildNodes()` method on the `product` element, which returns a `NodeList` object. The `NodeList` has a `getLength()` method, which tells us the node count, and an `item(int index)` method, which returns the node at the specified index within the list.
- Call the `product` element's `getFirstChild()` method, and then each child's `getNextSibling()` method in turn until it returns `null`.

Our code uses the second method.

To get the text node values, we use a helper method that collects the values of text nodes that are immediate children of a given element.

We're now ready to write our JSP page. Again, we'll cheat a little, knowing that we're about to develop a SAX version, and create a common base:

```
<%@ page session="false" %>
<%@ page import="com.jspcr.xmlsamples.*" %>
<%@ page import="java.io.*" %>
<%@ page import="java.net.*" %>
<%@ page import="java.text.*" %>
<%@ page import="java.util.*" %>
<%
    ProductList productList =
        (ProductList) request.getAttribute("productList");

    String parserType =
        (String) request.getAttribute("parserType");
%>
<html>
<head>
<title>
    (<%= parserType %>)
    Clemens-Altman Musical Instruments
</title>
```

```
<style>
body, td, th {
    font-family: Verdana;
    font-size: 9pt;
}
h1 { font-size: 130%; }
h2 { font-size: 110%; }
body { text-align: center; }
</style>
</head>
<body>
<h1>Clemens-Altman Musical Instruments</h1>
<h2>(Powered by <%= parserType %>)</h2>
<table border="1" cellpadding="3" cellspacing="0">
<tr>
    <th>Product Code</th>
    <th>Description</th>
    <th>Price</th>
</tr>
<%
    NumberFormat fmt = NumberFormat.getCurrencyInstance();
    for (Iterator it = productList.iterator(); it.hasNext(); ) {
        Product product = (Product) it.next();
        if (product.getManufacturer().equals("Clemens-Altman")) {
%>
<tr>
    <td><%= product.getCode() %></td>
    <td><%= product.getDescription() %></td>
    <td align="right"><%= fmt.format(product.getPrice()) %></td>
</tr>
<%
        }
    }
%>
</table>
</body>
</html>
```

Note that the JSP page operates with just interfaces—Product and ProductList. The concrete instance of the ProductList implementation class is passed in the request as an attribute. Also, the name of the parser type ("DOM" or "SAX") is passed as a request attribute so that it can be printed in the headings. Note as well that the JSP page does not need to import any XML classes; it doesn't know where its data comes from beyond knowing that the data comes from a ProductList object.

The actual front-end DOM-specific JSP is just this:

```
<%@ page session="false" %>
<%@ page import="com.jspcr.xmlsamples.*" %>
<%
    request.setAttribute("parserType", "DOM");
    request.setAttribute("productList", new DOMProductList());
%>
<jsp:forward page="ClemensAltman.jsp"/>
```

The results are shown in Figure 16-1.

The main advantage of DOM as a parsing model is it provides random access to all parts of the document structure. This is made possible by its biggest disadvantage, though—the entire document must be read and parsed before any part of it is accessible through the DOM API. For large documents, this overhead can be significant.

Figure 16-1.   *Product catalog search using XML DOM parser*

Parsing with SAX

A typical SAX-oriented application creates an instance of a SAX parser, registers the content handler, and then invokes the `parse()` method to start the parsing and callbacks. In this section, we'll develop the same product catalog example we did for DOM.

There's very little to do, given our foresight in creating the common parent classes. Here's the `SAXProductList` subclass of `AbstractProductList`:

```java
package com.jspcr.xmlsamples;

import java.io.*;
import java.net.*;
import java.util.*;
import javax.xml.parsers.*;
import org.xml.sax.*;
import org.xml.sax.helpers.*;

/**
 * An extension of AbstractProductList that loads data from
 * a SAX event stream
 */
public class SAXProductList extends AbstractProductList
{
    /**
     * SAX-specific implementation of loadProductList.
     */
    protected synchronized List loadProductList()
        throws IOException
    {
        ProductContentHandler handler = new ProductContentHandler();
        try {
            SAXParserFactory spf = SAXParserFactory.newInstance();
            SAXParser parser = spf.newSAXParser();
            parser.parse(inputURL, handler);
        }
        catch (SAXException e) {
            throw new IOException
                ("parsing exception: " + e.getMessage());
        }
        catch (ParserConfigurationException e) {
            throw new IOException
                ("parsing exception: " + e.getMessage());
        }

        return handler.getProductList();
```

```
   }

   /**
    * Content handler that constructs the list of product objects
    */
   private static class ProductContentHandler
      extends DefaultHandler
   {
      private ProductImpl product;
      private List productList;
      private StringBuffer buffer;

      /**
       * Called when parsing starts
       */
      public void startDocument()
         throws SAXException
      {
         productList = new ArrayList();
         product = null;
         buffer = new StringBuffer();
      }

      /**
       * Called when a start tag is encountered
       */
      public void startElement
         (String ns, String ln, String qName, Attributes attrs)
            throws SAXException
      {
         if (qName.equals("product")) {
            product = new ProductImpl();
            product.code = attrs.getValue("code");
         }
         buffer.setLength(0);
      }

      /**
       * Accumulates characters from text nodes
       */
      public void characters(char[] ch, int start, int len)
         throws SAXException
      {
         buffer.append(ch, start, len);
      }
```

```
/**
 * Called when an end tag is encountered
 */
public void endElement(String ns, String ln, String qName)
    throws SAXException
{
    String text = buffer.toString().trim();
    buffer.setLength(0);

    if (qName.equals("product-type"))
        product.type = text;
    else if (qName.equals("price"))
        product.price = Double.parseDouble(text);
    else if (qName.equals("manufacturer"))
        product.manufacturer = text;
    else if (qName.equals("description"))
        product.description = text;
    else if (qName.equals("product")) {
        productList.add(product);
    }
}

/**
 * Returns the constructed product list
 */
public List getProductList()
{
    return productList;
}
}
}
```

Like DOMBuilderFactory and DOMBuilder, SAXParserFactory and SAXParser can be invoked through JAXP:

```
SAXParserFactory factory = SAXParserFactory.newInstance();
SAXParser parser = factory.newSAXParser();
```

Recall that the SAX technique is to implement `ContentHandler` (or extend `DefaultHandler`) and provide callbacks for the parsing event methods of interest. We'll use an inner class to do that, having it build the product list and return it to the main class when asked. The JAXP `parse()` method registers our `ProductContentHandler` class as the content handler and then starts parsing:

```
parser.parse(inputURL, handler);
```

The `ProductContentHandler` class is interested in four events:

- **startDocument** This method is called when the parser starts reading the document. This allows us to initialize the objects we need.
- **startElement** At the beginning of a new `product` element, we need to create a `Product` object and store the `code` attribute in it.
- **characters** As text flies by, we accumulate it in a `StringBuffer`.
- **endElement** At the end of an element, we assign its value from the `StringBuffer`, if it's one of the product fields. If this is the end of a `<product>` element, we add the `Product` object we've constructed to the product list, clear our buffers, and wait for the next product to be parsed.

The JSP page is also a simple front end to get the SAX product list and pass it to `ClemensAltman.jsp`:

```
<%@ page session="false" %>
<%@ page import="com.jspcr.xmlsamples.*" %>
<%
    request.setAttribute("parserType", "SAX");
    request.setAttribute("productList", new SAXProductList());
%>
<jsp:forward page="ClemensAltman.jsp"/>
```

This differs from the DOM version only in that it uses `SAXProductList` instead of `DOMProductList`, and it passes a different string for the `parserType` attribute.

The resulting HTML table is shown in Figure 16-2.

SAX offers a number of advantages over DOM. It's much simpler and easier to learn, uses much less memory, and doesn't require an entire document to be loaded. Nearly all XML parsers have a SAX interface; fewer have a DOM interface. SAX is also well suited for reading ill-formed documents (such as most HTML).

Figure 16-2. *Product catalog search using an XML SAX 2.0 parser*

XSL Transformations with XSLT

As noted earlier, XML is designed purely to identify document structure, not document appearance. Obviously, though, XML and HTML are closely related, and XML documents can be converted to HTML. When this happens, style information can be added. This is the role of *Extensible Stylesheet Language (XSL)*.

XSL is a language for designing stylesheets. An XSL stylesheet systematically describes which formatting elements are applied to which elements in an XML source document to produce the desired HTML output. Not surprisingly, an XSL stylesheet itself is an XML document.

Although XSL was originally designed for stylesheet purposes, it became apparent that it could also be used for general XML structure transformations. This manipulation is performed by an *XSL transformation* processor *(XSLT)*. XSLT is defined in a W3C recommendation dated November 1999 (see http://www.w3.org/TR/xslt.html). Popular XSLT processors are available from the Apache Software Foundation (Xalan), Microsoft (MSXML), Michael Kay (Saxon), and James Clark (XT). Xalan is included in JDK 1.4 and later.

XSLT uses an XML document called an *XSL stylesheet* to describe what it modifies and how. In the stylesheet are one or more templates, which identify the particular XML elements they're designed to transform, and then provide a set of literals and nested XSL statements that indicate the format of the output. Some key XSLT instructions are listed in Table 16-7.

XSLT is a broad topic, and the subject of numerous books and articles. This book gives you only a basic introduction, just enough to let you read an XSL stylesheet, if you need to do so.

XSLT can create not only XML output, but HTML and ordinary text as well. Surprisingly, the text output feature turns out to be quite useful for generating source code.

Instruction	Description
`<xsl:stylesheet>`	The outermost document element in an XSL stylesheet. Required attributes are `xmlns:xsl` (the namespace for XSL tags) and `version`.
`<xsl:template>`	Identifies a template block. Optional attribute is `match`, which specifies which XML element the template matches. A rich variety of ways exists to express the match value. See the XSLT specification for details.
`<xsl:apply-templates>`	Causes the processor to seek other elements to match. Optional attribute is `select`, which specifies a subset of elements in the same language as the `<xsl:template>` `match` attribute.
`<xsl:value-of>`	Causes the processor to substitute the value of the specified element. An optional attribute is `select`, which operates the same as in `<xsl:apply-templates>`

Table 16-7. *Highlights of XSLT instructions*

XSLT in Action

We can use the same example in XSLT that we used to illustrate DOM and SAX. Here's the XSL stylesheet:

```
<?xml version="1.0"?>
<xsl:stylesheet
    xmlns:xsl="http://www.w3.org/1999/XSL/Transform"
    version="1.0">

  <xsl:output method="html" encoding="ISO-8859-1"/>

  <xsl:template match="/">
    <html>
      <head>
        <title>
          (XSLT) Clemens-Altman Musical Instruments
        </title>
        <style type="text/css">
<![CDATA[
body, td, th {
  font-family: Verdana;
  font-size: 9pt;
}
h1 { font-size: 130%; }
h2 { font-size: 110%; }
body { text-align: center; }
]]>
        </style>
      </head>
      <body>
        <h1>Clemens-Altman Musical Instruments</h1>
        <h2>(Powered by XSLT)</h2>
        <xsl:apply-templates select="products"/>
      </body>
    </html>
  </xsl:template>

  <xsl:template match="products">
    <table border="1" cellpadding="3" cellspacing="0">
      <tr>
        <th>Product Code</th>
        <th>Description</th>
```

```
              <th>Price</th>
          </tr>
          <xsl:apply-templates
              select="product[manufacturer='Clemens-Altman']"/>
      </table>
    </xsl:template>

    <xsl:template match="product">
    <tr>
       <td><xsl:value-of select="@code"/></td>
       <td><xsl:value-of select="description"/></td>
       <td align="right"><xsl:value-of select="price"/></td>
    </tr>
    </xsl:template>

</xsl:stylesheet>
```

The document element matches the / template, so the HTML used on either side of the HTML table is coded in the body of this template. In place of the table, there's a call back into the XSLT processor:

```
<xsl:apply-templates select="products"/>
```

The `products` template creates the table start and end tags and the table headings, then calls back into the XSLT processor to generate the table rows:

```
<xsl:apply-templates
         select="product[manufacturer='Clemens-Altman']"/>
```

The value of the `select` attribute indicates that any product elements having a `manufacturer` attribute with a value of `Clemens-Altman` will be matched.

So, as the document is parsed, each product element that matches the criteria is passed to the `product` template. This template stands for a single row in the table. It adds the `<tr><td>...</td></tr>` tags and fills them in with document element text:

```
<td><xsl:value-of select="@code"/></td>
<td><xsl:value-of select="description"/></td>
<td align="right"><xsl:value-of select="price"/></td>
```

In the next section, we'll see how this XSL stylesheet gets invoked.

JAXP Again

Like the DOM and SAX parsers, XSLT is represented by a wrapper layer in JAXP. There is a `javax.xml.transform.TransformerFactory` with a `newInstance()` method. This gives you a factory object on which you can call `newTransformer()` or `newTranformer(Source)`. The former is used to create a simple copy transformation (which is quite useful in writing XML to a file); the latter, for creating transformers based on a specific XSL stylesheet. There is a third method, `newTemplates(Source)`, that precompiles a stylesheet for efficient repeated use.

The heart of the JAXP interface for XSLT is the `Transformer` class. Its main method of interest is

```
public void transform(Source source, Result result)
```

The `Source` and `Result` interfaces define the input and output, respectively, of the transformation (the stylesheet is already embodied in the `Transformer` object, being specified in the `factory.newTransformer(Source)` method call). JAXP provides three implementations each for `Source` and `Result`: `DOMSource`/`DOMResult`, `SAXSource`/`SAXResult`, and `StreamSource`/`StreamResult`. These allow input from or output to a DOM tree, a SAX event stream, and an input or output stream, respectively. This gives you great flexibility in your processing capability.

An XSLT Filter

We'll employ JAXP to create an XSLT transformer that is suitable for use in a filter chain (see Chapter 10 for more about filters).

```
package com.jspcr.filters;

import java.io.*;
import java.net.*;
import java.util.*;
import javax.servlet.*;
import javax.servlet.http.*;
import javax.xml.parsers.*;
import javax.xml.transform.*;
import javax.xml.transform.dom.*;
import javax.xml.transform.sax.*;
import javax.xml.transform.stream.*;
import org.w3c.dom.*;
import org.xml.sax.*;
import org.xml.sax.helpers.*;

/**
```

```
* Filter that applies an XSLT transformation to an
* XML response stream.
*/
public class XSLTFilter implements Filter
{
    /**
     * Saved reference to config object so that
     * we can get the servlet context later
     */
    private FilterConfig config;

    /**
     * A factory object that creates instances of the precompiled
     * XSL stylesheet.
     */
    private Templates templates;

    /**
     * Called when the filter is placed into service.
     * @param config the filter configuration object
     * @exception ServletException if a fatal error occurs
     */
    public void init(FilterConfig config)
        throws ServletException
    {
        this.config = config;
        try {

            // Get the name of the XSL stylesheet from
            // the init parameter in web.xml

            String xsltPath = config.getInitParameter("stylesheet");

            // Get a transformer source object for this
            // stylesheet

            ServletContext context = config.getServletContext();
            URL xsltURL = context.getResource(xsltPath);
            String xsltSystemId = xsltURL.toExternalForm();
            Source xsltSource = new StreamSource(xsltSystemId);

            // Precompile the stylesheet

            TransformerFactory tf = TransformerFactory.newInstance();
```

```
        templates = tf.newTemplates(xsltSource);
    }
    catch (MalformedURLException e) {
        throw new UnavailableException(e.getMessage());
    }
    catch (TransformerException e) {
        throw new UnavailableException(e.getMessage());
    }
}

/**
 * Releases the template factory
 */
public void destroy()
{
    templates = null;
}

/**
 * Applies an XSLT transformation to the response
 * @param request the original request object
 * @param response the original response object
 * @exception IOException if an I/O error occurs
 * @exception ServletException if an application error occurs.
 */
public void doFilter(
        ServletRequest request,
        ServletResponse response,
        FilterChain chain)
    throws IOException, ServletException
{
    // Create a servlet response wrapper that will
    // buffer the response data so that it can be
    // fed to the XSLT processor

    BufferedResponseWrapper wrappedResponse =
        new BufferedResponseWrapper
            (response, config.getServletContext());

    // Pass the request on to the next entry in
    // the filter chain

    chain.doFilter(request, wrappedResponse);
```

```
// After the request is processed, retrieve
// the output from the wrapper object

String buffer = wrappedResponse.getBufferAsString();

// Create a transformation source and result

StringReader sr = new StringReader(buffer);
Source source = new StreamSource(sr);

StringWriter sw = new StringWriter();
Result result = new StreamResult(sw);

// Apply the XSL stylesheet to create the HTML

try {
    Transformer transformer = templates.newTransformer();
    transformer.transform(source, result);
}
catch (TransformerException e) {
    throw new ServletException(e.getMessage());
}

// Use the original response object to send
// converted results back to the requesting client

buffer = sw.toString();
response.setContentType("text/html");
response.setContentLength(buffer.length());
PrintWriter out = response.getWriter();
out.print(buffer);
out.flush();
    }
}
```

This is a fairly generic filter, which allows the XSL stylesheet name to be passed in an initialization parameter. The filter's init() method gets the value of this parameter and loads the stylesheet, precompiling it into a Templates object that is saved as an instance variable. Transformer objects are not reentrant, so we'll need to create new ones (or use a pool of instances) for each request.

The doFilter() method does six things:

1. Creates a servlet response wrapper that will be passed to the downstream entity (filter or Web resource endpoint). This is necessary because we need

to post-process the response to convert it from XML to HTML. We'll reuse the `BufferedResponseWrapper` class that we developed in Chapter 10 for this purpose.

2. Passes the request to the next entity in the chain.

3. After the request is processed, retrieves the XML as a string.

4. Creates a `StreamSource` object over this XML string and a `StreamResult` object that will be used to buffer the generated HTML.

5. Applies the XSLT transformation.

6. Sends the converted results back to the requesting client using the original response object.

Not surprisingly, the results look similar to those generated by the other two JSP pages, as seen in Figure 16-3.

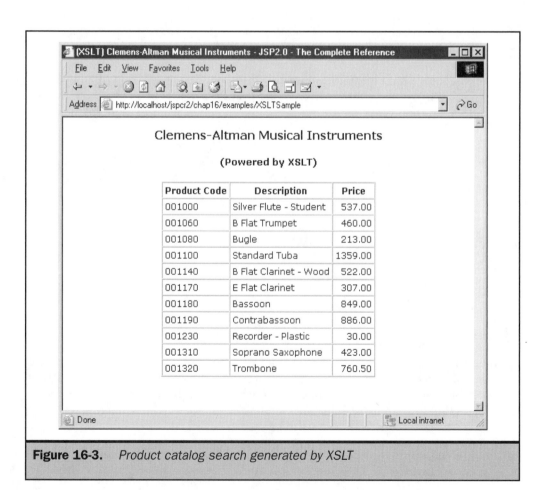

Figure 16-3. *Product catalog search generated by XSLT*

We've covered only a few of the capabilities of XSLT. As shy as I am about predicting future technology trends, I believe that XSLT's unique capabilities will make it a widely successful tool for a long time.

XML Syntax for JSP

The last XML topic we'll cover in this chapter is the alternative XML syntax for JSP pages. This is a little-known feature of JSP, but one that opens intriguing possibilities. The JSP specification provides true XML replacements for all the oddball <%, <%!, <%= JSP syntax. In this variant, our ClemensAltman.jsp looks like this:

```
<?xml version="1.0"?>
<jsp:root
   xmlns:jsp="http://java.sun.com/JSP/Page"
   version="2.0"
   >

   <!--  XML Syntax of ClemensAltman.jsp -->

   <jsp:directive.page session="false"/>
   <jsp:directive.page import="java.io.*"/>
   <jsp:directive.page import="com.jspcr.xmlsamples.*" />
   <jsp:directive.page import="java.net.*"/>
   <jsp:directive.page import="java.text.*"/>
   <jsp:directive.page import="java.util.*"/>
   <jsp:directive.page contentType="text/html"/>

   <jsp:scriptlet>

      ProductList productList =
         (ProductList) request.getAttribute("productList");

      String parserType =
         (String) request.getAttribute("parserType");

   </jsp:scriptlet>
<html>
<head>
<title>
   (<jsp:expression>parserType</jsp:expression>)
   Clemens-Altman Musical Instruments
</title>
<style>
```

```
<jsp:text>
<![CDATA[
   body, td, th {
      font-family: Verdana;
      font-size: 9pt;
   }
   h1 { font-size: 130%; }
   h2 { font-size: 110%; }
   body { text-align: center; }
]]>
</jsp:text>
</style>
</head>
<body>
<h1>Clemens-Altman Musical Instruments</h1>
<h2>(Powered by <jsp:expression>parserType</jsp:expression>)</h2>
<table border="1" cellpadding="3" cellspacing="0">
<tr>
   <th>Product Code</th>
   <th>Description</th>
   <th>Price</th>
</tr>
<jsp:scriptlet>
   NumberFormat fmt = NumberFormat.getCurrencyInstance();
   for (Iterator it = productList.iterator(); it.hasNext(); ) {
      Product product = (Product) it.next();
      if (product.getManufacturer().equals("Clemens-Altman")) {
</jsp:scriptlet>
<tr>
   <td>
      <jsp:expression>
         product.getCode()
      </jsp:expression>
   </td>
   <td>
      <jsp:expression>
         product.getDescription()
      </jsp:expression>
   </td>
   <td align="right">
```

```
    <jsp:expression>
        fmt.format(product.getPrice())
    </jsp:expression>
    </td>
</tr>
<jsp:scriptlet>
        }
    }
</jsp:scriptlet>
</table>
</body>
</html>


</jsp:root>
```

The mapping is fairly obvious. The document element is `<jsp:root>`, which identifies the JSP prefix with the `http://java.sun.com/JSP/Page` namespace and specifies that JSP version 2.0 is the minimum required level. If custom tags were used in this page, their namespace and prefix would be identified here as well. The `<%page %>` directives are converted to `<jsp:directive.page>` elements. Java code that would appear in scriptlets, expressions, and declarations is coded inside `<jsp:scriptlet>`, `<jsp:expression>`, and `<jsp:declaration>` elements, respectively. The remaining HTML template text passes through unmodified.

There are several issues to consider:

■ Since this is real XML, you need to observe all the rules. The HTML has to be XHTML. Your start and end tags have to match.

■ You can't have bare "<" and ">" characters in your HTML text, which makes ordinary `for (int j = 0; j < n; j++)` statements illegal. To get around that, you can either escape the "<" as "<" or enclose the whole block in a CDATA section: `<![CDATA[ for (int j = 0; j < n; j++) ]]>`.

■ If you need to embed an expression in your HTML, you have to wrap the whole tag in a `<jsp:text>` element, and escape the appropriate characters.

Beyond being simply a curiosity, this syntax is important in one particular context: validating custom tags. The `TagLibraryValidator` class has a `validate()` method that is invoked when the page is translated. It is passed a `PageData` object that has a `getInputStream()` method that supplies the XML representation of the page—whether it was originally written in the JSP or XML syntax. You can parse this input stream and perform sophisticated validations that are not feasible otherwise.

Summary

XML is becoming the universal language for structured data storage and interchange. Using human-readable text files and simple grammatical rules, XML captures not only data but metadata, information about the structure of the data. Hundreds of applications are being written or converted to use XML as their input and/or output. The XML specifications and those for its related technologies are managed by the World Wide Web Consortium, usually referred to as W3C.

To read XML, you need a parser. Two primary parser models are in general use:

- **Document Object Model (DOM)**   Models an XML document as a tree of nodes. The DOM API provides methods for navigating a DOM tree in an arbitrary order: forward, backward, through siblings.

- **Simple API for Java (SAX)**   Event-driven parser model that invokes callback methods in registered handlers.

XML can be transformed using an XSLT processor and an XSL stylesheet.

There's no question that XML applications will multiply greatly in the future. JSP can be an enabling technology for these applications.

The Complete Reference

Chapter 17

JSP Testing and Debugging

Debugging techniques are frequently glossed over in programming tutorials, but they are indispensable in application development. While programming can be systematic and code is easily borrowed from other programs, debugging is often viewed as a process of random trial-and-error changes that may or may not fix a problem.

The Web application environment presents its own unique difficulties. Because applications are split into server and client components, request handling involves multiple cooperating processes. As a result, errors are hard to reproduce, especially if they occur intermittently.

In this chapter, we'll see that testing and debugging can be as systematic as development. The chapter outlines basic testing and debugging techniques that can be applied and develops several tools that can be helpful.

Building a Mental Model

The key to systematic debugging is to understand how the application is designed to work. This means knowing what components are involved, how they interact, and what their expected behavior is. This makes it possible to isolate the failing component and determine what can account for the error.

Translation and Compilation

For example, you know a JSP page exists in three forms, as illustrated in Figure 17-1.

- **JSP Source Code**   This is what a developer creates—a .jsp file containing scriptlets, expression, directives, and HTML template code.

- **Generated Servlet Source Code**   When a JSP page is first requested or whenever it is requested after any changes to its .jsp file, the JSP container translates it into an equivalent Java servlet.

- **Compiled Servlet Class**   After the JSP page is translated into servlet source code, it is compiled to produce a Java .class file.

Errors can occur at any point during this process. A careful examination of the error message and a knowledge of where the intermediate forms exist can help us zero in on the cause.

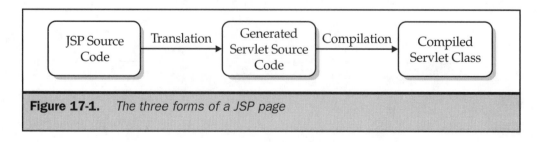

Figure 17-1.   *The three forms of a JSP page*

Note   *Careful reading of error messages is crucial, but you can't read them if they aren't there. Internet Explorer by default substitutes its own error page when a 500 level (internal servlet) error occurs. Presumably, this is intended to protect end users from frightening stack traces, but it makes things difficult for the developer. You can turn off this feature by selecting the Tools | Internet Options menu item, and then selecting the Advanced tab. A check box entitled "Show friendly HTTP error messages" is under the Browsing section of the tree. If you unselect this option, you can see full stack traces and any other data sent by a servlet exception.*

For example, suppose you have a custom tag named `timer` that keeps track of how long its body takes to execute. The tag handler is a class named `TimerTag`, which takes a snapshot of the current system time in its `doStartTag()` and `doEndTag()` methods and creates a scripting variable with the result.

```java
import javax.servlet.jsp.*;
import javax.servlet.jsp.tagext.*;
import java.io.*;
import java.net.*;
import java.util.*;

/**
 * A tag handler for a custom tag that keeps track
 * of how long its body takes to execute
 */
public class TimerTag extends TagSupport
{
    private long startTime;
    private long endTime;

    /**
     * Starts the timer
     */
    public int doStartTag() throws JspException
    {
        startTime = System.currentTimeMillis();
        return EVAL_BODY_INCLUDE;
    }

    /**
     * Stops the timer and calculates the elapsed time
     * in seconds. This is stored as a page context
     * attribute using the ID variable name
```

```
        */
     public int doEndTag() throws JspException
     {
        endTime = System.currentTimeMillis();
        double elapsed = (endTime - startTime)/1000.0;
        pageContext.setAttribute(getId(), new Double(elapsed));
        return EVAL_PAGE;
     }
  }
```

A typical use might be to see how long it takes to create a JDBC connection, as shown in the following JSP code:

```
<%@ page session="false" %>
<%@ page import="java.sql.*" %>
<%@ taglib prefix="debug" uri="/WEB-INF/tlds/debug.tld" %>
<debug:timer id="t1">
<%
   Connection con = null;
   try {
      Class.forName("sun.jdbc.odbc.JdbcOdbcDriver");
      con = DriverManager.getConnection("jdbc:odbc:usda");
   }
   finally {
      if (con != null)
         con.close();
   }
%>
</debug:timer>
Connecting to the database took <%= t1 %> seconds.
```

When this JSP page is run, it produces the following error message (reformatted a bit for legibility, as always):

```
org.apache.jasper.JasperException: Unable to compile class for JSP

An error occurred at line: 3 in the jsp file: /examples/Timer.jsp

Generated servlet error:
[javac] Compiling 1 source file
jspcr2_chap17\examples\Timer_jsp.java:55: cannot resolve symbol
```

```
symbol : class TimerTag
location: class org.apache.jsp.Timer_jsp
        TimerTag _jspx_th_debug_timer_0 = (TimerTag) ...
      ^
```

Looking at the message carefully, you can find several clues about the nature of the error. First, it reports the location of the JSP page. This tells you Tomcat was able to find the JSP source code. Next, the message text says *Jasper* (the Tomcat JSP translator) was unable to compile a JSP servlet class and gives the name of the generated .java source file. This means translation from .jsp to .java completed and the java compiler was invoked but failed. So you know this isn't a run-time error. This isn't due to a problem with the JDBC-ODBC driver, so it must be a compilation error with the generated servlet source code.

Having isolated the failing component, you can understand the rest of the error message. The generated servlet on line 55 creates an instance of TimerTag() and stores it in the _jspx_th_debug_timer_0 variable. This is the line that gets the error message "cannot resolve symbol". So the java compiler (not the JSP translator or the servlet engine) was unable to find a class. If you can figure out why, you're done.

The compiler might not find a class for several reasons. The class may not have been compiled, or its .class file may not exist in the classpath. But a careful examination of the error message points to a different reason. Notice exactly which class the compiler is working on: org.apache.jsp.Timer_jsp. Because this is a compile issue, you need to look at the .java file to determine the source of the problem. The location of this file is servlet engine–dependent. With Tomcat, it is under the work subdirectory of the Tomcat root. Working your way down through the Web application subdirectories, you find the servlet source file. The first few lines show what the problem is:

```
package org.apache.jsp;

import javax.servlet.*;
import javax.servlet.http.*;
import javax.servlet.jsp.*;
import org.apache.jasper.runtime.*;
import java.sql.*;

public class Timer_jsp extends HttpJspBase {
...
   TimerTag _jspx_th_debug_timer_0 = (TimerTag)
      _jspx_tagPool_debug_timer_id.get(TimerTag.class);
...
}
```

The generated servlet has a `package` statement and a number of `import` statements. From your general Java knowledge, you know classes can be referred to without their fully qualified package name if an `import` statement supplies the rest of the name. If none of the imported packages contain a referenced class name, the compiler assumes it's in the same package as the class being compiled. Therefore, the `TimerTag` class referred to on line 55 of the generated servlet (remember the error message?) is looked up in each of the imported packages, where it isn't found, and is then treated as if it were a class in the servlet's own package: `org.apache.jsp`. End of mystery.[1]

Now, how can you fix the error? One way is to supply an `import` statement for `TimerTag`, so that the java compiler knows not to try to associate it with any other package. You don't have access to the generated servlet, only to the JSP source, which means you could place this statement in your JSP:

```
<%@ page import="TimerTag" %>
```

While this would work, it's an unsatisfactory solution because it would have to be done in every JSP page that uses the tag. Apart from the problem of remembering to do this, it isn't even clear to the maintenance programmer why this class is being imported— there are no apparent references to it.

A better solution is to assign a package name to the tag handler. If the full class name is `jspcr.debug.TimerTag`, then line 55 becomes

```
com.jspcr.debug.TimerTag _jspx_th_debug_timer_0 =
    (com.jspcr.debug.TimerTag) ...
```

and no ambiguity occurs.

 A helpful way to separate compilation and run-time errors is to precompile the JSP page. The JSP specification requires compliant JSP containers to do this when a page is invoked with a request parameter named `jsp_precompile`. The JSP container translates the JSP page into servlet source code and compiles the servlet, but won't cause it to service the request. This needn't be done from a browser; it can be done from a batch Java application that simply creates a URL for the request (including the `jsp_precompile` parameter) and then calls the URL's `openStream()` method.

---

[1] I am indebted to Jim Adams, a coworker and veteran debugger, for his memorable insight on this issue: "It's always the classpath." Jim rightly observes that JSP debugging is not a matter of finding out *whether* your classpath is wrong, but exactly *how* you got it wrong. This narrows down the search considerably.

Testing in Isolation

Given that isolating the failing component is the key to debugging, making this easy to do is important. Walking through the mental flowchart and identifying both what *should* be happening and what is *actually* happening should be possible. When the problem area is isolated, it should be possible to test the failing component by itself, verifying each step of its operation.

To do this, you need to start from a known state. If you've changed several sections of code, recompiled some beans, and modified a deployment descriptor, you may well find the solution, but you may not see different results because of partial initializations and leftover classes. To avoid this, you can do the following:

- **Delete old copies of translated JSP servlets and classes.** A JSP file is translated only when it's newer than its corresponding servlet and class file, but modules it depends on may change without triggering its retranslation. Changes to files included with the `<%@ include %>` directive, for example, aren't guaranteed to cause the including JSP page to be retranslated. Some JSP containers do this, but the specification doesn't require it.

- **Delete serialized sessions.** Some JSP containers save sessions to persistent storage during shutdown and then restore them when the JSP container is started again. Tomcat, for example, writes serialized sessions to files named `SESSIONS.ser` in its work directory tree. If you make changes to classes and recompile them, you may have an old version of the class deserialized when you bring the servlet engine back up.

- **Restart the Web server and servlet engine.** While this may not be strictly necessary in all cases, this step lets you be certain all initializations are done properly. Changes to `web.xml` and tag library descriptors, for example, may be detected only during startup.

Once you're sure of the application state, you can provide it with known input and follow it through the process. The servlet log provides a central collection point for messages from the servlet engine, and from individual servlets and JSP pages. You can write a message to the log with the `log()` method, the same as you would use `System.out.println()`. Particularly in JSP pages, it's easy to add a few log messages, test, add a few more based on the results of that test, and so on. Writing messages to the servlet log provides a better execution trace than trying to write to the servlet output stream, which may be corrupted and may disappear before you can analyze it.

Debugging Tools

Most commercial *integrated development environments (IDEs)* provide some kind of debugger that enables you to step through the execution of a Java class, examining, and possibly changing, the values of variables. The JDK includes a command line debugger named jdb, which performs these same functions, more or less. While these tools can be useful, they have several drawbacks when used to debug JSP code.

To begin with, JSP pages don't map closely to their byte code equivalents. They may consist of scriptlets, directives, expressions, HTML, and custom tags. If you're really interested in line-by-line execution tracing, you would need to debug with the generated servlet source code, not the .jsp file.

In addition, JSP classes are loaded and run in a separate virtual machine controlled by the servlet engine, possibly linked to a Web server. To debug an individual class, you may have to start the whole servlet engine in debug mode. You need to verify that all the same classpath entries are active, the same ports are used, and so on. Given that you can even figure out how to do this, it tends to make the debug environment very different from the actual runtime environment. Likewise, substantial timing differences between the two environments may cause timeouts and race conditions that have nothing to do with the problem being debugged.

In practical terms, there is little you can do with a line-by-line debugger that you can't do with the log() method (or System.out.println(), for that matter). Any variable you might examine at a breakpoint can just as easily be written to the servlet log. You can stop execution at any point and produce a stack trace simply by throwing an exception. Given JSP's automatic compilation and the browser refresh button, you can probably do several iterations with new message points faster than you can start the IDE and bring up the servlet engine in debug mode.

In this section, we'll develop three tools that are less intrusive and better adapted to the HTTP request-handling environment. Used in conjunction with log() method for execution tracing, they can help both in isolating errors and verifying fixes.

Capturing Form Parameters

When an HTML form is used to send request parameters to a JSP or servlet, an obvious testing requirement is being able to know what parameters it sends and what their value is. This isn't always obvious. If a <select> element allows multiple selections, what is the value of the request parameter? If a text input element isn't filled in, will it be passed as a blank or null? What about check boxes that don't specify a value attribute?

An easy way to find out is to use a debugging JSP page that captures the request parameters and displays them as name/value pairs in tabular form. The following JSP page (Echo.jsp) shows how this can be done:

```
<%@ page session="false" %>
<%@ page import="java.util.*" %>
<html>
<head>
```

```
<title>Form Parameters</title>
<link rel="stylesheet" type="text/css" href="style.css"/>
</head>
<body>
<h1>Form Parameters</h1>
<table border="1" cellpadding="3" cellspacing="0">
<tr>
   <th width="200">Name</th>
   <th width="200">Value</th>
</tr>
<%
   Enumeration enames = request.getParameterNames();
   while (enames.hasMoreElements()) {
      String name = (String) enames.nextElement();
      String[] values = request.getParameterValues(name);
      if (values != null) {
         for (int i = 0; i < values.length; i++) {
            String value = values[i];
%>
<tr>
   <td><%= name %></td>
   <td><%= value %></td>
</tr>
<%
         }
      }
   }
%>
</table>
</body>
</html>
```

Echo.jsp gets a list of all the parameter names from the request object and then loops through the list and prints the name and value(s) of each one. The only wrinkle is that a parameter may have more than one value. For example, groups of check boxes can have the same name but different value attributes. The servlet API takes care of this, however, by providing a getParameterValues() method in the request object that returns an array of values.

Figure 17-2 shows an HTML form with several types of input elements. The JSP page that generates the form is listed here:

```
<%@ page session="false" %>
<html>
<head>
<title>Job Application</title>
<link rel="stylesheet" type="text/css" href="style.css"/>
</head>
<body>
<h1>Please Indicate Your Qualifications</h1>

<form action="Echo.jsp" method="POST">

<input type="hidden"
       name="locale"
       value="<%= request.getLocale() %>">

<table border="0" cellpadding="3" cellspacing="0">
   <tr>
      <td>
         <input type="checkbox" name="speed">
            Faster than a speeding bullet
         </input>
         <br/>
         <input type="checkbox" name="power">
            More powerful than a locomotive
         </input>
         <br/>
         <input type="checkbox" name="flight">
            Able to leap tall buildings with a single bound
         </input>
         <br/>
      </td>
   </tr>
   <tr>
      <td>
         Name: <input type="text" name="name"/>
               <input type="submit" value="Submit"/>
      </td>
   </tr>
</table>
```

```
</form>
</body>
</html>
```

This form enables job applicants to describe their qualifications using a set of check boxes. Additionally, the user's locale is captured as a hidden field, so responses can be sent in the user's preferred language.

Ordinarily, this form is processed by /dailyplanet/apphandler.jsp. To handle this input properly, apphandler.jsp needs to know the format in which the request parameters will be sent. Without peeking, would you know the default format of the check box values that don't specify a value attribute?

This is easy to determine. By substituting ACTION="Echo.jsp" for ACTION="/dailyplanet/apphandler.jsp", you can capture the output of the form and test it using several different browsers and combinations of values. If you do this for the form values in Figure 17-2, you get the table shown in Figure 17-3.

Echo.jsp can be enhanced to show more information about the request, such as the request headers, cookies, and request attributes. The main advantage of Echo.jsp is that it requires no change to the server-side component that processes the form. All it takes is a quick one-line change to the <form> element in the HTML document or JSP page that submits the form.

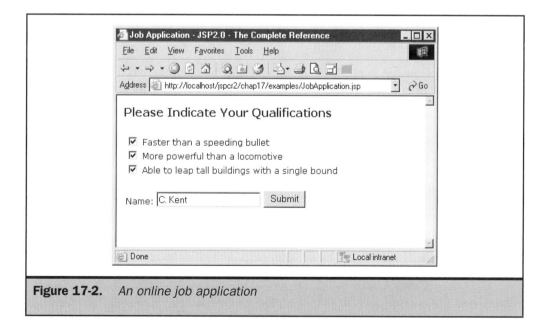

Figure 17-2. *An online job application*

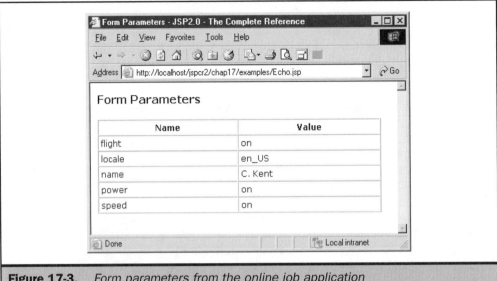

Figure 17-3.   *Form parameters from the online job application*

A Debugging Web Client

The Echo.jsp server enables you to see what the Web client produces. The other side
of the transaction is how the processing servlet or JSP page responds. Debugging the
server side component is easier when you can view its input and output in isolation,
rather than after a Web browser manipulates it.

This is easier than you might suspect. A Web client doesn't need to be a Web browser,
only something that can produce an HTTP request in ordinary ASCII form. Telnet invoked
on port 80 works perfectly well for this:

```
% telnet www.lyricnote.com 80
Trying...
Connected to www.lyricnote.com.
Escape character is '^]'.
GET / HTTP/1.0

HTTP/1.1 200 OK
...
```

Unfortunately, the default Telnet client on Windows systems is GUI-based and
awkward to use for this purpose. The GUI window doesn't scroll and automatically
clears its text after the request is processed. And the Windows client doesn't handle the
Unix line-ending convention properly.

Duplicating the HTTP request functionality with a standalone console-mode Java application is easy enough, however. WebClient.java, listed in the following, is a simple Web client designed to be called from a command line:

```java
package com.jspcr.debug.webclient;

import java.io.*;
import java.net.*;
import java.util.*;
import java.util.regex.*;

/**
 * A command-line interface to a Web server
 */
public class WebClient
{
    private String host;
    private int port;

    public WebClient(String host, int port)
    {
        this.host = host;
        this.port = port;
    }

    public void run() throws IOException
    {
        int contentLength = 0;

        // Open a socket to the Web host

        Socket socket = new Socket(host, port);

        // Set up to read input from the user
        // and echo it to Web host

        BufferedReader in =
            new BufferedReader(new InputStreamReader(System.in));

        PrintWriter out =
            new PrintWriter(socket.getOutputStream(), true);

        // The first line is the HTTP request
```

JSP APPLICATIONS

```
// e.g., "GET /path HTTP/1.0"

promptForRequest();
String line = in.readLine();
out.println(line);

// Read and echo any other headers, stopping
// when a blank line is encountered.

while (true) {
   promptForHeader();
   line = in.readLine();
   if (line == null)
      break;

   line = line.trim();
   out.println(line);
   if (line.equals(""))
      break;

   // Check for a Content-Length header

   Pattern p = Pattern.compile
      ("^\\s*([^:]+):\\s+(.*\\S)\\s*$");
   Matcher m = p.matcher(line);
   if (m.matches()) {
      String name = m.group(1);
      String value = m.group(2);
      if (name.equalsIgnoreCase("Content-Length"))
         contentLength = Integer.parseInt(value);
   }
}

// If a non-zero content length header was used,
// read and echo that many bytes to the Web host.

if (contentLength > 0) {
   promptForData();
   for (int i = 0; i < contentLength; i++)
      out.print((char) in.read());
   out.flush();
}

// The server is now working on the request.
```

```
        // Read its output and dump to stdout

        in = new BufferedReader(
            new InputStreamReader(socket.getInputStream()));

        out = new PrintWriter(System.out);

        while ((line = in.readLine()) != null) {
           out.println(line);
        }

        // Close files

        in.close();
        out.close();
        socket.close();
    }

    private void promptForRequest()
    {
        System.out.print("Request> ");
        System.out.flush();
    }

    private void promptForHeader()
    {
        System.out.print("Header>   ");
        System.out.flush();
    }

    private void promptForData()
    {
        System.out.print("Data>     ");
        System.out.flush();
    }
}
```

To run the WebClient class from a command line, we need a simple Main class:

```
package com.jspcr.debug.webclient;

import java.io.*;
import java.net.*;
```

```java
import java.util.*;

/**
 * Mainline for running the Web client
 */
public class Main
{
    /**
     * Reads command line parameters, creates a new
     * <code>WebClient</code> object, then invokes it.
     */
    public static void main(String[] args)
        throws IOException
    {
        // Default values

        String host = "localhost";
        int port = 80;

        // Use values from command line, if specified

        for (int i = 0; i < args.length; i++) {
            String arg = args[i];
            if (arg.equals("-h") || arg.equals("-help")) {
                showUsage();
                return;
            }
            else
            if (arg.equals("-host") && ++i < args.length)
                host = args[i];
            else
            if (arg.equals("-port") && ++i < args.length)
                port = Integer.parseInt(args[i]);
        }

        // Create and start the Web client

        new WebClient(host, port).run();
    }

    /**
     * Displays the calling syntax
```

```
    */
    private static void showUsage()
    {
        String[] text = {
            "usage: java -jar webclient.jar"
            + " [-host <hostName>]"
            + " [-port <portNumber>]",
        };
        for (int i = 0; i < text.length; i++)
            System.out.println(text[i]);
    }
}
```

The calling syntax from a command line is:

```
java -jar webclient.jar [-host <hostName>] [-port <portNumber>]
```

When WebClient is started, it opens a socket connection to the specified host (default is `localhost`), and then waits for an HTTP request and optional headers to be entered from the keyboard. Each line entered by the user is sent out over the socket. Input terminates when a blank line is entered. This signals to the HTTP server that no more headers will be sent and the request is complete, except possibly for data being sent with a POST request.

After the request is sent and processed, the server sends back a response, which is echoed to the console. Using the job application example from the preceding section, we can see a typical exchange might be:

```
C:\>java -jar webclient.jar

Request> POST /jspcr2/chap17/examples/Echo.jsp HTTP/1.0
Header>   Content-type: application/x-www-form-urlencoded
Header>   Content-length: 53
Header>
Data>     speed=on&power=on&flight=on&name=C.+Kent&locale=en_US

HTTP/1.1 200 OK
Content-Type: text/html;ISO-8859-1
Date: Thu, 12 Sep 2002 00:59:53 GMT
Server: Apache Coyote HTTP/1.1 Connector [1.0]
Connection: close
```

```
<html>
<head>
<title>Form Parameters</title>
<link rel="stylesheet" type="text/css" href="style.css"/>
</head>
<body>
<h1>Form Parameters</h1>
<table border="1" cellpadding="3" cellspacing="0">
<tr><th width="200">Name</th><th width="200">Value</th></tr>
<tr><td>locale</td><td>en_US</td></tr>
<tr><td>flight</td><td>on</td></tr>
<tr><td>name</td><td>C. Kent</td></tr>
<tr><td>power</td><td>on</td></tr>
<tr><td>speed</td><td>on</td></tr>
</table>
</body>
</html>
```

Tracing HTTP Requests

To troubleshoot a Web application effectively, you must be able to monitor how it makes requests and receives responses. We already saw that a Java class can act both as a Web client and a Web server. In this section, we'll develop a monitoring tool that performs both functions, acting as the middleman between the client and the server, as illustrated in Figure 17-4.

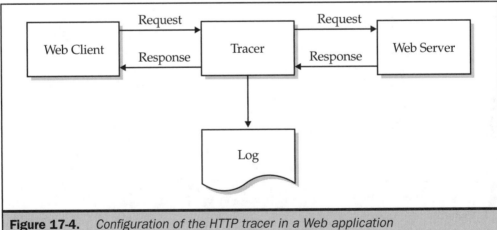

Figure 17-4. *Configuration of the HTTP tracer in a Web application*

When this tracer tool is plugged into a Web application, its server component listens for HTTP requests, logs their headers, and then forwards them to the real Web server. Its client component then receives the Web server's response, logs the headers, and sends the response back to the client. Neither the client nor the server is aware of the tracer's presence in the loop.

The tool consists of two main components:

■ A Web server proxy that listens for HTTP requests.

■ A request handler that copies the client request to the server and the response back to the client, logging headers in both directions.

Here's the first component (`Tracer.java`):

```java
package com.jspcr.debug.tracer;

import java.io.*;
import java.net.*;
import java.util.*;

/**
 * Acts as a proxy web server, capturing requests
 * and responses and echoing the headers to a
 * log stream.
 */
public class Tracer extends Thread implements Logger
{
    public static final int DEFAULT_PORT = 8601;

    private String host;
    private int port;
    private int tracerPort;
    private PrintWriter logWriter;

    public void run()
    {
        // Set defaults if not otherwise specified

        if (tracerPort == 0)
            tracerPort = DEFAULT_PORT;

        if (logWriter == null)
            logWriter = new PrintWriter(System.out);
```

```java
        // Start proxy server

        try {
            log("M: Opening tracer server on tracerPort "
                + tracerPort);
            ServerSocket server = new ServerSocket(tracerPort);

            // Loop forever

            while (true) {

                // Wait for connection

                log("M: Waiting for connections");
                Socket client = server.accept();
                log("M: Connection received from " + client);

                // Dispatch it to a request handler thread

                RequestHandler rh = new RequestHandler(client);
                rh.setLogger(this);
                if (host != null)
                    rh.setHost(host);
                if (port != 0)
                    rh.setPort(port);
                rh.start();
            }
        }
        catch (IOException e) {
            e.printStackTrace();
        }
    }

    // ==========================================
    //    Implementation of Logger
    // ==========================================

    /**
     * Writes a message to the log
     * @param message the message
     */
    public synchronized void log(String message)
```

```java
{
   logWriter.println(message);
   logWriter.flush();
}


// ==========================================
//    Property setters
// ==========================================

/**
* Sets the host.
* @param host the host.
*/
public void setHost(String host)
{
   this.host = host;
}

/**
* Sets the port.
* @param port the port.
*/
public void setPort(int port)
{
   this.port = port;
}

/**
* Sets the tracerPort.
* @param tracerPort the tracerPort.
*/
public void setTracerPort(int tracerPort)
{
   this.tracerPort = tracerPort;
}

/**
* Sets the logWriter.
* @param logWriter the logWriter.
*/
public void setLogWriter(Writer logWriter)
   throws IOException
```

```
    {
        this.logWriter = new PrintWriter(logWriter);
    }
}
```

Aside from its property setting methods, `Tracer` consists of two tasks:

- The `run()` method creates a `java.net.ServerSocket` and begins listening for client connections.
- When a connection is accepted, `run()` creates a request-handling thread to process the transaction. We'll examine this component shortly.

A log message is written for each of these steps.

To handle command line options and to start the process, we use a `Main` class:

```
package com.jspcr.debug.tracer;

import java.io.*;
import java.net.*;
import java.util.*;

/**
 * Mainline for the HTTP tracer tool
 */
public class Main
{
    public static void main(String[] args) throws IOException
    {
        String opt_host = null;
        String opt_port = null;
        String opt_tracerPort = null;
        String opt_log = null;

        try {

            // Parse command line arguments

            for (int i = 0, n = args.length; i < n; i++) {
                String arg = args[i];
                if (arg.equals("-h")) {
                    showUsage();
```

```
            return;
        }
        if (arg.equals("-host") && (i+1 < n))
            opt_host = args[++i];
        else if (arg.equals("-port") && (i+1 < n))
            opt_port = args[++i];
        else if (arg.equals("-tracerPort") && (i+1 < n))
            opt_tracerPort = args[++i];
        else if (arg.equals("-log") && (i+1 < n))
            opt_log = args[++i];
        else
            throw new IllegalArgumentException
            ("Unrecognized option " + arg);
    }

    // Verify that there is no port conflict

    int testTracerPort = (opt_tracerPort == null)
        ? Tracer.DEFAULT_PORT
        : Integer.parseInt(opt_tracerPort);

    int testHostPort = (opt_port == null)
        ? RequestHandler.DEFAULT_PORT
        : Integer.parseInt(opt_port);

    if (testTracerPort == testHostPort)
        throw new IllegalArgumentException
        ("Cannot assign port and tracerPort both to "
        + testHostPort);
}
catch (IllegalArgumentException e) {
    System.err.println(e.getMessage());
    return;
}

// Create the tracer and set its properties

Tracer tracer = new Tracer();
if (opt_host != null)
    tracer.setHost(opt_host);
if (opt_port != null)
    tracer.setPort(Integer.parseInt(opt_port));
```

```
      if (opt_tracerPort != null)
         tracer.setTracerPort
            (Integer.parseInt(opt_tracerPort));
      if (opt_log != null)
         tracer.setLogWriter(new FileWriter(opt_log));

      // Start it running

      tracer.start();
   }

   public static final void showUsage()
   {
      String[] text = {
         "",
         "usage: java -jar tracer.jar [options]",
         "",
         "where options are:",
         "",
         "-host          <hostName>  (default is localhost)",
         "-port          <hostPort>  (default is 80)",
         "-tracerPort    <localPort> (default is 8601)",
         "-log           <fileName>  (default is stdout)",
      };
      for (int i = 0; i < text.length; i++)
         System.out.println(text[i]);
   }
}
```

The Main class parses the command line, which supports four options:

■ **-host <*hostname*>** The name of the target Web server host. If not specified, this defaults to localhost.

■ **-port <*portnumber*>** The port number on the target Web server. The default is 80, which is the default HTTP port number.

■ **-tracerPort <*portnumber*>** The local port number on which the tracer itself runs. The default is 8601. This port number must be included in the URL to be traced. For example, if an HTML form has an ACTION attribute of http://www.lyricnote.com/search/ProductSearch.jsp, then it should be changed to http://www.lyricnote.com:8601/search/ProductSearch.jsp. This is the only change that must be made to hook up the tracer to any application.

■ **-log <*filename*>** The name of a file to which the HTTP headers is to be written. Log messages go to System.out if this option isn't specified.

After validating the command line options, the mainline creates a `Tracer` object, sets its properties, and starts it.

Both `Tracer` and `RequestHandler` write log messages. Because the log may be redirected by a command line option, each component needs a handle to the log output stream. You can accomplish this by defining a `Logger` interface that `Tracer` implements. `RequestHandler` is passed a reference to `Tracer` in its role as `Logger`. To make clear which component sent the message, each message begins with either `C:` for client, `S:` for server, or `M:` for the tracer middleman.

The second component of the tool, `RequestHandler`, acts as a Web client to the target Web server, passing it the request line, request headers, and any request data stream it obtains from the real Web client, logging headers as it goes. `RequestHandler` then turns around and copies the response line, response headers, and response data to the client.

```java
package com.jspcr.debug.tracer;

import java.io.*;
import java.net.*;
import java.util.*;

/**
 * A proxy HTTP server that handles a single request
 */
public class RequestHandler extends Thread
{
    public static final String DEFAULT_HOST = "localhost";
    public static final int DEFAULT_PORT = 80;

    private Socket client;
    private Logger logger;
    private String host;
    private int port;

    // =========================================
    //     Constructors
    // =========================================

    /**
     * Creates a new <code>RequestHandler</code>
     * for the specified client
     */
    public RequestHandler(Socket client)
    {
        this.client = client;
```

```
        }

        // =============================================
        //     Instance methods
        // =============================================

        /**
         * Copies the request from the client to the server
         * and copies the response back to the client.
         */
        public void run()
        {
            try {

                // Open a socket to the web server

                if (host == null)
                    host = DEFAULT_HOST;
                if (port <= 0)
                    port = DEFAULT_PORT;

                Socket server = new Socket(host, port);

                // Open I/O streams to the client

                InputStream cin =
                    new BufferedInputStream(client.getInputStream());
                OutputStream cout =
                    new BufferedOutputStream(client.getOutputStream());

                // Open I/O streams to the server

                InputStream sin =
                    new BufferedInputStream(server.getInputStream());
                OutputStream sout =
                    new BufferedOutputStream(server.getOutputStream());

                // Copy request line and headers from client to server,
                // echoing to logger if specified.  Stop after the
                // first empty line (end of headers)

                int contentLength = 0;
                StringBuffer sb = new StringBuffer();
```

```
for (;;) {

   // Read a byte from client
   // and copy it to server

   int c = cin.read();
   sout.write(c);

   // Ignore CR at end of line

   if (c == '\r')
      continue;

   // If LF, process the line

   if (c == '\n') {
      String line = sb.toString();
      sb = new StringBuffer();

      // Log the line

      logger.log("C: " + line);

      // If this is an empty line,
      // there are no more headers

      if (line.length() == 0)
         break;

      // If it is a content length header,
      // save the content length

      int p = line.indexOf(":");
      if (p != -1) {
         String key = line.substring(0, p).trim();
         String value = line.substring(p+1).trim();
         if (key.equalsIgnoreCase("content-length"))
            contentLength = Integer.parseInt(value);
      }
   }

   // Otherwise, append char to string buffer
```

```
      else
         sb.append((char) c);
   }
   sout.flush();

   // If content length was specified, read input stream
   // and copy to server

   if (contentLength > 0) {
      for (int i = 0; i < contentLength; i++) {
         int c = cin.read();
         sout.write(c);
      }
      sout.flush();
   }

   // Echo the response back to the client

   sb = new StringBuffer();
   while (true) {

      // Read a byte from server
      // and copy it to client

      int c = sin.read();
      cout.write(c);

      // Ignore CR at end of line

      if (c == '\r')
         continue;

      // If LF, process the line

      if (c == '\n') {
         String line = sb.toString();
         sb = new StringBuffer();

         // Log the line

         logger.log("S: " + line);

         // If this is an empty line,
```

```
                    // there are no more headers

                if (line.length() == 0)
                    break;
            }

            // Otherwise, append char to string buffer

            else
                sb.append((char) c);
        }
        cout.flush();

        // Copy remaining bytes to client

        int bytesCopied = 0;
        while (true) {
            int c = sin.read();
            if (c == -1)
                break;
            cout.write(c);
            bytesCopied++;
        }
        if (bytesCopied > 0)
            cout.flush();

        // Close streams and sockets

        cin.close();
        cout.close();
        client.close();

        sin.close();
        sout.close();
        server.close();
    }
    catch (IOException e) {
        e.printStackTrace();
    }
}


// ============================================
//    Property setters
```

```
// =============================================

/**
 * Sets the logger.
 * @param logger the logger.
 */
public void setLogger(Logger logger)
{
    this.logger = logger;
}

/**
 * Sets the host.
 * @param host the host.
 */
public void setHost(String host)
{
    this.host = host;
}

/**
 * Sets the port.
 * @param port the port.
 */
public void setPort(int port)
{
    this.port = port;
}
}
```

The heart of `RequestHandler` is its `run()` method, which does the following:

1. Opens a client socket to the Web server, and then the socket's input and output streams.

2. Opens input and output streams for the Web client.

3. Reads the request line and request headers, looking for a blank line that signals the end of the headers. As each header is read, it is logged and passed on to the Web server. If a `Content-Length` header is found, its value is noted so that the user-supplied POST data can be forwarded.

4. After the blank line at the end of the headers, if the content length is nonzero, the request handler reads that many bytes from the client input stream and copies them to the server.

The same process is then repeated in reverse for the server's response, except the `Content-Length` header is ignored and the server's output is read and copied until the end of the file.

An example of where the `Tracer` tool can be useful is HTTP authentication. Much of what makes this work happens under the covers of both the browser and the Web server. An examination of the HTTP headers can make it clear.

HTTP Basic Authentication works like this:

- A Web user requests a document protected by HTTP basic authentication.

- The Web browser formats an HTTP request and sends it to the Web server.

- The server refuses the request, setting the status code to 401 (Authorization Required) and sending a `WWW-Authenticate` header specifying the authentication type and the realm.

- The browser gets the 401 response code and searches its cache to see if the user has already logged in to this realm during this session. If the user hasn't logged in, the browser prompts for the user ID and password.

- The credentials, obtained either from this prompt or from the browser session cache, are Base64-encoded[2] and the original request is retransmitted, this time with an `Authorization` header.

- The server sees the `Authorization` header, verifies whether the user is authorized to retrieve the document, and then returns either the document or another 401 response line.

You can find a simple demonstration of this process in the Manager servlet included in the Tomcat distribution. Ordinarily, you invoke this from a Web browser with `http://localhost/manager/<command>`, where *<command>* is `list`, `start`, `stop`, or some other command. When you start the application, you are prompted for a user name and password, which you must have previously registered in the `$TOMCAT/conf/tomcat-users.xml` file. Here's what `Tracer` reports for the authentication dialog:

```
M: Opening tracer server on tracerPort 8601
M: Waiting for connections
M: Connection received from Socket
   [addr=/127.0.0.1,port=1427,localport=8601]
M: Waiting for connections
```

JSP APPLICATIONS

---

[2] Base64 encoding converts a byte stream to readable ASCII characters so that control characters in the bytes don't confuse the server. RFC 2068 describes the algorithm. Note, however, that this isn't encryption, only a character transformation that can be easily reversed. For this reason, HTTP Basic Authentication is not particularly secure and should be used only for applications where security is not critical, or where it is supplemented by SSL or some other encryption layer.

The tracer server starts by opening a server socket on port 8601. It blocks on the server socket's accept() method, waiting for clients to connect. Once a connection is received, the server starts a request handler in a separate thread and resumes listening for other client requests. Here's what the client side of the request looks like:

```
C: GET /manager/list HTTP/1.1
C: Accept: application/msword, application/vnd.ms-excel, ...
C: Accept-Language: en-us
C: Accept-Encoding: gzip, deflate
C: User-Agent: Mozilla/4.0 (compatible; Windows NT 4.0)
C: Host: localhost:8601
C: Connection: Keep-Alive
C:
```

with a final blank line to indicate no more headers follow. The request handler reads the request line and six headers, echoing them to the Web server. The Web server refuses the request, returning a 401 status code (Authorization Required) and a WWW-Authenticate header specifying that the authentication type is Basic and that the security realm is "Tomcat Manager Application":

```
S: HTTP/1.1 401 Unauthorized
S: Pragma: No-cache
S: Cache-Control: no-cache
S: Expires: Thu, 01 Jan 1970 00:00:00 GMT
S: WWW-Authenticate: Basic realm="Tomcat Manager Application"
S: Content-Type: text/html
S: Transfer-Encoding: chunked
S: Date: Thu, 12 Sep 2002 02:43:00 GMT
S: Server: Apache Coyote HTTP/1.1 Connector [1.0]
S:
```

Meanwhile, the Web browser has prompted the user for a user name and password for that realm, and it reissues the request:

```
M: Connection received from Socket
    [addr=/127.0.0.1,port=1429,localport=8601]
M: Waiting for connections

C: GET /manager/list HTTP/1.1
C: Accept: application/msword, application/vnd.ms-excel, ...
C: Accept-Language: en-us
C: Accept-Encoding: gzip, deflate
```

```
C: User-Agent: Mozilla/4.0 (compatible; Windows NT 4.0)
C: Host: localhost:8601
C: Connection: Keep-Alive
C: Authorization: Basic bm8td2F5Ompvc2U=
C:

S: HTTP/1.1 200 OK
S: Pragma: No-cache
S: Cache-Control: no-cache
S: Expires: Thu, 01 Jan 1970 00:00:00 GMT
S: Content-Type: text/plain
S: Transfer-Encoding: chunked
S: Date: Thu, 12 Sep 2002 02:43:21 GMT
S: Server: Apache Coyote HTTP/1.1 Connector [1.0]
S:
```

This time, the request includes an `Authorization` header with the Base64-encoded credentials. And this time, the server accepts the request and sends back the results.

`Tracer` is easy to use and wasn't particularly difficult to write, but it doesn't cover 100 percent of the HTTP protocol you might encounter. Most Web servers provide this functionality with similar tools. JRun has several tools, including one called `sniffer` that is similar to `tracer`, and Tomcat comes with a request dumper valve.

Summary

Testing and debugging are indispensable parts of application development. While programming is systematic and amenable to design patterns, debugging is often haphazard and performed by trial and error changes. This chapter highlighted two key aspects of a systematic debugging methodology:

- Building a mental model of the components and their interactions
- Isolating the failing component

Three tools that can assist in this methodology were presented:

- **Echo.jsp**   A JSP page that captures parameters produced by an HTML form
- **WebClient**   A standalone application that simulates a Web browser
- **Tracer**   A standalone application that intercepts and logs HTTP requests

With sufficient forethought and design for testability, debugging can be as systematic as application development.

Chapter 18

Deploying Web Applications

P rior to the Servlet 2.2 API specification, installing and configuring Web applications was very much a vendor-specific task. Apache JServ, for example, used both .properties files and files containing Apache directive extensions to configure its servlet zones and their attributes. Early versions of JRun came with a raft of .properties files used to indicate how many servers existed, what ports they used, their classpaths, what servlet aliases they recognized, which servlets should be preloaded, and so on. The JSWDK reference implementation used a custom XML format for this purpose.

A certain amount of diversity is inevitable because servlet containers are, after all, different implementations with their own particular features. But that part of the configuration task is limited. The part that describes and interacts with servlets themselves is fairly regular and can be standardized to great benefit. This is precisely what happened in connection with the introduction of Web applications in the Servlet API.

With version 2.4 of the Servlet API, there are two additional features:

1. The deployment descriptor is extensible. You can describe new syntax for entering configuration information directly in the web.xml file. Unless you have very specialized requirements, you may not need to use this capability—it's not for the faint of heart. The Servlet 2.4 specification is the best place to look for details.

2. The deployment descriptor is now described with an XML Schema, not a DTD. Although the schema may look intimidating, you only have to be able to read it, not write it. It's not particularly difficult to find syntax information in the schema that will tell you where to place elements in the web.xml file. You can find more details about XML Schema in Chapter 16.

To ease the pain of transition, Servlet 2.4–compliant containers are required to support versions 2.2 and 2.3 deployment descriptors as well.

This chapter describes the structure of a Web application and how to move it out of the development environment and into a production environment.

The Web Application Environment

A collection of cooperating resources mapped to a common area of the Web server namespace is referred to by the Servlet 2.4 and JSP 2.0 API specifications as a *Web application.* This collection may include servlets, JSP pages, HTML files, images, supporting classes, and configuration data.

For example, the LyricNote Web site might contain several Web applications:

- **products**   This would include the product catalog database, images, a search engine, a shopping cart application for customer orders, and Web pages that describe product categories.

- **support**   This application would provide JSP pages for customers to report problems and ask questions, defect tracking servlets, servlets for generating e-mail, and classes that interact with a knowledge base.

- **internal**   MIS applications such as conference room bookings, job postings, and company newsletters would live here, in a mixture of servlets, JSP pages, and ordinary HTML.

Directory Structure

A Web application has a prescribed directory structure that all compliant servlet containers understand. The structure is illustrated in Figure 18-1. The top level, or *application root*, contains HTML documents, JSP pages, images, and any other resources that make up the *content* of the application. Any number of subdirectories, which also contain application content, can be under the root, much like folders in the document tree of a Web server.

The root directory also contains a special directory named WEB-INF. This directory and its subdirectories aren't visible to application users. Instead, they contain servlets,

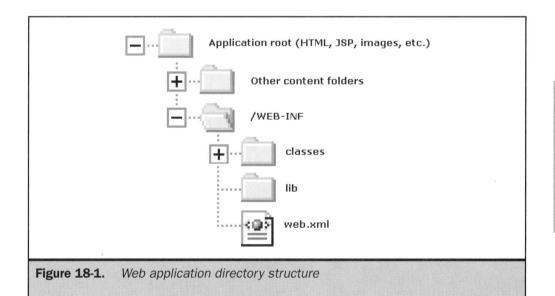

Figure 18-1.   *Web application directory structure*

classes, .jar files, and configuration data that make up the operational parts of the application. Three entries of note are in WEB-INF:

- **classes** This directory contains servlets and other classes. These classes are automatically found by the servlet class loader, as if they were in the application classpath. classes may have subdirectories that correspond to the package structure, the same as any other directory in a classpath.

- **lib** Similar to classes, but contains .jar files. Classes in any .jar file in this directory are automatically made available to the class loader without having to be listed explicitly in some classpath.

- **web.xml** This is an XML document referred to as the *deployment descriptor*. It has a rigorously defined vendor-independent structure and is used to configure the servlets and other resources that make up the Web application. We'll examine web.xml in greater detail later in this chapter.

Other files and subdirectories may occur in WEB-INF, although the Servlet API specification doesn't define any particular ones. One subdirectory commonly used is tlds, which contains Tag Library Descriptors for JSP custom tags. Because entries in this subdirectory are visible to application classes, but not to Web users, WEB-INF is often used for vendor-specific purposes. In general, WEB-INF is suitable for any data you want to use in a Web application while keeping it hidden from direct access by users.

Resource Mapping

Web servers have a document root directory that primarily contains HTML files. In Apache, for example, this is *<apache root>*/htdocs. Microsoft *Internet Information Server (IIS)* uses inetpub/wwwroot. When a URL is clicked in a Web browser, the browser separates it into its server and path components and generates an HTTP request to the server for the specified resource. The Web server, when it receives the request, extracts the path from the request header and translates it into a path relative to the document root directory. For example, if the URL is

```
http://www.lyricnote.com/products/index.html
```

the browser opens an HTTP connection to the www.lyricnote.com host and sends it a request starting with the line

```
GET /products/index.html HTTP/1.0
```

If the Web server is Apache and is installed at /usr/local/Apache, then the file sent back is

```
/usr/local/Apache/htdocs/products/index.html
```

If the server is Microsoft IIS and is installed at `c:\inetpub`, then the file requested is

```
c:\inetpub\wwwroot\products\index.html
```

A Web application also has a document root directory, as we've seen, but this root can be anywhere in the file system. The servlet container, when it recognizes that an HTTP request is for a servlet or JSP page, extracts the Web application name from the URL and maps the rest to a resource within that application. For example, if the URL is

```
http://www.lyricnote.com/products/contest/rules.jsp
```

then the servlet container creates a request for `/contest/rules.jsp` and passes it to the `products` Web application. Servlets are handled similarly. A URL like

```
http://www.lyricnote.com/products/servlet/Counter
```

gets passed to the `products` Web application as a request for the `Counter` servlet.

URLs used in a servlet or JSP page within an application to refer to another resource within the application don't use the application name. For example, if the `rules.jsp` page needs to include the output of the `Counter` servlet dynamically, it uses the statement

```
<jsp:include page="/servlet/Counter" />
```

not the statement

```
<jsp:include page="/products/servlet/Counter" />
```

The same applies to URLs used by `<jsp:include>`, the `<%@ include %>` directive, the `<%@ taglib %>` directive, and methods that create `RequestDispatcher` objects. The rule for interpreting these relative URLs is this:

- If the URL begins with `/`, it's interpreted as being relative to the application root directory.
- If it doesn't begin with `/`, it's interpreted as being relative to the current JSP page.

This brings up a subtle difficulty, however. URLs in a JSP page used as hyperlinks, form actions, style sheet links, or image sources are interpreted by the browser, not the server. If the LyricNote home page is a JSP page with a link to `/products/contest/rules.jsp`, the link cannot be hardcoded with the `products` application name. Why not? Because the application name isn't necessarily going to be `products`. This depends entirely on where the system administrator chose to install the Web application. It could have been mounted as `product_test` or `staging_area` or anything else. Only when the application is actually running can a JSP page know the name, which can be obtained from the `request.getContextPath()` method.

You can get around this problem in several ways. The JSP page can write every URL as a JSP expression concatenating `request.getContextPath()` with the rest of the URL, but this gets to be tedious and clutters up the code unnecessarily. A more elegant approach is to use the HTML `<base>` element to assign a context to the page:

```
<html>
<head>
<base href="http://www.lyricnote.com/products/">
</head>
<body>
<a href="contest/rules.jsp">View the contest rules</A>
</body>
</html>
```

With the `<base>` tag, the Web browser can interpret any nonabsolute URLs relative to the HREF attribute. Thus, `contest/rules.jsp` becomes `http://www.lyricnote.com/products/contest/rules.jsp`.

Of course, you aren't done yet. You still need to figure out the base element's HREF attribute at run time. The HREF attribute needs to be a complete URL, not just an absolute path from the server, so you need a number of details. The URL may start with `https`, if the connection uses SSL. A port number may be specified, not just the default port 80. Fortunately, the `request` object can provide all this information. The following scriptlet solves the problem in a general way.

```
<%
    String    scheme   = request.getScheme();
    String    server   = request.getServerName();
    int       port     = request.getServerPort();
    String    path     = request.getContextPath();

    StringBuffer sb = new StringBuffer();
    sb.append(scheme);
    sb.append("://");
    sb.append(server);
    if ((port != -1) && (port != 80)) {
        sb.append(":");
        sb.append(port);
    }
    sb.append(path);
    sb.append("/");
    String baseURL = sb.toString();
```

```
%>
<base href="<%= baseURL %>">
```

Note in particular that the base URL must end with a path separator "/". This means that the base URL and relative resource names when concatenated are exactly the same as the full, absolute URL.

The Servlet Context

Within a Web application, servlets and JSP pages can share data and functionality through a common object known as the *servlet context*. This is an object that implements the `javax.servlet.ServletContext` interface. The servlet context serves a number of useful purposes:

- **Object sharing**   Both servlets and JSP pages can store objects by name in the servlet context, so they can be retrieved by other servlets and JSP pages. These bindings persist as long as the application is active.

- **Initialization parameters**   Constants used throughout the application can be specified in the deployment descriptor and accessed through methods in the servlet context. This permits configuration details—such as database URLs and driver class names—to be specified outside any compiled Java code.

- **Request dispatching**   Servlets can forward requests to other servlets and JSP pages or include their output in the current output stream. The servlet context provides methods for creating request dispatchers using either a path or a servlet name.

- **Message logging**   The servlet context has access to the servlet log and can be used to write messages in a vendor-independent way.

In a JSP page, the servlet context object is automatically available in the `application` implicit variable. In a servlet, it can be obtained with the `getServletContext()` method.

The Web Archive (war) File

Described so far is the run-time structure of a Web application. For deployment, this structure must be collapsed into a single file called a *Web archive (war)* file. This is nothing more than a `.jar` file with a different extension (`.war`), whose top level corresponds to the root of the Web application. The `.war` file must also contain a `WEB-INF` directory with a `web.xml` file.

To use a concrete example, consider the `products` Web application, shown in Figure 18-2. Its root directory contains an `index.jsp` file and four content subdirectories: `contest`, `debug`, `images`, and `sounds`. In addition, it contains a `WEB-INF` directory

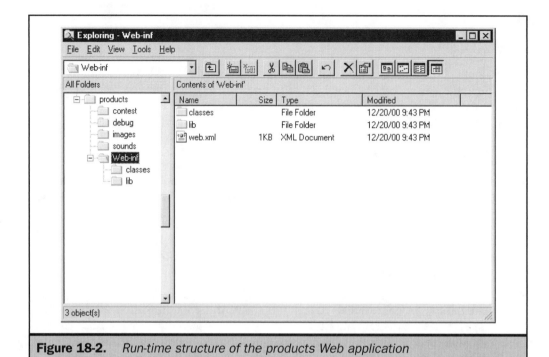

Figure 18-2.   *Run-time structure of the products Web application*

with the required `classes` and `lib` subdirectories, as well as the `web.xml` deployment descriptor.

To create the `.war` file, go to the `products` directory and use the JDK `jar` command line tool:

```
D:\lyricnote\products>jar -cvf products.war *
added manifest
adding: contest/(in = 0) (out= 0)(stored 0%)
adding: contest/contest.url(in = 184) (out= 125)(deflated 32%)
adding: contest/index.jsp(in = 1890) (out= 739)(deflated 60%)
adding: debug/(in = 0) (out= 0)(stored 0%)
adding: debug/AddProduct.jsp(in = 400) (out= 240)(deflated 40%)
adding: debug/AddProduct2.jsp(in = 543) (out= 292)(deflated 46%)
adding: debug/Example1.jsp(in = 153) (out= 119)(deflated 22%)
adding: debug/Example1.url(in = 76) (out= 78)(deflated -2%)
adding: images/(in = 0) (out= 0)(stored 0%)
adding: index.jsp(in = 782) (out= 392)(deflated 49%)
adding: sounds/(in = 0) (out= 0)(stored 0%)
adding: sounds/BIRDS.MID(in = 3494) (out= 1138)(deflated 67%)
adding: sounds/ITBGON.MID(in = 975) (out= 478)(deflated 50%)
```

```
adding: WEB-INF/(in = 0) (out= 0)(stored 0%)
adding: WEB-INF/classes/(in = 0) (out= 0)(stored 0%)
adding: WEB-INF/lib/(in = 0) (out= 0)(stored 0%)
adding: WEB-INF/web.xml(in = 46) (out= 37)(deflated 19%)
```

See the JDK documentation for complete details about the `jar` tool.

The resulting file `products.war` is ready to be deployed. All Servlet 2.4–compliant servlet containers are required to accept a `.war` file directly and construct the corresponding Web application. The specific means for installing the file are, as you might expect, vendor specific. Tomcat, the reference implementation, allows `.war` files simply to be dropped into the *<tomcat_home>*/webapps directory. When Tomcat is restarted, the `.war` file is then unpacked and validated, and the new application is available. Many servlet containers provide a GUI administration tool for this job. Tomcat features a Web application manager (shown in Figure 18-3) from which applications can be monitored, started, stopped, installed, and uninstalled.

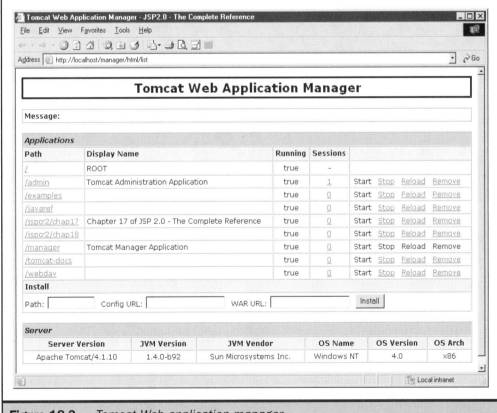

Figure 18-3. *Tomcat Web application manager*

The Deployment Descriptor—web.xml

The web.xml file in the WEB-INF directory is referred to as the *deployment descriptor*. This is an XML document in a strictly defined format that specifies the configuration of the Web application. Among other things, it can be used to describe

- Servlets aliases, mappings, and initialization parameters
- Session timeout limits
- Global parameters to be made available throughout the application
- Security configuration
- Mime types

Because this file is an XML document, its format is described with an *XML Schema*. The schema is named web-app_*x.y*.xsd, where *x.y* is the Servlet API specification version, such as 2.4. It is published by Sun Microsystems and can be downloaded at http://java.sun.com/xml/ns/j2ee/web-app_2_4.xsd.

The web.xml file looks like this:

```
<?xml version="1.0"?>
<web-app xmlns="http://java.sun.com/xml/ns/j2ee" version="2.4">
    ...
</web-app>
```

In the body of the <web-app> element are other elements that describe the application configuration. Table 18-1 lists the elements that can be used.

Note *The complete Servlet 2.4 deployment descriptor is extensible and can include a number of elements that are specific to other J2EE technologies. For more details on particular elements, see the Servlet 2.4 API specification.*

Note *Any elements used inside the <web-app> body must be specified exactly in the order listed. If multiple occurrences of an element are allowed, they must all occur together, not intermingled with other elements. For example, all <servlet> elements must occur before any <servlet-mapping> elements.*

Element	Contents
`<web-app>`	This is the top-level element. It may contain any of the following subelements, in the order shown: `<description>` (optional) `<display-name>` (optional) `<icon>` (zero or more) `<distributable>` (optional) `<context-param>` (zero or more) `<filter>` (zero or more) `<filter-mapping>` (zero or more) `<listener>` (zero or more) `<servlet>` (zero or more) `<servlet-mapping>` (zero or more) `<session-config>` (optional) `<mime-mapping>` (zero or more) `<welcome-file-list>` (optional) `<error-page>` (zero or more) `<jsp-config>` (optional) `<security-constraint>` (zero or more) `<login-config>` (optional) `<security-role>` (zero or more) `<env-entry>` (zero or more) `<ejb-ref>` (zero or more) `<ejb-local-ref>` (zero or more) `<resource-ref>` (zero or more) `<resource-env-ref>` (zero or more) `<message-destination-ref>` (zero or more) `<message-destination>` (zero or more) `<locale-encoding-mapping-list>` (optional) `<deployment-extension>` (zero or more)
`<description>`	A description of the parent element that can be used by administrative tools. This element can appear in several different contexts in this file.
`<display-name>`	A short name for the parent element (`<web-app>` or `<servlet>`), which can be used by administrative tools.
`<icon>`	Allows developer to specify the relative location within the application of icon files, in either JPEG or GIF format. These icons can be used by a GUI administration to represent the application. It may contain either of the following elements, or both: `<small-icon>` (optional) `<large-icon>` (optional)
`<small-icon>`	A 16 × 16 icon image filename.
`<large-icon>`	A 32 × 32 icon image filename.

Table 18-1. *Elements of the deployment descriptor*

Element	Contents
`<distributable>`	If specified, indicates this application is designed to run in multiple distributed servlet containers.
`<distributable>`	If specified, indicates this application is designed to run in multiple distributed servlet containers.
`<context-param>`	Defines an application-wide initialization parameter. Contains the following subelements: `<param-name>` (required) `<param-value>` (required) `<description>` (optional)
`<param-name>`	A parameter name.
`<param-value>`	A parameter value.
`<filter>`	Identifies a filter, the name of which must be unique in the Web application. Subelements are: `<description>` (optional) `<display-name>` (optional) `<icon>` (zero or more) `<filter-name>` (required) `<filter-class>` (required) `<init-param>` (required)
`<filter-name>`	Specifies the filter name.
`<filter-class>`	The fully-qualified name of the class that implements the filter.
`<filter-mapping>`	Associates a filter with a URL pattern. The filter name must match some filter name specified earlier in a `<filter>` element. Subelements are: `<filter-name>` (required) `<url-pattern>` (required) `<dispatcher>` (zero or more)
`<dispatcher>`	Used to indicate how the filter mapping should be applied with respect to request dispatcher actions. The legal values are FORWARD - apply filter to dispatcher forward() actions REQUEST - apply filter to dispatcher include() actions REQUEST - apply filter only to regular client calls (default) Multiple `<dispatcher>` elements can be specified in a filter mapping to get a combination of these attributes.
`<listener>`	Identifies an event listener. Subelements are: `<description>` (optional) `<display-name>` (optional) `<icon>` (zero or more) `<listener-class>` (required)
`<listener-class>`	The fully-qualified name of the class that implements the listener.

Table 18-1.   *Elements of the deployment descriptor* (continued)

Element	Contents
`<servlet>`	Defines a servlet and all its associated configuration. May contain the following subelements, in this order: `<icon>` (optional) `<servlet-name>` (required) `<display-name>` (optional) `<description>` (optional) `<servlet-class>` or `<jsp-file>` (must specify one or the other) `<init-param>` (zero or more) `<load-on-startup>` (optional) `<run-as>` (optional) `<security-role-ref>` (zero or more) `<deployment-extension>` (zero or more)
`<servlet-name>`	The name by which a servlet is known to the servlet container. Note, multiple `<servlet>` elements with different servlet names may specify the same servlet class. In that case, the servlet container creates multiple instances of the servlet. A servlet may call the `<getServletName()>` method in GenericServlet or ServletConfig to determine its name.
`<servlet-class>`	The fully qualified name of the servlet class.
`<jsp-file>`	The full path to a JSP file relative to the root of the Web application.
`<init-param>`	Defines a servlet initialization parameter. Contains the following subelements: `<param-name>` (required) `<param-value>` (required) `<description>` (optional)
`<load-on-startup>`	If specified, this element indicates the servlet should be preloaded when the servlet container starts. This means the servlet's init() method will be called and the servlet will then be available for requests. The value of this element (if any) can be an integer specifying the relative order in which this servlet should be started, if several exist.
`<run-as>`	Specifies an identity under which a component executes. Must contain a `<role-name>` subelement.
`<deployment-extension>`	Used to supply configuration data that is specific to a particular J2EE component.
`<servlet-mapping>`	Specifies which URL patterns should be mapped to which servlet names. Must contain the following subelements: `<servlet-name>` (required) `<url-pattern>` (required).

Table 18-1.   *Elements of the deployment descriptor* (continued)

Element	Contents
`<url-pattern>`	Indicates a pattern that must be matched by a substring of a URL for this servlet to be invoked. The pattern may include the wildcard character *.
`<session-config>`	Defines session configuration parameters. May include the `<session-timeout>` subelement.
`<session-timeout>`	The default number of minutes with no activity the servlet container allows before HTTP sessions are terminated.
`<mime-mapping>`	Defines the MIME type implied by a file extension. Must contain the following elements: `<extension>` (required) `<mime-type>` (required).
`<extension>`	A suffix of a filename that indicates its type. For example, png is used to indicate a Portable Network Graphics file.
`<mime-type>`	The MIME type associated with a particular file extension. For example, image/png is used to indicate a Portable Network Graphics file.
`<welcome-file-list>`	A list of zero or more `<welcome-file>` elements. When a request is made for a URL that is a directory, the servlet container tries each welcome file in turn.
`<welcome-file>`	The default file to be used to service a request in a directory if no filename is specified in the URL. Examples would be index.html or index.jsp.
`<error-page>`	Maps an HTTP response code or exception type to a servlet, JSP page, or HTML file that will be invoked by default when error occurs. Contains the following subelements: `<error-code>` or `<exception-type>` (one or the other is required) `<location>` (required)
`<error-code>`	An HTTP response code to be mapped to an error page.
`<exception-type>`	A fully qualified Java exception class name.
`<location>`	The URI of a servlet, JSP page, or HTML file used as an error page.
`<resource-ref>`	Contains information used to set up a J2EE resource factory. May contain the following subelements: `<description>` (optional) `<res-ref-name>` (required) `<res-type>` (required) `<res-auth>` (required).
`<message-destination-ref>`	A reference to a message destination, typically a JMS message queue.

Table 18-1. *Elements of the deployment descriptor* (continued)

Element	Contents
`<message-destination>`	A message destination, typically a JMS message queue.
`<res-ref-name>`	Specifies the name of a resource factory reference.
`<res-type>`	Specifies the Java class name of the data source associated with a resource factory.
`<res-auth>`	Indicates the source of the credentials supplied to a resource factory. There are two possible values: SERVLET—The Web application supplies the value programmatically. CONTAINER—Credentials supplied by the container.
`<security-constraint>`	Defines the security constraints to be applied to one or more resource collections. May contain the following subelements: `<web-resource-collection>` (one or more) `<auth-constraint>` (optional) `<user-data-constraint>` (optional)
`<web-resource-collection>`	Defines a set of resources in the Web application to which security constraints can be applied. May contain the following subelements: `<web-resource-name>` (required) `<description>` (optional) `<url-pattern>` (zero or more) `<http-method>` (zero or more)
`<web-resource-name>`	The name by which a Web resource can be referred to.
`<http-method>`	An HTTP method type (for example, GET, POST, and so forth).
`<user-data-constraint>`	Specifies how data transmitted to and from the application should be protected. May contain the following subelements: `<description>` (optional) `<transport-guarantee>` (required)
`<transport-guarantee>`	Allowed values are NONE—application doesn't require transport guarantees. INTEGRAL—requires that data cannot be altered in transit. CONFIDENTIAL—requires that data cannot be read in transit.
`<auth-constraint>`	Specifies a list of role names treated collectively in a `<security-constraint>` element. May contain the following subelements: `<description>` (optional) `<role-name>` (zero or more)
`<role-name>`	A name used to identify a role in which an authenticated user may be logged in. This is the same value specified in the `<request.isUserInRole()>` method to allow conditional execution of parts of a servlet by users in different roles.

Table 18-1.   *Elements of the deployment descriptor* (continued)

Element	Contents
`<login-config>`	Specifies the type of login configuration. May include the following subelements: `<auth-method>` (optional) `<realm-name>` (optional) `<form-login-config>` (optional).
`<realm-name>`	A realm name used in HTTP Basic Authentication.
`<form-login-config>`	Specifies the resources used in form-based login. Must contain the following subelements: `<form-login-page>` (required) `<form-error-page>` (required)
`<form-login-page>`	Specifies the name of a resource (HTML file, JSP page, servlet) that prompts for user name and password. This page must adhere to the following requirements: 1. The form must use METHOD="POST" and ACTION="j_security_check". 2. The user name field must be named j_username. 3. The password field must be named j_password.
`<form-error-page>`	Specifies the name of a resource (HTML file, JSP page, servlet) displayed when the form-based login isn't successful.
`<auth-method>`	Specifies the authentication method used. There are four legal values: BASIC DIGEST FORM CLIENT-CERT Not all servlet containers support all methods.
`<security-role>`	Declares a security role name valid for use in a `<security-constraints>` element. May contain the following subelements: `<description>` (optional) `<role-name>` (required)
`<security-role-ref>`	Creates a mapping between a role name and an alias for it. May contain the following subelements: `<description>` (optional) `<role-name>` (required) `<role-link>` (required) This allows servlets to use the role link in the request.isUserInRole() method and have that name equated to the actual role name. Thereafter, if the application is modified to use a different role name, the servlet needn't be modified.
`<role-link>`	A symbolic name used by a servlet to refer to an actual role name.

Table 18-1. *Elements of the deployment descriptor* (continued)

Element	Contents
`<env-entry>`	Used to define the J2EE environment entry. May contain the following subelements: `<description>` (optional) `<env-entry-name>` (required) `<env-entry-value>` (optional) `<env-entry-type>` (required)
`<env-entry-name>`	The J2EE environment entry name relative to the JNDI java:comp/env context.
`<env-entry-value>`	The value of the J2EE environment entry.

`<env-entry-type>`	Must be one of the following:
	`java.lang.Boolean`
	`java.lang.String`
	`java.lang.Integer`
	`java.lang.Double`
	`java.lang.Float`

`<ejb-ref>`	Defines a reference to an *Enterprise Java Bean (EJB)*. May contain the following subelements: `<description>` (optional) `<ejb-ref-name>` (required) `<ejb-ref-type>` (required) `<home>` (required) `<remote>` (required) `<ejb-link>` (optional)
`<ejb-ref-name>`	The JNDI name of an EJB reference.
`<ejb-ref-type>`	The Java class of the EJB.
`<home>`	The fully qualified name of the class that's the EJB's home interface.
`<remote>`	The fully qualified name of the class that's the EJB's remote interface.
`<ejb-link>`	The name of an EJB in an encompassing J2EE application to which this EJB is linked.

Table 18-1.   *Elements of the deployment descriptor* (continued)

Sample Deployment Descriptor

Table 18-1 looks formidable, but fortunately, most deployment descriptors use only a tiny fraction of the possible elements. The following listing shows a typical web.xml file:

```
<?xml version="1.0"?>
<web-app xmlns="http://java.sun.com/xml/ns/j2ee" version="2.4">
```

```
<context-param>
   <param-name>JDBC.DRIVER</param-name>
   <param-value>
      org.gjt.mm.mysql.Driver
   </param-value>
</context-param>

<context-param>
   <param-name>JDBC.URL</param-name>
   <param-value>
      jdbc:mysql://localhost/lyricnote
   </param-value>
</context-param>

<servlet>
   <servlet-name>Sample</servlet-name>
   <servlet-class>
      com.jspcr.servlets.SampleServlet
   </servlet-class>
   <init-param>
      <param-name>message</param-name>
      <param-value>Hello, world</param-value>
   </init-param>
</servlet>

<servlet>
   <servlet-name>daytime</servlet-name>
   <servlet-class>
      com.jspcr.services.daytime
   </servlet-class>
   <load-on-startup>1</load-on-startup>
</servlet>

</web-app>
```

This deployment descriptor contains four elements: two context parameters and two servlet declarations. The context parameters define constants available to all servlets and JSP pages in the Web application. In this case, they define a JDBC driver class and a database URL. Servlets and JSP pages can retrieve these values with the servlet context getInitParameter() method. Because this type of information frequently changes and, typically, varies in different installations, being able to describe it here rather than hard-coding it in a Java class is convenient.

Two servlets are defined. The first one, named `Sample`, refers to the `jspcr.servlets.SampleServlet` class and has one initialization parameter. This allows the servlet to be called with a URL similar to

```
http://www.lyricnote.com/products/servlet/Sample
```

without requiring the full servlet class name to be specified. The second servlet, named `daytime`, uses the `<load-on-startup>` element to cause it to be preloaded when the servlet container starts.

The Servlet 2.4 API specification provides other sample deployment descriptors. Likewise, most servlet containers come with examples of this file, as well as tools to manipulate it.

Summary

Web application deployment has become standardized and vendor-independent. The servlet specification describes a standard directory structure that contains the Web content, as well as configuration information and class directories. The configuration is specified in an XML document named `web.xml` and known as the *deployment descriptor*. The directory structure is mirrored in the *web archive (.war)* file format. Deploying a Web application and moving it from one servlet container to another usually requires little more than installing the `.war` file and invoking the servlet container's deployment tool.

Chapter 19

Case Study: A Product Support Center

577

O ur hypothetical Internet music store, LyricNote.com, sells a variety of musical products: sheet music, musical instruments, books on musical topics, gift items, and music software. Support for these products involves taking orders over the phone, checking order status, resolving billing questions, and providing technical support for software. The last item is the focus of this chapter.

In this case study, we'll develop a Web-based system for managing the product support center. Users of the system can report and track product defects, log comments about them, and route them to the appropriate parties.

In the interest of clarity, this application doesn't include all the validations, user controls, or management reporting that a real production system might have. It does, however, illustrate many of the techniques described throughout the book and provide a model for further development.

Process Flow

To start with, let's consider the environment in which the system is going to operate. The process flow is shown in Figure 19-1.

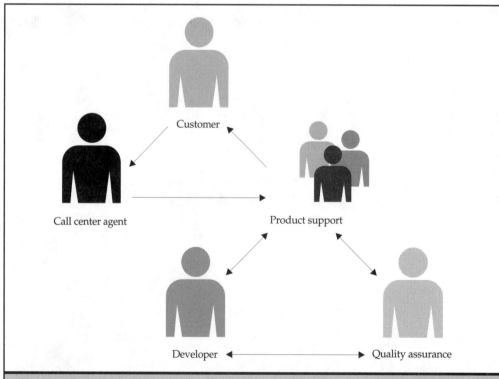

Figure 19-1. *Product support center process flow*

When a customer calls to report a software problem, the first available call center agent answers the phone. This *call center agent* may route the call to sales or customer service, if the problem isn't software-related. Otherwise, the agent verifies the customer is entitled to support, meaning the customer is a valid purchaser of the specified product. The agent creates a problem report and tells the customer to expect a call from product support.

The problem report is routed to the product support specialist for the product for which the defect is being reported. Each *product support specialist* has a queue of open problem reports, and when a new problem is received, the specialist calls the customer to get more details, trying to determine if this is a customer problem or a code problem. Customer problems may involve lack of required hardware or software, or failure to install the product properly. In these cases, the product support person helps the customer resolve the problem to the extent possible, and then closes the problem report.

If the problem is code-related, it may be that other customers have encountered it and a fix already exists. If so, the fix is documented in the knowledge base, which the product support person can search by appropriate keywords. The patch or procedure necessary to fix the problem is sent to the customer via e-mail or made available over the Web.

If the problem isn't found in the knowledge base, it's routed to the developer listed as the primary support for the product. The *developer* analyzes the problem and attempts to reproduce it. It may be the product is working as designed, in which case the defect is rerouted back to product support marked "not a bug." Otherwise, the developer tries to isolate the bug and to develop a fix. After unit testing the fix, the developer routes the problem to quality assurance. The problem report may be updated to indicate how to reproduce the problem and where to get the code patch necessary to fix it.

The *quality assurance* support person for the product receives the problem report from development and tests the fix. This is an integration test, in which the effect of the new code on existing systems is examined. If the fix introduces other problems or fails to pass all the established test cases, the problem is rerouted to development. Otherwise, the fix is routed to product support, so the customer can be contacted and supplied with the new code.

At any point, system users can look up the status of a particular problem, add comments to it, and route the problem to its next destination. To be most effective, each routing would be accompanied by e-mail sent to the new problem owner. That part isn't developed here, but can be done either with the Java Mail API or the Java Messaging Service (JMS).

To summarize, the system users and their functions are as follows:

Call center agent

- Verifies customer entitlement
- Enters new problems
- Can look up status of existing problems

Product support

- Receives incoming problem reports from call center
- Can view outstanding problems by product

- Interviews customer
- Updates problem status
- Adds comments
- Routes problem to development

Developer

- Receives problem reports from product support
- Can view outstanding problems by product
- Analyzes problem and develops fix
- Adds comments to problem report
- Routes problem to quality assurance

Quality assurance

- Receives problem reports and fixes from development
- Performs integration test
- Adds comments to problem report
- Routes fixed problems to product support
- May route problem back to developer if tests fail

In addition, management can view problem status at any time and can access reports showing quality statistics, such as time in queues, bugs reported per product, and outstanding bugs by developer. These reports aren't included in this application but could be developed from the problem database.

Data Model

Table 19-1 describes the database tables that contain all the data necessary to record and track problems.

Developing the System

JSP is a convenient development environment. Pages get automatically compiled when necessary and URLs map easily to directory locations. Inside a JSP page, you can use any mix of HTML and Java you like, which gives you a great deal of flexibility.

Unfortunately, these same advantages mean ordinary JSP applications don't scale well. As more Java code is embedded in JSP pages, keeping track of it becomes increasingly more difficult. Unlike Java classes that can be compiled and unit tested, JSP scriptlet code cannot easily be separated from its container. Being consistent over large stretches of Java-strewn HTML is also difficult. You may start out using beans to do most of the work,

Table Name	Description	Fields
customer	A list of customers who have bought LyricNote products	customerID customer name phone
product	A list of products and their support personnel	productID product name product support person lead developer lead tester
custprod	A list of customer/product pairs indicating which customer bought which product	customerID productID date purchased
problems	The main record of a reported problem	problemID description severity (1=high, 2=medium, 3=low) date reported date resolved (if closed) customerID productID
problog	A log of events in the life of a reported problem	problemID timestamp eventID comments
nextproblemid	A single-record table that contains the next unused problem ID	problemID
employees	Users of the system, including call center agents, product support, developers, and testers	employeeID name other fields (not used here)

Table 19-1.   *Tables in the Product Support Data Model*

and then find they don't do quite what you need, leading you to cheat with a little extra Java buried in the HTML. These problems are compounded if the application makes free use of the `<%@ include %>` directive.

What's needed in larger applications is a better way to separate code into components with clear responsibilities. For our product support system, we'll use the *Model-View-Controller (MVC)* design.

Model-View-Controller Architecture

The idea behind MVC is that the visual aspects of a system should be isolated from the internal workings, which, in turn, should be separate from the mechanism that starts and controls the internals. The MVC architecture was first prominently adopted by Smalltalk and its practitioners but is now a widely used design pattern. Figure 19-2 illustrates how MVC works.

The *model* refers to code that manages the abstract internal state and operations of the system. It handles database access and most business logic. The model has no visual component, providing instead an application programming interface that's accessible to other parts of the system. This makes it possible to write a driver program that can test and debug the model from a simple command-line interface.

In a chess game, for example, the model might consist of a set of objects representing the pieces and a simple 8 × 8 array to hold them. The model could have methods that indicate whose turn it is to move, that evaluate whether a given move is legal, and that move pieces from one array element to another. The model would *not* have code that provides any visual representation of the board.

The *view* is the presentation layer of the system. It does no database access and contains no business logic. What little nonvisual code the view has is limited to presentation logic, such as looping over an array of objects to be displayed. By design, a model can be associated with more than one view, perhaps a *graphical user interface*

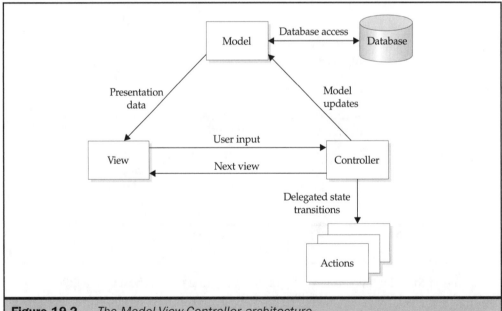

Figure 19-2. *The Model-View-Controller architecture*

(*GUI*) and a printed report. For example, a Web-based, two-player game could have one view for each player, both attached to the same model. This wouldn't require any changes to the model because the model is unaware of how it is being displayed.

In the case of the chess game, the view would contain code to draw the board and the pieces, list the moves, and show the clock. It wouldn't know anything about the rules of chess, whose turn it was, or even the locations of the pieces. The view would call methods in the model to keep track of all this. Even though GUI code is often complex, all a view has to worry about is its visual aspects. Testing and debugging is straightforward because a stub version of the model can be used to exercise all parts of the view.

The *controller* is what manipulates the model according to user input. Based on the current view, the state of the model, and the actions taken by the user, the controller calls the model API to update the model state and select the next view. Roughly speaking, the controller handles input *from* the user, whereas the view handles output going *to* the user.[1] The chess game might have two controllers—one that conveys the human player's moves, and one that chooses the computer's moves.

In this product support system, the model consists of ordinary Java classes (not servlets and not network-oriented). Simple JSP pages are used as the view and the controller is a single servlet with some supporting classes.

> **Note** *The Model-View-Controller architecture is the basis for the Jakarta Struts application framework. In a production environment, you would likely use such a framework. However, when you are first learning this approach, it is useful to develop something from scratch. That is the rationale for the detailed development outline in this chapter.*

Model Classes

Let's start by examining the product support system model. It consists of three sets of classes:

- Classes that represent business objects, roughly corresponding to tables in the database
- The application container and interface classes
- A testing framework

These classes collectively make up the `com.lyricnote.support.model` package. In addition to maintaining the application state, the model contains all the code that accesses the database, using a session-aware wrapper class to ensure that database resources are properly managed.

---

[1]   The role of the controller is sometimes handled by the view in a simpler Model-View architecture.

Business Objects

There are seven classes that encapsulate the business entities used in the data model:

- com.lyricnote.support.model.Customer
- com.lyricnote.support.model.Product
- com.lyricnote.support.model.CustomerProduct
- com.lyricnote.support.model.Employee
- com.lyricnote.support.model.Problem
- com.lyricnote.support.model.ProblemLog
- com.lyricnote.support.model.Event

The following sections list the source code for each of these classes and describe their operation.

Customer Class   The first class in the package is the Customer class, which represents a person or company that has bought LyricNote products and is eligible for product support. The class contains the customer name and phone number, as well as a unique customer identifier. The identifier is composed of the first four letters of the customer's last name, followed by the first and last letters of the customer's first name, ending with a two-digit unique numeric suffix. The class is shown in the following listing:

```
package com.lyricnote.support.model;

import java.io.*;
import java.sql.*;
import java.util.*;

/**
 * A person or company that has bought LyricNote products.
 */
public class Customer implements Serializable
{
    private String customerID;
    private String name;
    private String phone;

    /**
     * Factory method to create a customer record
     * from the current row of a result set.
     * @param rs a result set from the customer table
     * @exception SQLException if a database error occurs
     */
```

```java
public static Customer load(ResultSet rs)
   throws SQLException
{
   Customer customer = new Customer();
   String value = null;

   value = rs.getString(1);
   if (value != null)
      customer.setCustomerID(value);

   value = rs.getString(2);
   if (value != null)
      customer.setName(value);

   value = rs.getString(3);
   if (value != null)
      customer.setPhone(value);

   return customer;
}

/**
 * Returns the object as a CSV string
 */
public String toString()
{
   StringBuffer sb = new StringBuffer();

   if (getCustomerID() != null)
      sb.append(Model.quote(getCustomerID()));

   sb.append(",");
   if (getName() != null)
      sb.append(Model.quote(getName()));

   sb.append(",");
   if (getPhone() != null)
      sb.append(Model.quote(getPhone()));

   return sb.toString();
}

// ===========================================
// Property accessor methods
```

```
// ============================================

/**
 * Returns the customerID.
 */
public String getCustomerID()
{
    return customerID;
}

/**
 * Sets the customerID.
 * @param customerID the customerID.
 */
public void setCustomerID(String customerID)
{
    this.customerID = customerID;
}

/**
 * Returns the name.
 */
public String getName()
{
    return name;
}

/**
 * Sets the name.
 * @param name the name.
 */
public void setName(String name)
{
    this.name = name;
}

/**
 * Returns the phone.
 */
public String getPhone()
{
    return phone;
}
```

```
/**
 * Sets the phone.
 * @param phone the phone.
 */
public void setPhone(String phone)
{
    this.phone = phone;
}
}
```

In addition to the getter and setter methods for each property, the `Customer` class
contains a `toString()` method that returns a comma-separated-values string and a
class method named `load()`. The `load()` method creates a `Customer` object from a
`customer` table row in an SQL result set. This method is used in the model application
classes to simplify retrieving a collection of `Customer` objects from the database.

The `Model.quote()` method in the `toString()` method is discussed later in this
chapter in the "Application Objects" section.

Product Class   Next is the `Product` class, representing a row in the `product` table.
Its properties consist of a unique product identifier, the product name, and the employee
numbers of the product's primary support person, its lead developer, and its lead tester.
The class is shown in the following listing:

```
package com.lyricnote.support.model;

import java.io.*;
import java.sql.*;
import java.util.*;

/**
 * A software product supported by the Product
 * Support system.
 */
public class Product implements Serializable
{
    private String productID;
    private String name;
    private String productSupport;
    private String developer;
    private String tester;

    /**
     * Factory method to create a product record
```

```java
 * from the current row of a result set.
 * @param rs a result set from the product table
 * @exception SQLException if a database error occurs
 */
public static Product load(ResultSet rs)
   throws SQLException
{
   Product product = new Product();
   String value = null;

   value = rs.getString(1);
   if (value != null)
      product.setProductID(value);

   value = rs.getString(2);
   if (value != null)
      product.setName(value);

   value = rs.getString(3);
   if (value != null)
      product.setProductSupport(value);

   value = rs.getString(4);
   if (value != null)
      product.setDeveloper(value);

   value = rs.getString(5);
   if (value != null)
      product.setTester(value);

   return product;
}

/**
 * Returns the object as a CSV string
 */
public String toString()
{
   StringBuffer sb = new StringBuffer();

   if (getProductID() != null)
      sb.append(Model.quote(getProductID()));

   sb.append(",");
```

```java
   if (getName() != null)
      sb.append(Model.quote(getName()));

   sb.append(",");
   if (getProductSupport() != null)
      sb.append(Model.quote(getProductSupport()));

   sb.append(",");
   if (getDeveloper() != null)
      sb.append(Model.quote(getDeveloper()));

   sb.append(",");
   if (getTester() != null)
      sb.append(Model.quote(getTester()));

   return sb.toString();
}

// ==========================================
// Property accessor methods
// ==========================================

/**
 * Returns the product ID.
 */
public String getProductID()
{
   return productID;
}

/**
 * Sets the product ID.
 * @param product the product ID.
 */
public void setProductID(String productID)
{
   this.productID = productID;
}

/**
 * Returns the product name.
 */
public String getName()
{
```

```
      return name;
}

/**
 * Sets the product name.
 * @param name the product name.
 */
public void setName(String name)
{
    this.name = name;
}

/**
 * Returns the productSupport ID.
 */
public String getProductSupport()
{
    return productSupport;
}

/**
 * Sets the productSupport ID.
 * @param productSupport the productSupport.
 */
public void setProductSupport(String productSupport)
{
    this.productSupport = productSupport;
}

/**
 * Returns the developer.
 */
public String getDeveloper()
{
    return developer;
}

/**
 * Sets the developer.
 * @param developer the developer.
 */
public void setDeveloper(String developer)
{
    this.developer = developer;
```

```
   }

   /**
    * Returns the tester.
    */
   public String getTester()
   {
      return tester;
   }

   /**
    * Sets the tester.
    * @param tester the tester.
    */
   public void setTester(String tester)
   {
      this.tester = tester;
   }
}
```

Like the `Customer` class, `Product` contains getter and setter methods for each of
its properties, as well as the customized `toString()` method and the factory method
for loading a `Product` object from a result set row.

CustomerProduct Class   A key responsibility of the call center agent is to verify
customer entitlement, meaning the person reporting the problem is a valid customer and
has purchased the specified product. This is indicated by the existence of a record
linking the customer and product in the `custprod` table. The class corresponding to
this table is `CustomerProduct`, shown in the following listing:

```
package com.lyricnote.support.model;

import java.io.*;
import java.sql.ResultSet;
import java.sql.SQLException;
import java.util.*;

/**
 * A customer/product pair whose existence indicates
 * that the customer bought the specified product.
 */
public class CustomerProduct implements Serializable
{
```

```java
private String customerID;
private String productID;
private Date datePurchased;

/**
 * Factory method to create a customer/product record
 * from the current row of a result set.
 * @param rs a result set from the customer table
 * @exception SQLException if a database error occurs
 */
public static CustomerProduct load(ResultSet rs)
   throws SQLException
{
   CustomerProduct custprod = new CustomerProduct();

   custprod.setCustomerID(rs.getString(1));
   custprod.setProductID(rs.getString(2));
   custprod.setDatePurchased(rs.getDate(3));

   return custprod;
}

/**
 * Returns the object as a CSV string
 */
public String toString()
{
   StringBuffer sb = new StringBuffer();

   sb.append(getCustomerID());
   sb.append(",");
   sb.append(getProductID());
   sb.append(",");
   sb.append(Model.formatDate(getDatePurchased()));

   return sb.toString();
}

// ==========================================
// Property accessor methods
// ==========================================

/**
 * Returns the customerID.
```

```
*/
public String getCustomerID()
{
   return customerID;
}

/**
* Sets the customerID.
* @param customerID the customerID.
*/
public void setCustomerID(String customerID)
{
   this.customerID = customerID;
}

/**
* Returns the productID.
*/
public String getProductID()
{
   return productID;
}

/**
* Sets the productID.
* @param productID the productID.
*/
public void setProductID(String productID)
{
   this.productID = productID;
}

/**
* Returns the datePurchased.
*/
public Date getDatePurchased()
{
   return datePurchased;
}

/**
* Sets the datePurchased.
* @param datePurchased the datePurchased.
*/
```

```
public void setDatePurchased(Date datePurchased)
{
    this.datePurchased = datePurchased;
}


}
```

`CustomerProduct` has fields containing the customer ID, the product ID, and the date the product was purchased. This information comes from product registration mail-in cards, or manual input, not shown here.

Like the `Customer` and `Product` classes, `CustomerProduct` has getter and setter methods, a `toString()` method to create a comma-separated-values string, and a factory method for loading objects from the database.

Employee Class Associated with each product is a product support person, a lead developer, and a lead tester. Information about these employees is contained in the `employee` table and encapsulated in the `Employee` class, listed here:

```java
package com.lyricnote.support.model;

import java.io.*;
import java.sql.ResultSet;
import java.sql.SQLException;
import java.util.*;

/**
 * A LyricNote employee who uses the Product Support system.
 */
public class Employee implements Serializable
{
    private String employeeID;
    private String name;
    private Date dateHired;
    private boolean isManager;
    private String departmentID;
    private String title;
    private String email;
    private String phone;

    /**
     * Factory method to create an employee record
     * from the current row of a result set.
     * @param rs a result set from the employee table
```

```
 * @exception SQLException if a database error occurs
 */
public static Employee load(ResultSet rs)
   throws SQLException
{

   Employee employee = new Employee();

   employee.setEmployeeID(rs.getString(1));
   employee.setName(rs.getString(2));
   employee.setDateHired(rs.getDate(3));
   employee.setIsManager(rs.getBoolean(4));
   employee.setDepartmentID(rs.getString(5));
   employee.setTitle(rs.getString(6));
   employee.setEmail(rs.getString(7));
   employee.setPhone(rs.getString(8));

   return employee;
}

/**
 * Returns the object as a CSV string
 */
public String toString()
{
   StringBuffer sb = new StringBuffer();

   sb.append(getEmployeeID());
   sb.append(",");
   sb.append(Model.quote(getName()));
   sb.append(",");
   sb.append(Model.formatDate(getDateHired()));
   sb.append(",");
   sb.append(getIsManager());
   sb.append(",");
   sb.append(getDepartmentID());
   sb.append(",");
   sb.append(Model.quote(getTitle()));
   sb.append(",");
   sb.append(getEmail());
   sb.append(",");
   sb.append(getPhone());

   return sb.toString();
```

```
    }

    // ===========================================
    // Property accessor methods
    // ===========================================

    /**
     * Returns the employee ID.
     */
    public String getEmployeeID()
    {
        return employeeID;
    }

    /**
     * Sets the employee ID.
     * @param employeeID the employee ID.
     */
    public void setEmployeeID(String employeeID)
    {
        this.employeeID = employeeID;
    }

    /**
     * Returns the employee name.
     */
    public String getName()
    {
        return name;
    }

    /**
     * Sets the employee name.
     * @param name the employee name.
     */
    public void setName(String name)
    {
        this.name = name;
    }

    /**
     * Returns the dateHired.
```

```java
*/
public Date getDateHired()
{
    return dateHired;
}

/**
 * Sets the dateHired.
 * @param dateHired the dateHired.
 */
public void setDateHired(Date dateHired)
{
    this.dateHired = dateHired;
}

/**
 * Returns the isManager flag.
 */
public boolean getIsManager()
{
    return isManager;
}

/**
 * Sets the isManager flag.
 * @param isManager the isManager flag.
 */
public void setIsManager(boolean isManager)
{
    this.isManager = isManager;
}

/**
 * Returns the department ID.
 */
public String getDepartmentID()
{
    return departmentID;
}

/**
 * Sets the department ID.
```

```
* @param departmentID the department ID.
*/
public void setDepartmentID(String departmentID)
{
    this.departmentID = departmentID;
}

/**
 * Returns the title.
 */
public String getTitle()
{
    return title;
}

/**
 * Sets the title.
 * @param title the title.
 */
public void setTitle(String title)
{
    this.title = title;
}

/**
 * Returns the email.
 */
public String getEmail()
{
    return email;
}

/**
 * Sets the email.
 * @param email the email.
 */
public void setEmail(String email)
{
    this.email = email;
}

/**
 * Returns the phone.
 */
```

```
public String getPhone()
{
   return phone;
}

/**
* Sets the phone.
* @param phone the phone.
*/
public void setPhone(String phone)
{
   this.phone = phone;
}
}
```

Unlike some of the other tables, the `employee` table is used in more than just the product support system. For this reason, it contains more fields than are used in product support, as shown here:

- **employeeID**   A unique four-digit employee number
- **name**   The employee name
- **dateHired**   The employee's date of hire
- **isManager**   A boolean variable, which is true if the employee is a manager
- **departmentID**   The code of the department to which the employee belongs
- **title**   Job title
- **email**   E-mail address
- **phone**   Telephone extension

The `Employee` class has the `toString()` and `load()` methods, described earlier.

Problem Class   The heart of the system is the set of reported problems. In the database, each problem consists of two types of records: one that represents the problem as a whole, and another that represents each event in the life of the problem, from when it is reported until it's closed. The static problem data is contained in the `Problem` class, listed here:

```
package com.lyricnote.support.model;

import java.sql.*;
import java.util.*;
import java.util.Date;
```

```
import java.text.*;

/**
 * A software problem supported by the Problem
 * Support system.
 */
public class Problem implements java.io.Serializable
{
   private String problemID;
   private String description;
   private int severity;
   private Date dateReported;
   private Date dateResolved;
   private String customerID;
   private String productID;

   /**
    * Factory method to create a problem record
    * from the current row of a result set.
    * @param rs a result set from the problem table
    * @exception SQLException if a database error occurs
    */
   public static Problem load(ResultSet rs)
      throws SQLException
   {
      Problem problem = new Problem();

      problem.setProblemID(rs.getString(1));
      problem.setDescription(rs.getString(2));
      problem.setSeverity(rs.getInt(3));
      problem.setDateReported(rs.getTimestamp(4));
      problem.setDateResolved(rs.getTimestamp(5));
      problem.setCustomerID(rs.getString(6));
      problem.setProductID(rs.getString(7));

      return problem;
   }

   /**
    * Returns the object as a CSV string
    */
   public String toString()
   {
      StringBuffer sb = new StringBuffer();
```

```java
      sb.append(getProblemID());
      sb.append(",");
      sb.append(getDescription());
      sb.append(",");
      sb.append(getSeverity());
      sb.append(",");
      sb.append(Model.formatDateTime(getDateReported()));
      sb.append(",");
      sb.append(Model.formatDateTime(getDateResolved()));
      sb.append(",");
      sb.append(getCustomerID());
      sb.append(",");
      sb.append(getProductID());

      return sb.toString();
   }

   /**
    * Closes the problem
    */
   public void close()
   {
      setDateResolved(Model.toTimestamp(new Date()));
   }

   // =========================================
   // Property accessor methods
   // =========================================

   /**
    * Returns the problemID.
    */
   public String getProblemID()
   {
      return problemID;
   }

   /**
    * Sets the problemID.
    * @param problemID the problemID.
    */
   public void setProblemID(String problemID)
   {
      this.problemID = problemID;
```

JSP APPLICATIONS

```java
    }

    /**
     * Returns the description.
     */
    public String getDescription()
    {
        return description;
    }

    /**
     * Sets the description.
     * @param description the description.
     */
    public void setDescription(String description)
    {
        this.description = description;
    }

    /**
     * Returns the severity.
     */
    public int getSeverity()
    {
        return severity;
    }

    /**
     * Sets the severity.
     * @param severity the severity.
     */
    public void setSeverity(int severity)
    {
        this.severity = severity;
    }

    /**
     * Returns the dateReported.
     */
    public Date getDateReported()
    {
        return dateReported;
    }
```

```java
/**
 * Sets the dateReported.
 * @param dateReported the dateReported.
 */
public void setDateReported(Date dateReported)
{
    this.dateReported = dateReported;
}

/**
 * Returns the dateResolved.
 */
public Date getDateResolved()
{
    return dateResolved;
}

/**
 * Sets the dateResolved.
 * @param dateResolved the dateResolved.
 */
public void setDateResolved(Date dateResolved)
{
    this.dateResolved = dateResolved;
}

/**
 * Returns the customerID.
 */
public String getCustomerID()
{
    return customerID;
}

/**
 * Sets the customerID.
 * @param customerID the customerID.
 */
public void setCustomerID(String customerID)
{
    this.customerID = customerID;
```

JSP APPLICATIONS

```
    }

    /**
     * Returns the productID.
     */
    public String getProductID()
    {
        return productID;
    }

    /**
     * Sets the productID.
     * @param productID the productID.
     */
    public void setProductID(String productID)
    {
        this.productID = productID;
    }

    /**
     * Assigns a globally unique problem ID
     */
    public static synchronized String assignProblemID
        (Connection con) throws SQLException
    {
        String id = null;

        final String SQL_QUERY =
            "select problemID from nextProblemID";

        final String SQL_UPDATE =
            "update nextProblemID set problemID = ?";

        Statement stmt = con.createStatement();
        ResultSet rs = stmt.executeQuery(SQL_QUERY);
        if (!rs.next())
            throw new SQLException("No record found");
        id = rs.getString(1);
        rs.close();
        stmt.close();

        String nextID = incrementProblemID(id);

        PreparedStatement pstmt = con.prepareStatement(SQL_UPDATE);
```

```
        pstmt.setString(1, nextID);
        pstmt.executeUpdate();
        pstmt.close();

        return id;
    }

    /**
     * Helper method to generate the next problem ID
     * from the last one.
     */
    public static String incrementProblemID(String id)
    {
        char prefix = id.charAt(0);
        int suffix = Integer.parseInt(id.substring(1));
        DecimalFormat fmt = new DecimalFormat("00000000");
        String nextSuffix = fmt.format(suffix+1).substring(1);
        String nextID = prefix + nextSuffix;
        return nextID;
    }
}
```

A `Problem` object consists of the following fields:

- **`problemID`**   A unique problem identifier, assigned by the system.
- **`description`**   A brief description of the problem for display in the GUI.
- **`severity`**   The call center agent's assessment of how critical the problem is to the customer, with 1=high, 2=medium, 3=low.
- **`dateReported`**   The date and time at which the problem was reported to the call center.
- **`dateResolved`**   If the problem is closed, this contains the date and time at which it was closed. The value is `null` otherwise.
- **`customerID`**   The eight-character customer identifier.
- **`productID`**   The unique product identifier.

ProblemLog Class   The events in a problem's lifecycle are modeled by rows in the `problog` table, which contains the following columns:

- **`problemID`**   The problem identifier, to allow for joining the `problog` and `problem` tables.
- **`logtime`**   A timestamp generated by the database system. This, combined with the problem ID, constitutes the unique key for this problem log entry.

- **eventID** A three-character code indicating the nature of the problem log event. Event ID codes are taken from the event table which is described in the next section.
- **comments** Comments entered by the person making this log entry.

The system uses the ProblemLog class, shown in the following listing, to represent a row in the problog table:

```java
package com.lyricnote.support.model;

import java.io.*;
import java.sql.ResultSet;
import java.sql.SQLException;
import java.util.*;

/**
 * An update to a reported problem.
 */
public class ProblemLog implements Serializable
{
    private String problemID;
    private java.util.Date logTime;
    private String eventID;
    private String comments;

    /**
     * Creates an empty problem log record
     */
    public ProblemLog()
    {
    }

    /**
     * Factory method to create a problem record
     * from the current row of a result set.
     * @param rs a result set from the problem table
     * @exception SQLException if a database error occurs
     */
    public static ProblemLog load(ResultSet rs)
        throws SQLException
    {
        ProblemLog probLog = new ProblemLog();

        probLog.setProblemID(rs.getString(1));
```

```
      probLog.setLogTime(rs.getTimestamp(2));
      probLog.setEventID(rs.getString(3));
      probLog.setComments(rs.getString(4));

      return probLog;
   }

   /**
    * Returns the object as a CSV string
    */
   public String toString()
   {
      StringBuffer sb = new StringBuffer();

      sb.append(getProblemID());
      sb.append(",");
      sb.append(Model.formatDateTime(getLogTime()));
      sb.append(",");
      sb.append(getEventID());
      sb.append(",");
      sb.append(getComments());

      return sb.toString();
   }

   // ===========================================
   // Property accessor methods
   // ===========================================

   /**
    * Returns the problemID.
    */
   public String getProblemID()
   {
      return problemID;
   }

   /**
    * Sets the problemID.
    * @param problemID the problemID.
    */
   public void setProblemID(String problemID)
   {
      this.problemID = problemID;
```

JSP APPLICATIONS

```
    }

    /**
     * Returns the logTime.
     */
    public java.util.Date getLogTime()
    {
        return logTime;
    }

    /**
     * Sets the logTime.
     * @param logTime the logTime.
     */
    public void setLogTime(java.util.Date logTime)
    {
        this.logTime = logTime;
    }

    /**
     * Returns the eventID.
     */
    public String getEventID()
    {
        return eventID;
    }

    /**
     * Sets the eventID.
     * @param eventID the eventID.
     */
    public void setEventID(String eventID)
    {
        this.eventID = eventID;
    }

    /**
     * Returns the comments.
     */
    public String getComments()
    {
        return comments;
    }
```

```
/**
 * Sets the comments.
 * @param comments the comments.
 */
public void setComments(String comments)
{
    this.comments = comments;
}
}
```

Event Class   The event codes used in the problem log class are contained in the event table, which contains the following columns:

- **eventID**   The three-character event code
- **description**   The event description
- **isClosingEvent**   A boolean flag indicating whether this code is one that is used to close a problem

The values of the event table are as follows:

- **COM**   Comments
- **CSI**   Customer interviewed
- **RPS**   Routed to product support
- **RPD**   Routed to development
- **RQA**   Routed to test
- **DEF**   Deferred
- **CNB**   Closed, not a bug
- **CCP**   Closed, customer problem
- **CFX**   Closed, fixed

The last three events are closing events.

The system uses the Event class, shown in the following listing, to represent a row in the event table:

```
package com.lyricnote.support.model;

import java.io.*;
import java.sql.*;
import java.util.*;

/**
```

```
* An event in the life of a problem
*/
public class Event implements Serializable
{
   private String eventID;
   private String description;
   private boolean isClosingEvent;

   /**
    * Factory method to create an event record
    * from the current row of a result set.
    * @param rs a result set from the event table
    * @exception SQLException if a database error occurs
    */
   public static Event load(ResultSet rs)
      throws SQLException
   {
      Event event = new Event();
      String value = null;

      value = rs.getString(1);
      if (value != null)
         event.setEventID(value);

      value = rs.getString(2);
      if (value != null)
         event.setDescription(value);

      event.setIsClosingEvent(rs.getBoolean(3));

      return event;
   }

   /**
    * Returns the object as a CSV string
    */
   public String toString()
   {
      StringBuffer sb = new StringBuffer();

      sb.append(Model.quote(getEventID()));
      sb.append(",");
      sb.append(Model.quote(getDescription()));
      sb.append(",");
```

```java
        sb.append(isClosingEvent());

        return sb.toString();
    }

    // =========================================
    // Property accessor methods
    // =========================================

    /**
     * Returns the eventID.
     */
    public String getEventID()
    {
        return eventID;
    }

    /**
     * Sets the eventID.
     * @param eventID the eventID.
     */
    public void setEventID(String eventID)
    {
        this.eventID = eventID;
    }

    /**
     * Returns the description
     */
    public String getDescription()
    {
        return description;
    }

    /**
     * Sets the description
     * @param description the description
     */
    public void setDescription(String description)
    {
        this.description = description;
    }

    /**
```

```
 * Returns the isClosingEvent flag
 */
public boolean isClosingEvent()
{
    return isClosingEvent;
}

/**
 * Sets the isClosingEvent
 * @param isClosingEvent the isClosingEvent
 */
public void setIsClosingEvent(boolean isClosingEvent)
{
    this.isClosingEvent = isClosingEvent;
}

}
```

Application Objects

The business objects represent the individual entities known by the system. For the purposes of the model, other objects represent the application as a whole. Classes in this category include the following:

- com.lyricnote.support.model.Model
- com.lyricnote.support.model.WebModel

The following sections list the source code for each of these classes and describe their operation.

Model Class   During the operation of the system, the business objects reside in an application container class named Model. This class exposes an API that allows the controller to manipulate it and the view to extract data from it. One Model object exists for each user session, so model state is threadsafe.

Model is a fairly large class. Let's list a section at a time, so we can examine it in detail.

```
package com.lyricnote.support.model;

import java.io.*;
import java.sql.*;
import java.text.*;
import java.util.*;
import java.util.Date;
```

```
/**
* The model component in the Model-View-Controller architecture
* of the product support application. The model is designed
* to be used in a dedicated HTTP session with a single user,
* however, there is no HTTP-specific code. This allows the
* model to be tested by a batch driver.
*/
public abstract class Model implements Serializable
{
   // Class variables and constants

   public static final SimpleDateFormat DATE_FORMAT =
      new SimpleDateFormat("yyyy-MM-dd");

   public static final SimpleDateFormat DATE_TIME_FORMAT =
      new SimpleDateFormat("yyyy-MM-dd HH:mm:ss");

   // Instance variables

   private transient Connection con;
   private List customers;
   private String customerID;
   private List products;
   private String productID;
   private List problems;
   private String problemID;
   private List problemLogs;
   private Map eventMap;
```

Model is an abstract class for reasons we'll discuss in a moment. It contains static (class) variables used for formatting date and time values, and instance variables that represent the state of the application. These variables fall into the following categories:

- **Configuration fields**   These include the name of the file containing the next available problem ID number, the name of the JDBC driver used to access the database, the database URL, and the database connection object.

- **Customer fields**   The model supports an alphabetic search for customer names. The results of the most recent search are stored in a java.util.List of Customer objects. This list is exposed as a property and made available with the getCustomers() method. In addition, the model has a customerID property, which supplies an implicit ID for several methods that require it.

- **Product fields**   Like the customer fields, instance variables exist for the current product search results and the current product ID.

- **Problem fields**   The model has instance variables for the current list of `Problem` objects and the currently selected problem.

- **Problem log fields**   Likewise, there's a `java.util.List` for the list of `ProblemLog` objects associated with the current problem.

Next come the database handling methods:

```java
// =========================================
// Configuration and database methods
// =========================================

/**
 * Returns the current connection
 */
public Connection getConnection()
{
    return con;
}

/**
 * Sets the connection (visible only to subclasses)
 * @param con the connection
 */
protected void setConnection(Connection con)
{
    this.con = con;
}

/**
 * Opens a database connection.
 * @exception SQLException if the connection fails
 * or if it already exists
 */
public abstract void connect() throws SQLException;

/**
 * Closes the current connection
 */
public void disconnect() throws SQLException
{
    if (con != null)
        con.close();
}
```

```
/**
* Returns true if there is an active connection
*/
public boolean isConnected()
{
    return (con != null);
}
```

The model contains a set of methods that handle datasources. The first is
`assignProblemID()`. This is a class method that reads the next available problem ID
from a table in the database, and then rewrites the entry with an incremented number.
There are get and set methods for the problem ID filename.

Database connections are managed with three methods:

- void connect()
- void disconnect()
- boolean isConnected()

The connect() method opens a JDBC connection to the database. This method is
abstract, meaning that it must be implemented directly or indirectly by a Model subclass.
In a test environment, the connection logic may use a JDBC driver name and URL to
connect to the database, whereas a Web environment is more likely to use a JNDI
datasource. The disconnect() method closes the connection, and the isConnected()
method exposes a means for testing whether a database connection exists.

> **Note**   *The connect() and disconnect() methods provide the capability of connecting to
> a database, but they don't choose when and how to do so. In fact, the model itself has no
> logic for handling this. This is the task of the controller object, as we will see.*

After the database section comes a set of methods that operate on Customer objects:

```
// ==========================================
// Customer methods
// ==========================================

/**
* Returns the customer object corresponding to
* the current customer ID
* @exception SQLException if a database error occurs
*/
public Customer getCustomer()
    throws SQLException
{
```

JSP APPLICATIONS

```java
   // Verify that a connection exists

   if (!isConnected())
      throw new SQLException("No connection");

   // Verify that there is a current customer ID

   if (customerID == null)
      throw new SQLException("No customer ID");

   PreparedStatement pstmt = null;
   ResultSet rs = null;
   Customer customer = null;

   try {

      // Prepare the SQL statement

      final String SQL =
          "SELECT * "
        + "FROM customers "
        + "WHERE customerID=?";

      pstmt = con.prepareStatement(SQL);
      pstmt.setString(1, customerID);

      // Execute the query

      rs = pstmt.executeQuery();
      if (rs.next())
         customer = Customer.load(rs);
   }
   finally {
      if (rs != null)
         rs.close();
      if (pstmt != null)
         pstmt.close();
   }

   // Return the customer

   return customer;
}
```

```
/**
 * Returns the current customer search results
 */
public List getCustomers()
{
    return customers;
}


/**
 * Uses the specified customer search argument to query
 * the database for matching customers. Creates a list
 * of customer objects.
 * @param searchArgument the search argument
 * @exception SQLException if a database error occurs
 */
public void customerSearch(String searchArgument)
    throws SQLException
{
    // Verify that a connection exists and that
    // the search argument has been specified

    if (!isConnected())
        throw new SQLException("No connection");

    PreparedStatement pstmt = null;
    ResultSet rs = null;
    customers = null;

    try {

        // Prepare the SQL statement

        final String SQL =
            "SELECT * "
          + "FROM customers "
          + "WHERE name like ? "
          + "ORDER BY name";

        pstmt = con.prepareStatement(SQL);
        searchArgument = searchArgument.trim();
        searchArgument = "%" + searchArgument + "%";
        pstmt.setString(1, searchArgument);

        // Execute the query and copy the results
```

```
        // to a List

        rs = pstmt.executeQuery();
        customers = new LinkedList();
        while (rs.next()) {
            customers.add(Customer.load(rs));
        }
    }
    finally {
        if (rs != null)
            rs.close();
        if (pstmt != null)
            pstmt.close();
    }
}

/**
 * Returns the customerID.
 */
public String getCustomerID()
{
    return customerID;
}

/**
 * Sets the customerID.
 * @param customerID the customerID.
 */
public void setCustomerID(String customerID)
{
    this.customerID = customerID;
}
```

There are get and set methods for the current customer ID, and a method for retrieving from the database the `Customer` object having that ID. The `getCustomer()` method illustrates the function of the `Customer.load()` method in extracting a `Customer` object from a result set. The `customerSearch()` method selects `Customer` objects from the `customer` table whose name field matches a specified search argument. The resulting `java.util.List` is stored as an instance variable and can be retrieved with `getCustomers()`.

Following the `Customer` methods are the `Product` methods:

```java
// ==========================================
// Product methods
// ==========================================

/**
 * Returns the product object corresponding to
 * the current product ID
 * @exception SQLException if a database error occurs
 */
public Product getProduct()
    throws SQLException
{
    // Verify that a connection exists

    if (!isConnected())
        throw new SQLException("No connection");

    // Verify that a current product ID exists

    if (productID == null)
        throw new SQLException("No product ID");

    PreparedStatement pstmt = null;
    ResultSet rs = null;
    Product product = null;

    try {

        // Prepare the SQL statement

        final String SQL =
            "SELECT * "
          + "FROM products "
          + "WHERE productID=?";

        pstmt = con.prepareStatement(SQL);
        pstmt.setString(1, productID);

        // Execute the query

        rs = pstmt.executeQuery();
        if (rs.next())
            product = Product.load(rs);
    }
```

```java
   finally {
      if (rs != null)
         rs.close();
      if (pstmt != null)
         pstmt.close();
   }

   // Return the product

   return product;
}

/**
 * Returns the current product search results
 */
public List getProducts()
{
   return products;
}

/**
 * Uses the specified product search argument to query
 * the database for matching products. Creates a list
 * of product objects.
 * @param searchArgument the search argument
 * @exception SQLException if a database error occurs
 */
public void productSearch(String searchArgument)
   throws SQLException
{
   // Verify that a connection exists and that
   // the search argument has been specified

   if (!isConnected())
      throw new SQLException("No connection");

   PreparedStatement pstmt = null;
   ResultSet rs = null;
   products = null;

   try {

      // Prepare the SQL statement
```

```
        final String SQL =
            "SELECT * "
          + "FROM products "
          + "WHERE name like ? "
          + "ORDER BY name";

        pstmt = con.prepareStatement(SQL);
        searchArgument = searchArgument.trim();
        searchArgument = "%" + searchArgument + "%";
        pstmt.setString(1, searchArgument);

        // Execute the query and copy the results
        // to a List

        rs = pstmt.executeQuery();
        products = new LinkedList();
        while (rs.next())
            products.add(Product.load(rs));
    }
    finally {
        if (rs != null)
            rs.close();
        if (pstmt != null)
            pstmt.close();
    }
}

/**
 * Returns the productID.
 */
public String getProductID()
{
    return productID;
}

/**
 * Sets the productID.
 * @param productID the productID.
 */
public void setProductID(String productID)
{
    this.productID = productID;
}
```

Exactly parallel to the customer methods, product methods get and set the current product ID, retrieve the corresponding `Product` object, select products matching a search string, and retrieve the selection.

In like manner, there are methods that handle the customer entitlement records:

```java
// ============================================
// Customer/product methods
// ============================================

/**
 * Returns a list of CustomerProduct objects
 * for the current customer.
 * @exception SQLException if a database error occurs
 */
public List getCustomerProducts()
    throws SQLException
{
    // Verify that a connection exists

    if (!isConnected())
        throw new SQLException("No connection");

    // Verify that a current customer ID exists

    if (customerID == null)
        throw new SQLException("No customer ID");

    PreparedStatement pstmt = null;
    ResultSet rs = null;
    List list = null;

    try {

        // Prepare the SQL statement

        final String SQL =
            "SELECT * "
          + "FROM custprod "
          + "WHERE customerID = ? "
          + "ORDER BY datePurchased DESC";

        pstmt = con.prepareStatement(SQL);
        pstmt.setString(1, customerID);
```

```
    // Execute the query and populate the list

    rs = pstmt.executeQuery();
    list = new LinkedList();
    while (rs.next())
       list.add(CustomerProduct.load(rs));
}
finally {
    if (rs != null)
       rs.close();
    if (pstmt != null)
       pstmt.close();
}

// Return the list

return list;
}
```

When a customer ID has been selected and stored in the model, the custprod table can be searched for products purchased by that customer. The resulting list of CustomerProblem objects is sorted in descending order by date purchased and returned to the caller.

After CustomerProblem methods come the methods for handling problems:

```
// ==========================================
// Problem methods
// ==========================================

/**
 * Factory method to create a new problem record
 * and add it to the database. Expects the customer
 * ID and product ID to be set already.
 */
public void newProblem() throws SQLException
{
    if (getCustomerID() == null)
       throw new SQLException
       ("No customer ID");

    if (getProductID() == null)
       throw new SQLException
```

```
        ("No product ID");

    Problem problem = new Problem();

    problemID = Problem.assignProblemID(con);
    problem.setProblemID(problemID);
    problem.setDescription("");
    problem.setSeverity(2);
    problem.setDateReported(new Date());
    problem.setCustomerID(getCustomerID());
    problem.setProductID(getProductID());

    // Add to database

    PreparedStatement pstmt = null;
    try {
        final String SQL =
            "INSERT "
          + "INTO problems "
          + "VALUES(?, ?, ?, ?, ?, ?, ?)";

        pstmt = con.prepareStatement(SQL);
        pstmt.setString(1, problemID);
        pstmt.setString(2, problem.getDescription());
        pstmt.setInt(3, problem.getSeverity());
        pstmt.setTimestamp
            (4, Model.toTimestamp(problem.getDateReported()));
        pstmt.setNull(5, Types.TIMESTAMP);
        pstmt.setString(6, problem.getCustomerID());
        pstmt.setString(7, problem.getProductID());
        pstmt.executeUpdate();
    }
    finally {
        if (pstmt != null)
            pstmt.close();
    }
}

/**
 * Updates the problem record in the database
 * @param problem the problem object
 * @exception SQLException if a database error occurs
 */
public void updateProblem(Problem problem)
```

```java
      throws SQLException
{
   // Verify that a connection exists

   if (!isConnected())
      throw new SQLException("No connection");

   PreparedStatement pstmt = null;
   try {

      boolean resolved = problem.getDateResolved() != null;
      String SQL =
            "UPDATE problems "
         + "SET description=?,"
         + " severity=?";

      if (resolved)
         SQL += ",dateResolved=?";

      SQL += " WHERE problemID=?";

      // Prepare the SQL statement

      pstmt = con.prepareStatement(SQL);

      // Set the parameters - note that the columns may vary

      int col = 0;
      pstmt.setString(++col, problem.getDescription());
      pstmt.setInt(++col, problem.getSeverity());
      if (resolved) {
         Date dateResolved = problem.getDateResolved();
         Timestamp ts = Model.toTimestamp(dateResolved);
         pstmt.setTimestamp(++col, ts);
      }
      pstmt.setString(++col, problem.getProblemID());

      // Execute the update

      pstmt.executeUpdate();
   }
   finally {
      if (pstmt != null)
         pstmt.close();
```

```java
    }
}

/**
 * Returns the problem object corresponding to
 * the current problem ID
 * @exception SQLException if a database error occurs
 */
public Problem getProblem()
   throws SQLException
{
   // Verify that a connection exists

   if (!isConnected())
      throw new SQLException("No connection");

   // Verify that a current problem ID exists

   if (problemID == null)
      throw new SQLException("No problem ID");

   PreparedStatement pstmt = null;
   ResultSet rs = null;
   Problem problem = null;

   try {

      // Prepare the SQL statement

      final String SQL =
          "SELECT * "
        + "FROM problems "
        + "WHERE problemID=?";

      pstmt = con.prepareStatement(SQL);
      pstmt.setString(1, problemID);

      // Execute the query

      rs = pstmt.executeQuery();
      if (rs.next())
         problem = Problem.load(rs);
   }
   finally {
```

```
            if (rs != null)
               rs.close();
            if (pstmt != null)
               pstmt.close();
      }

      // Return the problem

      return problem;
}

/**
 * Returns the current problem search results
 */
public List getProblems()
{
   return problems;
}

/**
 * Uses the specified customer ID to query
 * the database for problems for that customer.
 * Creates a list of problem objects.
 * @exception SQLException if a database error occurs
 */
public void customerProblemsSearch(String customerID)
   throws SQLException
{
   // Verify that a connection exists

   if (!isConnected())
      throw new SQLException("No connection");

   PreparedStatement pstmt = null;
   ResultSet rs = null;
   problems = null;

   try {

      // Prepare the SQL statement

      final String SQL =
          "SELECT * "
        + "FROM problems "
```

```java
                + "WHERE customerID=?";

        pstmt = con.prepareStatement(SQL);
        pstmt.setString(1, customerID);

        // Execute the query and copy the results
        // to a List

        rs = pstmt.executeQuery();
        problems = new LinkedList();
        while (rs.next())
            problems.add(Problem.load(rs));
    }
    finally {
        if (rs != null)
            rs.close();
        if (pstmt != null)
            pstmt.close();
    }
}

/**
 * Uses the specified product ID to query
 * the database for problems for that product.
 * Creates a list of problem objects.
 * @exception SQLException if a database error occurs
 */
public void productProblemsSearch(String productID)
    throws SQLException
{
    // Verify that a connection exists

    if (!isConnected())
        throw new SQLException("No connection");

    PreparedStatement pstmt = null;
    ResultSet rs = null;
    problems = null;

    try {

        // Prepare the SQL statement

        final String SQL =
```

```
            "SELECT * "
          + "FROM problems "
          + "WHERE productID = ?";

      pstmt = con.prepareStatement(SQL);
      pstmt.setString(1, productID);

      // Execute the query and copy the results
      // to a List

      rs = pstmt.executeQuery();
      problems = new LinkedList();
      while (rs.next())
         problems.add(Problem.load(rs));
   }
   finally {
      if (rs != null)
         rs.close();
      if (pstmt != null)
         pstmt.close();
   }
}

/**
 * Returns the problemID.
 */
public String getProblemID()
{
   return problemID;
}

/**
 * Sets the problemID.
 * @param problemID the problemID.
 */
public void setProblemID(String problemID)
{
   this.problemID = problemID;
}
```

A newProblem() method creates a new problem record for the current customer and product, initializes it, and adds it to the database, and an updateProblem() method modifies it. There are methods for retrieving problems by customer and product, which store their results in a java.util.List that can be retrieved with getProblems().

Related to the problem methods are the problem log methods:

```
// =========================================
// ProblemLog methods
// =========================================

/**
 * Adds a new problem log entry
 * @param log a problem log object
 * @exception SQLException if a database error occurs
 */
public void addProblemLogEntry(ProblemLog log)
    throws SQLException
{
    // Verify that a connection exists

    if (!isConnected())
        throw new SQLException("No connection");

    PreparedStatement pstmt = null;

    try {

        // Prepare the insert SQL

        final String SQL =
            "INSERT "
          + "INTO problog "
          + "VALUES(?, ?, ?, ?)";

        pstmt = con.prepareStatement(SQL);
        pstmt.setString(1, log.getProblemID());
        pstmt.setTimestamp(2,
            Model.toTimestamp(log.getLogTime()));
        pstmt.setString(3, log.getEventID());
        pstmt.setString(4, log.getComments());

        // Execute the statement

        pstmt.executeUpdate();
    }
    finally {
        if (pstmt != null)
            pstmt.close();
```

```java
      }
}

/**
 * Uses the specified problem ID to query
 * the database for problem log entries for
 * that problem.
 * Creates a list of problem log objects.
 * @exception SQLException if a database error occurs
 */
public void problemLogSearch(String problemID)
   throws SQLException
{
   // Verify that a connection exists

   if (!isConnected())
      throw new SQLException("No connection");

   PreparedStatement pstmt = null;
   ResultSet rs = null;
   problemLogs = null;

   try {

      // Prepare the SQL statement

      final String SQL =
          "SELECT * "
        + "FROM problog "
        + "WHERE problemID = ?";

      pstmt = con.prepareStatement(SQL);
      pstmt.setString(1, problemID);

      // Execute the query and copy the results
      // to a List

      rs = pstmt.executeQuery();
      problemLogs = new LinkedList();
      while (rs.next())
         problemLogs.add(ProblemLog.load(rs));
   }
   finally {
      if (rs != null)
```

```
            rs.close();
        if (pstmt != null)
            pstmt.close();
    }
}

/**
 * Returns the problemLogs.
 */
public List getProblemLogs()
{
    return problemLogs;
}
```

The model has methods to add a log entry for a problem, to search for the log entries for an existing problem, and to retrieve the search results.

The employee records in the database are handled next:

```
// ===========================================
// Employee methods
// ===========================================

/**
 * Returns the employee object corresponding to
 * the specified employee ID
 * @param employeeID the employee ID
 * @exception SQLException if a database error occurs
 */
public Employee getEmployee(String employeeID)
    throws SQLException
{
    // Verify that a connection exists

    if (!isConnected())
        throw new SQLException("No connection");

    PreparedStatement pstmt = null;
    ResultSet rs = null;
    Employee employee = null;

    try {
```

```
    // Prepare the query SQL

    final String SQL =
        "SELECT * "
      + "FROM employees "
      + "WHERE employeeId = ?";

    pstmt = con.prepareStatement(SQL);
    pstmt.setString(1, employeeID);

    // Execute the query

    rs = pstmt.executeQuery();
    if (rs.next())
        employee = Employee.load(rs);
    }
    finally {
        if (rs != null)
            rs.close();
        if (pstmt != null)
            pstmt.close();
    }

    // Return the employee

    return employee;
}
```

Employee objects can be retrieved from the database by calling `getEmployee()`, passing it the employee ID. This is primarily useful for displaying employee names for the three support IDs in the `Product` object.

Event methods are next:

```
// =========================================
// Event methods
// =========================================

/**
 * Returns true if the specified event is valid.
 * @param eventID event ID code
 */
public boolean isValidEvent(String eventID)
```

```
{
   if (eventMap == null)
      loadEventMap();
   return eventMap.get(eventID) != null;
}


/**
 * Returns true if the specified event
 * is a closing event
 * @param eventID event ID code
 */
public boolean isClosingEvent(String eventID)
{
   if (eventMap == null)
      loadEventMap();
   Event event = (Event) eventMap.get(eventID);
   if (event == null)
      return false;
   return event.isClosingEvent();
}

private void loadEventMap()
{
   eventMap = new HashMap();
   Statement stmt = null;
   ResultSet rs = null;
   try {
      final String SQL = "select * from events";
      stmt = con.createStatement();
      rs = stmt.executeQuery(SQL);
      while (rs.next()) {
         Event event = Event.load(rs);
         eventMap.put(event.getEventID(), event);
      }
   }
   catch (SQLException e) {
      e.printStackTrace();
   }
   finally {
      try {
         if (rs != null)
            rs.close();
         if (stmt != null)
            stmt.close();
```

```
        }
        catch (SQLException ignore) {
        }
    }
}
```

The Event class is slightly different from the others in that it represents a static table, whose elements are not modified through the application. Model has two public methods that deal with the event table—one to determine whether a specified code refers to a valid entry in the table, and another that indicates whether the event is one that closes a problem. Both of these methods use a private loadEventMap() method to instantiate the table when it is first requested.[2]

The final set of methods consists of class methods that are used to convert dates to different formats, and to enclose a string in quotes if it contains one or more commas:

```
// ==========================================
//     Class methods
// ==========================================

/**
 * Formats a date using the default JDBC format
 */
public static String formatDate(Date d)
{
    return d == null ? "" : DATE_FORMAT.format(d);
}


/**
 * Formats a timestamp using the default JDBC format
 */
public static String formatDateTime(Date d)
{
    return d == null ? "" : DATE_TIME_FORMAT.format(d);
}


/**
 * Converts a java.util.Date to a java.sql.Timestamp
 */
public static Timestamp toTimestamp(Date d)
```

---

[2]   This technique is sometimes referred to as *lazy instantiation*.

```
{
    return (d == null)
        ? null
        : new Timestamp(d.getTime());
}


/**
 * Encloses a string in quotation marks
 * if it contains a comma.
 * @param s the string
 */
public static String quote(String s)
{
    if (s != null) {
        if (s.indexOf(",") > -1) {
            StringBuffer sb = new StringBuffer();
            sb.append('"');
            sb.append(s);
            sb.append('"');
            s = sb.toString();
        }
    }
    return s;
}
```

WebModel Class   If you read the Model class carefully, you'll note it contains no
Web-aware methods. This is deliberate. For testing purposes, you want to be able to run
the model using a simple command-line environment such as JUnit, so you don't want to
have javax.servlet or javax.servlet.http classes used anywhere in the model.
When it's run from the Web, however, you want the model to take advantage of a little
more knowledge about its environment. For this reason, we'll use a subclass of Model
that has this awareness.

WebModel implements three methods:

- **void connect()** gets a datasource from the Web container using JNDI and
  then uses it to obtain a database connection. It stores the connection as an
  instance variable by calling the setConnection() method.

- **void valueBound(HttpSessionBindingEvent event)** is one of two
  methods that form the HttpSessionBindingListener interface. It
  initializes the database connection by calling connect().

- **void valueUnbound(HttpSessionBindingEvent event)** is the other of the
  two HttpSessionBindingListener methods. This is where you perform the
  important function of closing the database connection when the session times out
  or is invalidated.

The WebModel class is shown here:

```
package com.lyricnote.support.model;

import java.sql.*;
import javax.naming.*;
import javax.servlet.*;
import javax.servlet.http.*;
import javax.sql.*;

/**
 * HTTP-specific subclass of Model.  Implements session
 * binding and unbinding.  Allows the database connection
 * to be disconnected when the session times out or is
 * invalidated.
 */
public class WebModel
    extends Model
    implements HttpSessionBindingListener
{
    /**
     * The JNDI string that specifies the data source.
     * Hard coded here; this could be supplied as an
     * input parameter.
     */
    public static final String DATASOURCE =
        "java:comp/env/jdbc/LyricNote";

    /**
     * Implementation of the abstract connect method
     */
    public void connect() throws SQLException
    {
        try {
            InitialContext ctx = new InitialContext();
            DataSource ds = (DataSource) ctx.lookup(DATASOURCE);
            Connection con = ds.getConnection();
            setConnection(con);
        }
        catch (NamingException e) {
            throw new SQLException(e.getMessage());
        }
    }
```

```
/**
 * Called when the model is bound to a session
 */
public void valueBound(HttpSessionBindingEvent event)
{
    // Connect to the database

    try {
        connect();
    }
    catch (SQLException e) {
        e.printStackTrace();
    }
}

/**
 * Called when the model is removed from a session
 */
public void valueUnbound(HttpSessionBindingEvent event)
{
    try {
        disconnect();
    }
    catch (SQLException e) {
        e.printStackTrace();
    }
}
```

Using the Model

This completes the development of the model component. In the early stages of
development, you want to write the Model and unit testing classes in tandem, so each
part of the model can be tested in isolation. When bugs are discovered, you can return
to the unit test environment to reproduce them without having to start and stop a Web
server or search through debugging entries in the servlet logs. This results in a more
reliable base for the rest of the application.

View Classes

The model could be attached to a standalone Java application. However, the product
support system is accessed by users in at least four roles: call center agents, product
support specialists, developers, and testers. In addition, management may want to

measure quality statistics, such as the average length of time a problem waits in a queue, the average number of customer callbacks needed to resolve a problem, and the number of defects outstanding for a particular product. For this reason, the best system operating environment is probably the company's intranet, and the presentation layer consists of JSP pages. In this section, we see how JSP pages can be used as the view to which the model is attached.

There are three general entry points into the system:

- **By customer** Call center agents on the phone with a customer first look up the customer ID by means of an alpha search of the `customer` table by customer name. After selecting a customer from the list of matches, the agent sees details about the customer, including the products this customer has purchased and the history of problems reported by the customer. From there, the call center agent can enter a new problem report or provide status about an existing one.

- **By product** Product support personnel, developers, and testers are all assigned to particular products rather than customers. Their initial view of the system, therefore, is by product. They can use an alpha search of the `product` table to find products by name, and from there, they can view the list of outstanding problems.

- **By problem** Any users of the system may already know the problem ID assigned to a particular defect. If they need to update the problem record, they can use a form that prompts for the specific problem ID.

In all three cases, the application eventually ends up showing a detailed view of a particular problem. From there, the user can update the problem description and severity, route the problem to another department, or close the problem. The last JSP view is then a confirmation screen showing what action was applied.

Figure 19-3 diagrams this application flow. Each of the rectangular boxes represents a particular JSP page. The circles represent controller actions, which we'll learn about shortly. For now, remember that controller actions are what cause changes in the model and cause the next view to be displayed. The arrows from the JSP view to the controller actions are labeled with the type of action the user takes with respect to the view: selecting from a list, entering a search argument, or clicking a submit button.

We'll examine each of the JSP view pages in more detail shortly. First, however, we need to look at some supporting classes.

Support Pages

Two sections of code are common to all the JSP view pages in this application. Rather than duplicate them in every JSP file, we'll store them in separate text files and include them with the `<jsp:include>` action.

SetBaseURL.jsp The first common section allows the application to specify URLs that are relative to the Web server root.

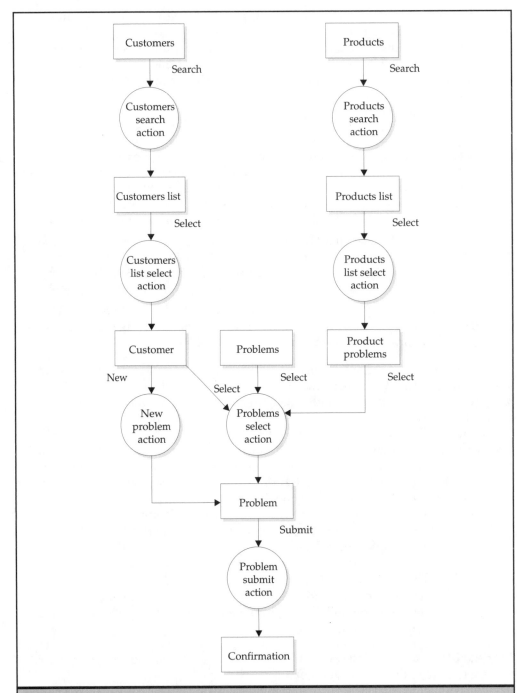

Figure 19-3. *View/controller interaction diagram*

```
<%@ page session="false" %>
<%@ page import="java.io.*" %>
<%@ page import="java.net.*" %>

<%-- Sets the base URL for the application so that relative
     references can be used in non-JSP elements --%>
<%
   StringBuffer sb = request.getRequestURL();
   String path = sb.toString();
   URL url = new URL(path);

   sb = new StringBuffer();
   sb.append(url.getProtocol());
   sb.append("://");
   sb.append(url.getHost());
   int port = url.getPort();
   if (port != -1) {
      sb.append(":");
      sb.append(port);
   }
   sb.append(request.getContextPath());
   sb.append("/");
   path = sb.toString();
%>
<base href="<%= path %>"/>
```

This code generates a one-line HTML element that specifies the base URL. Why is this necessary? Because our application generates <form>, <img>, and other HTML elements that refer to locations in the application file space. We can't hardcode the absolute path because we don't know the name by which the application will be deployed. Moreover, we can't easily use a relative URL because there is more than one relative starting point (JSP versus servlet). The <base> HTML element comes to the rescue, causing all relative URLs to be resolved according to the actual host name and Web application name used at runtime.

Note *If you look carefully at the URL, you'll see a trailing slash character. This is required, although it is not common practice in URL concatenation. HTML is not entirely consistent here.*

Banner.jsp We'll use a standard header to provide a common look and feel in all the JSP view pages. This header, stored in a file named Banner.jsp, contains an HTML table that includes the company logo and standard navigation links.

JSP APPLICATIONS

```
<%@ page session="false" %>

<%-- Displays the LyricNote logo and top menu --%>

<table border="0" cellspacing="3" cellpadding="3" width="500">
<tr>
<td><img src="images/logo.jpg"></td>
</tr>
<tr>
<td class="menucell" align="RIGHT">
<a class="menuitem" href="Problems.jsp">Problems</a>
<span class="menuitem">|</span>
<a class="menuitem" href="Products.jsp">Products</a>
<span class="menuitem">|</span>
<a class="menuitem" href="Customers.jsp">Customers</a>
</tr>
</table>
```

ErrorPage.jsp   A final supporting module is the error page, listed here:

```
<%@ page session="false" %>
<%@ page import="java.io.PrintWriter" %>
<%@ page isErrorPage="true" %>

<html>
<head>
<title>Error Page</title>
<jsp:include page="SetBaseURL.jsp" flush="false"/>
<link rel="stylesheet" href="style.css">
</head>

<body>
<h1>Error</h1>
The following error occurred:
<pre>
<%
    exception.printStackTrace(new PrintWriter(out));
%>
</pre>
</body>
</html>
```

ErrorPage.jsp does little more than display a stack trace for any uncaught exception. This is useful during system development but should probably be replaced by something more user-friendly in production.

JSP View Pages

Using Figure 19-3 as our road map, let's look at the nine individual JSP view pages:

- **Customers.jsp**   Prompts for customer search argument
- **CustomersList.jsp**   Selection list of customer search results
- **Customer.jsp**   Detail view of a single customer record; performs general layout, delegating the details to subsidiary pages invoked via <jsp:include>
- **Problem.jsp**   Detail view of a single problem record; likewise delegates to included pages
- **Confirm.jsp**   Confirmation screen shown after problem update
- **Products.jsp**   Prompts for product search argument
- **ProductsList.jsp**   Selection list of product search results
- **ProductProblems.jsp**   Selection list of problems for a product
- **Problems.jsp**   Prompts for a product ID

Customers.jsp   The initial entry point of call center agents is typically the customer search view, listed in the following code:

```
<%@ page session="true" %>
<%@ page errorPage="ErrorPage.jsp" %>
<%@ page import="com.lyricnote.support.model.*" %>


<jsp:useBean id="model"
             scope="session"
             class="com.lyricnote.support.model.WebModel"/>
<html>
<head>
<title>Customer Search</title>
<jsp:include page="SetBaseURL.jsp" flush="false"/>
<link rel="stylesheet" href="style.css">
</head>

<body>
<jsp:include page="Banner.jsp" flush="false"/>
<h1>Customer Search</h1>
<form method="POST" action="servlet/controller/Customers/Search">
```

```
<b>Customer name</b>:
<input type="TEXT" name="customerSearchArgument" size="20">
<input type="SUBMIT" value="Search">
</form>
</body>
</html>
```

After including the model initialization and banner code, this JSP page uses an HTML form to prompt for a customer name search string. If the call center agent is talking to a customer named Eleanor Wagner, for example, the agent may search for names containing the letter W, as shown in Figure 19-4. When the agent clicks the search button, the form is then submitted to a servlet that performs the search (which is discussed later in this chapter in the "Controller Classes" section).

Where does the database connection get initialized? It's not immediately obvious, but it's triggered by the <jsp:useBean> action, which creates a WebModel *object and binds it to the HTTP session. Recall that* WebModel *implements the* HttpSessionBinding Listener *interface. This means that its* valueBound() *method is called when it is bound to a session. In that method, we've included code that calls the* connect() *method.*

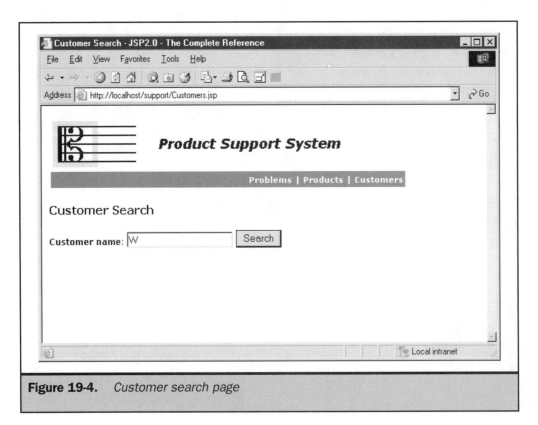

Figure 19-4.   *Customer search page*

CustomersList.jsp   The results of searching by customer name are stored in a
`java.util.List` in the model. The `CustomerList.jsp` page extracts the list and
displays it with the customer ID column as hyperlinks. The JSP source code is listed here:

```
<%@ page session="true" %>
<%@ page errorPage="ErrorPage.jsp" %>
<%@ page import="com.lyricnote.support.model.*" %>
<%@ page import="java.util.*" %>

<jsp:useBean id="model"
             scope="session"
             class="com.lyricnote.support.model.WebModel"/>
<html>
<head>
<title>Customers List</title>
<jsp:include page="SetBaseURL.jsp" flush="false"/>
<link rel="stylesheet" href="style.css">
</head>

<body>
<jsp:include page="Banner.jsp" flush="false"/>
<h1>Customers List</h1>
<table border="0" cellspacing="5" cellpadding="0">
<tr>
<th align="LEFT">Customer ID</th>
<th align="LEFT">Customer Name</th>
</tr>
<%
   List list = model.getCustomers();
   if (list != null) {
      Iterator it = list.iterator();
      while (it.hasNext()) {
         request.setAttribute("customer", it.next());
%>
<jsp:useBean id="customer"
             scope="request"
             type="com.lyricnote.support.model.Customer"/>
<tr>
<td>
<a href='<%=
   "servlet/controller/CustomersList/Select?customerID="
   + customer.getCustomerID() %>'>
<jsp:getProperty name="customer" property="customerID"/></a>
</td>
```

```
<td><jsp:getProperty name="customer" property="name"/></td>
</tr>
<% }} %>

</table>

</body>
</html>
```

The Web page with the list of customers whose names contain the letter W is shown in Figure 19-5.

Notice the technique used to access properties of the Customer object inside each loop iteration. The JSP page stores the object as a request attribute and then populates a JavaBean from it. This allows us to use the `<jsp:getProperty>` action to retrieve the name and customerID properties. We could have used scriptlets and operated on the iteration object directly, but that involves more Java code than we want to use in the JSP page. Even at that, there is more Java code than would be necessary if we used JSTL and the JSP expression language to access the list.

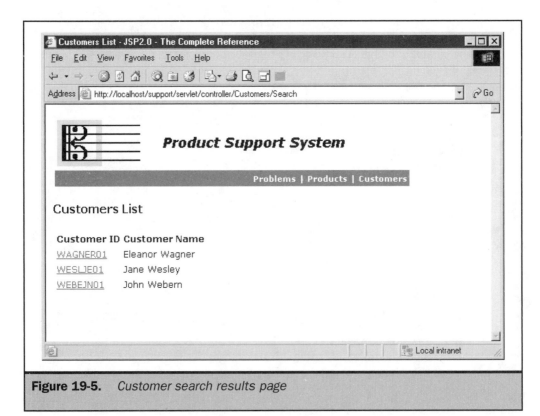

Figure 19-5. *Customer search results page*

The point is that JSP provides more than one way to do most things. This has been cited as a weakness by purists, since it allows Java code to proliferate inside the HTML, making things difficult for the Web designer. In my view, however, this is a strength because it provides flexibility in using whatever technique is appropriate to the scale of the application. Bad code can be written in any language.

Customer.jsp   After selecting Eleanor Wagner from the list, the call center agent sees the customer detail page, as illustrated in Figure 19-6. This page has three sections:

- **Top left** contains the customer ID, name, and phone number. This section is delegated to the `CustomerInfo.jsp` page.

- **Top right** has a list of products the customer has purchased. The list is in descending date of purchase order, and the product name is a hyperlink used to report a new problem. This is handled by `CustomerProductInfo.jsp`.

- **Bottom** is a history of problems reported by the customer. In this case, we see one problem, one that has already been resolved. This block is produced by the `CustomerProblemInfo.jsp` page.

The list of products enables the call center agent to determine the products for which Ms. Wagner is entitled to support.

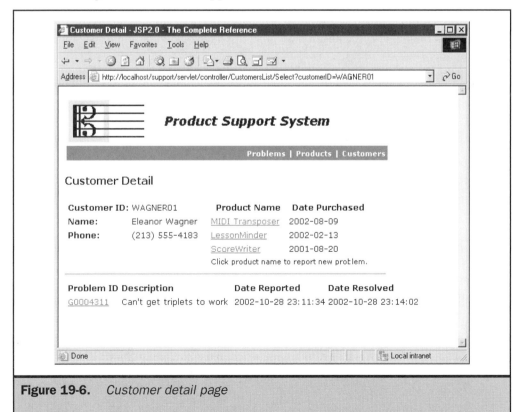

Figure 19-6.   *Customer detail page*

The source code for Customer.jsp is shown here:

```
<%@ page session="true" %>
<%@ page errorPage="ErrorPage.jsp" %>
<%@ page import="com.lyricnote.support.model.*" %>

<%-- Displays customer details, using included pages
     to do each major section --%>

<jsp:useBean id="model"
             scope="session"
             class="com.lyricnote.support.model.WebModel"/>
<%
   request.setAttribute("customer", model.getCustomer());
%>
<jsp:useBean id="customer"
             scope="request"
             type="com.lyricnote.support.model.Customer"/>
<html>
<head>
<title>Customer Detail</title>
<jsp:include page="SetBaseURL.jsp" flush="false"/>
<link rel="stylesheet" href="style.css">
</head>

<body>
<jsp:include page="Banner.jsp" flush="false"/>
<h1>Customer Detail</h1>
<table border="0" cellspacing="0" cellpadding="0">
<tr>
   <td valign="TOP">
   <jsp:include page="CustomerInfo.jsp" flush="false"/>
   </td>
   <td valign="TOP">
   <jsp:include page="CustomerProductInfo.jsp" flush="false"/>
   </td>
</tr>
</table>
<hr width="506" align="LEFT">
<jsp:include page="CustomerProblemInfo.jsp" flush="false"/>
</body>
</html>
```

The `CustomerInfo.jsp` page looks like this:

```jsp
<%@ page session="true" %>
<%@ page errorPage="ErrorPage.jsp" %>
<%@ page import="com.lyricnote.support.model.*" %>

<%-- Page included from Customer.jsp to display
     customer ID, name, and phone section --%>

<jsp:useBean id="customer"
             scope="request"
             type="com.lyricnote.support.model.Customer"/>

<table border="0" cellspacing="5" cellpadding="0">
<tr>
<td><b>Customer ID:</b></td>
<td>
<jsp:getProperty name="customer" property="customerID"/> 
</td>
<td rowspan="3"></td>
</tr>
<tr>
<td><b>Name:</b></td>
<td>
<jsp:getProperty name="customer" property="name"/> 
</td>
</tr>
<tr>
<td><b>Phone:</b></td>
<td>
<jsp:getProperty name="customer" property="phone"/> 
</td>
</tr>
</table>
```

This page plucks properties from the customer object bound to the request by the calling page.

The right-hand side of the page containing product information for this customer is produced by `CustomerProductInfo.jsp`:

```jsp
<%@ page session="true" %>
<%@ page errorPage="ErrorPage.jsp" %>
```

```jsp
<%@ page import="com.lyricnote.support.model.*" %>
<%@ page import="java.util.*" %>

<%-- Page included from Customer.jsp that displays
     list of products purchased by this customer --%>

<jsp:useBean id="model"
             scope="session"
             type="com.lyricnote.support.model.WebModel"/>

<jsp:useBean id="customer"
             scope="request"
             type="com.lyricnote.support.model.Customer"/>

<table border="0" cellspacing="5" cellpadding="0">
<tr>
   <th>Product Name</th>
   <th>Date Purchased</th>
</tr>
<%
   List products = model.getCustomerProducts();
   if ((products != null) && (products.size() > 0)) {
       Iterator it = products.iterator();
       while (it.hasNext()) {
          request.setAttribute("custprod", it.next());
%>
<jsp:useBean id="custprod"
             scope="request"
             type="com.lyricnote.support.model.CustomerProduct"/>
<%
   model.setProductID(custprod.getProductID());
   request.setAttribute("product", model.getProduct());
%>
<jsp:useBean id="product"
             scope="request"
             type="com.lyricnote.support.model.Product"/>
<tr>
<td>
<a href='<%=
```

```
    "servlet/controller/Customer/NewProblem"
        + "?customerID=" + custprod.getCustomerID()
        + "&productID=" + custprod.getProductID()
    %>'>
<jsp:getProperty name="product" property="name"/>
</a>
</td>
<td><%= Model.formatDate(custprod.getDatePurchased()) %></td>
</tr>
<% } %>
<tr>
<td class="fineprint" colspan="2">
Click product name to report new problem.
</td>
</tr>
<% } %>
</table>
```

The problem detail section is generated by `CustomerProblemInfo.jsp`:

```
<%@ page session="true" %>
<%@ page errorPage="ErrorPage.jsp" %>
<%@ page import="com.lyricnote.support.model.*" %>
<%@ page import="java.util.*" %>

<%-- Page included from Customer.jsp to display the
     list of problems reported by this customer --%>

<jsp:useBean id="model"
            scope="session"
            type="com.lyricnote.support.model.WebModel"/>

<table border="0" cellspacing="5" cellpadding="0">
<%
    List list = model.getProblems();
    if (list != null && list.size() > 0) {
%>
<tr>
```

```
        <th align="LEFT">Problem ID</th>
        <th align="LEFT">Description</th>
        <th align="LEFT">Date Reported</th>
        <th align="LEFT">Date Resolved</th>
    </tr>
    <%
        Iterator it = list.iterator();
        while (it.hasNext()) {
            request.setAttribute("problem", it.next());
    %>
    <jsp:useBean id="problem"
                 scope="request"
                 type="com.lyricnote.support.model.Problem"/>
    <tr>
    <td><a href=
        '<%= "servlet/controller/Problems/Select?problemID="
            + problem.getProblemID() %>'
        ><jsp:getProperty name="problem" property="problemID"/></a>
         
    </td>
    <td>
    <jsp:getProperty name="problem" property="description"/> 
    </td>
    <td><%= Model.formatDateTime(problem.getDateReported()) %></td>
    <td><%= Model.formatDateTime(problem.getDateResolved()) %></td>
    </tr>
    <%
        }
    }
    %>
    </table>
```

Problem.jsp Ms. Wagner reports she's having a problem with the ScoreWriter product. When she tries to enter *Db*, the software substitutes *C#* instead. The call center agent clicks the ScoreWriter hyperlink, which brings up the JSP view page shown in Figure 19-7.

After entering the description, the problem severity, and comments from the customer, the agent clicks the submit button to create the problem record.

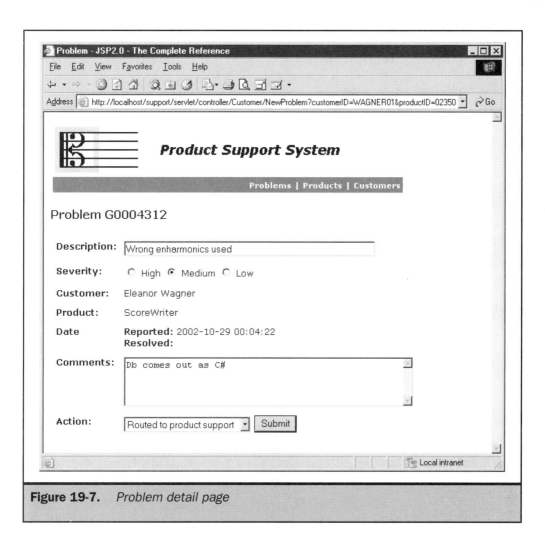

Figure 19-7.   *Problem detail page*

Listed here is the source code for `Problem.jsp`:

```
<%@ page session="true" %>
<%@ page errorPage="ErrorPage.jsp" %>
<%@ page import="com.lyricnote.support.model.*" %>
<%@ page import="java.util.*" %>
```

```jsp
<%-- Displays problem details, calling subpages
     to handle major sections --%>

<jsp:useBean id="model"
             scope="session"
             class="com.lyricnote.support.model.WebModel"/>
<%
   request.setAttribute("problem", model.getProblem());
%>
<jsp:useBean id="problem"
             scope="request"
             class="com.lyricnote.support.model.Problem"/>
<%
   model.setCustomerID(problem.getCustomerID());
   request.setAttribute("customer", model.getCustomer());
%>
<jsp:useBean id="customer"
             scope="request"
             class="com.lyricnote.support.model.Customer"/>
<%
   model.setProductID(problem.getProductID());
   request.setAttribute("product", model.getProduct());
%>
<jsp:useBean id="product"
             scope="request"
             class="com.lyricnote.support.model.Product"/>
<html>
<head>
<title>Problem</title>
<jsp:include page="SetBaseURL.jsp" flush="false"/>
<link rel="stylesheet" href="style.css">
</head>
<body>
<jsp:include page="Banner.jsp" flush="false"/>
<h1>Problem
   <jsp:getProperty name="problem" property="problemID"/>
</h1>
<jsp:include page="ProblemInfo.jsp"/>
<jsp:include page="ProblemHistory.jsp"/>
</body>
</html>
```

Again, the JSP is composed primarily of HTML layout code, with the detailed work being delegated to subpages. First, `ProblemInfo.jsp`, to list the problem attributes:

```jsp
<%@ page session="true" %>
<%@ page errorPage="ErrorPage.jsp" %>
<%@ page import="java.util.*" %>
<%@ page import="com.lyricnote.support.model.*" %>

<%-- Included from Problem.jsp to generate the
     problem details and update section --%>

<jsp:useBean id="problem"
             scope="request"
             type="com.lyricnote.support.model.Problem"/>

<jsp:useBean id="customer"
             scope="request"
             type="com.lyricnote.support.model.Customer"/>

<jsp:useBean id="product"
             scope="request"
             type="com.lyricnote.support.model.Product"/>

<form method="POST" action="servlet/controller/Problem/Submit">
<input type="HIDDEN"
       name="problemID"
       value="<jsp:getProperty name='problem'
                     property='problemID'/>">
<table border="0" cellspacing="5" cellpadding="3">
<tr>
<td><b>Description:</b></td>
<td>
<input type="TEXT"
       name="description"
       size="50"
       value="<jsp:getProperty name='problem'
                     property='description'/>">
</td>
</tr>
<tr>
<td><b>Severity:</b></td>
<td>
```

JSP APPLICATIONS

```
<input name="severity" type="radio" value="1"
   <%= problem.getSeverity() == 1 ? "CHECKED" : "" %>> High
<input name="severity" type="radio" value="2"
   <%= problem.getSeverity() == 2 ? "CHECKED" : "" %>> Medium
<input name="severity" type="radio" value="3"
   <%= problem.getSeverity() == 3 ? "CHECKED" : "" %>> Low
</td>
</tr>
<tr>
<td><b>Customer:</b></td>
<td><jsp:getProperty name="customer" property="name"/></td>
</tr>
<tr>
<td><b>Product:</b></td>
<td><jsp:getProperty name="product" property="name"/></td>
</tr>
<tr>
<td><b>Date</b></td>
<td>
<b>Reported:</b>
<%= Model.formatDateTime(problem.getDateReported()) %>
<br/>
<b>Resolved:</b>
<%= Model.formatDateTime(problem.getDateResolved()) %>
</td>
</tr>
<tr>
<td><b>Comments:</b></td>
<td>
<textarea name="comments" cols="50" rows="4">
</textarea>
</td>
</tr>
<tr>
<td><b>Action:</b></td>
<td>
<select name="eventID">
<option value="COM">Comments</option>
<option value="CSI">Customer interviewed</option>
<option value="RPS">Routed to product support</option>
<option value="RPD">Routed to development</option>
```

```
<option value="RQA">Routed to test</option>
<option value="DEF">Deferred</option>
<option value="CNB">Closed - not a bug</option>
<option value="CCP">Closed - customer problem</option>
<option value="CFX">Closed - fixed</option>
</select>
<input type="SUBMIT" value="Submit">
</td>
</tr>
</table>
</form>
```

Next, `ProblemHistory.jsp`, which generates the list of events in the history of this problem:

```
<%@ page session="true" %>
<%@ page errorPage="ErrorPage.jsp" %>
<%@ page import="java.util.*" %>
<%@ page import="com.lyricnote.support.model.*" %>

<%-- Included from Problem.jsp to display problem history --%>

<jsp:useBean id="model"
             scope="session"
             type="com.lyricnote.support.model.Model"/>

<jsp:useBean id="problem"
             scope="request"
             type="com.lyricnote.support.model.Problem"/>
<%
   model.problemLogSearch(problem.getProblemID());
   List problemLogs = model.getProblemLogs();
   if (problemLogs.size() > 0) {
%>
<table border="1" cellpadding="3" cellspacing="0">
<tr>
<th>Time</th>
<th>Event Code</th>
<th>Comments</th>
</tr>
```

```
<%
   Iterator it = problemLogs.iterator();
   while (it.hasNext()) {
      ProblemLog log = (ProblemLog) it.next();
%>
<tr>
<td><%= Model.formatDateTime(log.getLogTime()) %></td>
<td><%= log.getEventID() %></td>
<td><%= log.getComments() %> </td>
</tr>
<% } %>
</table>
<% } %>
```

Confirm.jsp   After the agent submits the problem record, a confirmation page (see
Figure 19-8) is produced, listing the problem ID assigned, the description, the severity,
the customer comments, and problem routing. The agent gives the problem ID to the

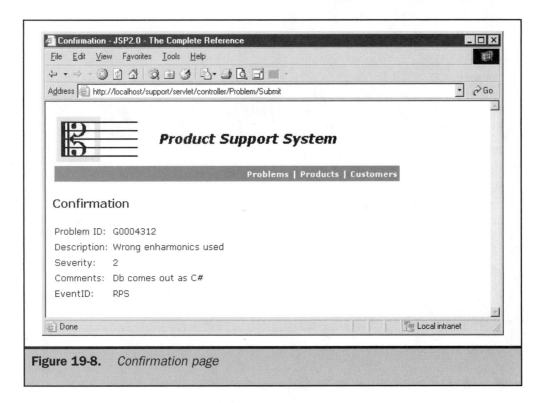

Figure 19-8.   *Confirmation page*

customer on the phone and informs her that ScoreWriter product support will call her back. The confirmation source code is listed here:

```jsp
<%@ page session="true" %>
<%@ page errorPage="ErrorPage.jsp" %>
<%@ page import="com.lyricnote.support.model.*" %>

<%-- Displays confirmation of problem update --%>

<jsp:useBean id="model"
             scope="session"
             type="com.lyricnote.support.model.WebModel"/>
<html>
<head>
<title>Confirmation</title>
<jsp:include page="SetBaseURL.jsp" flush="false"/>
<link rel="stylesheet" href="style.css">
</head>

<body>
<jsp:include page="Banner.jsp" flush="false"/>
<h1>Confirmation</h1>

<table border="0" cellpadding="3" cellspacing="0">
<tr>
   <td>Problem ID:</td>
   <td><%= request.getParameter("problemID") %> </td>
</tr>
<tr>
   <td>Description:</td>
   <td><%= request.getParameter("description") %> </td>
</tr>
<tr>
   <td>Severity:</td>
   <td><%= request.getParameter("severity") %> </td>
</tr>
<tr>
   <td>Comments:</td>
   <td><%= request.getParameter("comments") %> </td>
</tr>
<tr>
   <td>EventID:</td>
```

```
    <td><%= request.getParameter("eventID") %> </td>
</tr>
</table>

</body>
</html>
```

Products.jsp   Other users, such as product support personnel, developers, or testers, may start the application by looking for a particular product. Like the customer search page, there's a JSP view page (Products.jsp) for product search, listed here:

```
<%@ page session="true" %>
<%@ page errorPage="ErrorPage.jsp" %>
<%@ page import="com.lyricnote.support.model.*" %>

<%-- Prompts for a product search argument --%>

<jsp:useBean id="model"
             scope="session"
             class="com.lyricnote.support.model.WebModel"/>
<html>
<head>
<title>Product Search</title>
<jsp:include page="SetBaseURL.jsp" flush="false"/>
<link rel="stylesheet" href="style.css">
</head>

<body>
<jsp:include page="Banner.jsp" flush="false"/>
<h1>Product Search</h1>
<form method="POST" action="servlet/controller/Products/Search">
<b>Product name</b>:
<input type="TEXT" name="productSearchArgument" size="20">
<input type="SUBMIT" value="Search">
</form>
</body>
</html>
```

Like the customer search page, Products.jsp uses an HTML form to prompt for a search string. Figure 19-9 illustrates a search for products whose name contains the letter S.

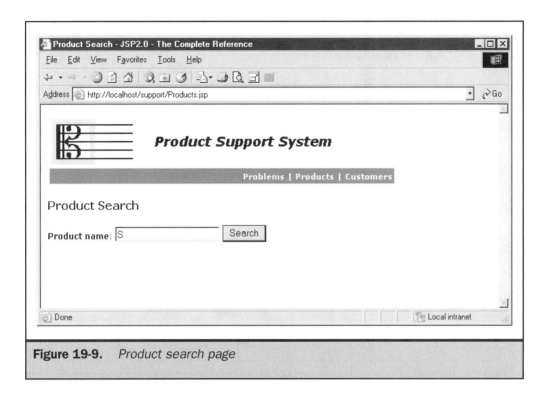

Figure 19-9.   *Product search page*

ProductsList.jsp   As Figure 19-10 shows, there are six product names containing the letter S. The `ProductsList.jsp` page displays the product IDs, product names, and the names of the support personnel assigned.

```
<%@ page session="true" %>
<%@ page errorPage="ErrorPage.jsp" %>
<%@ page import="com.lyricnote.support.model.*" %>
<%@ page import="java.util.*" %>

<%-- Displays the list of products matching the
     search argument --%>

<jsp:useBean id="model"
             scope="session"
             class="com.lyricnote.support.model.WebModel"/>
<html>
<head>
<title>Products List</title>
```

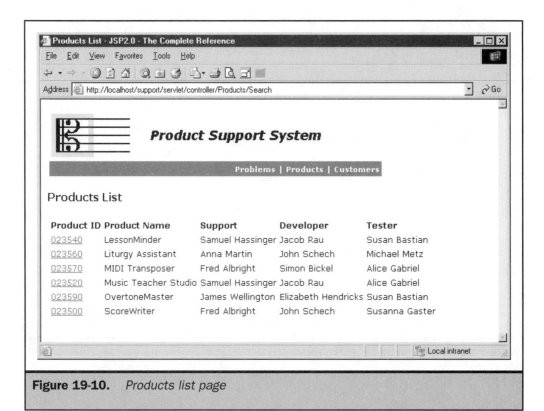

Figure 19-10. Products list page

```
<jsp:include page="SetBaseURL.jsp" flush="false"/>
<link rel="stylesheet" href="style.css">
</head>

<body>
<jsp:include page="Banner.jsp" flush="false"/>
<h1>Products List</h1>
<table border=0 cellspacing=5 cellpadding=0>
<tr>
<th align="LEFT">Product ID</th>
<th align="LEFT">Product Name</th>
<th align="LEFT">Support</th>
<th align="LEFT">Developer</th>
<th align="LEFT">Tester</th>
</tr>
<%
```

```
    List list = model.getProducts();
    if (list != null) {
        Iterator it = list.iterator();
        while (it.hasNext()) {
            request.setAttribute("product", it.next());
%>
<jsp:useBean id="product"
             scope="request"
             type="com.lyricnote.support.model.Product"/>
<tr>
<td>
<a href='<%=
    "servlet/controller/ProductsList/Select?productID="
    + product.getProductID()
    %>'><jsp:getProperty name="product" property="productID"/>
</a>
</td>
<td><jsp:getProperty name="product" property="name"/></td>
<td>
<%= model.getEmployee(product.getProductSupport()).getName() %>
</td>
<td>
<%= model.getEmployee(product.getDeveloper()).getName() %>
</td>
<td>
<%= model.getEmployee(product.getTester()).getName() %>
</td>
</tr>
<% }} %>

</table>
</body>
</html>
```

For each of the three employee IDs in the Product object, the JSP shows the corresponding employee name. It gets the Employee objects from the model's getEmployee() method and then invokes the Employee.getName() method to get the name.

ProductProblems.jsp   If the ScoreWriter link is selected, the list of problems for that product is displayed, as shown in Figure 19-11.

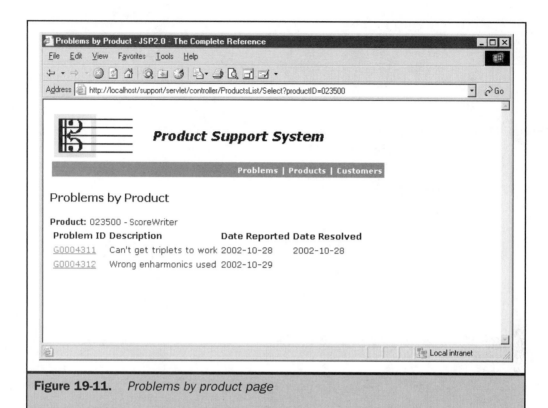

Figure 19-11. *Problems by product page*

```
<%@ page session="true" %>
<%@ page errorPage="ErrorPage.jsp" %>
<%@ page import="com.lyricnote.support.model.*" %>
<%@ page import="java.util.*" %>

<%-- Displays the list of problems associated with
     this product --%>

<jsp:useBean id="model"
             scope="session"
             class="com.lyricnote.support.model.WebModel"/>
<html>
<head>
<title>Problems by Product</title>
<jsp:include page="SetBaseURL.jsp" flush="false"/>
<link rel="stylesheet" href="style.css">
</head>
```

```
<body>
<jsp:include page="Banner.jsp" flush="false"/>
<h1>Problems by Product</h1>
<%
   request.setAttribute("product", model.getProduct());
%>
<jsp:useBean id="product"
             scope="request"
             type="com.lyricnote.support.model.Product"/>
<b>Product:</b>
<jsp:getProperty name="product" property="productID"/>
- <jsp:getProperty name="product" property="name"/>
<table border="0" cellspacing="5" cellpadding="0">
   <tr>
      <th align="LEFT">Problem ID</th>
      <th align="LEFT">Description</th>
      <th align="LEFT">Date Reported</th>
      <th align="LEFT">Date Resolved</th>
   </tr>
<%
   List list = model.getProblems();
   if (list != null) {
      Iterator it = list.iterator();
      while (it.hasNext()) {
         request.setAttribute("problem", it.next());
%>
<jsp:useBean id="problem"
             scope="request"
             type="com.lyricnote.support.model.Problem"/>
<tr>
<td><a href='<%=
   "servlet/controller/Problems/Select?problemID="
   + problem.getProblemID() %>'>
<jsp:getProperty name="problem" property="problemID"/></a></td>
<td><jsp:getProperty name="problem" property="description"/></td>
<td><%= Model.formatDate(problem.getDateReported()) %></td>
<td><%= Model.formatDate(problem.getDateResolved()) %></td>
</tr>
<% }} %>
</table>

</body>
</html>
```

As the listing of `ProductProblems.jsp` shows, the current `Product` object can be obtained from the model, as well as the list of problems for this product.

When the product support person for ScoreWriter (Fred Albright) calls the customer to get more details about the problem, he selects the problem number from the list by clicking the hyperlink. He then sees an updated version of the problem (see Figure 19-12). He enters the results of the customer interview in the comments section and submits the problem update. The new confirmation is shown in Figure 19-13.

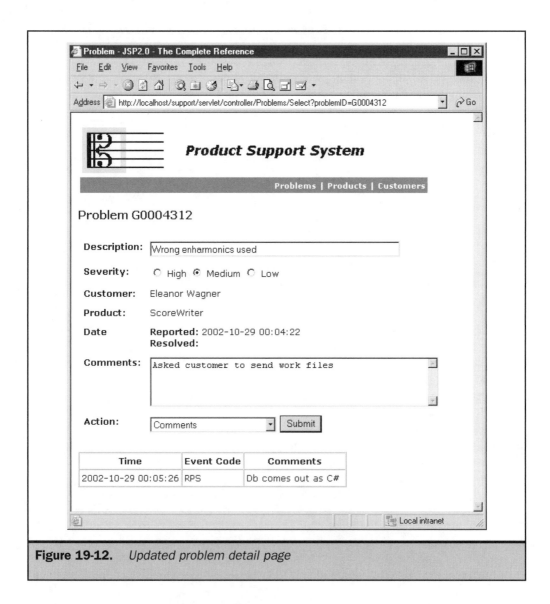

Figure 19-12. *Updated problem detail page*

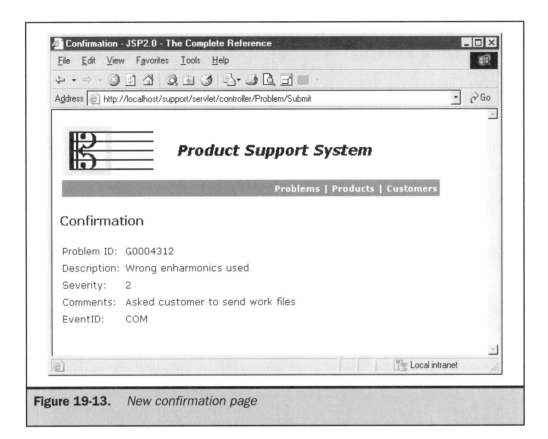

Figure 19-13. *New confirmation page*

Problems.jsp   If the problem ID is already known, a user can select the problem directly, using the JSP view shown in Figure 19-14.

The source code for `Problems.jsp` is similar to the customer and product search pages:

```
<%@ page session="true" %>
<%@ page errorPage="ErrorPage.jsp" %>
<%@ page import="com.lyricnote.support.model.*" %>

<%-- Prompts for a problem ID --%>

<jsp:useBean id="model"
            scope="session"
            class="com.lyricnote.support.model.WebModel"/>
<html>
<head>
```

```
<title>Problem Selection</title>
<jsp:include page="SetBaseURL.jsp" flush="false"/>
<link rel="stylesheet" href="style.css">
</head>

<body>
<jsp:include page="Banner.jsp" flush="false"/>
<h1>Problem Selection</h1>
<form method="POST" action="servlet/controller/Problems/Select">
<b>Problem ID</b>:
<input type="TEXT" name="problemID" size="8">
<input type="SUBMIT" value="select">
</form>

</body>
</html>
```

On further exploration of the problem, Fred Albright determines that it was due to a user input error. He enters a comment to that effect (see Figure 19-15) and closes the problem. The confirmation screen is shown in Figure 19-16.

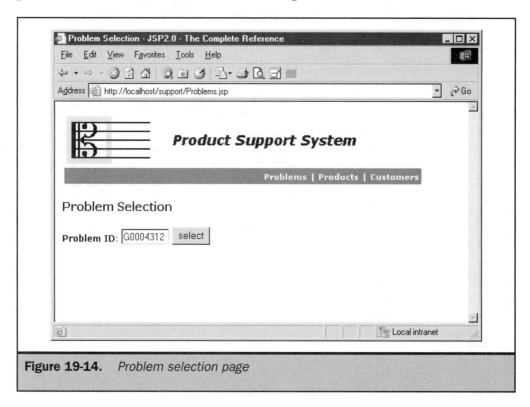

Figure 19-14. *Problem selection page*

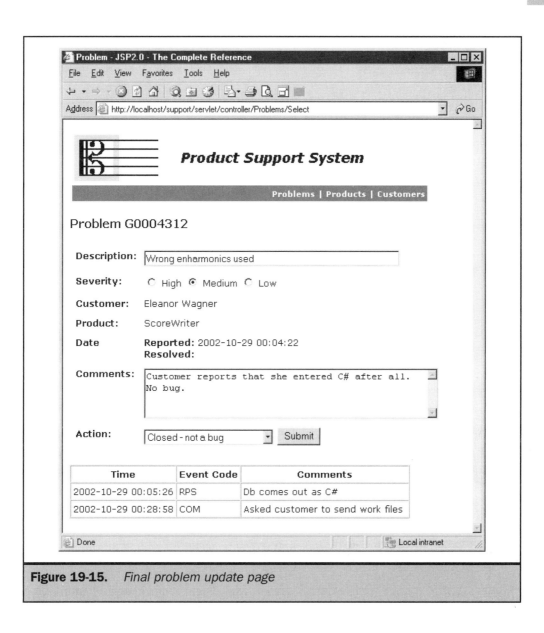

Figure 19-15.   *Final problem update page*

Controller Classes

The last component to develop is the controller, the part of the system that operates on the model according to user input and selects the next view. In the product support system, this function is performed by a single servlet, appropriately named `ControllerServlet`.

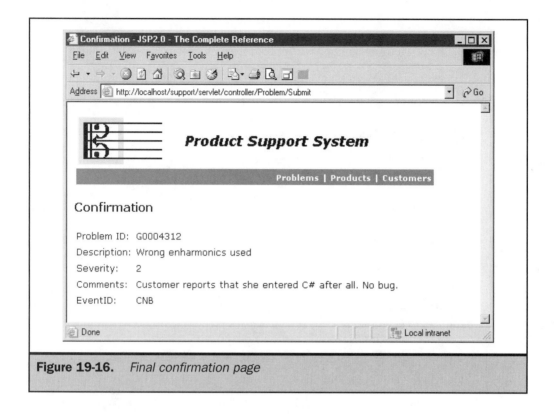

Figure 19-16. *Final confirmation page*

The controller functionality can be built a piece at a time by using small, customized action classes to handle each state transition, rather than hardcoding each action in the servlet.[3] The mechanism the controller uses to delegate to the action classes is explained next.

Each time the controller servlet is invoked, it needs to know two things:

- What is the current view?
- What action has the user selected from this view?

You may have noticed all the JSP view pages invoke the controller servlet with additional path information in the URL. This path information contains the name of the current view and a keyword describing the action the user selected. For example, from the `Customers.jsp` page, when the user enters a search string and clicks the search button, the form is submitted to the controller servlet with the path information `/Customers/Search`.

---

[3] This is the essence of the Jakarta Struts approach.

Some view pages have more than one possible user action. From the `Customer.jsp` page, the user can either click a product name to report a new problem or select an existing problem for update. In any event, the controller takes the view name and action keyword, concatenates them, and appends the word `Action`. The result is the name of the class that can handle the state transition.

The Action Base Class

Here is a listing of the abstract `Action` class:

```java
package com.lyricnote.support.controller;

import com.lyricnote.support.model.*;
import java.io.*;
import javax.servlet.*;
import javax.servlet.http.*;

/**
 * The base class for all state transitions
 */
public abstract class Action implements Serializable
{
    protected transient HttpServletRequest request;
    protected transient HttpServletResponse response;
    protected transient ServletContext application;
    protected Model model;

    /**
     * Executes the action. Subclasses should override
     * this method and have it forward the request to the
     * next view component when it completes processing.
     */
    public abstract void run()
        throws ServletException, IOException;

    /**
     * Sets the request.
     * @param request the request.
     */
    public void setRequest(HttpServletRequest request)
    {
        this.request = request;
    }
```

```
/**
 * Sets the response
 * @param response the response
 */
public void setResponse(HttpServletResponse response)
{
    this.response = response;
}


/**
 * Sets the servlet context.
 * @param application the application.
 */
public void setApplication(ServletContext application)
{
    this.application = application;
}


/**
 * Sets the model.
 * @param model the model.
 */
public void setModel(Model model)
{
    this.model = model;
}
}
```

`Action` contains instance variables for the servlet request and response, the servlet context, and the model itself. In addition to the getter and setter methods for these variables, there's an abstract method named `run()`. This method is the only one that must be implemented by the individual action handlers. The `run()` method calls model methods to effect the transition and then creates a request dispatcher and forwards the request to the next view.

Note that the servlet-related variables (`request`, `response`, and `application`) are marked `transient`. This is necessary because none of these classes are serializable.

The Controller Servlet

The controller servlet is the driver for all the state transitions. It maintains a cache in each session of action classes that have been invoked. When a request is made, the servlet checks the session action map to see if an instance of the class has already been loaded. If not, it extracts the view name and action keyword from the path information, concatenates them, and appends `Action` to the result to get the action class name. It then loads the class and creates an instance, storing this in the session action map. After ensuring a model already exists, the servlet then sets the request, response, application, and model properties in the action object and invokes its run() method.

Here is ControllerServlet:

```
package com.lyricnote.support.controller;

import com.lyricnote.support.model.*;
import java.io.*;
import java.sql.*;
import java.util.*;
import javax.servlet.*;
import javax.servlet.http.*;

/**
 * The controller component of the Model-View-Controller
 * architecure for the LyricNote problem reporting system
 */
public class ControllerServlet extends HttpServlet
{
    /**
     * Handles an HTTP GET request
     */
    public void doGet(
        HttpServletRequest request,
        HttpServletResponse response)
      throws ServletException, IOException
    {
        doPost(request, response);
    }

    /**
     * Handles an HTTP POST request
     */
    public void doPost(
        HttpServletRequest request,
        HttpServletResponse response)
      throws ServletException, IOException
    {
        HttpSession session = request.getSession();
        Map actionMap = (Map) session.getAttribute("actionMap");
        if (actionMap == null) {
            actionMap = new HashMap();
            session.setAttribute("actionMap", actionMap);
        }
```

```
ServletContext context = getServletContext();
try {

    // Get the state and event from the path info

    String pathInfo = request.getPathInfo();
    if (pathInfo == null)
        throw new ServletException
        ("Invalid internal state - no path info");

    // Load the action object that handles
    // this state and event

    Action action = (Action) actionMap.get(pathInfo);
    if (action == null) {

        // This is the first time the servlet has seen
        // this action. Get the state and event name
        // from pathInfo.

        StringTokenizer st =
            new StringTokenizer(pathInfo, "/");

        if (st.countTokens() != 2)
            throw new ServletException
            ("Invalid internal state - invalid path info ["
            + pathInfo + "]");

        String state = st.nextToken();
        String event = st.nextToken();

        // Form the class name from the state and event

        String className =
            "com.lyricnote.support.controller."
            + state + event + "Action";

        // Load the class and create an instance

        try {
            Class actionClass = Class.forName(className);
            action = (Action) actionClass.newInstance();
        }
        catch (ClassNotFoundException e) {
```

```
         throw new ServletException
         ("Could not load class " + className
        + ": " + e.getMessage());
      }
      catch (InstantiationException e) {
         throw new ServletException
         ("Could not create an instance of "
         + className + ": " + e.getMessage());
      }
      catch (IllegalAccessException e) {
         throw new ServletException
         (className + ": " + e.getMessage());
      }

      // Cache the instance in the action map

      actionMap.put(pathInfo, action);
   }

   // Ensure that a model exists in the session.

   Model model = (Model) session.getAttribute("model");
   if (model == null)
      throw new ServletException
      ("No model found in session");

   // Now execute the action. The action should perform
   // a RequestDispatcher.forward() when it completes

   action.setRequest(request);
   action.setResponse(response);
   action.setApplication(context);
   action.setModel(model);
   action.run();
}
catch (ServletException e) {

   // Use the JSP error page for all servlet errors

   request.setAttribute("javax.servlet.jsp.jspException", e);
   RequestDispatcher rd =
      context.getRequestDispatcher("/ErrorPage.jsp");

   if (response.isCommitted())
```

```
                    rd.include(request, response);
            else
                    rd.forward(request, response);
        }
    }
}
```

The sections that follow describe each of the action classes used in the product support system.

Action Classes

A review of Figure 19-3 shows that seven state transitions occur from one view to another. These transitions correspond to the following action classes:

- CustomersSearchAction
- CustomersListSelectAction
- CustomersNewProblemAction
- ProductsSearchAction
- ProductsListSelectAction
- ProblemsSelectAction
- ProblemSubmitAction

CustomersSearchAction Class   The run() method in this class is called to accept a customer search argument from the Customers.jsp view and invoke the customerSearch() method in the model. It then forwards the request to the JSP view page that displays the search results. A listing of CustomersSearchAction is shown here:

```
package com.lyricnote.support.controller;

import java.io.*;
import java.sql.SQLException;
import javax.servlet.*;
import javax.servlet.http.*;

/**
 * Searches the database for customers matching the
 * customer search argument
 */
public class CustomersSearchAction extends Action
```

```
{
    /**
     * Executes the action
     */
    public void run() throws ServletException, IOException
    {
        // Perform search

        String arg = request.getParameter("customerSearchArgument");
        if (arg != null) {
            arg = arg.trim();
            if (!arg.equals("")) {
                try {
                    model.customerSearch(arg);
                }
                catch (SQLException e) {
                    throw new ServletException(e.getMessage());
                }
            }
        }


        // Forward to customer list JSP

        final String next = "/CustomersList.jsp";
        RequestDispatcher rd =
            application.getRequestDispatcher(next);
        if (rd == null)
            throw new ServletException
            ("Could not find " + next);
        rd.forward(request, response);
    }
}
```

CustomersListSelectAction Class   The user selects a customer from the list by
clicking a hyperlink into the controller that carries the CustomerList view name and the
Select action keyword. In addition, the hyperlink URL has the customer ID appended as
a query string. From this information, the CustomersListSelectAction class does the
following:

- Extracts the customer ID parameter from the URL and stores it in the model
- Invokes the model's customer problems search method
- Forwards the request to the customer detail JSP view

Here's a listing of the action class:

```java
package com.lyricnote.support.controller;

import java.io.*;
import java.sql.SQLException;
import javax.servlet.*;
import javax.servlet.http.*;

/**
 * Gets detailed information for this customer
 */
public class CustomersListSelectAction extends Action
{
    /**
     * Executes the action
     */
    public void run() throws ServletException, IOException
    {
        // Get customer ID and store it in the model

        String customerID = request.getParameter("customerID");
        if (customerID == null)
            throw new ServletException
            ("No customer ID specified");
        model.setCustomerID(customerID);

        // Get the list of problems for this customer

        try {
            model.customerProblemsSearch(customerID);
        }
        catch (SQLException e) {
            throw new ServletException(e.getMessage());
        }

        // Forward to customer detail JSP

        final String next = "/Customer.jsp";
        RequestDispatcher rd =
            application.getRequestDispatcher(next);
        if (rd == null)
            throw new ServletException
            ("Could not find " + next);
```

```
        rd.forward(request, response);
    }
}
```

CustomerNewProblemAction Class   As noted previously, the Customer view has two possible actions: creating a new problem or updating an existing one. The new problem action is handled by the following action class:

```
package com.lyricnote.support.controller;

import java.io.*;
import java.sql.SQLException;
import javax.servlet.*;
import javax.servlet.http.*;

public class CustomerNewProblemAction extends Action
{
    /**
     * Executes the action
     */
    public void run() throws ServletException, IOException
    {
        // Get the customer ID and product ID

        String customerID = request.getParameter("customerID");
        if (customerID == null)
            throw new ServletException
            ("No customer ID");

        String productID = request.getParameter("productID");
        if (productID == null)
            throw new ServletException
            ("No product ID");

        // Create a new problem

        try {
            model.setCustomerID(customerID);
            model.setProductID(productID);
            model.newProblem();
        }
        catch (SQLException e) {
            throw new ServletException(e.getMessage());
```

```
        }

        // Forward to problem detail JSP

        final String next = "/Problem.jsp";
        RequestDispatcher rd =
            application.getRequestDispatcher(next);
        if (rd == null)
            throw new ServletException
            ("Could not find " + next);
        rd.forward(request, response);
    }
}
```

This action class does the following:

- Retrieves the customerID and productID parameters from the request generated by the view.
- Creates and initializes a new `Problem` object. It does so by invoking the `newProblem()` factory method in the model, which assigns a unique problem ID and writes the initial record in the database.
- Forwards the request to the problem detail view.

ProductsSearchAction Class   Like the customer search action, the product search action takes a search string from the request and calls a search method in the model, forwarding the request then to the `ProductsList.jsp` view.

```
package com.lyricnote.support.controller;

import java.io.*;
import java.sql.SQLException;
import javax.servlet.*;
import javax.servlet.http.*;

/**
 * Searches the database for products matching the
 * product search argument
 */
public class ProductsSearchAction extends Action
{
    /**
     * Executes the action
     */
```

```
   public void run() throws ServletException, IOException
   {
      // Perform search

      String arg = request.getParameter("productSearchArgument");
      if (arg != null) {
         arg = arg.trim();
         if (!arg.equals("")) {
            try {
               model.productSearch(arg);
            }
            catch (SQLException e) {
               throw new ServletException(e.getMessage());
            }
         }
      }

      // Forward to product list JSP

      final String next = "/ProductsList.jsp";
      RequestDispatcher rd =
         application.getRequestDispatcher(next);
      if (rd == null)
         throw new ServletException
         ("Could not find " + next);
      rd.forward(request, response);
   }
}
```

ProductsListSelectAction Class   When a product ID is selected, this action class stores it in the model and invokes the model's product problem search. The request is then forwarded to the ProductProblems.jsp view, which displays the results.

```
package com.lyricnote.support.controller;

import java.io.*;
import java.sql.SQLException;
import javax.servlet.*;
import javax.servlet.http.*;

/**
* Searches the database for products matching the
* product search argument
```

```
*/
public class ProductsListSelectAction extends Action
{
    /**
    * Executes the action
    */
    public void run() throws ServletException, IOException
    {
        // Get product ID and store it in the model

        String productID = request.getParameter("productID");
        if (productID == null)
            throw new ServletException
            ("No product ID specified");
        model.setProductID(productID);

        // Get the list of problems for this product

        try {
            model.productProblemsSearch(productID);
        }
        catch (SQLException e) {
            throw new ServletException(e.getMessage());
        }

        // Forward to product problems JSP

        final String next = "/ProductProblems.jsp";
        RequestDispatcher rd =
            application.getRequestDispatcher(next);
        if (rd == null)
            throw new ServletException
            ("Could not find " + next);
        rd.forward(request, response);
    }
}
```

ProblemsSelectAction Class   All three application entry points—customer, product, and problem—use a common problem select action, shown here:

```
package com.lyricnote.support.controller;

import java.io.*;
```

```
import java.sql.SQLException;
import javax.servlet.*;
import javax.servlet.http.*;

/**
 * Sets the current problem ID
 */
public class ProblemsSelectAction extends Action
{
    /**
     * Executes the action
     */
    public void run() throws ServletException, IOException
    {
        String problemID = request.getParameter("problemID");
        if (problemID != null) {
            problemID = problemID.trim();
            if (!problemID.equals("")) {
                model.setProblemID(problemID);
            }
        }

        // Forward to problem JSP

        final String next = "/Problem.jsp";
        RequestDispatcher rd =
            application.getRequestDispatcher(next);
        if (rd == null)
            throw new ServletException
            ("Could not find " + next);
        rd.forward(request, response);
    }
}
```

The action class simply stores the problem ID in the model and forwards the request to the problem detail page.

ProblemSubmitAction Class   The last action class needed is the one that accepts problem updates from the problem detail page. This class

- Retrieves the data entry fields from the requests.
- Retrieves the current `Problem` object from the model and updates its properties. If the event ID is one that indicates the problem should be closed, the `Problem` object's `close()` method is invoked.

- Updates the database record for the problem.
- Adds an entry to the problem log.
- Forwards the request to the next view—the confirmation.

```java
package com.lyricnote.support.controller;

import com.lyricnote.support.model.*;
import java.io.*;
import java.sql.SQLException;
import javax.servlet.*;
import javax.servlet.http.*;

/**
 * Submits a problem update
 */
public class ProblemSubmitAction extends Action
{
    /**
     * Executes the action
     */
    public void run() throws ServletException, IOException
    {
        // Get the parameters

        String problemID = request.getParameter("problemID");
        String description = request.getParameter("description");
        String severity = request.getParameter("severity");
        String comments = request.getParameter("comments");
        String eventID = request.getParameter("eventID");

        try {

            // Get the problem object from the model

            model.setProblemID(problemID);
            Problem problem = model.getProblem();

            // Update the problem object

            problem.setDescription(description);
            problem.setSeverity(Integer.parseInt(severity));
            if (model.isClosingEvent(eventID)) {
```

```
            problem.close();
        }
        model.updateProblem(problem);

        // Add a problem log record

        ProblemLog log = new ProblemLog();
        log.setProblemID(problemID);
        log.setLogTime(new java.util.Date());
        log.setEventID(eventID);
        log.setComments(comments);
        model.addProblemLogEntry(log);
    }
    catch (SQLException e) {
        throw new ServletException(e.getMessage());
    }

    // Forward to confirmation JSP

    final String next = "/Confirm.jsp";
    RequestDispatcher rd =
        application.getRequestDispatcher(next);
    if (rd == null)
        throw new ServletException
        ("Could not find " + next);
    rd.forward(request, response);
    }
}
```

JSP APPLICATIONS

Summary

This chapter brings together elements discussed throughout the book in a Web-based system for managing a product support center. The system supports the following process flow:

- A customer with a problem calls a toll-free number and speaks to a call center agent.

- The agent verifies the customer is entitled to support for the specified product, enters a problem report, gives the confirmation number to the customer, and routes the problem to product support.

- Product support calls the customer to determine whether it's a code problem or customer problem. If the problem turns out to be a code problem, for which no fix is currently available, it's routed to development.

- The responsible developer analyzes the problem. If the problem isn't a bug, the developer reroutes the problem to product support to inform the customer. If the problem is a bug, the developer codes and unit tests a fix and routes the problem to quality assurance.

- Quality assurance performs integration tests. If the fix needs more work, the problem is rerouted back to development. Otherwise, it's sent to product support, where the fix is forwarded to the customer and the problem is closed.

The data model required to support this system consists of relational database tables that represent customers, products, customer/product pairs, employees, problem reports, and problem log entries.

The system architecture employed is known as Model-View-Controller (MVC). This consists of three components:

- **Model**   The internal workings of the application, including database access and business logic. Has no visual code—can be operated by a simple command-line driver.

- **View**   The presentation layer that retrieves data from the model and displays it for the user's interaction.

- **Controller**   The component that accepts user input and operates on the model to change its state and present the next view.

The resulting system keeps complexity to a minimum by partitioning code to provide components that can be tested in isolation. This yields a robust, full-featured, and easy-to-extend application.

The
Complete
Reference

Appendix

Servlet 2.4 and
JSP 2.0 API

This appendix describes each class in the servlet packages:

- **javax.servlet** Classes and interfaces not specific to any particular protocol
- **javax.servlet.http** Classes and interfaces specific to the HTTP protocol
- **javax.servlet.jsp** Classes and interfaces that define the relationship between the servlet generated from a JSP page and the JSP container in which it runs
- **javax.servlet.jsp.el** Classes and interfaces that provide programmatic access to the Expression Language evaluator
- **javax.servlet.jsp.tagext** Classes and interfaces that support development of JSP tag extensions

For each class, the following sections are included:

- Class name
- Context (full name, type, superclass, interfaces implemented). No superclass or superinterface is listed if the class extends java.lang.Object.
- Class description
- Details of each constructor and method in the class

The classes are listed in alphabetical order.

Note *A number of classes and methods are marked "deprecated." This means that they are no longer recommended for use and will likely be discontinued in future versions.*

Package javax.servlet

This package contains classes and interfaces not specific to any particular protocol. These classes define the relationship between a servlet and the runtime environment provided by the servlet container.

Filter

Full Name:	javax.servlet.Filter
Type:	Interface

The set of methods that must be implemented by classes that perform filtering tasks on a request, a response, or both.

Methods

destroy

```
public void destroy()
```

Called by the servlet container when the filter is about to be taken out of service.

doFilter

```
public void doFilter(
    ServletRequest request,
    ServletResponse response,
    FilterChain chain)
throws IOException, ServletException
```

Called by the servlet container when a request is passed through this part of the filter chain.

init

```
public void init(FilterConfig filterConfig)
    throws ServletException
```

Called by the servlet container when a filter is initialized before any requests have been serviced.

FilterChain

Full Name:	javax.servlet.FilterChain
Type:	Interface

An interface provided by the servlet container that allows a filter to invoke the next element in the chain, which may be another filter or the servlet at the end of the chain.

Methods

doFilter

```
public void doFilter(
    ServletRequest request,
```

```
    ServletResponse response)
throws IOException, ServletException
```

This method should be called in a filter's doFilter() method to invoke the next filter element. A filter can also prevent a request from being processed by skipping the invocation of this method.

FilterConfig

Full Name:	javax.servlet.FilterConfig
Type:	Interface

An object that represents the environment in which a filter operates, including its name, servlet context, and any initialization parameters. Analogous to the ServletConfig object for servlets.

Methods

getFilterName

```
public String getFilterName()
```

Returns the filter name.

getInitParameter

```
public String getInitParameter(String name)
```

Given a parameter name, returns the value of the initialization parameter of that name, or null if the parameter is not defined.

getInitParameterNames

```
public Enumeration getInitParameterNames()
```

Returns an enumeration of the initialization parameter names.

getServletContext

```
public ServletContext getServletContext()
```

Returns the servlet context.

GenericServlet

Full Name:	`javax.servlet.GenericServlet`
Type:	Abstract class
Implements:	`javax.servlet.Servlet`
	`javax.servlet.ServletConfig`
	`java.io.Serializable`

A base class for servlets that do not use HTTP protocol–specific features. Generic servlet implements the basic features of all servlets, including initialization, request handling, and termination.

Constructors

GenericServlet

```
public GenericServlet()
```

Default constructor, which does nothing because this is an abstract class.

Methods

destroy

```
public void destroy()
```

Called by the servlet container when the servlet is about to be taken out of service. By default, does nothing except write a "destroy" message to the log.

getInitParameter

```
public String getInitParameter(String name)
```

Given a name, returns the value of the initialization parameter with that name, or `null` if the parameter is not defined in `web.xml`.

getInitParameterNames

```
public Enumeration getInitParameterNames()
```

Returns an enumeration of the initialization parameter names.

getServletConfig

```
public ServletConfig getServletConfig()
```

Returns the servlet configuration object, which was stored as an instance variable in the init() method.

getServletContext

```
public ServletContext getServletContext()
```

Returns the servlet context for the Web application containing this servlet.

getServletInfo

```
public String getServletInfo()
```

Returns human-readable information about this servlet. By default, returns nothing; must be overridden to be useful.

getServletName

```
public String getServletName()
```

Returns the servlet name, as defined in web.xml.

init

```
public void init() throws ServletException
```

A convenience method invoked by servlet(ServletConfig config).

init

```
public void init(ServletConfig config)
    throws ServletException
```

Called by the servlet container when the servlet is placed into service. Is passed an instance of the servlet configuration object, which provides access to the initialization parameters. This method should either save the configuration object as an instance variable so that it can be retrieved during the application, or call `super.init(config)`, which does so.

log

```
public void log(String msg)
```

Writes the specified message to the log, with this servlet's name prepended.

log

```
public void log(String message, Throwable t)
```

Writes the specified message to the log, with this servlet's name prepended and the root cause exception text appended.

service

```
public abstract void service(
    ServletRequest req,
    ServletResponse res)
throws ServletException, IOException
```

Called by the servlet container to pass a request to a servlet.

RequestDispatcher

Full Name:	`javax.servlet.RequestDispatcher`
Type:	Interface

An object used to pass requests from a client to any resource on the server.

Methods

forward

```
public void forward(
    ServletRequest request,
    ServletResponse response)
throws ServletException, IOException
```

Passes a request from a servlet to another servlet, JSP page, or HTML document. forward can be called only before the response has been committed.

include

```
public void include(
    ServletRequest request,
    ServletResponse response)
throws ServletException, IOException
```

Merges the content of another servlet, JSP page, or HTML document with the current output buffer. The included resource may not set any response headers.

Servlet

Full Name:	javax.servlet.Servlet
Type:	Interface

The set of methods that must be implemented by all servlets. Note that most servlets will extend either GenericServlet or HttpServlet, both of which provide default implementations of all methods.

Methods

destroy

```
public void destroy()
```

Called by the servlet container when the servlet is about to be taken out of service.

getServletConfig

```
public ServletConfig getServletConfig()
```

Returns the servlet configuration object, which was stored as an instance variable in the init() method.

getServletInfo

```
public String getServletInfo()
```

Returns human-readable information about this servlet.

init

```
public void init(ServletConfig config)
    throws ServletException
```

Called by the servlet container when the servlet is placed into service. Is passed an instance of the servlet configuration object, which provides access to the initialization parameters. This method should save the configuration object as an instance variable so that it can be retrieved during the application.

service

```
public void service(ServletRequest req, ServletResponse res)
    throws ServletException, IOException
```

Called by the servlet container to pass a request to a servlet.

ServletConfig

Full Name:	`javax.servlet.ServletConfig`
Type:	Interface

Used by the servlet container to pass information to a servlet during initialization.

Methods

getInitParameter

```
public String getInitParameter(String name)
```

Returns the value of the specified initialization parameter, or `null` if it does not exist.

getInitParameterNames

```
public Enumeration getInitParameterNames()
```

Returns an enumeration of the names of the servlet's initialization parameters, or an empty enumeration if none exist.

getServletContext

```
public ServletContext getServletContext()
```

Returns the `ServletContext` associated with the servlet.

getServletName

```
public String getServletName()
```

Returns the name of the servlet instance as recorded in the `web.xml` deployment descriptor.

ServletContext

Full Name:	`javax.servlet.ServletContext`
Type:	Interface

Defines the list of methods that are available to a servlet for communicating with its servlet container. The servlet context can store attributes that are available to all servlets in the application.

Methods

getAttribute

```
public Object getAttribute(String name)
```

Returns the application-level attribute with the specified name, or `null` if it does not exist. The object must be cast into the appropriate type.

getAttributeNames

```
public Enumeration getAttributeNames()
```

Returns an enumeration of the attribute names in the servlet context.

getContext

```
public ServletContext getContext(String uripath)
```

Returns the `ServletContext` object of another URL on the same server. The path must begin with "/" and will be interpreted as being relative to the Web server's document root.

getInitParameter

```
public String getInitParameter(String name)
```

Returns the specified initialization parameter.

getInitParameterNames

```
public Enumeration getInitParameterNames()
```

Returns an enumeration of the names of the servlet context's initialization parameters, or an empty enumeration if there are none.

getMajorVersion

```
public int getMajorVersion()
```

Returns the number to the left of the decimal point in the Servlet API version number.

getMimeType

```
public String getMimeType(String file)
```

Returns the MIME type of the specified file, or `null` if the MIME type is not known.

getMinorVersion

```
public int getMinorVersion()
```

Returns the integer to the right of the decimal point in the Servlet API version number.

getNamedDispatcher

```
public RequestDispatcher getNamedDispatcher(String name)
```

Returns a `RequestDispatcher` for the specified servlet, or `null` if the `RequestDispatcher` cannot be returned.

getRealPath

```
public String getRealPath(String path)
```

Given a URI path in the current servlet context, converts the path into the absolute filename to which it refers.

getRequestDispatcher

```
public RequestDispatcher getRequestDispatcher(String path)
```

Returns a `RequestDispatcher` for the specified resource, or `null` if it cannot be created. The path name must begin with "/" and is interpreted as being relative to the root of the servlet context.

getResource

```
public URL getResource(String path)
    throws MalformedURLException
```

Returns a URL for the specified resource, or `null` if it cannot be created. The path name must begin with "/" and is interpreted as being relative to the root of the servlet context.

getResourceAsStream

```
public InputStream getResourceAsStream(String path)
```

Returns an `InputStream` for the specified resource, or `null` if it cannot be created. The path name must begin with "/" and is interpreted as being relative to the root of the servlet context.

getResourcePaths

```
public Set getResourcePaths(String path)
```

Returns a `java.util.Set` of strings representing the paths to resources held in the Web application. The paths begin with a leading / and are relative to the root of the servlet context.

getServerInfo

```
public String getServerInfo()
```

Returns the name and version of the servlet container. The returned value is in the form servername/version_number.

[deprecated] getServlet

```
public Servlet getServlet(String name)
    throws ServletException
```

No longer supported, for security reasons. The servlet specification now requires the method to return `null`. See `HttpSessionListener` for an alternative approach.

getServletContextName

```
public String getServletContextName()
```

Returns the name of the Web application, corresponding to the `display-name` element for this `ServletContext` in the `web.xml` deployment descriptor.

[deprecated] getServletNames

```
public Enumeration getServletNames()
```

No longer supported, for security reasons. The servlet specification now requires the method to return `null`. See `HttpSessionListener` for an alternative approach.

[deprecated] getServlets

```
public Enumeration getServlets()
```

No longer supported, for security reasons. The servlet specification now requires the method to return `null`. See `HttpSessionListener` for an alternative approach.

[deprecated] log

```
public void log(Exception exception, String msg)
```

No longer supported. Use `log(String message, Throwable t)` instead.

log

```
public void log(String msg)
```

Writes the specified message to the servlet log.

log

```
public void log(String message, Throwable throwable)
```

Writes the specified message and a stack trace for a given `Throwable` to the servlet log.

removeAttribute

```
public void removeAttribute(String name)
```

Removes the attribute with the specified name from the servlet context.

setAttribute

```
public void setAttribute(String name, Object object)
```

Stores an object under the specified attribute name in this servlet context.

ServletContextAttributeEvent

Full Name: `javax.servlet.ServletContextAttributeEvent`

Type: Class

Extends: `javax.servlet.ServletContextEvent`

Used for notifications about changes to the attributes of the servlet context of a Web application.

Constructors

ServletContextAttributeEvent

```
public ServletContextAttributeEvent(
    ServletContext source,
```

```
String name,
Object value)
```

Constructs a `ServletContextAttributeEvent` from the specified context for the specified name and value.

Methods

getName

```
public String getName()
```

Returns the name of the attribute that changed.

getValue

```
public Object getValue()
```

Returns the value of the attribute that was added, removed, or replaced. The value depends on whether the attribute was added, changed, or deleted. For changes or deletions, it is the value of the old attribute. For additions, it is the value of the new attribute.

ServletContextAttributeListener

Full Name:	`javax.servlet.ServletContextAttributeListener`
Type:	Interface
Superinterface:	`java.util.EventListener`

Classes implementing this interface will receive notification of changes to the servlet context's attribute list.

Methods

attributeAdded

```
public void attributeAdded(
    ServletContextAttributeEvent scab)
```

Called when a new attribute is added to the servlet context.

attributeRemoved

```
public void attributeRemoved(
    ServletContextAttributeEvent scab)
```

Called when an existing attribute is removed from the servlet context.

attributeReplaced

```
public void attributeReplaced(
    ServletContextAttributeEvent scab)
```

Called when an existing attribute is replaced in the servlet context.

ServletContextEvent

Full Name:	`javax.servlet.ServletContextEvent`
Type:	Class
Extends:	`java.util.EventObject`

Event class for notifications about changes to the servlet context.

Constructors

ServletContextEvent

```
public ServletContextEvent(ServletContext source)
```

Creates a `ServletContextEvent` from the given context.

Methods

getServletContext

```
public ServletContext getServletContext()
```

Returns the `ServletContext` that changed.

ServletContextListener

Full Name:	`javax.servlet.ServletContextListener`
Type:	Interface
Superinterface:	`java.util.EventListener`

Classes implementing this interface will receive notification about changes to the servlet context.

Methods

contextDestroyed

```
public void contextDestroyed(ServletContextEvent sce)
```

Called when the servlet context is about to be shut down.

contextInitialized

```
public void contextInitialized(ServletContextEvent sce)
```

Called when the Web application is ready to process requests.

ServletException

Full Name:	`javax.servlet.ServletException`
Type:	Class
Extends:	`java.lang.Exception`

A generic servlet exception.

Constructors

ServletException

```
public ServletException()
```

Creates a new servlet exception.

ServletException

```
public ServletException(String message)
```

Creates a new servlet exception with the specified message.

ServletException

```
public ServletException(String message, Throwable rootCause)
```

Creates a new servlet exception that includes a message and the root cause exception.

ServletException

```
public ServletException(Throwable rootCause)
```

Creates a new servlet exception that includes the root cause exception.

Methods

getRootCause

```
public Throwable getRootCause()
```

Returns the root cause exception for the current servlet exception.

ServletInputStream

Full Name:	`javax.servlet.ServletInputStream`
Type:	Abstract class
Extends:	`java.io.InputStream`

An input stream a servlet can use for reading binary data from a client request. Typically retrieved with the `ServletRequest.getInputStream()` method.

Methods

readLine

```
public int readLine(byte b, int off, int len)
    throws IOException
```

Reads one line at a time from the input stream, starting at the specified offset. Reads bytes into an array until it reads the specified number of bytes or a newline character (also read into the array). Returns –1 if end of file is reached before the maximum number of bytes is read.

ServletOutputStream

Full Name:	`javax.servlet.ServletOutputStream`
Type:	Abstract class
Extends:	`java.io.OutputStream`

An output stream used to send binary data to a client. Typically retrieved with the `ServletResponse.getOutputStream()` method.

Methods

print

```
public void print(boolean b) throws IOException
```

Writes a boolean value to the client but no carriage return–line feed character at the end.

print

```
public void print(char c) throws IOException
```

Writes a character to the client but no carriage return–line feed at the end.

print

```
public void print(double d) throws IOException
```

Writes a double value to the client but no carriage return–line feed at the end.

print

```
public void print(float f) throws IOException
```

Writes a float value to the client but no carriage return–line feed at the end.

print

```
public void print(int i) throws IOException
```

Writes an int to the client but no carriage return–line feed at the end.

print

```
public void print(long l) throws IOException
```

Writes a long value to the client but no carriage return–line feed at the end.

print

```
public void print(String s) throws IOException
```

Writes a String to the client but no carriage return–line feed character at the end.

println

```
public void println() throws IOException
```

Writes a carriage return–line feed to the client.

println

```
public void println(boolean b) throws IOException
```

Writes a boolean value to the client followed by a carriage return–line feed.

println

```
public void println(char c) throws IOException
```

Writes a character to the client followed by a carriage return–line feed.

println

```
public void println(double d) throws IOException
```

Writes a double value to the client followed by a carriage return–line feed.

println

```
public void println(float f) throws IOException
```

Writes a float value to the client followed by a carriage return–line feed.

println

```
public void println(int i) throws IOException
```

Writes an int to the client followed by a carriage return–line feed character.

println

```
public void println(long l) throws IOException
```

Writes a long value to the client followed by a carriage return–line feed.

println

```
public void println(String s) throws IOException
```

Writes a String to the client followed by a carriage return–line feed.

ServletRequest

Full Name:	javax.servlet.ServletRequest
Type:	Interface

An interface that represents a client request to a servlet. The servlet container creates a `ServletRequest` object and passes it as an argument to the servlet's service method. Has methods for retrieving parameter names and values, attributes, and the input stream.

Methods

getAttribute

```
public Object getAttribute(String name)
```

Returns the value of the specified attribute, or `null` if no attribute of the specified name exists.

getAttributeNames

```
public Enumeration getAttributeNames()
```

Returns an `Enumeration` of the names of the attributes available to this request, or an empty `Enumeration` if the request has no attributes.

getCharacterEncoding

```
public String getCharacterEncoding()
```

Returns the name of the character encoding used in the body of this request, or `null` if the request does not specify a character encoding.

getContentLength

```
public int getContentLength()
```

Returns the length of the request body or –1 if the length is not known. In HTTP servlets, this is the same as the value of the CGI variable CONTENT_LENGTH.

getContentType

```
public String getContentType()
```

Returns the MIME type of the body of the request, or `null` if not known. In HTTP servlets, same as the value of the CGI variable CONTENT_TYPE.

getInputStream

```
public ServletInputStream getInputStream()
   throws IOException
```

Retrieves the body of the request as binary data. Either getInputStream() or getReader() may be called to read the body, but not both.

getLocale

```
public Locale getLocale()
```

Returns the preferred Locale in which the client will accept content, if specified. Otherwise, returns the default locale for the server.

getLocales

```
public Enumeration getLocales()
```

Returns an Enumeration of Locale objects in order of user preference, or an Enumeration containing one Locale, the default locale for the server, if the client indicates no preferred locale.

getParameter

```
public String getParameter(String name)
```

Returns the value of a request parameter as a String, or null if the parameter does not exist.

getParameterMap

```
public Map getParameterMap()
```

Returns a java.util.Map of the parameters of this request.

getParameterNames

```
public Enumeration getParameterNames()
```

Returns a java.util.Enumeration of the names of the parameters in this request, or an empty Enumeration if the request has no parameters.

getParameterValues

```
public String getParameterValues(String name)
```

Returns an array of `String` objects containing all the values of the given request parameter, or `null` if the parameter does not exist.

getProtocol

```
public String getProtocol()
```

Returns the name and version of the protocol the request uses. The value returned is in the form protocol/majorVersion.minorVersion. In HTTP servlets, this is the same as the CGI variable SERVER_PROTOCOL.

getReader

```
public BufferedReader getReader() throws IOException
```

Retrieves the body of the request as character data. Either `getInputStream()` or `getReader()` may be called, but not both.

[deprecated] getRealPath

```
public String getRealPath(String path)
```

No longer supported. See `ServletContext.getRealPath()`.

getRemoteAddr

```
public String getRemoteAddr()
```

Returns the Internet Protocol (IP) address of the client that sent the request. For HTTP servlets, same as the CGI variable REMOTE_ADDR.

getRemoteHost

```
public String getRemoteHost()
```

Returns the name of the client that sent the request, or the client's IP address if the name cannot be determined. For HTTP servlets, same as the CGI variable REMOTE_HOST.

getRequestDispatcher

```
public RequestDispatcher getRequestDispatcher(String path)
```

Returns a `RequestDispatcher` object for the resource located at the specified path. The difference between this method and `ServletContext` `.getRequestDispatcher()` is that this method can take a relative path.

getScheme

```
public String getScheme()
```

Returns the scheme used to make the request.

getServerName

```
public String getServerName()
```

Returns the server host name for the server receiving the request. In HTTP servlets, this is the same as the CGI variable SERVER_NAME.

getServerPort

```
public int getServerPort()
```

Returns the port number to which this request was sent. In HTTP servlets, this is the same as the CGI variable SERVER_PORT.

isSecure

```
public boolean isSecure()
```

Returns true if this request was made using a secure channel, such as https.

removeAttribute

```
public void removeAttribute(String name)
```

Removes the named attribute from this request.

setAttribute

```
public void setAttribute(String name, Object o)
```

Binds an attribute to this request under the given name.

setCharacterEncoding

```
public void setCharacterEncoding(String env)
    throws UnsupportedEncodingException
```

Specifies the character encoding used in the body of this request. Must be called before reading the request parameters or input data.

ServletRequestAttributeEvent

Full Name:	`javax.servlet.ServletRequestAttributeEvent`
Type:	Class
Extends:	`javax.servlet.ServletRequestEvent`

The event class used to notify a listener of changes to servlet request attributes.

Constructors

ServletRequestAttributeEvent

```
public ServletRequestAttributeEvent(
    ServletContext sc,
    ServletRequest request,
    String name,
    Object value)
```

Creates a new `ServletRequestAttributeEvent`.

Methods

getName

```
public String getName()
```

Returns the name of the changed attribute.

getValue

```
public Object getValue()
```

Returns the changed value.

ServletRequestAttributeListener

Full Name:	javax.servlet.ServletRequestAttributeListener
Type:	Interface
Superinterface:	java.util.EventListener

Classes implementing ServletRequestAttributeListener receive notifications by means of callback methods when there are changes to the attributes of any request in the application. It's hard for me to imagine why you would ever need to do this.

Methods

attributeAdded

```
public void attributeAdded(
    ServletRequestAttributeEvent srae)
```

Called after an attribute is added to some servlet request.

attributeRemoved

```
public void attributeRemoved(
    ServletRequestAttributeEvent srae)
```

Called after an attribute has been removed from some servlet request.

attributeReplaced

```
public void attributeReplaced(
    ServletRequestAttributeEvent srae)
```

Called when an attribute in some servlet request has been changed.

ServletRequestEvent

Full Name:	`javax.servlet.ServletRequestEvent`
Type:	Class
Extends:	`java.util.EventObject`

An event that is sent to servlet request listeners, allowing them to access the servlet request and servlet context.

Constructors

ServletRequestEvent

```
public ServletRequestEvent(
    ServletContext sc,
    ServletRequest request)
```

Creates a new `ServletRequestEvent`.

Methods

getRequest

```
public ServletRequest getRequest()
```

Returns a reference to the servlet request to which something happened.

getServletContext

```
public ServletContext getServletContext()
```

Returns a reference to the servlet context (application) of the servlet request to which something happened.

ServletRequestListener

Full Name:	`javax.servlet.ServletRequestListener`
Type:	Interface
Superinterface:	`java.util.EventListener`

An interface implemented by objects that need to be notified of changes in the state of a servlet request.

Methods

requestDestroyed

```
public void requestDestroyed(ServletRequestEvent sre)
```

Called when a servlet request is about to go out of scope.

requestInitialized

```
public void requestInitialized(ServletRequestEvent sre)
```

Called when a servlet request is about to go into scope.

ServletRequestWrapper

Full Name:	javax.servlet.ServletRequestWrapper
Type:	Class
Implements:	javax.servlet.ServletRequest

An implementation of `ServletRequest` that can be subclassed to extend the servlet container's implementation class.

Constructors

ServletRequestWrapper

```
public ServletRequestWrapper(ServletRequest request)
```

Creates a `ServletRequest` adapter for the given request object.

Methods

getAttribute

```
public Object getAttribute(String name)
```

Returns the value of the specified attribute, or `null` if no attribute of the specified name exists.

getAttributeNames

```
public Enumeration getAttributeNames()
```

Returns an `Enumeration` of the names of the attributes available to this request, or an empty `Enumeration` if the request has no attributes.

getCharacterEncoding

```
public String getCharacterEncoding()
```

Returns the name of the character encoding used in the body of this request, or `null` if the request does not specify a character encoding.

getContentLength

```
public int getContentLength()
```

Returns the length of the request body or –1 if the length is not known. In HTTP servlets, this is the same as the value of the CGI variable CONTENT_LENGTH.

getContentType

```
public String getContentType()
```

Returns the MIME type of the body of the request, or `null` if not known. In HTTP servlets, same as the value of the CGI variable CONTENT_TYPE.

getInputStream

```
public ServletInputStream getInputStream()
    throws IOException
```

Retrieves the body of the request as binary data. Either `getInputStream()` or `getReader()` may be called to read the body, but not both.

getLocale

```
public Locale getLocale()
```

Returns the preferred `Locale` in which the client will accept content, if specified. Otherwise, returns the default locale for the server.

getLocales

```
public Enumeration getLocales()
```

Returns an `Enumeration` of `Locale` object in order of user preference, or an `Enumeration` containing one `Locale`, the default locale for the server, if the client indicates no preferred locale.

getParameter

```
public String getParameter(String name)
```

Returns the value of a request parameter as a `String`, or `null` if the parameter does not exist.

getParameterMap

```
public Map getParameterMap()
```

Returns a `java.util.Map` of the parameters of this request.

getParameterNames

```
public Enumeration getParameterNames()
```

Returns a `java.util.Enumeration` of the names of the parameters in this request, or an empty `Enumeration` if the request has no parameters.

getParameterValues

```
public String getParameterValues(String name)
```

Returns an array of `String` objects containing all the values of the given request parameter, or `null` if the parameter does not exist.

getProtocol

```
public String getProtocol()
```

Returns the name and version of the protocol the request uses. The value returned is in the form protocol/majorVersion.minorVersion. In HTTP servlets, this is the same as the CGI variable SERVER_PROTOCOL.

getReader

```
public BufferedReader getReader() throws IOException
```

Retrieves the body of the request as character data. Either `getInputStream()` or `getReader()` may be called, but not both.

getRealPath

```
public String getRealPath(String path)
```

Returns `getRealPath(String path)`.

getRemoteAddr

```
public String getRemoteAddr()
```

Returns the Internet Protocol (IP) address of the client that sent the request. For HTTP servlets, same as the CGI variable REMOTE_ADDR.

getRemoteHost

```
public String getRemoteHost()
```

Returns the name of the client that sent the request, or the client's IP address if the name cannot be determined. For HTTP servlets, same as the CGI variable REMOTE_HOST.

getRequest

```
public ServletRequest getRequest()
```

Returns the wrapped request object.

getRequestDispatcher

```
public RequestDispatcher getRequestDispatcher(String path)
```

Returns a `RequestDispatcher` object for the resource located at the specified path. The difference between this method and `ServletContext.getRequestDispatcher()` is that this method can take a relative path.

getScheme

```
public String getScheme()
```

Returns the scheme used to make the request.

getServerName

```
public String getServerName()
```

Returns the server host name for the server receiving the request. In HTTP servlets, this is the same as the CGI variable SERVER_NAME.

getServerPort

```
public int getServerPort()
```

Returns the port number to which this request was sent. In HTTP servlets, this is the same as the CGI variable SERVER_PORT.

isSecure

```
public boolean isSecure()
```

Returns true if this request was made using a secure channel, such as https.

removeAttribute

```
public void removeAttribute(String name)
```

Removes the named attribute from this request.

setAttribute

```
public void setAttribute(String name, Object o)
```

Binds an attribute to this request under the given name.

setCharacterEncoding

```
public void setCharacterEncoding(String enc)
   throws UnsupportedEncodingException
```

Specifies the character encoding used in the body of this request. Must be called before reading the request parameters or input data are read.

setRequest

```
public void setRequest(ServletRequest request)
```

Sets the request object.

ServletResponse

Full Name:	javax.servlet.ServletResponse
Type:	Interface

Encapsulates all information about the response generated for a request, including response headers, the status code, and the output stream. HttpServletResponse extends this interface for HTTP-specific features.

Methods

flushBuffer

```
public void flushBuffer() throws IOException
```

Causes the buffer to be written to the client, thus committing the response.

getBufferSize

```
public int getBufferSize()
```

Returns the actual buffer size used in the response. If buffering is turned off, returns zero.

getCharacterEncoding

```
public String getCharacterEncoding()
```

Returns the name of the character set encoding for this response.

getContentType

```
public String getContentType()
```

Returns the content type.

getLocale

```
public Locale getLocale()
```

Returns the locale used by the response.

getOutputStream

```
public ServletOutputStream getOutputStream()
    throws IOException
```

Returns the `ServletOutputStream` for this response. Cannot be called if `getWriter()` has already been called for this response.

getWriter

```
public PrintWriter getWriter() throws IOException
```

Returns a `PrintWriter` for this response. Cannot be called if `getOutputStream()` has already been called for this response.

isCommitted

```
public boolean isCommitted()
```

Returns true if the response has already been committed, which implies that the response already had its status code and headers written.

reset

```
public void reset()
```

Clears any existing data in the response buffer as well as the status code and headers. If the response has been committed, throws an `IllegalStateException`.

resetBuffer

```
public void resetBuffer()
```

Clears any existing data in the response buffer. This method differs from `reset()` in that it does not clear the status code and headers. If the response has been committed, throws an `IllegalStateException`.

setBufferSize

```
public void setBufferSize(int size)
```

Sets the preferred buffer size for the response body. The servlet container will use a buffer at least as large as the size requested. The actual buffer size can be retrieved with `getBufferSize()`. Must be called before any body content is written, or it will throw an `IllegalStateException`.

setCharacterEncoding

```
public void setCharacterEncoding(String charset)
```

Sets the character encoding to the specified character set name.

setContentLength

```
public void setContentLength(int len)
```

Indicates to the client the length of the content written to the response.

setContentType

```
public void setContentType(String type)
```

Sets the content type.

setLocale

```
public void setLocale(Locale loc)
```

Sets the locale of the response. Must be called before `getWriter()`. The default locale is the one used by the server.

ServletResponseWrapper

Full Name:	`javax.servlet.ServletResponseWrapper`
Type:	Class
Implements:	`javax.servlet.ServletResponse`

A base class for subclasses that implement `ServletResponse`. Its default behavior is to invoke corresponding methods in the servlet container's `ServletResponse` implementation class.

Constructors

ServletResponseWrapper

```
public ServletResponseWrapper(ServletResponse response)
```

Creates a ServletResponseWrapper for the specified response object.

Methods

flushBuffer

```
public void flushBuffer() throws IOException
```

Causes the buffer to be written to the client, thus committing the response.

getBufferSize

```
public int getBufferSize()
```

Returns the actual buffer size used in the response. If buffering is turned off, returns zero.

getCharacterEncoding

```
public String getCharacterEncoding()
```

Returns the name of the character set encoding for this response.

getContentType

```
public String getContentType()
```

Returns the content type.

getLocale

```
public Locale getLocale()
```

Returns the locale used by the response.

getOutputStream

```
public ServletOutputStream getOutputStream()
    throws IOException
```

Returns the `ServletOutputStream` for this response. Cannot be called if `getWriter()` has already been called for this response.

getResponse

```
public ServletResponse getResponse()
```

Returns the wrapped `ServletResponse` object.

getWriter

```
public PrintWriter getWriter() throws IOException
```

Returns a `PrintWriter` for this response. Cannot be called if `getOutputStream()` has already been called for this response.

isCommitted

```
public boolean isCommitted()
```

Returns true if the response has already been committed, which implies that the response already had its status code and headers written.

reset

```
public void reset()
```

Clears any existing data in the response buffer as well as the status code and headers. If the response has been committed, throws an `IllegalStateException`.

resetBuffer

```
public void resetBuffer()
```

Clears any existing data in the response buffer. This method differs from `reset()` in that it does not clear the status code and headers. If the response has been committed, throws an `IllegalStateException`.

setBufferSize

```
public void setBufferSize(int size)
```

Sets the preferred buffer size for the response body. The servlet container will use a buffer at least as large as the size requested. The actual buffer size can be retrieved with `getBufferSize()`. Must be called before any body content is written, or it will throw an `IllegalStateException`.

setCharacterEncoding

```
public void setCharacterEncoding(String charset)
```

Sets the character encoding.

setContentLength

```
public void setContentLength(int len)
```

Indicates to the client the length of the content written to the response.

setContentType

```
public void setContentType(String type)
```

Sets the content type.

setLocale

```
public void setLocale(Locale loc)
```

Sets the locale of the response. Must be called before getWriter(). The default locale is the one used by the server.

setResponse

```
public void setResponse(ServletResponse response)
```

Saves a reference to the Response object being wrapped.

SingleThreadModel

Full Name:	javax.servlet.SingleThreadModel
Type:	Interface

An interface that can be implemented by a servlet to indicate to the servlet container that multiple threads cannot be used to access the service() method concurrently. This ensures that servlets will handle only one request at a time. There are no methods in this interface; it is simply a marker to indicate that it wants this behavior.

 Although this makes a single instance of the servlet thread-safe within its own service() *method, it does not prevent multiple instances from accessing external resources at the same time.*

Methods
None.

UnavailableException

Full Name:	javax.servlet.UnavailableException
Type:	Class
Extends:	javax.servlet.ServletException

A subclass of ServletException thrown by a servlet when it can no longer handle requests, either temporarily or permanently. Typically, this is used during init().

Constructors

[deprecated] UnavailableException

```
public UnavailableException(
    int seconds,
    Servlet servlet,
    String msg)
```

No longer supported.

[deprecated] UnavailableException

```
public UnavailableException(Servlet servlet, String msg)
```

No longer supported.

UnavailableException

```
public UnavailableException(String msg)
```

Creates a new exception with a message specifying that the servlet is permanently unavailable.

UnavailableException

```
public UnavailableException(String msg, int seconds)
```

Creates a new exception for the servlet with the specified error message indicating that the servlet is temporarily unavailable. Accepts an integer indicating the number of seconds the servlet is expected to be unavailable. If the number is zero or negative, no estimate is available.

Methods

getServlet

```
public Servlet getServlet()
```

No longer supported.

getUnavailableSeconds

```
public int getUnavailableSeconds()
```

Returns the length of time in seconds the servlet expects to be unavailable, or a negative number if the unavailability is permanent or of indeterminate length.

isPermanent

```
public boolean isPermanent()
```

Returns true if the servlet is permanently unavailable.

Package javax.servlet.http

This package contains classes and interfaces specific to the HTTP protocol. The primary class is javax.http.servlet.Servlet, which defines the methods used to process each HTTP method. Most servlets in the HTTP environment extend this class, directly or indirectly.

Cookie

Full Name:	`javax.servlet.http.Cookie`
Type:	Class
Implements:	`java.lang.Cloneable`

A cookie is a small collection of key/value pairs that a servlet sends to a requester. The requester (usually a Web browser) is asked to store the information locally and return it the next time it makes a request to the same URL. Servlet container can use cookies to store session information that is unique to a particular client. This usage is transparent to the servlet author. You can also explicitly send and receive cookies with the `HttpServletResponse.addCookie()` and `HttpServletRequest.getCookies()` methods, respectively. Note that users can refuse to accept cookies, so your application needs to handle this case.

Constructors

Cookie

```
public cookie(String name, String value)
```

Creates a new cookie with the specified name and value.

Methods

clone

```
public Object clone()
```

Returns a copy of the cookie. The number of calories is not affected.

getComment

```
public String getComment()
```

Returns the cookie comment.

getDomain

```
public String getDomain()
```

Returns the cookie domain name.

getMaxAge

```
public int getMaxAge()
```

Returns the maximum number of seconds that the cookie should be stored before it is deleted. Note that this is relative to the time that setMaxAge() was called, not the current time.

getName

```
public String getName()
```

Returns the cookie name. Note that there is no setName() method; you must set the cookie's name in the constructor.

getPath

```
public String getPath()
```

Returns the path under which the cookie is visible. A request for any URL in that path or any of its subdirectories will cause the cookie to be returned. See RFC 2109 for more information about cookie paths.

getSecure

```
public boolean getSecure()
```

Returns true if the user agent (browser) will return cookies using a secure protocol.

getValue

```
public String getValue()
```

Returns the cookie's value.

getVersion

```
public int getVersion()
```

Returns the cookie protocol version:

- **0**   Original Netscape specification
- **1**   RFC 2109 specification

setComment

```
public void setComment(String purpose)
```

Sets the cookie's comment field to the specified string.

setDomain

```
public void setDomain(String pattern)
```

Sets the cookie's domain. A domain can be used to restrict the cookie's visibility to a subset of servers in a particular addressing scheme. The domain name is converted to lowercase before it is stored. If no domain is specified, the cookie is returned only to the server that sent it. See RFC 2109 for details.

setMaxAge

```
public void setMaxAge(int expiry)
```

Specifies the length of time in seconds that the cookie should persist. A positive or zero value requests the browser to delete the cookie after the specified interval.

A negative value requests the browser to keep the cookie active only for the duration of the current browser instance.

setPath

```
public void setPath(String uri)
```

Specifies a path in which the cookie should be visible. If a path of `/servlet/abc` is specified, for instance, then the cookie will be returned along with any requests for a URL containing that path, e.g., `/servlet/abc/def`. If no path is specified, `/` is assumed. The path must include the servlet that sets the cookie. See RFC 2109 for more details about cookie paths.

setSecure

```
public void setSecure(boolean flag)
```

Tells the user agent (browser) whether to return the cookie using a secure protocol or not.

setValue

```
public void setValue(String newValue)
```

Sets the cookie's value to the specified string.

setVersion

```
public void setVersion(int v)
```

Sets the cookie protocol version:

- **0**   Original Netscape specification
- **1**   RFC 2109 specification

HttpServlet

Full Name:	`javax.servlet.http.HttpServlet`
Type:	Abstract class
Extends:	`javax.servlet.GenericServlet`
Implements:	`java.io.Serializable`

An abstract base class for servlets that operate in an HTTP environment. `HttpServlet` is a thin extension of `GenericServlet` that provides specific methods for HTTP GET, POST, PUT, DELETE, HEAD, OPTIONS, and TRACE requests. The `service()` method determines the HTTP request type and invokes the appropriate method. A typical `HttpServlet` subclass will override `doGet()`, `doPost()`, or both, but not `service()`.

Constructors

HttpServlet

```
public HttpServlet()
```

Default (empty) constructor. Performs no work. All servlet initialization should be performed in the `init()` method inherited from `GenericServlet`.

Methods

doDelete

```
protected void doDelete(
   HttpServletRequest req,
   HttpServletResponse resp)
      throws ServletException, IOException
```

Indirectly called by the Web container to handle an HTTP DELETE request.

doGet

```
protected void doGet(
   HttpServletRequest req,
   HttpServletResponse resp)
      throws ServletException, IOException
```

Indirectly called by the Web container to handle an HTTP GET request.

doHead

```
protected void doHead(
   HttpServletRequest req,
   HttpServletResponse resp)
      throws ServletException, IOException
```

Indirectly called by the Web container to handle an HTTP HEAD request.

doOptions

```
protected void doOptions(
    HttpServletRequest req,
    HttpServletResponse resp)
        throws ServletException, IOException
```

Indirectly called by the Web container to handle an HTTP OPTIONS request.

doPost

```
protected void doPost(
    HttpServletRequest req,
    HttpServletResponse resp)
        throws ServletException, IOException
```

Indirectly called by the Web container to handle an HTTP POST request.

doPut

```
protected void doPut(
    HttpServletRequest req,
    HttpServletResponse resp)
        throws ServletException, IOException
```

Indirectly called by the Web container to handle an HTTP PUT request.

doTrace

```
protected void doTrace(
    HttpServletRequest req,
    HttpServletResponse resp)
        throws ServletException, IOException
```

Indirectly called by the Web container to handle an HTTP TRACE request.

getLastModified

```
protected long getLastModified(HttpServletRequest req)
```

Returns the time (in milliseconds since January 1, 1970) at which the request object was created or last modified.

service

```
protected void service(
    HttpServletRequest req,
    HttpServletResponse res)
        throws ServletException, IOException
```

An HTTP-specific version of the `service()` method. This method need not be overridden; it already contains logic to delegate the request to `doGet()`, `doPost()`, etc., based on the HTTP method.

service

```
public void service(ServletRequest req, ServletResponse res)
    throws ServletException, IOException
```

A convenience method that converts a protocol-neutral request to an HTTP request, if possible, and then invokes the HTTP-specific `service()` method.

HttpServletRequest

Full Name:	`javax.servlet.http.HttpServletRequest`
Type:	Interface
Superinterface:	`javax.servlet.ServletRequest`

Encapsulates all information about an HTTP request: its parameters, attributes, headers, and input data.

Methods

getAuthType

```
public String getAuthType()
```

If the server uses an authentication scheme like BASIC or SSL, returns the name of this scheme; otherwise, returns `null`.

getContextPath

```
public String getContextPath()
```

Returns the portion of the request URI that specifies the servlet context (application). The path starts with but does not end with a "/" character.

getCookies

```
public Cookie getCookies()
```

Returns an array containing all of the Cookie objects the client sent with this request. Returns null if no cookies were sent.

getDateHeader

```
public long getDateHeader(String name)
```

Given a request header name, converts the corresponding header value into a Date object, which is returned as a long value (the number of milliseconds since January 1, 1970). If the specified request header does not exist, returns –1.

getHeader

```
public String getHeader(String name)
```

Returns the string value of the specified request header, or null if the named header is not found in the request.

getHeaderNames

```
public Enumeration getHeaderNames()
```

Returns an Enumeration of all the header names found in this request. If there are no headers, returns either null or an empty Enumeration, depending on the servlet container.

getHeaders

```
public Enumeration getHeaders(String name)
```

For headers that can occur multiple times in a request, this method will return an Enumeration of the header values.

getIntHeader

```
public int getIntHeader(String name)
```

Given a request header name, converts the corresponding header value into an integer and returns the integer value. If the specified request header does not exist, returns –1.

getMethod

```
public String getMethod()
```

Returns the HTTP method contained in the first line of the request, e.g., GET or POST.

getPathInfo

```
public String getPathInfo()
```

Returns the substring of the request URL that follows the servlet name, or null if there is no additional path information. Same as the CGI variable PATH_INFO.

getPathTranslated

```
public String getPathTranslated()
```

Returns the substring of the request URL that follows the servlet name converted to a real filesystem path, or null if there is no additional path information. Same as the CGI variable PATH_TRANSLATED.

getQueryString

```
public String getQueryString()
```

Returns the substring of the request URL that follows the "?", or null if there is no query string. Usually found only in GET requests. Same as the CGI variable QUERY_STRING.

getRemoteUser

```
public String getRemoteUser()
```

Returns the user name, if HTTP authentication is active and the user had logged in. Returns null otherwise. Same as the CGI variable REMOTE_USER.

getRequestedSessionId

```
public String getRequestedSessionId()
```

Returns the value of the session ID returned by the client. Usually the same as the current session, but may refer to an old expired session. Returns null if the request does not specify a session ID.

getRequestURI

```
public String getRequestURI()
```

Returns the substring of the request URL starting with the protocol name (e.g., http://) if present, and extending to but not including the query string (which starts with "?").

getRequestURL

```
public StringBuffer getRequestURL()
```

Reconstructs the entire URL used for the request. Includes the protocol, server name, port number (if other than the default), and filename. Does not include the query string.

getServletPath

```
public String getServletPath()
```

Returns the part of this request's URL that calls the servlet. This includes either the servlet name or a path to the servlet but does not include any extra path information or a query string. Same as the value of the CGI variable SCRIPT_NAME.

getSession

```
public HttpSession getSession()
```

A convenience method that returns the value of HttpSession.getSession(true).

getSession

```
public HttpSession getSession(boolean create)
```

Returns the current HttpSession object or creates a new one (if the create parameter is true). The returned value depends on whether the session already exists and whether the create parameter is true or false.

getUserPrincipal

```
public Principal getUserPrincipal()
```

If the user has been authenticated, returns a java.security.Principal object for the user. Otherwise, the method returns null.

isRequestedSessionIdFromCookie

```
public boolean isRequestedSessionIdFromCookie()
```

Returns true if the request session ID was received from a cookie as opposed to being sent as part of the request URL.

[deprecated] isRequestedSessionIdFromUrl

```
public boolean isRequestedSessionIdFromUrl()
```

No longer supported. Use isRequestedSessionIdFromURL() instead.

isRequestedSessionIdFromURL

```
public boolean isRequestedSessionIdFromURL()
```

Returns true if the requested session ID came in as part of the request URL as opposed to being sent from a cookie.

isRequestedSessionIdValid

```
public boolean isRequestedSessionIdValid()
```

Returns true if the request specifies the ID of a valid, active session.

isUserInRole

```
public boolean isUserInRole(String role)
```

Returns true if the authenticated user is included in the specified logical "role" in the deployment descriptor.

HttpServletRequestWrapper

Full Name:	`javax.servlet.http.HttpServletRequestWrapper`
Type:	Class
Extends:	`javax.servlet.ServletRequestWrapper`
Implements:	`javax.servlet.http.HttpServletRequest`

This class is a concrete implementation of `HttpServletRequest` that can be overriden in a servlet container–neutral way to provide additional functionality to the request object. By default, looks through to the corresponding servlet container–specific methods.

Constructors

HttpServletRequestWrapper

```
public HttpServletRequestWrapper(HttpServletRequest request)
```

Creates a request object wrapping the given request.

Methods

getAuthType

```
public String getAuthType()
```

If the server uses an authentication scheme like BASIC or SSL, returns the name of this scheme; otherwise, returns `null`.

getContextPath

```
public String getContextPath()
```

Returns the portion of the request URI that specifies the servlet context (application). The path starts with but does not end with a "/" character.

getCookies

```
public Cookie getCookies()
```

Returns an array containing all of the Cookie objects the client sent with this request. Returns `null` if no cookies were sent.

getDateHeader

```
public long getDateHeader(String name)
```

Given a request header name, converts the corresponding header value into a Date object, which is returned as a long value (the number of milliseconds since January 1, 1970). If the specified request header does not exist, returns –1.

getHeader

```
public String getHeader(String name)
```

Returns the string value of the specified request header, or `null` if the named header is not found in the request.

getHeaderNames

```
public Enumeration getHeaderNames()
```

Returns an `Enumeration` of all the header names found in this request. If there are no headers, returns either `null` or an empty `Enumeration`, depending on the servlet container.

getHeaders

```
public Enumeration getHeaders(String name)
```

For headers that can occur multiple times in a request, this method will return an `Enumeration` of the header values.

getIntHeader

```
public int getIntHeader(String name)
```

Given a request header name, converts the corresponding header value into an integer and returns the integer value. If the specified request header does not exist, returns –1.

getMethod

```
public String getMethod()
```

Returns the HTTP method contained in the first line of the request, e.g., GET or POST.

getPathInfo

```
public String getPathInfo()
```

Returns the substring of the request URL that follows the servlet name, or `null` if there is no additional path information. Same as the CGI variable PATH_INFO.

getPathTranslated

```
public String getPathTranslated()
```

Returns the substring of the request URL that follows the servlet name converted to a real filesystem path, or `null` if there is no additional path information. Same as the CGI variable PATH_TRANSLATED.

getQueryString

```
public String getQueryString()
```

Returns the substring of the request URL that follows the "?", or null if there is no query string. Usually found only in GET requests. Same as the CGI variable QUERY_STRING.

getRemoteUser

```
public String getRemoteUser()
```

Returns the user name if HTTP authentication is active and the user had logged in. Returns null otherwise. Same as the CGI variable REMOTE_USER.

getRequestedSessionId

```
public String getRequestedSessionId()
```

Returns the value of the session ID returned by the client. Usually the same as the current session, but may refer to an old expired session. Returns null if the request does not specify a session ID.

getRequestURI

```
public String getRequestURI()
```

Returns the substring of the request URL starting with the protocol name (e.g., http://) if present, and extending to but not including the query string (which starts with "?").

getRequestURL

```
public StringBuffer getRequestURL()
```

Reconstructs the entire URL used for the request. Includes the protocol, server name, port number (if other than the default), and filename. Does not include the query string.

getServletPath

```
public String getServletPath()
```

Returns the part of this request's URL that calls the servlet. This includes either the servlet name or a path to the servlet but does not include any extra path information or a query string. Same as the value of the CGI variable SCRIPT_NAME.

getSession

```
public HttpSession getSession()
```

A convenience method that returns the value of `HttpSession.getSession(true)`.

getSession

```
public HttpSession getSession(boolean create)
```

Returns the current `HttpSession` object or creates a new one (if the create parameter is true). The returned value depends on whether the session already exists and whether the create parameter is true or false.

getUserPrincipal

```
public Principal getUserPrincipal()
```

If the user has been authenticated, returns a `java.security.Principal` object for the user. Otherwise, the method returns `null`.

isRequestedSessionIdFromCookie

```
public boolean isRequestedSessionIdFromCookie()
```

Returns true if the request session ID was received from a Cookie as opposed to being sent as part of the request URL.

[deprecated] isRequestedSessionIdFromUrl

```
public boolean isRequestedSessionIdFromUrl()
```

Returns the value of the deprecated isRequestedSessionIdFromUrl() method on the wrapped request object.

isRequestedSessionIdFromURL

```
public boolean isRequestedSessionIdFromURL()
```

Returns true if the requested session ID came in as part of the request URL as opposed to being sent from a Cookie.

isRequestedSessionIdValid

```
public boolean isRequestedSessionIdValid()
```

Returns true if the request specifies the ID of a valid, active session.

isUserInRole

```
public boolean isUserInRole(String role)
```

Returns true if the authenticated user is included in the specified logical "role" in the deployment descriptor.

HttpServletResponse

Full Name:	javax.servlet.http.HttpServletResponse
Type:	Interface
Superinterface:	javax.servlet.ServletResponse

Encapsulates all information about the response generated for an HTTP request, including response headers, the status code, and the output stream.

Methods

addCookie

```
public void addCookie(Cookie cookie)
```

Writes a Set-Cookie header for the specified cookie.

addDateHeader

```
public void addDateHeader(String name, long date)
```

Writes a date header for an HTTP header that can have multiple values.

addHeader

```
public void addHeader(String name, String value)
```

Writes a general header for an HTTP header that can have multiple values.

addIntHeader

```
public void addIntHeader(String name, int value)
```

Writes an integer header for an HTTP header that can have multiple values.

containsHeader

```
public boolean containsHeader(String name)
```

Returns true if the response already contains a header with the specified name.

[deprecated] encodeRedirectUrl

```
public String encodeRedirectUrl(String url)
```

No longer supported. Use encodeRedirectURL() instead.

encodeRedirectURL

```
public String encodeRedirectURL(String url)
```

Supports session tracking by optionally appending the encoded session ID as a parameter in a URL intended to be used with `sendRedirect()`. This is not necessary if the client supports cookies. The servlet container makes this determination; it is always safe to filter URLs to be written through this method.

[deprecated] encodeUrl

```
public String encodeUrl(String url)
```

No longer supported. Use `encodeURL()` instead.

encodeURL

```
public String encodeURL(String url)
```

Supports session tracking by appending the encoded session ID as a parameter in the specified URL, if necessary. This is not necessary if the client supports cookies. The servlet container makes this determination; it is always safe to filter URLs to be written through this method.

sendError

```
public void sendError(int sc) throws IOException
```

Sets the HTTP status code to the specified value. The response object is committed after this method is called; any further writing to it has no effect.

sendError

```
public void sendError(int sc, String msg) throws IOException
```

Sets the HTTP status code to the specified value and sets the status message. The response object is committed after this method is called; any further writing to it has no effect.

sendRedirect

```
public void sendRedirect(String location) throws IOException
```

Sets the HTTP status code to 302 (moved temporarily) and writes a `Location` header with the specified value. The user agent (Web browser) will usually interpret this response and request the new URL automatically.

setDateHeader

```
public void setDateHeader(String name, long date)
```

Writes a response header with the specified name and a correctly formatted date value.

setHeader

```
public void setHeader(String name, String value)
```

Writes a response header with the specified name and value.

setIntHeader

```
public void setIntHeader(String name, int value)
```

Writes a response header with the specified name and a string-formatted integer value.

setStatus

```
public void setStatus(int sc)
```

Sets the status code for this response.

[deprecated] setStatus

```
public void setStatus(int sc, String sm)
```

No longer supported.

HttpServletResponseWrapper

Full Name:	javax.servlet.http.HttpServletResponseWrapper
Type:	Class
Extends:	javax.servlet.ServletResponseWrapper
Implements:	javax.servlet.http.HttpServletResponse

A concrete implementation of HttpServletResponse that can be extended to allow customization of the response object. By default, methods in this class look through to their counterparts in the servlet container's implementation class.

Constructors

HttpServletResponseWrapper

```
public HttpServletResponseWrapper(
    HttpServletResponse response)
```

Creates a response adapter wrapping the specified response.

Methods

addCookie

```
public void addCookie(Cookie cookie)
```

Writes a Set-Cookie header for the specified cookie.

addDateHeader

```
public void addDateHeader(String name, long date)
```

Writes a date header for an HTTP header that can have multiple values.

addHeader

```
public void addHeader(String name, String value)
```

Writes a general header for an HTTP header that can have multiple values.

addIntHeader

```
public void addIntHeader(String name, int value)
```

Writes an integer header for an HTTP header that can have multiple values.

containsHeader

```
public boolean containsHeader(String name)
```

Returns true if the response already contains a header with the specified name.

encodeRedirectUrl

```
public String encodeRedirectUrl(String url)
```

No longer supported. Use encodeRedirectURL instead.

encodeRedirectURL

```
public String encodeRedirectURL(String url)
```

Supports session tracking by optionally appending the encoded session ID as a parameter in a URL intended to be used with sendRedirect(). This is not necessary if the client supports cookies. The servlet container makes this determination; it is always safe to filter URLs to be written through this method.

encodeUrl

```
public String encodeUrl(String url)
```

No longer supported. Use encodeURL() instead.

encodeURL

```
public String encodeURL(String url)
```

Supports session tracking by appending the encoded session ID as a parameter in the specified URL, if necessary. This is not necessary if the client supports cookies. The servlet container makes this determination; it is always safe to filter URLs to be written through this method.

sendError

```
public void sendError(int sc) throws IOException
```

Sets the HTTP status code to the specified value. The response object is committed after this method is called; any further writing to it has no effect.

sendError

```
public void sendError(int sc, String msg) throws IOException
```

Sets the HTTP status code to the specified value and sets the status message. The response object is committed after this method is called; any further writing to it has no effect.

sendRedirect

```
public void sendRedirect(String location) throws IOException
```

Sets the HTTP status code to 302 (moved temporarily) and writes a Location header with the specified value. The user agent (Web browser) will usually interpret this response and request the new URL automatically.

setDateHeader

```
public void setDateHeader(String name, long date)
```

Writes a response header with the specified name and a correctly formatted date value.

setHeader

```
public void setHeader(String name, String value)
```

Writes a response header with the specified name and value.

setIntHeader

```
public void setIntHeader(String name, int value)
```

Writes a response header with the specified name and a string-formatted integer value.

setStatus

```
public void setStatus(int sc)
```

Sets the status code for this response.

[deprecated] setStatus

```
public void setStatus(int sc, String sm)
```

Invokes the deprecated `setStatus(int sc, String sm)` method in the servlet container–specific class.

HttpSession

Full Name:	`javax.servlet.http.HttpSession`
Type:	Interface

An `HttpSession` is a repository of named references to objects belonging to a user's browser session. This repository remains active in the server between user requests. A session has a unique session ID assigned by the server that the client keeps track of and passes back with each subsequent request. A session is created by calling the `HttpServletRequest.getSession(true)` or `HttpServletRequest .getSession()` method. The session ID is then passed to the client either by a cookie or as a parameter in a generated URL. The session is considered "new" until the client joins it, that is, until the client passes back the session ID in a subsequent request. The `isNew()` method can be used to determine this. Objects are stored in the session using the `setAttribute()` method and can be retrieved with `getAttribute()`. If an object in a session implements the `HttpSessionBindingListener` interface, it will be notified whenever it is bound to or unbound from a session.

Methods

getAttribute

```
public Object getAttribute(String name)
```

Returns the object with the specified name if it exists in the session, or `null` if it does not.

getAttributeNames

```
public Enumeration getAttributeNames()
```

Returns an `Enumeration` of the names of all the objects bound to this session.

getCreationTime

```
public long getCreationTime()
```

Returns the time the session was created in milliseconds from January 1, 1970.

getId

```
public String getId()
```

Returns the session identifier.

getLastAccessedTime

```
public long getLastAccessedTime()
```

Returns the time the session was last accessed in milliseconds from January 1, 1970.

getMaxInactiveInterval

```
public int getMaxInactiveInterval()
```

Returns the maximum number of seconds this session can remain active between requests. If the time interval is exceeded, the servlet container is permitted to terminate it.

getServletContext

```
public ServletContext getServletContext()
```

Returns the servlet context this session belongs to.

[deprecated] getSessionContext

```
public HttpSessionContext getSessionContext()
```

No longer supported.

[deprecated] getValue

```
public Object getValue(String name)
```

No longer supported.

[deprecated] getValueNames

```
public String getValueNames()
```

No longer supported.

invalidate

```
public void invalidate()
```

Closes the session, calling `valueUnbound()` for any `HttpSessionBindingListener` objects bound to the session.

isNew

```
public boolean isNew()
```

Returns true if a session has been created but the client has not yet issued a request with that session ID.

logout

```
public void logout()
```

Logs the user out of the Web server and invalidates all of this user's sessions.

[deprecated] putValue

```
public void putValue(String name, Object value)
```

No longer supported.

removeAttribute

```
public void removeAttribute(String name)
```

Removes a reference to an object in the session with the specified name. If the object implements the HttpSessionBindingListener interface, the servlet container calls its valueUnbound() method. Ignored if the specified value does not exist in the session.

[deprecated] removeValue

```
public void removeValue(String name)
```

No longer supported.

setAttribute

```
public void setAttribute(String name, Object value)
```

Stores a reference to an object in the session under the specified name. If the object implements the HttpSessionBindingListener interface, the servlet container calls its valueBound() method.

setMaxInactiveInterval

```
public void setMaxInactiveInterval(int interval)
```

Specifies the maximum number of seconds this session can remain active between requests. If the time interval is exceeded, the servlet container is permitted to terminate it.

HttpSessionActivationListener

Full Name:	javax.servlet.http.HttpSessionActivationListener
Type:	Interface
Superinterface:	java.util.EventListener

Objects can register to receive notification of session activation and passivation events by implementing this interface.

Methods

sessionDidActivate

```
public void sessionDidActivate(HttpSessionEvent se)
```

Will be called when the session has just been activated.

sessionWillPassivate

```
public void sessionWillPassivate(HttpSessionEvent se)
```

Will be called when the session is about to be passivated.

HttpSessionAttributeListener

Full Name:	javax.servlet.http.HttpSessionAttributeListener
Type:	Interface
Superinterface:	java.util.EventListener

Objects can register to receive notification of attribute add/remove events by implementing this interface. This is similar in concept to the HttpSessionBindingListener except that the object being bound to the session does not implement the interface. Instead, a class implementing this interface will get notification for all objects being bound or unbound.

Methods

attributeAdded

```
public void attributeAdded(HttpSessionBindingEvent se)
```

Will be called when an attribute has been added to a session.

attributeRemoved

```
public void attributeRemoved(HttpSessionBindingEvent se)
```

Will be called when an attribute has been removed from a session.

APPENDIX

attributeReplaced

```
public void attributeReplaced(HttpSessionBindingEvent se)
```

Will be called when an attribute has been replaced in a session.

HttpSessionBindingEvent

Full Name:	`javax.servlet.http.HttpSessionBindingEvent`
Type:	Class
Extends:	`javax.servlet.http.HttpSessionEvent`

An event object that is passed as a parameter to the `valueBound()` and `valueUnbound()` methods of an `HttpSessionBindingListener`. Using methods in the event object, the `HttpSessionBindingListener` can get the name by which it was bound and a reference to the `HttpSession` itself.

Constructors

HttpSessionBindingEvent

```
public HttpSessionBindingEvent(
    HttpSession session,
    String name)
```

Creates a new `HttpSessionBindingEvent` object for the specified session. The name parameter indicates the name by which the listening object was bound to the session.

HttpSessionBindingEvent

```
public HttpSessionBindingEvent(
    HttpSession session,
    String name,
    Object value)
```

Creates a new `HttpSessionBindingEvent` object for the specified session. The name parameter indicates the name by which the listening object was bound to the session, and the value parameter contains its value.

Methods

getName

```
public String getName()
```

Returns the name by which the object is known to the session.

getSession

```
public HttpSession getSession()
```

Returns the session to which the listener object was bound or unbound.

getValue

```
public Object getValue()
```

Returns the value of the attribute being added, changed, or deleted.

HttpSessionBindingListener

Full Name:	`javax.servlet.http.HttpSessionBindingListener`
Type:	Interface
Superinterface:	`java.util.EventListener`

Objects that implement this interface are notified when they are bound to or unbound from an HttpSession. The object must provide `valueBound()` and `valueUnbound()` methods, each of which have a `HttpSessionBindingEvent` parameter that allows the object to determine its name and the session to which it belongs.

Methods

valueBound

```
public void valueBound(HttpSessionBindingEvent event)
```

Called when an object is bound to a session.

valueUnbound

```
public void valueUnbound(HttpSessionBindingEvent event)
```

Called when an object is unbound from a session.

[deprecated] HttpSessionContext

Full Name:	`javax.servlet.http.HttpSessionContext`
Type:	Interface

For security reasons, this interface is no longer supported. The servlet specification says that it will definitely be removed in some later version.

Methods

[deprecated] getIds

```
public Enumeration getIds()
```

No longer supported.

[deprecated] getSession

```
public HttpSession getSession(String sessionId)
```

No longer supported.

HttpSessionEvent

Full Name:	`javax.servlet.http.HttpSessionEvent`
Type:	Class
Extends:	`java.util.EventObject`

Represents an event notification for changes to sessions in a Web application.

Constructors

HttpSessionEvent

```
public HttpSessionEvent(HttpSession source)
```

Creates a new session event from the specified source.

Methods

getSession

```
public HttpSession getSession()
```

Returns a reference to the session that changed.

HttpSessionListener

Full Name:	`javax.servlet.http.HttpSessionListener`
Type:	Interface
Superinterface:	`java.util.EventListener`

Classes that implement `HttpSessionListener` receive notification when sessions are created or invalidated.

Methods

sessionCreated

```
public void sessionCreated(HttpSessionEvent se)
```

Called when a new session is created.

sessionDestroyed

```
public void sessionDestroyed(HttpSessionEvent se)
```

Called when a session is invalidated.

[deprecated] HttpUtils

Full Name:	javax.servlet.http.HttpUtils
Type:	Class

A utility class providing methods useful in HTTP servlets. Deprecated since Servlet 2.3 because all the functionality is available in the servlet request classes.

Constructors

[deprecated] HttpUtils

```
public HttpUtils()
```

Creates a new HttpUtils object.

Methods

[deprecated] getRequestURL

```
public static StringBuffer getRequestURL(
    HttpServletRequest req)
```

Returns the entire URL used for the specified request. Includes the protocol, server name, port number (if other than the default), and filename. Does not include the query string.

[deprecated] parsePostData

```
public static Hashtable parsePostData(
    int len,
    ServletInputStream in)
```

Reads the servlet request input stream for the specified length and parses it into key/value pairs by calling parseQueryString().

[deprecated] parseQueryString

```
public static Hashtable parseQueryString(String s)
```

Given a query string containing URL-encoded parameters and values, returns a `Hashtable` containing the parsed names and values. In the hashtable, the parameter name is the key and the corresponding value is an array of strings. If the parameter occurs only once, the array length is one; otherwise, there are multiple entries in the array. See `java.net.URLEncoder` for specifics of how the decoding is done.

Package javax.servlet.jsp

This package contains classes and interfaces that define the relationship between the servlet generated from a JSP page and the JSP container in which it runs. For the most part, these classes are of interest only to JSP container developers, not JSP developers per se.

ErrorData

| Full Name: | javax.servlet.jsp.ErrorData |
| Type: | Class |

Supplies error information to an error page.

Constructors

ErrorData

```
public ErrorData(
    Throwable throwable,
    int statusCode,
    String uri,
    String servletName)
```

Creates a new `ErrorData` object with the specified exception, status code, request URI, and servlet name.

Methods

getRequestURI

```
public String getRequestURI()
```

Returns the request URI.

getServletName

```
public String getServletName()
```

Returns the servlet name.

getStatusCode

```
public int getStatusCode()
```

Returns the error status code.

getThrowable

```
public Throwable getThrowable()
```

Returns the root cause exception.

HttpJspPage

Full Name:	javax.servlet.jsp.HttpJspPage
Type:	Interface
Superinterface:	javax.servlet.jsp.JspPage

A subinterface of JspPage that is implemented by HTTP-specific classes generated by a JSP container. The JSP container will automatically create a _jspService() method that contains all the scriptlet code defined in the page. The JSP author should not override this method.

Methods

_jspService

```
public void _jspService(
   HttpServletRequest request,
   HttpServletResponse response)
throws ServletException, IOException
```

The body of the JSP page. The JSP author must not define this method, since it will be defined by the servlet code generated by the JSP container. _jspService() is where scriptlets are executed and where HTML template output is produced.

JspContext

Full Name:	`javax.servlet.jsp.JspContext`
Type:	Abstract class

An abstract base class that provides implementation for page context methods that are not specifically servlet-oriented.

Constructors

JspContext

```
public JspContext()
```

Creates a new `JspContext`.

Methods

findAttribute

```
public abstract Object findAttribute(String name)
```

Searches for the specified attribute in page, request, session, and application scope in that order and returns the value found or `null`.

getAttribute

```
public abstract Object getAttribute(String name)
```

Returns the attribute with the specified name.

getAttribute

```
public abstract Object getAttribute(String name, int scope)
```

Return the object having the specified name in the specified scope.

getAttributeNamesInScope

```
public abstract Enumeration getAttributeNamesInScope(
    int scope)
```

Enumerates the names of all the attributes in a given scope.

getAttributesScope

```
public abstract int getAttributesScope(String name)
```

Returns the scope where a specified attribute is defined.

getExpressionEvaluator

```
public abstract ExpressionEvaluator getExpressionEvaluator()
```

Returns an instance of an `ExpressionEvaluator`.

getOut

```
public abstract JspWriter getOut()
```

The current value of the out object (a `JspWriter`).

getVariableResolver

```
public abstract VariableResolver getVariableResolver()
```

Returns a `VariableResolver` that provides access to the implicit objects in this JSP context.

removeAttribute

```
public abstract void removeAttribute(String name)
```

Remove the attribute associated with the given name, looking in all scopes in the usual order.

removeAttribute

```
public abstract void removeAttribute(String name, int scope)
```

Remove the attribute having the specified name in the given scope.

setAttribute

```
public abstract void setAttribute(
    String name,
    Object attribute)
```

Sets the specified page attribute.

setAttribute

```
public abstract void setAttribute(
    String name,
    Object o,
    int scope)
```

Sets the specified attribte in one of the four scopes: application, session, request, or page.

JspEngineInfo

Full Name:	`javax.servlet.jsp.JspEngineInfo`
Type:	Abstract class

A class that provides information about the JSP container. An instance of this class is returned by the `JspFactory.getEngineInfo()` method. This class is designed primarily for use by JSP container developers.

Constructors

JspEngineInfo

```
public JspEngineInfo()
```

Creates a new `JspEngineInfo`.

Methods

getSpecificationVersion

```
public abstract String getSpecificationVersion()
```

Returns the JSP specification version supported by the JSP container.

JspException

Full Name:	`javax.servlet.jsp.JspException`
Type:	Class
Extends:	`java.lang.Exception`

The generic base class for JSP exceptions. A number of methods in the custom tags classes throw this exception.

Constructors

JspException

```
public JspException()
```

Creates a new `JspException` with no associated error message.

JspException

```
public JspException(String msg)
```

Creates a new `JspException` with the specified message.

JspException

```
public JspException(String message, Throwable rootCause)
```

Creates a new `JspException` with the specified message and associates the specified root cause exception with it.

JspException

```
public JspException(Throwable rootCause)
```

Creates a new `JspException` associated with the specified root cause exception.

Methods

getRootCause

```
public Throwable getRootCause()
```

Returns the exception that caused this `JspException`.

JspFactory

Full Name:	`javax.servlet.jsp.JspFactory`
Type:	Abstract class

A class that provides factory methods for creating the objects necessary to support the JSP environment. Includes a static method for assigning the default `JspFactory`.

Note | *This class is designed primarily for use by JSP container developers.*

Constructors

JspFactory

```
public JspFactory()
```

Creates a new `JspFactory`.

Methods

getDefaultFactory

```
public static synchronized JspFactory getDefaultFactory()
```

Returns the currently registered `JspFactory` object.

getEngineInfo

```
public abstract JspEngineInfo getEngineInfo()
```

Returns the `JspEngineInfo` object for this JSP implementation.

getPageContext

```
public abstract PageContext getPageContext(
    Servlet servlet,
    ServletRequest request,
    ServletResponse response,
    String errorPageURL,
    boolean needsSession,
    int buffer,
    boolean autoflush)
```

Returns the PageContext object. Calling this method causes the PageContext
.initialize() method to be invoked and causes the following attributes to be set:

- The requesting servlet
- The ServletConfig object for the requesting servlet
- The ServletRequest object
- The ServletResponse object
- The URL of the JSP's error page, if one was specified
- Whether the JSP needs an HTTP session
- The buffer size
- Whether the buffer should be autoflushed on overflow.

These resources are released when the releasePageContext() method is called.

 A call to this method is automatically generated by the JSP container and should not be coded by the JSP author.

releasePageContext

```
public abstract void releasePageContext(PageContext pc)
```

Releases the PageContext, including any resources obtained when
getPageContext() was invoked.

 A call to this method is automatically generated by the JSP container and should not be coded by the JSP author.

setDefaultFactory

```
public static synchronized void setDefaultFactory(
    JspFactory deflt)
```

Sets the default `JspFactory` object. Should be called only by the JSP container itself.

JspPage

Full Name:	`javax.servlet.jsp.JspPage`
Type:	Interface
Superinterface:	`javax.servlet.Servlet`

A subinterface of `Servlet` that is implemented by classes generated by a JSP container. The `jspInit()` and `jspDestroy()` methods can be overridded by the JSP author to perform what the `Servlet init()` and `destroy()` methods do.

Methods

jspDestroy

```
public void jspDestroy()
```

A method invoked when the generated JSP servlet is destroyed. If used, it must be defined within a JSP declaration. This method should be overridden instead of `destroy()`.

jspInit

```
public void jspInit()
```

A method invoked when the generated JSP servlet is initialized. If used, it must be defined within a JSP declaration. This method should be overridden instead of `init()`.

JspTagException

Full Name:	javax.servlet.jsp.JspTagException
Type:	Class
Extends:	javax.servlet.jsp.JspException

A subinterface of JspException used in tag handlers to indicate a fatal error.

Constructors

JspTagException

```
public JspTagException()
```

Creates a new JspTagException with no associated message.

JspTagException

```
public JspTagException(String msg)
```

Creates a new JspTagException with the specified message.

JspTagException

```
public JspTagException(String message, Throwable rootCause)
```

Creates a new JspTagException with the specified detail message and root cause exception.

JspTagException

```
public JspTagException(Throwable rootCause)
```

Creates a new JspTagException with the specified root cause exception.

Methods
None

JspWriter

Full Name:	`javax.servlet.jsp.JspWriter`
Type:	Abstract class
Extends:	`java.io.Writer`

A subclass of `java.io.Writer` that is used to write JSP output. Its role is primarily the same as `java.io.PrintWriter`. This class is instantiated by the generated `_jspService()` by calling the underlying servlet's `getWriter()` method, which makes it illegal later to call `getOutputStream()`. The out implicit variable is an instance of this class.

Methods

clear

```
public abstract void clear() throws IOException
```

Clears the page buffer. Throws an `IOException` if the buffer has already been cleared (i.e., if a full buffer of data has already been written to the output stream).

clearBuffer

```
public abstract void clearBuffer() throws IOException
```

Clears the page buffer. Does not throw an `IOException`.

close

```
public abstract void close() throws IOException
```

Flushes and closes the stream.

flush

```
public abstract void flush() throws IOException
```

Flushes the output stream.

getBufferSize

```
public int getBufferSize()
```

Returns the actual buffer size used.

getRemaining

```
public abstract int getRemaining()
```

Returns the number of unused bytes remaining in the buffer.

isAutoFlush

```
public boolean isAutoFlush()
```

Returns an indication of whether the JSP autoFlush flag is set.

newLine

```
public abstract void newLine() throws IOException
```

Writes the System line.separator string.

print

```
public abstract void print(boolean b) throws IOException
```

Prints a boolean value.

print

```
public abstract void print(char c) throws IOException
```

Prints a character.

print

```
public abstract void print(char s) throws IOException
```

Prints an array of characters.

print

```
public abstract void print(double d) throws IOException
```

Prints a double-precision floating-point value.

print

```
public abstract void print(float f) throws IOException
```

Prints a floating-point value.

print

```
public abstract void print(int i) throws IOException
```

Prints an integer value.

print

```
public abstract void print(long l) throws IOException
```

Prints a long integer value.

print

```
public abstract void print(Object obj) throws IOException
```

Prints an object using its `toString()` method.

print

```
public abstract void print(String s) throws IOException
```

Prints a string.

println

```
public abstract void println() throws IOException
```

Prints the System `line.separator` character(s).

println

```
public abstract void println(boolean x) throws IOException
```

Prints a boolean value followed by a newline.

println

```
public abstract void println(char x) throws IOException
```

Prints a character value followed by a newline.

println

```
public abstract void println(char x) throws IOException
```

Prints an array of characters followed by a newline.

println

```
public abstract void println(double x) throws IOException
```

Prints a double-precision floating-point number followed by a newline.

println

```
public abstract void println(float x) throws IOException
```

Prints a single-precision floating-point number followed by a newline.

println

```
public abstract void println(int x) throws IOException
```

Prints an integer followed by a newline.

println

```
public abstract void println(long x) throws IOException
```

Prints a long integer followed by a newline.

println

```
public abstract void println(Object x) throws IOException
```

Prints an object followed by a newline.

println

```
public abstract void println(String x) throws IOException
```

Prints a string followed by a newline.

PageContext

Full Name:	`javax.servlet.jsp.PageContext`
Type:	Abstract class
Extends:	`javax.servlet.jsp.JspContext`

`PageContext` is a wrapper object that encapsulates all the details of a single invocation of a JSP to handle a request. It contains methods to initialize and release the session, writer, request, and response objects. It also provides methods to set and retrieve attributes in the various namespaces accessible to the JSP. A `PageContext` object is created and initialized by the `JSPFactory` when its `getPageContext()` method is called and released when its `releasePageContext()` is called. These two method calls are automatically performed by code generated by the JSP container.

Constructors

PageContext

```
public PageContext()
```

Creates a new `PageContext`.

Methods

forward

```
public abstract void forward(String relativeUrlPath)
    throws ServletException, IOException
```

Calls the `forward()` method associated with a `RequestDispatcher` for this servlet. See `javax.servlet.RequestDispatcher` for details.

getErrorData

```
public ErrorData getErrorData()
```

Constructs and returns a new `ErrorData` object for the exception thrown by this page.

getException

```
public abstract Exception getException()
```

Returns the `Exception` object passed to an `ErrorPage`.

getPage

```
public abstract Object getPage()
```

Returns the servlet associated with this `PageContext`.

getRequest

```
public abstract ServletRequest getRequest()
```

Returns the `ServletRequest` associated with this `PageContext`.

getResponse

```
public abstract ServletResponse getResponse()
```

Returns the `ServletResponse` associated with this `PageContext`.

getServletConfig

```
public abstract ServletConfig getServletConfig()
```

Returns the `ServletConfig` associated with this `PageContext`.

getServletContext

```
public abstract ServletContext getServletContext()
```

Returns the `ServletContext` associated with this `PageContext`.

getSession

```
public abstract HttpSession getSession()
```

Returns the HttpSession for this request or null if no session exists.

handlePageException

```
public abstract void handlePageException(Exception e)
    throws ServletException, IOException
```

Used to process an unhandled exceptions thrown by the current page. Calls the ErrorPage if one is active.

 Although this method is not deprecated, handlePageException(Throwable t) is more general and should be used instead of this method.

handlePageException

```
public abstract void handlePageException(Throwable t)
    throws ServletException, IOException
```

Used to process an unhandled exceptions thrown by the current page. Calls the ErrorPage if one is active.

include

```
public abstract void include(String relativeUrlPath)
    throws ServletException, IOException
```

Calls the include() method associated with a RequestDispatcher for this servlet. See javax.servlet.RequestDispatcher for details.

include

```
public abstract void include(
    String relativeUrlPath,
    boolean flush)
throws ServletException, IOException
```

Calls the include() method associated with a RequestDispatcher for this servlet, passing it the specified flush attribute. See javax.servlet.RequestDispatcher for details.

initialize

```
public abstract void initialize(
    Servlet servlet,
    ServletRequest request,
    ServletResponse response,
    String errorPageURL,
    boolean needsSession,
    int bufferSize,
    boolean autoFlush)
throws IOException
```

Stores the `servlet, request, response, errorPageURL, needsSession, bufferSize,` and `autoFlush` attributes and makes the appropriate implicit variables available to the JSP. This method is called by the `getPageContext()` method and should not be called directly by the JSP author.

popBody

```
public JspWriter popBody()
```

Restores the `JspWriter` saved by the previous `pushBody()`, and updates the out implicit variable and the value of the `PageContext` "out" attribute.

pushBody

```
public BodyContent pushBody()
```

Saves the current `JspWriter` and creates a new `BodyContent` object, making it the value of the `PageContext` "out" attribute and the `out` implicit variable.

release

```
public abstract void release()
```

Performs the opposite of initialize, releasing the `PageContext` and the resources it acquired. This method is called by the `releasePageContext()` method and should not be called directly by the JSP author.

SkipPageException

Full Name:	`javax.servlet.jsp.SkipPageException`
Type:	Class
Extends:	`javax.servlet.jsp.JspException`

A subclass of `JspException` thrown by a simple tag handler to inform the calling page that an error occurred and the rest of the page should not be evaluated.

Constructors

SkipPageException

```
public SkipPageException()
```

Creates a new `SkipPageException`.

SkipPageException

```
public SkipPageException(String message)
```

Creates a new `SkipPageException` with the specified message.

SkipPageException

```
public SkipPageException(
   String message,
   Throwable rootCause)
```

Creates a new `SkipPageException` with the specified message and root cause exception.

SkipPageException

```
public SkipPageException(Throwable rootCause)
```

Creates a new `SkipPageException` with the specified root cause exception.

Methods
None

Package javax.servlet.jsp.el

This package contains classes and interfaces that provide programmatic access to the Expression Language evaluator.

ELException

Full Name:	javax.servlet.jsp.el.ELException
Type:	Class
Extends:	java.lang.Exception

Thrown when an error occurs during operation evaluation.

Constructors

ELException

```
public ELException()
```

Creates a new ELException with no detail message.

ELException

```
public ELException(String pMessage)
```

Creates a new ELException with the specified detail message.

ELException

```
public ELException(String pMessage, Throwable pRootCause)
```

Creates a new ELException with the specified detail message and root cause exception.

ELException

```
public ELException(Throwable pRootCause)
```

Creates a new ELException with the specified root cause exception.

Methods

getRootCause

```
public Throwable getRootCause()
```

Returns the root cause exception.

toString

```
public String toString()
```

Returns the exception as a formatted string.

ELParseException

Full Name:	javax.servlet.jsp.el.ELParseException
Type:	Class
Extends:	javax.servlet.jsp.el.ELException

An ELException thrown because of a parsing error.

Constructors

ELParseException

```
public ELParseException()
```

Creates a new exception with no detail message.

ELParseException

```
public ELParseException(String pMessage)
```

Creates a new exception with the specified detail message.

Methods
None

Expression

Full Name:	`javax.servlet.jsp.el.Expression`
Type:	Interface

An interface that represents a prepared expression, typically obtained from an `ExpressionEvaluator`.

Methods

evaluate

```
public Object evaluate(VariableResolver vResolver)
    throws ELException
```

Evaluates the specified expression and returns the result.

ExpressionEvaluator

Full Name:	`javax.servlet.jsp.el.ExpressionEvaluator`
Type:	Interface

An interface that specifies the two methods that must be implemented by an expression language evaluator.

Methods

evaluate

```
public Object evaluate(
    String expression,
    Class expectedType,
    VariableResolver vResolver,
    FunctionMapper fMapper,
    String defaultPrefix)
throws ELException
```

Parses and evaluates the string representation of an expression having the specified expected return type, a mapper to resolve any functions, a runtime variable resolver, and a default prefix used for functions with no prefix. Returns the object resulting from the evaluation.

parseExpression

```
public Expression parseExpression(
    String expression,
    Class expectedType,
    FunctionMapper fMapper,
    String defaultPrefix)
throws ELException
```

Parses and validates the string representation of an expression having the specified expected return type, a mapper to resolve any functions, and a default prefix used for functions with no prefix. Returns the Expression object constructed from the string.

FunctionMapper

Full Name: javax.servlet.jsp.el.FunctionMapper

Type: Interface

An interface that maps function names to Method objects.

Methods

resolveFunction

```
public Method resolveFunction(
    String prefix,
    String localName)
```

Given a function prefix and function name, returns the Method object that performs the function's operation.

VariableResolver

Full Name: javax.servlet.jsp.el.VariableResolver

Type: Interface

An interface that allows an ExpressionEvaluator's default variable resolver to be overridden.

Methods

resolveVariable

```
public Object resolveVariable(String pName, Object pContext)
    throws ELException
```

Resolves the specified variable in the specified context.

Package javax.servlet.jsp.tagext

This package contains classes and interfaces that support development of JSP tag extensions. In general, they outline the tag lifecycle, defining callback methods that can be implemented to interpret, validate, and execute custom actions.

BodyContent

Full Name:	javax.servlet.jsp.tagext.BodyContent
Type:	Abstract class
Extends:	javax.servlet.jsp.JspWriter

BodyContent is a subclass of javax.servlet.jsp.JspWriter but differs from its superclass in that its contents aren't automatically written to the servlet output stream. Instead, they're accumulated in what amounts to a string buffer. After the tag body is completed, the original JspWriter is restored, but the BodyContent object is still available in doEndTag() in the bodyContent variable. Its contents can be retrieved with its getString() or getReader() methods, modified as necessary, and written to the restored JspWriter output stream to be merged with the page output.

Methods

clearBody

```
public void clearBody()
```

Resets the BodyContent buffer to empty. This can be useful if the body is being written to the enclosing writer in doAfterBody().

flush

```
public void flush() throws IOException
```

Overrides the `JspWriter.flush()` method so that it always throws an exception. Flushing a `BodyContent` writer isn't valid because it isn't connected to an actual output stream to which it could be written.

getEnclosingWriter

```
public JspWriter getEnclosingWriter()
```

Returns the writer object (possibly another `BodyContent`) next higher in the stack.

getReader

```
public abstract Reader getReader()
```

Returns a reader for the body content after it has been evaluated. This reader can be passed to other classes that can process a `java.io.Reader`, such as `StreamTokenizer`, `FilterReader`, or an XML parser.

getString

```
public abstract String getString()
```

Returns a string containing the body content after it has been evaluated.

writeOut

```
public abstract void writeOut(Writer out) throws IOException
```

Writes the body content to the specified output writer.

BodyTag

Full Name:	`javax.servlet.jsp.tagext.BodyTag`
Type:	Interface
Superinterface:	`javax.servlet.jsp.tagext.IterationTag`

An extension of the `IterationTag` interface that adds new methods having to do with body handling.

Methods

doInitBody

```
public void doInitBody() throws JspException
```

A lifecycle method called after setBodyContent(), but just before the body is evaluated. If the body is evaluated multiple times, this method is called only once.

setBodyContent

```
public void setBodyContent(BodyContent b)
```

Invoked by the JSP servlet after the current JspWriter has been pushed and a new BodyContent writer has been created. This occurs just after doStartTag().

BodyTagSupport

Full Name:	javax.servlet.jsp.tagext.BodyTagSupport
Type:	Class
Extends:	javax.servlet.jsp.tagext.TagSupport
Implements:	javax.servlet.jsp.tagext.BodyTag

A useful base class that implements all the methods of BodyTag. Tag handlers can extend BodyTagSupport and override only those methods that need to be changed.

Constructors

BodyTagSupport

```
public BodyTagSupport()
```

Creates a new BodyTagSupport object.

Methods

doAfterBody

```
public int doAfterBody() throws JspException
```

Invoked at the end of each evaluation of the body. Returns `Tag.SKIP_BODY` by default. If you override this method, you should return either `Tag.SKIP_BODY` or `IterationTag.EVAL_BODY_AGAIN`.

doEndTag

```
public int doEndTag() throws JspException
```

Invoked at the end of the scope of a custom tag. Returns EVAL_PAGE by default but can be overridden by an implementation that returns SKIP_PAGE.

doInitBody

```
public void doInitBody() throws JspException
```

A lifecycle method called after `setBodyContent()`, but just before the body is evaluated. If the body is evaluated multiple times, this method is called only once. By default, this implementation does nothing.

doStartTag

```
public int doStartTag() throws JspException
```

See `doStartTag()` in the `Tag` interface. This implementation returns EVAL_BODY_BUFFERED.

getBodyContent

```
public BodyContent getBodyContent()
```

Returns the current `BodyContent`, which is the writer associated with the current `out` variable.

getPreviousOut

```
public JspWriter getPreviousOut()
```

Returns the surrounding `JspWriter`.

release

```
public void release()
```

Releases the tag handler state.

setBodyContent

```
public void setBodyContent(BodyContent b)
```

Stores a reference to the BodyContent object.

DynamicAttributes

Full Name:	javax.servlet.jsp.tagext.DynamicAttributes
Type:	Interface

An interface implemented by tags that accept dynamic attributes. The tag library descriptor must also indicate that the tag accepts dynamic attributes.

Methods

setDynamicAttribute

```
public void setDynamicAttribute(
    String uri,
    String localName,
    Object value)
throws JspException
```

Callback method that is invoked by the Web container when an attribuute not declared in the tag library descriptor is passed to the tag.

FunctionInfo

Full Name:	javax.servlet.jsp.tagext.FunctionInfo
Type:	Class

Wrapper for the name, class, and signature of a function in a tag library descriptor.

Constructors

FunctionInfo

```
public FunctionInfo(
    String name,
```

```
      String klass,
      String signature)
```

Creates a new `FunctionInfo` object with the specified name, class, and signature.

Methods

getFunctionClass

```
public String getFunctionClass()
```

Returns the function class name.

getFunctionSignature

```
public String getFunctionSignature()
```

Returns the function signature.

getName

```
public String getName()
```

Returns the function name.

IterationTag

Full Name:	`javax.servlet.jsp.tagext.IterationTag`
Type:	Interface
Superinterface:	`javax.servlet.jsp.tagext.Tag`

An extension of the `Tag` interface that defines semantics for repeated evaluation of the tag body.

Methods

doAfterBody

```
public int doAfterBody() throws JspException
```

A lifecycle method called after the body has been evaluated, but while the `BodyContent` writer is still active. This method must return either EVAL_BODY_AGAIN or SKIP_BODY. If the return code is EVAL_BODY_AGAIN, the body is evaluated again and `doAfterBody()` is called again.

JspFragment

Full Name:	`javax.servlet.jsp.tagext.JspFragment`
Type:	Interface

Provides support for JSP fragments, which are the body of a SimpleTag or JSP attribute, or blocks of code that are declared as JSP fragments in the tag library descriptor.

Methods

invoke

```
public void invoke(Writer out)
    throws JspException, IOException
```

Runs the JSP fragment, sending its output to the specified writer.

JspTag

Full Name:	`javax.servlet.jsp.tagext.JspTag`
Type:	Interface

A marker interface implemented by `Tag` and `SimpleTag`. This allows tags of all kinds to be identified by a common characteristic. This interface specifies no methods.

Methods
None

PageData

Full Name:	`javax.servlet.jsp.tagext.PageData`
Type:	Abstract class

A class that can be listed in the tag library descriptor as a validator for a JSP page. Provides a method for reading the XML document that corresponds to the JSP page.

Constructors

PageData

```
public PageData()
```

Creates a new `PageData`.

Methods

getInputStream

```
public abstract InputStream getInputStream()
```

Returns an input stream representing the JSP page as an XML document.

SimpleTag

Full Name:	`javax.servlet.jsp.tagext.SimpleTag`
Type:	Interface
Superinterface:	`javax.servlet.jsp.tagext.JspTag`

A simplified version of a tag handler that supports only one lifecycle method: `doTag()`.

Methods

doTag

```
public void doTag() throws JspException, IOException
```

Called by the generated servlet code to perform the tag's function.

getParent

```
public JspTag getParent()
```

Returns the parent tag object.

setJspBody

```
public void setJspBody(JspFragment jspBody)
```

The body of the simple tag is passed here as a `JspFragment` object.

setJspContext

```
public void setJspContext(JspContext pc)
```

Stores the `JspContext` parameter as a protected instance variable.

setParent

```
public void setParent(JspTag parent)
```

Sets the parent tag reference.

SimpleTagSupport

Full Name:	`javax.servlet.jsp.tagext.SimpleTagSupport`
Type:	Class
Implements:	`javax.servlet.jsp.tagext.SimpleTag`

Basic implementation of the `SimpleTag` interface.

Constructors

SimpleTagSupport

```
public SimpleTagSupport()
```

Creates a new `SimpleTagSupport`.

Methods

doTag

```
public void doTag() throws JspException, IOException
```

Invokes the tag handling logic.

findAncestorWithClass

```
public static final JspTag findAncestorWithClass(
    JspTag from,
    Class klass)
```

Looks up the first ancestor of this tag that is of the specified class.

getJspBody

```
public JspFragment getJspBody()
```

Returns the JSP fragment that is the body of this tag.

getJspContext

```
public JspContext getJspContext()
```

Returns the JSP context object.

getParent

```
public JspTag getParent()
```

Returns the parent tag object.

setJspBody

```
public void setJspBody(JspFragment jspBody)
```

Saves the body of the tag as a JspFragment.

setJspContext

```
public void setJspContext(JspContext pc)
```

Stores the provided JSP context in the protected jspContext field.

setParent

```
public void setParent(JspTag parent)
```

Sets the parent tag attribute.

Tag

Full Name:	`javax.servlet.jsp.tagext.Tag`
Type:	Interface
Superinterface:	`javax.servlet.jsp.tagext.JspTag`

A set of lifecycle methods that must be implemented by custom tag handlers.

Methods

doEndTag

```
public int doEndTag() throws JspException
```

Called when the end tag has been encountered. The return code indicates whether the JSP implementation servlet should continue with the rest of the page (EVAL_PAGE) or not (SKIP_PAGE). The method can throw a `JspException` to indicate a fatal error.

doStartTag

```
public int doStartTag() throws JspException
```

Called after the page context, parent, and any attributes coded on the start tag have been set. The return code indicates whether the JSP implementation servlet should evaluate the tag body (EVAL_BODY_INCLUDE or BodyTag.EVAL_BODY_BUFFERED) or not (SKIP_BODY). The method can throw a `JspException` to indicate a fatal error. BodyTag.EVAL_BODY_BUFFERED is valid only if the tag handler implements `BodyTag`.

getParent

```
public Tag getParent()
```

Returns the parent tag (the closest enclosing tag handler), or `null` if there is no parent tag.

release

```
public void release()
```

Guaranteed to be called before page exit. Allows the tag handler to release any resources it holds and reset its state so that it can be reused, if necessary.

setPageContext

```
public void setPageContext(PageContext pc)
```

The generated servlet calls this method first before requiring the handler to do anything else. The implementing class should save the context variable so that it is available at any point in the tag lifecycle. From the page context, the tag handler can access all the JSP implicit objects and can get and set attributes in any scope.

setParent

```
public void setParent(Tag t)
```

Sets the parent tag. Enables a tag handler to find the tag above it in the evaluation stack. Called immediately after `setPageContext()`.

TagAdapter

Full Name:	`javax.servlet.jsp.tagext.TagAdapter`
Type:	Class
Implements:	`javax.servlet.jsp.tagext.Tag`

Provides a wrapper implementation for a `SimpleTag` that makes it operate as a classic `Tag` handler.

Constructors

TagAdapter

```
public TagAdapter(SimpleTag adaptee)
```

Creates a new `TagAdapter` for the specified `SimpleTag`.

Methods

doEndTag

```
public int doEndTag() throws JspException
```

Specified here to satisfy the tag interface, but not designed to be called. Throws an exception if invoked.

doStartTag

```
public int doStartTag() throws JspException
```

Specified here to satisfy the tag interface, but not designed to be called. Throws an exception if invoked.

getAdaptee

```
public JspTag getAdaptee()
```

Returns the simple tag that is wrapped by this adapter.

getParent

```
public Tag getParent()
```

Returns the parent tag object.

release

```
public void release()
```

Specified here to satisfy the tag interface, but not designed to be called. Throws an exception if invoked.

setPageContext

```
public void setPageContext(PageContext pc)
```

Specified here to satisfy the tag interface, but not designed to be called. Throws an exception if invoked.

setParent

```
public void setParent(Tag parentTag)
```

Specified here to satisfy the tag interface, but not designed to be called. Throws an exception if invoked.

TagAttributeInfo

Full Name: javax.servlet.jsp.tagext.TagAttributeInfo

Type: Class

A class providing translation-time information on the attributes of a tag.

Constructors

TagAttributeInfo

```
public TagAttributeInfo(
    String name,
    boolean required,
    String type,
    boolean reqTime)
```

Creates a new TagAttributeInfo. Intended to be called only from code in the TagLibrary object.

TagAttributeInfo

```
public TagAttributeInfo(
    String name,
    boolean required,
    String type,
    boolean reqTime,
    boolean fragment)
```

Creates a new TagAttributeInfo, possibly with a JSP fragment. Intended to be called only from code in the TagLibrary object.

Methods

canBeRequestTime

```
public boolean canBeRequestTime()
```

True if this attribute can hold a request-time value.

APPENDIX

getIdAttribute

```
public static TagAttributeInfo getIdAttribute(
    TagAttributeInfo a)
```

Utility method that searches an array of `TagAttributeInfo` objects for the attribute that is named "id".

getName

```
public String getName()
```

Returns the attribute name.

getTypeName

```
public String getTypeName()
```

Returns the attribute type as a string.

isFragment

```
public boolean isFragment()
```

Returns true if this attribute is for a JSP fragment.

isRequired

```
public boolean isRequired()
```

Returns true if the attribute is required.

toString

```
public String toString()
```

Returns a string representation of the attribute information.

TagData

Full Name:	`javax.servlet.jsp.tagext.TagData`
Type:	Class
Implements:	`java.lang.Cloneable`

Contains translation-time information about the attributes of a tag. Intended for use by JSP containers only.

Constructors

TagData

```
public TagData(Hashtable attrs)
```

Creates a new `TagData` object from a hashtable.

TagData

```
public TagData(Object atts)
```

Creates a new `TagData` object from a two-dimensional array of attribute/value pairs.

Methods

getAttribute

```
public Object getAttribute(String attName)
```

Returns the attribute having the specified name. Can also return REQUEST_TIME_VALUE if the value must be specified at request time, or `null` if the attribute was not specified in the tag.

getAttributes

```
public Enumeration getAttributes()
```

Returns an `Enumeration` of the attributes.

getAttributeString

```
public String getAttributeString(String attName)
```

Returns the attribute's value object in string form.

getId

```
public String getId()
```

Returns the value of the id attribute, if it was specified.

setAttribute

```
public void setAttribute(String attName, Object value)
```

Sets an attribute to the specified value.

TagExtraInfo

Full Name:	javax.servlet.jsp.tagext.TagExtraInfo
Type:	Abstract class

A tag that needs to define variables or perform validation on its attributes must define a class that extends the TagExtraInfo class. This subclass is associated with the custom tag in the tag library descriptor.

Constructors

TagExtraInfo

```
public TagExtraInfo()
```

Creates a new TagExtraInfo.

Methods

getTagInfo

```
public final TagInfo getTagInfo()
```

Returns the TagInfo for this class.

getVariableInfo

```
public VariableInfo getVariableInfo(TagData data)
```

Based on the list of attribute names and values in the data parameter, constructs an array of `VariableInfo` objects that describe the name, type, existence, and scope of each scripting variable to create.

isValid

```
public boolean isValid(TagData data)
```

Returns true if the attributes referred to in the `TagData` parameter are valid.

setTagInfo

```
public final void setTagInfo(TagInfo tagInfo)
```

Supplies the `TagInfo` to this class.

validate

```
public ValidationMessage validate(TagData data)
```

Returns an array of error messages, or `null` if the tag data is valid. By default, there is a single error message that simply says that the tag data is invalid. Subclasses should override this method to provide meaningful behavior.

TagFileInfo

Full Name:	`javax.servlet.jsp.tagext.TagFileInfo`
Type:	Class

Information about a tag file in a tag Library.

Constructors

TagFileInfo

```
public TagFileInfo(
    String name,
```

```
String path,
TagInfo tagInfo)
```

Creates a new `TagFileInfo` object for the specified `.tag` filename, path, and `TagInfo` description object.

Methods

getName

```
public String getName()
```

The action name of this tag.

getPath

```
public String getPath()
```

The path to the `.tag` file that implements this action, relative to either the tag library descriptor or the current directory (for an implicit tag file).

getTagInfo

```
public TagInfo getTagInfo()
```

Returns tag information, based on directives in the `.tag` file.

TagInfo

Full Name:	`javax.servlet.jsp.tagext.TagInfo`
Type:	Class

An object representation of a `Tag` element in the tag library descriptor.

Constructors

TagInfo

```
public TagInfo(
    String tagName,
    String tagClassName,
```

```
    String bodycontent,
    String infoString,
    TagLibraryInfo taglib,
    TagExtraInfo tagExtraInfo,
    TagAttributeInfo attributeInfo)
```

Creates a new `TagInfo` object from a tag library descriptor in JSP 1.1 format.

TagInfo

```
public TagInfo(
    String tagName,
    String tagClassName,
    String bodycontent,
    String infoString,
    TagLibraryInfo taglib,
    TagExtraInfo tagExtraInfo,
    TagAttributeInfo attributeInfo,
    String displayName,
    String smallIcon,
    String largeIcon,
    TagVariableInfo tvi)
```

Creates a new `TagInfo` object from a tag library descriptor in JSP 1.2 format.

TagInfo

```
public TagInfo(
    String tagName,
    String tagClassName,
    String bodycontent,
    String infoString,
    TagLibraryInfo taglib,
    TagExtraInfo tagExtraInfo,
    TagAttributeInfo attributeInfo,
    String displayName,
    String smallIcon,
    String largeIcon,
    TagVariableInfo tvi,
    boolean dynamicAttributes)
```

Creates a new `TagInfo` object from a tag library descriptor in JSP 2.0 format.

Methods

getAttributes

```
public TagAttributeInfo getAttributes()
```

Returns an array describing the attributes of this tag, or `null` if there are no attributes.

getBodyContent

```
public String getBodyContent()
```

Returns the `bodycontent` attribute of this tag as specified in the tag library descriptor.

getDisplayName

```
public String getDisplayName()
```

Returns the tag's display name attribute.

getInfoString

```
public String getInfoString()
```

Returns the info element for this tag as specified in the tag library descriptor.

getLargeIcon

```
public String getLargeIcon()
```

Returns the name of the large icon associated with this tag.

getSmallIcon

```
public String getSmallIcon()
```

Returns the name of the small icon associated with this tag.

getTagClassName

```
public String getTagClassName()
```

Returns the name of the tag handler class.

getTagExtraInfo

```
public TagExtraInfo getTagExtraInfo()
```

Returns the name of the tag extra information class.

getTagLibrary

```
public TagLibraryInfo getTagLibrary()
```

Returns a reference to the `TagLibraryInfo` object for this tag.

getTagName

```
public String getTagName()
```

Returns the tag name.

getTagVariableInfos

```
public TagVariableInfo getTagVariableInfos()
```

Returns the `TagVariableInfo` objects associated with this `TagInfo`.

getVariableInfo

```
public VariableInfo getVariableInfo(TagData data)
```

Returns a reference to the `VariableInfo` object for this tag.

hasDynamicAttributes

```
public boolean hasDynamicAttributes()
```

Return true if this tag supports dynamic attributes.

isValid

```
public boolean isValid(TagData data)
```

Returns the results of evaluating the isValid() method of the associated TagExtraInfo class.

setTagExtraInfo

```
public void setTagExtraInfo(TagExtraInfo tei)
```

Stores a reference to the TagExtraInfo for this tag.

setTagLibrary

```
public void setTagLibrary(TagLibraryInfo tl)
```

Sets the TagLibraryInfo property.

validate

```
public ValidationMessage validate(TagData data)
```

Invokes the validation logic specified in the TEI (if present).

TagLibraryInfo

Full Name:	javax.servlet.jsp.tagext.TagLibraryInfo
Type:	Abstract class

A class that encapsulates information associated with a taglib directive and its underlying TLD (tag library descriptor).

Methods

getFunction

```
public FunctionInfo getFunction(String name)
```

Returns the `FunctionInfo` object describing the specified function in the tag library descriptor.

getFunctions

```
public FunctionInfo getFunctions()
```

Returns an array of `FunctionInfo` objects describing the functions defined in this tag library descriptor.

getInfoString

```
public String getInfoString()
```

Returns the info property from the tag library descriptor.

getPrefixString

```
public String getPrefixString()
```

Returns the prefix assigned in the `taglib` directive.

getReliableURN

```
public String getReliableURN()
```

Returns the `reliableURL` property from the tag library descriptor.

getRequiredVersion

```
public String getRequiredVersion()
```

Returns the minimum required JSP container version.

getShortName

```
public String getShortName()
```

Returns the short name property from the tag library descriptor.

getTag

```
public TagInfo getTag(String shortname)
```

Returns the `TagInfo` object associated with a given tag name.

getTagdir

```
public String getTagdir()
```

Returns the value of the `tagdir` attribute used in the `taglib` directive.

getTagFile

```
public TagFileInfo getTagFile(String shortname)
```

Given a short name, returns the associated `TagFileInfo` objects.

getTagFiles

```
public TagFileInfo getTagFiles()
```

Returns all associated `TagFileInfo` objects.

getTags

```
public TagInfo getTags()
```

Returns an array of `TagInfo` objects for all tags defined in this tag library.

getURI

```
public String getURI()
```

Returns the value of the `uri` attribute from the `taglib` directive.

TagLibraryValidator

Full Name: `javax.servlet.jsp.tagext.TagLibraryValidator`

Type: Abstract class

A validator class that can be associated with a JSP page in the tag library descriptor. The validator operates on the XML document representation of the JSP page.

Constructors

TagLibraryValidator

```
public TagLibraryValidator()
```

Creates a new `TagLibraryValidator`.

Methods

getInitParameters

```
public Map getInitParameters()
```

Returns the initialization parameters.

release

```
public void release()
```

Releases validation data used by this validator.

setInitParameters

```
public void setInitParameters(Map map)
```

Provides initialization key/value parameters to the validator.

validate

```
public ValidationMessage validate(
    String prefix,
    String uri,
    PageData page)
```

Validates the JSP page, returning either an array of error messages or `null`, if the page is valid.

TagSupport

Full Name:	`javax.servlet.jsp.tagext.TagSupport`
Type:	Class
Implements:	`javax.servlet.jsp.tagext.IterationTag`
	`java.io.Serializable`

A concrete implementation of the `Tag` interface. Tag handlers can extend this class and implement only those methods that need to be changed.

Constructors

TagSupport

```
public TagSupport()
```

Creates a new `TagSupport` object.

Methods

doAfterBody

```
public int doAfterBody() throws JspException
```

Invoked after the tag body is evaluated.

doEndTag

```
public int doEndTag() throws JspException
```

Called when the end tag has been encountered. The return code indicates whether the JSP implementation servlet should continue with the rest of the page (EVAL_PAGE) or not (SKIP_PAGE). The method can throw a `JspException` to indicate a fatal error. The `TagSupport` implementation returns EVAL_PAGE.

doStartTag

```
public int doStartTag() throws JspException
```

Called after the page context, parent, and any attributes coded on the start tag have been set. The return code indicates whether the JSP implementation servlet should evaluate the tag body (EVAL_BODY_INCLUDE or BodyTag.EVAL_BODY_BUFFERED) or not (SKIP_BODY). The method can throw a `JspException` to indicate a fatal error. BodyTag.EVAL_BODY_BUFFERED is valid only if the tag handler implements `BodyTag`. The `TagSupport` implementation returns SKIP_BODY.

findAncestorWithClass

```
public static final Tag findAncestorWithClass(
    Tag from,
    Class klass)
```

Searches the stack of parent tags for the nearest tag handler of the specified class. This enables an "inner" tag to access information in its enclosing tags.

getId

```
public String getId()
```

Returns the value of the `id` attribute of this tag.

getParent

```
public Tag getParent()
```

Returns the immediate parent tag of this tag handler instance.

getValue

```
public Object getValue(String k)
```

Returns the object stored in this tag handler under the given name.

getValues

```
public Enumeration getValues()
```

Returns an enumeration of the names of the values stored in this tag handler.

release

```
public void release()
```

Guaranteed to be called before page exit. Enables the tag handler to release any resources it holds and reset its state so that it can be reused, if necessary.

removeValue

```
public void removeValue(String k)
```

Removes the value stored in this tag handler under the specified name, if any.

setId

```
public void setId(String id)
```

Sets the id attribute for this tag.

setPageContext

```
public void setPageContext(PageContext pageContext)
```

The generated servlet calls this method first before requiring the handler to do anything else. The implementing class should save the context variable so that it is available at any point in the tag lifecycle. From the page context, the tag handler can access all the JSP implicit objects and can get and set attributes in any scope.

setParent

```
public void setParent(Tag t)
```

Sets the parent tag. Enables a tag handler to find the tag above it in the evaluation stack. Called immediately after setPageContext().

setValue

```
public void setValue(String k, Object o)
```

Stores the object under the specified name in the tag handler.

TagVariableInfo

Full Name:	javax.servlet.jsp.tagext.TagVariableInfo
Type:	Class

A class that encapsulates tag variable information extracted from a tag library.

Constructors

TagVariableInfo

```
public TagVariableInfo(
    String nameGiven,
    String nameFromAttribute,
    String className,
    boolean declare,
    int scope)
```

Creates a new TagVariableInfo object.

TagVariableInfo

```
public TagVariableInfo(
    String nameGiven,
    String nameFromAttribute,
    String className,
    boolean declare,
    int scope,
    String fragment)
```

Creates a new TagVariableInfo object with a JSP fragment.

Methods

getClassName

```
public String getClassName()
```

Returns the value of the <variable-class> element in the tag library descriptor.

getDeclare

```
public boolean getDeclare()
```

Returns the value of the <declare> element in the tag library descriptor.

getFragment

```
public String getFragment()
```

Returns the JSP fragment.

getNameFromAttribute

```
public String getNameFromAttribute()
```

Returns the value of the <name-from-attribute> element in the tag library descriptor.

getNameGiven

```
public String getNameGiven()
```

Returns the value of the <name-given> element in the tag library descriptor.

getScope

```
public int getScope()
```

Returns the value of the <scope> element in the tag library descriptor.

TryCatchFinally

Full Name:	javax.servlet.jsp.tagext.TryCatchFinally
Type:	Interface

An additional interface that can be implemented by tag handlers to enable them to be called in the catch and finally blocks of the tag invocation.

Methods

doCatch

```
public void doCatch(Throwable t) throws Throwable
```

This method is invoked in the catch block if an exception occurs while evaluating the body of a tag.

doFinally

```
public void doFinally()
```

This method is invoked in the finally block if an exception occurs while evaluating the body of a tag.

ValidationMessage

Full Name:	javax.servlet.jsp.tagext.ValidationMessage
Type:	Class

A validation message resulting from an error found while validating a tag. The JSP container internally assigns a jsp:id attribute to every element of the XML view of a page. The TagLibraryValidator can use this id to indicate the invalid element, and the JSP container can in turn use this to give precise information about the location of the error.

Constructors

ValidationMessage

```
public ValidationMessage(String id, String message)
```

Creates a new ValidationMessage with the specified text. The id may be null if the message applies to the page as a whole, or it can be a specific jsp:id attribute.

Methods

getId

```
public String getId()
```

Returns the jsp:id attribute passed to this object.

getMessage

```
public String getMessage()
```

Returns the localized validation message.

VariableInfo

Full Name:	`javax.servlet.jsp.tagext.VariableInfo`
Type:	Class

A data structure that provides configuration information about scripting variables created by a custom tag. Use primarily in the `getVariableInfo()` method of a `TagExtraInfo` subclass.

Constructors

VariableInfo

```
public VariableInfo(
    String varName,
    String className,
    boolean declare,
    int scope)
```

Creates a new `VariableInfo` object preloaded with the variable name, class name, declare flag, and scope.

Methods

getClassName

```
public String getClassName()
```

Returns the class name.

getDeclare

```
public boolean getDeclare()
```

Returns the boolean attribute representing whether the variable should be declared or not.

getScope

```
public int getScope()
```

Returns the integer representing the variable scope.

getVarName

```
public String getVarName()
```

Returns the variable name.

Index

Symbols

INTERNATIONAL CONTACT INFORMATION

AUSTRALIA
McGraw-Hill Book Company Australia Pty. Ltd.
TEL +61-2-9900-1800
FAX +61-2-9878-8881
http://www.mcgraw-hill.com.au
books-it_sydney@mcgraw-hill.com

CANADA
McGraw-Hill Ryerson Ltd.
TEL +905-430-5000
FAX +905-430-5020
http://www.mcgraw-hill.ca

**GREECE, MIDDLE EAST, & AFRICA
(Excluding South Africa)**
McGraw-Hill Hellas
TEL +30-210-6560-990
TEL +30-210-6560-993
TEL +30-210-6560-994
FAX +30-210-6545-525

MEXICO (Also serving Latin America)
McGraw-Hill Interamericana Editores S.A. de C.V.
TEL +525-117-1583
FAX +525-117-1589
http://www.mcgraw-hill.com.mx
fernando_castellanos@mcgraw-hill.com

SINGAPORE (Serving Asia)
McGraw-Hill Book Company
TEL +65-863-1580
FAX +65-862-3354
http://www.mcgraw-hill.com.sg
mghasia@mcgraw-hill.com

SOUTH AFRICA
McGraw-Hill South Africa
TEL +27-11-622-7512
FAX +27-11-622-9045
robyn_swanepoel@mcgraw-hill.com

SPAIN
McGraw-Hill/Interamericana de España, S.A.U.
TEL +34-91-180-3000
FAX +34-91-372-8513
http://www.mcgraw-hill.es
professional@mcgraw-hill.es

**UNITED KINGDOM, NORTHERN,
EASTERN, & CENTRAL EUROPE**
McGraw-Hill Education Europe
TEL +44-1-628-502500
FAX +44-1-628-770224
http://www.mcgraw-hill.co.uk
computing_neurope@mcgraw-hill.com

ALL OTHER INQUIRIES Contact:
Osborne/McGraw-Hill
TEL +1-510-549-6600
FAX +1-510-883-7600
http://www.osborne.com
omg_international@mcgraw-hill.com

Designed for people. Not clocks.

People learn at their own pace. That's why our Beginner's Guides provide a systematic pedagogy. Real-world examples from seasoned trainers teach the critical skills needed to master a tool or technology.

Osborne Beginner's Guides: Essential Skills—Made Easy

Solaris 9 Administration: A Beginner's Guide
Paul A. Watters, Ph.D.
ISBN: 0-07-222317-0

UNIX System Administration: A Beginner's Guide
Steve Maxwell
ISBN: 0-07-219486-3

Dreamweaver MX: A Beginner's Guide
Ray West & Tom Muck
ISBN: 0-07-222366-9

HTML: A Beginner's Guide, Second Edition
Wendy Willard
ISBN: 0-07-222644-7

Java 2: A Beginner's Guide, Second Edition
Herbert Schildt
ISBN: 0-07-222588-2

UML: A Beginner's Guide
Jason Roff
ISBN: 0-07-222460-6

Windows XP Professional: A Beginner's Guide
Martin S. Matthews
ISBN: 0-07-222608-0

Networking: A Beginner's Guide, Third Edition
Bruce Hallberg
ISBN: 0-07-222563-7

Linux Administration: A Beginner's Guide, Third Edition
Steve Graham
ISBN: 0-07-222562-9

Red Hat Linux Administration: A Beginner's Guide
Narender Muthyala
ISBN: 0-07-222631-5

Windows .NET Server 2003: A Beginner's Guide
Martin S. Matthews
ISBN: 0-07-219309-3

9 proven learning features:

1 Modules
2 Critical Skills
3 Step-by-Step Tutorials
4 Ask the Experts
5 Progress Checks
6 Annotated Syntax
7 Mastery Checks
8 Projects
9 Network Blueprints

McGraw